PSYCHOLOGY
OF
ADOLESCENCE

PRENTICE-HALL INTERNATIONAL, INC. *London*

PRENTICE-HALL OF AUSTRALIA, PTY. LTD. *Sydney*

PRENTICE-HALL OF CANADA, LTD. *Toronto*

PRENTICE-HALL OF INDIA (PRIVATE) LTD. *New Delhi*

PRENTICE-HALL OF JAPAN, INC. *Tokyo*

SIXTH EDITION

PSYCHOLOGY
OF
ADOLESCENCE

Karl C. Garrison

Professor of Education
University of Georgia

PRENTICE-HALL, INC. *Englewood Cliffs, New Jersey*

136.7354
G242p2

© 1934, 1940, 1946, 1951, 1956, 1965 by

PRENTICE-HALL, INC.
Englewood Cliffs, New Jersey

Current printing (last digit):
12 11 10 9 8 7 6 5 4

LIBRARY OF CONGRESS CATALOG CARD NUMBER
65-12167

Printed in the United States of America
C-73494

PREFACE

This sixth edition contains findings from recent studies of adolescents. The quantity of recently published data has made it possible to re-evaluate and often reinforce the materials presented in the previous edition.

Many students of adolescent psychology who have used the fifth edition have verified that the present organization of chapters furnishes an efficient and usable book for both the learner and the teacher. However, the impact of changing cultural forces on adolescents has led me to expand the Introduction to include a chapter, "The Adolescent and His World."

The aim of this edition, like that of the previous ones, is twofold. My experience has led me to believe, first, that its content and method will be welcomed by the many college students who are still in the later stages of adolescence. Special attention has been given in this edition to the developmental tasks and problems of adolescents, particularly to the concept of the *self*. This book is also designed to be of value to those entrusted with the care and guidance of adolescents. Parents—engrossed in domestic duties or in vocational and avocational pursuits—and even teachers often forget their own teen-years. Adults should relate the observations of present-day teen-agers to those of their own adolescent years for greater understanding.

The materials have been selected to introduce the reader to basic experimental studies dealing with adolescents, and thus lay the foundation for a critical appreciation of new studies that are constantly appearing. The general student will find the facts in the text supplemented by specific references to sources in the bibliographies that follow the chapters. The more advanced student should find the sources named in the footnotes additionally helpful in his development of new techniques of study as well as an analytical view of new findings and principles in the field.

The original volume had its inception in my mind while I was an advanced student in genetic psychology at Peabody College. Here, I first became familiar with Hall's writings and was impressed by the biological conception of individual development and the scientific study of the growing child. Throughout this edition, I have consistently adhered to certain fundamental principles of growth and development that I formulated during my years of study and teaching courses in adolescent psychology.

The present approach to understanding the adolescent takes the total personality into consideration; it views the individual as a product of heredity and environment, the interaction of which began with the fertilization of the egg at conception, and it evaluates the "whole situation" in which the individual develops and operates. The adolescent is coming to be regarded as a unified personality that can be neither catalogued by statistical procedures nor stereotyped by special tests. This does not mean that tests and statistics have no place in studying adolescents; they have a very important place. But the important thing is getting a more accurate picture of the adolescent growing and developing in accordance with his genetic constitution and the various environmental forces that have affected him from birth.

I have drawn heavily from recent scientific studies and from current source materials. Thus youth activity in this country, surveys of various aspects of the life of adolescents, clinical studies of adolescents, longitudinal studies, and representative research studies in related fields are reviewed, and are acknowledged by references. Apart from these acknowledgments however, it is difficult to give adequate credit to all the sources to which I am indebted. From correspondence and personal contacts as well as from published materials, I have secured valuable information and special help. I should like to express my thanks to these associates as well as to the writers and publishers who have permitted the use of quotations and special data from certain studies. Special acknowledgment is due, moreover, to many students of adolescent psychology who have offered suggestions since the publication of the original edition in 1934, the revised edition in 1940, the third edition in 1946, the fourth edition in 1951, and the fifth edition in 1956.

K.C.G.

Athens, Ga.

CONTENTS

Chapter 4

Chapter 5

Chapter 6

Part Three

PERSONALITY AND ADJUSTMENT IN ADOLESCENCE

Chapter 7

Chapter 8

Chapter 9

Chapter 10

Chapter 11

Chapter 12

Part Four

SOCIAL FORCES AFFECTING THE ADOLESCENT

Chapter 13

Chapter 14

Chapter 15

Chapter 16

Chapter 17

Chapter 18

Part Five

THE END OF ADOLESCENCE

Chapter 19

APPENDICES

INDEXES

PSYCHOLOGY
OF
ADOLESCENCE

PART ONE

INTRODUCTION

1

THE ADOLESCENT AGE

The attention focused on adolescents since the turn of the century is without parallel in history. Books, articles, and a growing number of products aimed especially at adolescence all point to a new interest in the change from child to man. Because of this attention, many people tend to look upon adolescence as a period separate from other periods of life. However, attempts to describe human development in terms of discrete stages are fraught with difficulty. Although we speak about the preadolescent, adolescent, and postadolescent stages of development, these are not discrete periods; the range and dimension of each are at best only loosely defined.

DEFINITIONS OF ADOLESCENCE

Various concepts of adolescence account for different viewpoints and emphasis in the study of the psychology of adolescence. However, all psychologists agree that the stage of adolescence lies somewhere between childhood and adulthood. They further define adolescence as a period of change: physical, emotional, and social.

Adolescence as a period of physiological change. The most important physiological changes that signify the beginning of adolescence involve the sex glands. The hormones from the sex glands bring the reproductive organs to maturity, and the individual becomes potentially capable of reproduction. This point in life is called puberty. The first menstruation marks puberty for girls, but there is no single criterion to indicate puberty for boys. Among criteria frequently used are the occurrence of first ejaculation, the appearance of axillary (underarm) and pubic hair, and other secondary sexual characteristics. Girls tend to judge a boy's sexual maturity by facial and body hair and by change of voice; boys judge girls' sexual maturity in terms of figure and breast development. Regardless of the method used for determining puberty it is generally recognized that boys mature about two years later than girls. This is discussed more fully in the chapters (3 and 4) dealing with physiological and physical development.

Whereas puberty refers to a datable time signaling the beginning of adolescence, pubescence refers to a period of time during which a constellation of changes are taking place. Among the changes taking place are those involving metabolic rate, blood pressure, pulse rate, skeletal growth, voice pitch, and pubic hair. According to Shuttleworth, changes occur in the following sequence:

> In girls, the order is: enlargement of the breasts; appearance of straight, pigmented pubic hair; age of maximum growth; appearance of kinky pubic hair; menarche; and growth of axillary (underarm) hair. In boys, the order is: beginning growth of the testes, first pubic hair (straight, pigmented), early voice changes, first ejaculation, kinky pubic hair, age of maximum growth, axillary hair, marked voice changes, and development of the beard.[1]

Based on a study of the behavior of 200 boys as they passed through pubescence, Dimock concluded, "Changes that take place in the development of the adolescent are probably not so numerous, so radical, so far-reaching or so abrupt as was assumed in the earlier psychology of adolescence."[2] His conclusion has been verified by more recent studies. Adolescent growth is continuous rather than periodic, gradual rather than cataclysmic in nature.

The range of puberty for girls may vary as much as 10 or more years. This is indicated in Figure 1-1, which shows the distribution and

Figure 1-1

PERCENTAGE DISTRIBUTIONS AND AVERAGE MENARCHEAL AGES OF 357 MOTHERS AND THEIR DAUGHTERS (*Reproduced from Figure 113 of F. K. Shuttleworth, "The Adolescent Period,"* Monographs of the Society for Research in Child Development, *1938, Vol. 3, No. 3*)

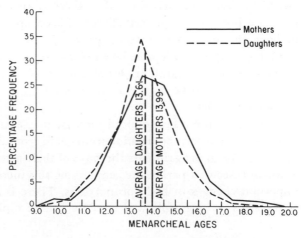

average menarcheal ages for 357 mothers and their 680 daughters.[3] There is no clearly defined method for determining puberty among boys. In a study reported by Ramsey, complete histories were obtained from personal interviews of 291 boys between the ages of 10 and 20 years.[4] These boys were from the middle or upper socio-economic strata of a midwestern city. The different phases of the sexual development of the boys at different age levels are shown in Table 1-1. These data indicate that not all of these sex characteristics appear in a boy at the same time; however, the 13-year level seems to be the modal period for the appearance of each of these characteristics, with a distribution range for each characteristic from 10 to 16 years.

Table 1-1

PERCENTAGE OF EACH AGE GROUP OF BOYS SHOWING DIFFERENT ASPECTS OF SEXUAL DEVELOPMENT

(After Ramsey)

Age group	Ejaculation	Voice change	Nocturnal emission	Pubic hair
10	1.8	0.3	0.3	0.3
11	6.9	5.6	3.7	8.4
12	14.1	20.5	5.3	27.1
13	33.6	40.0	17.4	36.1
14	30.9	26.0	12.9	23.8
15	7.8	5.5	13.9	3.3
16	4.9	2.0	16.0	1.0

Physical symptoms of early adolescence. Studies of the physical growth of boys and girls show that there is an increased rate of growth in height just prior to puberty. Since puberty appears in girls earlier than in boys, the accelerated rate of growth in height occurs earlier among girls. This is quite noticeable when one observes a group of girls and boys in the seventh and eighth grades of our schools. These girls at the ages of 12, 13, and 14 will be on the average as tall as or taller than the boys of the same age level.

There is also a pronounced increase in the rate of growth in weight just prior to puberty. Some adolescents gain from 20 to 30 pounds during the year. The girls again pass the boys of their age level in weight during a two- or three-year period. Accompanying this increased growth, one finds important changes in body proportions. There is at first a rapid growth of the arms and legs, followed later by a more rapid growth of the trunk of the body. The hands, feet, and nose seem to play an important part in adolescent development. By the time the boy is 13 or 14 years of age his hands and feet have achieved a large percentage of their total development at maturity.

One of the earliest indications of the development of the girl during the preadolescent stage is the development of the breasts. The mammary nipple usually does not project above the level of the surrounding skin structures until the third year after birth. The nipple after this stage shows a slight elevation above the surrounding structures. There is no further pronounced change for the average girl until about the tenth year, when the so-called "bud" stage appears. This is soon followed by the development of the "primary" breast, resulting mainly from an increase in the fat surrounding and underlying the papilla (nipple) and adjacent skin area.

Adolescence as a psychological phenomenon. The adolescent period has been described as an in-between period. The transition from childhood to adulthood is not sudden. During this transition period the individual displays many childlike characteristics, even though he is striving to be grown-up in nature. Observations of, and experiences with, individuals during the "teen" period reveal that there is a fairly distinct time during which the individual cannot be treated as a child, and actually resents such treatment. Yet this same individual is by no means fully mature, and cannot be classed as an adult. During this transition from childhood to adulthood, therefore, the subject is referred to as an adolescent.

The adolescent is torn, often violently, between acting as a child and acting as a man. G. Stanley Hall splendidly portrayed adolescence as a period of "storm and stress" in a vivid and striking description of this stage of life with all its specific characteristics, gradations, and peculiarities.[5] Just three years before his death, he pointed out the irony of the 1920's word, "flapper." "Flapper" was the expression applied to the daring, bold teen-age girls and young women of the day, yet Hall noted that the definition of the term was "[one] yet in the nest, and vainly attempting to fly while its wings have only pin feathers."[6] His conception of adolescence caught the attention of all who came into contact with his writings, which were, in fact, so impressive that they dominated the thinking of most American students of adolescent psychology for a number of years.

Adolescence as a sociological phenomenon. Many factors are involved in a sociological definition of adolescence. Numerous social rituals and ceremonies are introduced during this stage, some of which are described later in the chapter. Society no longer regards the individual as a child, and brings to bear its educational forces most heavily to train him for adult living.

Although physical changes deeply rooted in man's nature determine adolescence, social forces also act to shape this phase of life, especially in the West: educational plans, work opportunities, and age of marriage are factors that have an important bearing on the end of adolescence and the beginning of adulthood. For example, the recent increased period of education has augmented childhood dependency and consequently lengthened adolescence. Among families of lower social status, a boy is accepted into adulthood at 16 or 17, but in families of higher social status he remains in school and is financially dependent upon his family until he is 21 or older. It might be stated that the beginning of adolescence is to a marked degree a physical and physiological phenomenon, whereas the end of adolescence is mainly emotional-social.

THE ADOLESCENT AS A BIO-CULTURAL PRODUCT

The beginning of adolescence is fundamentally a period of physical change. Growth furnishes the physical basis for emotional, social, intellectual, and economic maturity. If a child did not increase in stature, his muscles become stronger, his sex organs develop, his brain mature, and if his internal organs did not increase in size and efficiency to meet the needs of the body, there would be no adolescence. Adulthood could never be achieved.

Are the problems of adolescent boys and girls a result of the nature of adolescents or of the culture in which they live and grow? All societies and all cultures recognize the changing status of the child as he approaches adulthood, but they do so in different ways. A study of the problems and adjustments of adolescents in cultures very different from our own may help in answering this question.

Puberty in different cultures. An outstanding difference between our culture and other cultures is that at puberty in some cultures there are ceremonies that usher boys and girls into manhood or womanhood, whereas in our culture there exists an in-between period during which a person is considered neither a child nor an adult.[7] The lengthy period between childhood and adulthood is one of the prime characteristics of adolescence in American society.

In our culture, adolescence is a period when new heterosexual relationships are formed. Although there is no strict taboo about boys and girls playing together at an early age, they tend to separate into different games and activities. A different relationship may be noted as they mature physically and sexually.

In Samoa, boys and girls are strictly separated from age 9 or 10 until after puberty. The opposite sexes may not touch each other, sit together, eat together, address each other familiarly, or in any way really associate with each other. At puberty, the taboos between the sexes are lessened. After two or three years, these separate groups of boys and girls tend to disappear and sexual relations usually begin. Premarital sexual relations are accepted by the Samoan society except in the case of the Taupo, who is the princess of the village and must remain a virgin until she marries.[8]

In the Arapesh society a boy's father selects a bride for his son, then takes her into his home and "grows her" for his son. The girl grows up with her future husband and treats him and his brothers as she would her own brothers. There is no taboo on the association of boys and girls. However, during the preadolescent period sexual relations are forbidden. The boy's parents act as chaperones, protecting the girl. They may relax their strictness on her after the first menstruation period ceremony has been performed. The couple drifts from a brother-sister relationship into marriage.

In Pondoland there is no strict separation of the sexes at any time, although boys and girls are separated by the fact that men and women eat apart and do many other things separately. Marriages are officially arranged by the parents, but only after the boy and girl have agreed to the match. Subordination of individual desires to those of the group is emphasized. Parents feel very responsible for their children, and children have little choice in what they will do, since they all get married and live in a hut in the boy's father's domain.

Puberty ceremonies. Several authors, among whom G. Stanley Hall is prominent, have given us full and vivid descriptions of puberty ceremonies among the more primitive tribes. In connection with puberty ceremonies, Ruth Benedict stated:

> In order to understand puberty institutions, we do not most need analyses of the necessary nature of *rites de passage;* we need rather to know what is identified in different cultures with the beginning of adulthood and their methods of admitting to the new status. Not biological puberty, but what adulthood means in that culture conditions the puberty ceremony.[9]

In other words, the physiological facts of adolescence are socially interpreted. Furthermore, the interpretation of puberty in the male's life cycle differs from that in the female's. In most primitive cultures the adult prerogatives of men are greater than those of women, and consequently it is more common for societies to take special note of this period in the lives of boys than in the lives of girls. However, the puberty rites for boys and girls may be celebrated in the same tribe in identical ways. This may be noted in the rites for adolescents in the interior of British Columbia, where the purpose is to provide training for manhood and womanhood and work. In Africa and Australia, more attention is directed toward the boy. Among such cultures the most elaborate and important ceremonials are those which transfer the youth to the society of men and thus to the tribal life. Sometimes physical ordeals inflicted by adult members of the group are involved. The boy must accept the ordeal stoically to prove his courage and manhood. The ceremony brings the adolescent boy to man's estate and to full participation in the activities of the men of the tribe.

Puberty rites for girls are designed primarily to promote marriage. Among tribes of central Africa, the girl is segregated, sometimes for several years, fed sweets and fatty foods, and allowed no physical activity. During her stay at the fatting-house she is taught her future duties, and at the end of this period she is ready for marriage. No special treatment is accorded the bridegroom. When a Takuma maiden reaches the age of 12 or 13, long pubertal ceremonies are held for her introduction into womanhood.[10] After three months of isolation the Takuma maidens are brought out on the third day of the festival. They must submit to much torture during this stage of their development. However, they yield unprotestingly, believing they cannot attain womanhood without the suffering. Afterwards, they may marry.

Certain practices saturated with particular moral and religious connotations are handed down through tribal ceremonies. Among the Yahgan of South America, a prominent part of their ceremony consists of group singing and dancing, usually late at night. The songs are communications to an evil spirit, *Yetaita,* who must be kept away.

All these ceremonies serve as a means of welcoming the adolescents into adulthood with no regard to why certain practices ever started or why they still exist. The pubertal ceremony, recognizing the adolescent status of youth, has tremendous significance for the adolescent, his parents, and the members of the community or tribe. It marks the transition from childhood and signals a change in the attitude of the parents and society toward the youth. Through the pubertal ceremony the taboos, prohibitions, and customs of the society are preserved, and the authority of the older members of the society is maintained. Such ceremonies tend to inhibit the adolescent from usurping the privileges and powers of his elders and from aspiring to overthrow the existing order of things.

Some informal rites of modern civilization. Probably the most noticeable of the modern practices is the introduction of the young lady into "society." This usually takes place during the latter part of the adolescent period and signifies to the world—and particularly to the young men —that a daughter is about to enter woman's estate. Among the upper social class the initiate-to-be is frequently given a "house" or "coming-out" party, or makes her debut at a debutante ball. Among lower and most middle-class groups, growing up is usually less formal; adolescents are simply given more privileges and responsibilities than they had as preadolescents. The individual is frequently required to play both a child's and an adult's role. Both boys and girls are admitted to a greater variety of adult life and activities. Obtaining a driver's license, the gift of an automobile, commencement (a significant term) exercises at high school, the finishing school, the linking of the self with the church—these are all more or less socialized events related to the entrance into maturity.

It has been suggested that this recognition is informal, and that the youth has not wholly put away childish things. Yet the world at large, as well as the individual concerned, is advised of a person's becoming a matured social being. On the other hand, we must not ignore the fact that practices to which we have referred are mainly those of the more financially fortunate families.

A survey of the life habits of people from a lower social stratum will show that many such observances are absent, and that today there is little here to indicate to the world and to the developing youth that the adult group, with its privileges and responsibilities, is receiving a new member. Frequently the "initiation" lessons are given by uncouth and unworthy elders. Often, indeed, the home is a very poor agent for developing and setting forth a responsible social being; and as a result of its neglect, inadequacy, or general unwholesomeness, undesirable psychological traits appear in the young.

Postadolescence is legally recognized through compulsory school laws, legal age for voting and marriage, and the age for securing a driver's license. However, technological developments and increased educational demands have created situations that have in many ways aggravated the problems of adolescents.

Teen-ager's role in American culture. Adolescence is characterized in our culture as a period of transition—a period when the individual faces new and frequently difficult problems. Concerning this, Lawrence Frank has stated:

> . . . the second decade of life—the teen ages—are necessarily difficult and problematic because the child is being transformed into the adult, physically, intellectually, culturally, and socially. In that process the boy and girl must relinquish much of their previously learned patterns of action, speech, belief and feelings, and learn new patterns as they struggle to master their life tasks.[11]

The adolescent assumes the roles he must assume by the nature of his biological inheritance, his developing personality, his socio-economic opportunities, and cultural demands and expectations. Unlike primitive youth, who is the product of a group within a single relatively static culture, the American adolescent moves in a "ring of cultures." These are alike with respect to basic human needs but are different by virtue of varying beliefs, sentiments, and customs. The adolescent in the United States lives in a society committed to the freedom and dignity of the individual, to equal opportunities for all, and to the security and general welfare of the nation as a whole.[12]

The adolescent is a member of a variety of groups large and small, formal and informal. His activities and role in each vary considerably from group to group. As he moves into new and different groups his role is frequently uncertain, and he often feels insecure as he attempts to cope with the expectations and demands of the respective groups. In our democratic society he finds an absence of consistent patterns of behavior and a lack of clearly defined goals and purposes among the different groups. He finds himself going around in circles as he whirls through these "rings upon rings of cultures" in the short-lived orbital space commonly called the "teen age."

There are, however, many teen-agers who do not participate in the teen-age culture; these are the 4,419,000 in the civilian labor force, the

Table 1-2

PERCENTAGE OF TEEN-AGERS IN SCHOOL BY SEX, 1959

	14–15 years old	16–17 years old	18–19 years old
Males	97.8	84.8	45.6
Females	97.0	81.0	29.2

904,000 in the armed services, and the 1,206,000 who are married.[13] Table 1-2 shows the percentage by age of teen-agers still in school and thus able to participate in the teen-age culture. Further investigation shows that those who leave school as they grow older are adolescents of the lower socio-economic classes. They usually find a job, enter the armed services, or get married. They may share some aspects of the teen-age culture, but generally they are expected to perform in an adult manner; they become a part of the adult culture. They are, then, a part of the teen-age culture only in their early teens. On the other hand, persons from a higher socio-economic background participate in the teen-age culture until they reach adulthood; hence the teen-age culture is a culture of the leisure class.

The concept of individual differences is important in understanding adolescents. Generalizing from averages to individual cases is dangerous. When we consider the average adolescent we are dealing with a nonexisting person, a statistic.

It is important, however, to consider in general some of the major adjustment problems faced by the adolescent in American culture. The reader will also need to consider further the problems faced by the adolescent born and reared in other dynamic and complex cultures. For example, problems confronting the adolescent growing up in America may also be found in West Germany, since the latter, through its economic growth, industrialization, and perhaps the influx of American personnel, has created a culture similar to ours in its complexity.

METHODS OF STUDYING ADOLESCENTS[14]

The methods of studying adolescents reflect philosophical and scientific trends in other areas of learning, especially in education and psychology. The variety of problems involved and the varying conditions under which these problems are studied call for different modes of attack. The methods used by different investigators depend upon the nature of the problem, materials and subjects available, and training and experience of the investigators. The methods here described are not by any means exhaustive but are representative.

Adolescent diaries. G. Stanley Hall made use of diaries for gathering data about the nature, interests, and activities of adolescents, since the adolescent period is characterized by a pronounced interest in diaries of various activities. For instance, high school annuals have great appeal to students, who persist in writing in each other's books.

Adolescent diaries frequently reveal a great deal about the aspirations and problems of their authors that cannot be obtained from other sources. Such autobiographical material is, however, subject to a certain amount of error. The errors arise from the sampling of those who keep diaries and from the selection of materials within the diary. Adolescent girls are more prone to keep diaries than adolescent boys. Also, boys and girls considered self-oriented are more likely to keep diaries than those who are others-oriented, since the self-oriented person is so concerned with himself that he likes to write about himself and thus analyze himself. Materials included in diaries frequently border on the dramatic yet overlook many significant events. Trivial events are emphasized, but more important events are forgotten or deemed inconsequential.

Anthropological studies. Studies of adolescents in primitive cultures made by Margaret Mead and other anthropologists referred to earlier in this chapter have furnished useful data about the nature of adolescence and the influence of cultural forces on adolescent development and behavior. Comparisons of cultural practices provide a wide range of possible explanations for the characteristics and problems of adolescents in our own culture and thus help to furnish a basis for understanding. Studies of patterns of living in different social classes and among different ethnic and cultural groups within the same society have also furnished valuable information about the influences of varying conditions upon adolescent development and behavior. For example, the study by Havighurst and Taba of adolescents in a midwestern community called Prairie City furnished convincing evidence that different cultural forces and customs influence development.[15]

These studies make use of careful observations, reports from adolescents, and interviews with those concerned with the education and guidance of adolescents. There are, however, certain dangers involved in drawing conclusions from cross-cultural comparisons. One cannot infer that what is a successful theory for one culture will be successful for an entirely different culture. Also, one cannot rely completely on the accuracy of reports from adolescents or adults concerned with the guidance of adolescents. Generalizations and inferences made by the investigators should be studied with a certain amount of caution, since they frequently bring their own experiences and biases into their interpretations.

Retrospective reports from adults. During the past decade a number of researchers have made use of data gathered from adults. The adult is asked to think back upon his adolescent years and to give some desired information. This method may be thought of as a questionnaire procedure, since it usually involves the use of questions on certain problems or areas. It seems rather safe to say that older subjects are more willing to give a true account of their adolescent years than most adolescents, since an appraisal of their present status is not involved. However, forgetfulness can be an important source of error. Also, many early experiences have become highly colored over the years. However, like diaries, these reports have some value when used with caution and understanding.

The experimental method. The experimental method was introduced in early psychological studies in an attempt to make psychology an exact science. This method attempts to answer a question or solve a problem by carefully testing it out. In physics, to solve problems relative to the refraction of light, careful measurements must be made. This method of studying problems has been generally regarded as the most accurate one for arriving at their solutions. However, there are problems for which this method is not suitable. Two general types of experimental methods are used in studying problems in educational and child psychology: the single group and the parallel group. The first method studies a single individual or a group of individuals under laboratory or controlled conditions. For example, if we wished to study the radio and television interests of a group of adolescents, it would be necessary to gather data regarding a group of adolescents by observations, interviews, questionnaires, or some other technique. Other adolescent phenomena that could be studied by this method include (1) the effect of puberty upon pulse rate and blood pressure, (2) change of interest as a result of certain experiences at school, and (3) the relationship between emotional instability and classroom behavior problems of a group of adolescents.

The parallel group method makes use of two or more groups in studying a problem. The parallel groups should be equivalent except for the factor being studied. Problems in adolescent psychology that have been studied by this method include, (1) the relative effects of puberty upon the interests and behavior of adolescents, (2) a comparison of the influence of autocratic and democratic leadership upon the behavior and activities of adolescents, and (3) the effects of a guidance program upon the vocational choices of adolescents.

The experimental method, like the cross-sectional and the longitudinal methods, makes use of various techniques for gathering data on adolescents. The techniques most commonly used for gathering data include observations, the written questionnaire, personal interviews, tests and rating devices, anecdotes, and projective techniques.

The normative survey. Much of the available data on adolescents is based upon cross-sectional studies. An example of the early use of this method for studying children and adolescents is that of measuring the height and weight of all the children in the public schools of a particular city or area. Averages are then computed for the different age groups. When these averages are plotted on a chart and lines are drawn connecting the different points, a curve, which may be regarded as an average growth curve, is obtained. This makes it possible to compare the growth of an individual child with that of the average. However, certain weaknesses such as are presented in Chapter 3 and in subsequent chapters, appear in this method.

Following the development of intelligence tests, a number of experimenters began studying areas of growth other than that of height and weight. In such studies, groups of children and adolescents are observed under similar conditions, with respect to a certain characteristic. Comparisons are then made between these groups, age for age, grade for grade, and the like.

Longitudinal studies. Longitudinal studies correct some of the outstanding weaknesses present in the cross-sectional method. These have been used in many recent studies of child and adolescent development. The normative survey (referred to also as cross-sectional) method furnishes data that make it possible to construct growth curves for a number of developmental factors and tasks. They do not, however, furnish an accurate picture of the growth pattern or curve of an individual child. Longitudinal studies make use of repeated measurements or observations of the same individuals over relatively long periods. This method has been used extensively in studying the adolescent growth curves for height and weight, blood pressure and pulse rate during adolescence, change of interests with adolescence, social development during adolescence, change of attitudes, educational growth, or dating activities at different periods of growth.

Although the longitudinal method gives a more nearly accurate picture of how individuals grow and develop than does the cross-sectional method, there are certain weaknesses in this method that the student should be able to recognize. In the first place, a considerable amount of time is spent in gathering data. Much of the data in school or elsewhere may not be available throughout the entire study. This, then, presents a problem of selection. Also, it is possible for a special event or condition to affect the particular group being studied, a factor that would classify the group as not typical or not representative of adolescent groups. Thus, the effect may be a result of the cultural happening rather than of the particular age of the individuals in the group. Thirdly, the repetition of a test is likely to have its effect upon the individuals. The fact that the group is an experimental group being tested periodically is likely in itself to have some effect upon the results. Careful students of adolescent psychology should be aware of the fact that the method used in collecting information may in itself have an important bearing on the results.

The clinical method. The clinical method studies a single individual, intensively, by all the means available. This is usually known as a case study. The complete cycle of a case study includes:

1. Determination of the status of the phenomenon under investigation

2. Collection of data relating to the circumstances associated with the given phenomenon

3. Identification of the causal factors

4. Application of remedial measures

5. Follow-up to determine the effectiveness of the corrective measure.[16]

Problem cases suitable for study by the clinical procedure are (a) the withdrawal or shy adolescent, (b) the juvenile delinquent, (c) the educationally retarded adolescent, and (d) the socially maladjusted adolescent.

Each of these techniques has its place in research but, at the same time, each has definite limitations. It is not the province of this discussion to present these limitations, except to point out that any technique in the hands of an individual who does not know how to use it, or how to interpret correctly the results obtained from its use is of little value. Thus, each of these techniques is limited in its value not only by the nature of the instrument being used but also by the training and experience of the student using it.

SUMMARY

Since the appearance of the momentous work of G. Stanley Hall, much has been said about the age of adolescence. There are many who would consider this period of life as separate and distinct from other periods, holding it up as a dramatic stage that justifies all the phrases and titles that have been built up around it. We hear the expressions "Flaming Youth," "Coming-out Parties," "The Age of Accountability," and the like. These are merely terms used to express ideas formerly thought of in connection with various puberty ceremonies. The importance of this transition period was recognized by the early primitive tribes, but the conception of the nature of the transition was not in harmony with the notions presented by modern students of adolescent psychology. The notion that the adolescent age is a problem age is seriously open to question. It does appear, however, that this is an age when the individual is confronted with many problems, resulting largely from the social and economic demands of his culture.

The American adolescent growing up in a democratic society committed largely to the Judeo-Christian ethic yet made up of different dynamic complex groups with varying demands and expectations finds himself reacting to a "ring of cultures." Of the 19 million teen-agers in this country, approximately 12.5 million are enrolled in our schools and participate in the teen-age culture. The point of view presented throughout the text is that, given a favorable environment, much of the tension and strain of adolescence will be eliminated.

Students of adolescent psychology have made use of various methods and techniques for gathering data on the development, activities, and problems of teen-age boys and girls. These studies have provided valuable data for use in interpreting the growth, development, and special characteristics of adolescents.

THOUGHT PROBLEMS

1. Look up several definitions of adolescence and note the points of similarity in each. (See Appendix A for a bibliography.)
2. What is meant by puberty ceremonies? Do you notice any points of similarity between the various ceremonies? Show how they frequently represent different purposes. Show also how differences in the practices represent different folkways or general cultural patterns.
3. What factors are associated with the time of the beginning of pubescence? How would you account for the fact that pubescence is earlier today than it was a generation or more ago?
4. What is the educational and social significance of the age differences in the

physical and physiological developments associated with adolescence as suggested by Figure 1-1 and Table 1-1?

5. An annotated bibliography of popular literature involving adolescents is presented in Appendix C. Read one or more of these books along with your readings from this text. Note the characteristics of the individuals involved, and the problems encountered by the adolescent. Has the writer presented a description of the adolescent and his problems which is in harmony with the materials presented throughout this book?

6. Study the methods listed in this chapter for collecting data on adolescents. List several problems that would make use of each of these methods.

7. What are some of the causes that have led some to think of adolescence as a "storm and stress" period of life? Do you find evidences for this in a consideration of your own adolescent years?

8. Some have suggested that the period of adolescence could be made less trying by relieving sex taboos and encouraging earlier marriages along the lines followed in Samoa, as described by Margaret Mead. Would the advantages, if any, outweigh the disadvantages? Just what would you suggest in this connection?

9. Do you think that modern society should grant all the rights and privileges of adulthood to adolescents? Give reasons for your answer.

SELECTED REFERENCES*

Grinder, Robert E., and Strickland, Charles E., "G. Stanley Hall and the Social Significance of Adolescence," in *Studies in Adolescence* (Robert E. Grinder, ed.). New York: The Macmillan Company, 1963.

Hall, G. S., *Adolescence: Its Psychology and Its Relations to Physiology, Anthropology, Sociology, Sex, Crime, Religion, and Education.* New York: Appleton-Century-Crofts, Inc., 1904, Vol. I., Chaps. 1, 2, and 13.

Horrocks, John E., *The Psychology of Adolescence*, 2nd ed. Boston: Houghton-Mifflin Company, 1962, Chap. 1.

Mead, Margaret, *From the South Seas; Studies of Adolescence and Sex in Primitive Societies.* New York: William Morrow & Co., Inc., 1939, p. 1072. This is a one-volume edition of three anthropological works: *Coming of Age in Samoa, Growing Up in New Guinea,* and *Sex and Temperament.*

Miller, N., *The Child in Primitive Society.* New York: Coward-McCann, Inc., 1928.

Rogers, Dorothy, *The Psychology of Adolescence.* New York: Appleton-Century-Crofts, Inc., 1962, Chap. 1.

Seidman, Jerome M., ed., *The Adolescent—A Book of Readings,* 2nd ed. New York: Holt, Rinehart & Winston, Inc., 1960, Chap. 3.

Stone, L. Joseph and Joseph Church, *Childhood and Adolescence.* New York: Random House, 1957, Chap. 10.

NOTES

[1] Frank K. Shuttleworth, "The Physical and Mental Growth of Boys and Girls Age Six to Nineteen in Relation to Age at Maximum Growth," *Monographs of the Society for Research in Child Development,* 4, No. 3 (1939).

---

* A selected annotated bibliography on the psychology of adolescence is presented in Appendix A.

2 H. S. Dimock, *Rediscovering the Adolescent* (New York: Association Press, 1937), p. 266.

3 H. N. Gould and M. R. Gould, "Age of First Menstruation in Mother and Daughter," *Journal of the American Medical Association,* **98** (1932), 1349-52.

4 G. V. Ramsey, "The Sexual Development of Boys," *American Journal of Psychology,* **56** (1943), 217-23.

5 G. Stanley Hall, *Adolescence* (New York: Appleton-Century-Crofts, Inc., 1904), I, xiii.

6 G. Stanley Hall, "Flapper Americana Novisscina," *Atlantic Monthly,* **129** (1922), 771-80.

7 Margaret Mead, *From the South Seas* (New York: William Morrow & Co., Inc., 1939).

8 *Ibid.*

9 Ruth Benedict, *Patterns of Culture* (Boston: Houghton Mifflin Company, 1934), p. 24.

10 Harald Schultz, "Takuma Maidens Come of Age," *National Geographic Magazine,* **116** (November, 1959), 629-49.

11 Lawrence K. Frank, "Needs and Problems of Adolescents in the Area of Emotional Health," *The High School Journal,* **35** (December, 1951), 66.

12 Clara M. Olson, "The Adolescent: His Society," *Review of Educational Research,* **24** (February, 1954), 5-8.

13 Jessie Bernard, "Teen-age Culture: An Overview," *The Annals of the American Academy of Political and Social Science* (November, 1961), pp. 1-12.

14 A detailed presentation of the different methods of studying adolescents is beyond the scope of this chapter. For a more complete survey of methods of studying children and adolescents, the reader is referred to J. E. Anderson, "Methods of Child Psychology," L. Carmichael (ed.), *Manual of Child Psychology,* revised ed. (New York: John Wiley & Sons, Inc., 1954), Chap. 1.

15 Robert J. Havighurst and Hilda Taba, *Adolescent Character and Personality* (New York: John Wiley & Sons, Inc., 1949).

16 C. V. Good, "Methods of Research and Problem Solving in Education," *Journal of Educational Research,* **84** (1940), 81-89.

2

THE
ADOLESCENT
AND HIS
WORLD

Adults, especially since World War II, frequently describe adolescents as irresponsible, pleasure loving, and mixed-up. Such opinions are, no doubt, a result of the adolescent's increased leisure-time activities, his mischief and crime, and his behavior patterns, referred to as adolescent culture. As Hess and Goldblatt pointed out, his position in American society is not clear: ". . . it is loosely defined at both entry and transition points and offers a set of vague and often conflicting roles. The age behaviors expected of adolescents by adults are viewed by society with ambivalence and anxiety. With the possible exception of old age, no other phase of individual development is so clearly marked by negative connotations and lack of positive sanctions."[1]

Must there be a conflict between the adolescent and society? Anthropologists have pointed out that there are cultures where this conflict does not appear to exist; however, in such cultures those personality characteristics which we associate with adolescence do not appear. It has been postulated that "tensions and frictions develop between the generations to the extent to which social roles, values, and relationships in the new generation deviate from those of the preceding generation."[2] In other words, tension between the generations is not a result of human nature as such, but a consequence of the rate of social change. Since Western society is, above all, a society of change, conflict between our society and the growing child is inherent in the development of personality. If parents, teachers, and others concerned with guidance are to understand the behavior of the adolescent, they must not only take account of our changing world but also understand the way in which the adolescent himself views the world and his own problems.

ADOLESCENCE IN A PERIOD OF TRANSITION

Adults should be particularly aware of the fact that conditions today are very different from what they were just a decade ago. Change is the watchword of our time. We think in terms of change. We measure our progress on the basis of change, thus confusing change with progress. We now face opportunities never known before, but we also face challenges and problems for which we have no ready-made answer. The changing world has perhaps affected adolescents more than any other group in our society.

The effects of automation. The physicist defines work in terms of energy output. The economist defines it in terms of material output, rather than energy output. Although today's laborer produces prodigiously, he no longer does work as the physicist defines it. The machine has more and more taken over the "back-breaking" tasks, work that man once did. Automation has also shifted jobs from man to the machine. Mechanization and standardization have eliminated the satisfaction of certain basic needs once obtained through work, such as the desire to create and to have a sense of personal worth. Now, increased emphasis is being given to means other than the specific job for satisfying these basic psychological and social needs. The feeling of importance in being a part of a large organization contributing to society and a feeling of accomplishment through advancement have become important in today's work, since machines have taken away much of the satisfaction of manual output.

The increase of free time which comes with automation threatens to present a real problem to the modern adolescent, since there is considerable evidence that juvenile delinquency is closely related to the great amount of leisure time left for him in technically advanced civilizations. He is no longer called upon to help on the farm, to work in the stores and factories, or to assist in tasks at home. Modern means of production along with many labor saving devices have relieved him of these tasks. He no longer feels himself to be an important part of the family economy except as a consumer, and he tends to lose his sense of purpose.

Increased period of schooling. Closely related to problems growing out of automation are problems stemming from the increased period of schooling required by modern society. The great majority of youth of the future will not only complete high school but will also seek training beyond the high school level. Thus, the adolescent will remain in the protective custody of the school a considerable part of his life. He can anticipate a longer period of dependency on others than he could a generation ago. Our child labor and compulsory school-attendance laws force dependency upon the adolescent, whether he wishes it or not. For most young people adolescence has become, in its external circumstances, an extension of childhood rather than a short passage to adulthood.

It has been suggested that as a result of prolonged dependency a young person will find so much satisfaction in a secure home life that he will lose his desire to become independent. Never having faced responsibility for himself and others, he will be poorly equipped to accept adult responsibilities. Hence he will remain dependent upon others if they are available. If they are not, he will flounder into adulthood, unable to cope with the demands imposed upon him because his pattern of behavior is serviceable only to a child.[3] However, if parents and other adult leaders recognize the adolescent's basic needs for accepting responsibility and achieving independence, and gradually give him opportunities to satisfy these needs, when the time comes he will have no trouble assuming the role of an adult.

Increased urbanization—suburbia. Census figures show that the majority of our population lives within 150 to 160 metropolitan areas. The attitudes and values of adolescents today are determined more than ever by the city rather than by the farm; boys and girls look to the city for their amusements, ways of dressing, models for action, and ideals.

The last decade has seen important changes in the structure of the city and, consequently, in the neighborhood and family. The central area of the city has given way to slums, apartments, and expansions of different kinds of businesses. Around the fringes and far out into the countryside we find "suburbia" with its shopping centers, churches, schools, and commercial recreational centers, where people of all faiths and viewpoints are brought together. Here, children and adolescents are confronted with conflicting moral and religious viewpoints. The home and church are thus frequently faced with the problem of combatting the forces and conditions that would challenge and in many cases disrupt adolescents' faith.

The ever-increasing "togetherness" of suburbia's adults—everyone cooks out one night, or goes to the country club dance another, everyone spends Sunday at the lake, all wives take the shoppers' special to town—has had its impact on the youth of suburbia and on the intimacy and initiative of the individual family as a governing unit. Many more social and emancipatory problems have developed from the high standard of living for adolescent "suburbanites" who have more freedom from parental control, are more demanding and yet not needed, and have much more leisure time yet do nothing.

Importance of things. In a panel of high school students discussing the goals of life, one student pointed out that she felt a goal most people seek is happiness. An alert and energetic high school junior replied, "Why should you seek happiness? That doesn't make you any money!" Surveys show that "the making of more money" is the main motivating factor that causes young people to seek an increased amount of education. Visiting students from many Asiatic countries often express amazement at the high standard of living in the United States and at the goals of students who seek happiness and satisfaction through the acquisition of *things*.

The American adolescent today lives and functions in a society where material values are considered of utmost importance, as a result of American ingenuity, mass production, and salesmanship. When adolescents have their own television sets, radios, telephones, and subscriptions to glamour magazines, yet neglect the aesthetic and the sublime, it follows that one of the most urgent tasks confronting the home, church, and schools today is to destroy the twentieth-century myth that the accumulation of wealth and the attainment of widespread luxuries are the most important goals of man. There is need to remember that "man does not live by bread alone." The way materialistic values in American life affect the personal and social lives of adolescents helps provide an understanding of some of our youth's problems.

Conflict in values. Many leaders recognize the value to be derived from interaction with people of different backgrounds and beliefs. However, such contact may result in confusion, particularly in cases where religious faith has not been nourished. If an individual grows up in a community where the religion of his parents predominates he would not be likely to experience serious conflicts. The adolescent needs more than a religious background as a guide; he needs faith and the convictions that go with it, especially now. Conflicts in values characterize life today: many people are less certain about the line between right and wrong; they have no firm beliefs. Young people feel insecure in such an era, yet they still seek the purpose of life and the kinds of behavior that will lead to the highest fulfillment of such a purpose.

DEVELOPMENTAL TASKS OF THE ADOLESCENT

In a given society there are certain roles expected of individuals at different stages of life. The processes of growing to fulfill such roles have been termed "developmental tasks."[4] There are two major forces that interact to set forth these tasks: the expectations of society, or the "cultural patterns" in which the individual grows and learns, and the changes that take place in the individual organism as a result of maturation. The cultural expectations vary within a particular society from home to home and with different communities. There are, however, certain developmental tasks encountered by the great majority of American children and adolescents. The major developmental tasks of late childhood, early adolescence, and late adolescence are presented in Table 2-1.

In studying the materials of Table 2-1 the reader should keep in mind that these tasks may be grouped in different ways and that their achievement is gradual and continuous in nature. Some appear during the early adolescent years, whereas others appear during late adolescence or postadolescence. Much of the material of forthcoming chapters will deal with problems related to the achievement of these tasks.

Achieving an appropriate dependence-independence pattern. It is during the adolescent years that boys and girls establish close relationships with others and develop increased independence from parents. To retain affection for the parents without continued dependence upon them is the desired goal. Teen-agers desperately want to break away from close parental control, yet they feel a strong need for parental guidance. They want freedom in making plans, choosing friends, buying clothes, and spending money, but at the same time, they need the security of a close and happy home relationship. The resolution of this conflict is made difficult when parents are very strict and authoritative, allowing little freedom for their children.

Remmers and Radler noted from an extensive poll of young people that "only 10 per cent of the high school students think parents give them more advice than they need. But 33 per cent say they would like to have more parental counsel than they are getting."[5] Although much friction frequently exists in the family during the time adolescents are attempting to develop independence, the great majority of boys and girls accomplish this task successfully.

Achieving an appropriate affectional pattern. An individual must feel accepted and loved during his early childhood in order to feel secure in his social relations during late childhood and adolescence, to attain emotional stability during marriage, and to enable him to more satisfactorily meet frustrations and difficulties throughout life. Although the adolescent finds much gratification in achievement, he finds even more in the affectional relations within his home and among his peers. Close affectional patterns established with a relatively small number of persons provide the necessary feeling of being wanted.

Achieving a sense of belonging. Learning to interact with others of a group is an important developmental task of early childhood. The child must not only interact, but he must also feel that he belongs, is liked by, and accepted as a part of a group. Although at first the child usually learns to interact with groups of his own sex, he must later learn to live with others of both sexes. The task of learning to get along with agemates of both sexes continues throughout the high school years and into college years or employment. It is closely related to the task of learning

Table 2-1

IMPORTANT DEVELOPMENTAL TASKS OF LATE CHILDHOOD, EARLY ADOLESCENCE, AND LATE ADOLESCENCE OF AMERICAN CHILDREN AND ADOLESCENTS

Task	Late Childhood	Early Adolescence	Late Adolescence
Achieving an appropriate dependence-independence pattern	Growth in self-identification. Accepting physical characteristics, aptitudes, and abilities	Establishing independence from adults in self identification and emotional independence	Establishing self as an independent person. Making own decisions on matters concerning self
Achieving an appropriate affectional pattern	Forming friendships with peers on sharing basis	Accepting self as a person worthy of affection	Building a strong affectional bond with another person
Achieving a sense of belonging	Establishing peer loyalty and identification	Accepting and adjusting to special groups with whom identified	Accepting an adult role in different groups
Acquiring an appropriate sex role	Identifying with peers of the same sex	Learning role in heterosexual situations	Becoming attached to a member of the opposite sex. Preparing to accept future sex role
Developing intellectual skills and concepts	Developing concepts and skills essential for everyday living	Developing intellectual, language, and motor skills essential for individual and group participation	Developing intellectual, language, and motor skills and understanding for assuming civic responsibility
Developing conscience, morality, and a set of values	Acquiring moral concepts and elementary values	Acquiring moral concepts and values as guides to behavior	Acquiring standards and ethical concepts. Acquiring a philosophy of life

the appropriate sex role and is important in relation to successful social relations during later years.

Acquiring an appropriate sex role. In our culture the child tends to identify himself with his own sex at an early age, largely on the basis of dress and play activities, particularly the toys with which he plays. During late childhood there is a tendency to identify with peers of the same sex, although actual antagonism toward members of the opposite sex appears only where cultural patterns tend to promote such behavior.

At pubescence the difference between the sexes becomes greater. Each sex develops characteristics distinctly masculine or feminine, characteristics peculiar to and necessary for the part sex plays in the process of life. Sometimes girls find it difficult to determine just what society expects of them, especially since the role of women in our society is in a state of transition. Unlike their Pilgrim sisters, they can choose between following a career and raising a family.

The task of learning the appropriate sex role involves the acceptance and learning of socially approved adult male and female roles. Generally, most boys and girls find it easy to accept their respective sex roles, although accurate and honest information about sex is badly needed by all adolescents. One major problem faced by teen-agers is the directing of the sex drive into culturally desirable channels. Here, sex education and guidance should be most helpful.

Developing intellectual skills and concepts. The growing adolescent must acquire sufficient intellectual skills and concepts to enable him to function effectively and harmoniously in the social order. The increasing complexity of our social order has brought with it additional educational demands. Thus, educational attainments are essential both for effective living and for making a living. The adolescent must not only acquire certain intellectual skills and concepts, but he must also acquire a better understanding of himself as a growing person and come to accept his possibilities and limitations.

Attaining economic independence. Another task important for adolescent boys, and increasingly more so for girls, is that of attaining economic independence. In our society a person's occupation is of prime importance; most parents encourage their children to remain in school and to prepare for some vocation that will provide financial security and a favorable social status. Usually, the adolescent is free to select an occupation within the limits imposed by his inherited characteristics and by his financial ability to prepare for such an occupation.

Thus, the choice of and preparation for a vocation is a developmental task which becomes increasingly important as the individual matures and nears the end of his schooling. Studies show that occupational planning and preparation are chief concerns of a majority of adolescents.

However, there is necessarily a period of delay between the desire for adult status and its fulfillment, so that the paralyzing force of anxiety often appears.

Developing conscience, morality, and a set of values. The infant must lean entirely on external standards of right and wrong. The goal, however, is for internal discipline gradually to replace external controls. Young adolescents may not be consciously struggling with the problem of developing a "philosophy of life," but they are concerned with ethical and moral problems and are constantly trying to fit into their lives the moral and ethical values passed on to them throughout earlier years from their parents and others. As they grow up, they must acquire a better understanding of the meaning of life and the role of religion in daily living.

Unless the adolescent develops some standard or system of values, he will be without a stable guide to help him in making the decisions he will be required to make later. The kinds of choices he makes are extremely important in relation to his future adjustments and happiness, and much of what he does as an adult and a citizen in a democratic society will be the result of the philosophy of life developed during his adolescent years.

THE ADOLESCENT VIEWS HIMSELF

Faced with the task of growing up in a progressive, dynamic society, how then does the adolescent view himself, and how in turn is he viewed by the adult? Many methods have been used for gaining insight into the adolescent's private world. One of the most informative and most sound is that of having adolescents write compositions describing themselves. Although there are obvious limitations to data obtained from unstructured compositions, the writing can furnish useful information about the thoughts and feelings uppermost in the minds of a representative sampling of adolescents at the time of writing.

Over 2000 compositions on "How It Feels to Be Growing Up" were obtained by Strang from adolescents of a wide range of ability and socioeconomic background, grades 7-12.[6] The dominant feelings expressed in the compositions are summarized in Table 2-2.

The common point of view expressed did not support the belief that adolescence is a period of "stress and strain"; some of the students referred to it as a "nice" period, a "time for fun," and the like. However, many expressed the desire for more independence, a concern about education, vocation, the future, and other practical problems. Significantly, only 4.4 per cent mentioned reluctance to lose their childhood depend-

Table 2-2

DOMINANT FEELINGS EXPRESSED BY ADOLESCENTS IN COMPOSITIONS,
"HOW IT FEELS TO BE GROWING UP"

(*Strang*)

Rank	Category	Per cent
1. Concern with boy-girl relationships		33.4
2. Feeling of increasing independence and self-direction		27.6
3. Concern about vocation of future		26.4
4. Concern with social relationships		25.6
5. Concern with marriage and raising a family		23.1
6. Awareness of increased responsibilities		19.9
7. Feelings about religion or morality		17.6
8. Concern about school success or grades		17.5
9. Problems of sibling relationships		14.9
10. Dissatisfaction with school experiences		12.9
11. Interest in sports		12.3
12. Concern with larger social problems (national, international)		10.5
13. Concern with clothes or appearance		10.3
14. Feels "good," it is "fun," it is a "nice" time of life		9.4
15. Feeling of frustration that independence is not recognized		8.4
16. Viewpoint that adults do not "understand" adolescents		6.1
17. Problems about money		6.1
18. Suggestion of reluctance to lose dependence		4.4
19. Awareness of increasing acceptance in the adult world		4.1
20. Concerns with military service		3.6

ence and 8.4 per cent expressed a feeling of frustration because adults fail to recognize their growing need for independence.

Especially interesting were the viewpoints of specific individuals. The self-concepts covered a range from that of an individual who considered himself "a good person" to one who admitted being selfish and having "an ugly disposition." The criteria involved in self-concepts also varied widely. Some showed much concern about physical appearance, others were particularly concerned with health, and many indicated home conflicts, school problems, or difficulties in making friends. Many expressed a desire for less timidity, popularity with their classmates, greater independence from home ties, or more opportunity to accept responsibility.

A study by Wilson reported that more girls than boys think the teens are a happy time of life.[7] One reason for this is that parents, especially fathers, frequently make greater demands on boys. Many more boys than girls have passed through periods of maladjustment and have thus had some of the drive and enthusiasm for the enjoyment of life taken out of them. Girls in their teens are, according to Wilson, happy because they find conquest of the male an exciting experience, and in their striving to be physically attractive, most feel that they succeed.

Teen-age girls look forward to their twenties when they hope to be married but are afraid they will be trapped by the demands of home-making, motherhood, work, or all three. Teen-age boys look forward unreservedly to their twenties as the period when the chase by girls will have ended and they will have proved their ability to establish and provide for their own homes and families, although a large percentage of boys, especially from urban areas, expect their wives to work after marriage.

Unique self-concept patterns. The adolescent must develop a realistic yet compassionate self-concept in order to lead a stable and useful life. He must learn to accept his own capabilities, then shape his aspirations accordingly. Those unable to see themselves realistically seek various forms of escape from the real world. For example, a young boy may say, "I am not very popular with the gang because I live too far away from them," rather than "because I am too selfish."[8]

Self-acceptance is to a great extent dependent on intellectual abilities. In a comparison by Strang of two eighth grade classes in the same school, one made up of poor learners, the other of able learners, the former's self-assessment and hopes for the future were way beyond what their abilities would indicate, whereas the latter's aims were almost entirely realizable.[9] Both groups mentioned the varied factors that enter into self-concepts: physical characteristics, clothes, attitudes of age-mates toward them, interests, educational plans, and future vocation. Both mentioned their good and bad traits, but the intelligent group seemed to be more realistic than the other.

The able learners looked upon themselves more as average than superior, as for instance in the following: "I think that I am what might be regarded as a normal person. Perhaps other people may think of me as shy or timid. I just like to watch television. Most of the time I enjoy my schoolwork." Individuality seemed to be the key feature of the group as a whole. Each person seemed to be smart in his own way or to display unique interests. This group frequently ran into difficulty with teachers in an effort to maintain individuality.

Adolescents are to a marked degree dependent upon their peers for self-concepts. The adolescent personality is so pliable that the tastes and values of contemporaries become an unquestioned norm which must be followed for group approval, without which the adolescent cannot accept himself. One who is not considered a part of his peer group has serious doubts about himself; similarly, a person unsure of himself lacks confidence even in his apparent acceptance by others.

The self-accepting adolescent is likely to be more forthright in recognizing himself as one who at times is troubled, sexually excited, anxious, uncertain, or angry, without always compulsively pretending to himself and to others that he is serene, assured, and in control. Although he is more honest with himself, the self-accepting adolescent is, as Jersild noted, likely to persist longer against difficulties than the self-rejecting adolescent.

The growing independence and physical strength of the adolescent make it especially important that self-concepts be crystallized, that childlike concepts be reinterpreted in the light of new autonomy,[10] and that the hiatus between the ideal and the real self be breached.[11] The adolescent failing to achieve self-acceptance will find it difficult to cope with his environment.

There is perhaps no period of life more difficult than the adolescent period—the transition stage of life.[12] The adolescent is often not only misunderstood by adults, but also by himself. This will be shown in case studies presented throughout subsequent chapters. The brief case study of Tom, with whom the writer has had close contact, illustrates how an adolescent can be an enigma to himself.

> Tom was slightly late in reaching physical maturity, although he was above average mentally and got better than average grades in school. He developed a keen desire for a repeater shotgun. Over his mother's protest, Tom was given the gun for Christmas. During the next several months he seemed to get much pleasure in going hunting with a good friend of his, a young man his own age.
>
> Most of the usual habits and characteristics common to a large percentage of adolescents were to be found in Tom. He was rather careless; he would forget to clean his gun after hunting, despite his father's continuously calling this to his attention. He would wear a good shirt to school and forget about his clothing and enter into some tumbling or play activities, even though his mother had warned him on many occasions not to. He would leave the lights on in the basement, although he had been reminded of this a number of times. At times he would join with the family; at other times he would prefer to remain in his room listening to the radio or would rather go to the movies with his friends. Just two years before, he seemed to be very fond of his family, his father in particular, and spent a great deal of time with him, yet Tom no longer wished to go with him to watch a practice ball game; he preferred other activities—watching television and playing with his friends. Tom himself could not understand why he changed in some of his interests and activities as rapidly as he did, and why he always forgot things. Thus, Tom, a normal adolescent boy, was understood neither by his family nor by himself.

ADOLESCENCE AND THE SOCIAL STRUCTURE

The status of adolescence in American society. The preadolescent attempts to break away from childhood and begins to think of himself as an independent agent. The preadolescent girl is especially anxious to take on the ways of her older counterparts; she wants to wear lipstick, dress up in high heels, and even go out on dates. Likewise, the preadolescent boy strives to prove his masculine nature; he may smoke, brag, or swear in order to prove his "grown-up" characteristics.

Hess and Goldblatt once attempted to ascertain the status of the adolescent in American society.[13] They used a rating scale consisting of 20 pairs of adjectives to obtain evaluations of adolescent and adult reputations. Each pair of adjectives was set up in a seven-point scale, with seven the highest or most desirable point in the scale and one the lowest. The subjects, consisting of 32 teen-agers and 54 parents, were asked to use the scale in making ratings on the "average teen-ager" and the "average adult."

The results of the study, presented in Table 2-3, indicated a significant similarity between the adolescents and adults in the ratings given the different items of the scale. There was, however, an indication that adolescents tended to idealize adults; they rated adults on all of the traits as more desirable than the adults rated themselves. Three trends in the data relevant to parent-adolescent relationships were pointed out by the investigators: "the agreement between the two groups in their evaluation of teen-agers, the perceptual distortions of both groups in predicting the response of the other group, and the immense status difference between the groups that teen-agers believe exists in the minds of adults."[14]

Social demands upon adolescents. Frank has emphasized the importance of social demands on the attitudes and behavior of adolescents. With the development into adolescence, the individual must face a *new self*, with added physical and mental abilities and an emerging sex drive.[15] Also, he must learn to adapt to a society in which his role in the group has changed. New demands are made upon him. Once excused from many acts because of immaturity, he is now expected to assume the role of an adult. He is expected to remain in school, study hard, make difficult educational and vocational decisions, and conform to adult behavior standards. Concerning the effects of the new social demands made upon adolescents Barclay states:

"He is likely to feel—or be made to believe he should feel—a deepening sense of responsibility for himself and for others, an increased realization of the value of work to the world and to his own future. He must begin making his way toward emotional and economic independence; and yet, so long is the preparation period for adulthood today, he must somehow manage to gain increasing freedom and grow in self-management while still dependent in every vital aspect of life."[16]

The role of sex. In all societies the initial status of the child is that of a member of a kinship unit. In early childhood the sexes are usually not sharply differentiated, although in some cultures a relatively sharp segregation of children begins very early. Our own society is conspicuous for the extent to which children of both sexes are in many fundamental respects treated alike during the early years. The primary distinction within the group of dependent siblings involves age differences.[17]

Girls at all ages beyond infancy are likely to be relatively more docile than boys and to conform to adult expectations, to "be good." Boys, on the other hand, are apt to be stubborn and defiant of adult authority. Equality of privileges and responsibilities, graded mainly by age rather than sex, is extended to a certain degree throughout the whole

Table 2-3

RATINGS OF ADOLESCENTS AND ADULTS

Traits	Ratings by adolescents		Ratings by adults	
	Teen-agers	Adults	Teen-agers	Adults
Neat-untidy	4.81	5.88	3.98	5.00
Patient-impatient	2.94	4.72	2.48	3.69
Cooperative-uncooperative	4.59	5.38	4.45	4.84
Serious-frivolous	4.50	5.56	4.80	5.20
Responsible-irresponsible	4.62	6.22	4.87	5.24
Courteous-rude	4.81	5.81	4.44	4.86
Mature-immature	4.62	6.06	3.98	5.02
Cautious-impulsive	2.69	5.44	2.72	4.78
Consistent-inconsistent	3.56	5.44	3.57	4.18
Grateful-ungrateful	4.81	5.72	4.59	4.82
Reliable-unreliable	5.19	5.97	4.98	5.10
Stable-unstable	4.35	5.47	4.45	4.76
Moral-immoral	5.16	5.53	5.98	5.46
Self-directed–easily influenced	3.72	5.28	4.18	4.32
Respectful-disrespectful	4.78	5.75	4.50	5.22
Unspoiled-spoiled	3.97	5.03	3.70	4.31
Considerate-inconsiderate	4.44	5.62	4.22	4.78
Self-controlled–wild	4.59	5.88	4.62	5.34
Thoughtful-thoughtless	4.66	5.66	4.09	5.24
Loving-angry	4.81	5.69	4.83	5.14
Means	4.38	5.60	4.27	4.71

life cycle, based mainly on individual ability to assume responsibility and on class status.

Youth culture. During the early years of adolescence there appears a set of behavior patterns which involves a complex combination of age grading along with sex-role identification. It is then that each sex must begin behaving according to the pattern set forth for it. Such behavior patterns begin to take shape within the youth social culture that exists in America, distinct from the adult culture, yet an adaptation of its norms and behavior. It accepts the patterns of competition and individual success, social class position, conformity, sex glamour, and parental family life with its formal morality and material subsistence. On the other hand, it has a solidarity and concealment of behavior; a withdrawal from adult socializing agencies; modification of adult behavor, appearance, and dress; a sex code of its own that permits progressive intimacies; and a language all its own. Youth's high degree of conformity is based on an adolescent biological need to be accepted and identified with the group, but it is excessively synthesizing a dominant cultural pattern of compulsive conformity.

SUMMARY

Today's adolescent is growing up in a world radically different from that of his forebears. Mass production, automation, urbanization, materialism, and a great conflict in values have all changed our society greatly and created new problems for the growing child. He is no longer an economic necessity at home, but is more dependent than ever before, and dependent for a longer time since he requires a longer period of education. Material change is reflected in moral change, a change which leaves youth without a definite set of values to grasp.

Against this changing background, the adolescent must still accomplish the age-old task of growing up; he must adjust to his parents, establish friendships, acquire an appropriate sex role, develop intellectually, attain economic independence, and evolve a set of values.

Adolescents see the period until adulthood as beset with problems, but generally enjoy themselves, the girls more than the boys. Adults seem to have more respect for their children than is generally supposed. As they mature, young people tend to create a culture of their own, a microcosmic adult culture.

THOUGHT PROBLEMS

1. Consider the developmental tasks presented in Table 2-1. Present a full discussion of the nature and problems of one of these tasks at different age levels.
2. What are some methods used by investigators to study the self-concepts of adolescents? Criticize these methods.
3. How would you account for the greater docility of girls than boys? Illustrate this from your observations.
4. What are the major conclusions to be drawn from Table 2-2? What are the educational implications of these conclusions?
5. Just what do you understand the term "youth culture" to mean? How would you account for the distinct youth culture found among adolescents in the United States?
6. Show how *automation* has aggravated the problems of adolescents.

7. How would you account for the *increased period of schooling* which has become a part of our civilization? How has this increased the problems of adolescents?

8. How has *urbanization* affected adolescent culture? Look up materials bearing on this.

9. What are the major conclusions to be drawn from Table 2-3? What are the implications of these findings for adult leaders of teen-agers?

SELECTED REFERENCES

Cole, Luella, *Psychology of Adolescence,* 6th ed. New York: Holt, Rinehart & Winston, Inc., 1964, Chap. 1.

Coleman, James S., *The Adolescent Society.* New York: The Free Press of Glencoe, Inc., 1961, Chaps. 1 and 2.

Friedenberg, Edgar Z., *The Vanishing Adolescent.* Boston: Beacon Press, 1959.

Hemming, James, *Problems of Adolescent Girls.* London: William Heinemann, Ltd., 1960, Chap. 1.

Jersild, Arthur T., *The Psychology of Adolescence,* 2nd ed. New York: The Macmillan Company, 1963, Chap. 2.

Josselyn, Irene M., *The Adolescent and His World.* New York: Family Service Association of America, Chap. 3.

Rogers, Dorothy, *The Psychology of Adolescence.* New York: Appleton-Century-Crofts, Inc., 1962, Chap. 2.

Seidman, Jerome M., ed., *The Adolescent—A Book of Readings,* 2nd ed. New York: Holt, Rinehart & Winston, Inc., 1960, Chap. 2.

Smith, E. A., *American Youth Culture; Group Life in Teen Age Society.* New York: The Free Press of Glencoe, Inc., 1961, Chap. 1.

Staton, Thomas F., *Dynamics of Adolescent Adjustment.* New York: The Macmillan Company, 1963, Chap. 6.

Strang, Ruth, *The Adolescent Views Himself.* New York: McGraw-Hill Book Company, 1957, Chap. 2.

NOTES

[1] Robert D. Hess and Irene Goldblatt, "The Status of Adolescents in American Society: A Problem in Social Identity," *Child Development,* 28 (1957), 459-68.

[2] Walter B. Simon, "Youth and Authority," *The Toronto Education Quarterly,* 2 (Spring, 1963), 9-13.

[3] Irene M. Josselyn, "Are We Prolonging Youth's Dependence?" *National Parent Teacher,* 51 (1957), 4-6.

[4] Robert J. Havighurst, *Developmental Tasks and Education* (Chicago: University of Chicago Press, 1948), p. 86.

[5] H. H. Remmers and D. H. Radler, *The American Teen-ager* (The Bobbs-Merrill Company, Inc., 1957), pp. 87-88.

[6] Ruth Strang, "Adolescent Views on One Aspect of Their Development," *Journal of Educational Psychology,* 46 (1955), 423-32.

[7] Frances M. Wilson, "More Girls than Boys Think Teens Best Years," *Science News Letter,* 68 (1957), 265.

[8] Arthur T. Jersild, *The Psychology of Adolescence* (New York: The Macmillan Company, 1957), Chap. 17.

9 Ruth Strang, *The Adolescent Views Himself* (New York: McGraw-Hill Book Company, 1957), pp. 89-96.

10 Thomas F. Staton, *Dynamics of Adolescent Adjustment* (New York: The Macmillan Company, 1963), Chap. 6.

11 Dorothy Rogers, *The Psychology of Adolescence* (New York: Appleton-Century-Crofts, 1962), Chap. 2.

12 Sister M. Paul, O.S. F., "Understanding the Adolescent," *Catholic School Journal,* **60** (1960), 21.

13 Hess and Goldblatt, *op. cit.*

14 *Ibid.,* p. 467.

15 L. K. Frank, Introduction: Adolescence as a Period of Transition," *Forty-third Yearbook of the National Society for the Study of Education, Part 1* (Chicago: Department of Education, University of Chicago, 1944), Chap. 1.

16 Dorothy Barclay, "Adolescents in Suburbia," *Journal of the National Educational Association,* **48** (January, 1959), 11.

17 Talcott Parsons, "Age and Sex in the Social Structure of the United States," *American Sociological Review,* **7** (October, 1942), 604-16.

PART TWO

GROWTH
AND
DEVELOPMENT
IN
ADOLESCENCE

3

PHYSIOLOGICAL GROWTH AND DEVELOPMENT

INTRODUCTION: THE NATURE AND SIGNIFICANCE OF GROWTH

The growth of an individual from birth to maturity constitutes a considerable amount of time—almost one-third of the normal life span. Simple physiological growth, then, plays a tremendously important part in a person's development. The materials of the next two chapters are designed to give the student a better understanding of the conditions of growth and their effect on personality, through presentation of data from various genetic studies.

Change goes on constantly in living cells—as once said, "life is a process of changing." The growing child is constantly faced with new and different forces of two special types. The one is organic, and is in essence the physiological process occurring in all living organisms; energy is being made available through the metabolic processes related to food assimilation and is released through activity. The other force is man's external environment, which continuously stimulates a reaction. Concerning the effect of these forces, Boswell states:

Each living organism, in relation to internal as well as to external changes and conditions, tends to maintain itself as an integrated whole, as do also social organisms and a wide range of animate things. Each is, then, not merely something happening, but is a complex, integrated, and unified system of activities. Thus, definite internal changes are taking place within each living being in accordance with its character and mode of life; and all its vital mechanisms, however varied, combine to maintain a uniform dynamic state or "field" within each individual, in the face of fluctuating conditions of internal or external stimulation.[1]

Thus, it may be noted that the development of the individual is a result of conditions set forth in the germ plasm and environmental stimulation continuously operating on the growing organism.

How development occurs. The individual is constantly affected by the environment. From the moment the egg is fertilized until death, we may say that a person is always responding to stimuli. His behavior may very well be considered as composed of a series of responses to a continuous series of successive situations. We speak of the action of the environment upon the individual, but we do not mean exactly what the statement implies. The individual has hereditary characteristics, limits that will confine his development whatever the environmental conditions may be, yet he always reacts to the stimulus. He cannot be considered an inert, static thing merely being impressed by its surroundings; he is active toward the environment, and activity toward a situation tends to change the meaning of a situation so that it is never again the same for him. Not only does activity toward a situation tend to give meaning to the situation, but it also develops characteristic ways of behaving—habits. By regulating the environment, the individual's reactions—and thus his development—may to some extent be controlled.

Only by definition can we separate the individual and his environment. There is a continuous interaction between them so long as the individual survives. Any statement regarding the individual that takes account of his biological nature must emphasize this mutual relationship. It may be stated thus: *the individual may be conceived of as protoplasm capable of maintaining itself by responding to a changing environment; during life, many of these responses become fixed or characteristic, so that we may consider an individual as a bit of protoplasm possessing more or less definite patterns of response.* Or, if we desire to think of him purely in terms of action, we may say: *the individual is a relational sum-total of behavior patterns developed in protoplasm in response to environment—* in which sense the individual is considered neither as protoplasm nor as environment but as the result of the reaction of the one to the other.

Importance of studying physical development. The momentous work of G. Stanley Hall, referred to in Chapter 1, gave very little attention to the physiological changes occurring in adolescence. Physiologists of his day did not understand the differences between children, adolescents, and adults in the functioning of the organism. Today, it is generally recognized that the young child is not a miniature adult; likewise, that the adolescent is neither a child nor an adult in his physiological reactions. Physical development during adolescence must therefore be studied by itself.

Longitudinal studies are the best means for supplying a valid index of the rate and periodicity of physiological growth during adolescence. However, since reliable and interpretable data on changes in body chemistry are difficult to obtain, only a small number of such studies have been conducted. Nonetheless those that have been made supply not only purely scientific data, but also a basis for understanding and guiding growing boys and girls. For example, a study of the physiological differences in the rate of development of the sexes gives one a better perspective on the earlier changes of interest among girls during their passage from childhood or helps in planning a physical education program. Mental hygiene problems, behavior disorders, and other maladjustments can also be better understood by studying a pupil's physical development.

Physiological changes. Children often suffer from the "tyranny of the norm," an expectation that at a certain chronological age they will be a "normal" size and will have "normal" physical abilities. There is, however, no "normal" physical development commensurate with each age level. Each person's growth is not dependent on his chronological age, but rather on *physiological age,* the extent of sexual development. Changes in height, weight, metabolism, and strength all hinge on the occurrence of puberty. The wide individual differences in the time of the onset of puberty and in rates of change should be recognized. The materials presented throughout this chapter are not for the purpose of providing a standard to judge physiological development of the individual, but to emphasize how boys and girls may vary greatly from the average and still stay within the range of natural development.

Endocrine factors in relation to development. The pituitary gland is by far the most important organ in relation to growth. Two hormones in particular from this gland are especially influential. One is the growth hormone, which enables the healthy, well-nourished child to attain his normal body size. If there is a deficiency of this hormone, normal growth will be retarded, and a form of pituitary dwarfism will result. On the other hand, if an excess is produced during the growing period, pituitary gigantism will follow. The other pituitary hormone of special importance in maturation is the gonad-stimulating hormone. A deficiency of this hormone durng preadolescence would interfere with the normal growth and development of the ovaries or testes; an oversupply would tend to produce precocious sexual development. The importance of properly timed action of the growth and gonad-stimulating hormones has been pointed out by Greulich:

> If the testes or ovaries begin to function at the requisite level too early in life, growth is arrested prematurely and the child ends up abnormally short. If, on the other hand, the adequate production of the ovarian and testicular hormones is unduly delayed, growth, particularly that of the limbs, continues

for too long a period and the characteristic bodily proportions of the eunuch are attained. It appears, therefore, that normal growth and development are contingent upon the reciprocal and properly timed action of pituitary [growth] and gonadal hormones.[2]

A number of studies have been conducted relating to gonadotrophic hormone secretion in children. In general these studies indicate that excretion of the hormone in early childhood in both sexes is too slight to be detected by the methods used; measurable amounts first appeared in the urine during adolescence. Greulich and others reported on the results of 120 urinary gonadotrophin assays performed on 64 boys:

> The results show that with advancing age and with advancing developmental status there is a general tendency for gonadotrophin to increase in amount from the undetectable levels of early childhood to levels more characteristic of the adult. There is as yet no direct evidence as to the biological nature of this gonadotrophin; on the other hand, it does not seem likely that it differs from the hormone found in the urine of the adult male. . . . it seems reasonable to suppose that the primary changes of puberty, namely an increase in size of the testes and the initiation of spermatogenesis, are related to the action of this gonadotrophin upon the seminiferous tubules.[3]

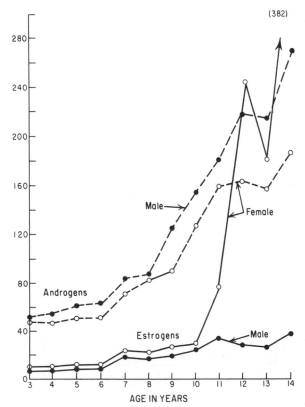

Figure 3-1

AGE CHANGES IN EXCRETION OF SEX HORMONES. THE FEMALE SEX HORMONE, PRODUCED BY THE OVARY, IS THE CHIEF ESTROGENIC HORMONE

(*After Nathanson, et al.*)

Nathanson and others have reported somewhat similar results.[4] Average curves for boys and girls are presented in Figure 3-1. Note that before the ages of 10 or 11, both boys and girls excrete measurable amounts of male and female hormones. The increase of female sex hormones in the girl leads to the growth of breasts at menarche, and the increase of male hormones in the boy produces significant changes.

The female reproductive organs do not begin to function suddenly at menarche. At the time of the first menstruation the ovarian glands have attained only 30 per cent of their mature size, and their functional efficiency is low. A somewhat comparable but more prolonged period of sexual development occurs with boys. The adolescent must continuously adjust to these changes in the balance of his glandular secretions, since the development of the reproductive powers is progressive. Aspects of these adjustments may be noted in his social-sex development and changed interests.

The pubescent period. Data on sexual development of a group of 97 girls, based on a study made by Bryan, are presented in Table 3-1.[5] The immaturity point is defined as the age at which the girls have begun to show changes associated with sexual development. From a further analysis of the data Bryan found the average age of beginning breast development to be approximately 10.7 years; of pubic hair, 11.5 years; of axillary hair, 12.5 years; and of menarche 13.1 years.

Table 3-1

PERCENTAGE OF GIRLS SHOWING SEXUAL MATURITY IN DIFFERENT CATEGORIES

(*Bryan*)

Age at last birthday	Number of girls	Per cent immature with respect to:			
		breast	pubic hair	axillary hair	menarche
9	11	82	100	100	100
10	22	50	82	95	100
11	17	35	53	71	94
12	21	0	15	62	71
13	26	4	4	16	35

Sexual maturation seems, however, to be related to living standards. In the highly developed countries of Western civilization the mean age at menarche has steadily declined in the past century at a rate of approximately four months each decade. In 1959 the mean age of menarche for London schoolgirls was 13.1 years.

Burrell and others made a study of different races of girls to determine possible genetic influences on the age of menarche.[6] They found, however, that incidence of menarche was heavily dependent on living conditions. For example, 47,420 Bantu schoolgirls were divided into two groups: those from poor and those from comparatively wealthy homes. The latter group underwent menarche significantly earlier than the former, as shown in Table 3-2. The researchers also found that the mean age for well-nourished Burmese and Assamese girls was 13.2.

Table 3-2

DISTRIBUTION OF AGE AT MENARCHE OF BANTU GIRLS FROM POOR AND COMPARATIVELY WEALTHY HOMES
(*Burrell*, et al.)

Per cent at menarche	10	25	50	75	90
Age in years from poor homes	13.6	14.5	15.4	16.3	17.2
Age in years from comparatively wealthy homes	13.4	14.2	15.2	15.8	16.6

In the West Indies, menarche among the Negroes occurs later than in the United States. Yet there is no significant difference between the mean age of menarche of the Negro girl in the United States and that of the white girl.[7] Also, Negro girls mature earlier today than formerly; hence it seems safe to conclude that living standards do play an important part in determining the age of menarche.

The problem of determining the exact age of puberty is more difficult for boys than for girls. No clear-cut line of demarcation such as that provided by the menarche in girls is present for determining the exact period of puberty for boys. Ellis reports a study that compared the percentage of Nigerian school boys with a group of boys in Great Britain who had reached puberty.[8] The Nigerian school boys represent a select group and may be thought of as having living standards comparable to boys in Great Britain. Any method of classifying boys in terms of pubescence must be somewhat subjective, since one stage of development passes gradually rather than abruptly into the next; however, the grading system used by Ellis served to separate the great majority of cases into three groups. A total of 333 Nigerian boys aged 9 to 18 were examined and compared with a control group of 662 boys examined in Great Britain. The per cents of boys graded as pubescent in each year of age are given in Table 3-3. No significant differences appear in the age of pubescence for these two groups. The median ages when 50 per cent of the boys are pubescent, or more mature, was 13.14 for the boys in Great Britain and 12.95 for the boys in Nigeria.

Blood pressure, heart, and pulse rate. The growth of the heart, like

Table 3-3

PUBESCENCE IN NIGERIAN SCHOOLBOYS
COMPARED TO THAT OF A CONTROL GROUP IN
GREAT BRITAIN

(*Ellis*)

Age group	Per cent pubescent*	
	Nigeria	Great Britain
9–10	6	0
10–11	6.5	5.0
11–12	21.2	13.5
12–13	40.8	35.8
13–14	38.9	43.7
14–15	48.5	39.2
15–16	18.7	29.5
16–17	16.7	18.2
17–18	0	11.4

* The sum of the per cents for each group is more than 100, since the period of pubescence includes a period of more than one year for most of the boys. Thus, many boys are counted more than once. The criteria used for grading were: *nonpubescent* when pigmented pubic hair was entirely absent and genital development infantile; *pubescent* when pigmented pubic hair and/or early but incomplete genital development was present; and adolescent or *postpubescent* when both growth of pubic hair and genital development were advanced.

that of other organs of the body, follows a course of its own. During the adolescent years its weight nearly doubles, and its transverse diameter, as shown in Figure 3-2, increases by almost one-half.[9] During most of childhood, boys' hearts are a little larger than girls; then from approximately 9 to 14, girls' are larger. From 13 on, boys' hearts continue to grow at a rapid pace, girls' very slowly.

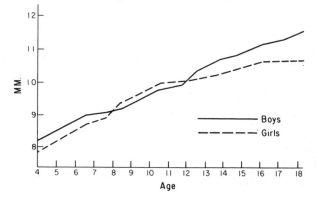

Figure 3-2

GROWTH IN THE TRANS-
VERSE DIAMETER OF
THE HEART FROM AGES
4 TO 18

(*Marsh*)

The veins and arteries do not follow the same growth pattern as that of the heart. Prior to adolescence they grow quite rapidly, whereas they show little growth during adolescence, when the heart is growing rapidly. Thus, the preadolescent may be said to have a relatively small heart with large arteries. Changes during adolescence in the relative ratio of the size of the heart to the arteries are reflected in changes in blood pressure.[10] During early childhood, blood pressure is nearly the same in both sexes, but between the ages of 10 and 13 blood pressure is higher in girls than in boys; after the age 13 the pressure of boys exceeds that of girls, the difference increasing with age. This is an example of the general trend toward an earlier incidence of maturity among girls, a trend which has been observed in connection with other developmental characteristics.

An exaggerated fear still exists that the adolescent will overtax his heart through exertion and is usually founded on a belief in the lack of harmony between the development of the heart and that of the blood vessels. This idea was pointed out as early as 1879 by Beneke.[11] He pointed out that the volume of the heart increases in proportion to the body weight; the circumferences of the aorta and the pulmonary artery increase in proportion to the body length. These observations are essentially correct but the interpretations and generalizations based on them are misleading. For example, as late as 1931 a text translated from the German stated:

> . . . the heart of an adult man is three times the size of the child's, while the proportionate circumference of the aorta (close to the heart) remains the same. . . . We can readily see that no system of exercise can meet the first principles of practical hygiene, unless it recognizes the physiological condition described.

The volumetric capacity of the aorta and other blood vessels is proportional to the *area* of the cross section of the aorta rather than to the circumference.

The California Growth Studies, begun in 1932, have furnished useful and valuable data about the development and characteristics of adolescents.[12] One such study measured in various ways every six months a sample of 215 cases selected from the fifth and sixth grades of six elementary schools. These studies revealed that with the beginning of menstruation a pronounced change occurred in pulse rate, systolic blood pressure, and oxygen consumption.[13] The results of this analysis for a total of 52 cases are presented in Figure 3-3.

Both the lungs and the liver show a pronounced increase in growth during adolescence; between the ages of 10 and 14 for girls, one or two years later for boys.

Age changes in basal metabolism. Probably the most striking non-sexual physiological change appearing at the time of puberty is the rather

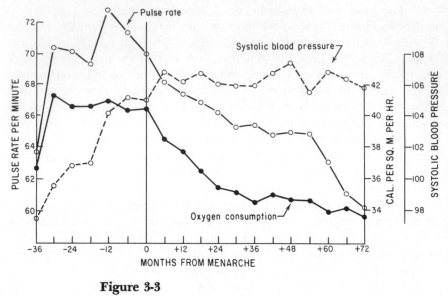

Figure 3-3

BASAL FUNCTIONS AS RELATED TO MATURITY
(*Shock*)

sudden decline in basal metabolism.[14] This decline presents quite a contrast with the change in blood pressure pointed out earlier; there is little change registered in blood pressure after the menarche, yet there is a continuous decrease in basal metabolism throughout the teen years for both boys and girls. This is shown in Figure 3-4, which is based upon materials from the California study. Over one-half the cases illustrated in the figure showed a pronounced decrease.

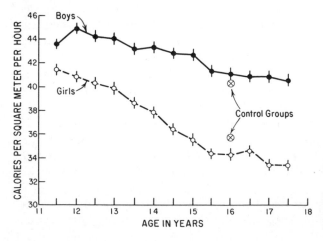

Figure 3-4

AGE CHANGES IN BASAL METABOLISM FROM REPEATED TESTS ON THE SAME SUBJECTS (SMOOTHED DATA) (*After Shock*)

Individual curves show a marked increase just before or at puberty, followed by a conspicuous decrease. This is shown, in Case C9, for an adolescent girl in Figure 3-5. The adolescent decline is followed by a recovery to an adult level which is then maintained. There are, however, cases which do not conform to this pattern. The individual slump in

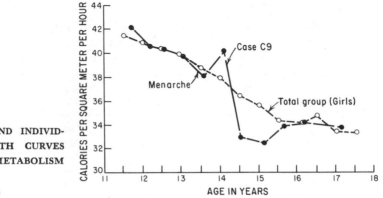

Figure 3-5

AVERAGE AND INDIVIDUAL GROWTH CURVES OF BASAL METABOLISM FOR GIRLS

(*After Shock*)

metabolic rate exists among both boys and girls, and should be taken into consideration by those concerned with the guidance of adolescents. For example, the adolescent who appears sluggish in his activities may be suffering from a low metabolic rate.

The digestive system. Pronounced changes in the organs of digestion also occur during adolescence. The stomach increases in size and capacity and undergoes qualitative changes. The increased size of his stomach, along with his greater need for food caused by rapid growth, is closely related to the adolescent's strong cravings for food. This craving persists throughout the adolescent years, and adolescents are able to assimilate amounts of food that they could not earlier.

When the child is adding three inches to his height, his calcium need will perhaps be twice as high as during the period following puberty. He will also need about three times the protein required in adult life in order to attain optimum storage of nitrogen in the muscle tissues and achieve a normal metabolism. Caloric needs of the average adolescent are presented in Table 3-4.[15]

Nutrition requirements vary according to the height, weight, volume of muscle and bone tissue, and metabolic rate of the individual. In general, changes in nutritional needs and actual assimilation of food elements that make up muscle and bone parallel the growth rate, and since the latter varies from one person to another, food requirements also vary.[16] Burke and others noted wide calcium intake variations in adolescents of the same sex.[17] Usually the individual appetite acts as a natural guide to fulfilling nutritional requirements.[18] Often, however, girls do not eat a sufficient number of calories, in an attempt to change their figures, and boys indulge themselves with too many carbohydrates; both in disregard of teachings about health and balanced diets.

Table 3-4

NUMBER OF CALORIES PER DAY NEEDED BY TYPICAL ADOLESCENT BOYS AND GIRLS, ACCORDING TO AGE
(After Johnston)

| Age | Calories required | | Age | Calories required | |
	Girls	Boys		Girls	Boys
10	2000	2000	15	2500	3000
11	2100	2200	16	2400	3200
12	2200	2400	17	2400	3400
13	2300	2600	18	2400	3600
14	2400	2800	19	2400	3800

SPECIAL GROWTH CHARACTERISTICS AND PROBLEMS

The skin glands. Marked changes take place in the structure of the skin and in the activity of the skin glands as the individual matures sexually; the soft, delicate skin of childhood gradually becomes thicker and coarser, and the pores become enlarged, a development closely related to adolescent skin disturbances and blemishes.

There are three different kinds of skin glands, each of which is distinctly separate from the others. They are (1) the *merocrine glands,* which are scattered over most of the skin surfaces of the body, (2) the *apocrine sweat glands,* which are limited primarily to the armpits, mammary, genital, and anal regions, and (3) the *sebaceous glands,* the oil-producing glands of the skin.

a. *Merocrine and apocrine sweat glands.* The merocrine and apocrine sweat glands of the armpits become increasingly active during adolescence, even before the growth of axillary hair. Their secretion is fatty and has a pronounced odor that is usually not detectable in boys prior to puberty but becomes more pronounced during the early adolescent years. Among girls the apocrine sweat glands appear to undergo a cycle of secretory activity during the menstrual cycle.

b. *Sebaceous glands.* The increased size and activity of the sebaceous glands during puberty is thought to be closely associated with skin disturbances during adolescence. There is a disproportion between the size and activity of these glands and the size of the gland ducts that begins at puberty, so that they frequently become plugged with dried oil and turn black as a result of oxidation in the dried oil upon exposure to the air. These plugged gland ducts are generally referred to as blackheads, and are most often found on the nose and chin. The glands continue to function, even though the opening has been blocked, and raised pimples then appear on the surface of the skin.

There has been considerable talk about acne being caused by certain foods, particularly sweets. Although some individual cases are aggravated by chocolates, nuts, or some other specific food, the most important thing about nutrition is for the individual to eat three nourishing meals each day with food particularly rich in proteins, minerals, and vitamins.

The sebaceous glands are also associated with hair follicles, and are absent from the skin in some regions where there is a lack of hair, such as on the palms of the hands. During puberty the sebaceous glands are associated with disproportionately small hairs. This causes a temporary maladjustment, and is regarded as the major reason for acne. There is some evidence that an excess of male hormones may also be an important factor in the causation of acne.

There is evidence that emotional upsets are closely associated with acne. For example, a boy may have a bad case of acne after a violent argument with his father. Again, the chemical imbalance resulting seems to provide for an overstimulation of the oily glands of the skin. Washing the affected part several times each day is usually recommended to help reduce acne. However, too violent a scrubbing, strong soaps, and intense squeezing or pinching of blackheads only aggravate the condition. Acne sometimes presents a problem that should receive the attention of a specialist.

Distribution of subcutaneous fat. During childhood there is a pronounced reduction in the amount of fat over the thorax, abdomen, and back. The reduction is less marked in girls, and the fat over the abdomen continues to increase during childhood. After about the tenth year, the fat gradually increases in boys. In later years, the amount of fat over the back, the thorax, and especially the abdomen increases in girls more than in boys.

A study by Reynolds furnished certain quantitative information about the amount and distribution of subcutaneous fat in various regions of the body.[19] Means and medians for different age levels, measurements based on results obtained from six individual tissue areas, are presented in Figure 3-6. There were, of course, some differences in growth patterns for the different areas; however, in general, the similarities were striking. A second observation resulting from this study showed consistent sex differences; girls displayed a pattern of greater fat thickness than boys, in all six areas. The steady rise, during the period studied, in mean values for girls, and the drop at adolescence in boys were in harmony with results obtained by other investigators. The drop in the curves for girls at the upper age limits may be accounted for by the small number of cases in these age groups or by the problem of selection.

Changes in hair. Changes occur in the hair as well as in the skin during early adolescence. Three kinds of hair succeed each other during one's life span: *lanugo,* unpigmented hair, which appears during the last three months of intra-uterine life; *vellus,* down hair, which replaces lanugo and persists during infancy and childhood; and *terminal,* which replaces the childhood hair and becomes the dominant type in the adult. This re-

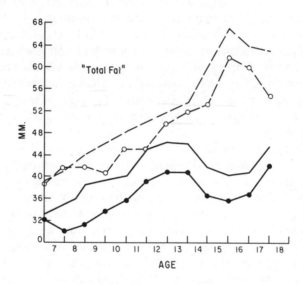

Figure 3-6

MEANS (BOYS, SOLID LINES; GIRLS, BROKEN LINES) AND MEDIANS (BOYS, SOLID CIRCLES; GIRLS, MIXED CIRCLES) FOR TOTAL FAT BREADTH *(Reynolds)*

placement is greatly accelerated during puberty and continues at a less rapid rate throughout adult life.

There is also a distinct change in the shape of the hairline on the forehead as the individual begins to mature. This has been referred to as a secondary sexual characteristic. The hairline of immature boys and girls follows an uninterrupted bow-like curve, as illustrated in the upper row of Figure 3-7. In mature males, the curved hairline is interrupted by a wedge-shaped recess on each side of the forehead. Greulich and others found this characteristic to be a late rather than an early developmental feature.[20]

a. *Facial hair.* There are no marked sexual differences during childhood in the vellus of the upper lips, cheeks, and chin. Among boys, the downy hairs at the corners of the upper lip become noticeable beginning with puberty. This development extends medially from each corner of the upper lip, and eventually forms a mustache of rather fine hair which is perceptibly larger, coarser, and darker than the vellus hair it replaces.

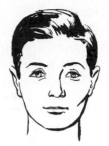

Figure 3-7

ADOLESCENT CHANGES
IN HAIRLINE AND FA-
CIAL CONTOURS

The mustache becomes progressively coarser and more heavily pigmented as the individual passes through adolescence. During the period when the mustache is developing, the vellus over the upper part of the cheeks increases in length and diameter. It persists as long, coarse down until the juvenile mustache is fairly well developed. Somewhat later, a thin growth of long, rather coarse, pigmented hairs appears along the sides and lower parts of the chin and on the upper part of the face just in front of the ears. These, too, gradually become coarser and more heavily developed, eventually forming a beard.

b. *Pubic hair.* Pubic hair is a secondary sex characteristic that appears during puberty. However, not until the growth of the genitals is well under way does the terminal hair appear to replace the vellus. It has been customary to associate the amount and extension of terminal hair over the body with the degree of masculinity in terms of sexual potency; however, there is no indication that a close association exists.

c. *Axillary hair.* The axillary hair does not usually appear until the development of the pubic hair is nearly complete. The transition from vellus to terminal hair in the axilla is quite similar to changes in hair in other regions of the body, and the amount of axillary hair appearing is closely associated with the development of other body hair. Among boys,

Table 3-5

ITEMS OF SELF-DESCRIPTION CHECKED BY 10 PER CENT OR MORE OF 580
TENTH-GRADE BOYS AND GIRLS, WITH AMOUNT OF EXPRESSED CONCERN
(*After Frazier and Lisonbee*)

Boys			*Girls*		
Item of description	*Per cent check-ing*	*Per cent of con-cern*	*Item of description*	*Per cent check-ing*	*Per cent of con-cern*
Blackheads or pimples	57	51	Blackheads or pimples	57	82
Lack of beard	34	2	Heavy eyebrows	24	11
Heavy eyebrows	27	1	Freckles	23	24
Scars, birthmarks, moles	20	13	Oily skin	22	52
Irregular teeth	17	39	Scars, birthmarks, moles	22	30
Heavy lips	14	5	Glasses	21	31
Protruding chin	13	6	High forehead	19	8
Ears stick out	13	6	Too round face	19	21
Oily skin	12	27	Too homely	18	42
Freckles	12	—	Dry skin	16	43
Heavy beard	11	13	Irregular teeth	16	42
Glasses	11	23	Thin lips	15	13
Dark skin	10	4	Low forehead	13	3
Receding chin	10	4	Too long nose	11	23
Gaps in teeth	10	26	Too big nose	11	44
Too long nose	10	8	Receding chin	10	13
Too thin face	10	15	Odd-shaped nose	10	23
Too large ears	10	8			

the development of terminal hair on the limbs and trunk begins during the early stages of adolescence, with growth rather rapid at first. Terminal hair on the limbs begins to appear first on the upper part of the forearm, later on the sides of the lower arms, and then on the back of the hands.

After the transition from long down to terminal hair has made considerable progress, a similar process begins on the distal half of the leg. It gradually extends upward toward the knee. The extension of the hair-covered areas from the centers on the trunk and limbs proceeds at different rates of speed in different boys, and the amount of hair developed will vary considerably from individual to individual. By the age of 18 or 19 the growth of hair on the arms is fairly heavy for the majority of boys. Also, there is a moderate growth of terminal hair over the legs, thighs, and buttocks as well as a varying amount on the ventral surface of the trunk.

Special problems related to physiological growth. The physiological changes associated with adolescence present conditions the individual has not yet met and, in many cases, is ill-prepared to meet. For the girl, the period of the menarche can be a real problem when she has not been prepared for it, or, if she is prepared, when too much concern has been shown over it. Some groups overemphasize the seriousness of the changes appearing at this time—thus causing the girl to limit her activities unnecessarily.

Skin blemishes and acne as well as body odors disturb many boys and girls of this age. In fact, Frazier and Lisonbee found, as shown in Table 3-5, that the main concern of over half a group of tenth-graders was their poor skin. Some tend to go to an extreme in the use of perfumes, lotions, and other toilet articles in an effort to combat these problems.

The appearance of axillary hair is in some cases a source of disturbance for girls; the lack of hair on the arms and legs is regarded by many boys as a weakness. The growth of hair on the chin and upper lip presents one more problem for the adolescent boy: he must learn to shave.

SUMMARY

In recent years we have witnessed an increased attention to the physiological changes that occur during the adolescent years. Since growth in height and weight is easy to observe and measure, it is but natural that it would have first received the attention of students of adolescent psychology. Pronounced individual differences appear in the change of pulse rate, blood pressure, and glandular secretions so that it is safer to evaluate the individual's development in terms of measurements made during the growing years than to rely upon the norm or average.

There is ample evidence that the endocrines play an important role in physiological changes taking place during adolescence. They pave the way and initiate many changes connected with the sex drive as well as physical growth. The California longitudinal studies of physiological changes and other studies provide valuable data for arriving at a clearer understanding of the nature and characteristics of these changes in relation to various internal and external forces and conditions.

In our society, many problems, interwoven with customs and conventions, emerge as these physiological changes appear. A number of the most pronounced difficulties connected with these changes that adolescents face have been presented in this chapter. As a partial summary to this chapter, it is worth while to point out that these problems are *real,* and are not to be ignored or to be looked upon with ridicule or scorn by adults. Owing to the transition state of the adolescent, he is not always able or ready to accept these changes.

THOUGHT PROBLEMS

1. How is the pituitary gland related to gonadal stimulation?
2. What are some of the more pronounced physiological changes that take place with the onset of pubescence in girls? In boys?
3. Discuss the nature and amount of change in metabolism that takes place with age.
4. What are the different skin glands? Why are these especially important during the adolescent period?
5. Observe several children between the ages of eight and seventeen. What changes in the hairline appear with advancing age level?
6. Interpret the data presented in Figure 3-9 showing a comparison of premenarcheal and postmenarcheal girls in total strength. What is the general significance of these data?
7. What factors largely determine the nutritional needs of an adolescent? Evaluate the diet selected by some adolescent of your acquaintance in the light of his needs.
8. What relationship exists between the growth of the arteries, the heart, and pulse rate? How are these related to blood pressure? What sex differences have been noted?
9. List criteria useful in evaluating the physiological growth of adolescents. What uses can be made of such evaluations?
10. What sex differences appear in the growth of subcutaneous fat during childhood and adolescence? What are the social and educational implications of these differences?

SELECTED REFERENCES

Cole, L., *Psychology of Adolescence*, 6th ed. New York: Holt, Rinehart & Winston, Inc., 1964, Chaps. 5 and 6.

Greulich, W. W., R. I. Dorfman, H. R. Catchpole, C. I. Solomon, and C. S. Culotta, "Somatic and Endocrine Studies of Puberal and Adolescent Boys," *Monographs of the Society for Research in Child Development*, 1942, Vol. VII, No. 3.

Horrocks, John E., *The Psychology of Adolescence*, 2nd ed. Boston: Houghton-Mifflin Company, 1962, Chap. 11.

Rogers, Dorothy, *The Psychology of Adolescence*. New York: Appleton-Century-Crofts, Inc., 1962, Chap. 7.

Seidman, Jerome M., ed., *The Adolescent—A Book of Readings*, 2nd ed. New York: Holt, Rinehart & Winston, Inc., 1960, Chap. 4.

Stolz, H. R. and L. M. Stolz, *Somatic Development of Adolescent Boys*. New York: The Macmillan Company, 1951.

Stone, L. Joseph and Joseph Church, *Childhood and Adolescence*. New York: Random House, 1957, Chap. 11.

Strang, Ruth, *The Adolescent Views Himself*. New York: McGraw-Hill Book Company, 1957, Chap. 6.

Thompson, H., "Physical Growth," in *Manual of Child Psychology*, 2nd ed., editor L. Carmichael. New York: John Wiley & Sons, Inc., 1954, Chap. 5.

NOTES

1 F. P. Boswell, "Trial and Error Learning," *Psychological Review*, 54 (1947), 290.

2 W. W. Greulich, "Physical Changes in Adolescence," *Forty-third Yearbook of the National Society for the Study of Education, Part 1* (Chicago: Department of Education, University of Chicago, 1944), Chap. 2, p. 16. (Quoted by permission of the Society.)

3 W. W. Greulich, R. I. Dorfman, H. R. Catchpole, C. I. Solomon, and C. S. Culotta, "Somatic and Endocrine Studies of Puberal and Adolescent Boys," *Monographs of the Society for Research in Child Development*, 7, No. 3 (1942), 62.

4 I. T. Nathanson, L. E. Towne, and J. C. Aub, "Normal Excretion of Sex Hormones in Childhood," *Endocrinology*, 28 (1941), 851-65.

5 A. Hughes Bryan, "Methods for Analyzing and Interpreting Physical Measurements of Groups of Children," *American Journal of Public Health*, 44 (1954), 766-71. Copyright 1954 by the American Public Health Association, Inc.

6 J. W. Burrell, M. J. R. Healy, and J. M. Tanner, "Age at Menarche in South Africa Bantu Schoolgirls Living in the Transki Reserve," *Human Biology*, 33 (1961), 250-61.

7 Comradge L. Henton, "A Comparative Study of the Onset of Menarche among Negro and White Children," *The Journal of Psychology*, 46 (1958), 65-73.

8 R. W. B. Ellis, "Age of Puberty in the Tropics," *British Medical Journal*, 1 (1950), 85-96.

9 Based on data from M. M. Marsh, "Growth of the Heart Related to Bodily Growth During Childhood and Adolescence," *Journal of Pediatrics*, 2 (1953), 382-404.

10 H. G. Richey, "The Blood Pressure in Boys and Girls Before and After Puberty," *American Journal of Diseases of Children*, 42 (1931), 1281-1330.

11 F. W. Beneke, *Uber das Volumen des Herzens und die Weite der Arteria pulmonalis und Aorta ascendas* (Marburg: V. Theodore Kay, (1879).

12 H. E. Jones, "California Adolescent Growth Study," *Journal of Educational Research*, 31 (1938), 561-67.

13 N. W. Shock, "Physiological Changes in Adolescence," *Forty-third Yearbook of the National Society for the Study of Education, Part 1*, (Chicago: Department of Education, University of Chicago, 1944), Chap. 4, pp. 59-60.

14 *Ibid.*, pp. 61-63.

15 *Public Health Reports*, 70 (1955), 176.

16 J. A. Johnston, "Nutritional Problems of Adolescence," *American Medical Association Journal*, 137 (1948), 1587-88.

17 Bertha S. Burke, Robert B. Reed, Anna S. Vandonberg, and Harold C. Stuart, "A Longitudinal Study of the Calcium Intake of Children from One to Eighteen Years of Age," *American Journal of Clinical Nutrition*, 10 (1962), 79-88.

18 J. W. Maroney and J. A. Johnston, "Caloric and Protein Requirements and Basal Metabolism of Children from Four to Fourteen Years Old," *American Journal of Diseases of Children*, 54 (1937), 29.

19 E. L. Reynolds, "The Distribution of Subcutaneous Fat in Childhood and Adolescence," *Monographs of the Society for Research in Child Development*, 15 (1950), 1-189.

20 W. W. Greulich, R. I. Dorfman, H. R. Catchpole, C. I. Solomon, and C. S. Culotta, "Somatic and Endocrine Studies of Puberal and Adolescent Boys," *Monographs of the Society for Research in Child Development*, 7, No. 3 (1942).

4

PHYSICAL
AND
MOTOR
DEVELOPMENT

One of the most apparent changes taking place during the adolescent period is the accelerated rate of physical growth that occurs just before puberty and continues at a lesser rate throughout the early years of adolescence. To the adult this growth spurt and the accompanying problems are somewhat humorous, but to the adolescent they are often disconcerting. The adolescent boy, accustomed to throwing his legs across the arm of a chair, suddenly finds the chair arm breaking under his extra weight and the dynamic movements of the legs. Zachry has pointed out how growth presents problems to the adolescent and how it becomes necessary for him to adjust to increased size and resulting temporary clumsiness in motor activities.[1] This chapter is concerned with physical growth and adolescent problems connected with it.

PHYSICAL DEVELOPMENT DURING ADOLESCENCE

Physical development—methods of study. In general, three methods have been used in the study of the physical development of children. The first in point of historical interest and frequency of use is the study of weight-height-age relationships. A study of either weight or height alone gives very little information, because children of the same sex, age, race, and environmental conditions vary greatly. Although when only individual measurements are considered, weight is the one more generally used, it is probably a less reliable measure of physical development than height. A child may become heavy simply as a result of fat accumulation with no real growth in the number of tissue cells. Or just the opposite may happen: he may lose weight because he is using up adipose tissue, yet at the same time increasing the number of tissue cells.

Measurements of height furnish a much more accurate index of growth because they indicate it in terms of the length of the skeleton. However, bones may grow in thickness, bone cavities decrease in size, and chemical constituents may alter greatly without any increase in length.

Early height-weight charts failed to take into consideration differences in body build. Concerning their use, Simmons and Todd concluded in an analysis of stature and weight from 3 months to 13 years, "The stature-weight relationship is shown to be too low for employment of

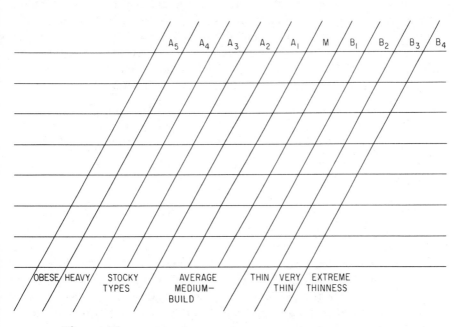

Figure 4-1

THE PHYSIQUE CHANNELS USED IN THE WETZEL GRID CHART
FOR EVALUATING PHYSICAL FITNESS IN TERMS OF BODY BUILD

either measure as a criterion of the other." However, because physical measurements are easily made and objective, they offer great possibilities, and various attempts have been made to devise valid height-weight tables that would take into account body build. Dearborn and Rothney devised an equation for the prediction of body weight that they found to be 21 per cent more efficient than the ordinary height-weight chart in the case of boys aged 14 to 18, and 20 per cent more efficient for girls of the same age.[2] Wetzel developed a gridlike chart, shown in Figure 4-1, that takes into account seven types of body build.[3] Weight is first plotted against height in order to obtain estimates of a child's shape and size, then size is plotted against age. Such a graph furnishes a continuous basis for determining the rate and direction of a child's physical growth, considered normal as long as the child advances steadily in his own channel.

The second method of study is by means of repeated measurements —longitudinal studies. Baldwin and others made such studies early and were thus able to plot continuous growth curves as well as group averages.

The third method is by determining anatomical age, the stage of development of the skeletal system. *Skeletal age* can be measured since, with the increase in height and weight of adolescence, there is a regular change in the composition of the bones (in the osseous and cartilaginous materials). Also, there is evidence that the skeletal development of the child provides a good basis for determining his general physical development and for predicting his mature size. Bayley concludes from studies at the Institute of Child Welfare, University of California:

> When expressed as per cent of a child's eventual natural size, his growth is seen to be very closely related to the development and maturing of his skeleton. . . . It appears that growth in size is closely related to the maturing of the skeleton. At a given skeletal age we may say that a child has achieved a given proportion of his eventual adult body dimensions. Consequently, mature size can be predicted with fair accuracy if a child's present size and skeletal age are known.[4]

Thus the carpal bone of the wrist has been extensively used as a means of determining anatomical development. The *anatomic index* is used as the unit of measurement; for example, an index of 10 indicates that 10 per cent of the area of the wrist shows ossification. The child's age at the time of eruption of the permanent teeth has also been used as an indicator of anatomical development, so that dental age scales are possible.

Growth in height and weight. Any table of averages of children's growth is likely to be misleading, since children of the same age vary enormously in their rate of development. However, such tables do provide indications of growth trends, which, as mentioned before, seem to center around and be dependent on the onset of puberty.

Just prior to the advent of puberty, the rate of growth in height increases. Nicolson and Hanley reported that the average chronological age at which the largest increment in standing height occurs is 11.5 years for girls and 13.8 years for boys.[5] The average yearly increments for weight show a somewhat different picture. Beginning around the fifth year there is a gradual and progressive increase in gain each year. Table 4-1 reveals that the average 13-year-old girl is both heavier and taller than her male contemporary.[6]

Table 4-1

AVERAGE STANDING HEIGHT AND WEIGHT OF
BOYS AND GIRLS DURING THE TEEN YEARS
(*Martin*)

	Males		Females	
Age	Height (inches)	Weight (pounds)	Height (inches)	Weight (pounds)
13	60.7	98.9	61.3	102.2
14	63.6	113.7	62.9	113.6
15	66.6	128.1	63.5	117.2
16	67.9	136.6	63.9	120.8
17	69.0	145.3	64.1	122.0
18	69.3	150.3	64.4	123.0

The only adequate way to measure acceleration in growth is with longitudinal studies extending a few years before and after the advent of puberty. Over two decades ago this was done in a study that throws considerable light on growth acceleration, although only 60 girls were examined.[7] The greatest increase in height and weight occurred during the year before puberty. Anthropometrical data on 1817 girls, ages 6 to 17 years, and on 1884 boys, ages 6 to 18 years, who attended the Laboratory Schools of the University of Chicago were analyzed to compare rates of growth, weights, heights, and height-weight relationships. The subjects were divided into three maturity groups on the basis of objective criteria. General conclusions were:

1. Differences in the height-weight relationship suggested differences in the body build of the three groups.
2. Statements concerning overweight or underweight should not neglect consideration of maturity.
3. Growth as measured by height and weight is slightly accelerated before puberty.
4. No significant differences were found in the heights of different female maturity groups after 15 years or in those of the different male maturity groups after 17 years.
5. Girls maturing before 13 years of age were, as a group, heavier at each age from 6 to 17 years than those who matured later, and those who matured between their thirteenth and fourteenth birthdays were heavier at all ages than those who matured after their fourteenth birthdays.
6. Boys who matured before their fourteenth birthdays were heavier than those who matured later, and those who matured between the fourteenth and fifteenth birthdays were heavier at all ages than those who matured after their fifteenth birthdays.[8]

These data are in harmony with results obtained from other such studies.

Anatomical development. The ossification of the bones (skeletal age) proceeds gradually, but is rather advanced at the beginning of adolescence. Early studies by Baldwin and others revealed that after age 5 or 6, girls show more advanced ossification than boys.[9] At 13, when the rate of development slows considerably, about 70 per cent of the area of the girl's wrist shows ossification. A sex difference also appears on dental age scales, presented in Figure 4-2.

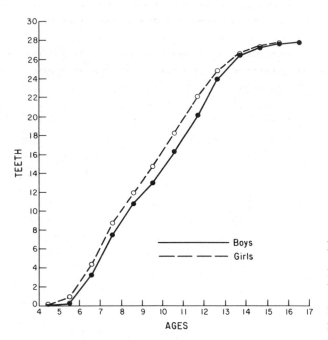

Figure 4-2

AVERAGE NUMBER OF ALL PERMANENT TEETH (EXCEPT THIRD MOLARS) ERUPTED AT SPECIFIED AGES

Both skeletal age and tooth eruption are closely tied to the onset of puberty. Normal skeletal development will not occur in the absence of adequately functioning gonads. In fact, the relation of skeletal age to maturation is so close that an X-ray film of the hand and wrist during preadolescence may be used for predicting the time of occurrence of menarche.[10] Simmons and Greulich demonstrated the close correspondence in a study of girls aged 7 to 17. The results appear in Figure 4-3.

A study of somatic and endocrine changes associated with puberty and adolescence among boys was carried on over a period of several years at Yale University.[11] The skeletal status of 476 private school boys was compared with the degree of development of their primary and secondary sexual characteristics. The boys were divided into five *maturity groups*

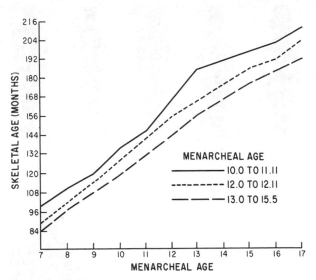

Figure 4-3

MEAN SKELETAL AGE OF
GIRLS 7 TO 17 YEARS OF
AGE IN THREE MEN-
ARCHEAL GROUPS
(Simmons and Greulich)

representing successive stages in sexual maturity from prepuberty to late adolescence. Skeletal age increased with advancing maturity regardless of chronological age.

Sexual development and body proportion. Differences in rate of growth and age of sexual maturity produce varied body builds, but certain proportional changes are common to all. Figure 4-4 sketches the nature of these changing proportions with growth toward maturity. Arms and legs grow in length and become firmer; hands and feet become larger. Shoulders of the boy and hips of the girl widen, as shown in Figures 4-5 and 4-6.

Boynton presents thirteen measurements of growth increments for anthropometric characteristics based on retests from ages 5.5 years to 16.5 years inclusive.[12] His data show that although the 5.5-year-old boy is 65 per cent as tall as he probably will be at 17.5 years, he weighs only 33 per cent as much and has only 18 per cent of the strength of grip he will possess 12 years later. The brain of the child at birth weighs a little less than one pound. The number of cell bodies is apparently complete, but the neurones increase in size and richness of terminal endings up to the period of physical maturity.

With respect to weight and strength of grip, the average girl 5.5 years old has approximately one-third of her 17-year development, but her height, shoulder width, and ankle circumference are already three-fourths developed. Although the average girl is not completely grown in some respects at 17.5 years, certain elements of growth are complete by the age of 15.5 years. Most of the early disproportions in growth are smoothed out as the individual reaches normal maturity.

As shown in Figure 4-7, girls who reached maturity early were ad-

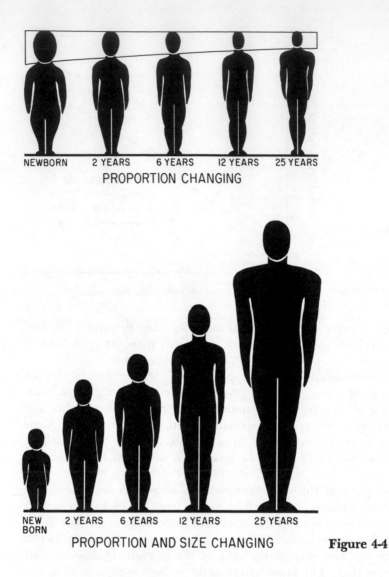

NEWBORN　2 YEARS　6 YEARS　I2 YEARS　25 YEARS

PROPORTION CHANGING

NEW BORN　2 YEARS　6 YEARS　I2 YEARS　25 YEARS

PROPORTION AND SIZE CHANGING　　**Figure 4-4**

vanced in their growth prior to puberty and grew more during their period of rapid growth than did those who reached maturity late.[13] The same trend was noted for boys. According to Shuttleworth, early-maturing boys tend to be slightly taller than the average at adulthood, whereas early-maturing girls show a slight tendency to be short.[14] However, the correlation between height and age at menarche is .15, insufficient to justify any widespread generalization.

Boys who mature early sexually tend to have relatively broad hips and narrow shoulders, whereas for those who develop late, the opposite is true. Also, boys of a rugged, muscular build mature more rapidly than the delicately constructed.

60

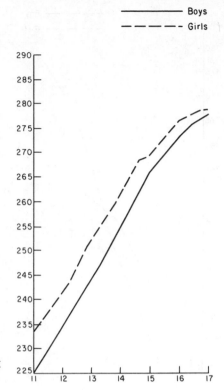

——————— Boys
— — — — Girls

Figure 4-5

GROWTH IN HIP WIDTH
(MILLIMETERS)

Jacobsen found that women with a relatively early menstrual onset tend to develop a more "feminine" adult body structure than those with a late onset. In a study of somatometric and functional data obtained from 300 adult Norwegian nurses ranging in age from 20 to 37, he noted significant differences in length and fat factors between the early-and late-maturing groups; the former had smaller length factor, the latter a smaller fat factor.[15]

Kralj-Cereck collected data from girls born in the northeastern region of Slovenia, where they lived the majority of the time from birth until menarche.[16] He divided the girls into three groups: Baroque—"pyknic," broad, feminine; Renaissance—medium; and Gothic—"linear" or "boyish," angular. Statistical comparisons of the three groups showed that the Baroque type had their first menstrual period earlier than Renaissance girls, and Gothic girls had the latest menstrual onset.

When we consider these conclusions about the relation between physique and skeletal maturation along with results from studies of the relation between socio-economic status and skeletal maturation, the findings become very confusing. The relationship between physique and rate

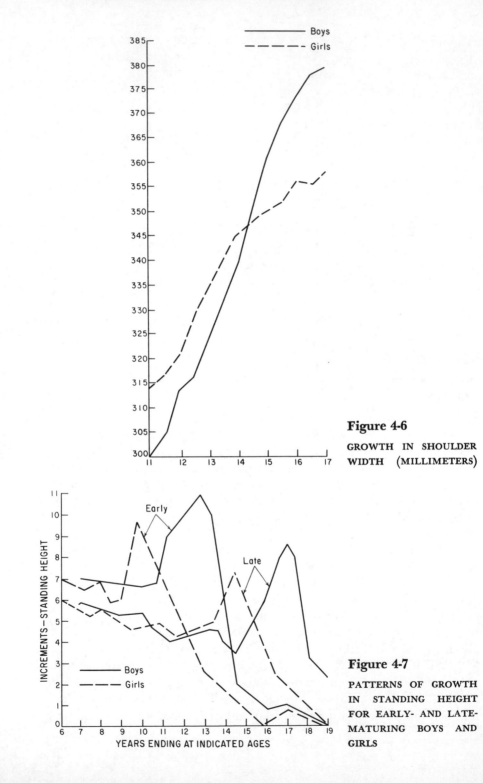

Figure 4-6

GROWTH IN SHOULDER WIDTH (MILLIMETERS)

Figure 4-7

PATTERNS OF GROWTH IN STANDING HEIGHT FOR EARLY- AND LATE-MATURING BOYS AND GIRLS

of maturation is presumably genetically determined, yet all the evidence suggests that adverse environmental conditions slow the rate of growth and reduce final adult height. The results of a study by Dupertius and Michael suggest that for mesomorphs and ectomorphs the somatotype remains relatively constant throughout childhood. However, differences in growth patterns for each type have been noted. The investigators conclude:

> . . . The shorter, heavier, mesomorphs were found to grow faster and to mature earlier. The peak of their puberal spurt in both height and weight occurs on the average about one year earlier than it does among the ecto-morphs. The overall growth period for the ectomorphs appears to cover a longer span of years whereas the attainment of adult stature for the meso-morphs is achieved in a shorter length of time, and the process of growth seems to be more intensified particularly during adolescence.[17]

MOTOR DEVELOPMENT DURING ADOLESCENCE

Age and motor performance. Motor performance reaches its peak during the adolescent years, except for complex performances requiring years of practice and excessive strength. Still, some have described the adolescent period as an "awkward age" because of apparently awkward movements made by many adolescents. However, there is a biological principle that functional capacity must follow physiological or structural growth, and individuals actually reach their peak in motor skills during this period. Two factors seem to account for any awkwardness that may appear among adolescents. The adolescent is growing rapidly; he is expanding his physical activities, doing many things that he has never done before requiring motor coordination. Any period of life when one is called upon to learn many new motor coordinations will involve awkward movements.

As with body shape, body strength and agility are closely related to sexual maturity. Muscular development in the studies that follow is plotted in average chronological age, but it must be kept in mind that the ages also indicate stages of sexual development. It must also be remembered that the lower performance of girls is partly due to their mechanical disadvantage; the arms and legs are proportionally shorter than boys', the trunk larger, pelvis broader, and the femur is attached to the pelvis at an oblique angle.

The California Adolescent Growth Study found some interesting facts about development of strength.[18] Figure 4-8 compares growth in right-hand strength in two groups of girls representing contrasting extremes in age at menarche. Among these girls, the earlier-maturing group showed a rapid rise in strength before age 12. The later-maturing group was relatively retarded in strength, but the two groups eventually reached

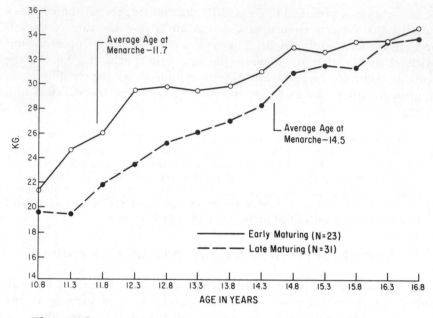

Figure 4-8

MANUAL STRENGTH DEVELOPMENT OF GIRLS IN TWO MATURITY GROUPS
(*After Jones*)

the same level. Significantly, the greatest increase in strength occurred near the time of menarche.

In comparison with the group means for strength of grip, each of the early-maturing boys studied was above the norm in strength at ages 13 to 16; whereas the late-maturing boys tended to fall below the norm at these ages. Results for boys and girls classified as early-, average-, and late-maturing, are presented in Table 4-2. The early- and late-maturing groups represented approximately the 20 per cent at each extreme of a normal public school distribution at the different age levels; the average group consisted of those whose maturational level was approximately that of the norm for their age level. Jones states: "It is apparent that the three curves are more or less parallel, with some divergence of the early- and late-maturing groups between the ages of 13 and 15, and with a later convergence which, however, fails to bring them together at the end of the series of measures."[19] A further study of the results of the table shows that the early-maturing girls, although stronger at the age of 13, failed to maintain their superiority in subsequent years, and actually dropped below that of the average-maturing group, just as they did in their height and weight. Thus, precocious sexual development of girls appears to be associated with an early arrest in physical and motor development; this is not true for boys.

MacCurdy found further evidence connecting strength and sexual maturation in adolescent boys.[20] He stated that strength grows gradually

Table 4-2

MEAN SCORES FOR EARLY-, AVERAGE-, AND LATE-MATURING
BOYS AND GIRLS* (K.G., RIGHT GRIP)

(*After Jones*)

	Per cent of boys			Per cent of girls		
Age	Early N = 16	Average N = 28	Late N = 16	Early N = 16	Average N = 24	Late N = 16
11.0	27.1	24.0	22.7	21.1	20.9	20.6
11.5	29.3	25.9	25.2	24.4	23.2	21.2
12.0	29.3	26.9	26.0	26.1	25.8	22.5
12.5	31.3	28.4	27.0	29.1	26.8	23.7
13.0	33.3	30.4	28.1	30.3	28.8	25.7
13.5	37.6	32.5	30.0	29.3	30.3	26.8
14.0	44.2	34.3	30.2	29.7	30.7	26.4
14.5	47.1	38.6	33.3	31.0	32.2	28.4
15.0	50.0	43.0	36.3	32.5	33.3	31.4
15.5	52.2	47.6	41.1	33.4	35.2	32.7
16.0	54.3	49.0	43.9	33.4	35.8	32.4
16.5	55.9	50.9	48.4	34.7	36.1	34.4
17.0	57.2	53.5	51.3	34.3	36.5	34.8
17.5	....	55.8	54.3	33.9	37.8	35.3

* The boys are classified on the basis of skeletal maturing, the girls on the basis of age at menarche.

to age 12, then quite rapidly, reaching a maximum for most boys around the eighteenth birthday. McCloy confirmed the fact that the most rapid increase in strength for boys was between ages 13 and 16; for girls between 12 and 14. Boys increased only slightly after age 17; most girls actually decreased after their fifteenth birthday.

Jokl and Cluver studied the development of physical fitness among a group of children from 5 to 20 years of age.[21] In endurance, measured by the 600-yard run, both boys and girls improved from age 6 to 13. The improvement up to 13 years was about the same for both sexes; but afterwards boys continued to improve, whereas girls actually lost in efficiency, so that from 17 to 20 the girls' ability was about that of 6- to 8-year-olds. Their decline in efficiency was reflected not only in their running time, but also in their pulse rate, respiration, and fatigue. It seems likely that the early decline in motor ability among girls is a result of their way of life: that is, they show an increased interest in social activities at a fairly early age, and a lack of interest in athletics and other forms of muscular activity as they grow older.

Sex differences. Significant sex differences that became greater at each age level were found in all the performances studied by Espenschade. The greatest gap recorded was in the distance throw, although differences in the broad jump became as great among the older adolescents. Sex differences in the Brace test were studied for the falls of 1934 and 1937. In 1934, 16 of the 20 tests comprising the Brace study were taken by more than 90 per cent of both boys and girls. A larger percentage of girls than boys passed six of these tests, although the differences were not statistically significant, except for one event—the agility and control test.

In order to secure additional comparable data and also to extend the age range, 325 girls and 285 boys, ages 10.5 to 16 years, were given the Brace test again in 1943-45 during the school day. The items in the test were classified as: agility, control, strength, and static balance. The test consisted of 20 items selected to include a wide variety of coordinations not frequently practiced. A comparison of the scores of boys and girls on the different tests showed that only slight differences appeared in total scores or in measures of the various classes until 13.8 years, when boys began to excell in all events and increased their superiority rapidly at each successive age level. The most striking difference between the boys and girls was in the "push-up" test, one of the tests of strength. The greatest similarity noted was in the "sit, then stand again, with arms folded and feet crossed" test, a control test. Girls made their best showing in the control tests, their poorest in the tests of agility and strength. The following is a summary of the results:

1. The increment pattern for boys of total scores on the Brace test battery is similar to that of adolescent growth in standing height. Scores for girls show little change after the thirteenth year.

2. The stunts of the Brace test battery were placed in four general classes according to the predominant type of muscular action demanded. Additional elements necessary for performance were noted. "Dynamic balance," especially, is important in many events.

3. Boys show an increase in ability to perform events of all classes. The rate of growth is greater after 14 years of age than before and appears to be more rapid in "agility" than in "control."

4. All tests for boys in which "dynamic balance" is a factor show a marked "adolescent lag." . . .

5. Girls improve in "agility" up to 14 years, then decline. In "control" and in "flexibility and balance," little change can be seen over the age range studied. . . .[22]

Although strength and motor coordination increase with age, the bones and joints reach their peak of flexibility at a relatively early age.

One study measured the flexibility of 12 areas of the body in 300 girls ranging in age from 5.5 to 18.5 years. The girls showed greatest flexibility of the shoulder, knee, and thigh at age 6. Head rotation was most flexible at age 9; the remaining eight areas at age 12. Although individual differences were observed in the degree of flexibility among girls of the same age group, the figures indicate that it is highest during childhood and early adolescence, so that for education in motor skills, exercises requiring a high degree of flexibility should be started during the preschool years and continued during the elementary school years to reach the potentially highest level.

Relationship of strength to other traits. Significant relations have been reported by various investigators between dynamic and static strength and certain physical measurements. Dynamic strength is strength in action —in field events or other sports, whereas static strength is sheer strength of pull—in grip or lifting—and is frequently measured by means of dynamometric tests. Some interesting similarities in the operation of these two aspects of motor performances are revealed in the results of a study by Bower and reported by Jones.[23] Correlations were obtained among a group of boys between these aspects of strength and chronological age; skeletal age, based on assessments of X-rays of the hand and knee; height; an evaluation of "good looks"; and intelligence, based on an average mental age obtained from the results of two forms of a group intelligence test. These correlations are presented in Table 4-3. An interesting feature of the results of the table is that whereas chronological age and physical measurements correlate highest with total strength, more closely related to the gross motor scores are popularity and "good looks." This is to be expected, when one realizes the prestige value of motor performances among adolescent boys. The low correlation between motor performances and intelligence is also significant.

Table 4-3

MOTOR PERFORMANCE CORRELATIONS WITH
OTHER DEVELOPMENTAL TRAITS—BOYS

Variable	Total strength (grip, pull, thrust)	Gross motor scores (track events)
Chronological age	.39 ± .06	.18 ± .07
Skeletal age	.50 ± .055	.36 ± .06
Height	.65 ± .04	.40 ± .06
Popularity	.30 ± .07	.39 ± .06
"Good looks"	.21 ± .07	.38 ± .06
Intelligence	− .17 ± .07	.05 ± .08

Physical fitness. Adolescents and adults alike depend on machines to do their work, carry them from place to place, and entertain them while they relax. The general practice has become, "Don't run if you can walk, don't walk if you can stand, and don't stand if you can sit." Walking several miles to school and to church over muddy or snow-covered roads is a part of the past that no other form of exercise has replaced. Also, much of the time now spent watching television was formerly spent doing different chores that helped keep muscles fit. Even athletics have changed: they have become so highly specialized that the typical adolescent must be a spectator. Less than one per cent of the average American youth's time is spent on physical education, and only a fraction of that time is in vigorous activities that produce physical fitness.[24]

The ill effects of such habits appeared in comparisons of American boys and girls with their European counterparts on different physical fitness tests and attracted the attention of our national leaders. A study reported by Ikeda compared the physical fitness of children aged 9 to 12 in Iowa and Tokyo.[25] There were 172 girls and 178 boys from Iowa, 221 girls and 174 boys from Tokyo. The Iowa girls and boys were taller, heavier, and had longer legs than the Tokyo children of the same age, yet the Japanese exceeded the Iowans in all but the sit-up test.

A summary of findings from a checklist of the activities of the groups showed that the Tokyo children pursued various physical activities more than the Iowa children, although the physical education classes in Tokyo were larger with less desirable facilities. The explanation of this, no doubt, lies in the differences in culture and in living standards. The Tokyo children must walk to school and have different customs of entertainment and recreation.

Competitive athletics for preteen-agers. It is quite natural for 10-, 11-, and 12-year-olds to want to engage in play activities similar to those pursued by adults. Thus, the play interests of children are largely determined by the activities of adolescents and adults. There has, however, been great controversy, much on an emotional and immature level, over the effects of premature competition in athletics by children.

That vital lessons are learned through competitive athletics seems quite certain. Furthermore, such activity furnishes the badly needed motivation and means for youngsters to secure exercise and develop good coordination and physical fitness. However, certain dangers are inherent in some athletics. Since during the preadolescent period there are wide variations in body build, physiological maturity, and strength, age groupings are often unfair and dangerous: the immature boy of 10 or 11 years is no match for a physiologically more mature opponent of the same age. This is clearly shown in a study by Hale.[26] He found that the majority of boys of the 1955 Little League World Series (ages 10-12) were adolescent, not preadolescent, as their chronological age would indicate. In eliminations involved in making the team and in competition between various teams the more mature boy was at a distinct advantage.

When athletic contests are not controlled and directed toward the best interests of the participants, they may become harmful. It may be stated as a fundamental principle that junior high school boys and girls should not engage in as heavy an athletic schedule as senior high school boys and girls. Even in the case of senior high school boys and girls, highly competitive forms of strenuous activity may, when poorly administered, be harmful to physical development and to mental activity. Junior and senior high school students may get so excited over winning a game that, when they lose, an upset stomach, loss of appetite, or even diarrhea results.

Too often the money available for physical education and athletics is spent on athletic contests which affect the physical development of only a small minority of the student body. Many schools have attempted to increase the benefits of the athletic program by emphasizing intramural contests, or by intelligent guidance of the athletic program in harmony with the best interests of the participants. The importance of a complete recreational program for adolescents will be emphasized further in connection with social growth, character formation and juvenile crime prevention.

Any program concerned with the improvement of health must take into consideration the weight of the individual children. First, a thorough health examination is essential to any efforts toward the modification of weight. It may be expected that 10 to 15 per cent of adolescents from an average group will require some attention to their weight. Weight problems are closely related to diet, a complicated factor, since many considerations enter into the eating habits of adolescents. The problem, therefore, is not always as simple as it might appear at first. It has been found that efforts directed toward the improvement of diet are most beneficial when the individual is able to record and observe his own progress. Thus, the adolescent should be given systematic guidance and instruction in methods of controlling his diet in order to improve his weight standard and his health.

Good posture habits. The importance of good posture habits in maintaining the organs of the body in their correct position and in enabling them to function at maximum efficiency has been stressed by physicians in recent years. Charts have been devised, exercises recommended, and clinics held, all in an effort to provide for the development of good posture among children, adolescents, and adults. Although training should begin in early childhood, adolescence is the period when so many bad posture habits are formed. There are several reasons why adolescents are susceptible to incorrect habits. First, much of the energy from food during the adolescent years is used up in providing for growth. Thus the adolescent is inclined to slump from a tired feeling. Secondly, the adolescent years are active years. Adolescents use a great deal of energy in their social, recreational, and play activities. This, again, brings on a feeling of tiredness and the tendency to slump. Thirdly, the individual may feel self-conscious over his long legs, or general height, leading him to assume an unhealthy posture in an effort to hide his height or gangliness. This is much more prevalent among girls than among boys. If proper posture is not acquired during childhood or adolescence, it will never be acquired.

An appraisal of posture is not a simple matter; individual differences in body build must be taken into consideration. Where teachers are available—usually teachers in physical education and health—measurements and careful evaluations based upon observations may be made. Where such help is not available, other means should be used to get a more accurate appraisal of posture, for example, a simple check to see that the individual stands erect, with the head, trunk, hips, and legs well aligned. Also, all children should be observed for sagging shoulders, correct manner of walking, and lateral curvatures.

SOME GROWTH CHARACTERISTICS AND PROBLEMS

Changes in voice. Closely connected with muscular development are the obvious changes of voice in early adolescence. They are much more evident in boys and constitute one of the external signs of the advent of puberty. They are the effect of the rapid growth of the larynx, or the "Adam's apple," and a corresponding lengthening of the vocal cords that stretch across it. The cords approximately double their former length with a consequent drop of an octave in pitch. Girls' voices are not subject to such an outright transformation; at maturity, they are little, if at all, lower than in childhood, although fuller and richer. Boys' voices not only change pitch but also increase in volume, and often become more pleasant in quality. They require two or more years to achieve control in the lower register, and during that time the roughness of their tones are often embarrassing. They are mortified by unexpected squeaks which punctuate bass rumblings. Such whimsical "breakings" cause them to feel they are making themselves ridiculous—an opinion that is often confirmed, unfortunately, by the mirth with which others greet their vocal vagaries.

The voice change, however, is not an accurate index for use in studies of the development of a boy, since there is no satisfactory way of evaluating it objectively. It could be studied if a recording device were used for comparing the depth and other qualities of the voice at varying stages of development. In this connection, it should be pointed out that it is the progressive deepening of the voice, rather than the absolute pitch, that is significant as an indication of progress toward maturity, since the voices of young men at maturity will vary widely in pitch and other qualities.

A difference in rate of physiological maturity may be a source of anxiety to the adolescent. When Bill's pal, Henry, suddenly surpasses him in physical development, develops a bass voice, and begins to shave, Bill may wonder whether he is normal. The difference between his own appearance and that of his friend may become so pronounced that he begins to seek other friends, and may even resort to behavior not socially acceptable in an effort to prove himself.

For boys, motor ability is often directly related to emotional health since the former is closely associated with athletic prowess, aggressiveness,

Table 4-4

PER CENTS OF 580 TENTH-GRADE BOYS AND GIRLS GIVING CERTAIN DESCRIPTIONS OF THEIR PHYSIQUES AND PER CENTS EXPRESSING CONCERN ABOUT THE CHARACTERISTICS DESCRIBED

(*After Frazier and Lisonbee*)

Descriptions	Per cent so describing themselves		Per cent expressing concern	
	Boys	Girls	Boys	Girls
Thin	21	16	22	48
Heavy	13	30	3	55
Short	26	27	39	22
Tall	28	22	4	49
Development early	19	24	6	15
Development slow	17	13	40	36

and leadership. Although excellence in tennis, swimming, skating, and dancing usually leads to peer approval and prestige for girls, they are usually not so concerned with athletic ability. In a seven-year longitudinal study of boys, the 10 highest in strength had greater social prestige and fewer adjustment problems, whereas the 10 lowest suffered from a lack of social prestige, lower status, and feelings of inferiority.[27]

Adolescent concerns with physique. The unevenness of growth of different parts of the body and individual variances in rate of growth and time of onset of puberty often present difficulties. For example, asynchrony of development is often a problem for girls. Also, the lag in the increase in the size of the muscles presents a problem to boys. The adolescent boy is particularly conscious about lack of height; the opposite may be an extremely disturbing condition for the adolescent girl. This fact is brought out in the results of a study reported by Frazier and Lisonbee, presented in Table 4-4.[28] Over one-half the girls expressed a concern over being too tall, whereas almost one-half the boys were concerned with being too short. However, most thought themselves average in maturation.

Both boys and girls are in many cases frustrated because of their lack of "sex appropriate physique". The phrase should perhaps be "sex appropriate face and figure" for girls, to differentiate clearly from the health, strength, and muscular abilities so prominent in the appropriate physique concept among boys. For the girl, too much muscular strength is regarded as undesirable, and the rugged appearance of a healthy individual is looked upon as masculine rather than feminine. In connection with any frustration existing, girls are more likely to do something about the condition than boys. They are much more willing to diet in order to have an appropriate figure. However, boys often exert great effort and endure continued exercise in order to develop a masculine physique. It seems likely, then, that even temporary deviations from the "sex appropriate" development may produce significant problems of adjustment for adolescent boys and girls.

The attitudes of parents, teachers, and classmates toward masculine traits in growing boys frequently create difficult problems for the pre-adolescent, particularly the late maturer. The standard of the norm or average is sometimes imposed without a consideration of basic differences in rate of development. Boys with a late onset of puberty may be disturbed by serious doubts about their own physiological development and adequacy, although they are well within the limits of normality. On the other hand, Schofield noted that an apparent or actual delay in age of onset of sexual maturation, the failure of the growth spurt in pubescence or inadequacy of masculine development may lead to a variety of personality conflicts and psychosomatic complaints during the teen years.[29] In more serious cases application of psychotherapy or psychiatric therapy may be needed.

Physical growth and personality adjustment. The normal physical growth of adolescents plays an important role in their personality adjustments. American society has developed a concept of the ideal shape for a person. The boy or girl whose physical make-up does not meet this ideal will, in many cases, be timid, self-conscious, or withdrawn from the group.

Early- and late-maturing boys were rated independently by three judges for each of nine significant drives: autonomy, social acceptance, achievement, recognition, abasement, aggressiveness, helpfulness, control, and escape.[30] It was found that high drives for social acceptance and aggression were more characteristic of late-maturing boys than of early-maturing boys. On the other hand, early-maturing girls are often maladjusted, particularly since the average girl matures a year or more ahead of the average boy anyway.

Many cruel jokes are told about one whose body does not conform to the ideal. It may be he is a late maturer or that he has a malfunction of the pituitary gland. A boy may lack broad shoulders or terminal hair or have feminine characteristics and to avoid ridicule because of his physique or to avoid being referred to as a "sissy," he becomes opposed to cleanliness, politeness, and conformity. Commonly preadolescent boys from the lower social class go dirty, unkempt, and are rude to female teachers merely to exert a sense of masculinity. A girl goes to extremes in order to make her physique appear to conform to the ideal standard set forth for the female.

The physically handicapped adolescent. The effects of being physically handicapped are frequently intensified during adolescence. The developing social-sex drive, the needs for independence, and the growth from the dependency of childhood toward the realization of adulthood present difficult adjustment problems for the handicapped teen-ager. He frequently grows into adolescence unprepared to meet the new demands that are geared toward helping him function independently. Often, he identifies closely with the mother, resulting in a low self-concept and little identification with the father. Such a situation is especially difficult for the adolescent boy. The case of Arnold illustrates the problems of the emotionally disturbed, blind adolescent.

Arnold, age 18, had been known to our agency for approximately 10 years. Diagnosis: Retrolental Fibroplasia. Initially his mother requested simple services, i.e., talking back machines, recreation, etc. Both parents were well educated, successful, and set high standards for their son. The mother had previously sought help at a time when there was no direct service for blind children in the area, and hence had to work out her conflicts and problems the best she could. At the time of the contact, she was seeking direct material advice as to what to do, while running away from the kind of involvement that would help her understand the why's of her own behavior and Arnold's. She was full of self-blame, and seemed to be using this as a defense against further self-involvement. The parents' attitude was one of forcing him to develop up to their expectations and not according to his readiness.

After Arnold graduated from high school, where he attended special classes, he came to the rehabilitation center for evaluation and training, so that he might prepare for the goal that his parents had set for him—college.

Arnold was a likeable person, but otherwise ill prepared for coping with life. He had little ability to comprehend even the most simple concepts of his environment. Although his intelligence was bright-normal he had not been allowed or given the opportunity to learn what goes on around him daily, i.e., he had little concept of what a city block was, what a head of lettuce looks like, etc. Nor did he have too much curiosity about himself or his environment. He did not even know the color of his hair or eyes. Arnold expressed hostility toward his parents and seemed to blame much of his shortcomings on them. Although there was some reality in this, he also used it to avoid taking any responsibility on himself.

Arnold had great difficulty in special conceptualization and [had] poor coordination. Progress was limited in travel but although he might sometimes get lost coming from the railroad station to the rehabilitation center, he could use the public systems to get there. This was a new experience for him.[31]

Physical handicaps and adjustment. The physically handicapped child is faced not only with the general problems common to those of his age, but also with the more specific problems resulting from his particular disability. Cruickshank and Norris reviewed research bearing on this general problem.[32] They noted the following relations of physical disability to social and emotional adjustments:

1. The crippled child fears his disability.

2. Physically handicapped children believe they have more fears and guilt feelings than normal children.

3. Physically handicapped adolescents demonstrate better relations with their mothers than with their fathers.

4. The physically handicapped child sometimes refuses to face reality (often denies his handicap).

5. The adjustment of the physically handicapped is less mature in nature than that of the normal.

It should be pointed out, however, that a physical handicap may or may not lead to maladjustments, depending upon environmental circumstances. The crippled adolescent boy will be handicapped when attending his class dance; he will not meet frustrations in ordinary classroom procedures or at the soda fountain. Thus, a particular impairment may or may not be a source of frustration. The attitude of the subject will affect his social adjustments. If he accepts the fact that he is handicapped and thus different from others in one respect, he is less likely to be emotionally and socially maladjusted.

SUMMARY

Growth begins with the fertilization of the egg cell, and birth merely extends the sphere of activity. Many factors determine the nature, direction, and amount of development that will take place. Certain biological laws enable us to predict development when it occurs in average environmental conditions. Although varying circumstances may alter the direction and amount of development, the growing child is a unified whole, and the nature of development of one part of the body must be considered in connection with its relation to other parts. Even though there is a lack of uniformity in the growth of different parts of the body, a continuous, interrelated form of growth is ever-present.

Height-weight charts, the anatomical index, dental age norms as well as other physical measurements have been used in the study of the growth process. Repeated measurements made on boys and girls from year to year show a distinct sex difference in the age for the onset of puberty and accelerated growth. The preadolescent decline in the general rate of growth followed by the adolescent spurt is about one and one-half years earlier on the average for girls than for boys. However, individual growth curves show that this will vary considerably with different individuals of the same sex. There is a wide variation in the age of the onset of puberty, as well as the variation referred to in the general physical development. Variations in growth may be affected by such extraneous factors as exercise, living conditions, and diet. Since growth is affected by so many factors, it becomes very difficult to set forth simple formulae or predictive procedures to estimate it for different stages of life.

A summary of the results from the developmental studies reported at the University of Iowa, at Harvard, and at the University of California present a good review of the materials presented in this chapter:

1. There is a period of relatively slow growth prior to the prepubertal growth spurt.

2. A prepubertal spurt in growth is from 1½ to 2 years earlier for girls than for boys. In the case of girls the twelfth year frequently is the time at which they make their largest annual gain in height.

3. A decrease in rate of growth following puberty.

4. Sufficient consistency in stature rank in the group during elementary-school years for competent prediction in the classifications "tall" and "medium," and to a lesser extent in the classification "short."

5. Individual differences are prevalent and important. An individual's growth rate not only differs from other children; it also develops irregularly. Although there are important general trends, there appears to be slight uniformity in the development of his various traits and abilities. The result of this variability in growth is that in the intermediate grades —Grades 5, 6, and 7—there are, in general, a few pupils who are still in the stage of fairly uniform rate of growth, many who are at the beginning of the prepubertal growth spurt, and a small number who have passed through the accelerating phase and are beginning to slow down in their rate of growth.

Many and diverse problems related to physical growth appear among adolescents. Some of these stem from differences in rate of growth, others stem from the wide variations in abilities and appearance among adolescents, while others grow out of cultural expectations. Physical prowess and courage are expected of boys, while these are of less importance for girls. In fact, too much muscular strength and a too adventurous spirit is not regarded in many groups as ideal for the girl.

THOUGHT PROBLEMS

1. Consider your own adolescent years. What problems related to physical development appeared in your life at this stage?
2. Summarize briefly the sex differences presented in this chapter in motor ability at age 13.25. How would you account for the early cessation and actual decline in many cases of motor development of girls during the adolescent years?
3. What are the different methods used in the study of physical development? Give the advantages of each.
4. If they are available, study some data on physical development secured from a group of students, and note the variations existing. How do these variations relate to their interests? To their personalities?
5. In your observations, have you detected in yourself a spurt in growth with the onset of adolescence? What other pronounced changes occurred rather rapidly?
6. What is the significance of the lack of uniformity in growth discussed on pages 56 and 63?
7. What are the different methods of measuring anatomical development? Which of these do you regard as the most accurate? Which most useful in general? Give reasons for your answers.
8. What are some physical growth features that present adjustment problems for boys? For girls?
9. Miss Queen, a seventh-grade teacher in the North Street School, has been studying the height and weight of her pupils.
   a. What would you expect her to find in the way of sex differences?
   b. She finds that five boys and six girls are several pounds in weight below the norm for their height. What should be her next step? What are some factors she should consider?
10. Outline a physical education or recreational program that will reach all the boys and girls of a high school.
11. Give advantages and disadvantages of competitive athletics as an aspect of the physical education program.

SELECTED REFERENCES

Cole, Luella, *Psychology of Adolescence,* 6th ed. New York: Holt, Rinehart, & Winston, Inc., 1964, Chap. 4.

Garn, Stanley M., "Growth and Development," in *The Nation's Children,* ed. Eli Ginzberg. New York: Columbia University Press, Vol. II.

Greulich, W. W. and S. I. Pyle, *Radiographic Atlas of Skeletal Development of the Hand and Wrist.* Stanford, Calif.: Stanford University Press, 1950, pp. 1-29.

Horrocks, John E., *The Psychology of Adolescence.* Boston: Houghton-Mifflin Company, 1962, Chap. 12.

Jones, H. E., *Motor Performance and Growth*. Berkeley, Calif.: University of California Press, 1949.

Jourard, Sidney M., *Personal Adjustment*. New York: The Macmillan Company, 1958, Chap. 12.

Rogers, Dorothy, *The Psychology of Adolescence*. New York: Appleton-Century-Crofts, Inc., 1962, Chap. 3.

Seidman, Jerome M., ed., *The Adolescent—A Book of Readings*, 2nd ed. New York: Holt, Rinehart & Winston, Inc., 1960, Chap. 4.

Stolz, H. R. and L. M. Stolz, *Somatic Development of Adolescent Boys*. New York: The Macmillan Company, 1951.

Strang, Ruth, *The Adolescent Views Himself*. New York: McGraw-Hill Book Company, 1957, Chap. 6.

Thompson, H., "Physical Growth," in *Manual of Child Psychology* (2nd ed.), editor L. Carmichael. New York: John Wiley & Sons, Inc., 1954, Chap. 5.

NOTES

[1] C. B. Zachry and M. Lighty, *Emotions and Conduct in Adolescence* (New York: Appleton-Century-Crofts, Inc., 1940).

[2] W. F. Dearborn and J. W. M. Rothney, "Basing Weight Standards upon Linear Bodily Dimensions," *Growth*, 2 (1938), 197-212.

[3] N. C. Wetzel, "Physical Fitness in Terms of Physique, Development, and Basal Metabolism," *Journal of the American Medical Association*, 116 (1941), 1187-95.

[4] N. Bayley "Skeletal Maturing in Adolescence as a Basis for Determining Percentage of Completed Growth," *Child Development*, 14 (1943), 44-45.

[5] A. Nicolson and C. Hanley, "Indices of Physiological Maturity; Deviations and Interrelationships," *Child Development*, 24 (1953), 3-38.

[6] W. E. Martin, *Children's Body Measurements for Planning and Equipping Schools*, Special Publication No. 4 (Washington, D.C.: U.S. Department of Health, Education, and Welfare), 1955.

[7] G. E. Van Dyke, "The Effect of the Advent of Puberty on the Growth in Height and Weight of Girls," *School Review*, 38 (1930), 211-21.

[8] H. G. Richey, "The Relation of Accelerated, Normal, and Retarded Puberty to the Height and Weight of School Children, *Monographs of the Society for Research in Child Development*, No. 8 (1937), pp. 1-67.

[9] B. T. Baldwin, L. M. Bresby and H. V. Garside, "Atomic Growth of Children, A Study of Some Bones of the Hand, Wrist, and Lower Forearm by Means of Roentgenograms," *University of Iowa Studies in Child Welfare*, 4, No. 1 (1928).

[10] W. W. Greulich, "The Rationale of Assessing the Developmental Status of Children from Roentgenograms of the Hand and Wrist," *Child Development*, 21 (1950), 33-44.

[11] W. W. Greulich, R. I. Dorfman, H. R. Catchpole, C. I. Solomon, and C. S. Culotta, "Somatic and Endocrine Studies of Puberal and Adolescent Boys," *Monographs of the Society for Research in Child Development*, 7, No. 3 (1942).

[12] P. Boynton and J. Boynton, *Psychology of Child Development* (Minneapolis: Educational Publishers, Inc., 1938), p. 114.

[13] N. Bayley and R. D. Tuddenham, "Adolescent Changes in Body Build," *Forty-third Yearbook of the National Society for the Study of Education, Part 1* (Chicago: Department of Education, University of Chicago, 1944), 33-55.

[14] F. L. Shuttleworth, "The Physical and Mental Growth of Girls and Boys Age Six to Nineteen in Relation to Age at Maximum Growth," *Monographs of the Society for Research in Child Development*, 4, No. 3 (1939).

[15] Lennart Jacobsen, "On the Relationship between Menarcheal Age and Adult Body Structure," *Human Biology*, 26 (1954), 127-32.

16 Lea Kralj-Cereck, "The Influence of Food, Body Build, and Social Origin on the Age at Menarche," *Human Biology,* 28 (1956), 393-406.

17 C. Wesley Dupertius and N. Michael, "Comparison of Growth in Height and Weight Between Ectomorphic and Mesomorphic Boys," *Child Development,* 24 (1953), 212-13.

18 H. E. Jones, "The Development of Physical Abilities," *Forty-third Yearbook of the National Society for the Study of Education, Part 1* (Chicago: Department of Education, University of Chicago, 1944), Chap. 6.

19 H. E. Jones, *Motor Performance and Growth* (Berkeley, Calif.: University of California Press, 1949), pp. 56-57.

20 H. L. MacCurdy, *A Test for Measuring the Physical Capacity of Secondary School Boys* (New York: Harcourt, Brace & World, Inc., 1953).

21 E. Jokl and E. H. Cluver, "Physical Fitness," *Journal of the American Medical Association,* 116 (1941), 2383-89.

22 E. Espenschade, "Development of Motor Coordination in Boys and Girls," *Research Quarterly, American Physical Education Association,* 18 (1947), 30-43.

23 H. E. Jones, *Motor Performance and Growth,* Chap. 2.

24 Max Eastman, "Let's Close the Muscle Gap!" *The Reader's Digest,* 79 (1961), 125

25 Nameko Ikeda, "A Comparison of Physical Fitness of Children in Iowa, U. S. A. and Tokyo, Japan" (Ph.D. Dissertation, State University of Iowa, 1961).

26 John L. Reichert, "Competitive Athletics for Preteen-age Children," *Journal of the American Medical Association,* 166 (1958), 1704. Report is based upon personal communication from C. Hale to John L. Reichert.

27 H. E. Jones, *Motor Performance and Growth.*

28 A. Frazier, and L. K. Lisonbee, "Adolescent Concerns with Physique," *School Review,* 58 (1950), 397-405.

29 William A. Schofield, "Inadequate Masculine Physique as a Factor in Personality Development of Adolescent Boys," *Psychosomatic Medicine,* 12 (1950), 49-54.

30 Paul H. Mussen and Mary C. Jones, "The Behavior Inferred Motivations of Late- and Early-maturing Boys," *Child Development,* 29 (1958), 61-67.

31 Georgiana Wagner, "The Caseworker Faces the Adolescent," *The New Outlook,* 55 (1961), 299-302.

32 William M. Cruickshank and Howard J. Norris, "Adjustment of Physically Handicapped Adolescent Youth," *Exceptional Children,* 21 (1955), 282-88.

33 See "Pupil Personnel, Guidance, and Counseling," *Review of Educational Research* (Washington, D.C.: American Educational Research Association, 1939), 9, 148.

5

INTELLECTUAL
DEVELOPMENT

INTELLIGENCE: ITS MEANING AND MEASUREMENT

During the past several decades there has been a continuously mounting tide of research which has not only provided valuable information about the nature of mental growth, but has also opened up new areas for further study. No clear-cut principles of mental growth during the adolescent years has yet been presented, although the results of research do indicate certain characteristics of mental development. In any consideration of mental growth during adolescence, it is helpful for the student to recognize (1) that an evaluation of mental growth must take into consideration the varied experiences of the individual; (2) that mental growth during the adolescent years cannot be divorced from that during infancy and childhood; and (3) that mental growth is an integral part of the total development of the individual.

The discussion in this chapter will be confined mainly to the adolescent stage of life. Moreover, since many problems relating to mental development are highly controversial, the materials presented here are given in the spirit of what scientific studies tend to point out. Some of the major problems to be studied are the meaning of intelligence or mental ability, problems encountered in the attempt to measure intelligence, concepts of mental growth, development of individual mental abilities, and factors related to mental growth.

Concepts of intelligence. The concepts of the nature of intelligence held by early students of psychology were quite simple. Intelligence was conceived by many as a general mental power or a multiplicity of mental powers that could be measured on a vertical scale by a single score. These scores were either divided by chronological age and the resultant quotient called the intelligence quotient (IQ), or transmuted into mental ages. (A child's mental age, according to the early Binet tests and revisions of his test, was expressed in terms of the average age of children making that test score.) Any significant changes in an individual's IQ from year to year were regarded as exceptions. Thus, the theory of "the constancy of the IQ" was developed and generally accepted.

Thorndike suggested that in considering intelligence three levels or kinds of intelligent activity may be observed: *abstract, mechanical,* and *social.*[1] Abstract intelligence is one's ability to use and understand symbols, such as words and ideas. Mechanical intelligence is one's ability to understand and deal with objects, such as guns or lawn mowers. Social intelligence is the ability to understand and deal successfully with social events, particularly those involving decision making in human relations. At a later date Stoddard offered a functional and more precise definition of intelligence as the ability to perform difficult, complex, and abstract activities with speed, adaptiveness to a goal, social value, and inventiveness, and to maintain such activities under conditions that demand a concentration of energy and a resistance to emotional forces.[2]

Goddard defines intelligence as the bringing together of past experiences to solve immediate problems and to anticipate future ones.[3] A distinction should be made between intelligence as an inherited potential ability and intelligence as measured by intelligence tests. Actually the only intelligence we know anything about is that manifested in some performance or on some mental test. It might be more accurate to refer to an individual's intelligence test score rather than to his intelligence, since the latter is largely an abstraction. Intelligence as used in this chapter and in subsequent discussions refers to that which is determined from intelligence test scores.

Mental growth. The data available about mental growth are those obtained from administering intelligence tests to the same individual or group of individuals repeatedly for a number of years. Freeman and Flory reported results from the Chicago growth study, in which tests were administered to several hundred children over a period of years.[4] Many individuals were retested at the age of 17 or 18 years when they graduated from the University of Chicago Laboratory Schools, and some were later retested in college. A composite of four standardized tests consisting of (a) vocabulary, (b) analogies, (c) completion, and (d) opposites was used. The growth curves drawn from the raw scores showed mental development continuing well beyond the age of 17 or 18 years. There was, furthermore, some evidence from these studies that children of average ability might continue intellectual growth to a somewhat later age than the brighter pupil. The disparity in rate of growth, however, is in all likelihood a result of the average environment's failure to stimulate brighter pupils. The Minnesota studies of the mental growth of children from 2 to 14 years of age had similar results.[5]

Since each person develops at a unique rate, curves made from studies of individual mental growth vary greatly in shape; a plateau period frequently appears that will vary in duration from one individual to another. Some variations may be observed in Figure 5-1.[6] The curves show further that some children forge ahead and maintain their relatively advanced position after the early years, whereas others grow slowly and tend to fall further and further behind. Compared to the adolescent years, the early years are a period of rapid growth.

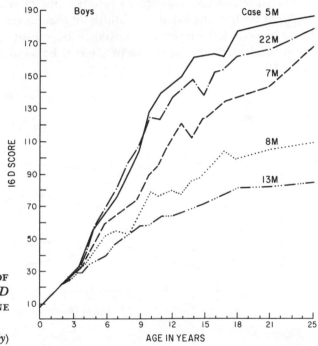

Figure 5-1

INDIVIDUAL CURVES OF INTELLIGENCE (16 *D* UNITS) FOR 5 BOYS, ONE MONTH TO 25 YEARS (*Berkeley Growth Study*)

Constancy of mental growth. There has been much controversy over the general nature of mental growth curves that has centered around the constancy of the IQ. Recent studies, however, offer evidence that mental growth is affected by a number of factors. Terman retested gifted children after a six-year interval, and concluded:

> Making due allowances for complicating factors in measuring IQ constancy, one can hardly avoid the conclusion that there are individual children in our gifted group who have shown very marked changes in IQ. Some of these changes have been in the direction of IQ increase, others of them in the direction of decrease. The important fact which seems to have been definitely established is that there sometimes occur genuine changes in the rate of intellectual

growth which cannot be accounted for on the basis of general health, educational opportunity, or other environmental influences.[7]

Correlations between test scores obtained one or more years apart are far from perfect. Significant fluctuations are likely to occur in a large percentage of cases. The extent of such changes will depend upon such factors as the circumstances that have appeared in the child's life during the interim (such as emotional problems, illness, change of environment, opportunity for schooling, motivation). In the guidance study at the University of California mental test scores were obtained from 252 children at specified ages between 21 months and 18 years.[8] The scores were analyzed to show the extent of stability of mental test performance during this age period. Performance constancy depended partly on the age at testing and partly on the length of interval between tests. That is, predic-

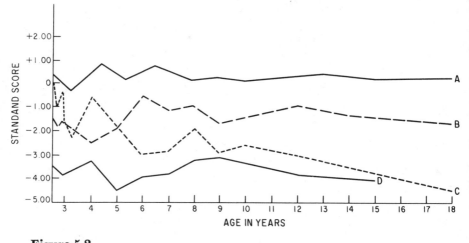

Figure 5-2

STABILITY OF IQ'S ON REPEATED MEASUREMENT OF THE SAME INDIVIDUALS

tion could be reliable over short age periods and more so after the preschool years. A study of individual cases showed that the IQ's of about 60 per cent of the group changed 15 or more points. The IQ's of 9 per cent changed 30 or more points. Illustrative cases of results on repeated measurements of the same individuals are presented in Figure 5-2. These show the great amount of instability of IQ's during the early years. Prediction of IQ's at age 18 based on 6-year-old mental test scores should be made with extreme caution.

Mental growth during adolescence. Anderson pointed out that suitable tests for the measurement of intelligence are not available for the preschool child.[9] He reported correlations from the Harvard growth data slightly in excess of .50 between mental test scores at the 7- and 16-year levels. Some of the discrepancies found in growth curves of this study may be observed from the comparison of those shown in Figure 5-3.[10] Mental

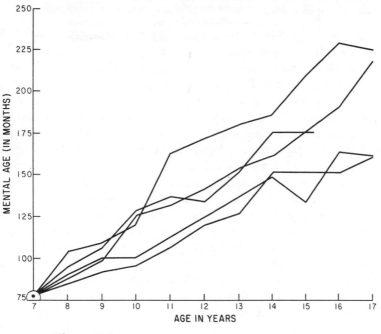

Figure 5-3

DIVERGING INDIVIDUAL MENTAL GROWTH CURVES

age curves of this figure are based on Harvard growth data for five boys with IQ's of 92 whose scores were the same at the age of 7. The progressive divergence of these curves, with the IQ's at the 17-year age level ranging from below 80 to 110, suggested that repeated measurements must be made if accurate classifications are to be maintained, although the fact that different tests were used and that these were group tests may account in part for these variations.

Some evidence was presented from earlier studies indicating that rise of mental growth curves is accompanied by a rise in physical growth curves.[11] More recent studies have not supported any connection between the two. It was suggested in Chapter 3 that individuals from homes with good living standards tended to mature earlier than those from homes of unfavorable living standards; these same general environmental conditions also have an important influence on intelligence test scores. Bersch, Lenz, and Maxwell obtained intra-pair correlations between intelligence and height of two groups of twins. They concluded:

"For both the German and the Scottish twin samples the intra-pair correlations between physical and mental measurements are of the order of zero. This is compatible with the hypothesis under investigation, namely, that there is no intrinsic biological relation between physical and intellectual development and that the observed tendency for more intelligent children to be better developed physically is a function of common environment."[12]

In a study by Stone and Barker, 175 postmenarcheal and 175 premenarcheal girls of the same chronological age were compared with respect to Otis intelligence test scores, personality, and socio-economic status of their parents.[13] The postmenarcheal girls made a mean score on the intelligence test which was 2.25 points higher than that made by the premenarcheal girls, but the difference was not statistically reliable. The Pressey interest-attitude test scores and the Sullivan test for developmental age showed the postmenarcheal girls to be more mature than the premenarcheal of the same chronological age. The two groups were from families of about the same socio-economic status, and did not show a difference in their general personality traits as measured by the Bernreuter Personality Inventory. Apparently, then, pubescence has much more significance as a physiological change affecting various glandular secretions—especially those relating to sexual characteristics—and the rate of growth in height, weight, and other physical measurements than it has as a criterion for mental growth. Physical and emotional changes are much more closely related to the onset of puberty than are the more specific mental abilities.

Age of cessation of mental growth. The age at which individuals cease to grow in intellectual ability has been studied by a number of students of child and adolescent development. Early investigations estimated that the limit of mental growth was reached somewhere between the thirteenth and sixteenth year. Later investigators have gradually raised the estimated year upward into the early twenties. A study of this problem conducted by Jones and Conrad, particularly appropriate since it contained a sufficient sample of subjects in the late teens and early twenties to furnish a complete picture of the nature of the mental growth until maturity, reported that the rate of mental growth was most rapid during the early years.[14] This rate slowed gradually until around age 16, after which there was a continued deceleration until the highest point was reached between age 19 and 20.

After reviewing earlier studies of this problem and analyzing retest scores made by approximately 1000 individuals, Thorndike concluded that ability to achieve on a standard test of intelligence continues to increase until and probably beyond age 20.[15] He points out, however, that this conclusion is based upon data for individuals in school. One should be careful in making generalizations from this finding to adolescents who drop out of school. Although the final answer to the question of the age of cessation of mental growth is not complete, studies tend to agree that mental test scores on standard paper-and-pencil tests continue to increase beyond the teen years. However, at higher levels of difficulty, group tests of mental ability become increasingly weighted with vocabulary and information exercises; thus, it appears likely that most of the increase in this later period consists chiefly in an increase in information and vocabulary, rather than an increase of potential ability resulting from maturation.

Certain broad generalizations emerge from further analysis of the results of these studies. The first is that intelligence is much more responsive to environmental changes than had previously been conceived. For practical purposes of education, it is the environmental stimulation or, in many cases, the lack of early environmental stimulation that sets the limits to a child's mentality.

The second is that hereditary constitution probably sets certain limitations. When children have been placed in an environment sufficiently stimulating, hereditary limitations begin to effect pronounced differences. As long as we are dealing with children who have not had such an environment, we shall find that responses to ordinary intelligence test items improve as a result of better environmental conditions.

GROWTH OF DIFFERENT INTELLECTUAL ABILITIES

Guilford has presented five major intellectual abilities: cognition, memory, convergent thinking, divergent thinking, and evaluation. These are described as follows:

"Cognition means discovery or rediscovery or recognition. Memory means retention of what is cognized. Two kinds of productive-thinking operations generate new information from known information and remembered information. In divergent-thinking operations we think in different directions, sometimes searching, sometimes seeking variety. In convergent thinking the information leads to one right answer or to a recognized best or conventional answer. In evaluation we reach decisions as to goodness, correctness, suitability, or adequacy of what we know, what we remember, and what we produce in productive thinking."[16]

With advancement from childhood into and through adolescence there is an increased stability of patterns of mental abilities, shown in the results of a study by Meyer, presented in conjunction with another study.[17] Meyer concluded: "These studies clearly demonstrate (a) increasing stability of test patterns with age and (b) increasing differentiation of the primary abilities with age."[18] This would seem to result from training and practice. The individual with a high score in numerical ability will probably make considerable use of this ability, and thus increase it. On the other hand, if he has a low verbal score, he will probably shun activity

Table 5-1

CORRELATION BETWEEN TWELFTH-GRADE PRIMARY
MENTAL ABILITIES SCORES AND THE EIGHTH-GRADE
SCORES ON THE CORRESPONDING TESTS AND ON
THE TOTAL

(*Meyer*)

Twelfth-grade Scale	Eighth-grade Corresponding Scale	Eighth-grade Total Score
Verbal	.81	.74
Numerical	.73	.34
Spatial	.66	.67
Reasoning	.75	.61
Word Fluency	.43	.33
Total		.82

that requires use of words, and as a result his verbal ability will not increase at the same rate.

The development of memory ability. Some have described childhood as the "golden age of memory" and adulthood as the age of reasoning. Studies of the growth of different mental functions show, however, that memory, reasoning ability, critical thinking, interpretive ability, and other mental functions grow continuously, in an orderly manner. There are a number of reasons why certain misconceptions have developed about the memory ability of children. In the first place, much of that memorized by children is mechanical. On that basis, the child competes favorably with adults. Children have not developed a wide range of associations and understandings; therefore, they are compelled to rely largely upon mechanical memories, and are not distracted by meaningful elements that may appear in the situation. Furthermore, children are more limited in the scope of their mental activity and spend considerable time in going over certain materials. The developmental curve for memory ability is somewhat similar in nature to that of other mental functions; it increases with age and experience.

The problem of the influence of age upon the learning of poetry and nonsense syllables was studied by Stroud and Maul.[19] The subjects consisted of 172 grade-school children, 26 ninth-grade students, and 23 college freshmen. The average chronological ages ranged from 7.7 years to 18.1 years. The different groups were approximately equal in average IQ. The growth with age in the ability to memorize poetry is shown in Figure 5-4. The memory curve for nonsense syllables was found to be similar to that shown for poetry, and a high correlation existed between memory ability and mental age.

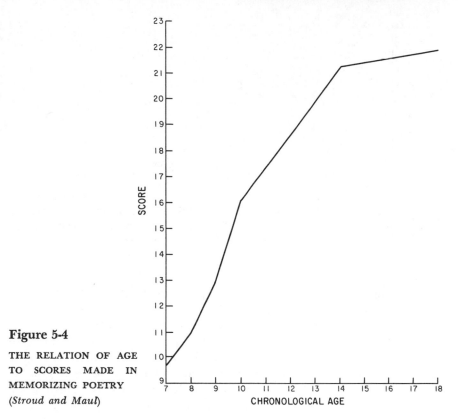

Figure 5-4

THE RELATION OF AGE
TO SCORES MADE IN
MEMORIZING POETRY
(*Stroud and Maul*)

Vocabulary growth. Studies by Terman, Thorndike, and others have shown a constant and continuous growth in the size of vocabulary during childhood and adolescence. Studies of the qualitative aspects of vocabulary reveal also a change in the character of word definitions. Feifel and Lorge tested 900 children aged 6 to 14, all slightly above the average in intelligence except at age 14.[20] They administered the vocabulary test of Form L of the Stanford revision of the Binet tests to these children, and the definitions given were studied for their completeness and qualitative nature. The results are presented in Figure 5-5. It is apparent that children at the 6- and 7-year age level define by giving the use and description of the object most often; *orange* would be "something to eat." The explanation type of response is used very little at this age, but appears to grow slowly and continuously in use until the 13-year age level. The decline noted at the 14-year age level may be partially accounted for by the lower intelligence of this group in comparison with that of the other groups. The synonym type of response, although seldom used by the 6- and 7-year-olds, is used quite frequently by children around the ages of 9 and 10, and continues to grow in use throughout the following years. The decline in the dem-

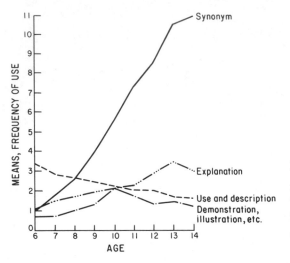

Figure 5-5

MEAN FREQUENCY OF USE OF FOUR QUALITATIVE CATEGORIES BY AGE

(Feifel and Lorge)

onstrational and illustrative types of response during the adolescent years may be attributed to the growth in the size of vocabulary and the ability to symbolize things and events in terms of opposites and similarities.

Quantity concepts. Piaget noted in his studies of the development of quantity conceptions in children that abstract responses to mass, weight, and volume appeared in a regular sequence related to age.[21] A number of studies have confirmed in part the results obtained by Piaget. Elkin tested 469 junior high school students for their conceptions of mass, weight, and volume.[22] The results showed, "(a) of the students tested, 87 per cent had attained an abstract conception of mass and weight, but only 47 per cent had attained an abstract conception of volume; (b) the percentage of students having an abstract volume conception increased significantly between the ages of 12 and 18; (c) a significantly higher percentage of boys than girls attained an abstract conception of volume; (d) there was a low but positive correlation of IQ with attainment of the volume conception."[23]

Growth of concepts of casual relations. With increased mental development, the ability of the growing individual to understand causal relations increases. In the study of children's concepts by Deutsche, two types of analyses of children's causal thinking were made—quantitative and qualitative.[24] Questions of causality were selected and tried out with children as subjects. From these preliminary trials, final forms of the tests were developed. Form I consisted of questions based upon demonstrations of experiments in the classroom. Form II consisted of questions without experiments. Quantified scores, based on the adequacy of the answer as an explanation of the phenomenon, were derived for each of the questions. Phenomenistic answers such as, "The wind makes the wind blow," comprised from 30 to 40 per cent of the answers at age 8, and approximately 10 per cent at ages 15-16. There was, on the other hand, a striking increase from age 8 to ages 15-16 in logical deduction answers. Very little change with age was noted in dynamic causality and mechanical causality answers.

Imagination and critical thinking. Although teachers and parents recognize changes in the imaginative and critical abilities with age, a study of their development during childhood and adolescence is made difficult by the lack of good instruments and techniques for measuring these mental functions. One aid is that the imagination of adolescents is reflected in their poems, stories, drawings, music, constructive activities, and dances. Vernon has offered evidence that children are unable to fully understand and interpret a series of pictures prior to age 11.[25] The interpretation given to a picture by a preadolescent will be determined not only by his mental development but also by previous experiences he has had with elements presented in the picture.

Tests designed to measure critical thinking in science were given to approximately 1000 pupils in grades 10, 11, and 12 of the San Francisco Bay area.[26] Differences in scores on the tests indicate that the skills measured by these tests may be taught, and if pupils are to be taught to think they must first be taught to recognize problems, then learn sound methods for the solution of such problems. This implies, then, that knowledge or information is essential for critical thinking. The lack of improvement in the ability of the adolescent to do critical thinking may result from one or more of the following:

(a) failure to comprehend the problem,
(b) lack of information about the problem, and
(c) inappropriate method of organizing information dealing with the problem.

Insight and interpretations. The pattern of development in the ability to interpret simple literary materials is shown in Figure 5-6.[27] Materials for this study consisted of five selections from very simple poetry. The pupils were given the selections along with five statements on each selection, one statement being the corrct answer to the question. The following poem was correctly interpreted by three-fourths of the sixth-grade pupils tested:

Oh, the Wee Green Apple

I ate a small green apple;
It tasted good, and yet—
I wish that small green apple
And I had—never met.

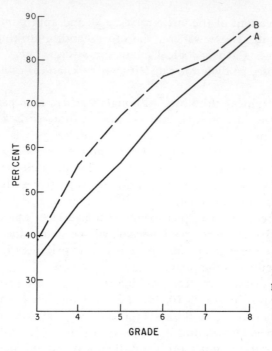

Figure 5-6

THE AVERAGE PER CENT OF PUPILS GIVING THE CORRECT INTERPRETA- TION TO THE FIVE LIT- ERARY SELECTIONS (A) AND THE PER CENT OF PUPILS GIVING THE COR- RECT INTERPRETATION TO A SINGLE LITERARY SELECTION (B) *(Pyle)*

QUESTION: Why does he wish that he had never met the apple?

1. The green apple made him sick.
2. The apple was sour.
3. The apple had worms.
4. Because he was not hungry.
5. Because green apples are not good for children.

The data for Graph A of Figure 5-6 were secured by obtaining the average per cent of pupils at each grade level giving the correct interpretations to the five selections. Grape B shows the pattern of development of pupils from the third through the eighth grade in their ability to give a correct interpretation to the poem about the green apple. The rapid development in the ability to give correct interpretations to literary selections is most significant; however, it should be noted that important variations in ability exist at each grade level.

In the study by Shaffer, approximately 150 children in each grade from 4 through 12 were tested for their ability to interpret cartoons.[28] There was a continuous increase with age in the general merit of interpretations. This is shown in Figure 5-7. Four fairly distinct types of responses were observed: *repetitions, descriptions, concrete interpretation,* and *abstract interpretation*. Repetition occurred irregularly in the earlier

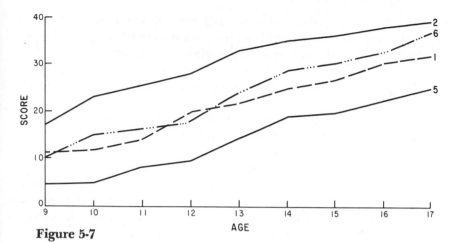

Figure 5-7

MEAN SCORE BY AGES FOR INTERPRETING CARTOONS 1, 2, 5, AND 6
(*After Shaffer*)

age levels studied. One implication of this study is that cartoons may be successfully used for teaching at the junior high school level.

This study shows that the ability to interpret cartoons of a complex nature occurs considerably later than for simpler cartoons. Immature perception characterizes early childhood. The child notes things in large units; careful classifications are wholly lacking, e.g., the horse may be called a big dog. Increased maturity and experience enable the adolescent to make discriminations and offer more accurate and realistic interpretations.

Intelligence and creativity. Although it is true that children with high intelligence test scores are in general superior in a number of abilities, especially verbal abilities, there are many with little more than average intelligence who have a special ability or talent. Tiebot and Meier conducted a study to determine the relationship of intelligence to artistic ability.[29] The study with children from the first seven grades yielded the conclusion: "Artistic ability is a special ability in the sense of being only somewhat related to general intelligence, as measured by established tests." In their study of artistically superior individuals, they found that both professionally recognized and high school artists had higher than average IQ's.

Getzels' and Jackson's studies showed significant differences in character between adolescents exceptionally high in intelligence but not equally high in creativity and those exceptionally high in creativity but not equally high in intelligence.[30] Significant differences also appeared in the fantasy production of the two groups. The highly creative adolescents expressed more imagination, humor, and originality in their themes. They were also more rebellious and less given to conformity, which led to more conflict with their teachers at school and their parents at home.

MENTAL GROWTH CORRELATES

Relationship between mental and physical growth. There is recent evidence that a large number of subnormal children suffer from physical defects and afflictions. One of the most complete studies bearing on this shows that subnormal boys grow more slowly than normal children and that the degree of physical abnormality or deficiency is related to the degree of mental deficiency.[31] The results of this study were further corroborated by a study conducted in Los Angeles, comparing the physical characteristics of 900 educationally backward children with those of 2700 mentally normal children.[32] In spite of the medical care and services supplied to these subnormal children, there was a higher incidence of physical defects of every kind among them than among the children of normal intelligence.

The social-class structure. Continued exposure to differential environmental conditions, found in different social-class groups, favors the development of certain abilities and discourages the development of others. Most of the tasks to be learned at school are more closely related to the background of middle-class than of lower-class children. Consequently, middle-class children tend to excel in the tasks. This was indicated in a study by Janke and Havighurst.[33] All available 16-year-old boys and girls in a Midwestern community were given intelligence tests, performance tests, reading tests, and mechanical aptitude tests. The following conclusions were drawn from an analysis of the results of these tests:

1. Boys and girls from families of higher social status tended to do better in all the tests than boys and girls of lower social position, with the exception of the Mechanical Assembly Test, where there was no reliable social class difference between the boys.

2. Urban boys and girls tended to do better than rural boys and girls, but not statistically so.

3. No significant sex differences were noted.

Most of the widely used tests of intelligence are geared to the experiences of the child from the middle and high socio-economic class. Also, the definition of intelligence itself is stated in terms of learning and problem solving of materials found in middle-class situations. The school program promotes the values of the middle-class and rewards those children who adhere to them. Thus, the lower-class child is at an extreme disadvantage in the performance of many school tasks.

Mental growth and personality development. The relationship between certain personal characteristics and mental growth was studied at the Fels Research Institute, where extensive longitudinal data were available on a sample of 140 children.[34] The investigators concluded that an accelerated or decelerated rate of mental growth "did not appear to be related to any specific areas of ability as measured by the performances on the different types of items." There appears to be a general accelerator-decelerator factor present regardless of the child's own special competence, often described as curiosity or "eagerness to learn." This study supports the viewpoint that eagerness, curiosity, and a favorable self-concept aid mental and educational growth.

School achievement in relation to intelligence. When one considers the nature of intelligence tests and traditional achievement tests, it seems that a significant relationship should exist between achievement and intelligence. Layton and Swanson obtained correlations between scores on the items of the *Differential Aptitude Test* and high school rank, presented in Table 5-2, that indicated such a relationship.[35] The correlations varied with a number of factors but usually ranged between .30 and .75.

Table 5-2

CORRELATIONS OF THE ITEMS ON THE
DIFFERENTIAL APTITUDE TEST WITH
HIGH SCHOOL RANK
(*After Layton and Swanson*)

Verbal reasoning	.56
Numerical ability	.57
Abstract reasoning	.45
Space relations	.36
Mechanical reasoning	.29
Clerical speed and accuracy	.32

Evidence from studies has confirmed the hypothesis that a well-made test of verbal and mathematical ability furnishes useful information about a student's academic promise. Such predictions would be greater if the program of studies and the standards of grading were more uniform. Figure 5-8 illustrates the kind of relationship found between the verbal scores on the *Scholastic Aptitude Test* and college freshmen grades under favorable conditions. The chart indicates, as expected, that the higher the student's SAT score, the better the chances of satisfactory or honor work in college.[36] Colleges have succeeded in greatly reducing the failure rate among students enrolled through their selective admissions policies, and this would affect the relationship that might be expected between SAT

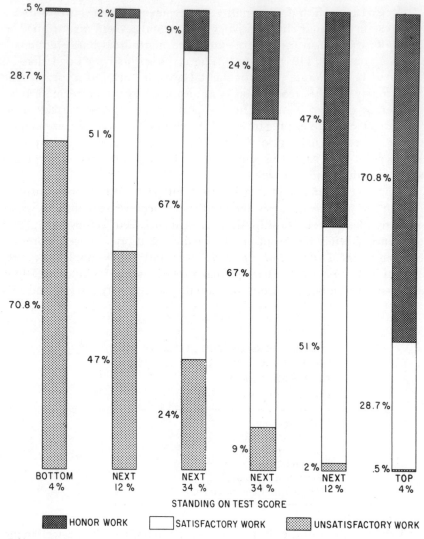

Figure 5-8

RELATION BETWEEN STANDING ON SCHOLASTIC APTITUDE TEST AND STAND-
ING ON COLLEGE FRESHMAN GRADES UNDER FAVORABLE CONDITIONS
(*Educational Testing Service*)

scores of students actually admitted to college and grades obtained during
the freshman year.

Some problems related to mental growth. Mental growth is usually
accompanied by increased social and intellectual demands. This presents
some difficult, baffling problems for adolescents who are ill-prepared

through lack of guidance and experience to make choices and assume responsibility. Some of these problems are discussed in later chapters dealing with guidance.

A common source of worry to the adolescent is the question of whether he will be successful in meeting intellectual requirements. Passing examinations, making satisfactory marks in school, and being admitted to college are among the common preoccupations and aspirations of pupils in the upper grades of our schools. The urgency of these demands is often unrelated to the values and aspirations the individual has set for himself; however, the adolescent does not want to be regarded as a failure by his parents, teachers, and peers who hold up school success as the criterion of real success. Thus, many types of problem behavior and personal and social maladjustments are traceable to failure in school.

Studies of adolescent groups reveal that intelligence is no guide to personal adjustment. There are a number of factors responsible for this, some of which are suggested in the following statement:

> These are the child's absolute level of intelligence: the level of intelligence required in the activities toward which he is being pointed, through the ambitions of his family and friends; the social pressures which arise from such ambitions; his own "felt needs" and level of aspiration; and his actual achievement. These factors are interconnected in a variety of ways and a great variety of complex patterns may result.[37]

SUMMARY

Many of the early notions about the nature of intelligence and the mental growth curve have been modified or discarded as a result of more recent research. It is now generally recognized that most group intelligence tests are culturally biased in favor of the middle-class child. Thus, one finds a significant correlation between scores on these tests and middle-class conditions or factors present in the life activities of children. Intelligence test scores furnish data about the manifestation or functioning of intelligence in dealing with special problems. Thus, scores on these tests are influenced by the nature and amount of experience of the individuals concerned.

A mental-growth characteristic of special interest relates to the age of maturity, or limit of mental growth. Problems of maturation, learning, and motivation affect scores on intelligence tests. Also, the nature of the test materials may be the important factor in accounting for differences found. Individual growth curves presented in this chapter show that the special characteristics of mental growth are not uniform from individual to individual. The close relation between intelligence test score and size of vocabulary during adolescence indicates that mental ability is closely related to the ability to learn materials of an abstract and symbolic nature. Although mental growth, like other aspects of growth, is gradual and continuous in nature, research studies indicate that it tends to proceed rapidly during the early years of life with a slowing down in rate during the teen years. Whether the growth during the latter teen years into the twenties is a gain in actual mental ability or one of mental content is a matter of controversy. However, it is quite likely that many extraneous factors reduce the accuracy of the rates and limits derived for mental growth at any given period.

THOUGHT PROBLEMS

1. What experiences have you had with intelligence tests? On the basis of your experience, what do you consider they are actually measuring?
2. To what extent is mental development related to the age of pubescence? To physical maturity?
3. What do the various experiments appear to indicate relative to intelligence? What are the various correlations that have been obtained?
4. How is mental ability related to learning? How should this relation affect the curriculum prior to adolescence?
5. How would you account for the relation between mental and physical development? What is the educational significance of this relation?
6. What mental expansion in yourself took place as you reached adolescence?
7. Compare curves of growth in memory and reasoning. What would you conclude from such a comparison?
8. What is the relationship between school achievement and intelligence? How would you account for this relationship?
9. What are the educational implications of the materials presented relative to mental growth during late childhood and adolescence?
10. Differentiate *potential* and *functional* intelligence. What factors sometimes operate to obscure a child's potential intelligence?

SELECTED REFERENCES

Anderson, J. E., *The Psychology of Development and Personal Adjustment.* New York: Holt, Rinehart & Winston, Inc., 1949, Chaps. 8 and 9.

Cole, Luella, *Psychology of Adolescence,* 6th ed. New York: Holt, Rinehart & Winston, Inc., 1964, Chaps. 8 and 9.

Coleman, James S., *The Adolescent Society.* New York: The Free Press of Glencoe, Inc., 1961, Chap. 9.

Goodenough, Florence L., "The Measurement of Mental Growth in Childhood," in *Manual of Child Psychology,* 2nd ed., L. Carmichael, ed. New York: John Wiley & Sons, Inc., 1954, Chap. 8.

Horrocks, John E., *The Psychology of Adolescence,* 2nd ed. Boston: Houghton-Mifflin Company, 1962, Chap. 14.

Johnson, Eric W., *How to Live Through Junior High School*. Philadelphia: J. B. Lippincott Co., 1959, Chap. 3.

Rogers, Dorothy, *The Psychology of Adolescence*. New York: Appleton-Century-Crofts, 1962, Chap. 5.

Seidman, Jerome M., ed., *The Adolescent—A Book of Readings*, 2nd ed. New York: Holt, Rinehart & Winston, Inc., 1960, Chap. 6.

Strang, Ruth, *The Adolescent Views Himself*. New York: McGraw-Hill Book Company, 1957, Chap. 7.

NOTES

[1] E. L. Thorndike, "Intelligence and Its Uses," *Harper's Magazine*, **140** (1929), 227-35.

[2] G. D. Stoddard, "On the Meaning of Intelligence," *Psychological Review*, **48** (1941), 250-60.

[3] H. H. Goddard, "What Is Intelligence?" *Journal of Social Psychology*, **24** (1946), 68.

[4] F. N. Freeman and C. D. Flory, "Growth in Intellectual Ability as Measured by Repeated Tests," *Monographs of the Society for Research in Child Development*, **2** (1937), 116.

[5] Florence L. Goodenough and K. M. Mauer, "The Mental Growth of Children from Two to Fourteen Years: A Study of the Predictive Value of the Minnesota Preschool Scales," *University of Minnesota Child Welfare Monograph Series*, No. 19 (1942).

[6] Nancy Bayley, "On the Growth of Intelligence," *American Psychologist*, **10** (1955), 814.

[7] L. M. Terman, *Genetic Studies of Genius*, **3** (1930), 30.

[8] M. P. Honzig, J. W. Macfarlane, and L. Allen, "The Stability of Mental Test Performance Between Two and Eighteen Years," *The Journal of Experimental Education*, **17** (1948), 309-24.

[9] J. E. Anderson, "The Prediction of Terminal Intelligence from Infant and Preschool Tests," *Intelligence: Its Nature and Nurture. Thirty-ninth Yearbook of the National Society for the Study of Education, Part 1* (Chicago: Department of Education, University of Chicago, 1940), Chap. 13, pp. 385-403.

[10] Harold E. Jones and Herbert S. Conrad, "Mental Development in Adolescence," *Adolescence. Forty-third Yearbook of the National Society for the Study of Education, Part 1* (Chicago: Department of Education, University of Chicago, 1944), Chap. 8, p. 159.

[11] Ethel M. Abernethy, "Correlations in Physical and Mental Growth," *Journal of Educational Psychology*, **16** (1925), 438-66, 539-46.

[12] O. F. Bersch, W. Lenz, and J. Maxwell, "The Correlation Between Mental and Physical Growth in Twins," *British Journal of Educational Psychology*, **31** (1961), 267.

[13] C. P. Stone and R. G. Barker, "Aspects of Personality and Intelligence in Postmenarcheal and Premenarcheal Girls of the Same Chronological Age," *Journal of Comparative Psychology*, **23** (1937), 439-45.

[14] Harold E. Jones and Herbert S. Conrad, "The Growth and Direction of Intelligence," *Genetic Psychology Monographs*, **13** (1933), 223-98.

[15] Robert L. Thorndike, "Growth in Intelligence During Adolescence," *Journal of Genetic Psychology*, **72** (1948), 11-15.

[16] J. P. Guilford, "Three Faces of Intellect," *American Psychologist*, **14** (1958), 470.

[17] William J. Meyer, "The Stability of Patterns of Primary Mental Abilities Among Junior High and Senior High School Students," *Educational and Psychological Measurements*, **20** (1960), 795-800.

[18] *Ibid.*, p. 800.

[19] J. B. Stroud and P. Maul, "The Influence of Age upon Learning and Retention of Poetry and Nonsense Syllables," *Journal of Genetic Psychology*, **42** (1933), 242-50.

[20] H. Feifel and L. Lorge, "Qualitative Differences in the Vocabulary Responses of Children," *Journal of Educational Psychology*, **41** (1950), 1-18.

21 Jean Piaget, *The Child's Conception of Numbers* (London: Kegan, Paul Trench & Co., 1952). First published in Switzerland, 1941.

22 David Elkin, "Quantity Conceptions in Junior and Senior High School Students," *Child Development,* **32** (1961), 551-60.

23 *Ibid.*, p. 559.

24 J. M. Deutsche, *The Development of Children's Concepts of Causal Relation* (Minneapolis: University of Minnesota Press, 1937).

25 M. D. Vernon, "The Development of Imaginative Construction in Children," *British Journal of Psychology,* **39** (1948), 102-111.

26 T. B. Edwards, "Measurement of Some Aspects of Critical Thinking," *Journal of Experimental Education,* **18** (1950), 268.

27 W. H. Pyle, "An Experimental Study of the Development of Certain Aspects of Reasoning," *Journal of Educational Psychology,* **26** (1935), 539-46.

28 L. F. Shaffer, "Children's Interpretations of Cartoons," *Contributions to Education,* No. 429 (Teachers College, Columbia University, 1930).

29 Tiebot and N. C. Meier, "Artistic Ability and General Intelligence," *Psychological Monographs,* **48** (1936), 95-125.

30 J. W. Getzels and P. W. Jackson, "The Highly Creative and Highly Intelligent Adolescent: An Attempt to Differentiate," Paper read at the American Psychological Association Convention, Washington, D.C. (September, 1958).

31 C. D. Flory, "The Physical Growth of Mentally Deficient Boys," *Monographs of the Society for Research in Child Development,* **1** No. 6 (1936).

32 M. Goldwasser, "Physical Defects in Mentally Retarded School Children," *California and Western Medicine,* **47** (1937), 310-15.

33 L. L. Janke and R. J. Havighurst, "Relation between Ability and Social Status in a Midwestern Community. II: Sixteen-year-old Boys and Girls," *Journal of Educational Psychology,* **36** (1945), 499-509.

34 Lester W. Sontag, Charles T. Baker, and Virginia L. Nelson, "Mental Growth and Personality Development: A Longitudinal Study," *Monographs of the Society for Research in Child Development,* **23,** No. 2 (1958).

35 Wilbur L. Layton and Edward O. Swanson, "Relationship of Ninth Grade Differential Aptitude Test Scores to Eleventh Grade Test Scores and High School Rank," *Journal of Educational Psychology,* **49** (1958), 153-55.

36 *Educational Testing Service Annual Report 1961-1962* (1963), p. 41.

37 H. S. Conrad, F. N. Freeman, and H. E. Jones, "Differential Mental Growth," *Forty-third Yearbook of the National Society for the Study of Education, Part 1* (Chicago: Department of Education, University of Chicago, 1944), p. 180.

EMOTIONAL
AND
SOCIAL
GROWTH

THE NATURE AND DEVELOPMENT OF EMOTIONAL BEHAVIOR

Emotions and behavior. The changed concepts of the nature of the child and adolescent have brought with them different methods and objectives in schools and socializing agencies. There has been a shift from consideration of the intellectual, moral, or social side of the child to that of development of the total personality. An increased understanding of the development and significance of the emotions in the growing personality is of utmost importance to those concerned with guidance. Many people tend to regard the emotions as a stereotyped pattern of expression appearing with certain forms of stimulation. However, "the present tendency is to recognize that emotional components are in some form and to some degree present in all behavior."[1]

Emotional development, although treated in this chapter as a separate topic from that of physical development, must not be considered without reference to physical development. The case of Jo, reported by Zachry in a study of adolescents, illustrates how impossible it is to isolate certain elements as "physical" and others as "emotional." Presented here, the case shows the necessity of considering all the factors that enter into the nature of an individual at any particular stage of life.[2]

Jo's sister was soon to be married and his brother had just started to work, but Jo, 12 years old and the youngest child, was not particularly interesting to any member of the family. He had not been doing well in his school work, especially in arithmetic. One morning at breakfast he ate heartily; he had oatmeal with cream, eggs, bacon, jam, and milk. At the thought of an arithmetic test he was to take that morning, he felt a queer, twitchy feeling of excitement in his stomach. He walked slowly to school, thinking more about the test. His stomach felt strange. He had a vague feeling, hardly a thought, that if he were sick, he would not have to go to school. The arithmetic test came to mind again, and he suddenly found it hard to keep breakfast down.

Shortly after his arrival at school, he was sick. He was sent home with a clear conscience to have a day in bed. The principal telephoned his mother, who immediately became concerned. She put Jo to bed in the guest room and lavished him with attention such as he had not experienced since he was a small boy. His sister showed him her wedding presents; before going out in the evening, his brother had a talk with him, an event that had not occurred for months; and his father spent the evening reading to him.

The upset stomach had a high value: no arithmetic test, and solicitude from all the people from whom he had been wishing attention for some time. The next time Jo was faced with a difficult situation and there was a queer feeling in his stomach, there was no hesitation. He was immediately sick.

The development of the emotions. According to Bridges the emotional reactions of the infant are not highly differentiated, but the most common response to emotional stimuli is that of general bodily agitation or excitement.[3] Out of this general excitation develop, during the first several months, the differential responses of distress and delight. Here we note the negative and positive forms of emotional responses that have commonly been recognized and given varied classifications. Anger, disgust, fear, and jealousy emerge at an early age from distress; elation, affection for others, and joy grow out of delight. The different ages for the appearance of different forms of behavior during emotional episodes show that crying, screaming, restlessness, and struggling appear during the first four months of life and may be regarded as general bodily agitation caused by some sort of overstimulation. Following infancy the child passes through a period of growth, coordinating and integrating each new stage with that which has gone before. Emotional development is not great, due to the slow rate of growth of the internal organs of the body controlled by the autonomic nervous system, and thus closely identified with the emotional life.

Most of our fears or angers are acquired ways of responding to various situations. Most of our other emotional patterns are the results of learning and maturation—few of the stimuli that cause fear or anger among adults will frighten an infant. Since emotions are learned, the child or adolescent should be guided in the development of desirable emotional patterns, thus enabling one to avoid the inefficiency, embarrassment, and annoyance that uncontrolled emotions produce.

The word *emotion* was derived from the Latin word *emovere*, "to move out." It is usually defined as a stirred-up state or condition, but should not be regarded as a name for a type of response that is entirely different from nonemotional behavior. Behavior is a continuous, complex process involving simultaneous activity in many parts of the body. Emotion, instinct, and habit do not designate distinctly different types of behavior; they are merely abstractions which are necessary for convenience of study. Emotional behavior is an *emotion* in pure form only within a textbook. The same is true of a conditioned reflex, or a *habit*. However, emotional elements intensify, inhibit, and otherwise modify the behavior in process at any given time and are integral parts of the whole pattern of behavior; they comprise what is sometimes called one's *emotional tone*.

Earlier, James, Lange, Cannon, and others were concerned with the physiological center of emotional responses. Today psychologists recognize that the visceral responses are important components of the emotions. Although the term was recognized by earlier students, Lindsey clearly defined and described emotional responses by *activation*.[4] Strong emotion represents one end of a continuum of activities, and sleep represents the other, at which time there is a minimum activation.

Internalized and externalized emotional responses. A careful study of early childhood emotions shows that activation is both external and internal; however, important changes in the proportion of internal and external activation appear with growth. One of the most important problems of the dynamics of emotions is determining just this proportion. The galvanic skin response (GSR) is sometimes used as a measure of internalized emotional responses, and observed overt behavior is used for estimating externalized emotional responses. Jones reports that children who are most overtly excitable are least reactive on the galvanic test.[5] It is thus suggested that the increase of apparent emotional control with age may indicate a shift from externalized to internalized patterns of responses. This results in a large measure from the suppression of overt emotional behavior, since it tends to bring social disapproval and punishment.

In the Adolescent Growth Study at the University of California a series of observations on a group of children were made from age 12 to age 18.[6] These records included ratings of personal expressiveness and of various social traits. A series of experiments were conducted in which polygraphic records of palm-to-forearm skin-resistance changes, pulse rates, and respiration changes in a mild stress situation of a free association test were secured. A comparison of the overt behavioral characteristics of 40 cases, evenly divided at each extreme (high reaction and low reaction) in the average magnitude of GSR, furnished data, presented in Figure 6-1, concerning the relationship of internalized and externalized emotional responses during adolescence.[7] The first and most striking fact noted was that the high-reactive group showed significantly less overt emotional behavior than the low-reactive group. They were less talkative, less animated, displayed less attention-seeking behavior, and were less assertive

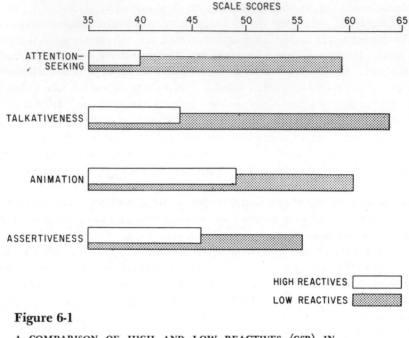

Figure 6-1

A COMPARISON OF HIGH AND LOW REACTIVES (GSR) IN
SOCIAL BEHAVIOR (PSYCHOLOGISTS' RATINGS)
(*After Jones*)

in their social behavior. From 85 to 95 per cent of the high reactives
excelled the average of the low reactives as more calm, more cooperative,
more deliberate, more good natured, and more responsible.

EMOTIONAL MANIFESTATIONS OF ADOLESCENTS

A significant change in the orientation of the individual to his
environment occurs at puberty. This change is clearly revealed in the
changed interests that appear at this age, and will be elaborated in Chapter
9. Also, the overt manifestations of emotions become less intense; the reactions of the child to thrills and dangers in the movies become more
subdued. Children and preadolescents tend to react violently to thrill and
danger in movies or on television, whereas they are relatively unresponsive
to love-making scenes. Four or five years later, with the ripening of the
sex impulse, the story will likely be very different.

Adolescent fears. Fear of animals and other tangible things in the
immediate environment appears to decrease as the child develops from
age 5 to age 12; fear of the dark, of being left alone at night, and the

unknown increases. With growth into adolescence, social fears are very important. However, a study by Hicks and Hayes shows that 50 per cent of a group of 250 junior high school students reported they were still afraid of something: in order of frequency reported, snakes, dogs, the dark, storms, accidents, high places, strange noises, and being alone at home; many childhood fears persist into adolescence and, on good evidence, even throughout life. Older adolescents become more concerned over social approval, failure in school, being disliked, and other relations with their peers. The fears of adolescents may be roughly classified into three groups:

1. *Fears of material things.* These include many of the early childhood fears of dogs, snakes, storms, and the like.

2. *Fears relating to the self.* These include death, failure in school, personal inadequacy, and the like.

3. *Fears involving social relations.* These include embarrassment at social events, when meeting with a more mature group or with people in general, and at parties, dates, and the like.

The frustration-aggression hypothesis. Available evidence favors the viewpoint that anger is a result of the frustration of some goal-seeking activity. For example, when one withholds the bottle from the hungry baby anger appears in the form of aggressive behavior. The student becomes angry when he is ejected from the team; the college girl becomes angry

Table 6-1

FRUSTRATIONS AND ANGER IN MEN AND WOMEN
COLLEGE STUDENTS

(*After Meltzer*)

	Men (Per cent)	Women (Per cent)
Thwarting of self-assertion:		
Defense reactions to persons	29	45
Aggressive reactions to persons	7	19
Defense reactions to things	47	26
Thwarting of organic needs	6	5
Complex situational thwarting	12	5

when her dinner date fails to appear; the auto salesman becomes angry when someone severely criticizes his product and he loses a sale.

Meltzer gathered significant data from college students on situations or conditions causing anger during a period of one week.[9] In about 86 per cent of the situations listed, frustrations were involved. A very small percentage of the frustrations presented in Table 6-1 involved organic needs. The majority of college men's frustrations dealt with things; 64 per cent of college women's dealt with persons.

Worries of adolescents. A careful study of the sources of children's worry reveals that fear is its foundation. As the child passes from preschool to elementary school age, considerable anxiety over failure appears. Also, as the child grows in understanding and reacts to different social situations, he develops anxieties and fears relative to his status in the group, although earlier fears about bodily injury are not suddenly eliminated. For example, Zeligs found that sixth-graders were most frequently worried about matters pertaining to bodily injury, health, grades, and promotion in school.[10]

Specifically, growth into adolescence is accompanied by anxieties on the part of many boys and girls connected with appearance, popularity, the future, and boy-girl relationships. Remmers and Taliana made a study in which some 2500 high school students were asked to write anonymous letters and essays about their most pressing problem.[11] The results suggest strongly that teen-agers could hardly be called light-hearted. The letters showed that the two areas of greatest concern were family relationships, 22 per cent, and school, 21 per cent. Next in frequency came worries about the future—choosing a career, the draft, college, and so on, 15 per cent. This was followed by boy-girl relationships, 14 per cent; personal concern, 12 per cent; getting along with other people, 7 per cent; problems of a general nature, 5 per cent; and health, 2 per cent.

Some of the letters also gave reasons for these problems. For example, in the "School" category there was the adolescent's desire to be himself and, at the same time, the conflicting desire to fit in with the group. When the high school youngster writes about himself, he sometimes discloses an awareness that may well lead to desirable self-insight. Under "Getting Along with Others" many replies gave evidence of the individual-group conflict. "They don't understand me!" is a recurrent theme in the letters grouped under "Home and Family." Under the "Boy Meets Girl" category, girls were particularly worried about how much they should "neck" or pet.

As can be seen in Table 6-2, younger adolescents worry more than older adolescents about achievement at school and about personal characteristics.[12] Guilt feelings and a guilty conscience also ranked high among the worries of the younger adolescents. On the other hand, acceptance by others, especially by girls, and money for dates were consistent worries of the older boys. The category of apprehensions about war, natural disasters, personal accidents, and personal health was used for the younger, but not for the older adolescents; however, the early adolescents were not concerned. It seems likely that war and personal accidents would concern late adolescents more.

Table 6-2

THINGS EARLY ADOLESCENT AND ADOLESCENT BOYS WORRY ABOUT MOST

(*Survey Research Center Institute*)

Worries	11–13 Years (per cent)	14–16 Years (per cent)
Achievement	65	57
Passing, getting through school	35	20
Doing well in school	14	16
Winning the game, making the team	8	7
Vocational choice	3	5
General achievement	2	3
Doing well on a job	1	2
Other	2	4
Acceptance by Others	16	29
Girls	10	21
Peer acceptance	4	8
Parental acceptance and approval	2	—
Reality Pressures	16	23
Money for dates	5	14
Getting parents' permission for activities	2	4
Draft	1	4
Crisis in family	1	2
Anticipation of family crisis	4	2
Family finances	*	1
Marriage	1	—
Other	2	2
Personal Characteristics	19	11
Being grown up too quickly	1	*
Self-conscious, awkward	1	*
Physical characteristics, weakness, appearance	4	3
Guilt feelings, guilty conscience	11	5
Other	2	3

* Less than one per cent.

Expression of sympathy. The development of the ability to "sympathize" or express sympathy is a result of maturation and experience. The small child may cry when the mother cries, but he does not understand why. In a study of adolescent boys by Loran it was found that those from low socio-economic conditions were less sensitive to the feelings of others than were boys from good socio-economic conditions.[13] However, no differences were found among adolescent girls. The lack of sympathy among boys of low status probably stems from the economic struggle and keen competition they encounter, forcing them to suppress any show of sympathy and adopt the atittude of "every man for himself." Sympathy is important to good interpersonal relations during childhood and adolescence. In Loran's study, it was noted that the most sensitive adolescents were more popular with their peers than the less sensitive. They displayed a greater interest in books and activities that dealt with idealistic, aesthetic, and sympathetic themes.

HABITS AND CONTROL

Emotional and social development. Many factors in the child's physical and social environment affect his emotional and social development. Although class status does not leave the same emotional imprint on all individuals, there are certain experiences common enough to the different members of a class group to warrant consideration. In an analysis of over 100 Negro adolescents from the deep South, Davis and Dollard found that parents from the lower-class group relied upon physical punishment to a much greater degree than did parents from the higher-class groups.[14] Furthermore, children from slum areas engage in fights more than children from better living conditions. Thus, readily giving way to emotions is often part of the underprivileged child's normal social behavior.

However, not all children from the lower class group lack emotional control. Davis and Dollard found that children differed more widely within each class than from class to class. Thus, home conditions as well as biological factors operated to produce significant differences in emotional expressions within each class. There are unquestionably happy homes with little emotional tension in all class groups, just as there are unhappy, quarrelsome homes filled with tension in all class groups.

The results of a study by Henton show that, from the onset of their menses, Negro girls experienced more intense emotions than did white girls.[15] The socio-economic level of white girls' parents was higher than that of the Negro girls'. It is quite likely that the white girls' mothers were more alert in preparing their daughters for pubescence than were the mothers of the Negro girls. The need for sex education and guidance is clearly implied in these results. The adolescent's emotional habits are, therefore, affected by many factors.

Habits as drives to action. The importance of habits in the study of the adolescent cannot be overemphasized. In considering emotionality and the drive to action, however, one must not oversimplify. Social and emotional habits are in their formative stage during later adolescence.

Many mannerisms appear, manifested in isolation from the individual's general habit patterns—which, in fact, are often inconsistent and changeable. The extent to which a habit pattern once built up becomes a drive to action will depend mainly on the extent to which it becomes integrated in the individual's general habit patterns and finally becomes automatic.

It has been found that attentive repetition of an act tends to make for automaticity of the act. Habits are continuous rather then periodic; a habit once formed is never completely eradicated from man's neural structure, for all changes which are effected must be built upon the structural patterns existing at the time in the individual. James recognized this in his well-nigh classic statement:

> Every smallest stroke of virtue or of vice leaves its never so little scar. The drunken Rip Van Winkle, in Jefferson's play, excuses himself for every fresh dereliction by saying, "I won't count this time!" Well! he may not count it, and a kind Heaven may not count it; but it is being counted none the less. Down among his nerve-cells and fibers the molecules are counting it, registering and storing it up to be used against him when the next temptation comes. Nothing we ever do is, in strict scientific literalness, wiped out. Of course this has its good side as well as its bad one. As we become permanent drunkards by so many separate drinks, so we become saints in the moral, and authorities and experts in the practical and scientific spheres, by so many separate acts and hours of work.[16]

Changes may become automatic in nature, but the old habit system operates under special emotional conditions when rational behavior is lacking. Even volition must be studied in terms of learning and can best be thought of in terms of man's habit system. All these habit patterns, which tend to contribute to the efficiency of the human mechanism, become potent drives for the initiation and direction of action. (We shall consider this subject further in connection with the development of attitudes and social behavior.)

SOCIAL DEVELOPMENT

Social development cannot be considered apart from other aspects of development. Its close relationship with emotional development, physiological changes, intellectual activities, and one's concept of the self may be observed in any adolescent group of boys and girls. Important and significant changes in social behavior occur during the adolescent years, usually more pronounced during the early period of adolescence than during the latter years, when a more definite pattern of behavior exists and a more consistent and stable philosophy of life is being realized.

Importance of social interaction. It was suggested in Chapter 2 that an important developmental task of adolescents is to learn to live with their age-mates. They use various methods to obtain approval from and establish good relations with their peers. Adolescent group activities have been found most important to the development of social patterns of behavior. To be successful, they must either have a simple, direct action purpose or have a variety of social experiences in learning to understand each other, both of which will call for social interaction, the only means of learning to understand and get along with others.

Children are directed into their sex role at a very early age and become conscious of sex differences before they enter school; however, their attitudes toward members of the opposite sex will be closely related to their training and experiences, which serve to identify them with their sex group. Considerable attention has been given the identification of adolescent boys and girls with their masculine and feminine roles. Lynn presented the following generalizations on sex identification:

1. With increasing age males become relatively more firmly identified with the masculine role, while females become relatively less firmly identified with the feminine role.

2. A larger proportion of females than males show preference for the role of the opposite sex.

3. A larger proportion of females than males adopt aspects of the role of the opposite sex.

4. Males tend to identify with a cultural stereotype of the masculine role, whereas females tend to identify with aspects of their mothers' roles specifically.[17]

Broadened social experiences. A striking characteristic of the American child's social development is an ever-widening circle of friends and range of social experiences, illustrated by an examination of the location of a child's friends at different stages in his development. First he becomes acquainted with children of the neighborhood or community served by the elementary school he attends, although his best friends will most likely be made up of children from his immediate neighborhood—proximity is the most important factor in the choice of friends. As he grows up and enters the later elementary school years or the junior high school, he begins to form an increasing circle of friends with common interests and similar social status.

Adolescents' best friends are dispersed over a relatively wide area, although proximity still remains an important factor in the making of friends throughout life. In general, experiences in high school bring adolescents from scattered geographic areas and different backgrounds together, increasing the dispersion of friends. These contacts have desirable as well as undesirable effects on the social, emotional, and moral development of adolescents.

The maturing sex drive. As a full-fledged drive, sex does not mature until puberty. The manner in which a preadolescent reacts to a sex situation or problem will depend largely upon the attitudes toward sex formed during his earlier years. There will be important differences in the social-sex pattern for different groups and for different members of the same group. For example, boys with several sisters are likely to regard sex somewhat differently from those without sisters. In an effort to arrive at a better understanding of the development of the social-sex patterns of boys and girls, Campbell conducted a careful study in 1939 of boys and girls in the Merrill-Palmer recreational clubs.[18] The results showed a gradual and continuous development from timidity in the presence of members of the opposite sex at ages 11 or 12 to an intense interest and less timidity at 16 or 17. At all age levels the sex pattern for girls revealed a greater maturity than that for boys of the same age. However, later studies and current literature have revealed a faster maturing of the social-sex behavior patterns. Social blossoming has dropped down the age ladder.

Social-sex behavior of preadolescents. A review of research on social-sex behavior of preadolescents shows the emergence of new norms in cross-sex relationships among boys and girls in the 10 to 12 year age range. The old pattern of avoidance is still present among some groups, but the emerging new pattern has changed the traditional concept of a natural antagonism of boys toward girls during the early teen years. The change is borne out in the results of a 1958 study by Broderick and Fowler in a Southeastern urban community among fifth to seventh graders, upper-lower to upper-middle in social class status.[19] Table 6-3 shows the percentage of children who chose at least one of four friends across sex lines. Comparing these data with those obtained from preadolescents in the

Table 6-3

FREQUENCY OF CHOOSING AT LEAST ONE FRIEND OF THE
OPPOSITE SEX, BY GRADE*

Grade	*Per cent*			*Total number*
	One or more cross-sex choices	*No cross-sex choices*	*Total*	
5	51.9	48.1	100.0	108
6	41.8	58.2	100.0	79
7	37.7	62.3	100.0	77
Total	44.7	55.3	100.0	264

* Each child had up to four choices. The units in this table are children.

twenties and thirties one finds a remarkable thawing of the antagonisms of boys and girls toward each other.

There has also been an increase in romantic interest among preadolescents. Romance has perhaps always been an element for some pre-adolescents, although in the past, a 12-year-old girl was very reluctant to admit that a cretain boy was attractive to her and a 12- or 13-year-old boy preferred to pretend that girls were obnoxious to him even if he did have a covert interest in a particular girl. In the study by Broderick and Fowler, the great majority of children in each of the grades studied (fifth, sixth, and seventh) claimed to have a sweetheart. The percentage of children claiming to have a sweetheart did not change appreciably from grade to grade, but Broderick offers evidence, shown in Figure 6-2, from a later

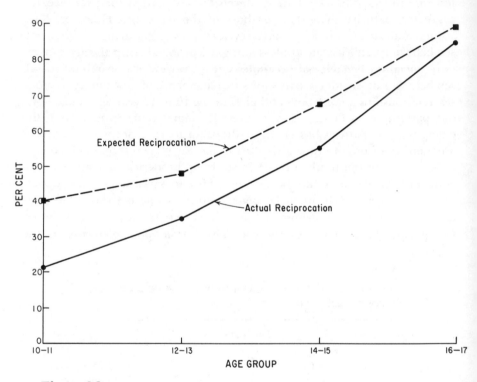

Figure 6-2

EXPECTED AND ACTUAL RECIPROCATION
(Broderick)

study conducted in four Pennsylvania communities that the nature of the relationship changed: the relationship between expected and actual reciprocation became closer with advancement in age.[20]

In both studies experience with kissing was found to be fairly common, varying to some degree with social class and the area in which the study was conducted. One of the most convincing evidences of growth in preadolescent interest in the opposite sex was the choice of friends for three activities: walking, eating, and attending movies. The preadolescents were asked to rank the desirability of a companion of the same sex, a companion of the opposite sex, or of no companion at all in the three activities. The results are presented in Table 6-4. The majority of sixth and seventh graders felt that when walking or going to the movies a companion of the opposite sex was to be preferred to no companion or a companion of the same sex. Both sexes were more conservative when choosing an eating companion, although almost half the seventh graders preferred an eating companion of the opposite sex.

Several factors may explain the lessened antagonism toward the opposite sex on the part of present-day preadolescents. The overlapping and flexibility now present in sex roles makes it easier for boys and girls to plan, work, and play together. The increased amount of social events at school, church, and other community institutions has enabled boys and girls to gain a better understanding of each other and has resulted in many common interests.

Table 6-4

PREFERENCE FOR OPPOSITE SEX COMPANION
IN THREE SITUATIONS, BY GRADE AND SEX

		Per cent	
		Prefer opposite sex companion	
Situation	*Grade*	Boys	Girls
Eating	5th	35.0	30.9
	6th	34.9	31.4
	7th	46.2	47.4
Walking	5th	49.0	50.9
	6th	69.8	51.4
	7th	71.8	68.4
Movie	5th	58.5	45.5
	6th	68.2	51.4
	7th	74.3	65.7

Also, an increased equality in performance at school and in social status makes it no longer necessary for the boy to attempt to prove his superiority, so that there is no need to be hostile toward the opposite sex. In our middle-class culture, both are working toward similar goals.

Physical maturation and social behavior. It is a common observation that the 12- or 13-year-old girl advanced in her physical development displays an interest in boys, whereas the girl retarded in her physical development displays little interest in boys. A study reported by Ames, as part of a longitudinal study of 40 males and 40 females, dealt with the long-term relation between rate of maturation of the 40 boys during adolescence and various measures of social participation during adulthood.[21] Physical maturity was determined on the basis of skeletal age. Scores of skeletal age divided by chronological age during the fourteenth to the seventeenth years of life were averaged for each individual to obtain an index of his relative rate of maturation. Ratings of the adolescent social behavior of the subjects were also available. Significant positive correlations were obtained between level of maturation and social ratings, indicating that adolescents advanced in rate of physical maturation were inclined to be advanced in their adult social behavior, whereas those retarded in rate of physical maturation were also likely to be retarded in their social development.

Changes in sex-appropriateness of behavior during adolescence are also related to physical maturation. Girls advanced in their physical maturation attempt to play a feminine role advanced for their age level. This may be observed in their manner of dress, make-up, behavior, and growing interest in boys. Zuk's analysis of behavior of adolescent boys and girls during the postadolescent years (15-17) revealed the following:

1. Sex-appropriate behavior increased significantly in girls from 16 to 17 years. Boys showed no comparable increase during this period.

2. Sex-appropriate behavior tended to be more stable in girls from year to year than boys. For both sexes, however, such behavior was more stable during the sixteenth year than during the fifteenth year.

3. Behavior which was sex-appropriate and more popular with boys tended also to be relatively more popular with girls and vice versa.

4. Sex-appropriate behavior was shown to be related in reasonable directions but in low degree with social, physical, intellective, and temperament factors.

5. The sex-appropriateness of adolescent behavior was shown to vary widely from one area to another. . . .[22]

The fifth conclusion has widespread implications: one should be careful in making generalizations from data on adolescent behavior, such as those presented by Broderick and Fowler. One can generalize from one group to another, to the extent that sex-appropriate behavior is based upon physiological maturation and to the extent that sex-appropriate behavior is a result of similar cultural forces and conditions. Much of the behavior and growth data on adolescents has been obtained from middle-class cultural groups, making it hazardous to apply such data to lower-class cultural groups. However, as pointed out in Chapter 2, there are many educational forces operating to furnish adolescents with what might be termed a universal American culture.

Mass means of communication have been a potent force in informing adolescents from different social classes and subcultures of the manner of dress considered most appropriate for different occasions. Studies show that, in general, there is little difference in the habits of dress and type of clothing worn by adolescent girls in different economic groups. The major difference usually lies in the more expensive clothes and greater number of luxury items worn by those in better economic circumstances; however, girls from all economic levels attempted to conform to the group stlye of dress and make-up.

Leadership among adolescents. In the study of leadership, it is essential that we recognize the importance of individual variation, not merely in native or acquired intelligence, but in the whole range of physical, emotional, and social variability. Often a prevailing social status may provide opportunity for leadership otherwise not at hand. In another social dimension, physical force may be important. The control of others, in some types of activities, demands brute strength. For example, leadership in some forms of athletics will usually be found among those superior in strength, motor coordination, and speed of reaction. This was revealed in one study in which a group of 447 boys aged 13 and 14 were classified according to leadership criteria and according to sexual maturity.[23] A comparison was then made of the proportion of leaders found among the mature and immature boys. Three types of leadership were noted: elective, appointive, and athletic. Only in athletic leadership did mature boys show a consistent superiority over immature boys. Physical maturity did not have a significant influence upon elective or appointive leadership at the 13- or 14-year level.

Some studies show that leaders are younger than nonleaders while other studies show exactly the opposite.[24] Chronological age cannot be regarded as a factor which is correlated with leadership in any uniform direction or degree. Lack of consistency in the findings may result, however, from a failure to define leadership or a failure to recognize different kinds of leadership, calling for different characteristics. In general, the average adolescent who occupies a position of leadership exceeds the average member of his group in the following respects: (a) intelligence, (b) scholarship, (c) dependability in exercising responsibility, (d) activity and social participation, (e) socio-economic status, (f) drive, endurance, and vigor of mind and body (g) initiative, self-confidence, and self-control, (h) adaptability and insight, and (i) past achievements.

The qualities and skills required in a leader are determined to a large extent by the demands of the situation in which he is to function as a leader; the adolescent chosen may not be a "born" leader, yet he is fit to take charge according to the estimates of his peers. Leadership and "followership" appear, then, to be a working relationship among members of the group; the relationship is changeable and flexible according to the types of activities and the membership involved.

Social consciousness during adolescence. Cooley was one of the first of the modern sociological writers to emphasize that man is dependent upon his fellows in a large measure for his thoughts, emotions, and modes of behavior.[25] He formulated the term *social consciousness*. According to Cooley and others, the consciousness of any single individual is nothing more than the consciousness of the many social groups with which he has come in contact. The dawning social consciousness appearing during the preadolescent stage is an important factor in the development of problems of a social nature at this period. Timidity, moodiness, temper outbursts, and daydreaming tendencies frequently result. If we consider the average adolescent girl in her junior year in high school, we will find an individual bound by certain group standards, ideals, and general attitudes. The home and playmates have given her lessons in loyalty, service, cooperation, and interest in others. School studies have brought her into contact with peoples of other countries and with deeds of men of the past and given her a wider and deeper appreciation of direct experience. Her religion, her politics, her pride of family and state, and her respect for the opinions of others have been molded by her social group. However, she is constantly meeting new social groups, many of which have ideals and attitudes somewhat different from those previously met; and here, Cooley points out, since the individual's standards as built up through contact with different social groups may not be harmonious, conflicts are likely to develop. Thus the adolescent in a new situation is often referred to as "green" or "square" or some other name which would indicate his failure to understand and thus enter into the behavior of the new social group.

PROBLEMS RELATED TO SOCIAL DEVELOPMENT

The desire for conformity. The normal adolescent, though idealistic in his attitudes, is a slave to group conformity. His ardently poetic and religious ideals are seldom carried over into everyday activities. If his group frowns upon noble ideals, he will frown upon such ideals; if the group keeps late hours, he is bent upon keeping late hours; and if the group swears and uses slang, he will do the same. The attitude of conformity is one of the most important motivating forces at this period of life.

Problems in socialization. Adolescent girls have social problems more frequently than boys. Too little social life, lack of friends, wanting to learn how to dance, spending money for social activities, the desire for a new dress and the like are problems experienced by a great many adolescents.

Since boys and girls do not develop uniformly, there will be a variation in their desires for social experiences. And, although social participation is essential for healthy social development, they should not be pushed into such experiences until they are socially and emotionally ready for them. There is, likewise, a corollary to this proposition, namely, that adolescents should not have the activities in which they desire to participate closed to them when they have reached the stage of development suitable to such participation. If social activities are provided periodically by the home, the church, the school, and other organizations concerned with the social development of children, there will be opportunities for the latter gradually to take part in them. Some of a particular age-group will be mere onlookers on certain occasions, but gradually the desire to play an active role will emerge, and later on they will begin to take some part in social activities; later still, there will probably be full-fledged and unanimous participation.

Differences in physiological maturity. In the middle period of adolescence early maturing tends to be advantageous to boys, whereas it is a disadvantage to girls.[26] The average girl matures earlier than the average boy anyway; for a girl to mature earlier than most puts her at a disadvantageous extreme. She is conspicuously large in comparison to other girls and boys of her age. The case of Louise shows how difficult such a situation can be.[27]

> Louise, a 12-year-old girl, was much taller than the other girls of her age and grade. Her intelligence quotient of 90 had made it difficult for her to do satisfactory work in school and consequently she was retarded in her school work. Although she was in a grade where most of the children were one year younger, she was still unable to do satisfactory work, especially in reading. This was accounted for in part by her inferior cultural home background. The poverty of the home did little to overcome an unhappy home situation and tended to make her still more unattractive to the others of her class, since she was usually poorly and untidily dressed.
>
> The teacher recognized her problems and showed a very sympathetic and understanding attitude toward them. Louise recited from her seat entirely and was never called upon to go to the blackboard for fear that this would embarrass her. Furthermore, Louise did not like to march in line with the other members of the class. Although the teacher was rather formal in conducting her class work, she was lenient in allowing Louise to remain in the room and complete certain tasks while the other students were going out of the room in the line. However, the teacher's efforts did not solve Louise's problems. For, in fact, the problem was more than one of self-consciousness. Her self-consciousness developed into a defiant attitude. Louise came to feel that if she did not wish to do certain things that she should be excused from doing them.
>
> At the end of the school year, Louise, now 13 years of age, was promoted to the seventh grade. The seventh-grade teacher was informed of Louise's problems, and was thus in a position to profit from some of the well-meaning mistakes of the former teacher. The teacher set as her goal the bringing about of a better social adjustment on the part of Louise. Through visits to the home she was able to enlist some cooperation from the parents. Fortunately for Louise, one of the neighbors employed her to remain with their children, as a "sitter." This provided her with some spending money and gave her needed

confidence in her ability and worth. At the end of the year considerable improvement was noted in her socialization.

On the other hand, the early-maturing girl is frequently the envy of her slower-maturing age-mates who are anxious to begin dating. Boys find that early maturing places them on par with girls and ahead of most boys in physical development. This gives the boy an advantage in his social relations with girls. Late-maturing boys, usually unable to compete successfully in athletics and many social activities, frequently turn to individual pursuits such as academic work at school in an effort to satisfy the need to succeed.

Based on data gathered on 731 girls enrolled in the sixth, seventh, eighth, and ninth grades in a suburban community, Faust presents the following generalizations about the relation between developmental maturity and prestige among their classmates:

> . . . When all of the prestige-lending traits of a given grade are considered as a whole, it appears that prestige is more likely to surround those in the sixth grade who are developmentally "in phase" (prepuberal), whereas during the junior high school years being ahead of the group developmentally seems to be an advantage. While prepuberal status may be hazardous for girls in junior high school, it is not considered "immature" nor undesirable in sixth grade. A prepuberal girl in sixth grade is developmentally "in phase" with the great majority of her classmates, while a prepuberal girl in ninth grade is a "developmental isolate." A girl's level of physical maturity is not only relative to the development of others in the class, but it is seen against a background of developmental differences within the whole school. Being at the prepuberal level of development seems to lend different qualities to the composite picture of an individual in elementary school than it does to one in the junior high school grades."[28]

Social adjustment and class status. Wherever large groups of individuals come together there appears some sort of class structure whose characteristics depend largely on the factors that operate to produce class groupings. (Certain carefully devised procedures have been developed for the evaluation of class status in America.[29] Also, it has been observed that outstanding class differences exist in the social goals, mores, attitudes, and patterns of behavior of children and adolescents from different social classes. Some differences in middle-class and lower-class expectations are presented in Table 6-5. Considerably more anxiety appears among middle-class than among lower-class parents in connection with education, thrift, sexual behavior, manners, and respect for law. The lower class is more honest and frank in social situations; the middle class is more tactful.

The personal and social effects of the class status in which the individual is reared have been studied by a number of investigators. According to Neugarten's study, social class seems to operate differently in affecting the reputation scores at the fifth- and sixth-grade level and at the high school level.[30] At the fifth- and sixth-grade level, upper-class

Table 6-5

COMPARISON OF MIDDLE-CLASS AND LOWER-CLASS EXPECTATIONS FOR CHILDREN
AND ADOLESCENTS

(After Neugarten)

Middle Class	Lower Class
Anxious for children to finish high school	Parents somewhat indifferent toward children finishing high school
Emphasis upon postponement of marriage in order to secure an education	Likelihood of early marriage and responsibility for a family
Early taboo on sexual interests	Relatively few taboos on sexual interests
Recreation is organized and supervised	Recreation of children not closely supervised by parents
Children given an allowance and encouraged to save money	Children allowed to spend what money they have as they please
Interest in school grades and graduation from high school is inculcated	Indifference toward good grades and high school graduation shown
Aggression must be controlled; children discouraged from fighting	Children, especially boys, encouraged to "fight for their rights"
Respect for law and policeman is taught	Fear of law and policeman is taught
Tact in social situations is practiced	Honesty and frankness in social situations are practiced
Stress put on education and upward social mobility	Stress put on getting a job and accepting financial responsibility
Child learns proper etiquette—manner of social intercourse	Little emphasis placed on proper etiquette

status carries with it almost automatically a favorable reputation score, while membership in the lower class usually results in an unfavorable reputation score. At the high school level, upper-class status insures the individual that he will be given attention and consideration, whether his reputation is favorable or unfavorable. At this age level the lower-class child either drops out of school or takes on the behavior and values of his middle-class associates and thus tends to lose his lower-class characteristics.

Cultural expectations. The relation between physical maturation and sex-appropriate behavior has an important bearing on cultural expectations. Sex-appropriate behavior for boys is more limited in scope than what is regarded as sex-appropriate for girls. The boy must show physical prowess, courage, and other characteristics regarded in American culture as masculine. On the other hand, the girl must display effeminate behavior. She may or may not be courageous; she may be regarded as a tomboy and still be accepted by her age-mates, but boys must refrain from being classified as "sissy" if they are to get along with age-mates. In spite of their relative freedom in sex-appropriate behavior, girls tend to conform more rigidly than boys to the cultural image generally projected for them. The results of the study by Zuk, referred to earlier, indicate that behaviors associated with popularity for each sex tended to be quite stable during the three-year period of adolescence studied.

Failure in socialization. Bonney's study was designed to determine the type of individual generally well accepted socially.[31] Two methods of gathering data were used in this study: (a) trait ratings, on the part of both teachers and pupils, and (b) the pupil's choice of friends—a method referred to as a sociometric test. One fact emerging from this study is that the most popular children are more aggressive and overt in their responses. It was found that the highest social recognition does not go to children who are submissive and docile, but that to be well accepted, the child or adolescent needs to possess positive attributes that will make him count in the group, i.e., a strong personality, enthusiasm, friendliness, and marked abilities. Extreme introversion and daydreaming or antisocial tendencies are quite likely to arise when there is a failure in the socialization process.

During adolescence increased barriers to free social intercourse develop. Along with the development of social consciousness, consciousness of differences in color, religion, national background, and social class increase tremendously. These become increasingly important factors in the choice of friends, choice of dates, and membership in cliques. Deviated personalities begin to be observed to a large degree as the individual makes wider social contacts. The adolescent's physiological development, new contacts, heightened emotions, and enlarged mental life create a new self, and this new self seeks an expression that needs sympathetic guidance if it is to develop along desirable lines.

SUMMARY

The growth and development of the child into adolescence are accompanied by glandular changes closely related to the emotional life. The heightened emotional states during this period of life have constantly been recognized as a part of the nature of adolescents; however, in addition to a heightened emotional state at this time, there is also an expansion of the emotions into the social realm. Fears and angers related to social situations become very important; self-conscious feelings about one's own adequacy appear; and the adolescent becomes especially concerned over the approval of his peers. This increased fear is also observed in connection with classroom situations. Fear of reciting in class, fear of failure, and fear of ridicule become more pronounced at this age level.

Emotional devèlopment, no less than the development of motor abilities, is dependent upon maturation and learning. The relationship of emotional development to social development may be observed in the early emotional and social responses of the infant child to the mother. Emotional and social growth are clearly entwined in the social responses of the child at each stage of his social development.

It has been emphasized throughout this chapter that development into adolescence is accompanied by an increased interest in personal appearance, one's peers, and social activities involving members of the opposite sex. The extent to which the adolescent is able to make satisfactory social adjustments will depend upon a number of factors, including the operation of the developmental process during his earlier years. This is in harmony with the statement quoted from Conradi, which emphasizes the concept that growth and development are gradual in nature. There is, therefore, a necessity for boys and girls to have had opportunities to develop through social participation at the various stages in life. Such participation must always be on the level of the child's maturity and past experiences, if it is to be most effective.

With the onset of adolescence there is an increased interest in participating in such activities as clubs, team games, and so forth. If adolescents have had the opportunities for normal development under favorable guidance, they will constantly seek the companionship of members of the opposite sex as well as of their own. Social qualities become quite pronounced in speech, conduct, and common motor expressions. In the development of a social being there must, of course, be contact with others, but other elements are essential, such as: (1) some important activity in common, for example, a language, symbol, creed, or aim; (2) the effect of suggestion by the activities of others; (3) an acquaintance, unity, or some general interfeeling and intercommunication.

THOUGHT PROBLEMS

1. Just what do you understand the term *social development* to mean? What do you consider the most important factors affecting a child's social development?
2. What type of activities characterize the play and recreational lives of 10-year-old boys? Of 10-year-old girls? Of 13-year-old boys? Of 13-year-old girls?
3. Consider some pal of yours during your early teen years. What factors entered into your selecting the particular person as a pal? Is this in harmony with the materials on this problem presented in this chapter?
4. How is language related to social development? Will language training speed up social development or the socializing process? Explain.

5. Look up the James-Lange theory of emotions. What evidence have you observed that would support this theory?
6. List some principles of emotional control. Which of these have you found most useful in your life?
7. How would you account for the changes in attitudes of preadolescents toward members of the opposite sex as shown in the study by Broderick and Fowler? What is the significance of these changes?
8. Present a brief paper or discussion on the qualities that contribute to *leadership* and to *followership* among adolescents. What is the teacher's obligation in this connection?
9. What are the major agencies concerned with social development of adolescents? Evaluate the effectiveness of three of these in light of your own experiences.
10. Study carefully the materials dealing with social-sex development. What outstanding sex differences appear in these results? Account for some of the most outstanding differences.

SELECTED REFERENCES

Anderson, J. E., "Changes in Emotional Response with Age," in *Feelings and Emotions,* ed. M. L. Reymert. New York: McGraw-Hill Book Company, 1950, Chap. 34.

Cole, Luella, *Psychology of Adolescence,* 6th ed. New York: Holt, Rinehart & Winston, Inc., 1964, Chaps. 12, 13.

Coleman, James S., *The Adolescent Society.* New York: The Free Press of Glencoe, Inc., 1961, Chap. 8.

Malm, M. and O. G. Jamison, *Adolescence.* New York: McGraw-Hill Book Company, 1952, Chap. 5.

Rogers, Dorothy, *The Psychology of Adolescence.* New York: Appleton-Century-Crofts, 1962, Chap. 4.

Seidman, Jerome M., ed., *The Adolescent—A Book of Readings,* 2nd ed. New York: Holt, Rinehart & Winston, Inc., 1960, Chap. 5.

NOTES

[1] H. E. Jones, H. S. Conrad, and L. B. Murphy, "Emotional and Social Development and the Educative Process," *Thirty-eighth Yearbook of the National Society for the Study of Education, Part 1* (Chicago: Department of Education, University of Chicago, 1939), Chap. 18, p. 363. Quoted by permission of the society.

[2] C. B. Zachry and M. Lighty, *Emotions and Conduct in Adolescence* (New York: Appleton-Century-Crofts, 1940), pp. 69-70.

[3] K. M. B. Bridges, "Emotional Development in Early Infancy," *Child Development,* 3 (1932), 324-41.

[4] D. B. Lindsey, "Emotion," in *Handbook of Experimental Psychology,* ed. S. S. Stevens (New York: John Wiley & Sons, Inc., 1951).

[5] H. E. Jones, "The Study of Patterns of Emotional Expression," in *Feelings and Emotions,* ed. E. L. Reymert (New York: McGraw-Hill Book Company, 1950), Chap. 13.

[6] H. E. Jones, "Principles and Methods of the Adolescent Growth Study," *Journal of Consulting Psychology,* 3 (1939), 172-80.

[7] H. E. Jones, "The Study of Patterns of Emotional Expression," in Reymert, *op. cit.,*

p. 165. By permission of McGraw-Hill Book Company. Copyright (1950) by McGraw-Hill Book Co.

8 J. A. Hicks and M. Hayes, "Study of the Characteristics of 250 Junior High School Children," *Child Development,* 9 (1938), 219-42.

9 H. Meltzer, "Students' Adjustments in Anger," *Journal of Social Psychology,* 4 (1933), 285-309.

10 Rose Zeligs, "Children's Worries," *Sociological and Social Research,* 24 (1939), 23-32.

11 H. H. Remmers and L. E. Taliana, "What Youth Worries About and Why," *National Parent Teacher,* 52 (1957), 7-10.

12 *A Study of Boys Becoming Adolescents* (Ann Arbor, Mich.: Survey Research Center, Institute for Social Research, University of Michigan, 1960), pp. 173-74. A report of a national survey of boys on the 11 to 18 year age range for the National Council, Boy Scouts of America.

13 W. Loran, "A Study of Social Sensitivity (Sympathy) Among Adolescents," *Journal of Educational Psychology,* 44 (1953), 102-12.

14 A. Davis and J. Dollard, *Children of Bondage: The Personal Development of Negro Youth in the Urban South* (Washington: American Council on Education, 1940).

15 Comradge L. Henton, "The Effect of Socio-economic and Emotional Factors on the Onset of Menarche among Negro and White Girls," *Journal of Genetic Psychology,* 98 (1961), 255-64.

16 William James, *Psychology, Briefer Course* (New York: Holt, Rinehart & Winston, Inc., 1892), p. 150.

17 David B. Lynn, "A Note on Sex Differences in the Development of Masculine and Feminine Identification," *Psychological Review,* 66 (1959), 126-35.

18 E. H. Campbell, "The Social and Sex Development of Children," *Genetic Psychology Monographs,* 21 (1939), 461-552.

19 Carlfred B. Broderick and Stanley E. Fowler, "New Patterns of Relationships between the Sexes among Preadolescents," *Marriage and Family Living,* 23 (1961), 27-30.

20 Carlfred B. Broderick, "Social-sexual Development in a Suburban Community." Prepublication data supplied by Broderick, Pennsylvania State University, 1963.

21 Robert Ames, "Physical Maturing among Boys as Related to Adult Social Behavior," *California Journal of Educational Research,* 8 (1957), 69-75.

22 G. H. Zuk, "Sex-appropriate Behavior in Adolescence," *Journal of Genetic Psychology,* 93 (1958), 31-32.

23 A. J. Latham, "The Relationship between Pubertal Status and Leadership in Junior High School Boys," *Journal of Genetic Psychology,* 78 (1951), 185-94.

24 Ralph M. Stogdill, "Personal Factors Associated with Leadership: A Survey of the Literature," *Journal of Psychology,* 25 (1948), 35-71.

25 C. H. Cooley, *Human Nature and the Social Order* (New York: Charles Scribner's Sons, 1902).

26 Mary Cover Jones, "A Study of Socialization Patterns at the High School Level," *Journal of Genetic Psychology,* 93 (1958), 87-111.

27 The case of Louise was cited by the author in *The Psychology of Exceptional Children,* revised ed. Copyright 1950 by The Ronald Press Company.

28 Margaret S. Faust, "Developmental Maturity as a Determinant in Prestige of Adolescent Girls," *Child Development,* 31 (1960), 180.

29 See W. L. Warner, M. Meeker, and K. S. Eells, *Social Class in America: A Manual of Procedure for the Measurement of Social Status* (Chicago: Science Research Associates, Inc., 1949). This procedure is still valid, although certain weightings given to specific items of the scale may have changed slightly since the book was written. A scale was developed for determining social class. Since status symbols have changed, certain items of the scale should be altered so as to encompass present-day class symbols.

30 B. L. Neugarten, "Social Class and Friendship among Children," *American Journal of Sociology,* 51 (1946), 305-12.

31 M. E. Bonney, "Personality Traits of Socially Successful and Unsuccessful Children," *Journal of Educational Psychology,* 34 (1943), 449-72.

PART THREE

PERSONALITY AND ADJUSTMENT IN ADOLESCENCE

7

CHANGE
OF
INTERESTS
WITH AGE

INTERESTS: THEIR NATURE AND DEVELOPMENT

The meaning of interests. It has already been pointed out that the adolescent is in no sense a passive agent in a constant environment. His mode of action is determined not only by the environment but by the specific direction, in accordance with changes that have been wrought in the neuromuscular system during the earlier years of experience, of the energies of the organism. Interest, then, is the purposive response in the individual such that certain desires and strivings are channeled toward realization.

The word *interest* is derived from the Latin word *interesse,* which means "to be between," "to make a difference," "to concern," "to be of value." Interest has been described as that "something between" that secures some desired goal, or is a means to an end *that is of value to the individual* because of its usefulness, pleasure, or general social and vocational significance. During a state of interest, certain parts of the environment are singled out, not merely because of such objective conditions of attention as *intensity, extensity, duration, movement,* but because changes have been established in the neuromuscular system that cause the organism to favor some reactions to the exclusion of others. The term interest has ordinarily been used in describing or explaining the latter condition. Interest is directly related to voluntary attention; when interest is not present, attention tends to fluctuate readily.

Adolescence is the period of varied and peculiar interests. It should be noted, first, that all interests grow out of life experiences, which tend to guide and direct the development of further interests. In attempting to build some interest in the life of the child, one should realize that it must be established according to the laws of learning, just as other habit patterns are formed. Over a long period of careful observations it becomes evident that different individuals have preferred characteristic ways of reacting to a specific phase of their environment. When the adolescent reads a book instead of playing a game, we know that a special type of interest, in itself a drive to a special type of action, is present. When a boy pursues a game for its own sake or for the amusement and fun that he gets from the exercise, then his interest is referred to as intrinsic or as "an end unto itself." On the other hand, when a boy goes into athletics in order to keep himself fit or to develop certain desirable character traits, we have an example of extrinsic interests, or a means to arrive at some desirable element. Athletics, reading a book, driving an automobile, and practically any activity we might consider may be of either an intrinsic or an extrinsic type of interest.

> This differentiation in the nature of interests is a matter of importance to parents, teachers, or boys' workers who wish to regulate the overflow of restlessness in boyhood and youth. An individual responds to an intrinsic interest, to the pleasure which his palate will take, for instance, in a fine dinner, more readily than to a plain meal which is good for his health. At the same time, adolescence may also be rightly thought of as the period when individuals begin to look with a longer horizon upon the experiences of daily living as a means to an end. Wise adults are accustomed to look beyond the immediate gratification yielded by an activity to discover its values.[1]

The growth of interests. The early interests of the child are centered on purely personal relations. When he sees an unknown animal, he will ask, "What is it? Will it bite?" These questions are not scientific in nature; neither are they prompted by the ideal of scientific inquiry; nevertheless, they do give evidence of an interest in the structure, behavior, and life history of the animal that represents the beginning of a scientific interest in life, especially the life of animals. Interest is dependent on experience, but also on native ability.

The physical growth of the individual with its accompanying visceral and glandular changes has an important bearing on the development of new and varied interests, as pointed out earlier in connection with the emotional and social changes that take place in the transition from childhood into adolescence. Children take considerable interest in games of all types, especially those involving physical or motor action. Changes in these interests occur gradually; they are closely related to the pace of physical growth. An investigation of the interests of fifth- and sixth-graders from different geographical regions of the United States was conducted by Amatora.[2] Ten categories accounting for more than 90 per cent of their freely expressed interests emerged from the study. By means of weighted scores, presented in Table 7-1, the total strength of each interest category was determined. Foremost among the ten categories were scores for the possession of objects; in all four groups, preadolescents expressed a greater interest in the possession of objects than in anything else. Next on the list were interests in good life, vocation, relatives, and travel in descending order.

Although very slight sex differences appeared in the broad categories of interests, an analysis of the interests making up each category revealed important sex differences. Table 7-2 presents an analysis of boys' and girls' interests in ownership of objects. Both sexes wanted a bicycle. Boys displayed less interest in clothes than girls, and more in guns, athletic equipment, boats, trains, and airplanes, revealing the extent to which the latter are identified with the masculine role.

Table 7-1

COMPOSITE SCORES FOR EACH INTEREST CATEGORY FOR 629
PREADOLESCENT BOYS AND GIRLS

(*Amatora*)

Category	Boys			Girls			Sexes combined
	Grade 5	Grade 6	Average	Grade 5	Grade 6	Average	
Things owned	13.7	15.3	14.8	12.7	11.2	11.9	13.3
Good life	4.7	9.2	6.5	6.0	8.9	7.4	7.0
Vocation	2.3	8.4	5.3	3.3	8.8	6.1	5.7
Relatives	2.4	4.2	3.3	4.2	5.4	4.3	3.8
Travel	1.1	2.2	1.6	1.4	3.2	2.3	2.0
School	2.3	1.9	1.6	2.2	1.4	1.8	1.7
Pets	1.9	1.8	1.8	1.7	1.3	1.5	1.6
Money	1.0	2.0	1.4	0.8	0.9	0.8	1.1
Education	0.1	1.6	0.8	0.2	1.5	0.9	0.8
Health	0.4	0.3	0.3	0.5	0.7	0.6	0.5
Miscellaneous	3.8	6.6	5.2	6.3	8.3	7.3	6.2

Interests of children and adolescents are also revealed in their wishes studied by Cobb.[3] He noted a high frequency of wishes for material objects and possessions that decreased with age and was replaced by an incidence of wishes for more general and inclusive benefits for self and others. There was also a tendency for wishes to be predominantly extrovert rather than introvert with few wishes related to shortcomings. Boys showed a greater interest in personal achievement and possessions, girls in social and family relations.

Interest in personal appearance. With the onset of adolescence both

Table 7-2

ANALYSIS OF BOYS' AND GIRLS' INTERESTS IN OWNERSHIP OF OBJECTS
(*Amatora*)

	Boys Grade 5	Grade 6	Average	Girls Grade 5	Grade 6	Average
	Grade 5	Grade 6	Average	Grade 5	Grade 6	Average
Bicycle	27.6	28.9	28.2	29.1	25.5	27.3
Car	14.6	6.6	10.6	4.0	3.6	3.8
House	4.9	7.3	6.1	7.3	5.5	6.4
Clothes	3.0	2.6	2.8	12.1	8.2	10.2
Guns	11.4	7.2	9.3	0.0	0.0	0.0
Balls	3.3	7.2	5.2	1.8	3.6	2.7
Athletic Equipment	5.7	5.3	5.5	0.0	0.0	0.0
Watch	1.6	0.7	1.2	4.0	3.6	3.8
Boats	4.1	3.9	4.0	0.0	0.0	0.0
Train	4.1	3.3	3.7	0.0	0.0	0.0
Swimming pool	0.6	1.3	1.0	3.6	5.5	4.5
Skates	0.9	0.6	0.7	4.1	7.3	5.7
Dolls	0.0	0.0	0.0	4.0	4.6	4.3
Books	0.8	2.1	1.4	1.6	1.8	1.7
Airplane	2.7	3.3	3.0	0.0	0.0	0.0
Food	3.3	2.3	2.8	1.8	1.2	1.5
Radio	0.8	2.2	1.5	1.1	2.7	1.9
Fishing equipment	3.2	1.3	2.3	0.0	0.0	0.0
Animals	1.2	2.6	1.9	1.3	1.8	1.5
Record player	0.5	0.7	0.6	2.4	1.8	2.1
Television	0.8	1.3	1.1	2.4	0.9	1.7
Sled	0.0	0.0	0.0	0.6	0.9	0.7
Piano	0.8	0.7	0.7	1.4	3.6	2.5
Games	0.8	0.7	0.7	1.9	1.8	1.9
Miscellaneous	2.8	7.9	8.4	15.5	16.1	15.6
Total	100.0	100.0	100.0	100.0	100.0	100.0

boys and girls become enormously interested in their appearance. The teen-age girl, especially, spends a great deal of time in front of the mirror experimenting with new hairdos, or adjusting articles of clothing. Their clothes become part of a symbol for the self. Shop windows, fashion shows, and department stores take on new significance. There is perhaps no greater joy for the adolescent girl than that experienced in the wearing of a stylish, new party dress.

Once uninterested in his personal appearance, except when his parents or friends brought it to his attention, the adolescent boy can now be seen combing his hair and washing his neck. He turns his attention to well-groomed hair and nails without being constantly reminded of those things by his mother. By examining and recognizing the nature of these interests one can obtain a more accurate portrait of the teen years and the dawning social consciousness than through perhaps any other means available. Conflicts with parents resulting from such interests are discussed in Chapter 13.

SCHOOL-RELATED INTERESTS

Reading interests. Adolescents satisfy a demand for adventure through reading. Possibly the two media for reading most preferred are comic books and magazines. Comic books decrease in popularity during the adolescent years, although their appeal continues into adulthood. As adolescents mature they manifest an increased interest in biographical and travel sketches. In general, girls, due largely to advanced maturity, tend to broaden their interest from adventure and mystery to romantic novels earlier than boys.

A study of reading interests by Witty showed that a relatively small percentage of high school pupils reported a liking for poetry, plays, or essays.[4] Girls at all grade levels expressed a greater liking for poetry, humor, and plays than did boys. Likewise, romance and career stories were frequently chosen by girls but not by boys. Boys at all grade levels expressed a preference for adventure, mystery, science fiction, and Westerns. Boys' reading interests were generally broader than girls'. These results, in harmony with those obtained by others, have educational implications that should be carefully considered. For example, science and adventure books could be designed for reading classes to catch the interest of boys who are poor readers.

Different choices of books by boys and girls are also reflected in magazines. Any consideration of periodicals for the home or school must recognize this difference in taste. The magazines found in school libraries have been chosen largely from the woman's world, because, in part at least, they are usually chosen by a woman or by a committee made up of female schoolteachers.

Three types of American periodicals are increasing in popularity: the digest, the news magazine, and the picture magazine. In Witty's study, high school pupils consistently ranked *Life* and *Look* among their favorites. The *Saturday Evening Post* also had a high rating at all grade levels among boys; *Seventeen* among girls. They also read news periodicals such as *Time* and *Newsweek,* indicating that high school students are interested in what is happening in the world. The fact that high school pupils are better informed today than in the past would tend to accentuate their interest in world happenings, domestic problems, and world affairs.

The comic book, in its present form, is the most recent and in many cases the most widespread of all the leisure verbal activities pursued by preadolescents and adolescents. They have, however, been subjected to considerable criticism. Some consider them the inspirer of bad deeds; their art has been described as a "hodge-podge of blotched lines and clashing colors," and the content has been referred to as "sadistic drivel." However, some educators recognize their appeal and have attempted to turn their method of presentation into a channel for developing more worthy concepts and ideals. Case studies show that the bright as well as the dull, the privileged as well as the underprivileged read comic books. With age, however, there is a gradual and continuous decrease of interest in them. As the individual moves into the postadolescent stage, pronounced sex differences become evident, well illustrated in the cases of Karl and Joan:

> At the age of 7 Karl showed a great deal of interest in cartoons displaying activities of animals and children. By the age of 10 he was keenly interested in super activities of men, who were oftentimes made heroes; with the outbreak of World War II, he became interested in constructing comics of his own and at the age of 11 developed a series of comics entitled *Flying Tommy*.
>
> Karl was always very successful in his school work and had a reading ability two years advanced for his age. At 12 he seemed to lose interest in most comic magazines, but showed an increased interest in a number of comic strips. There was a significant relationship observed between these changes of interest in the comics and the development and change of interest in the radio, movies, and play activities.
>
> From early childhood Joan displayed an interest in doll play, animals, and stories involving animals. By the age of 9 she became interested in nursing activities and used her dolls as patients. She displayed considerable creativeness in her care of the doll patients.
>
> Joan was advanced in her school work and in physiological development. She began reading romance stories when she was 11½. She lost her interest in dolls but continued to study science in order to ultimately work as a nurse or technician in a hospital.

Interests in school subjects. General conclusions of various studies on interest and ability do not reflect the individual's capacity in comparison with that of others, so much as they do his hierarchy of abilities. The individual is likely to be most interested in those things he can do best; but this "best" does not of necessity mean superiority over others in the specified task. Interests grow out of experiences that are satisfying, so that students will be more interested in those school subjects that bring forth satisfaction than in those less satisfying. Thus, the student who does his best in English is probably more interested in English than in any other subject.

A questionnaire consisting of 45 items was employed by Tierney for evaluating the interests of secondary school pupils in different aspects of geography.[5] Although age and sex differences were observed, he noted that interest in physical and economic geography was relatively high, whereas interest in cartographic geography was relatively low, especially among girls. This is another example of adolescent boys' interest in schoolwork related to their goals and values. Boys more than girls are interested in the economic aspects of geography or science. Their interest in the physical aspects of geography rather than cartographic geography is in harmony with their interest in travel and the out-of-doors.

The study of children's school interests by Jersild and Tasch showed that, at all grade levels, children liked a certain area of study best.[6] Nature study and natural science were mentioned infrequently in the earlier grades but showed a gain in popularity at the junior and senior high school levels. The results of this study (presented in Table 7-3) show, however, a decline of interest in the academic and educational features of school life, and an increased interest in social aspects: sports, games, discussion clubs, and student council. Lentke's analysis of German adolescents' interests in school subjects showed boys to be more interested in mathematics, physical education, and sciences; whereas girls preferred languages.[7] Senior high school boys continued to select more science subjects than language subjects, and girls continued to show a preference for languages. Neither showed an interest in music or citizenship to an appreciable degree.

Table 7-3

WHAT I LIKE BEST IN SCHOOL

(After Jersild and Tasch)

Category	Ages 9–12		Ages 12–15		Ages 15–18	
	Boys	Girls	Boys	Girls	Boys	Girls
Sports, games, physical education	13.3	9.5	30.6	33.2	34.8	34.4
Areas of study, subject matter	69.7	76.3	44.4	60.1	41.3	45.5
Art activity or appreciation: music, painting, drawing	11.1	14.8	10.0	15.9	16.2	13.8
Crafts, mechanical arts	.3	0	19.8	0	15.5	.4
Discussion clubs, student council	1.3	.8	1.0	.5	3.6	6.4
People: both pupils and teachers	2.5	6.1	4.1	5.6	6.0	11.4

Vocational interests. The exact age at which genuine vocational interests appear is not known, but they may be observed in hobbies, such as butterfly or leaf collecting or in school interests and activities. Terman noted in a longitudinal study of a group of intellectually gifted individuals that 58 per cent of those who in childhood had expressed a preference for engineering, actually became engineers.[8] Roe noted that the most frequent early interests of eminent social scientists studied were literature and the classics, not directly related to social science as such, but dealing with human relations as noted in literature and the classics.[9] He found also that half of a group of twenty eminent biologists displayed an interest in natural history as children.

Early vocational interests are frequently manifested at a later stage in avocational interests and hobbies. This may be noted in the case of the boy who displayed an early interest in animals, studied medicine, became a successful physician, and then moved outside town to operate a small ranch. The girl who displayed an early interest in political science may at a later stage participate actively in party politics. Thus, childhood and adolescent interests can well be thought of as a part of the individual's total personality.

Musical preferences. Studies of adolescent radio and television interests show that girls prefer music to a greater degree than boys do. This results in part from boys' wider range of interests. Rogers made a study of children's musical preferences that yielded some worthwhile findings relative to (a) their preferences at succeeding grade levels and (b) factors related to musical preferences.[10] He administered a 57-item musical preference test involving excerpts from different categories of music to 635 pupils in grades 4, 6, 9, and 12 from six different school systems. The major conclusions from this study were:

1. There is an overwhelming preference for popular music at all grade levels and by all groups regardless of type of school, sex, or socioeconomic status.

2. There is a corresponding and sharp decrease in children's preferences for classical music as they grow older regardless of sex, type of school, or socio-economic status.

3. With increased age, children exhibit a tendency to conform more and more to a single pattern of musical preferences; that is, there are much greater differences at the fourth-grade level than there are at the twelfth-grade level, even though the pattern is similar.

4. Physical maturity is a factor, though indirectly, in determining musical preferences . . . .

5. Socio-economic status is an important factor in children's musical taste. While this is not so strong, there is a consistently larger number of choices for classical music among the children from the upper-class group, even among twelfth grade pupils.

6. No significant differences are found between the musical preferences of children from rural and suburban backgrounds.

The school and the expansion of interest. Schools offer the adolescent the opportunity, among other things, to expand his social contacts, to achieve status, and to prepare himself for a normal adult life. Not all adolescents can master academic subjects, but the majority can learn to live a reasonably normal life according to the training and influence the school implants within them.

The friendships made in school during this period have a marked bearing upon the shaping of character and personality and the stabilizing of adulthood. Records and charts show that such friendships are based primarily on common interests, illustrated in the activities of any adolescent one knows: he is obviously drawn toward a fellow athlete, musician, or craftsman. Moreover, the frequency of such associations will determine the duration of these interests, and here the school promotes recurring association by means of its many avenues of approach to these varied interests.

Loyalty, too, has its foundation in the school. It is first directed toward the adolescent's classmates and teachers, but soon embraces the entire school in the form of school spirit. The school does not complete its function when it merely *teaches* loyalty, honesty, and democracy; these lessons are realized only when they are put into practice in all the organizations of the school. The result proves to be a stepping-stone to good citizenship, through loyalty to community and, ultimately, loyalty to country. It is to this end that many activities taking place outside the classroom function most effectively. These activities have often been referred to as extracurricular; they are, however, an important part of the school's program. Such activities have been classified in various ways. Hausle suggests a four-division classification as follows: "(1) Athletics—interscholastic and intramural; (2) Clubs—subject, hobby, welfare, honorary; (3) Semi-curricular activities—those for which a school may grant subject-credit; (4) Citizenship activities—service."[11]

INTERESTS IN PLAY AND SOCIAL ACTIVITIES

The increased amount of leisure time has brought with it many and diverse problems, particularly acute during the adolescent years, when many are not interested in school activities and find nothing challenging to them in the other institutions of the community in which they live. Many communities are aware of these problems and are making provisions for the needs of adolescents during the time when they are not in school and are not employed in some useful pursuit.

Interest in play. Witty found that swimming was the favorite outdoor sport of girls in grades 9 through 12.[12] It ranked third in interest among the boys at the same level. Baseball and football were preferred by most boys in high school. This does not mean that these are the activities that most boys participate in, since many are spectators rather than participants. The favorite indoor sport for both boys and girls is basketball, although indoor swimming, and skating are well-liked by a large percentage of teen-agers, especially those from the middle class.

The different studies of play activities at different ages show that (a) play is a continuous process rather than an activity confined to the period of childhood; (b) there is an enormous overlapping in play interests for individuals of the same age but of different sex, of different social groups, or different intelligence levels.

a. *Strength and play participation.* Van Dalen reports a study of the participation of adolescent boys in play activities.[13] Strength tests were administered to 348 boys in the seventh, eighth, and ninth grades. A comparison of the frequency and amount of participation of the high and low physical-fitness index groups showed that the boys in the high groups engaged in more play activities and devoted more time to play than did the low groups. This was true for all types of activities except for the reading and constructive categories. In the latter, the low physical-fitness index group exceeded by a minimum of ten times the boys of the high group.

Another study by Van Dalen dealt with differences in participation in play activities of junior high school girls at the extremes in muscular strength.[14] Strength index and physical-fitness index were used as a basis for determining the strength of the girls. The frequency of participation of girls in the high-strength group was more than six times that of the girls of the low-strength group; the number of play activities was three times that of the low-strength group. Girls in the latter group played games that were somewhat individualistic in nature and distinctly of a lower degree of organization than those of the high-strength group.

b. *Sex differences.* The differences among communities suggest that sex alone is not responsible for the nature of play, but that customs, environmental conditions, size of the group, and educational level affect it. In general, however, girls' games are not so rough as boys' and less likely to be controlled by such rigid rules.

Girls begin to lose interest in athletics, even in swimming, during the eleventh and twelfth grades. This may be partially accounted for by their increased interest in grooming, dating, and various social activities. Boys, later and to a lesser extent, also show a change in interest as they reach the junior and senior years in high school; talking about things, sharing ideas, interpersonal relations, and socialization in general become more important in their recreational activities. Interest in being spectators rather than participants increases among both boys and girls.

Team activities. Some team activities do, however, develop to satisfy certain *felt* needs that have a biological basis but are socialized in accordance with the expanding social life of the individual. Interest in team games tends to supplement rather than supplant earlier individualistic play interests. At this period, many games have a greater social element than before. The sexes are beginning to mingle and to develop interests of a sexual-social nature; girls now become loyal to boys' teams, and boys to those of the girls. Also at this period of life, games for both boys and girls become more formal in nature, and definite rules are laid down in order better to standardize the playing.

Athletics seem to be the most popular type of activity in the average high school. Baseball, basketball, and other games that do not require expensive equipment and prolonged periods of training are usually found in the smaller high schools; however, an increased number of small high schools are providing indoor space for team activities. Furthermore, there is a tendency on the part of the small high school toward interscholastic rather than intramural participation.

Interest in competitive team activities among adolescents and post-adolescents is encouraged not only through high school contests, but also through programs sponsored by the American Legion and other organizations, which have aided in creating a national interest in baseball as well as in other types of athletics. The values to be derived from participating in athletics are many and diverse, and not the least of these is the development of permanent interests that have recreational and mental hygiene value throughout the later years of life.

Since participation in athletics usually increases muscular development, and since muscular development is not considered feminine, girls are less interested in athletics, especially as they reach adolescence and wish to remain feminine. This is a problem that must be reckoned with by those concerned with girls' athletic programs.

Interest in conversation. Although many preadolescents and adolescents find it difficult to carry on a conversation with adults, they find it easy to talk with their friends. Conversation or what might be called "gab-sessions" has become the main out-of-school activity of a large percentage of adolescents to the extent that lengthy telephone conversations of adolescents have become a source of concern for parents and others who are likely to want to use the phone. Just getting together in a group and talking about the things that interest or disturb them gives them an important feeling of security. Girls talk most about parties, clothes, dates, and social happenings at school. Boys display a greater interest in jokes, sports, the automobile, and girls. There is, however, a shift in conversational topics among boys as they progress through high school; world affairs begin to take on added importance.

OUT-OF-SCHOOL INTERESTS

The out-of-school activities of adolescents reflect their interests. The corner drug store, movies, and television are focal points for many adolescents. In a survey conducted by Gallup and Hill one-third of the high school and college students interviewed stated that they had not read a book in the four months preceding the interview.[15] This may refer to leisure-time reading, since most students have some required reading for their schoolwork. Adolescent interests in group activities do not increase the solitary business of reading.

Home interests. In a study reported by Amatora, seventh- and eighth-graders were asked to list their first, second, and third choice of home interests.[16] The first choice and the average of the first, second, and third choices of the boys and girls are shown in Table 7-4. Twenty-three categories of interests emerged for the 351 boys, 21 for the 323 girls. The findings lead to the conclusion that there are definite home pastimes

Table 7-4

ANALYSIS OF HOME INTERESTS OF SEVENTH- AND EIGHTH-GRADERS

(*Amatora*)

Category	Boys		Girls	
	First	Average	First	Average
Family	10.6	9.1	12.0	8.5
Television	34.4	21.9	21.7	17.2
Hobbies	5.6	7.2	4.2	7.1
Radio	3.3	5.9	4.0	4.7
Food	3.9	4.7	1.6	2.5
Work	4.2	5.5	7.8	10.4
Play	4.5	6.8	2.2	3.8
Music	0.9	0.7	3.4	3.7
Friends	0.8	0.6	0.6	1.5
Baby sit	0.2	0.8	5.6	4.2
Animals	4.6	5.9	3.0	3.3
Sleep	1.4	2.7	0.3	0.9
Bike rides	1.9	1.7	1.6	0.9
Sports	6.2	5.1	1.3	1.5
Trips	2.0	1.8	1.8	0.8
Garden	2.0	3.8	2.8	2.7
Read	4.0	4.8	4.7	6.8
Room	2.2	1.9	0.6	1.9
Games	1.9	3.0	1.2	3.0
Hikes	0.3	0.6	—	—
Park	1.7	0.9	—	—
Cook	1.4	1.6	14.6	9.1
Pray	0.0	0.4	0.9	0.7
Miscellaneous	2.0	3.5	4.1	4.8

among adolescents that vary considerably with social class and other cultural conditions.

Amatora's study indicates that adolescent interest in home activities is greater than many parents and other adults realize. Although there seems to be a decrease in interest in home activities during the teen years, closer study reveals that most adolescents are genuinely interested in their home. Special materials bearing on this are presented in Chapter 13. This interest persists longer to the extent that needs for affection, belonging, and security are satisfied.

Interest in movies. Children's movie attendance is largely confined to week-ends and evenings. Due to a great amount of school social activity, those of high school age attend movies less frequently than fifth-, sixth-, and seventh-graders but customarily go with a date on Friday night. Boys prefer athletics to movies; girls do not. Later, girls show a preference for dancing and dates over movies.

Witty determined the favored television, movie, and radio programs of 1200 pupils in grades 9 through 12 by means of a questionnaire.[17] The subjects were taken from schools in Evanston, Illinois, and Gary, Indiana. The data on movie attendance were gathered during the latter part of November and early December, 1958, and during January, 1959. A pronounced similarity was noted in the favorite programs in grades 9 and 10 and in grades 11 and 12. These favorites indicate the interest of high school students in sex, youth, romance, and adventure. These interests tend to parallel reading interests in that girls show greater interest in romance than boys while boys display a greater interest in adventure than girls.

A German study found that adolescents aged 13-15 years most frequently spent their spare time in sports, reading, and games (in order of listing).[18] Motion pictures and television seemed to attract most adolescents with low concentration ability, less spontaneity, less endurance and persistence, and lack of self-confidence. One should not, however, generalize too readily from this, a German study, to conditions elsewhere such as in the United States. Nevertheless, one could hypothesize that adolescents unsuccessful at school or elsewhere may seek escape and attain vicarious satisfaction from attending motion pictures, watching television and other activities that do not require direct and active participation.

Interest in radio and television. Types of radio and television programs preferred by boys and girls at different age levels are similar to those of reading activities and the movies. Interest in children's programs wanes with the onset of pubescence; instead detective and mystery stories, romance, and dance music command attention. The growth of interest in dance and popular music is especially marked among senior high school students. Witty's report on the favorite TV programs of junior high school pupils in 1960 revealed that boys more than girls preferred sports, mystery and adventure.[19] It is interesting to note that programs preferred by teachers are among those preferred by pupils. Such preferences are often a clue to the behavior and aspirations of teen-agers.

Many youngsters watch television for hours from lack of opportunity to engage in other activities that would challenge their abilities and interests. In Battin's study conducted some years ago boys and girls of high school age reported that they spent an average of 19 hours a week before a television set, less than the amount reported by youngsters in the late elementary school years.[20]

Many parents complain that their children listen to the radio or watch television while studying. Witty discovered that pupils study while listening to the radio more frequently than while viewing television. However, pupils claimed that they received more help from television than from the radio.[21]

SIGNIFICANCE OF ADOLESCENT INTERESTS

Expanding interests. The child's general satisfaction with himself and his surroundings gives way during adolescence to problems, difficulties, and maladjustments. Once indifferent to matters not immediately related to pleasure and pain, he now has an intense curiosity and self-consciousness, and a real concern with the social and ethical standards of adults. Curiosity may show itself in different ways, but it is subject to ready perversion if in unwholesome surroundings. This is true especially of impulses and interests that are maturing and becoming more and more important in the adolescent. Satisfaction and complacency are often suddenly replaced by a restlessness leading toward idealistic behavior or anti-social activities. After years of egocentric activities, the adolescent is thrown into contact with others that brings about new purposes and interests in special activities leading to definite results, whether in his play or in his work. His expanded interests necessitate further stimulation, inspiration, and guidance.

Sex differences. Early adolescent boys and girls have widely varying interests. The answers made by a large sample of 11- to 13-year-olds to the question, "If someone wanted to start a new club or group for boys (girls) like you, what things should the club do?" show that only 11 per cent of the boys, but almost 60 per cent of the girls wanted social activities to be included in the program of the club.[22, 23] As shown in Table 7-5 girls were especially interested in homemaking activities; boys in sports, games, and outdoor activities. It should be pointed out that 41 per cent of the 13-year-old boys and 44 per cent of the girls thought that the club should consist of both boys and girls. A summary of opinion of boys and

Table 7-5

ACTIVITIES PROPOSED FOR HYPOTHETICAL CLUB

Activities	Boys 11–13 Years (per cent)	Girls 11–13 Years (per cent)
Social activities	11	58
Sports and games	57	39
Outdoor activities	36	27
Hobbies, arts and crafts	15	18
Educational activities	10	15
Service, citizenship	5	10
Organizational activities	37	12
Homemaking activities	–	45
Other	4	3
Don't know	4	5
Not ascertained	–	2

girls aged 14-16, presented in Table 7-6, shows that more girls than boys dated and that the former preferred coed clubs and social activities to a greater degree than boys.[24] Again, boys wanted sports and games and outdoor activities significantly more than the girls; boys and girls have different notions as to what activities should be pursued in a club, and a balanced program would be needed in any club for both sexes.

Table 7-6

SUMMARY OF SEX DIFFERENCES IN ACTIVITIES AND INTERESTS

Item	Proportion Boys 14–16	Girls 14–16
1. Proportion Who Date	.59	.72
2. Preference for Club		
a. Prefer like-sexed	.42	.27
b. prefer coed	.37	.53
3. Activities Suggested for Club		
a. social activities	.33	.83
dances	.13	.30
parties	.13	.27
b. sports and games	.76	.33
c. outdoor activities	.48	.14
d. arts and crafts	.13	.03

The findings of three investigations of adolescent interests are reported by Fleming, Digaria, and Newth.[25] To a greater extent than was anticipated similarities were found in the interest patterns of both sexes throughout adolescence. Also differences between age groups were not found to be significant, making it difficult to predict interest patterns from a knowledge of sex, age, or educational classification. Interest in abstract things was high at all ages, but girls consistently showed a greater interest in people than boys. These findings for the English are the same for middle-class adolescents in the United States. It is when we study specific interests that differences become apparent. Boys show a greater interest in physical health, safety, and money, and are driven towards attaining a successful career more than girls. The latter display a greater interest in clothes and personal attractiveness in general, but are not interested in accomplishment; they are more passive and receptive, usually more introverted.

Interests and abilities. Thorndike was one of the first to investigate the ties between interest and ability.[26] He had a group of 344 college students rank their interests during elementary school, high school, and college in seven different school abilities. Correlations were computed between the individual's order of interest and his order of abilities, and were found to be .89 each. Bernard O. Nemoitin investigated the relation between interest and achievement by means of a questionnaire and the use of school records.[27] He found that the degrees of relationship between ability in high school courses "liked best," "liked second best," "disliked most," "disliked next as much," and average ability for high school courses were expressed by the correlation coefficients, $.60 \pm .04$, $.49 \pm .04$, $.58 \pm .04$, and $.57 \pm .04$, when the data obtained from 150 high school seniors were considered. The relationship between interest and ability was found to become more variable and hence less reliable as the degree of interest considered moved from the extremes.

Interest is always a powerful motivation for learning. Successful teachers know that when work appeals to student interests it seems easier. When a pupil is interested in a task, his attention remains more nearly in the marginal context and does not fluctuate far from the general pattern; interest focuses attention within a marginal field. It is selective as well as a driving force. Attitude can also affect learning. When different attitudes are set up by different purposes, the same person will exhibit marked differences in the amount learned.

It might be said that "interest breeds ability and ability breeds interest." It is not likely that one could be interested in a task if he knew nothing whatsoever about it.

However, it cannot be concluded that a student is of especially high ability merely because of his interest. In the first place, individuals vary:

the student might be interested in one subject more than in any other and have relatively better ability in it than in most others, but still have very little absolute ability. A boy may display a keen interest in baseball, but may not be able to make the team. It is, however, likely that he will play baseball better than any other form of athletics. There have indeed been some confused conclusions drawn about the relation between interest and ability. It is always safer to consider the individual's ability in the field of his intense interest in relation to his own abilities in other activities, than to compare it with that of others.

Social class influences. Interests are partially determined by cultural background. A study reported by Knapp, Brimner, and White[28] revealed that even esthetic preferences depend on economic station: middle-class adolescents prefer tartans with a complex design and without saturated color or striking contrast, whereas lower-class adolescents and younger children prefer designs of simple massive pattern, saturated color, and strong contrasts.

Since sex differences in interests are not so pronounced among middle-class as among lower-class parents, and since the home is the model of behavior for the child and adolescent, the teen-ager from the middle-class home does not have a masculine or feminine role so strictly delineated as the lower-class teen-ager's. This was indicated in the results of a study by Pierce-Jones.[29] He noted that the adolescent of high status background was less interested in outdoor and mechanical activities and more strongly attracted to literary, esthetic, persuasive, and scientific pursuits than his low status age-mates. In another project a sample of 40 father-son pairs was drawn from a local community for study.[30] The pairs were given the *Strong Vocational Interest Blank,* a free association personality test, the *Thorndike Vocabulary Test,* a general information questionnaire, and a role expectancy questionnaire. The results supported those of previous studies, indicating that boys tended to follow their fathers' vocational interests, rarely deviating from class lines.

Stability of interest. An outstanding characteristic of the adolescent period is the change in interests that appears during a relatively short period of time. Stability of interest is a function of intelligence: according to the genetic case study of interests conducted by Mackaye with adolescent subjects, early fixation and permanence of interests were most commonly found among those of inferior intelligence; the interests of more intelligent subjects were more unstable in nature.[31] Wishful thinking is oftentimes the basis of vocational interests, and they often show very little relation to actual ability. This is especially true for interests formulated without benefit of experience.

Considerable work has been done in the development of interest inventories for use in educational and vocational guidance. The *Kuder*

Preference Record is now the most widely used inventory for evaluating pupil interests.[32] Through results of this test a profile of interest scores may be made in ten broad areas: outdoor activities, mechanical, computational, scientific, persuasive, artistic, literary, musical, social service, and clerical. Other well-known and useful tests in this category mentioned before are the *Strong Vocational Interest Blanks for Men and Women*[33] and the *Lee-Thorpe Occupational Interest Inventory*.[34] More research has been done with the Strong Blanks than with any of the others, especially in industry.

In a study conducted by Crumrine data were available for 250 high school students who had completed the *Kuder Preference Record* at the ninth-grade level and again at the twelfth-grade level.[35] A tabulation of the per cent of cases in which the highest areas of interest at the ninth-grade level were also the highest at the twelfth-grade level is presented in Table 7-7. High ranking interests at the ninth-grade level tended to remain high at the twelfth-grade level, although changes in rankings of specific interest areas appear for the majority of students. These changes, however, were not likely to be extreme as is evidenced by the fact that 80 per cent of the highest ranking area of the ninth-grade level were among the three highest ranking areas at the twelfth-grade level. A comparison of the rankings of the areas of least interest at the ninth-grade

Table 7-7

CONSTANCY OF THREE HIGHEST AND THREE LOWEST
INTERESTS FROM GRADE NINE TO GRADE TWELVE

(*After Crumrine*)

Highest area of interest that remained highest	52%
Highest that remained in highest three	80
Second highest that remained in highest three	71
Third highest that remained in highest three	51
Lowest area of interest that remained lowest	43
Lowest that remained in lowest three	76
Second lowest that remained in lowest three	65
Third lowest that remained in lowest three	50

level that remained among the lowest three areas at the twelfth-grade level yielded somewhat similar results. Combinations of areas of least interest tended to remain in the lowest areas. For example, 64 per cent of the cases of the three lowest areas in grade 9 were among the three lowest at grade 12.

The results of these studies indicate that specific interests during the high school period are not necessarily permanent. The persistence of an interest will depend largely upon its foundation, and the extent to which it is rooted in the activities and experiences of the adolescent. This may be noted in the case of Louise.

> Louise was above average in intelligence, talented in music, enjoyed Sunday School, and at the age of 16 was in charge of a Sunday School class for younger girls. Her mother wanted her to go into the field of music. However, Louise was very fond of and respected a sister who was a graduate nurse. At the time of her freshman year in high school, she was most interested in music, nursing, and church work of some type, in order of rank. By her senior year her interest in nursing had waned, and she took part in various musical activities at high school, playing an important role in the Music Club. Her interest in music continued along with a general interest in church activities. Louise made her own plans about going to college: she entered a coeducational college about 40 miles from her home, and decided at the end of her freshman year to take courses that would prepare her for teaching in the elementary school and at the same time, take music courses. The interests present were those that had begun at an early age and were deeply rooted in her experiences and ability.

Problems of adjustment in relation to changing interests. Boys and girls whose interests and values coincide with their playmates' encounter no difficulty with changing interests. However, for children whose physiological development is accelerated, an interest in less mature and less social games is a thing of the past; they may seek connections in the church or in special neighborhood activities where there are others with more mature interests. A wholesome and friendly home relationship may help the individual to adjust during this stage. If there are several others at school who also have more mature interests, the advanced child may acquire close chums or join in the formation of small cliques.

Then, there is the person who is less mature in his or her interests than the rest of the group. He oftentimes develops an attitude of indifference toward the activities of the group as a whole but may be able to find comfort and needed friendship in activities with other less mature members; in which case, he will not be seriously affected by the time lag in maturity. Such friendships should be encouraged at this stage.

However, it is for the individual who has advanced at an average rate of physiological development but who, for some social or cultural reason, is unable to participate in the activities of the group, that the problem is more serious. Racial, religious, or social conflicts between the practices or ideals of the home and those of the group may be responsible for such a condition. An individual who, because of some such condition, is unable to change his pattern of interests in harmony with the interests of the growing boys and girls with whom he is thrown, in and out of school, is going to be faced with a difficult adjustment problem likely to affect his school work, his attitude toward his home, and other phases of his personal and social life.

SUMMARY

Many problems of growing up are closely related to changes in interests. The early interests of adolescents are personal in nature; but the social and emotional changes that appear at this stage are reflected in the development of interests in others and especially a changed attitude and feeling toward members of the opposite sex.

The play life of adolescents involves more team spirit and group action than was the case during the preadolescent stage. Adolescent boys continue to show an interest in adventure, but the adventures are less fantastic and are more closely connected with present-day living conditions and problems. Changes in interests with age are reflected in preferences for movies, television programs, and sports. It should not be inferred, however, that these changes are sudden and complete. Much inconsistency will be found in the interests and behavior of adolescent boys and girls. Their interest in a movie of an adventurous nature involving some romance may be followed by interests in make-believe activities resembling those of the 10- or 11-year-old individual. Differences will be found in the interests of boys and girls, with girls showing a more mature interest; this is in keeping with their advanced physiological development. Also, differences will be found in the interests and activities of adolescents from different social-class structures. There is much evidence that differences in social-class structure are very important in affecting differences in interests during childhood and adolescence.

The adolescent's interests lead in many directions and may change considerably in a short time. When they are not expressed in reality they usually appear in his daydreams, wishes, and imagination. It is essential that parents and teachers have a knowledge of adolescent interests, so that they may aid him better to understand himself and direct or guide him toward a more complete fulfillment of his aspirations and possibilities.

THOUGHT PROBLEMS

1. Point out the significance of adolescents' interests in magazines.
2. Discuss the range of adolescent interests as compared with the interests of the 8-year-old child.
3. What interests have been somewhat permanent in your own life? Why?
4. Show how a knowledge of the nature of adolescents' interests is of special value to a school teacher; to a scoutmaster.
5. How do you account for the intense interest of preadolescents in comic books? Note the extent to which this appears to hold over into adolescence and postadolescence.

6. Note the significant changes in school interests that occur with an increase in age. What are the implications of these changes that might be important to the teacher?

7. Study the case of Louise presented in this chapter. In what ways has the early interest in music persisted? How has this affected Louise's choice of a career?

8. What games or activities interested you most when you were 10-12, 14-16, 18-20 years of age? Note the changes of interests. Were these changes sudden or gradual? How would you account for the changes?

9. How does pubescence affect the interests of growing boys and girls? What are the implications of these changes for the development of a good recreational program at school or in the community?

SELECTED REFERENCES

Cole, Luella, *Psychology of Adolescence,* 6th ed. New York: Holt, Rinehart & Winston, Inc., 1964, Chap. 10.

Coleman, James S., *The Adolescent Society.* New York: The Free Press of Glencoe, Inc., 1961, Chap. 8.

Hollingshead, A. B., *Elmtown's Youth.* New York: John Wiley & Sons, Inc., 1949, Chaps. 12 and 15.

Horrocks, John E., *The Psychology of Adolescence,* 2nd ed. New York: Holt, Rinehart & Winston, Inc., 1960, Chaps. 17 and 18.

Rogers, Dorothy, *The Psychology of Adolescence.* New York: Appleton-Century-Crofts, Inc., 1962, pp. 202-12.

Seidman, Jerome M., ed., *The Adolescent—A Book of Readings,* 2nd ed. New York: Holt, Rinehart & Winston, Inc., 1960, Chap. 15.

NOTES

[1] W. R. Boorman, *Developing Personality in Boys* (New York: The Macmillan Company, 1929), p. 41. Quoted by permission of the publishers.

[2] Sister M. Amatora, "Interests of Preadolescent Boys and Girls," *Genetic Psychology Monographs,* **61** (1960), 77-113.

[3] Henry V. Cobb, "Role-wishes and General Wishes of Children and Adolescents," *Child Development,* **25** (1954), 161-70.

[4] Paul Witty, "A Study of Pupils' Interests, Grades 9, 10, 11, 12," *Education,* **82** (1961), 100-110.

[5] C. D. Tierney, "The Interests of Secondary School Children in Different Aspects of Geography," *The British Journal of Educational Psychology,* **32** (1962), 87-89.

[6] A. T. Jersild and R. J. Tasch, *Children's Interests* (New York: Bureau of Publications, Teachers College, Columbia University, 1949), p. 138.

[7] H. M. Lentke, "Eine Erhebung an höheren Schulen über das Interesse an den Schulfächern insbesondere an der Biologie," *Psychol. Beitr.,* **2** (1956), 308-26.

[8] L. M. Terman, "Scientists and Nonscientists in a Group of 800 Gifted Men," *Psychological Monographs,* **68,** No. 378 (1954).

[9] A. Roe, *The Making of a Scientist* (New York: Dodd, Mead & Co., 1952).

[10] Vincent R. Rogers, "Children's Musical Preferences," *Elementary School Journal,* **57** (1957), 433-35.

[11] E. C. Hausle, "Objectives of a Program of Extracurricular Activities in High School," *Recreation,* **34** (1940), 361.

[12] Paul Witty, *op. cit.*

13 D. B. Van Dalen, "A Differential Analysis of the Play of Adolescent Boys," *Journal of Educational Psychology*, 41 (1947), 204-13.

14 D. B. Van Dalen, "A Differential Analysis of the Play of Junior High School Girls," *Journal of Educational Research*, 43 (1949-50), 22-31.

15 G. Gallup and E. Hill, "Youth: The Cool Generation," *Saturday Evening Post* (December 22, 1961), pp. 63-80.

16 Sister M. Amatora, "Free Expression of Adolescents' Interests," *Genetic Psychology Monographs*, 55 (1957), 173-219.

17 Paul Witty, "A Study of Pupils' Interests, Grades 9, 10, 11, 12," *Education*, 82 (1961), 39-44.

18 Hans Thomae, "Beziehungen zwischen Freizeitverhalten sozialen Faktoren und Persönlichkeitsstruktur," *Psychol. Rdsch.*, 11 (1960), 151-59.

19 Paul Witty, "Televiewing by Children and Youth," *Elementary English*, 38 (1961), 103-13.

20 T. C. Battin, *"TV and Youth* (National Association of Radio and Television Broadcasters, 1954).

21 Paul Witty, "A Study of Pupils' Interests, Grades 9, 10, 11, 12," *Education*, 82 (1961), 39-44.

22 *A Study of Boys Becoming Adolescents* (Ann Arbor, Mich.: Survey Research Center, Institute for Social Research, University of Michigan, 1960). A report for the National Council, Boy Scouts of America, of a national survey of boys in the 11 to 13 year age range.

23 E. Douvan and C. Kaye, *Adolescent Girls*, (Ann Arbor, Mich.: Survey Research Center, Institute for Social Research, University of Michigan, 1957). A nationwide study of girls between 11 and 18 years of age.

24 Douvan and Kaye, *op. cit.*, p. 239.

25 C. M. Fleming, D. F. Digaria, and H. G. R. Newth, "Preferences and Values among Adolescent Boys and Girls," *Educational Research*, 2 (1960), 221-24.

26 E. L. Thorndike, "Early Interests: Their Permanence and Relation to Abilities," *School and Society*, 5 (1917), 178-79.

27 B. O. Nemoitin, "Relation between Interest and Achievement," *Journal of Applied Psychology*, 16 (1932), 59-73.

28 Robert H. Knapp, Janet Brimner, and Martan White, "Educational Level, Class Status, and Aesthetic Preference," *Journal of Social Psychology*, 50 (1959), 277-84.

29 John Pierce-Jones, "Vocational Interest Correlates of Socio-economic Status in Adolescence," *Educational and Psychological Measurement*, 19 (1959), 65-72.

30 Paul L. Metzgu, "An Investigation of Some Correlates of Vocational Interest Similarity between Fathers and Sons," *Dissertation Abstracts*, 19 (1958), 1116-17.

31 D. L. Mackaye, "The Fixation of Vocational Interest," *American Journal of Sociology*, 33 (1927), 353-70.

32 Published by Science Research Associates, Chicago, Illinois.

33 Published by Stanford University Press, Stanford, California.

34 Published by California Test Bureau, Los Angeles, California.

35 W. M. Crumrine, *An Investigation of the Stability of Interests of High School Students* (Master's Thesis, University of Michigan, 1949).

8

GROWTH IN ATTITUDES AND BELIEFS

THE DEVELOPMENT AND MODIFICATION OF ATTITUDES

The term *attitude* has been adopted to express a phase of development more complex than factual learning. Attitudes are inclinations, prejudices, or preconceived notions and feelings toward things, persons, situations, and issues.[1] We speak of one's attitude toward racial or religious groups, or toward fundamental social and economic issues such as price controls, reciprocal trade agreements, and public versus private development of power. Although attitudes are more passive than interests, they are extremely important in determining action.

Newcomb offers a functional definition of attitude used as a basis for much of the discussion presented in this chapter.

> An attitude is not a response but a more or less persistent set to respond in a given way to an object or situation. The concept of attitude relates the individual to any aspect of his environment which has positive or negative value for him.[2]

The development of attitudes. Attitudes depend on situations around which we have constructed various habit patterns and built up various images and concepts; it has been constantly observed that physical and social contacts result in the establishment of conscious adjustments and reaction tendencies. The child born and reared in a social world is continually subject to ever-changing social stimuli; socially, he becomes what his environment makes him. G. H. Mead points out that we learn who we are and the kind of person we are from the reaction of other people to us.[3] This learning begins at an early stage, so that by puberty the individual has acquired notions about *self* and others like and different from himself. Racial and religious attitudes, then, seem to be acquired as a part of the individual's attitude toward himself and as one of the areas of definition of his relationship with others.

Attitudes and beliefs are "soaked up" from the milieu in which the child develops. They are a result of all the physical and social stimulation he has encountered. As boys and girls mature, their attitudes and beliefs develop and change, a result of the influence of their families, community mores, religion, and peer culture. Results of the Purdue University polls of young people conducted under the general direction of H. H. Remmers show that students become more realistic and perhaps less idealistic in their attitudes as they grow toward maturity.[4] This may be noted in their responses to the question: To what extent do you believe social classes exist in America? Their responses are presented in Table 8-1. As students progress from grade 9 to grade 12 they appear to recognize more fully that social classes exist. There is, furthermore, a more general acceptance of social classes and cliques as the individual reaches his senior year in high school.

Table 8-1

RESPONSE OF HIGH SCHOOL STUDENTS TO THE QUESTION: "TO WHAT EXTENT DO YOU BELIEVE SOCIAL CLASSES EXIST IN AMERICA?"

(After Remmers, et al.)

Response	Grades (percentage)			
	9	10	11	12
They do not exist	10	7	5	2
They exist but differences among them are slight	55	54	58	61
They exist and differences among them are large	35	39	37	37

The Self-concept. As the individual matures, he learns more about himself than he does about external situations, since he tends to apply the general conclusions of his many learnings to himself. This conglomeration of learning, of self-knowledge, is called the self-concept. It is actually a pattern of attitudes, rather than knowledge, and is learned in the same way as other attitudes. It is the integration of the individual's countless learning experiences that strongly influences his perception and motivation in new experiences or situations and, in fact, actually shapes these new experiences to conform to the already established pattern.

The self-concept can, of course, be seen in the adolescent's notion about the type of person he would like to be. In a study by Crane, pupils from 12 to 15 years of age were asked to write an essay on, "The Sort of Person I Would Like to Be When I Grow Up."[5] Boys wanted money and a good job; girls, good looks and a kind disposition. There was greater agreement among the girls than among the boys. No significant changes in the stereotype appeared after age 13, indicating that certain values held by the individual are stabilized by then.

In order to determine how the estimate of one's own attribute might affect the estimate of the desirability of that attribute, Finnenbaum instructed college students to estimate their own height and weight and to rate the desirability of given heights and weights.[6] A consistent and significant positive correlation was found between estimates of average standing and judgments of optimum standing for one's estimate of his own position on an attribute. This is an important determiner of the evaluation he places on that attribute. This is most important in considering the adolescent's values—his evaluations of grades, athletic ability, popularity, good looks, manners, and other attributes.

The development of intergroup attitudes. Perhaps the most important attitudes of children are those which they develop toward members of the various groups which make up our society. These are called intergroup attitudes. They determine the extent to which a child can work effectively with others on common problems or toward a common goal; they determine the nature of the operation of the socialization process.

Children bring their prejudices to school with them. Since intergroup attitudes are affected by experiences with different groups, it is very important for children to be guided in such contacts. Martin has set forth four principles that, if applied by the skillful teacher or adult leader, would lead to the development of desirable intergroup attitudes:

"Principle I. That program is most desirable which accepts the child as he is and provides recognition of accepting behavior on the part of each child toward every other child.

Principle II. That program is most desirable which leads to an understanding on the part of the child of the reason why different people live as they do.

Principle III. That program is most desirable which fosters interaction among representatives of different groups, with every representative being of equal status.

Principle IV. That program is most desirable which makes it possible for each child to achieve success, but not at the expense of others."[7]

Prejudices shown by children and adolescents. Social, religious, and racial prejudices existing in a particular community are acquired at a relatively early age, so that by the time the child reaches the first grade at school these are already operating. They appear as part of the development of the concept of *self*. Early in their lives children are confronted with the word "American," and identify themselves as Americans. Likewise, children develop attitudes toward different American groups and identify themselves with one of the groups. A study by Radke-Yarrow and Miller dealt with the meaning of the word *American* to 275 children and adolescents from grades 5 through 12.[8] The subjects of this study, pre-

Table 8-2

RESPONSES OF STUDENTS BY GRADES TO THE QUESTION: "WHAT ARE AMERICANS LIKE?"

(*After Radke-Yarrow and Miller*)

Response	Percentage of Children Grades			
	5–6 (N-50)	7–8 (N-68)	9–10 (N-95)	11–12 (N-62)
Democratic ideology, patriotism				
Have many freedoms	12	22	24	10
Government by people	4	3	1	3
People loyal to government	14	36	13	11
Kinds of people				
Mixed nationalities	2	7	8	8
White people	6	2	1	0
Rich and poor	4	3	1	3
Comparison with other people				
Like others	28	25	7	13
Different from others	0	2	1	2
Better than others	4	12	12	16
A powerful nation	2	3	3	8
Personal characteristics				
Ambitious, energetic, achieving	20	19	31	46
Kind, honest, friendly	64	65	41	31
Clean	4	4	5	0
Educated, intelligent	4	12	14	19
Carefree	0	2	4	16
Religious	0	6	1	0
Value money, material possessions	4	6	11	13
Criticism of personal characteristics	6	16	15	21

dominantly Protestant, were from a small midwestern town. There were no Negroes nor members of the Jewish faith in the group.

The responses of the pupils to the question are given in Table 8-2. An American is considered ambitious and energetic, with many freedoms.

A belief in the superiority of the American people in comparison with others grows from grade 5 to grade 12. Although there were few derogatory descriptions, the number of personal descriptions increased with age, indicating an increased understanding of desirable and undesirable personal characteristics.

Varied amounts of hostility and anxiety according to Davis, all dependent on a person's subculture, may be observed among different individuals or groups.[9] The individuals from different social-status classes view quite differently social problems and social reality. In general, the middle class believes in the *status quo,* whereas the lower class, although conservative in many areas, is more radical. There is a close relationship existing between socialization in our culture and socially directed anxiety. Conformity tends to allay these anxieties, and leads to an intolerant attitude toward those who are different. This attitude serves as a support. Thus, among the young, rigid conformity to the group and prejudice against minorities are likely to be greatest among those adolescents who feel most insecure.

A review of writings on the development of ethnic attitudes reveals no consistent pattern or trend in development during adolescence. Ethnic attitudes are not crystallized during the early period of adolescence, although several trends have been listed by Wilson:

1. There is a tendency for level of prejudice to increase with age through adolescence.
2. Level of prejudice tends to be stable over the later ages of adolescence.
3. There is a tendency for perceived norms to become stabilized at some time in adolescence.
4. The degree of consistency among an individual's responses to a given ethnic group during adolescence increases.[10]

PUBESCENCE AND CHANGED ATTITUDES

With the onset of puberty there is an increase in sex hormones that brings about an increased sexual tension. The maturing individual learns that associations with members of the opposite sex are rewarding in that they both produce and relieve sexual tension. However, in our society these adolescent drives are not ordinarily relieved through direct sexual behavior but through substitute behavior. These substitute forms of behavior, which appear with the onset of puberty, differentiate the responses of more physiologically mature adolescents from those less mature.

The changed attitude appearing at this time is emphasized in a study by Jones and Bayley, a study in which comparisons were made between two groups of boys approximately equal in chronological age but two years apart in skeletal development.[11] The early-maturing boys from 12 to 17 were all more natural and unaffected than the average. As expected, the early-maturing boys displayed a greater interest in personal grooming and had better personal appearance than the late-maturing boys.

There are also pronounced changes in attitudes and interests among girls with the onset of pubescence. These changes, appearing at an earlier age for girls than for boys, aggravate the socializing problem in the seventh, eighth, and ninth grades. Girls select books of romance; in their social activities they prefer those activities involving both sexes; they tend to shun sports and strive to play the feminine role.

In order to determine the effect of the menarche, Stone and Barker studied interests and attitudes in 1000 girls of two large junior high schools of Berkeley, California.[12] These girls were matched with respect to chronological ages and social status, but were significantly different in physiological development—one group postmenarcheal, the other premenarcheal. More postmenarcheal than premenarcheal girls of the same chronological age indicated an interest in and favorable attitude toward the opposite sex. The postmenarcheal girls were more interested in adornment and display of the person; they engaged in daydreaming and imaginative activities of such types to a greater degree; they indicated less interest in participation in games and activities requiring vigorous activity. There was, however, no noticeable difference found in the extent to which the two groups rebelled against or came into conflict with family authority. These comparisons indicate a growing interest in adult activities, an increased independence, and an increased interest in the opposite sex, as a result of forces associated with the menarche.

Information and attitudes about sex. Fleege obtained data from 2000 boys attending Catholic high schools about where they received their first information about sex, and from what source or sources they had received subsequent information on this subject.[13] The results revealed that fathers and mothers ranked fifth and sixth, respectively, among the sources from which these boys received their first information. Over onehalf of the boys received their first knowledge from companions, and 34.6 per cent obtained theirs from the street. Results from other studies show that girls, even those from the lower cultural class, receive their information about sex from parents to a much greater degree than boys. In general, children and adolescents receive their information about love and marriage mainly from their homes.[14] Results from a recent survey of several thousand families, presented in Figure 8-1, show that television, other children, and movies are also important sources of information. Better educated parents, television, and other media of communication have furnished present-day adolescents with more, and more wholesome information about sex than their counterparts of several decades ago. However, adolescents from the lower cultural class still receive most of their information about sex from companions, the street, and lewd maga-

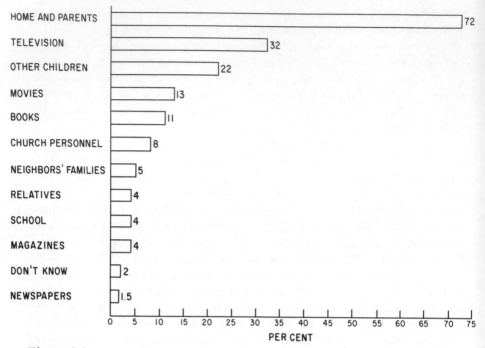

Figure 8-1

SOURCES OF CHILDREN'S IDEAS OF LOVE AND MARRIAGE
(*Duvall*)

zines. Thus, the results from any survey of this problem will be affected by the status of the subjects studied.

A large number of studies lend support to the viewpoint that the character of sex attitudes depend largely upon the manner and sources from which the adolescent received his information. In the study by Fleege, of the boys who received their information about sex from such sources as companions and the street, 53.5 per cent thought that its effects were bad; whereas, of the boys who obtained their information from wholesome sources, 80 per cent thought the effects were good. A wide range of attitudes toward sex, shown in Table 8-3, was found among the 2000 boys.[15]

Sexual maturation evokes different attitudes among boys and girls. Girls worry more than boys. In American society, sex is a topic of conversation more common among adolescent boys than girls. A comparison of results obtained by Fleege with those obtained earlier by Sister Knoebber from 3000 Catholic high school girls indicates that boys regard matters of petting and related activities less seriously than girls.[16]

Table 8-3

ATTITUDES OF BOYS TOWARD SEX

(After Fleege)

Whenever the thought of sex comes to my mind, I usually find myself
regarding it as:

Something that puzzles me	31.0%
A power of creation we share with God	22.5
Something sacred	21.2
Something dirty and vulgar	20.3
A source of thrills	16.6
Something disgusting	12.5
An ever-present opportunity for pleasure	12.3
Something mysterious	12.0
Lots of fun	11.5
Something fearful	6.1

Attitudes toward authority. Attitudes toward authority, ranging
from conformity to rebelliousness, were evaluated and studied by Tuma
and Livson in three interpersonal situations for a sample of boys and
girls at ages 14, 15, and 16.[17] In general, girls proved to conform more
than boys, but they consistently tended to increase their degree of conformity from age 14 to 16 in the three situations studied, whereas boys
showed no clear age trend, except that there was a decided decline in
conformity at age 16. These age trends are shown in Figure 8-2.

A negative relation was found between boys' conformity and socio-
economic ratings. In contrast, no significant relationships were found between the girls' conformity and socio-economic indices. In lower-class and
lower-middle-class families parents are more likely to instill in their children the importance of obedience and acceptance of their status—and thus
of authority. Upper-middle-class families encourage high aspirations and
a nonacceptant attitude toward existing patterns and conditions.

SCHOOL ATTITUDES

The adolescent brings with him to the classroom certain attitudes
and interests formulated at home, on the playground, in school, at church,
and elsewhere. The teacher who fails to take into account the various cultural forces that have operated in the development of a particular child's
attitudes and interests will be unable to understand him and the problems he encounters.

Attitudes toward classmates. Among the attitudes formulated by
junior and senior high school students are certain notions about the activ-

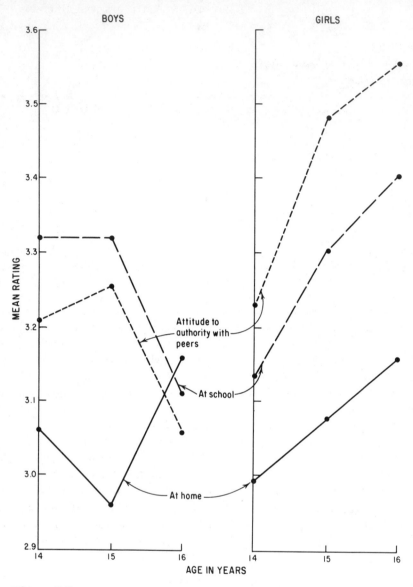

Figure 8-2

MEAN RATINGS OF DEGREE OF CONFORMITY IN THREE SITUATIONS AS
A FUNCTION OF AGE
(*Tuma and Livson*)

ities of their classmates. The results of the California studies, presented
in Table 8-4, show some of the special likes and dislikes of adolescents in
this connection.[18] No consistent sex differences were observed in the responses to these items.

154

Table 8-4

ASPECTS OF SCHOOL LIFE DISLIKED BY ADOLESCENTS: ATTITUDES TOWARD
CLASSMATES

Aspect	H5 L6		H8 L9		H11 L12	
	Boys	Girls	Boys	Girls	Boys	Girls
Classmates who plan games or hikes or parties and then won't let others in on the fun	45	32	20	25	15	7
Groups or gangs or crowds that won't have anything to do with pupils outside of these groups	42	31	21	26	11	26
Having some of the pupils start a club which they won't let others into	39	31	17	14	8	6
Having the classmates you like most turn out to be stuck-up	46	44	24	22	30	11
One's classmates are snobbish and stuck-up	39	44	27	37	30	21
Having certain pupils run everything in the school	61	49	38	43	27	46
Classmates whispering and making fun of one behind one's back	55	47	20	26	23	10
Having a few pupils in the school make fun of some of the other pupils	46	42	18	25	10	15
Being laughed at when one recites in class	39	35	35	35	23	21
Being called nicknames	18	11	3	8	0	0

The attitudes of adolescents toward their classmates are also reflected in their degree of acceptance of the members making up their group. Brown noted that the greater the number of school organizations to which students belong, the greater is the likelihood of their being in the high-acceptance group of their classmates.[19] Thirty-seven items were assembled for each of the 200 most-accepted and for each of the 200 least-accepted students of the Anderson (Indiana) High School. Over 40 per cent of the low-acceptance group in the study belong to no school organization. Students from the low socio-economic class take a less active part than other students in club activities as well as in most other extra-class activities. Thus, these students are often left out of many school functions and are frequently found among the low-acceptance group.

Attitudes toward the teacher. The attitude toward a teacher assumed by adolescents oftentimes represents a group attitude. The attitude toward a teacher taken by leaders of certain gangs or cliques may become the model for most other adolescents to follow. Sometimes a community may place a teacher in a favorable or unfavorable role and thus influence the actions of adolescents. However, adolescents are more honest and forthright in their appraisal than parents. Adolescents have in many cases taken a fair attitude toward a teacher who was being unfairly maligned by members of the community.

Table 8-5

ASPECTS OF THE SCHOOL SITUATION DISLIKED BY ADOLESCENTS: TEACHERS AND DISCIPLINE

Aspect	H5 L6		H8 L9		H11 L12	
	Boys	Girls	Boys	Girls	Boys	Girls
Being punished for things you do not do	69	58	69	56	59	36
Teachers who are not interested in their pupils	30	26	38	33	34	44
Teachers who make you feel embarrassed before the class	51	46	54	67	46	60
Teachers who mark you down because they do not like you	49	39	68	65	58	54
Examinations that are unfair	35	25	65	51	62	49
Too many teachers' pets	61	42	49	39	38	22
Teachers who have the wrong opinion about you	30	28	52	51	51	36

In the California growth study 71 boys and 72 girls completed an inventory consisting of 50 items entitled "Things You Do Not Like About School."[20] This inventory was checked annually by these boys and girls for seven consecutive years. Items from the school situation involving teacher-pupil relations are presented in Table 8-5. The numbers of pupils checking the items at the first checking (H5 L6), the fourth checking (H8 L9), and the seventh checking (H11 L12) are presented as a basis for comparing these boys and girls at the preadolescent or early adolescent years, the adolescent stage, and the postadolescent stage. At all of these stages of development both boys and girls showed a strong dislike for unfair practices on the part of teachers. Boys were slightly more inclined than girls to check the various items, except for the one relating to being embarrassed by the teacher before the class.

These studies reveal that many adolescents dislike school. Materials bearing on this in relation to school dropouts will be presented in Chapter 16. However, the majority of adolescents attain success and satisfaction through the wide range of activities provided in the modern school program. Unfavorable attitudes of adolescents toward school result from teachers who lack an understanding of adolescents, a school curriculum out of harmony with the interests and goals of many adolescents, and procedures of an authoritarian nature that fail to furnish the students with opportunities to preserve and enhance the ego.

RELIGIOUS ATTITUDES AND BELIEFS

The average adolescent today, when confronted with the popular question "What is religion?" may give any number of strange and incoherent answers. There is little likelihood that any two young people will give an identical definition. Strange though it may seem, this is to be expected, since religion is more than a mere definition to be mechanically learned and carried from generation to generation. We find, however, that there are certain fundamental principles and concepts upon which the religious experience of the adolescent is based.

Studies have been made of the religious development of adolescents from diaries, letters, and poems; these, together with results from questionnaires, have given valuable insights into the development of the religious self. Little can be learned from a study of the religion of childhood, as such, since felt and understood religious experiences do not ordinarily appear until puberty. The religious community and the temperament of the individual determine whether the development shall be continuous or catastrophic, leading to conversion. Sex, nature, and love influence religious development, but do not exclusively determine it.

In one investigation a group of girls between the ages of 15 and 17 were questioned about when and where they first experienced a feeling of reverence.[21] The meaning of reverence was made clear to them before asked. The project was so developed that the girls freely gave information and recognized that such experiences did not need to relate to a certain formal religious creed or program. Of the 148 girls questioned, 22 stated that they had never had any emotional experience that could be called "reverence"; 68 girls stated that such feelings arose at a time when they suddenly came to realize the beauty and wonder of nature; only 31 girls, or 21 per cent, reported their first feeling of reverence or awe to be connected with some religious observance. Some of the girls expressed reverence toward some person they had known—in some cases this approached what is usually termed pity—while others reported reverence toward special types of music or some masterpiece of art. The results suggest that reverence tends to be aroused toward anything that is impressive, beautiful, or extremely thought- and emotion-provoking.

The period of conversion. The adolescent period is characterized by various physiological changes that have very definite influences on the individual's psychic development. This period has already been described as one in which there is manifested a marked expression of self-consciousness, as well as a marked development of social consciousness. This development of a social consciousness, during which the child comes to be looked upon as a social rather than as an egocentric individual, tends to follow naturally the realization of life's purposes and the consciousness of perfected physical and mental powers. "In cases of normal development the religious teaching and impressions of childhood now come to a head, and are invested with a reality and significance they formerly lacked."[22]

Conversion means change—a modification of the goals and directions of one's life. The nature of the conversion experience may be as varied as life itself. The type of conversion is influenced by the nature of our religious institutions. A theology of crisis tends to produce experiences of crisis. A crisis in one's life may produce a religious crisis. This form of conversion appears more frequently among certain evangelical groups, whereas other groups attempt to bring forth a gradual religious awakening and growth. Three types of religious conversions were earlier noted by Clark: (1) definite crisis (in emotions and attitudes); (2) emotional stimulus (less intense, with no special change or transformation recalled); and (3) gradual awakening.[23]

The more radical awakening tends to occur between the ages of 15 and 17, whereas the gradual awakening comes considerably earlier. The conversion is likely to be more revolutionary in nature when the crisis is deferred. Conversion among adolescents today even in evangelical circles is not likely to involve a violent crisis, but instead include an acceptance of the teachings of the church and a series of decisions on the road toward the development of a philosophy of life.

If the individual is awakened and stimulated to further thought and activity with a positive emphasis on new loyalties, group welfare, and proper habits of conduct, there will probably be a healthier and more balanced growth in the social, educational, and religious life. It is when the sins of the past are recounted and the natural sex and various social tendencies are criticized so vehemently that we find morbid fears developing and becoming prime factors in the development of emotional instability and perversions. Statistics of conversion as well as various testimonies show that girls are more affected by the emotional appeal in religious life, whereas boys are more attracted by codes of honor, ethical sanction, and group activity.

Change of religious beliefs during adolescence. As the child grows, his concept of God takes on an added and to some degree changed meaning; his understanding of his relationship to God becomes more inclusive and less concrete in nature; and his concept of the "brotherhood of man" is enlarged in scope. These changed concepts are a part of the development of the *total self,* and affect changes in emotional, personal, and social behavior patterns.

In a study of the religious beliefs and problems of adolescents by Kuhlen and Arnold, a questionnaire was prepared that listed 52 statements representing various religious beliefs.[24] The subject completing the questionnaire was instructed to mark each statement according to whether he *believed it, did not believe it,* or *wondered about it.* Responses were secured from 547 (257 boys and 290 girls) sixth-, ninth-, and twelfth-grade pupils. These three groups were chosen since the sixth-grade group is largely prepubescent (especially boys; many girls are pubescent or near pubescent), the ninth-grade group pubescent, and the twelfth-grade group postpubescent. Approximately three-fourths of the pupils were Protestants, 22.85 per cent were Catholic, and several were either of Jewish faith or indicated no church attendance.

The findings were analyzed by determining what proportion of each group checked each statement. The results from this study are analyzed in Table 8-6. Significant changes appear in the religious beliefs of boys and girls as they reach adolescence and grow into maturity: of the 52 statements included in the study, statistically significant changes appeared in 36. A pronounced change appears in the attitude toward the Scriptures as shown by the responses to the statements, "Every word in the Bible is true," and "It is sinful to doubt the Bible." The responses to a number of the statements provide evidence for the assumption that a greater tolerance toward different religious beliefs and practices appears with increased maturity of the growing individual.

Factors related to adolescent beliefs. It has already been suggested that the preadolescent has accepted quite completely the beliefs he has been taught in the home and by religious teachers. However, as early as 12 or 13 some degree of doubt and oftentimes opposition begins to be manifested, as is revealed in Table 8-7. Certain investigators have sought to determine the factors related to the development of religious beliefs. MacLean found a negative correlation between chronological age and accepted beliefs.[25] Girls' revolt against accepted beliefs comes later than boys'. It is found less frequently and is probably not so inclusive. The general relationship between the educational and economic level of the home and the acceptance of definite religious beliefs is negative, as is also that between intelligence and acceptance of beliefs.

What relationship exists between one's conception of God and one's behavior? In order to throw some light on this problem, Mathias constructed the *Idea-of-God Test.* The purpose of the test as expressed by Mathias was "(1) to draw out an individual's social attitudes concerning God, and (2) to crystallize the person's viewpoint of God from the angle

Table 8-6

CHANGES IN SPECIFIC RELIGIOUS BELIEFS DURING ADOLESCENCE AS SHOWN BY
THE PERCENTAGE OF 12-, 15-, AND 18-YEAR-OLD CHILDREN WHO CHECKED
VARIOUS STATEMENTS INDICATING (A) BELIEF, (B) DISBELIEF, OR (C)
UNCERTAINTY (WONDER)

(After Kuhlen and Arnold)[*]

Statement	Believe			Disbelieve			Uncertain		
	12	15	18	12	15	18	12	15	18
God is a strange power working for good, rather than a person	46	49	57	31	33	21	20	14	15
God is someone who watches you to see that you behave yourself and who punishes you if you are not good	70	49	33	18	37	48	11	13	18
I know there is a God	94	80	79	3	5	2	2	14	16
Catholics, Jews, and Protestants are equally good	67	79	86	9	9	7	24	11	7
There is a heaven	72	45	33	15	27	32	13	27	34
Hell is a place where you are punished for your sins on earth	70	49	35	16	21	30	13	27	34
Heaven is here on earth	12	13	14	69	57	52	18	28	32
People who go to church are better than people who do not go to church	46	26	15	37	53	74	17	21	7
Young people should belong to the same church as their parents	77	56	43	13	33	46	10	11	11
The main reason for going to church is to worship God	88	80	79	6	12	15	4	7	6
It is not necessary to attend church to be a Christian	42	62	67	38	23	24	18	15	8
Only our soul lives after death	72	63	61	9	11	6	18	25	31
Good people say prayers regularly	78	57	47	9	29	26	13	13	27
Prayers are answered	76	69	65	3	5	8	21	25	27
Prayers are a source of help in times of trouble	74	80	83	11	8	7	15	10	9
Prayers are to make up for something that you have done that is wrong	47	24	21	35	58	69	18	17	9
Every word in the Bible is true	79	51	34	6	16	23	15	31	43
It is awful to doubt the Bible	62	42	27	18	31	44	20	26	38

[*] Discrepancies between the total of "Believe," "Not Believe," and "Uncertain" and 100 per cent represent the percentages that did not respond to the statements.

of available information regarding the universe and its mysteries, as we conceive them."[26]

Correlations were obtained between 16 factors, referred to as background factors, and composite *Idea-of-God* scores. Correlations were posi-

Table 8-7

PER CENT OF 13-YEAR-OLD CHILDREN MARKING THE STATEMENTS TRUE (N-646)

(*After MacLean*)

1. Religion consists of obeying God's laws	70%
2. God is simply imagination	21
3. We learn about God through dreams and visions	28
4. God made us, the animals, the stars, and the flowers, and everything in the world	82
5. God knows everything we say or do	78
6. God cares what we do	89
7. God has a good reason for what happens to us, even when we cannot understand it	92
8. God protects from harm those who trust him	70
9. God cares whether we repent of our sins or not	82
10. God hears and answers our prayers	85
11. True prayer consists of thinking of the wonderful ways of God in the world	66
12. It is possible to get things by prayer	31
13. The soul lives on after the body dies	71

tive but low, the highest being between moral knowledge and scores on the *Idea-of-God Test*. Correlations were also obtained between fifteen factors, referred to as behavior patterns, and composite *Idea-of-God* scores. All correlations were again positive but low, the three highest having as second members high motives (.28), self-functioning (.25), and school deportment (.21). It appears, therefore, that certain background factors, as well as personal factors, tend to be associated with high composite concepts of God. However, this does not mean that one is the cause of the other; but rather "that what have been designated as desirable concepts of God tend to be found in those pupils who come from homes with church affiliation and who have a good cultural background, and in individuals of high intelligence, moral knowledge, and social attitudes."[27] Also, the results support the theory that good conduct, independent action, and church and club participation tend to be associated with desirable concepts of God.

Adolescent doubts. Many adolescents, especially those whose early training has been dogmatic in nature, become very skeptical of all problems not concrete and not specific in nature. As the growing, developing youth increases his realm of knowledge and develops better habits of thinking, he is led to question many of the things he had formerly accepted uncritically: In a study of the religious attitudes and beliefs of young people Ross estimates that whereas about three-fourths of those questioned accepted various orthodox religious beliefs and doctrines, only about 16 per cent seemed to manifest the firmness of belief, zest, and security of conviction that is expected of a genuinely religious person.[28] Early faith, so firmly entrenched, receives a serious setback when the child learns that the answers to many of his questions are not based upon almost obvious facts.

This critical attitude has its beginning with the child's first observations that the things he has been taught are not wholly in harmony with facts observable in later life. New and broader experiences and the acquirement of certain scientific principles contradictory to early learning often aid in destroying faith in other early teachings. The development of doubt continues and may find further support in the behavior and attitude assumed by those who have a powerfully suggestive influence on the child.

Functional peculiarities of beliefs and attitudes are at this stage of life quite prevalent. The adolescent may desire to stay away from church for some social reason; therefore he comes to doubt the value of the work of the church as well as the general honesty of the leaders. This doubting may serve further to effect the satisfaction of a desire that has been blooming, or justify some need already existing. During adolescence there are usually several elements that combine to augment doubts extremely.

How should doubts be treated? In the first place, it should be recognized that doubting is not confined to the religious sphere of life. Neither should anyone be misled into believing that doubting is a universal trait and therefore an instinct. The adolescent does not need to clutch to a dogma or creed: he needs to find himself, and to interrelate in his own thinking the processes of the universe with the general plan of life. An anchorage in an open sea in a storm is analogous to the type of treatment usually given the individual during this stage.

The effects of conflicting group membership. The child increasingly enters into multiple group membership, with the likelihood that he will belong to groups with conflicting attitudes, values, and mores. The adolescent from a home representing a minority is the one most likely to find himself in conflict with his peers, especially as he feels the need for peer approval.

For many children and adolescents one of these areas of disagreement is religious beliefs; for example, conflict may occur in connection with interfaith dating activities or in other social activities. Rosen conducted a study with 50 Jewish adolescent boys and girls enrolled in high school—the issue of conflict concerned a practice of traditional Judaism, the use of kosher meat.[29] Two questions were asked of the adolescents: "When you get married are you going to use kosher meat in your home?" and "Is kosher meat now used in your home?" Adolescents who plan to use kosher meat, and parents who use kosher meat were labeled "observants." Some comparisons, presented in Table 8-8, show that a significant relationship exists between the attitude of the adolescent's membership group and his own. Also, adolescents of observant parents are proportionately more likely to follow their parents' practice.

This study emphasizes the impact of parents and peers on the behavior and attitudes of adolescents. The peer group furnishes the adoles-

Table 8-8

THE RELATION OF ADOLESCENT'S ATTITUDE TO THAT OF PARENTS AND
PEER GROUP

(After Rosen)

Adolescent attitude	Parent attitude		Peer group attitude	
	Observant	*Nonobservant*	*Observant*	*Nonobservant*
Observant	60%	32%	80%	23%
Nonobservant	40	68	20	77
Total	100	100	100	100
Total number	25	25	20	30

cent with a sense of belonging when conflicting loyalties appear and gives him a source of security and status when he is faced with the task of attaining emotional independence from the family.

SOCIAL FORCES AFFECTING ADOLESCENTS

The home and attitudes. There is a rather widespread notion that the youth of each generation revolt against the ideas of their parents and of their parents' generation. A study by Remmers and Weltman was undertaken to gather data bearing on such a hypothesis.[30] The *Purdue Opinion Poll for Young People* was available for gathering data in this study. A representative sample of 88 sons, 119 daughters, 207 fathers, 207 mothers, and 89 teachers from 10 school communities in Indiana and Illinois was used. Comparisons and interrelations obtained between the responses of parents and children, daughters and sons, and teachers and pupils showed that a high degree of community of attitudes exists between parents and children. The strength of this relationship varied, however, with the general nature of the attitude object. The correlations, presented in Table 8-9, show a closer relationship between mother and father and son and daughter than between parents and children. This reveals some tendency for those of one generation to agree more closely than individuals a generation apart in age. However, the close correlation between the attitudes of parents and those of adolescents, and the lower correlation between the attitudes of teachers and those of pupils indicate that home influences are most important factors affecting the attitudes of adolescent boys and girls. The importance of the home in the formation of attitudes is borne out further by the results of a rather comprehensive study at Teachers College, Columbia University.[31] As a part of the Citizenship Education Project the attitudes and political preferences of more than 6000 eleventh-grade students were studied. The findings supported results from earlier studies that revealed a close relationship between students' attitudes and parents' attitudes. Eighty-three per cent of the adolescents preferred the political party of their parents. This percentage would perhaps be even higher in most rural areas or where there is a more traditional school program, since these conditions do not contribute as freely to growth in independent thinking.

Importance of class structure. It was pointed out in Chapter 6 that class status is important in connection with the socialization of adolescents. This is further shown in a study of the moral beliefs of the youth of Prairie City by Havighurst and Taba.[32] They report that class struc-

Table 8-9

CORRELATIONS OF PROPORTIONS OF AGREEMENT RESPONSES ON SIXTEEN ITEMS FROM THE PURDUE OPINION POLL

(After Remmers and Weltman)

Parents vs. children	.86 ± .01
Mothers vs. fathers	.96 ± .03
Daughters vs. sons	.93 ± .05
Daughters vs. mothers	.87 ± .05
Daughters vs. fathers	.80 ± .07
Sons vs. mothers	.80 ± .07
Sons vs. fathers	.82 ± .06
Teachers vs. pupils	.65 ± .11
Teachers vs. parents	.65 ± .11
Children in grades 9 and 10 vs. parents	.90 ± .04
Children in grades 11 and 12 vs. parents	.79 ± .07
Children in grades 9 and 10 vs. children in grades 11 and 12	.96 ± .01

ture affects the adolescent's sense of honesty and responsibility, but not his loyalty, moral courage, and friendliness. During adolescence the individual learns his class role in manners, social activities, prejudices, attitudes toward peers, and the like. At school the child of a lower-class status is often faced with the fact that he is not wholly accepted by those of his age level, or, if accepted, he is given a rather minor role in the various activities. To be accepted he must take on the attitudes and values of a middle-class culture, which the high schools tend to promote.

Haire and Morrison investigated the way school children of high and low socio-economic status perceive problems of labor-management relations.[33] Four semiprojective tests were developed and administered to 755 students in grades 7, 8, 9 and 11. Adolescents in the lower socio-economic group tended consistently to be much more strongly prolabor, to show more undifferentiated approval of the workers involved, to agree with them on issues, and to identify with them. Both groups moved in the direction of a prolabor attitude as they became older.

A questionnaire designed to measure youth's attitude toward industrial relations was administered by the Purdue Opinion Panel to a nationally representative sample of high school students.[34] The youths polled showed very little knowledge of industrial relations and respected union and management leaders equally. In general they assumed a pessimistic attitude toward the future of collective bargaining and tended to favor government interference in labor disputes.

In general, where differences exist between the attitudes of adolescents and their parents, adolescents are more willing to break with tradition and the *status quo*. It is at this point that their idealistic nature and less deep-seated prejudices may be observed.

Socio-cultural differences. In a study of socio-cultural differences in attitudes and values reported by Lehmann, 2983 freshmen entering Michigan State University in the fall of 1958 were given a battery of tests and inventories designed to measure beliefs, rigidity, and values.[35] They were also given a 26-item biographical background questionnaire. Since there were significant sex differences in the three affective measures used, the data were analyzed separately for males and females. A rather complete statistical analysis of the data yielded the following conclusions:

1. Males are significantly more stereotypic and dogmatic than females. Whereas females tend to regard more highly the constellation of values embracing sociability, relativistic moral attitudes, and place more emphasis on living for today, males regard more highly the value constellation of the meaning of work and responsibility, puritan morality, and an emphasis on the future. Males also had higher scores on the political, theoretical, and economic scales of the Allport-Vernon-Lindzey Study of Values while females had significantly higher scores on the social, religious, and aesthetic scales. In addition, there is no significant difference between the sexes on a measure of personality rigidity.

2. Catholic students, as a group, are more stereotypic and dogmatic than either Protestants or Jews. In addition, Catholic students also have significantly higher mean traditional value scores. Jewish students, on the other hand, are more emergent in their value orientation. When comparisons were made among the different Protestant sects, it was found that the Presbyterian males and females [are] least stereotypic while the Baptist males and females are most dogmatic and have the highest mean traditional value scores. . . .

3. The mean scores of students who attended a parochial high school indicate that they are more stereotypic, more dogmatic, and have higher tradi-

tional value scores than students who attended either a private or public high school.

4. There is no significant difference in attitudes and values between those students whose parents are native-born and those whose parents are foreign-born.

5. The group of students whose parents only attended or completed high school have a significantly higher mean traditional value score and are more stereotypic than those students whose parents attended or completed college.

6. Males and females who have lived a major portion of their life on a farm have higher mean traditional value scores than those students who come from a predominantly urban environment. Whereas the most stereotypic group of males come from a farm, their female counterparts come from a city with a population of 25,000-100,000. Somewhat the same pattern holds for dogmatism, in that females who come from a city with over 100,000 population are the most dogmatic group, while the most dogmatic males live a major portion of their lives on a farm.

7. Students who come from homes where the father is in the laboring class and the parents have only a grade or high school education are, as a group, more stereotypic and have higher mean traditional value scores than those students who come from homes where the parents attended college and the father is an executive or professional man.[36]

Although it is generally recognized that attitudes are instilled early in life and are most easily modified during childhood, they are affected by education, even as late as the college years. This is clearly shown in a study of the impact of college training by Freedman[37] and in a study of international awareness in freshmen, sophomores, juniors, and seniors by Garrison.[38] Garrison's study shows that the greatest change occurs between the freshman and sophomore years in college. The results of these and other related studies suggest that with increased education we might expect significant changes in attitudes toward national and world problems.

The role of the school. The public high school is often the only place where the child is furnished the opportunity for learning certain middle-class motivational patterns. Teachers frequently misunderstand and resent the slum child's show of aggression in name-calling, cursing, and fighting. The parents of many lower-class children teach their children to "stand up for their rights," and when the child is losing a scuffle to a larger opponent, the father and mother are prepared to back up their teachings by joining the fight. The writer recalls such a fight between two 10-year-olds. When the smaller and weaker of the two was getting the worst of the fight, the father called to an older son to aid. This set off a melee in which a number of adults and children were involved. In the lower-class culture, if a boy does not try to be a good fighter, he will not receive the approval of his father, nor will he be accepted by his peers: the boy learns to fight and to admire fighters.

The middle-class boy is likely to be looked upon as a "sissy" by the lower-class boy. His sex role is not so different from that of girls as is the case for the lower-class boy. Furthermore, he displays greater interest than the lower-class boy in sedentary pastimes such as reading, music, and art, frequently considered feminine.

Kitano's studies of first and second generation Japanese in the United States, show that added education furnishes the adolescent with literary, historical, and scientific figures as models for patterning attitudes and behavior; those with less education tend to emulate parents, grandparents, relatives, and important figures in the local community.[39]

Youth and the church. To arrive at sound conclusions about the part the church plays in the lives of young people is not a simple task. The obvious difficulties are aggravated by the fact that it is impossible to isolate the church as a single factor in the experience and background of youth. It is quite possible, of course, to discover the conditions under which the youth of different church groups are living, and also to find out whatever differences may exist in the ways that they react to current problems. However, to presume to measure the extent to which these differences are due to dissimilarities in religious backgrounds and affiliations is not only unscientific but highly dangerous. Differences which, on the surface, may appear to be basically religious in character are, in fact, profoundly affected by such factors as race, nationality, locality of residence, and educational attainment.

Youths tend to accept the religion of their parents. In the Maryland study over four-fifths (81.1 per cent) of the youth with some church affiliation had adopted the faith of both their parents. When both parents had church affiliations, but when there was a difference between the persuasion of the father and mother, there was more than twice as strong a tendency to accept the faith of the mother. The proportion of youth who had adopted a belief different from that of either parent was quite negligible: 4.2 per cent for the Catholic youth, 2 per cent for the Protestants, and none for the Jewish.

The O'Reillys noted significant differences in the religious beliefs of college students who acknowledged membership in the Catholic church, as well as some interesting relationships between these beliefs and attitudes toward minorities.[40] The subjects of their study consisted of 92 white males in a Catholic liberal arts college for men in a southern city and 120 white females in a Catholic liberal arts college for women in the same city. The results supported the hypothesis that those prejudiced against minority groups tend to cluster together. The evidence of a relationship between religious attitudes and prejudice is supported further by intercorrelations between these variables:

	Correlations	
	Men	*Women*
Anti-Semitism and anti-Negro scores	.69	.68
Anti-Semitism and religion	.39	.31

One should not generalize too quickly from these results. Perhaps a distinction should be made between religious attitudes involving a humanitarian point of view and religious attitudes that are narrower in scope.

In one study college students were asked to check various influences that they believed might have affected their religious viewpoints.[41] The results, presented in Table 8-10, show the importance of parental influence, personal influence of others, fear and insecurity, and conformity with tradition. The principal sex difference involved greater susceptibility of women toward the influence of gratitude, mystical experience, and aesthetic appeal. Thus, it appears that the influence of culture in defining the role of women may have an important bearing on their religious beliefs and practices.

Table 8-10

PERCENTAGE REPORTING VARIOUS TYPES OF
INFLUENCES UPON THEIR RELIGIOUS LIFE
(After Allport, Gillespie, and Young)

	Harvard (Men)	Radcliffe (Girls)
Parental influence	51	34
Fear of insecurity	43	46
Personal influence of others	36	43
Conformity with tradition	35	27
Aesthetic appeal	25	41
Church teachings	24	34
Gratitude	23	42
Reading	20	24
Studies	17	19
Sorrow or bereavement	17	26
A mystical experience	10	21
Sex turmoil	8	8

Intellectual development and attitudes. Intellectual maturity, as an integral part of the total maturity of a growing child, is accompanied by pronounced changes in attitudes. As the child grows into adolescence, he becomes more discriminating in the choice of friends. At this time prejudices formed earlier at home and in the neighborhood become more generalized. Attitudes take on a fuller meaning and reveal an increased complexity. Many things of an abstract and nonpersonal nature become more significant and personal. Proof of a close relation between intelligence and the development of social attitudes and habits is demonstrated in studies of this problem.[42] The *Furfey Developmental Age Test* was given to 26 boys, median age 11 years, and to 24 girls, median age 11 years, of superior intelligence. There was a considerable variation in maturity shown for the different items. The highest maturity was revealed on the items concerned with choice of books to read, future vocations, and things to think about.

A study by Epstein with high school juniors and seniors as subjects showed that social and political attitudes could be changed by experience.[43] The students were given a social- and political-attitudes questionnaire consisting of 45 items, then only the senior class was taken on an extensive field trip to visit certain government projects. Following an interval of three weeks both the junior and senior classes were given the questionnaire a second time. The responses of the senior class changed significantly; the responses of the junior class stayed the same.

The results of another survey conducted among high school students showed that students similar in many ways, but different in the amount of information possessed about world affairs, expressed significantly different opinions on international issues on all but 1 of 16 questions.[44] The well-informed group was more optimistic, more international-minded, better able to make decisions on the questions, less eager to go to war over minor incidents, and less given to emotional solutions to international problems.

The influence of education upon the formation and direction of attitudes will depend largely upon the emotional climate in which the learning takes place. High school students will be influenced more by a teacher whom they admire than by one whom they dislike or take a neutral attitude toward. The teacher who is able to present a problem in such a way as to motivate students to think critically about it will stimulate them and influence their attitudes to a greater degree than the teacher who merely enlists their attention while he recites facts about an issue or problem. Thus, the extent to which the schools influence the attitudes of the students depends upon the teacher's personality and his rapport with the students.

The effects of movies, radio, and television. The various studies that have been made dealing with the influence of motion pictures on children's attitudes indicate that they can be a potent force in conditioning or reconditioning certain attitudes. The introduction of television sets into a large percentage of homes has increased enormously the possibilities of their molding and changing existing attitudes. Furthermore, the changes they make are not likely to be temporary.

Studies of movies after World War I showed that movies favorable to the German people were effective in building more favorable attitudes toward the Germans. In one study the effects of the motion picture, *Gentleman's Agreement,* on attitudes toward Jews was studied.[45] An experimental and a control group of college students were used as subjects in this study. An essay-type questionnaire consisting of five items was administered. There was a change in the average attitudes indicating greater tolerance for Jews on the part of the group that viewed the picture. However, not all students of this group registered such a change; a few showed greater prejudice and intolerance after seeing the picture. During the period there was no appreciable change in test scores of a control group that did not see the picture. Since the adolescent is more impressionable than the college student, one would expect an even greater change in his attitude during this period following the attendance at the movie or televiewing.

SUMMARY

The home, school, and community environments are the breeding grounds of attitudes. If the outstanding attitudes of the adolescent's social environment have been hostile, unfriendly, and distrustful he will view people in this manner. The adolescent brings with him to his group certain attitudes. The attitudes of the individual toward himself, others, and current problems furnish a measure of his emotional and intellectual maturity as well as a perspective of his past experiences.

Attitudes toward members of the opposite sex are profoundy affected by the physiological maturity of the individual. The home, school, church, and peers are the major sources of information about sex and determine in a large measure the adolescent's attitudes toward sex.

Interest in religious problems, religious convictions, and changes in life outlooks appear in the lives of many adolescents as they grow toward maturity. The mental and social development of adolescents are closely related to a religious awakening and changed attitudes. During adolescence, belief is strongest only to be followed in postadolescent years by doubts. Doubting grows out of wider social and intellectual contacts, and in this the adolescent needs sane, reliable, and honest guidance. It appears that adolescents are eager to find something of value in religion and are often disillusioned. Such a condition may lead to cynicism, doubt, and withdrawal from religious activities. But this is not always true; many a youth in his teens has ascended to heights of religious experience unsurpassed even by adults. When ideals are established and integrated in these religious experiences, there is an increased permanency in the dynamic force in operation. Ideals represent an integration of behavior units into a larger pattern, which comes to be a vital force in determining conduct. Additional materials bearing on this will be presented in Chapter 9.

Attitudes of adolescents develop out of their social milieu. Various studies referred to in this chapter support the following conclusions about their development:

1. There is a close relationship between the attitudes of adolescents and those of their parents.

2. The attitudes of adolescents reflect their social-class status.

3. Deep-seated prejudices appear reasonably early in the lives of individuals.

4. Intellectual development tends to contribute to the development of more liberal attitudes.

5. The adolescent's church affiliation and interests have an important bearing on his attitudes and beliefs.

THOUGHT PROBLEMS

1. How would you account for the findings of Tuma and Livson that girls in general show a higher degree of conformity than boys?
2. Show how the effects of conflicting group membership frequently present problems relative to attitudes, beliefs, and firmness of convictions?
3. What are the effects of puberty on the development of attitudes? Did you note any pronounced change in attitudes that occurred in your life during this period?
4. Write out a frank and accurate account of the genesis and development of your own religious attitudes from childhood up to the present time.
5. Is it conceivable that religion will ever be stripped of its contrasting and varying creeds and points of view? Would this be desirable? Give reasons for your answer.
6. What are the effects of movies on attitudes? Can you cite any change in attitudes observed by you as a result of the movies?
7. Why are religious doubts prevalent during adolescence? What can be done to minimize the frequency or seriousness of religious doubts?
8. Compare your attitudes toward various groups with your knowledge of and experiences with each of the groups. What are some conclusions that you might draw from this comparison?
9. Rate yourself for your attitudes toward other races, religions, and nationalities. Can you account for the differences in attitudes toward the various groups?
10. If you belong to a minority group or have ever been placed in a situation where you were regarded as a member of a minority group, list incidents in which you felt you were being discriminated against. What were your general reactions to this discrimination?

SELECTED REFERENCES

Bettleheim, B., and M. Janowitz, *Dynamics of Prejudice*. New York: Harper & Row, Publishers, 1950, Chaps. 2, 3, and 6.

Cole, Luella, *Psychology of Adolescence,* 6th ed. New York: Holt, Rinehart & Winston, Inc., 1964, Chaps. 20 and 21.

Fleege, U. H., *Self-Revelation of the Adolescent Boy*. Milwaukee: Bruce Publishing Co., 1945, Chap. 13.

Havighurst, R. J. and H. Taba, *Adolescent Character and Personality*. New York: John Wiley & Sons, Inc., 1949, Chap. 8.

Horrocks, John E., *The Psychology of Adolescence,* 2nd ed. Boston: Houghton Mifflin Company, 1962, Chap. 19.

Knoebber, Sister M., *Self-Revelation of the Adolescent Girl*. Milwaukee: Bruce Publishing Co., 1936.

Rogers, Dorothy, *The Psychology of Adolescence*. New York: Appleton-Century-Crofts, 1962, Chap. 6.

Seidman, Jerome M., ed., *The Adolescent—A Book of Readings,* 2nd ed. rev. ed. New York: Holt, Rinehart & Winston, Inc., 1960, Chaps. 16 and 17.

Wattenberg, William W., *The Adolescent Years*. New York: Harcourt, Brace & World, Inc., 1955, Chap. 17.

NOTES

1 L. L. Thorndike, "Attitudes: I. Their Nature and Development," *Journal of General Psychology,* 21 (1939), 367-99.

2 T. M. Newcomb, "Studying Social Behavior," *Methods of Psychology,* T. G. Andrews, ed. (New York: John Wiley & Sons, Inc., 1948).

3 G. H. Mead, *Mind, Self, and Society* (Chicago: University of Chicago Press, 1934).

4 H. H. Remmers, R. E. Horton, and S. Lysgaard, "Teen-age Personality in Our Culture," *The Purdue Opinion Poll, Report No. 32* (Lafayette, Ind.: Purdue University Studies, Purdue University, 1952).

5 A. R. Crane, "Stereotypes of the Adults Held by Early Adolescents," *Journal of Educational Research,* 50 (1956), 227-30.

6 Samuel Finnenbaum, "Own Position in Relation to Estimates of Average Standing and Desirability for More and Less Self-comparable Objects," *Journal of Personality,* 29 (1961), 195-204.

7 William E. Martin, "Some Ways to Develop Desirable Intergroup Attitudes in Children," *Journal of the National Education Association,* 43 (1954), 219-20.

8 M. Radke-Yarrow and J. Miller, "Children's Concepts and Attitudes about Minority and Majority American Groups," *Journal of Educational Psychology,* 40 (1949), 449-68.

9 A. Davis, "Socialization and Adolescent Personality," in *Readings in Social Psychology* (rev. ed.), eds. G. E. Swanson, *et al.* (New York: Holt, Rinehart & Winston, Inc., 1952).

10 W. Cody Wilson, "The Development of Ethnic Attitudes in Adolescence," in *Studies in Adolescence,* ed. Robert E. Grinder (New York: The Macmillan Company, 1963), p. 265.

11 M. C. Jones and N. Bayley, "Physical Maturity among Boys as Related to Behavior," *Journal of Educational Psychology,* 41 (1950), 137.

12 C. P. Stone and R. G. Barker, "The Attitudes and Interests of Premenarcheal and Postmenarcheal Girls," *Journal of Genetic Psychology,* 54 (1939), 27-72.

13 U. H. Fleege, *Self-revelation of the Adolescent Boy* (Milwaukee: Bruce Publishing Co., 1946), p. 272.

14 Evelyn M. Duvall, "Where Do They Get Their Ideas of Love and Marriage?" *The Parent Teachers Association Magazine,* 56 (1962), 10-14.

15 U. H. Fleege, *op. cit.,* p. 284.

16 Sister M. Knoebber, *The Self-revelation of the Adolescent Girl* (Milwaukee: Bruce Publishing Co., 1936).

17 Elias Tuma and Norman Livson, "Family Socio-economic Status and Adolescent Attitudes to Authority," *Child Development,* 31 (1960), 387-99.

18 H. E. Jones, *Development in Psychology* (New York: Appleton-Century-Crofts, 1948).

19 D. Brown, "Factors Affecting Social Acceptance of High School Students," *School Review,* 42 (1954), 151-56.

20 *U. C. Inventory I: Social and Emotional Adjustment.* Revised form for presentation of the cumulative record of an individual, with group norms by items for a seven-year period. (University of California at Berkeley.)

21 O. Kupy, *The Religious Development of Adolescents,* trans. William Clark Trow (New York: The Macmillan Company, 1928).

22 W. H. Selbie, *The Psychology of Religion* (London: Oxford University Press, 1926), p. 176.

23 E. T. Clark, *The Psychology of Religious Awakening* (New York: The Macmillan Company, 1929).

24 R. G. Kuhlen and M. Arnold, "Age Differences in Religious Beliefs and Problems during Adolescence," *Pedagogical Seminar and Journal of Genetic Psychology,* 65 (1944), 291-300.

25 A. H. MacLean, "The Idea of God in Protestant Religious Education," *Contributions to Education,* No. 410 (Teachers College, Columbia University, 1930).

26 W. D. Mathias, "Ideas of God and Conduct," *Contributions to Education,* No. 874 (Teachers College, Columbia University, 1943), 43.

27 *Ibid.,* p. 75.

28 M. G. Ross, *Religious Beliefs of Youth* (New York: Association Press, 1950).

29 Bernard C. Rosen, "Conflicting Group Membership: A Study of Parent-Peer Group Cross-Pressures," *American Sociological Review,* 20 (1955), 155-61.

30 H. H. Remmers, and N. Weltman, "Attitude Inter-Relationship of Youth, Their Parents, and Teachers," *Journal of Social Psychology,* 26 (1947), 61-67.

31 N. Young, F. Mayans, and B. R. Corman, "The Political Preferences of Adolescents," *Teachers College Record,* 54 (1952-53), 340-44.

32 R. J. Havighurst and H. Taba, *Adolescent Character and Personality* (New York: John Wiley & Sons, Inc., 1949), p. 95.

33 Mason Haire and Florence Morrison, "School Children's Perceptions of Labor and Management," *Journal of Social Psychology,* 46 (1957), 179-97.

34 R. D. Franklin, S. G. Graziano, and H. H. Remmers, *Report of Poll 59 of the Purdue Opinion Panel: Youth Attitude Toward Industrial Relations* (Lafayette, Ind.: Purdue University Division of Educational Reference, 1960).

35 Irvin J. Lehmann, "Some Socio-cultural Differences in Attitudes and Values," *Journal of Educational Psychology,* 36 (1962), 1-9.

36 *Ibid.,* pp. 5-6.

37 Mervin B. Freedman, *The Impact of College,* No. 4 (Washington: Department of Health, Education, and Welfare, New Dimensions in Higher Education, 1960).

38 Karl C. Garrison, "Worldminded Attitudes of College Students in a Southern University," *Journal of Social Psychology,* 54 (1961), 147-53.

39 Harry Kitano, "Differential Child-rearing Attitudes between First and Second Generation Japanese in the United States," *Journal of Social Psychology,* 53 (1961), 13-19.

40 C. T. O'Reilly, "Religious Beliefs of College Students and Their Attitudes toward Minorities," *Journal of Abnormal and Social Psychology,* 49 (1954), 378-80.

41 G. W. Allport, J. M. Gillespie, and J. Young, "The Religion of the Post-war College Student," *Journal of Psychology,* 26 (1948), 3-33.

42 R. L. Thorndike, "Performance of Gifted Children on Tests of Developmental Age," *Journal of Psychology,* 9 (1940), 337-43.

43 L. J. Epstein, "Attitudinal Changes Attendant upon Variations in Experience," *Journal of Educational Research,* 34 (1941), 453-57.

44 B. Shinberg, "The Relationship Between Information and Attitudes of High School Students on Certain International Issues," *Studies in Higher Education,* No. 68 (Lafayette, Ind.: Purdue University Studies, Purdue University, 1947-50).

45 I. C. Rosen, "Effect of the Motion Picture 'Gentleman's Agreement' on Attitudes Toward Jews," *Journal of Psychology,* 26 (1948), 525-36.

9

IDEALS, MORALS, AND RELIGION

Men and Nations Can Be Reformed Only in Their Youth; They Become Incorrigible as They Grow Old.

ROUSSEAU

There are many who despair of the frank self-expression of modern youth and its refusal to be blindly obedient to present-day customs and teachings. The notion that present-day adolescents have relinquished moral standards is heard each generation. This was reflected in a statement by Reverend D. Silliman Ives over 100 years ago.

> . . . I cannot suppress the humiliating conviction that even Pagan Rome, in the corrupt age of Augustus, never witnessed a more rapid and frightful declension in morals nor witnessed among certain classes of the young a more utter disregard of honor, of truth, and piety, and even the commonest decencies of life.[1]

Attitudes toward mores and institutions. The attitude of the adolescent toward the mores and institutions of his society can be characterized as acceptance, adherence, conformity, rejection, or belligerence. The lower-class adolescent may be under pressure from friends of his own social level to drop out of school, to spend money, and even to engage in sexual irregularities.[2] He usually receives little pressure from his parents to remain in school, since they see little value in schooling beyond a certain level. The attitudes and values of the class to which an individual belongs exert considerable pressure, and are most important in the formation of particular ideals and values.

The middle-class child acquires somewhat orthodox attitudes. He must not be too critical of the sacred dogmas and violate the moral codes of society, lest he meet with social disapproval and perhaps punishment. However, in our society there is perhaps a larger permissible range of variation in attitudes and moral concepts than in primitive cultures, consequently the adolescent is in a position to be more critical of parental viewpoints and not be considered dangerously radical or a heretic.

The role of discipline. Children and adolescents need to live according to certain standards, to live a well-disciplined life. In the first place they have a feeling of security if they know where their limits are and live according to such limits. Secondly, if they live according to their limits of freedom they are less likely to sense a feeling of guilt from having broken them. Third, when they obey rules and regulations, they are praised by their parents, stimulating them to continue to discipline themselves and live an orderly life. Fourth, such living helps to protect and enhance the ego by proving to the self that he controls his impulses in accordance with standards. This is important at all stages of life. Discipline in connection with antisocial behavior in school and in the home is usually thought of as related to the milder forms of antisocial behavior. Thus, the breaking of some rule at school, the infringement upon the good will of some other member of the home or school, many acts of mischief, and other forms of behavior are considered undesirable and punishable. Needless to say, the method of punishment has varied considerably from period to period. Not quite a century ago a rather detailed plan of discipline was established in our secondary schools. The following is a partial list of punishments that were in effect in an academy in Stokes County, North Carolina, in 1848.[3]

1. Boys and girls playing together	4	lashes
2. Quarreling	4	"
7. Playing at cards at school	10	"
9. Telling lies	7	"
14. Swearing at school	8	"
16. For misbehaving to girls	10	"
19. For drinking liquors at school	8	"
22. For wearing long finger nails	2	"
31. For blotting your copy book	2	"
33. For wrestling at school	4	"
35. For not making a bow when going out to go home	2	"
43. For not saying "Yes sir" or "No sir," etc.	2	"
45. For not washing at playtime when going to books	4	"
46. For going and playing about the mill or creek	6	"

Modern conceptions of child training lay stress on the fact that morality is not developed by rules, creeds, dogmas, or the establishment of specific amounts of punishment for various acts of mischief. The disciplinary act must strike deep into the innermost life and feelings of the individual and lead him to recognize that the antisocial behavior act will not be tolerated. But too often discipline is looked upon as a punishment for getting caught or as a form of vengeance.

The development of moral behavior of a group of children was studied by Havighurst and others at the University of Chicago over a period of eight years.[4] These children were observed from the time they were 9 years old until they were 18 years of age. At the end of this period of study, ratings on the moral development of these children were made and then compared with different facts about the subjects. The relation of severity and consistency of discipline to good character development was studied, with the observation that severity of discipline bore no relation to character development. Some of the children who had been severely disciplined had good character whereas others had poor character.

However, they found a close relation between consistency of discipline and character. The coefficient of correlation obtained between character ratings and consistency of discipline was .62. Thus, it appears that discipline can be successful or unsuccessful, depending largely upon the spirit in which it is administered and the consistency of parents in administering it.

Too often discipline is concerned with procedures for compelling the child or adolescent to act in certain prescribed ways dictated by the parent or teacher, with little consideration of the method used or its effects upon the individual concerned. Bad habits are not usually formed overnight; neither are they likely to be broken in so short a period. Like other forms of behavior patterns, changes in conduct follow the general laws of learning and occur gradually. Parents often express amazement at the sudden onset of some maladaptive form of behavior on the part of the growing boy or girl, but usually it has not been so sudden as it appears. The parent has simply failed to understand the other habits that have gone before. Discipline, if it is to be of value, must (1) be administered in terms of the past life of the child, (2) be based upon understanding rather than emotions, (3) be understood by the subject concerned, (4) relate to the behavior act from which it resulted rather than to the one administering the act, and (5) follow immediately after the act. Discipline should always have as its end self-control.

Need for guidance. Greater freedom and increased responsibility should come with growth and development. Thus, there is a constant need for guidance rather than unlimited freedom or an autocratic control. Better adjusted boys and girls can be given greater freedom than those more poorly adjusted. However, there are many cases in which the latter have had too much restraint and are in need of greater freedom, but since they have been given no opportunity to accept responsibility, they need guidance. When pupils are given increased responsibility and freedom under guidance better social and personal adjustments result.

Concerning the adolescent's need for the acquisition of standards of right and wrong that are acceptable in and appropriate to the adult society around him Gardner states:

> . . . We are all aware of the needs from society's point of view in this respect. What I would emphasize is the adolescent's need for inner controls, and I am not speaking only of morality or right and wrong in regard to sexual behavior. I am speaking of social morality—the rightness or wrongness of acts in all the roles that the individual must play in his association with all others in society. Even more so does he need agreed-upon standards that are "meetable," i.e., that he can meet in the sense that they do not repeatedly tear his personality to pieces through the anxieties and insecurities attendant upon impossibility of attainment.[5]

THE MORAL SELF

We encounter several important questions as we study the moral life of the adolescent: (1) What are the desirable attitudes that the home, school, church, and other agencies should strive to establish? (2) What specific habit patterns, when integrated, tend to produce such ideals and attitudes? (3) How can these specific habits best be acquired and integrated into a general attitude?

Moral development. The most important place in a list of environmental factors influencing moral behavior for most children is the home. "Children who have immoral surroundings, whose struggle to exist involves corrupt practices, whose whole horizon is dark with foreboding shadows cannot have healthy social attitudes."[6] During the earlier period of life the individual is amoral. Whatever his conduct may be, it is largely the result of simple forces that have played upon and thus conditioned his behavior during the earlier years of life. As he grows, he develops inner standards, often called the "voice of conscience," which serve as a guide to him in his actions.[7] Psychoanalysts have referred to this as the *superego*, which represents in the person the mores and standards of the parents, other associates, and the culture of the society in which he lives.

Many of the impressions, feelings of guilt, and anxieties which govern behavior lie deep within the unconscious part of the mind, the subconscious. Children must have affection, security, and effective guidance during their developmental years since the subconscious is so susceptible to both good and bad influences.

How moral behavior is learned. Tom is now in the sixth grade. He has a record of lying and stealing during his past years at school. Mrs. Keener, a teacher of the old school blames the lack of discipline in the home for Tom's dishonesty. Miss, Simpson, who is well acquainted with Tom's father asserts that Tom learned this from his father. On the other hand, Miss Hovis who recently enrolled in classes in mental hygiene of school children talks of Tom's needs that are not being met at home or at school.

The explanations offered for Tom's behavior though somewhat different, are alike in that they imply that this is a form of learned behavior. The problem then arises as to how such behavior is learned.

Havighurst and Taba state that character is learned (1) through reward and punishment, (2) through unconscious imitation, and (3) through reflective thinking.[8] Teaching a child dogmas, creeds, or rules of conduct is insufficient. If he is to develop good moral habits he must be given rewards for good conduct and punishment for undesirable conduct. He must learn by specific example.

Children tend to develop habits similar to those practiced by their parents and other adults with whom they are closely associated perhaps because their behavior meets with approval when they conform. Through reflective thinking the child applies past experiences to problems involving moral behavior. This is not likely to operate effectively for the child below average in intelligence except for problem situations where parents or teachers help the child make such applications. The adolescent is more mature mentally and has usually had a wider range of experiences than the child. Thus, he is able to draw on past experiences to help him meet problems involving morals. However, at all stages guidance is needed in making applications.

Adolescent conscience. The child inhibits responses regarded by his parent or other authority-figure as wrong because he has learned that he will thus be rewarded. As he grows older, he inhibits an increasing number of responses because they are frequently unpleasant or may lead to anxiety. The values he has encountered in his environment and training have become internalized, and the "voice of conscience" exerts an important role in the control of his behavior. Without the help of consistent standards the adolescent cannot develop healthy conscience controls. Erickson says about adult leaders:

> The strength a young person finds in adults at this time—their willingness to let him experiment, their eagerness to confirm him at his best, their consistency in correcting his excesses, and the guidance they give him—will co-determine whether or not he eventually makes order out of necessary inner confusion and applies himself to the correction of disordered conditions. He needs freedom to choose, but not so much freedom that he cannot, in fact, make a choice.[9]

The place of the church. Varied opinions are expressed about the place of the church in character development. Despite claims frequently made by church leaders some studies have served to question the value of church attendance in the development of character and the reduction of juvenile delinquency. To what extent is the church reaching young people? What part is religion playing in their lives? How can it be more effective in helping adolescents develop useful behavior patterns and a sound philosophy of living? An answer to these questions is not easy. In the first place the church frequently fails to reach the underprivileged adolescent. The nature of the youth programs at church is closely related to home and community conditions. Thus, it is extremely difficult to separate the influences of these varied forces and conditions affecting the lives and behavior of adolescents.

In Table 9-1 the frequency of offenses committed by boys claiming regular church attendance is compared with those whose attendance is reported as occasional, seldom, or never. A careful analysis of the home background of those who went to church and those who did not must be made before one can conclude that it is the church that reduces the likelihood of delinquency. This study, however, supports the general hypothesis that church attendance is a way of life in a total complex or field, and generally reduces tendencies toward delinquent behavior. Different religious programs, no doubt, have different effects, but a program built upon sound educational and psychological principles and designed to satisfy the needs of adolescents is most effective.

The role of the school. The failure of the junior and senior high schools to adjust their programs to the interests and abilities of the in-

Table 9-1

RELATIONSHIP BETWEEN REGULARITY OF CHURCH ATTENDANCE AND OFFENSES CHARGED AGAINST BOYS INTERVIEWED ON COMPLAINT BY DETROIT POLICE, 1946

(After Wattenberg)

Charge	Total	Regular attendance	All others	Ratio Regular	:	Others
Assaults	45	20	25	10	:	13
Sex offenses	48	24	24	10	:	10
Robbery	25	8	17	10	:	20
Burglary	263	105	158	10	:	15
Larceny	468	207	261	10	:	12
Auto thefts	96	50	46	10	:	10
Drunk	26	12	14	10	:	11
Disorderly	90	33	57	10	:	18
Traffic offenses	42	19	23	10	:	12
Miscellaneous	604	260	344	10	:	13
Total	1,707	738	969	10	:	13

creasing number of pupils is their worst fault. This failure is probably a result of a false application of our democratic ideal. *It should be the aim of the school to give the child the opportunity to develop those abilities he possesses, rather than to set up a great educational ladder to fit the abilities of all.*

The case of an adolescent boy who was pushed beyond his ability by well-meaning and intelligent parents, described by Slattery, illustrates a common failure of both parents and schools:

> Rodger had an IQ of about 80, but his father, a high school principal, wanted his son to be a white collar worker and was blind to the fact that the boy could not make high school. Owing to his father's position, the high school covered up Rodger's failure by giving him passing grades. The further Rodger went in high school, the more at sea he became.
>
> Rodger did possess a fair degree of mechanical ability and great interest along mechanical lines. Bewildered by academic subjects and frustrated in his efforts to express his natural tendencies, Rodger expressed his interest in an underhanded fashion.
>
> He began by stealing animal traps and concealing the identity of the other boy's traps by taking them apart and assembling parts of various traps to make a new one. Success along these lines encouraged him to more ambitious thefts. Gossip did not reach the father until his position was threatened. The father was beside himself with rage. . . . It took a great deal of persuasion to induce this father to send his son to a trade school, but when he did, the behavior difficulties of the boy abated.[10]

Chapter 16 presents some findings showing that dissatisfaction with school is the most important reason for pupils leaving high school. For many pupils, dropping out of school is the beginning point of a delinquent career. Some factors and conditions that make schools ineffective in dealing with potential delinquents may be listed as follows:

1. Some teachers are not properly qualified to detect the needs of adolescents.

2. Some teachers are not properly qualified to deal with problems when they appear among the pupils.

3. Teachers are often overloaded and are unable to give the individual attention needed in a good educational program.

4. The classroom program is not always conducive to the motivation of good behavior.

5. Curriculum materials are too often meaningless or empty verbalism for many pupils.

6. The extraclass activities are not organized and administered in harmony with the needs and interests of the individual pupils.

7. The school does not furnish the special assistance needed by teachers in detecting and dealing with potential delinquents.

8. The program of the school is not sufficiently integrated into the life of the community to be effective in developing good moral concepts and behavior.

The neighborhood. The social environment of adolescents is not restricted to the home and the school; another primary determinant, the neighborhood, also exerts a powerful influence. It was pointed out in an earlier chapter that the school grade and neighborhood were the great determining factors in the choice of chums. Yet the neighborhood is not only an important factor in the choice of playmates; its ideals in connection with the community are forces that determine to a large degree the behavior activities of growing boys and girls. There is a close relation between overt delinquent behavior and specific personal and environmental factors. Within recent years attempts have been made to take boys who are "criminals in the making" and train them into good future citizens. Illustrative cases show that efforts have not been in vain; however, too often conclusions relative to a program are based upon faith or wishful thinking fortified by one or more cases of boys whose lives were directed into more useful channels.

The attitudes of juvenile delinquents are largely a result of the attitudes of others, particularly adults, toward them. Thus, work among teen-age delinquents must begin with an effort to change their attitudes by instilling in them understanding of the good faith and motives of the adult society. One of the most noteworthy studies of the art of winning the confidence of youthful offenders is the Harlem Street Clubs Project.[11] The results of this project dispelled the notion that the delinquent is naturally tough, courageous, and filled with hostility. These are more often defense mechanisms operating as a result of tensions built up through failure at school, at home, in social situations, or in some other phase of life.

As a result of the efforts of those working with the Harlem teen-age gangs, four highly organized and apparently hostile but self-conscious gangs were changed into somewhat respectable street clubs.[12] Those working with these clubs have, through their insight into the nature of boys and through their offer of genuine friendship, found that so-called juvenile gangs become law-abiding youthful clubs.

Recreation or delinquency. There is much in common between juvenile recreation and juvenile delinquency, especially in the early stages of delinquency. That delinquency is often a form of play may be observed in such acts as: boys annoying or teasing smaller boys by partially undressing them in a city park; boys releasing the brakes of automobiles parked on a hillside and watching them coast down the hill and crash into another car; girls scattering pastry over a teacher's desk; girls hiding or destroying stamps or seals which the teacher has in her desk; pupils co-operating in stealing apples from the fruit vendor by having one pupil hold the attention of the attendant with some annoying act, while the others steal the apples.

These acts may satisfy the need for achievement better than most conventional activities at home or school. The situation becomes most complicated when there is some reward, such as an apple for the hungry adolescent with a big appetite. This furnishes reinforcement for the act.

Both recreation and delinquency are largely group activities, although they are sometimes carried on alone. However, these groups are different insofar as they reflect traditional customs of the community and its general welfare. Recreation is constructive in nature, whereas delinquency is destructive. Delinquency is a violation of the law; recreation is carried on within the spirit of the law. Random play may develop into acts of delinquency or wholesome recreation. For example, boys and girls may use an old abandoned building as a little theater. They may secure lumber, build a stage, and invite their parents and friends to the opening performance. On the other hand, the abandoned building may be a place where immoral practices occur, or where loot from thefts is hidden.

There is nothing inherent in either the building or the adolescents that could be classed as vile or delinquent. The important variable lies in the education and guidance given these boys and girls at home, in school, and at church. Where the forces influencing them have been favorable, desirable activities may be expected and vice versa. After habits of delinquency have developed, the problem becomes more difficult. New habits, new attitudes, and changed goals must be established.

Recreation facilities are being developed more and more, and it has been well demonstrated that activities directed through recreational programs will do much toward thwarting the adolescent pranks and mischief that may not appear bad in themselves but are often quite costly and, still worse, too often have dire consequences. The ways in which some communities direct the energies of boys and girls are well illustrated in connection with Halloween activities. The mischief associated with the mystic orange-and-black traditions has in many cases been very expensive as well as annoying. Many cities organize costume parades, various types of contests, and directed games.

IDEALS AND VALUES

Ideals and values differ from attitudes in their ever-present, imperative nature. It was suggested earlier that the adolescent has an indefinite number of attitudes and that these are often most inconsistent. Ideals are fewer in number—broad guiding principles of behavior. They tend to give stability and direction to one's life.

Ideals and the adolescent. The integration of behavior units into a general scheme or pattern, the development therefrom of a potent force that acts as a drive or tendency toward further activity, has been referred to in connection with habits as drives to behavior. It is in this integration of the various units of behavior that ideals arise and thus influence the behavior of the individual. During the early days of life, ideals pass through a formative stage. The individual's experiences are narrow and his ideals very elementary, involving mainly the welfare and pleasure of the ego. Ideals, like attitudes, are soaked up from the milieu in which the child lives and learns. The home, church, school, and other youth-serving agencies powerfully affect development of desirable attitudes in the boys and girls whom they serve. Concerning their work, Havighurst and others have pointed out that ". . . youth-serving agencies influence the ideals of youth as much or more through the presence and behavior of teachers, clergy, and youth-group leaders as through their verbal teaching."[18]

Values—their meaning and importance. Any attempt to completely separate attitudes, ideals, and values would be misleading. Values refer to what we regard as important rather than what we know. They are organizing factors within the personality and are especially important in relation to morals and character. They may best be understood from a brief description of the six types of men, presented by Spranger.[14] These six types are: (1) the *theoretical*—the individual who regards theories and knowledge as all-important; (2) the *esthetic*—one who places a high premium on beauty and loveliness; (3) the *economic*—one who cherishes things because of their material or economic value; (4) the *social*—one who places considerable importance upon the social factors; (5) the *political*—the person who has a strong desire for power and control; and (6) the *religious* —the person who finds satisfaction and joy in his relationships with the whole of life's experiences and purposes. These values have been organized into a measurable test by Allport and Vernon, and considerable research has evolved from these and other attempts to measure an individual's values.

The importance of values in character formation has been emphasized by a number of investigators. Leckley has postulated that after values are integrated into the personality they act as barriers to the acceptance of new ones which might be in opposition to them.[15] This is necessary if the personality is to remain consistent and somewhat stable. Four prevailing sets of conditions are set forth by Leckley: (1) new values that are in opposition to those already accepted by the individual may be rejected; (2) new values may be so modified that they are no longer in opposition to the accepted values; (3) new values that are in opposition to old values may be ignored and thus not incorporated into the value system; and (4) old values may be modified in such a way that the new values are incorporated into the total value-system.

The relationship between value patterns of college students and economic status, level of education, and size of home town was shown in a study by Woodruff.[16] Groups of individuals with similar socio-economic backgrounds engaged in similar educational or vocational pursuits tend to have similar value patterns.

Developmental sequence of ideals and values. Ideals and values are a function of the socialization process. In an attempt to generalize the changes in values occurring between 12 and 15, Tryon states:

> During the period between ages 12 and 15, values for girls have undergone some revolutionary changes; values for boys have undergone relatively minor changes, mainly in terms of slightly shifted emphases. For the 12-year-old girl, quiet, sedate, nonaggressive qualities are associated with friendliness, likeableness, good humor and attractive appearance. Behavior which conforms to the demands and regulations of the adult world is admired. Tomboyishness is tolerated. At the 15-year level, admiration for the demure, docile, rather prim, lady-like prototype has ceased. Instead, many of the criteria for the idealized boy such as extroversion, activity, and good sportsmanship are highly acceptable for the girl. The ability to organize games for parties involving both sexes and the capacity to keep such activities lively and entertaining is admired. In addition, the quality of being fascinating or glamorous to the other sex has become important, but is looked upon as relatively specific or unrelated to other desirable qualities. At the 12-year level, the idealized boy is skillful and a leader in games; his daring and fearlessness extend beyond his social group to defiance of adult demands and regulations. Any characteristic which might be construed as feminine by one's peers, such as extreme tidiness, or marked conformity in the classroom, is regarded as a weakness. However, some personableness and certain kindly, likable qualities tend to be associated with the more highly prized masculine qualities. At fifteen years, prestige for the boy is still in a large measure determined by physical skill, aggressiveness, and fearlessness. Defiance of adult standards has lost emphasis; though still acceptable and rather amusing to them, it tends to be associated with immaturity. In addition, much greater emphasis is placed on personal acceptability, suggesting the effectiveness of rising heterosexual interests. In fact *Unkempt-Tidy,* related to this constellation, is the only trait among the twenty on which the boys completely reversed their evaluation.[17]

In studying the sex differences revealed by these data, one is impressed by the lack of consistent ideals in girls over this relatively short period of three years. These data tend to support the theory that the behavior of the female of the species is characterized by expediency, design, irresoluteness, and caprice. A plausible explanation for the phenomenon, which appears early in the social development of boys and girls, is that social activities place a greater demand upon girls than upon boys for flexibility, capacity to readjust ideals, and ability to reorient themselves to new goals.

The role of the school. The wide variations in values found among high school pupils present difficult problems to teachers and others concerned with the educational program for adolescents. A large percentage of adolescents from lower-class homes are not interested in the values of good grades and a high school diploma, which the schools hold up to them as an incentive to remain in school, study hard, and graduate. The problem of motivating these boys and girls presents a real challenge to the high school teacher.

Not all teachers are equally effective in helping pupils clarify their values and formulate other values. In the first place, teachers themselves do not always have clearly defined and consistent values. Also, certain misconceptions and lack of understanding about the needs and problems of adolescents hinder teachers in their efforts. If teachers are to be effective in the teaching of values to adolescents, they must (1) have fairly clearly defined values themselves, (2) be consistent in their values, (3) respect the value patterns of all the pupils whom they encounter, (4) recognize that value patterns are best learned from examples rather than from mottoes and rules, (5) recognize that a learning situation involving value patterns will not be equally effective for all pupils, (6) understand the operation of the learning process in the development of value patterns, and (7) understand the adolescent as a dynamic product of the interrelation of heredity and environment.

The scholastic achievements of adolescents have an important bearing on their values. In one study a group of mathematically gifted ado-

Table 9-2

VALUE JUDGMENT SCORES OF MATH-
EMATICALLY GIFTED ADOLESCENTS
RANKED IN DESCENDING ORDER

(*Kennedy*)

Value	Score	Evaluation
Theoretical	49.8	High
Economic	41.3	Median
Religious	39.5	Median
Political	38.7	Median
Esthetic	36.4	Median
Social	34.2	Low

lescents was given the *Allport-Vernon-Lindzey Study of Values*.[18] Six categories of values were obtained: theoretical, economic, religious, political, esthetic, and social. The group mean rating for each value is presented in descending order in Table 9-2. It should be pointed out that, because of the nature of the test, a high score on one value necessarily causes a low score on another. The results do give, however, a basis for judging the relative standing of the different values in the lives of mathematically gifted adolescents; they scored highest on theoretical values and lowest on social values.

THE ROLE OF RELIGION

Religion is a complex phenomenon, not easily defined. To many Americans it means churches. Actually these are only external signs of the operation of religion as a social institution. Probably the best way of understanding religion is to list the needs with which it deals. It was apparently born out of the human need to understand the operation of the forces of nature, and to give life meaning and purpose. All religions declare a priority on selected beliefs and patterns of living. There is, however, a lack of agreement among the different religions about specific behavior patterns. This tends to present difficult problems to many adolescents. Adolescents are also confronted with contradictions in our culture between early home teaching, scientific outlook, and a traditional religious viewpoint. Adolescents learn many facts about the world of today, but often have only vague notions about the meanings and purposes of these experiences. It was suggested earlier that an important developmental task of adolescents is that of developing a philosophy of life.

Religious needs of adolescents. Individuals wonder about the meanings and purpose of life. They feel the need for bringing their life experiences together to arrive at some satisfying solution to the problems, contradictions, and conflicts of everyday living. A nationwide poll of high school students revealed that the typical student prays daily.[19] It is at this age that individuals affiliate themselves with the church and make other important decisions involving religion and morals.

Adolescents find themselves in a world where there are different standards of conduct for drinking, ways of making money, petting, and the like. The adolescent needs help and guidance in arriving at a set of values and standards to guide him in life. Certainly at the present time in our culture, adolescents are largely dependent upon religion to help them.

Despite the fact that church attendance tends to drop off during the adolescent years, interest in moral and religious problems remains high. This was shown in one study of the moral and religious problems of 1000 students from different grade levels.[20] The results, presented in Table 9-3 show a pronounced growth of interest in questions about courtship and marriage. Questioning about right and wrong, religion, God, and the church continued throughout the high school years.

Table 9-3

QUESTIONS ASKED BY ADOLESCENTS AND POSTADOLESCENTS
(After Burkhart)

Nature of Question	Number of questions asked		
	Grades 7, 8, 9	Grades 10, 11, 12	College
Habits of behavior	619	367	247
Religion, God, and the church	584	467	271
Self-improvement	538	1,298	369
Right and wrong	347	819	139
Courtship and marriage	334	1,457	1,183

A need of youth that can best be satisfied through religion is that for emotional direction and sensitive understanding. Much of the character-building work being done for adolescents is too artificial and too highly organized to be effective. The adolescent needs deeply rooted convictions and loyalties to certain ideals that will give stability and force to his character. Character building that does not take into consideration the importance of the education of the emotions will be largely ineffective, lacking the dynamic force essential for self-control. The emotions have been aptly described as "the modes of physiological integration through which we meet relatively critical situations."[21] Character based upon impulses and physiological drives that have not been internalized by teachings such as one finds in a religious atmosphere will lack the fundamental principles essential for generalizations so as to encompass the needs and welfare of others.

Religious education. The present situation in our society of the role of religion in education is (1) an increasing recognition of the importance of spiritual values and the role of religion in the development of these values and (2) confusion as to how religion can be integrated into a total educational program. Some would raise the question: "Why should education be concerned with religion?" A number of reasons may well be offered in answer. Perhaps the fact that Western civilization is imbedded with the philosophy, teachings, and traditions of Judeo-Christian religion is itself a sufficient reason. One of the reasons given by Van Dusen should furnish an adequate answer to this question. He states: "Religion has to do with the most elemental, the most universal, and in the end, *the most important issues of human existence*—its origin, its nature, its meaning and purpose, its destiny, especially with the determination and inescapable events which mark and moved each person's life—birth, love, parenthood, death."[22] Adolescents are seeking the purpose of life and the kinds of behavior that will lead to the highest fulfillment of such a purpose. Their education will be inadequate if it fails to help them find the answer, and if it does not provide a basis for them to judge attitudes, ideals, and behavior.

Hilliard conducted a survey on the influence of religious education upon the development of moral ideas.[23] The subjects included 174 adolescents ages 12, 15, and 18. The most important conclusion from this survey seems to be that "while the majority of adolescents experience considerable dissatisfaction in regard to earlier ideas and teachings about the divine 'sanctions' of morality, they continue to look to religious education and religion itself to assist them in the development and maintenance of their moral ideas and standards of conduct." Thus, sound and timely religious education is likely to interest adolescents. Religious leaders must realize that religious growth, like other aspects of growth, is gradual and continuous. They should help adolescents meet the developmental tasks referred to in Chapter 2 and should be especially concerned with helping teen-agers develop a more unified philosophy of life. They can help, since the real development of religious opinions is not made by scholars but by the daily life and experience of the common people. Contact with any life situation tends to develop new interpretations of so-called spiritual matters. New standards of living mean the visualization of new meanings in religion. In this connection, Kuhlen and Arnold have set forth two conclusions from their study that should be of interest to those concerned with religious education:

> First, those issues represented by statements which are increasingly "wondered about" as age increases may give clues as to appropriate topics for consideration in the teen years in both Sunday School classes and young people's groups. Second, beliefs discarded by children as they grow older may well be studied for their implications for teaching at earlier ages. Children's concepts regarding religion are more concrete and specific than are those of adults, the latter tending to be abstract and general. This change represents the normal growth of concepts. It would seem desirable that the specific and concrete beliefs taught to children be beliefs compatible with the more abstract adult views, and not beliefs later to be discarded because of incompatibility.[24]

SOME FUNDAMENTAL PRINCIPLES

The juvenile delinquent has the same basic needs as the nondelinquent. Achievement, self-esteem, and social approval are just as important in his life as in the lives of nondelinquents. Mentally and physically handicapped adolescents feel the same needs. The attitudes, ideals, and behavior of the adolescent must be interpreted in terms of his needs and life problems as he views them, and those concerned with the guidance and training of adolescents must take into consideration these basic needs.

Satisfying activities. The adolescent acts to defend the self, especially when the ego is attacked either directly or indirectly. The manner in which he meets a problem situation will depend largely upon how he has successfully met similar situations in the past. Various types of rewards are frequently offered to reinforce certain forms of behavior. When undesirable behavior is satisfying to the individual it will reinforce such behavior and thus lead to the establishment of an undesirable behavior pattern. Reinforcements may be of an abstract nature involving the ideals, and beliefs of peers or adults. The individual desires the approval of the group. Desires are established in part through a conditioning and directing of the natural impulses of the individual along lines in harmony with the ideals set forth by the group. Desires can and should be guided; but this guidance cannot best secure its end unless the desires are established in relation to situations for which there is an ultimate reward or form of satisfaction.

Adolescents should gradually learn through experience that anti-social conduct leads to their own misery and unpleasant experiences. It appears likely that one of the chief difficulties met by preadolescent and adolescent boys is the lack of men who understand boys and their problems and are able to win their confidence and admiration. Men teachers, physical education and recreational directors, 4H Club leaders, vocational agriculture teachers, boys' counselors, and others who work closely with boys have opportunities to influence their ideals and attitudes significantly. They meet these boys at a period when masculine contacts are desperately needed.

Developing morals and ideals. There is much evidence that Sunday school and classroom instruction, which have relied largely upon verbal teachings, have been ineffective in meeting the moral demands of modern life. Moral development, like the development of social habits and attitudes, will be most effective when it takes place in connection with situations arising naturally in the classroom or on the playground. The Sunday school can teach appreciation of one another and respect for the rights and feelings of others; but if this is done in a vacuum, and children see no relation between such teachings and the problems they meet on the street, at school, and in the park, the teaching will be so much babbling. Inconsistencies in moral concepts between parents, other adults, and his peers are a source of confusion to the adolescent and cause him concern and uncertainty. Milner states:

> The practice of our society's leaders and schoolteachers to confuse *what ought to be* or what we wish were so with *what actually is,* has contributed to much confusion, disillusionment and cynicism among our teen-agers, especially among teen-agers of ethnic and social-status groups whom we tacitly discriminate against socially and economically.[25]

Another essential in moral teachings is the harmonious correlation of all agencies affecting the moral life of boys and girls. The concepts presented in the home, on the playground, in school, and at church are usually too unrelated to have any great functional significance. The program of the church is in so many cases too far divorced from the other interests of the child, and the materials presented are too archaic to have any meaning for him in connection with present-day living. What seems to be needed is a positive approach to morals. Or, as Fleege states, "It would seem that too much emphasis has been placed on impurity and not enough on purity. The virtue has been left in the shadow while the failings have been paraded across the stage."[26]

The adolescent is likely to resent authoritative control. The self-conscious attitude so clearly displayed at this stage of life marks him as an individual on the alert, watching for someone to consider him as a child and thus boss him around. He is idealistic in nature and expects the teacher to play fair with him in his activities; he may question many of the procedures of the teacher for this reason. His personal manner of regarding everything as directed toward the self is a factor that should be watched. He is impulsive, oversensitive, and impressionable to mistreatment or unfair dealings. His needs and desires should be guided; but those concerned with his education and guidance should have an understanding of his characteristics and a genuine interest in his moral development.

Building spiritual values. The modern school emphasizes the growth of the total child, and is concerned with his total development—including spiritual development. Through associating with his peers and teachers under ideals set forth for living together in the school community, the child learns to live with others, to have consideration for their feelings, rights, and happiness, to gain satisfaction from achievement by the self or the group, to understand the orderliness of nature, and to recognize and accept ideals for guiding his daily activities. He learns how he can be helpful and how others can be helpful to him. He builds a framework of values from which to judge himself and his peers.

The nature of the values a child acquires must not be left to chance. The individual pupil has many needs in common with lower forms of life. In addition, he has insights, aspirations, and possibilities for learning and development that are distinctly human. Because of this he is capable, through experience, of acquiring habits of initiative and responsibility relative to his own behavior. This gives him a measure of self-control not to be found among lower forms of life. Ideals of honesty, fair play, and consideration for the feelings of others are acquired through experiences with others in situations in which such ideals are guiding forces. In this connection, Sister Mary Phelan asked a group of parochial school pupils: "Who is your ideal? Why have you chosen this ideal?"[27] Over 60 per cent of the responses at ages 11 to 18 involved either religious, historical, or contemporary public figures. This is in harmony with results obtained by Hill with public school children as subjects, except that the former chose a greater number of religious persons.[28]

Concerning the teaching of character Peck, Havighurst, and others have stated:

> . . . In short, in teaching character as in teaching intellectual knowledge, no one can teach what he does not know. In character education this includes much more than intellectual knowledge, alone; it requires that the "teacher" of character personally possess genuinely mature feelings, attitudes, and ethical behavior, or no success can be attained.[29]

These studies furnish evidence that moral and character development of adolescents are clearly influenced by association with people who are in positions of prestige and leadership. The implications of this for the churches, schools, and other youth-serving agencies are clear. The presence and behavior of teachers, clergy, and various youth-group leaders have an important influence on the ideals and thus the moral and character development of adolescents.

SUMMARY

The religious needs of adolescents should be given special consideration in a sound and functional program of character and moral development. Environmental factors are important in the development of the child's and the adolescent's religion. Thus, important differences will be found in the religious attitudes and values of adolescents from different homes and from different religious backgrounds. It is not possible to evaluate the relative contributions of the neighborhood, school, church, and agencies outside the home and immediate neighborhood on the moral development of children and adolescents. Each is part of their world, and thus influences their moral development. However, the personal contacts and participation usually found in group activities tend to make them a very dynamic and realistic force in the development of morals and character. It is from capable and understanding leaders of these groups that adolescents often find their ideals and learn worth-while values.

The adolescent must be taught to have respect for himself and his abilities. He must come to realize that he has a definite contribution to make to society. If there are physical defects, he must learn to overcome these—not to overcompensate or use some defense mechanism in an effort to cover them up. The mental-hygiene principles set forth in Chapter 12 should be followed if he is to develop the ability to function harmoniously in his social relations. Guidance and control should have as their function the bringing out of those qualities and assets of the individual that will be of greater service to the self and society.

THOUGHT PROBLEMS

1. Just how is the control of the adolescent's behavior activities related to mental hygiene? To moral and religious growth? Illustrate.
2. Why is the cooperation of all agencies essential if juvenile crime is to be more closely controlled? What are some of the agencies that would be involved?
3. Give an illustration, from your own observation, of how juvenile mischief has been directed into more wholesome channels through the development of recreational activities for adolescents.
4. Show how self-realization is important in the development of a well-adjusted individual. What are some needs of the adolescent, if he is to develop a wholesome attitude toward himself and others?
5. What do you understand the term *spiritual values* to mean? Can you see any relation between spiritual values and attaining a consistent and unified philosophy of life? Explain.
6. What purposes does religion serve in the lives of adolescents? Which of these were paramount in your life during adolescence?
7. In what ways are recreation and delinquency alike? In what ways are they different?
8. What opportunities for socialization among young people are furnished by your church or some church with which you are acquainted? Do you think they are adequate? If not, what else would you suggest?
9. Consider the six values listed in this chapter. Rank these in order of their importance to you in your choice of the following:
   a. Your best friend
   b. Vocation
   c. Automobile, or some other possession
   d. Place where you would like to work
   e. Vacation
10. List five or six major problems of a moral nature that adolescents face in our present-day culture. What conditions tend to aggravate the solution of these problems?

SELECTED REFERENCES

Baker, H. J., "Spiritual Values Give Life Its Highest Meaning," *Nineteenth Yearbook of the Elementary School Principal,* 1947, Vol. XXVII.

Chave, E. J., *A Functional Approach to Religious Education.* Chicago: University of Chicago Press, 1947.

Clark, Walter H., *The Psychology of Religion.* New York: The Macmillan Company, 1958.

Havighurst, R. J. and H. Taba, *Adolescent Character and Personality.* New York: John Wiley & Sons, Inc., 1949.

Jourard, S. M., *Personal Adjustment*. New York: The Macmillan Company, 1958, Chap. 2.

Peck, Robert F. and Robert J. Havighurst, *The Psychology of Character Development*. New York: John Wiley & Sons, Inc., 1960.

NOTES

1 *The York Times*, January 5, 1865.

2 See, for example, A. Davis and J. Dollard, *Children of Bondage* (Washington: American Council on Education, 1940), pp. 281-82.

3 C. L. Coon, *North Carolina Schools and Academies: A Documentary History* (State Document, 1915), p. 763.

4 R. J. Havighurst, "The Function of Successful Discipline," *Understanding the Child*, 21 (1952), 35-44.

5 George E. Gardner, "Present-day Society and the Adolescent," *American Journal of Orthopsychiatry*, 27 (1957), p. 510.

6 E. J. Chave, *Personality Development in Children* (Chicago: University of Chicago Press, 1937), p. 270.

7 Wesley A. Smith, "Conscience and Conflict: The Moral Force in Personality," *Child Development*, 28 (1957), 469-76.

8 R. J. Havighurst and Hilda Taba, *Adolescent Character and Personality* (New York: John Wiley & Sons, Inc., 1949), pp. 6-7.

9 Erik H. Erickson, "Youth and the Life Cycle," *Children* (March-April, 1960), p. 47.

10 R. J. Slattery, "Spotting the Maladjusted Pupil," *The Nation's Schools*, 30 (1942), 45-46.

11 *Working with Teen-Age Gangs* (New York: Welfare Council of New York City, 1950).

12 D. H. Stott, *Saving Children from Delinquency* (New York: Philosophical Library, Inc., 1953), Chap. 4.

13 R. J. Havighurst, M. Z. Robinson, and M. Dorr, "The Development of the Ideal Self in Childhood and Adolescence," *Journal of Educational Research*, 40 (1946-47), 257.

14 E. Spranger, *Lebensformen* (Halle, Germany: Niemeyer, 1928). This has been translated into English under the title of *Types of Men*.

15 P. Leckley, *Self-Consistency* (New York: The Island Press, 1945).

16 A. D. Woodruff, "A Study of the Directive Factors in Individual Behavior" (Ph.D. Thesis, University of Chicago, 1941).

17 C. M. Tryon, "Evaluation of Adolescent Personality by Adolescents," *Monographs of the Society for Research in Child Development*, 4 (1939), 77-78.

18 Wallace A. Kennedy, "A Multidimensional Study of Mathematically Gifted Adolescents," *Child Development*, 31 (1960), 655-66.

19 H. H. Remmers, M. S. Myers, and E. M. Bennett, *The Purdue Opinion Panel: Some Personality Aspects and Religious Values of High School Youth* (Lafayette, Ind.: Purdue University Division of Educational Reference), 10, No. 2.

20 From R. A. Burkhart, *Understanding Youth* (Nashville, Tenn.: Abingdon Press, 1938). Copyright 1938 by Roy A. Burkhart. By permission of Abingdon Press.

21 D. A. Prescott, *Emotion and the Educative Process* (Washington: American Council on Education, 1938), p. 59.

22 H. P. Van Dusen, "What Should be the Relation of Religion and Public Education?" *Teachers College Record*, 56 (1954), 3-4.

23 F. H. Hilliard, "The Influence of Religious Education upon the Development of Children's Moral Ideas," *British Journal of Educational Psychology*, 29 (1958), 50-59.

24 R. G. Kuhlen and A. Arnold, "Age Differences in Religious Beliefs and Problems during Adolescence," *Pedagogical Seminar and Journal of Genetic Psychology*, 65 (1944), 297.

25 Esther Milner, *The Failure of Success* (New York: The Exposition Press, Inc., 1959), p. 29.

26 U. H. Fleege, *Self-Revelation of Adolescent Boys* (Milwaukee: Bruce Publishing Co., 1944), p. 286.

27 Sister M. Phelan, "An Experimental Study of the Ideals of Adolescent Boys and Girls," *Catholic Monograph*, No. 193 (1936).

28 D. S. Hill, "Personification of Ideals of Urban Children, *Journal of Social Psychology*, 1 (1930), 379-93.

29 Robert F. Peck, Robert J. Havighurst, *et al., The Psychology of Character Development* (New York: John Wiley & Sons, Inc., 1960), p. 190.

10

THE
ADOLESCENT
PERSONALITY

PERSONALITY: ITS NATURE AND CHARACTERISTICS

It is the province of this chapter to describe the adolescent personality (although no effort is made here to indicate that all adolescents represent a particular type), to note factors affecting the development of personality, and to point out the special needs of adolescents.

The term *personality* is frequently used in our present-day terminology to refer to man's behavior and characteristics. It has been used widely and loosely by the layman, the personality expert, the orator, and the psychologist. The layman looks upon it in terms of qualifying adjectives such as "good," "pleasing," and "odd," whereas the personality expert considers it somewhat like a pair of gloves or a stylish hat—something that can be bought for five dollars or more and worn effectively with a few hints on how to wear it. Orators—and some psychologists—have clothed the term in a sort of mysticism and abstraction similar to that which surrounds the terms *ego, soul,* and *spirit*. In such a case it does not yield readily to definition or even to adequate description.

Three phases of personality cause much apparent disagreement between psychologists. They are really points of view. What is true of one of these aspects may or may not be true of another. They are like the inside and outside of a cup, aspects of the same thing. First, there is the social aspect, or the stimulus effect a person has on other people. "John has a good personality" means that John has had a favorable effect on some other person. This aspect of personality is the sum total of all those things about a person that affect other people. Acquaintance rating scales are ways of measuring this aspect of personality. The social aspect of a personality simply means that it affects other people.

Second, there is the reaction or response aspect of personality, or how a person acts and what he does. Some personalities are emotional in reaction whereas others are calm and "intellectual." Personality is often defined as the sum-total of one's reaction patterns. A person who reacts to a wide range of situations with jovial and felicitous behavior is said to have a happy or jovial personality. Some people are said to have aggressive personalities, others "sourpuss" personalities, others dignified personalities, others temperamental personalities—all depending on the way they react or behave in certain situations. Any personality may be studied from the response or behavioral aspect.

A third aspect of personality is the inside, or cause or "why" aspect. It is the psychological nature of the person that causes him to act unsocial, let us say, and thus affect other people unfavorably. People do not like a person (the social aspect) because he is unfriendly (the response aspect) which, in turn, is because he has negativistic attitudes (the cause aspect) developed in childhood. In other words, we may study John Doe's personality from the viewpoint of his friends, or from the viewpoint of what he does, or from the viewpoint of why he acts in whatever way he does. All three aspects are important and yet none of them alone describe the whole of personality. Neither the outside, nor the inside, nor the structure of a cup can be called the cup. The cup is all its aspects. Likewise, John Doe's personality is most certainly how he affects other people; it is unquestionably his behavior or how he acts; it is just as surely his attitudes, his feelings, his "inner state." No aspect definition, nor aspect measurement will give more than an aspect understanding of personality. How we affect other people, how we are affected by things and events in life, and our deepest thoughts, feelings, and attitudes—are all interesting aspects of our personalities. But personality must not be identified with any one of these aspects. It is all of them—and more. It is the whole man, his inherited aptitudes and capacities, his past learnings of all kinds, as well as the integration and synthesis of these factors (aptitudes and learning) into behavior patterns peculiar to and characteristic of that individual.

Personality characteristics or factors. Although personality is generally regarded as a functioning, interrelated whole, there are significant differences in the manifestations of the characteristics, traits, or factors that comprise the whole personality pattern. Thus, behavior can be described in terms of the functioning of the various traits or factors that make up personality. Trait names describe forms of behavior but fail to furnish information relative to the reasons for such behavior. Why, for instance, does the adolescent frequently act differently from his accustomed behavior at home when he is with his peers? Although the situation in which he finds himself influences his behavior, certain traits are deep-rooted in his personality structure. Many terms have been used that represent personality traits. Furthermore, these traits vary in strength. On the basis of a factor analysis study of personality traits, Cattell arrived at certain personality dimensions applicable to the age range 10-16 years. These have been referred to as the "primary personality factors." These factors are:

Emotional sensitivity	*versus*	Toughness
Nervous tension		Autonomic relaxation
Neurotic, fearful		Stability of ego strength
Will control		Relaxed casualness
Impatient dominance, cyclothymia		Withdrawal schizothymia
Socialized morale		Dislike of education
Independent dominance, energetic conformity		Quiet eccentricity
Surgency		Desurgency, intelligence[1]

The personality of an individual depends not only upon the manifestation of these traits, but also upon the integration of such traits. By integration is meant the general organization of traits into a larger unit of behavior, with some traits becoming subordinate to others in such an organization. There has developed a rather general recognition that personality is concerned with the individual as a unit. This has been emphasized by Woodworth; he emphasizes that a study of personality deals with behavior in its totality.[2] Many people lose sight of the integrative nature of personality in their study of the individual; this is especially in evidence in the classification of all individuals with the same educational achievement as similar in personality. The same error is made with regard to criminals, professional groups, people of the same intelligence, and so forth. It is only when two individuals have absolutely identical heredity, identical training, and identical organic conditions that one could expect various personality elements to be integrated into identical personality patterns.

The growing nature of personality. One can expect changes in the personality of an individual during pubescence. Mental maturity is reached during adolescence. Physical growth, which was discussed in Chapter 4, is rather rapid early in this period, but there are some rather abrupt organic changes involved. The thymus gland ceases to function, the sex glands begin to function, and thus a new endocrine balance is established. The child's egocentric nature thus takes on a social form, correlated with the changed endocrine self. The child is now held responsible for acts committed by the self; society looks upon the personality as a growing social force, and now sees not Smith's child but Mr. Smith's young daughter. The impression the growing individual makes upon others and the attitudes adults take toward him are quite different.

Again, it is interesting to note the personality of an individual as we observe it in different situations. The writer has in mind a 14-year-old girl, whom for convenience we shall call Edna. She is very disobedient at home, especially in response to her mother's requests, and the mother thinks of her as "a little smarty." In the presence of her older sister in social situations Edna is quite submissive and timid, but with the boys and girls in the eighth grade at school Edna is quite sociable, and is liked by all. Not only do we notice different behavior patterns when Edna is in three different situations, but even when she is "performing" in any one of these situations we are likely to notice at least a partial exhibition of these other personality characteristics. Thus, personality cannot be considered apart from the situation in which the various traits are exhibited. Some situations will call forth some traits, whereas another situation may call forth a very different pattern of traits. The combination of traits present in a particular situation will depend upon many variables, such as maturity, sex, habit systems, health, present attitude, general social pattern, and so forth.

Personality types. Man always wants to classify individuals as special types; they can then be catalogued and more readily described. This simplification has furnished the following two-way classifications: introverts—extroverts; dominant—submissive; and theoretical—practical. However, most people represent a mixture of components and cannot be divided according to a two-way grouping. Furthermore, variations are of a continuous nature, going from one extreme to the other, rather than of a discontinuous nature represented by types.

Various attempts have been made to discover the relationship of body build to temperament and other variations in personality. Kretschmer's classification furnishes a basis for dividing personality into the following types, based upon physical structure:[3]

Body Build	*Personality Characteristics*
Asthenic or slender build	Withdrawal tendencies
Pyknic or broad build	Volatile, outgoing, assertive tendencies

Sheldon's studies followed those of Kretschmer. One of the major purposes of his studies was to determine the pattern relationship between physique and temperament. He proposed three major types, although he recognized that most individuals are not clear body types but rather a mixture of types.[4] The three components listed by Sheldon and his collaborators are the *endomorphs,* the *mesomorphs,* and the *ectomorphs.* Those individuals characterized as endomorphs have highly developed internal organs and undeveloped external body structures. They are inclined to be fat, and are definitely not of the muscle-and-bone type. The mesomorphs show superior development of the muscles, bones, and connective tissue. The ectomorphs are fragile and delicate in nature.

Sheldon brought forth a tripolar classification parallel to his three large groups of body build types. His first group, the *viscerotonia,* is characterized, in the extreme cases, by general relaxation, sociability, love of comfort, extreme liking for food, and enjoyment of people. The second group, the *somatotonia,* is primarily a muscular type, and is characterized by vigorous bodily activity and the exertion of muscular activity and strength. The third, the *cerebrotonia,* is inhibitory; he is secretive and tends to hold the self in restraint. The individual may be rated on a 7-point scale for each of the primary body dimensions. In addition to the variables listed, there are others, such as intelligence and sexuality.

Sheldon and Stevens found that ectomorphs tended to be slightly more intelligent that mesomorphs.[5] Such a relation, if confirmed in other studies, may result in part at least from the different interests and activities pursued by individuals of differing physique. Boys with greater strength and better coordination tend to pursue games involving physical and motor abilities to a greater degree than boys and girls with less strength and motor coordination.

Measurements devised for the study of personality have revealed that certain trait clusters tend to appear together. Perhaps the most functional classification of personality types is that developed by the Committee on Human Development of the University of Chicago and presented by Havighurst and Taba.[6] Groupings of 16-year-olds were used. The clinical conference methods used in this study consisted of analyzing the data, observing similarities among certain subjects of their study, and grouping together similar subjects. A profile of personality and character factors that characterized each of the groups was then developed. This is shown in Table 10-1 for the five types developed in this analysis. The fact that 31 per cent of the group could not be placed in any of the five types is additional evidence for the contention that individuals do not fall into clear-cut types.

The materials of Table 10-1 are useful in observing adolescents and in noting the factors associated with certain character and personality qualities. They also provide a summary of the effects of peers, the family social status, community forces, and the school on the personality and character of adolescents.

It has also been observed that special abilities have a bearing on the adolescent's personality. For example, Kennedy noted that an interesting characteristic of mathematically gifted adolescents was their independence with regard to how they spent their out-of-class time.[7] "Though they

played some individual sports and some musical instruments, they completely resisted any regimented activity in the way of planned recreation.
In fact, irregularity would seem to have been the rule, with a high drive
level continually displayed and an occasional spurt of frenzied mental
activity."

Table 10-1

PERSONALITY PROFILES OF ADOLESCENTS*

(After Havighurst and Taba)

Personality types	Social personality	Social adjustments with age-mates	Personal adjustments
Self-directive	Ambitious Conscientious Orderly Persistent Introspective	Leader Active in school affairs Awkward in social skills	Self-doubt Self-critical Some anxiety, but well controlled Concerned about moral principles Moves away from people Lack of warmth in human relations Gains security through achievement
Adaptive	Outgoing Confident Positive, favorable reaction to environment	Very popular Active in school affairs Social skills well developed Popular with opposite sex	High on all adjustment measures Self-assured No signs of anxiety Unaggressive Moves toward people
Submissive	Timid Does not initiate action Avoids conflicts	Follower Nonentity Awkward in social skills	Self-doubts Self-critical Submissive to authority Unaggressive
Defiant	Openly hostile Self-defensive Blames society for failure	Unpopular Hostile to school activities	Hostile to authority Impulsive Inadequately socialized Moves against people
Unadjusted	Discontented Complaining Not openly hostile	Unpopular Hostile or indifferent to school situations	Aggressive impulses Feelings of insecurity

* Other traits listed in the profile are character reputation, moral beliefs and principles, family
environment, intellectual ability, and school achievement.

The persistence of the personality pattern. Children manifest differences in personality characteristics that set one child apart from another not only at the beginning of life but also during growth into adolescence and adulthood. A 13-year follow-up study of 28 adolescents who were given the *Symonds Picture Story Test* and the *Rorschach* lends support to the theory that certain personality characteristics persist.[8] The themes in the stories at both testings showed a marked persistence of certain features, and behavior ratings indicated a high degree of consistency in overt personality. Studies conducted with more mature subjects had similar results. In a study by Roberts and Fleming, 25 college women were selected from a large list of 100 cases.[9] Case studies as well as statistically treated group data indicated that home relationships were most important in the development of personality traits, and that whereas there was some fluctuation of traits, in general there was more persistence than change. Ausubel states:

> Once organized on a stable basis, distinctive personality structure, like any developmental equilibrium tends to remain intact in the absence of substantial cause for change. The child does not start from scratch in each new situation, but brings with him a precipitate of all past learnings. He attempts to maintain the same orientations, habits, adjustive mechanisms, and modes of striving and interacting with others that he used before. Even if change occurs in the objective properties of a situation (e.g., parent attitudes), habitual apperceptive sets may be strong enough in certain cases to force altered stimulus content into preconceived perceptual molds (perceptual constancy).[10]

The stability of personality factors makes it easier to predict personality development during childhood and adolescence. The fact that the child and adolescent brings with him his past to new and different situations makes it easier for him to adjust to such situations, although past habits may have to be altered because of the changed situation. Thus, new situations frequently present difficult problems of adjustment to the adolescent.

SELF-CONCEPT OF ADOLESCENTS

The nature of the adolescent's self-concept is so important that we shall examine it along with personality characteristics. Additional materials bearing on the self-concepts of adolescents will be presented in subsequent chapters dealing with adolescent adjustment and mental hygiene.

Development of self-concept. The self-image emerges from an interaction of physiological and sociological factors in the development of the individual. A case history presented by Brandt illustrates such interaction.[11]

. . . Betty Burrows was 14 years old and in the ninth grade of a junior high school. She was 5 feet 8 inches tall and weighed 137 pounds. She had menstruated at 11 and at 14 had about completed the growth cycle. Physically she had reached womanhood. Yet her parents treated her as a little girl. According to Betty's report her mother thought she still ought to be playing with dolls. Her father thought it sinful for her to attend movies or dances. In gym classes at school she was encouraged to dance with ninth grade boys who were several inches shorter than she. Boys and girls whose interests and development were equivalent to hers had long since left junior high school. Her mental capabilities were superior but her school grades were mediocre. She expressed little interest in schoolwork. She was forced to drop art, the only course in which she seemed interested. Deriving no satisfaction from a highly restrictive environment which was completely out of step with her development level, Betty resorted to "nonacceptable" ways of gaining attention and enhancing herself. She seemed to take delight in shocking people. One day she reportedly drank a Coke after taking aspirin because she heard this would make her drunk. Either she actually became drunk or she put on a good enough act to convince people of it. She upset the school nurse another day by volunteering to bring a marijuana plant to class for the project on narcotics.

An early maturer caught in a web of home and school pressures geared only to chronological age, Betty formed pictures of herself and the world about her that were anything but conducive to sound development. The following statements, which she made to a guidance counselor near the end of the year, illustrate some of the worries and concerns that made up her developing self-organization: "I am taller than you but I don't believe I look any taller. I quit letting them measure me when I got to be 5 feet 8 so I don't know exactly how tall I am and I don't want to. . . . They think I am nuts around here but honestly sometimes I think I will go crazy cooped up with all those little kids all day. Sometimes I run every step of the way home at noon and every step of the way back because I think I will pop if I don't."

Fortunately, the school counselor understood Betty's predicament and began accepting her as the mature young woman she actually was. Adjustments were made in Betty's high school program the next year with the result that she eventually became a popular, successful student. Fear of being peculiar and concern over her growth were alleviated as she received acceptance and understanding from the counselor. In other words, the change in her self-concept brought about an adjustment.

Concept of the physical self. Physical and psychological factors are interrelated in all behavior. The concept of the self in adolescence is largely influenced by physical experience because the body has greater realism than other aspects of personality.[12] This is true not only because it is visible, but also because of early training by parents in the development of modesty and cleanliness. The body has a special significance because it is the medium of personality—not only physical, but also emotional, intellectual, and social. This may be noted further in relation to the task of playing one's sex role. In Western culture the physical self is closely related to the appropriate sex role.

One of the chief problems of a growing person is the constant integration of personality characteristics and bodily states and changes. He must continuously adjust to bodily changes and reorganize his thoughts and feelings about himself in light of these changes. There are numerous social-emotional problems related to organic growth. The growth process itself is sometimes disturbing: a boy may feel like a "bull in a china shop" with his sudden increase in size; girls may be frightened by their first menses.

Influences on the self-concept. As early as 1934, George H. Mead described the self-concept as emerging directly from the behavior of others toward the individual and indirectly from physical and mental attributes of the individual himself.[13] A study by Smith and Lebe has an important bearing on this problem.[14] Forty-two boys, aged 12 to 15 were used in studying the relative effects of physiological development and experience on their concepts of heterosexual development and emancipation. Physiological growth status was obtained from ratings of pubic hair development, whereas chronological age provides a measure of the quantity of experiences along with the years of maturity. The following findings and conclusions appeared from comparisons made:

1. Pre-pubescent and post-pubescent boys differed significantly in certain projective aspects of the human figure drawing. "Adequate sex-rôle identification was assumed from the fact that all subjects drew the male figure first. Post-pubescent as compared with pre-pubescent males appeared to project their stronger feelings of sexual virility or masculinity into the males they drew by their excessive attention to hair. Pre-pubescent as compared with post-pubescent males appeared to express their need for proving masculinity and achieving the body-image by their excessive use of masculine objects such as cigars, pipes, cigarettes, scars, masks, and adam's apples."[15]

2. The findings presented in Table 10-2 indicate that measures of self-attitudes in the area of heterosexual development are more dependent on chronological age and experience than on sexual maturation.

3. The findings also indicate that adolescent emancipation from

Table 10-2

CORRELATIONS BETWEEN PUBESCENT MATURITY RATINGS OF BOYS AND CHRONOLOGICAL AGE WITH SELF-CONCEPTS OF HETEROSEXUAL DEVELOPMENT AND EMANCIPATION STATUS

Maturity measure	Self-concept of heterosexual development	Self-concept of emancipation status
Pubic hair maturity ratings	.17	.27
Chronological age	.37	.40

parental ties and concept of independence from parents are more closely related to age and experiences than to physiological maturity.

Mussen and Jones disclosed that in the group they studied early-maturing boys are more self-confident than late-maturing boys.[16] They found that late-maturing boys were likely to have stronger feelings of inadequacy, feelings of being rejected and dominated, more dependency needs, and a negative attitude toward parents. Only a few of the early-maturing boys had these same feelings. Most of the latter appeared self-confident, independent, and capable of playing adult roles in interpersonal relationships. Perhaps these attitudes resulted to some extent from the actions of classmates. The early maturer got a more favorable rating from his classmates than did the late maturer.

A study of three junior high curriculum organizations by Shannon indicates that there is a relationship between the child's class schedule and his self-concept.[17] The three organizations studied were the departmental structure, the self-contained classroom design, and the block-departmental pattern. Shannon found that in the situations he investigated, the self-contained classroom appears to develop more self-acceptant attitudes than the others. In this respect the departmental design appeared to be less successful than the other two.

A direct but unclear relation appears to exist between academic achievement and self-concept. Shaw indicates that male achievers feel more positive about themselves than male underachievers.[18] He states, however, that female underachievers are ambivalent with regard to their feelings toward themselves. This is perhaps related to the fact that the female's role is not so clearly defined as the male's.

The ideal self. The ideal self is shown in both aspirations and identifications. The concept in either case has been found useful in studying the development of character and personality. To the Freudians the origin of the ego-ideal is a result of identification with individuals that the child loves, admires, or fears. It is a process of identification through which the child takes on the attributes of such persons. The social psychologists, on the other hand, regard the ideal self as a term for the roles or aspirations that continuously affect the individual's life. A study by Havighurst and others dealt with the development of the ideal self during childhood and adolescence.[19] Boys and girls from 8 to 18 years were asked to write an essay on the person whom they would like most of all to be like when they grew up. This did not have to be a real person, but they were asked to describe the character, appearance, and activities of such a person. The responses of both boys and girls fell mainly into four categories: parents, glamorous adults, attractive and familiar young adults, and composite imaginary characters. Parent substitutes, such as teachers and older adults, were less frequently named. An age sequence was noted, the trend being for the individual to move outward from the family circle toward the composite imaginary figure. The researchers concluded:

> The final and mature stage of the ego-ideal is the composite of desirable characteristics drawn from all of the persons with whom the individual has identified himself during his childhood and adolescence.[20]

In a study by Crane, members of gangs between the ages of 10 and 14 were asked to list the person they would most wish to resemble as adults.[21] An analysis of the answers in relation to family and peer relationships indicated that once the young adolescent begins to link himself with the adult male pattern the close identification with the gang tends to drop off. In cases where no satisfactory identification is achieved, there is likely to occur a preponderance of antisocial behavior. After the age of 12, girls tend to identify themselves with someone outside the family circle, usually female. The boys frequently identify themselves with some hero or important figure. Again, an age sequence similar to that of the previous study mentioned was found.

Sex differences. Bowman noted that boys and girls obtained significantly higher mean self-concepts in the sixth and eighth grades than in the fourth and sixth grades.[22] Girls revealed higher mean self-concepts than boys at all grade levels studied perhaps because boys are more realistic than girls in their evaluations of themselves, especially when adjective check lists or ratings are used. Boys showed more variability in their self-concepts.

Some interesting and significant sex differences have been noted in a study of the person considered by boys and girls as their ideal self.[23] As seen in Table 10-3, the boys listed material things such as money and property more frequently than girls, whereas the girls frequently listed

Table 10-3

COMPARISON OF CHARACTER AND PERSONALITY TRAITS MENTIONED BY BOYS AND GIRLS

(After Havighurst, et al.)

	Boys *N = 158*	*Girls* *N = 168*
Material values—money, clothes, property	34	3
Good looks, good appearance, neat, clean	21	51
Good personality, stereotypes, popular	21	20
Friendly, lots of friends, courteous, polite, can take a joke	31	22
Honest, responsible, industrious, church-goer, kind	42	51
Cooperative, helpful, patient	5	18
Self-sacrificing, working for social justice, human brotherhood, altruism	4	3

good looks, cooperativeness, and helpfulness as most desirable characteristics. Both boys and girls regarded honesty, industriousness, and responsibility as very desirable character and personality traits. It has constantly been noted that pupils of secondary school age will accept almost any qualities in their teachers so long as the latter are fair and sincere in their relationships.

PERSONALITY CHARACTERISTICS OF ADOLESCENTS

Pictures of American youth have appeared from studies of beatniks, delinquents, fraternity and sorority groups, and other special groups. Are these really typical of American youth? If not, what is the average American youth like? The Gallup Poll was commissioned by the *Saturday Evening Post* to find an answer to this question.[24] More than 3000 young Americans ranging in age from 14 to 22 were interviewed. The sampling consisted of an approximately equal number of boys and girls from different backgrounds. Here are the conclusions:

> No one can say that the American youth is going to hell. He's not. But he is a pampered hothouse plant and likes it that way. The beatnik is a rarity; the delinquent is a minority.
>
> Our typical youth will settle for low success rather than risk high failure. He has little spirit of adventure. He wants to marry early—at twenty-three or twenty-four—after a college education. He wants two or three children and a spouse who is "affectionate, sympathetic, considerate and moral"; rarely does he want a mate with intelligence, curiosity or ambition. He wants a little ranch house, an inexpensive new car, a job with a large company, and a chance to watch TV each evening after the smiling children are asleep in bed.
>
> He is a reluctant patriot who expects nuclear war in his time and would rather compromise than risk an all-out war. He is highly religious yet winks at dishonesty. He wants very little because he has so much and is unwilling to risk what he has. Essentially he is quite conservative and cautious. He is old before his time; almost middle-aged in his teens.
>
> While he has high respect for education, he is critical of it—as he is about religion—and he is abysmally ignorant of the economic system that has made him what he is and of the system that threatens it.
>
> In general, the typical American youth shows few symptoms of frustration, and is almost unlikely to rebel or involve himself in crusades of any kind. He likes himself the way he is, and he likes things as they are.[25]

Kvaraceus has pointed out that most American adolescents do not contribute much to the creative arts, although they have potentials for creativeness.[26] This, he attributes to their preoccupation with sex, sports, and different fun-making activities. It appears, therefore, that the increased leisure time for adolescents has accentuated rather than lessened this tendency.

Emotional response patterns. The findings of the Adolescent Growth Study at the University of California, referred to in Chapter 6, indicate that the nature of personality is related to the amount of internalized or externalized emotional responses. Those adolescents of the Adolescent Growth Study having the greatest constancy of mood displayed the most intense internal responses to emotionally toned situations. Comparisons of the responses of high and low reactive groups to emotionally-toned stimuli on physiological tests for classmate ratings on certain traits are

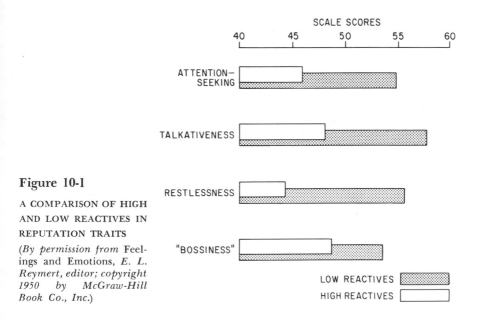

Figure 10-1

A COMPARISON OF HIGH AND LOW REACTIVES IN REPUTATION TRAITS

(By permission from Feelings and Emotions, *E. L. Reymert, editor; copyright 1950 by McGraw-Hill Book Co., Inc.)*

presented in Figure 10-1.[27] The low reactive group displayed more vigorous overt and social responses and tended to be less popular with their classmates than the high reactive group. One might postulate that frank and ready overt expressiveness helps to maintain good personal adjustments, whereas socialized inhibition of overt responses tends to lead to internal emotional tensions.

Contrasting phases of adolescent personality. Some elements characteristic of adolescent personality tend to make the individual unstable in nature; these elements are here referred to as "contrasting phases." G. Stanley Hall recognized the importance of emotion in adolescent life, and in one of his writings says: "Youth loves intense states of mind and is passionately fond of excitement."[28] Here we find a valid expression of the contrasting states of vitality and lassitude so characteristic of adolescents. Pleasure and pain are sometimes close together; tears and laughter may closely follow each other; elation and depression; egocentrism and sociability; ascendancy and submissiveness; selfishness and altruism; radicalism and conservatism; heightened ambitions and loss of interest—these contrasts in moods typify this period of life. Individual reactions are more transitory, unpredictable, and unstable; different traits predominate under different conditions; changes are likely to be very marked. However, as the individual has more and more social experiences, his manners of reaction change and his personality characteristics are increasingly modified and made more stable.

Anyone who studies the problems of young people becomes familiar with these common manifestations of behavior: Habit patterns have not fully developed, work in school is not steady, playground activities vary, general attitude toward the school is easily changed. Bronner makes the following observation:

> Today's enthusiasms may become matters of boredom before long. The desire one day may be to become a missionary, and ere long this has been completely forgotten and the goal of life is to be a dancer. Many an adolescent has said, "I don't know what I want to be. One day I think I want to be one thing and the next day something else, only I want to be someone great."[29]

The newly developed interests and broadened outlook of boys and girls as they reach maturity and come into contact with social reality cause this flightyness. Changes in outlook take place more rapidly than habit systems change, develop, and become integrated into a unified personality.

Adolescent instability. Emotional expression, as we have seen, is largely a matter of habit, and from such habits develop behavior patterns characteristic of extroversion or introversion. As attested by giggling, impulsiveness, yelling, loud talking, and other symptoms of instability, extroversion is more universal than introversion. Habits of introversion are likely to be present in individuals who are reaching maturity with poorly developed social and emotional habits. Just how truly such conditions are a result of training is quite evident as we observe many adolescents with varying backgrounds who are socially well-adjusted, wholesome in attitude, courteous in manners, and stable in the exhibition of various habit systems.

Far too many children, as they reach adolescence, are expected to assume the places of adults with only the training that would enable them to follow authority blindly. These individuals have not been given the opportunity for the development of habits of initiative and responsibility so essential in the ordinary pursuits of adult life; they are "too young" to do the things adults are doing and "too old" to act and play as children do. For many individuals this is, therefore, a period of bewilderment. If the individual desires to run and play the "kid-like" games, he is laughed at; if he offers his advice and counsel too freely to the adult group, he is reminded that he is still a child. Naturally, a sort of training that will enable the individual to adjust his earlier habit patterns to those of the adult group will aid him to develop desirable social habits and attitudes.

To what extent are adolescent worries, doubts, and fears associated with moodiness? This problem was investigated by Fleege, when he asked 2000 Catholic high school boys the question: "Do you ever get into moods when you can't seem to cheer up to save yourself?"[30] Seventy-five per cent of the boys replied "Yes." The alleged causes for the moodiness experienced are listed in Table 10-4. A prime cause of moodiness during adoles-

Table 10-4

ALLEGED CAUSES FOR FEELINGS OF SADNESS AND DEPRESSION ACCORDING TO 2000 HIGH SCHOOL BOYS

(*After Fleege*)

Cause	No. of Boys	Per Cent
Difficulties in studies and school, low marks, failure	298	14.9
Troubles in the home, arguments, debts, parental attitude	192	9.6
Disappointments, things go wrong	179	9.0
Sins, sex, self-abuse, guilty conscience, mistakes, wrong conduct	163	8.2
Deprivations, lack of social opportunities, curtailment of liberties	106	5.3
Sickness, death, mishap	103	5.2
Hurt feelings: because of a remark or because I have hurt those of others	102	5.1
Misunderstandings, quarrels with friends	102	5.1
Personality difficulties, inferiority complex, personal defects, lack of ability	80	4.0
Girl-friend troubles	65	3.2
Miscellaneous: nothing to do, worries, fears, lack of sleep, my future, etc.	117	5.8
No answer, or the statement "I don't know"	451	22.6

cence is self-consciousness about faults, weaknesses, and failures. However, only one boy out of seven indicated that he was frequently depressed. Disappointment, deprivations, and feelings of guilt as well as self-consciousness cause sadness and depressed states. On the basis of information presented in earlier chapters about the fears, worries, and anxieties of adolescent girls, one would expect the amount of moodiness experienced by high school girls to be in excess of that experienced by the high school boys.

Adolescent idealism. Adolescents are idealistic. They are unwilling to admit that nothing can be done to better existing conditions. Later, their idealism is tempered by a recognition of the realities of conditions and by the felt need to conform to existing conditions and standards.

The rigid adolescent personality results from the lack of experiences in which the individual is able to make choices and accept responsibility. Such an adolescent is frequently out of touch with reality and is unable to adjust to changed conditions. This does not mean that the adolescent should not have standards; rather, he needs to know the realistic limitations of his behavior.

INFLUENCES AFFECTING PERSONALITY

Noticeable differences in behavior and appearances have been observed at birth, and, although particular behavior patterns may not appear at this stage, the potential qualities necessary for their development are there, since the basic elements and potentials for personality development are contained in the genes at the time of conception.[31]

Personality differences during childhood appear when we apply the concepts of continuity and unity to personality study. Continuity refers to the similarities in appearance, speech, and emotional behavior at different points of childhood and adolescence. Unity implies the degree of harmony in the speech, emotional behavior, motor activities, and intellectual processes of the child. Continuity emphasizes passage of time in the child's development, whereas unity emphasizes the dynamics of the individual's behavior at a specific time. They are further related to such involuntary forms of behavior as the circulation of the blood, glandular secretions, and the digestion of foods.

Physiological conditions and personality. Greenberg and Gilliland found a relation between basal metabolism and personality.[32] They derived correlations between basal metabolism and personality traits of college students as measured by the *Humm-Wadsworth Temperament Scale* and the *Minnesota Multiphasic Personality Inventory* and discovered that metabolism rate with the neurotic triad had positive correlations; metabolism with the psychotic triad, negative. By extension, the extratensive personality would be expected to have a higher metabolic rate than the introversive personality.

Early childhood influences. Goldfarb presents Rorschach data obtained on an experimental group and a control group of boys and girls, ranging in age from 10 to 14 years.[33] The experimental group had entered an institution at a mean age of 4.5 months and remained there for an average of 3 years and 3 months. They were transferred to foster homes after spending slightly more than three years there. The control group was equated with the experimental (institution) group in terms of age and sex. The mothers of both groups were similar in national background and educational status.

The findings revealed significant differences in personality between the groups:

> In contrast to the foster home children, the institutional children tend to be (1) less mature, less controlled, less differentiated, more impoverished, and (2) more passive and apathetic, less ambitious, and less capable of adjustment related to conscious intention or goal.[34]

The adolescent institutionalized during early childhood lacks warmth in social relationships and finds it difficult to form close friendships.

Rate of maturity. Differences have been observed in the expressive behavior of early- and late-maturers: ratings of early- and late-maturers for "animation" and "eagerness" are presented in Figure 10-2.[35] The late-

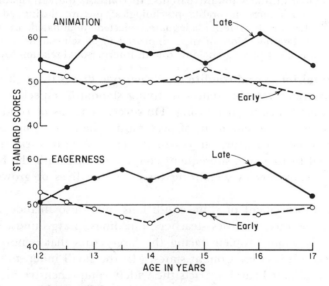

Figure 10-2

MEAN STANDARD SCORES FOR EARLY- AND LATE-
MATURING GROUPS, IN EXPRESSIVE TRAITS
(*Jones and Bayley*)

maturers are consistently above the average for the group on both of these traits, as well as on such traits as energy, talkativeness, and laughter. Two factors have been offered to account for the deviate position of the late-maturers. The first is that their childish tendencies persist. Secondly, they feel inferior because of their immaturity. The immature 14-year-old boy may be expressing, through his excessive activity, not only his more child-like nature, but may also be using this activity to gain the attention of others and thus compensate for his less favored physical status. It will be noted in Chapter 18 that this is sometimes an important factor in juvenile delinquency.

Inferences from projective materials furnish additional evidence of the influence of rate of maturity on personality. Data from the *Thematic Apperception Test* were used in the California Growth Study to obtain an expression of more covert self-conceptions. Complete physical growth data was available on 33 boys aged 17 who took the test. Concerning the influences of late maturity the investigators conclude:

> Analysis of the data of the present study indicates that this situation may have adverse effects on the personalities of the physically retarded. These boys are more likely to have negative self-conceptions, feelings of inadequacy, strong feelings of being rejected and dominated, prolonged dependency needs, and rebellious attitudes toward parents. In contrast, the early-maturity boys present a much more favorable psychological picture during adolescence. Relatively few of them felt inadequate, rejected, dominated, or rebellious toward their families. More of them appeared to be self-confident, independent, and capable of playing an adult role in interpersonal relationships.[36]

Cultural forces and conditions. When one drives through a city he becomes aware of vast differences in living standards, especially as these differences are reflected in housing. However, in terms of conditions or forces affecting the development of personality, the latter is not so important as the different cultural forces in the city. Some of these influences are discussed further in a subsequent chapter dealing with the neighborhood and community as socializing forces in the lives of growing boys and girls.

The improvement of slum conditions must also include improvement in educational facilities—teachers, buildings, playgrounds, libraries, etc. This is a major problem facing the large cities that is not acute in small independent cities. Conant states: "In the small independent cities and the consolidated rural districts the widely comprehensive high school functions as an effective instrument of democracy. All the youth in the community are enrolled and there is a variety of elective programs. . . . Any school that enrolls most of the youth in the community can be said to be comprehensive."[37] However, one does not find in the great metropolitan area the sense of social and economic cohesion that one finds in a small city. Various studies show that vast differences exist in the average scholastic aptitude scores of children from the more prosperous suburban area and the slum area of our cities. A significant amount of this difference can be eliminated either by changing the nature of the tests (which will likely lower their validity) or improving the educational conditions surrounding the child reared in the slum area.

Differences in cultural forces appear in other aspects of the adolescent's personality than that of academic aptitude. It has been noted that aspirations, interests, attitudes, values, and moral standards differ with different social-class groups. These are reflected in the recreational interests, ambitions, behavior, and interpersonal relations of teen-agers with each other and with the adult world. A study by Veness[38] dealt with the outlook on life of 1300 boys and girls ranging in age from thirteen plus to seventeen plus, from less privileged homes in England. These were school leavers from two counties, one in the west of England, and the other in the vicinity of London. The study dealt with two main spheres of life, *family* and *work*. The findings revealed little ambition among these boys and girls, picturing them as dull and uninteresting. The quotations from these youngsters indicated a lack of romanticism about marriage. This is, of course, somewhat a contrast with what one finds in suburban or slum areas in large cities in the United States. Such differences in personality reflect differences in culture.

SUMMARY

In all the various definitions of personality there appears, first, the notion of a *totality* of elements; in the second place, a general recognition of the *interrelation* of these various elements into a unified pattern. Furthermore, there is emphasis upon the *interaction* of these elements in the relationship between the individual subject and other persons. The totality may be made up of an abundance of some traits, a lack of others. Again, there may be a lack of harmonious interrelation of traits—conflicting values, or actually conflicting traits. Or, there may be a breakdown in the desirable interaction of the individual's personality traits and the characteristics of others. The latter is sometimes referred to as "personality clashes."

Since the period of adolescence is one in which personality traits are developing and finding expression in many directions, it becomes a period fraught with many problems and difficulties. It might be stated as a fundamental principle that *any period in life in which there is an undue physiological, social, or emotional stress for which the individual is not prepared, is a period at which mental abnormalities may and do appear, or at which those already in existence become more socially significant.*

The adolescent is faced with a changing physical self which he must now accept. He is also reaching that stage of maturity where he must accept his limitations and assets. The period from 10 to 13 appears to be crucial for the development of desirable personality and socialization patterns. It is during this period that a disorganization of the earlier personality structures and a stronger attraction to peers appear.

The effects of the social environment upon the aspirations, ideals, and behavior of adolescents have been emphasized in this chapter. Boys place a greater premium on material values, while girls are more social-minded. There is a tendency for the general personality pattern of childhood to persist, even though a certain amount of disorganization and reorientation appears with the onset of adolescence. The needs of adolescents are not wholly different from those of preadolescents, except perhaps for those relating to the sex drive. Certain personality needs are manifested by all adolescents, although their exact nature and potency will vary considerably from person to person.

THOUGHT PROBLEMS

1. Look up several definitions of personality, other than the ones presented in this chapter. Show how one's definition will affect his general treatment of this subject.

2. Why is it very difficult to measure personality traits? What experiences have you had with personality evaluations? What uses can be made of results from such evaluations? What cautions should be observed?

3. What are the educational implications of the notion presented in this chapter that "each personality is unique"?

4. Look up several definitions of the *self*. How does one's notion of the *self* affect his personality development? How does one acquire his self-concept?

5. Can you cite evidence from your own life or someone with whom you are well acquainted for the persistence of basic personality characteristics. How do you account for any significant changes that might have occurred?

6. Explain the possible effects of lack of social stimulation during early childhood upon the personality during adolescence.

7. What personality types have you encountered? Why do people try to pigeonhole people into types?

8. Show how differences in constitutional elements have affected the personality development of two boys or two girls of your acquaintance.

9. What is the significance of the findings from the study by Symonds and Jensen of 28 adolescents? What changes have occurred in your personality since you finished high school? How would you account for these changes?

10. How would you classify your own personality? Do you consider yourself as (1) a social type or (2) an emotional type; (3) a conforming type or (4) an inquiring type; (5) a self-confident type? What difficulties do you encounter in attempting such a classification?

11. Select two adolescents of approximately the same age and in the same grade at school. Show how their personality differences have probably been influenced by different social-group memberships.

SELECTED REFERENCES

Allport, Gordon W., *Pattern and Growth in Personality*. New York: Holt, Rinehart & Winston, Inc., 1961.

Frank, L. K., *et al*, "Personality Development in Adolescent Girls," *Monographs of the Society for Research in Child Development*, 1951, Vol. XVI, No. 53.

Havighurst, R. J. and H. Taba, *Adolescent Character and Personality*. New York: John Wiley & Sons, Inc., 1949, Chaps. 9 and 24.

Horrocks, J. E., *The Psychology of Adolescence*. Boston: Houghton Mifflin Company, 1951, Chap. 14.

Jersild, Arthur T., *The Psychology of Adolescence*, 2nd ed. New York: The Macmillan Company, 1963, Chap. 18.

Rogers, Dorothy, *The Psychology of Adolescence*. New York: Appleton-Century-Crofts, 1962, Chap. 6.

Ross, M. G., *Religious Beliefs of Youth*. New York: Association Press, 1950.

Schneiders, A. A., *The Psychology of Adolescence*. Milwaukee: Bruce Publishing Co., 1951, Chap. 16.

Seidman, Jerome M., ed., *The Adolescent—A Book of Readings*, 2nd ed. New York: Holt, Rinehart & Winston, Inc., 1960, Chaps. 16 and 17.

Wattenberg, W. W., *The Adolescent Years*. New York: Harcourt, Brace & World, Inc., 1955, Chap. 16.

Whiting, J. W. and I. L. Child, *Child Training and Personality: A Cross-Cultural Study*. New Haven: Yale University Press, 1953.

NOTES

[1] R. B. Cattell, *et al.*, *Handbook for the Junior Personality Quiz* (Champaign, Ill.: Institute for Personality and Ability Testing, 1953), pp. 8-10.

[2] R. S. Woodworth, *Contemporary Schools of Psychology* (New York: The Ronald Press Company, 1948), pp. 251-52.

[3] E. Kretschmer, *Physique and Character* (New York: Harcourt, Brace & World, Inc., 1925).

[4] W. H. Sheldon, S. S. Stevens, and W. B. Tucker, *The Varieties of Human Physique* (New York: Harper & Row, Publishers, 1942).

[5] W. H. Sheldon and S. S. Stevens, *The Varieties of Temperament: A Psychology of Constitutional Differences* (New York: Harper & Row, Publishers, 1942).

[6] R. J. Havighurst and H. Taba, *Adolescent Character and Personality* (New York: John Wiley & Sons, Inc., 1949), Chap. 11. The materials of Table 9-2 are reprinted by permission of the author and publisher.

[7] Wallace A. Kennedy, "A Multidimensional Study of Mathematically Gifted Adolescents," *Child Development*, 31 (1960), 664-65.

[8] P. M. Symonds and Arthur R. Jensen, *From Adolescent to Adult* (New York: Columbia University Press, 1961).

[9] K. E. Roberts and V. Fleming, "Persistence and Change in Personality Patterns," *Monographs of the Society for Research in Child Development*, 8, No. 3 (1943).

[10] David P. Ausubel, *Theory and Problems of Child Development* (New York: Grune & Stratton, Inc., 1958), p. 99. By permission of David P. Ausubel and Grune & Stratton, Inc.

[11] Richard M. Brandt, "Self: Missing Link for Understanding Behavior," *Mental Hygiene*, 41 (1957), 24-33. By permission of The National Association for Mental Health.

[12] See C. B. Zachry and M. Lighty, "Changing Body and Changing Self," *Emotions and Conduct in Adolescence* (New York: Appleton-Century-Crofts, 1940), Chap. 2.

[13] George H. Mead, *Mind, Self and Society* (Chicago: University of Chicago Press, 1934).

[14] Walter D. Smith and Dell Lebe, "Some Changing Aspects of the Self-concept of Pubescent Males," *Journal of Genetic Psychology,* 88 (1956), 61-75.

[15] *Ibid.,* p. 73.

[16] P. H. Mussen and M. C. Jones, "Self-conceptions, Motivations and Interpersonal Attitudes of Late and Early Maturing Boys," *Child Development,* 28 (1957), 243-56. This and other articles from *Child Development* used by permission of the Society for Research in Child Development.

[17] R. L. Shannon, "Student Self-acceptance and Curriculum Organization in the Junior High School," *National Association of Secondary School Principals Bulletin,* 44 (1960), 35-38.

[18] M. C. Shaw, *et al.,* "Self-concepts of Bright Underachieving High School Students as Revealed by an Adjective Check List," *Personnel and Guidance Journal,* 39 (1960), 193-96.

[19] R. J. Havighurst, M. Z. Robinson, and M. Dorr, "The Development of the Ideal Self in Childhood and Adolescence," *Journal of Educational Research,* 40 (1946-47), 241-57.

[20] *Ibid.,* p. 248.

[21] A. R. Crane, "Preadolescent Gangs: A Socio-psychological Interpretation," *Journal of Genetic Psychology,* 86 (1955), 275-79.

[22] Oliver D. Bowman, "A Longitudinal Study of Selected Facets of Children's Self Concepts as Related to Achievement, Intelligence, and Interests" (Ph.D. Dissertation, University of Georgia, 1963).

[23] Havighurst, Robinson, and Dorr, *op. cit.*

[24] George Gallup and Evan Hill, "Youth: The Cool Generation," *Saturday Evening Post,* 234 (December 30, 1961), pp. 63-80.

[25] *Ibid.,* p. 64.

[26] William C. Kvaraceus, "The Behavioral Deviate in the Secondary School Culture," *Phi Delta Kappan,* 40 (November, 1958), 102-4.

[27] H. E. Jones, "The Study of Patterns of Emotional Expressions," in *Feelings and Emotions,* E. L. Reymert, ed. (New York: McGraw-Hill Book Company, 1950), pp. 166-67.

[28] G. Stanley Hall, *Adolescence,* Vol. 2 (New York: Appleton-Century-Crofts, 1904), Chap. 10.

[29] A. F. Bronner, "Emotional Problems of Adolescence," *The Child's Emotions* (Chicago: University of Chicago Press, 1930), p. 230.

[30] U. H. Fleege, *Self-revelation of the Adolescent Boy* (Milwaukee: Bruce Publishing Co., 1945), p. 321.

[31] B. Klopfer, "Personality Differences between Boys and Girls in Early Childhood," *Psychological Bulletin,* 36 (1939), 538.

[32] Paul Greenberg and A. B. Gilliland, "The Relationship between Basal Metabolism and Personality," *Journal of Social Psychology,* 35 (1952), 3-7.

[33] W. Goldfarb, "Effects of Early Institutional Care on Adolescent Personality: Rorschach Data," *American Journal of Orthopsychiatry,* 14 (1944), 441-47.

[34] *Ibid.,* p. 446.

[35] M. C. Jones and N. Bayley, "Physical Maturing among Boys as Related to Behavior," *Journal of Educational Psychology,* 41 (1950), 129-48.

[36] Mussen and Jones, *op. cit.,* p. 255.

[37] James B. Conant, *Slums and Suburbs* (New York: McGraw-Hill Book Company, 1961), p. 4.

[38] Thelma Veness, *Studies in Individual Differences* (London: Methuen & Co., Ltd., 1962).

11

PERSONAL
AND
SOCIAL
ADJUSTMENTS

NEEDS: THEIR OPERATION DURING ADOLESCENCE

The concept of needs, brought forth in previous chapters, explains the adjustments made by the individual.

The hierarchy of needs theory. Maslow proposed a useful list of needs derived from experimental studies, observations, and clinical experience.[1] According to his theory, needs tend to have a sequency of priority; when needs of low priority have approached gratification, those at the next higher level become prepotent. The concept of purpose, which makes human needs different from animal needs, determines the order of needs. As presented by Maslow it is, in order of priority: (1) physiological needs, (2) safety needs, (3) belongingness and love needs, (4) status or esteem needs, and (5) self-actualization needs. Any attempt to separate the needs into discrete categories meets with difficulty. Although authorities are not in complete agreement over the classification, they recognize that personal-social needs are very important during adolescent years but that basic physiological needs must first be satisfied.

The needs of the adolescent. Physiological needs are particularly important during the early years of life, although they are not, by any means, absent at later periods: The sex drive ripens during and continues after the adolescent years. Actually, the nature and presence of personal needs can be deduced only from observations of behavior, and behaviors observed are so varied that it is largely a matter of choice as to how they are classified. Personal and social needs are not manifested in a similar manner among all groups of adolescents, so that it is difficult to determine their origin. It is generally recognized that cultural forces operate with the biological nature of the maturing individual to develop needs. Concerning this, Lewin stated:

> The needs of the individual are, to a very high degree, determined by social factors. The needs of the growing child are changed and new needs induced as a result of the many small and large social groups to which he belongs. His needs are much affected, also, by the ideology and conduct of those groups to which he would like to belong or from which he would like to be set apart. The effects of the advice of the mother, of the demand of a fellow child, or of what the psychoanalyst calls *superego,* all are closely interwoven with socially induced needs. We have seen that the level of aspiration is related to social facts. We may state more generally that the culture in which a child grows affects practically every need and all his behavior and that the problem of acculturation is one of the foremost in child psychology.
>
> One can distinguish three types of cases where needs pertain to social relations: (1) the action of the individual may be performed for the benefit of someone else (in the manner of an altruistic act); (2) needs may be induced by the power field of another person or group (as a weaker person's obedience to a more powerful one); (3) needs may be created by belonging to a group and adhering to its goals. Actually, these three types are closely interwoven.[2]

An analysis of needs and conditions of adolescence shows that the individual, though physically mature, is compelled to delay the natural expression of certain drives that play a large part in his everyday activities because civilization has lengthened the training period of life, but human biological development has not slowed accordingly. The adolescent's natural drives, which up to this period have found a greater freedom of outlet, are checked and modified by the cultural forces that he encounters in his various activities.

Categories of adolescent needs. Lucas and Horrocks constructed a questionnaire to investigate categories of needs that consisted of 90 items.[3] It was used on 725 adolescents, aged 12 through 18. The results were scored according to a key prepared for the 12 postulated needs included in that questionnaire. Through factor analysis five identifiable needs emerged as somewhat independent clusters. These were: (1) recognition-acceptance, (2) heterosexual affection and attention, (3) independence-dominance with regard to adults, (4) conformity to adult expectations, and (5) academic achievement.

The recognition-acceptance need appears early, as may be observed in the efforts of preadolescents to gain the attention of those whom they admire among both their peers and adults. Needs for heterosexual affection and attention appear during the adolescent years and have an important bearing on the personal and social adjustment of teen-agers. The independence-dominance need, evident during the adolescent years, is a source of conflict between the adolescent and parents or other adult authority-figures.

In American culture the adolescent boy's need for mastery is more conscious and overt than the girl's. We note this in his play, for example in driving an automobile, and in his work. The girl's efforts at mastery are far more subtle. She may try to gain favor by wearing stylish clothes that give her the desired feminine physique: she may use cosmetics to indicate her social development; or she may respond to social situations so as to win favor from other members of the group. Conflicts frequently appear when the needs relating to acceptance and mastery among peers do not conform to the same needs in the adult culture.

The need for self-fulfillment. At the top of Maslow's hierarchy of needs is that for self-actualization, the desire on the part of the individual to bring into use what he can do potentially. It may be observed in a boy's whistling or a girl's hopping and skipping. It must be remembered, however, that its emergence rests upon prior satisfaction of the physiological, safety, love, and esteem needs. It is particularly important in relation to school tasks but is not confined to the intellectual processes; It frequently finds expression through club activities, athletic performances, church or religious activities, and activities at home or in the community. However, efforts to satisfy this need are not likely to be displayed by the adolescent whose physiological needs have not been adequately cared for or by one who lacks self-confidence because his need for achievement and self-esteem has not been met.

The hierarchy order presented by Maslow is not to be regarded as a fixed order in which there are discrete needs. One can readily see a fusion of needs in most of the social and recreational activities of adolescents. This hierarchy of needs does, however, give the parent, teacher, and others working with adolescents a general guide so that they may furnish teen-agers with opportunities to use initiative and accept responsibilities in harmony with cultural expectations and demands and thus may encourage self-fulfillment.

ADOLESCENT PROBLEMS

A number of investigators have studied adjustment problems of adolescents at different age levels and from different cultural backgrounds. The results of these studies have furnished useful information to those concerned with the education and guidance of adolescents. Methods most frequently used consist of interviews, written essays, and problem checklists.

The use of problem checklists. A number of problem checklists have been used in studying the problems of adolescents. The *SRA Youth*

Inventory was constructed under the auspices of the Purdue University Opinion Poll for Young People with the cooperation of many high schools and over 15,000 teen-agers throughout the country.[4] The 298 questions making up the inventory were developed from essays submitted by hundreds of students stating in their own words the problems that bothered them most. The needs and problems of these boys and girls were studied and classified into eight major areas. Norms for boys and girls were then developed, based on a national sample of 2500 cases. The number of items in each category, the mean, and the standard deviation of the total scores for each area of the inventory are presented in Table 11-1.

A summary by Remmers of four cross-cultural studies conducted at Purdue University in which the SRA Inventory was used revealed some interesting differences in the problems of adolescents from different cultural backgrounds.[5] The results, shown in Table 11-2, suggest that Ameri-

Table 11-1

NUMBER OF ITEMS IN EACH AREA, MEAN, AND STANDARD DEVIATION FOR THE NATIONAL SAMPLE OF 2500 CASES OF THE SRA YOUTH INVENTORY

Area	*No. of items*	*Mean*	*Standard deviation*
My school	33	7.38	4.49
After high school	37	12.05	7.09
About myself	44	9.42	6.10
Getting along with others	40	10.40	6.32
My home and family	53	5.76	6.59
Boy meets girl	32	6.64	4.98
Health	25	3.94	2.77
Things in general	34	6.36	5.06

can youngsters are significantly more concerned about learning to read better than the West German youngsters, whereas the Germans were more concerned about how to prepare for tests. All of the problems listed in Table 11-2 were taken more seriously by Indian youngsters. Notwithstanding these differences, substantial correlations were obtained between the rankings of the seriousness of the problems by the different groups studied. The data presented in this study support the following conclusions:

1. Teen-agers' self-perceived problems can be comparably measured across widely different cultures.

2. The high internal consistency coefficients indicate that the SRA Inventory is a reliable measuring instrument.

3. There is a high degree of similarity of rankings of problem areas across different cultures with the similarity greater for similar cultures.

4. What to do after high school is a major concern especially for American and West German teen-agers.

5. Although the relative rankings of problem areas are highly correlated, the amount and intensity of concern vary greatly across cultures.

Table 11-2

COMPARATIVE PERCENTAGES OF SOME "MOST SERIOUS PROBLEMS"

Item	American		German		Indian	
	Boys	Girls	Boys	Girls	Boys	Girls
1. I want to learn how to read better.	17	15	6	4	55	53
2. I wish I knew how to study better.	36	36	35	32	68	79
3. I need to learn how to prepare for tests.	4	8	27	28	50	70
19. I wish my teachers would give me encouragement.	9	8	9	10	61	63
35. I wish I understood science better.	19	19	11	17	57	60
37. I worry about getting good grades.	25	23	33	42	58	65
44. I want to know more about what people do in college.	16	21	36	24	60	56
49. I wish I could afford college.	23	21	22	42	53	57
59. What career should I pursue?	19	16	28	32	56	54
81. I feel guilty about things I've done.	12	16	9	11	55	62
118. I want people to like me better.	20	20	5	8	69	65
120. I wish I could carry on a pleasant conversation.	16	15	15	15	69	65
122. I want to make new friends.	24	29	30	25	60	60
123. I need to develop more self-confidence.	22	28	18	28	62	69
142. I need to learn to be a "good sport" in games.	5	6	8	3	60	57
160. It bothers me that some kids are left out of things.	18	27	19	23	50	53
161. I wish I had a quiet place at home where I could study.	12	16	16	11	62	65
182. I wish I could be of more help to my family.	16	17	24	24	65	71
278. Is there any way of eliminating slums?	10	15	22	25	55	58
280. How can I learn to use my leisure time wisely?	12	12	17	18	51	51

A problem checklist devised by Mooney has been widely used with high school and college students.[6] The items making up the checklist for high school students are classified into 10 areas; each area contains 30 items. The 10 areas are:

Health and physical development
Finances, living conditions and employment
Social and recreational activities

Courtship, sex, and marriage
Social-psychological relations
Morals and religion
Home and family
The future: vocational and educational
Adjustment to school work
Curriculum and teaching procedures

The *Mooney Problem Checklist* was used by Smith in assessing problems of rural and urban senior high school Negroes. Smith stated, "The three problems that were of major concern to rural youth were (1) finances, living conditions, and employment; (2) adjustment to school work; and (3) the future: vocational and educational. Among urban students the important problems were (1) adjustment to school work; (2) curriculum and teaching precedures; and (3) personal-psychological relations."[7] Both groups were in agreement that social-psychological relations were among the least problems present. Rural students had on the average 33.15 problems, whereas urban adolescents checked 52.68 problems on the average. The results of this study indicate that cultural conditions and the nature of community life influence adolescent problems.

Problems related to physical growth and health. Cultural demands combined with physical changes frequently create problems for teen-agers, especially those who may deviate in their developmental pattern from that which is regarded as normal. However, adolescents are little concerned with general health problems; Remmers concludes from cross-cultural studies of adolescents that health problems for teen-agers of different cultures are of minimal concern. It is thus difficult for teachers to impress the importance of health upon high school youngsters. However, in America, boys are more interested in health problems than girls, since the male is supposed to be strong, healthy, and vigorous.

Conformity to adult expectations. Parental expectations for their children vary with culture and social class. The importance of middle-class expectations in relation to adolescent aspirations and behavior has been shown from a number of studies. Encouragement of individuality directed in harmony with both the development of the individual and group welfare is highly desirable. However, encouragement of sheer eccentricity, without regard to individual development, is not useful; to refuse to wash, comb, or shave is not an indication of personal worth or individual effort. Adolescents should be guided in the development of worthwhile standards. They should be encouraged to live by these standards even though this may not always conform to the activities of a particular group.

The relationship of personality patterns and conformity of tenth and eleventh grade boys was studied by Wilson.[8] Often nonconformity brought with it such qualities as irritability, high anxiety, chronic derogatory attitudes, and inability to establish effective relationships with peers.

Problems related to the self-concept. Considerable discrepancies frequently appear between one's self-concept and his ideal self. The difference between the two has been used as a basis for determining the extent of frustrations and maladjustments. Frequently compensatory defense mechanisms and excessive emotionality are directly related to the person's attempt to defend the self-concept and to bridge inadequacies in life activities. While some adjustive difficulties may stem from feelings of exaggerated superiority, in most cases apparent and external reactions of superiority are efforts to hide or deny feelings of inferiority. Inferiority may be experienced by persons on all levels of life but is a widespread adolescent phenomenon.

Brownfain's findings support the hypothesis that individuals with stable self-concepts are better adjusted than individuals with unstable self-concepts.[9] The former also have a higher level of self-esteem as measured by their ratings on the inventory of items defining self-acceptance. They were found to be freer of inferiority feelings, better liked by others, and displayed less evidence of compensatory defensive behavior.

Personal and social problems. Personal and social problems loom large in the lives of teen-agers. As pointed out in Chapter 2, boys and girls at this age must adjust to conditions imposed by a society which is in the process of rapid transition. Frequently they are faced with personal and social problems that are not only new to themselves but are different from those faced by their parents and other adults upon whom they depend for guidance.

The changed physiological self, new experiences, and increased cultural demands change the meaning of many forces within the adolescent world. Emotionally charged events are re-evaluated in terms of their social significance, especially during the transition to a heterosexual outlook. Many home and school problems are related to personal problems that appear at this time, as illustrated in the case of a 13-year-old boy cited by Pearson.

> A boy of 13 was deeply in love with a girl in his classroom. The love affair was a fantasy one as is usual at this age, and he expressed his feelings only very occasionally and, in private, to the girl, who only reciprocated slightly. He did express his feelings of love through writing verse, which he never showed to her or to anyone. One day a friend of his found the book in which he kept his poetry and read a verse or two aloud mockingly. The author became overwhelmed by shame and embarrassment and was for several days tormented by these feelings to such a degree that he was unable to do any of his school work.[10]

Adolescent problems involving religion. In some cases adolescents develop a peculiar state of hyperconscientiousness. Conscience, instead of being a friendly adviser, turns into an inquisitive persecutor and devotes itself to the task of producing an increasing sense of guilt, aggravated by serious doubts. One of the phases of the study by Kuhlen and Arnold dealt with problems involving religion.[11] Each student was asked to respond to 18 problems by encircling an *N, S,* or *O,* depending upon whether the particular problem *never* bothered him, *sometimes* troubled him, or *often* troubled him. The results for three age groups are presented in Table 11-3. There were no differences in the average number of problems checked by the three groups. Thus, these findings do not substantiate the hypothesis commonly presented that adolescence is an age with increased religious problems. However, certain age trends were noted with respect to specific problems. A study of the mean problem scores for the Catholic groups showed that Catholic boys and girls had lower scores in both "wonders" and problems than did non-Catholics.

Certain age trends may be observed from a further study of Table 11-3. More than 50 per cent of the 18-year-old group indicated that the following problems troubled them often or sometimes: dislike church service, failing to go to church, getting help on religious problems, wanting communion with God, wanting to know the meaning of religion, Heaven and Hell, sin, conflicts of science and religion, and wondering what becomes of people when they die. A significant change was found for those problems marked by an asterisk: the most pronounced change was with the problem of disliking church services. Youth is naturally skeptical, and sometimes its doubts become very disturbing. The apparent conflict between science and religion may serve as a storm center around which this turmoil rages. In some cases the inner disturbance follows a spectacular conversion which, the youth finds, has failed to solve all his psychic, social, and religious difficulties; in other cases this confusion is produced by the conflict between sexual urges and high spiritual ideals.

The introverted youth naturally tends toward troubled religious reflection, often leading to psychic depression or even to melancholy, a condition that demands the closest attention of parents, teachers, and psychiatrists. Adolescent melancholy should never be neglected on the assumption that this condition will readjust itself; it often does, but its inherent threat is too great to be taken lightly.

When adolescents become introspective in a religious sense, they should be encouraged immediately to seek help from a religious adviser. Of all the forms of spying on one's self, that of a religious nature is the most dangerous. Introspection can lead a young man to imagine not only that he has some grave physical disease, but also that he is one of the most wretched sinners on the face of the earth. A youth in this dilemma should be put on a proper program of physical hygiene and mental medicine, with suitable guidance in the acquisition of ideals and a more harmonious philosophy of life.

The church has an important function in connection with the sex life of adolescents. Many well-intentioned religious enthusiasts misinterpret the sex drive. They look upon it as sinful and shameful, so that many

Table 11-3

FREQUENCY WITH WHICH PARTICULAR RELIGIOUS PROBLEMS EXIST AT VARIOUS AGES THROUGH ADOLESCENCE AS SHOWN BY PERCENTAGE OF DIFFERENT AGE GROUPS WHO CHECKED EACH PROBLEM AS SOMETIMES OR OFTEN PRESENT

(After Kuhlen and Arnold)

	Problem age		
	12	*15*	*18*
Having a different religion from other people	34	25	27
Disliking church service	35	47	60*
Being forced to go to church	30	31	27
Disliking parents' religion	11	8	12
Failing to go to church	67	67	67
Changing my idea of God	27	32	31
Losing faith in religion	37	44	35
Doubting prayer will bring good	37	44	35
Getting help on religious problems	53	54	56
Choosing a religion	21	20	15
Parents objecting to church membership	23	14	11*
Wanting to know the meaning of religion	53	48	60
Wanting communion with God	59	47	57
Heaven and Hell	53	53	66*
Sin	71	62	72
Conflicts of science and religion	42	50	57*
Being teased about my religious feelings	26	22	18
Wondering what becomes of people when they die	67	56	80*
Number of cases	174	243	130

° Note change.

individuals have considered themselves possessed by evil spirits or by unwholesome ideas when the drive appeared. Margaret Mead's studies of the Samoans, a people not primitive, yet not so advanced as our present Western civilization, show that when this drive is dealt with more frankly and with less hypocrisy, there are fewer conflicts, and also that adolescents do not have to pass through the "storm and stress" period. If a storm appears, it is because they have not been prepared for a natural manifestation of the sex drive. There is evidence that the youth of today is facing this in a much franker manner than ever before in our civilization.

SOURCES OF ADOLESCENT FRUSTRATION

The possibilities of frustration increase with maturity. It has been suggested by Laycock that as they grow, all children must find outlets for their needs through one or more of the following areas of human activity: (1) relationships, (2) work, (3) recreation, (4) community service, (5) misbehavior or delinquency, and (6) neurotic traits and illness.[12] Any condition that offers a threat to the satisfaction of one's needs is a possible source of frustration. The operation of some of the major sources of frustration among adolescents will be described in greater detail at a later point in this chapter.

Deutsche has emphasized the importance of biological development and the associated psychological component of the increased drive toward independence during adolescence.[13] The immature child accepts the fact that his parents will protect him from dangers and will provide for his physical needs. This has been true for him since birth. The adolescent, however, feels the urge to explore and to use his own drives that have appeared or become intensified as part of his biological structure. He is, furthermore, encouraged in this by institutional forces that furnish opportunities for him to express these urges in a socialized manner.

Such explorations plunge the adolescent into a world outside the domain and protection of the parents. He is on his own, without constant guides and reinforcements from his parents. Josselyn stated:

> By his urge toward independence, the adolescent exposes himself to new and conflicting situations that are beyond the sphere of his adaptive resources, while at the same time he must reject formerly acceptable parental aid in meeting even the usual experience. As a result he is periodically threatened by failure with a resultant loss of confidence in himself.[14]

Cultural demands. The sex code operates differently for the sexes, although the so-called double standard does not apply today in the same manner that it applied several generations ago. The societal code requires that the girl take on a feminine sex role and at the same time places restrictions upon her that sometimes make it difficult for her to do so. This tends to make the inner acceptance of the sex role a frustrating and complex one for the adolescent girl.

Our culture allows boys to express their emotionality to a greater degree than girls, except for the act of crying.[15] Crying on the part of the adolescent boy is looked upon as an indication of weakness. The code demands greater conformity from girls, so they must express their emotions in conformance with fairly clearly defined mores. This is observed in the attitude of parents toward their "sassy" 11-year-old son, whom they regard as "all boy." However, the "sassy" 11-year-old girl is regarded as "a spoiled child." As a result, girls attack the problems of growing up in a more thoughtful and careful manner, and rely to a greater degree upon expediency. Girls seem to grow up by evolution, boys by revolution.

Urbanization has added to the difficulties of adjustment of adolescents. Paul Milton Smith compared the personality characteristics of rural and urban Southern Negro junior high school pupils by means of the *California Test of Personality* and the *Mooney Problem Checklist*.[16] No significant differences were observed in their general characteristics and adjustments made to home and school. However, urban students had significantly more problems than rural students; girls from both groups had more problems than boys. The urban students were especially concerned with problems of adjustment to schoolwork, teaching procedure, and personal-psychological relations. The added school problems of urban pupils may be closely related to the size and impersonal relations of urban schools. All too often, the pupil of the large school becomes a number rather than a personality: he may be assigned to a section where he knows very few pupils; his teacher becomes involved in paperwork and has little appreciation and less understanding of the home and community background of the individual pupils.

The effects of the home. The social adjustments of children living in a tenement area were studied by Boder and Beach.[17] The object of their study was to learn to what extent children on a given street in a large city varied in social adjustment, and to trace some of the factors that may have led to differences among them. By selection of one small street with fairly uniform housing conditions, certain of the most undesirable social and economic factors were held constant; and since all the children of the neighborhood were included in the study, some of the difficulties in attributing causal significance to certain factors were avoided. The outstanding conclusion that emerged was that parental attitudes toward the children were the main determinants in adequate social adjustment on the part of the children. Maladjustment in parental attitudes appeared to produce rather specific types of reactions in the children. Most of the families in which the children were shy, retiring, or generally socially inadequate had mothers that were—by one means or another—in complete control of the household. Some of them achieved dominance by psychosis or neurosis, others by native ability or by providing the family with economic support. For the most part they overprotected their children, either through excessive solicitude or by undue control of their activities. The fathers were either easy-going, quiet, submissive men or were no longer living at home. On the other hand, the children who were unsupervised and neglected through the mother's laxness or were subjected to the father's violent temper escaped the tense, quarrelsome atmosphere of their homes and became the mischief-makers of the neighborhood.

A large percentage of children come from underprivileged home conditions. That such conditions are not conducive to favorable development and learning is borne out by the large percentage of such children found among the educationally retarded, school dropouts, truants, and delinquents. The anxieties built up in the home or in some community activity become a source of frustration when such anxieties are beyond the scope of likely or possible fulfillment. Often the child from the upper-lower-class group has built up ambitions for his education and for the future which are practically impossible to attain. Likewise a boy or girl from the middle-class group may have only average ability, but because of the expectations of the family and friends he may have developed an anxiety to reach a level equal to that attained by an older and more capable brother or sister.

Another source of frustration among adolescents is that of achieving emotional independence from the home and family ties. This problem is often made difficult by the failure of parents to realize that boys and girls grow up. The results of parental domination may be observed in the case of a 13-year-old boy described by Mohr.

> The parents of a boy aged 13 complained of his lack of responsibility. He was argumentative, would accept nothing readily from his parents. He argued constantly with his younger brother and with his friends. He was impatient unless his friends would do just what he wanted to do. He did rather poorly in his school work, did not concentrate, "fiddled around." He was rather slender and did poorly in athletics. He whined, acted silly when the mother had company, so that she was ashamed of him and sent him from the room; seemed generally unhappy; spent a great deal of time reading; was unpleasant about family outings; did not even like to accept when the father invited him to go to a motion picture with the father and the younger brother; always felt abused and identified with the underdog.
>
> The picture as seen from the boy's point of view is interesting. Though 13, he had never been allowed to come into town by himself and was accompanied to the office by the mother until she was sure he had learned the way. The boy complained that there was too much arguing with the mother and when he got irritated with her the father chimed in on her side. His father offered to take him to motion pictures and insisted even when there was no picture which the boy cared to go to. He finally went because his father would be angry or the father's feelings would be hurt. His mother insisted that he come in to greet her friends when she had visitors, but she watched him all the time to see how he behaved and he knew that she did not want him to stay. When he decided he would like to have a party, the mother first insisted that he have all the children in his room and it took him two days to convince her that would be too many. Then the mother wanted certain children of her own friends invited, but he knew that they would not have a good time because they went to different schools and "the kids do not know them." Finally

he got it down to just one girl that mother insisted on, though he knew that the others would not want her and he did not think that she would have a good time.[18]

Class culture. The conflict of social-class culture has come to be recognized as an important source of frustration and personality difficulties among adolescents. The social class of a child's family determines not only the neighborhood in which he lives and the neighborhood group with which he plays, but also his goals, aspirations, and social skills. Although there are frustrations among individuals from all economic groups, the frustrations of adolescents from impoverished homes have greater social significance, since they usually lead to crime; more socially acceptable outlets are usually found by those in better circumstances. Heinz made a study of class status and adjustment problems of junior high school pupils.[19] He found that class status was most important in pupil adjustment to the curriculum and administration and in the social life of girls. He noted that at this time "isolates" among girls appeared in large numbers.

School adjustments. All too often the program of instruction in high school fails to provide for the need for achievement and self-enhancement of the individual pupil. The worst occurs when a student is forced to take certain courses distasteful to him in order to graduate, with no consideration for the materials in terms of the pupil's needs and aims. Such a situation is shown in Figure 11-1.[20]

Using 350 high school students as subjects, Resnick investigated the relationship between average marks and various factors of adjustment, such as school environment, socio-economic status, aspects of mental health, and results from psychometric instruments.[21] The relationship between grades and the scores on the psychometric instruments showed, for the most part, that pupils earning higher grades also made higher mean scores, indicating a more satisfactory personal adjustment. Intercorrelations of subtests of the Symonds Adjustment Questionnaire are presented in Table 11-4. The highest was between adjustment to the administration and adjustment to teachers, the lowest between adjustment to the administration and adjustment to home and family. A study reported by Gronlund and Holmlund showed that sociometric ratings obtained at the sixth-grade level were useful in predicting pupils' adjustments in high school.[22] (Sociometric ratings may be obtained by having pupils of a given class or grade make choices of their best friends or list three people whom they would like to go on a picnic with. Those pupils most frequently listed have the highest sociometric rating; those least mentioned, the lowest.) They conclude: "Pupils with high sociometric status tend to complete high school, have a relatively high rank in their graduating class, participate frequently in high school clubs and varsity sports, and hold a disproportionately large number of leadership positions in high school." However, these activities characterize students from the middle rather than the low class in our social structure.

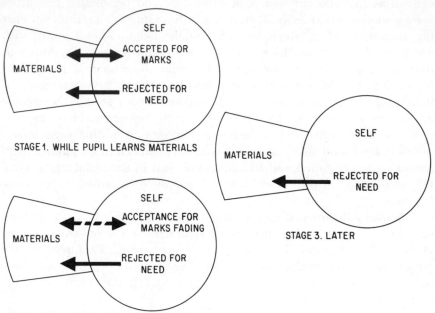

Figure 11-1

SCHEMATIC DIAGRAM SHOWING HOW YOUTH MAY ACCEPT LEARNING FOR IMMEDIATE SELF-ENHANCEMENT, BUT NOT FOR THE MORE FUNDAMENTAL LONG-TERM SELF-ENHANCEMENT

Mental retardation and adjustment. It has already been suggested that the child unable to do sataisfactory school work is a potential problem case. This is to be expected in an environment that places a premium on scholastic aptitude or intelligence. In a study of social acceptance of mentally retarded pupils, Martin used 561 boys and 605 girls from grades 5, 6, 7, and 8 as subjects.[23] She directed two questions toward determining the degree of acceptance and isolation and two toward indicating the degree of rejection. By weighing the points received on the two acceptance questions a social acceptance score was obtained for each pupil. Likewise, a rejection score was obtained by combining the weight of the two rejection questions. The results are presented in Table 11-5. They show a constant decline in acceptance score with a decline in intelligence, indicating that intelligence is important for the social acceptance of children in regu-

Table 11-4

INTERCORRELATIONS OF SUBTESTS OF THE SYMONDS ADJUSTMENT
QUESTIONNAIRE
(*Resnick*)

		Variables				
	2	3	4	5	6	7
Adjustment in relation to the curriculum	.35	.44	.48	.44	.38	.41
Adjustment in relation to the social life of the school		.36	.43	.46	.28	.28
Adjustment in relation to the administration			.51	.48	.34	.35
Adjustment in relation to the teachers				.42	.40	.29
Adjustment in relation to other pupils					.46	.46
Adjustment in relation to home and family						.48
Adjustment in relation to personal life						

lar classes. The results presented in Table 11-6 show that intelligence is important for the child's acceptance even when socio-economic status is controlled. Needless to say one should not generalize too widely from these results, since different prestige factors are likely to operate in different groups or situations. Skill in sports, dramatics, music, or some other spe-

Table 11-5

TOTAL ACCEPTANCE SCORES MADE BY PUPILS AT
THE VARIOUS INTELLIGENCE LEVELS
(*After Martin*)

Intelligence levels	N	Per cent	Mean
110 and above	49	17	.9
100–109	48	16	.6
90–99	33	12	.4
80–89	13	5	−.4
70–79	85	29	−1.1
60–69	56	19	−1.3
50–59	6	2	−1.6

cial ability may be extremely important for social acceptance among some adolescent groups and not in others.

Academic failure is a source of frustration for many students in high school. This may be observed in the case of a seventh-grade student, known as Anne, who came to the writer's attention.

Table 11-6

TOTAL ACCEPTANCE AND REJECTION SCORES MADE BY
PUPILS IN THE RETARDED AND CONTROL GROUPS IN THE
LOWER, MIDDLE, AND UPPER SOCIO-ECONOMIC GROUPS
(*After Martin*)

Level	Group	N	Mean acceptance	Mean rejection
Lower	Retarded	86	1.1	1.5
	Control	86	.6	—.5
Middle	Retarded	26	—1.5	1.9
	Control	26	.5	—.3
Upper	Retarded	33	—1.1	1.4
	Control	33	.4	—.3

Anne's report card, which she carried home, was what has generally been termed quite poor. The father was very much irritated over the poor showing in mathematics and social studies, and made some strong threats. Certain week-end privileges were taken from the girl, and she was required to spend more time with her studies. The girl seemed to withdraw from her classmates and indulged in considerable daydreaming. Little improvement was noted in her grades, and the father became all the more concerned and proceeded to visit the school principal about the matter, as he had earlier threatened to do. The principal looked up her record on the cumulative records and noted that she had never made good grades. He also observed that on one intelligence test she made a score which gave her an IQ of 86 while on a later test her IQ was listed as 82. The principal reminded her father that the girl's past work was not superior, and that he was perhaps expecting too much from her. The mother appeared to sense the problem better than the father, and brought the case to the attention of a psychologist. The below-normal intelligence was verified from administering the *Stanford Revision of the Binet Tests* to the girl. Tests of reading ability revealed a low comprehension score. The mother was told that the girl was definitely not of the academic type and should not be expected to make good and superior grades in school. A second visit to the psychologist by the mother, accompanied by the father, cleared up some points of confusion created from the traditional report card sent to the parents.[24]

REACTION TO THWARTING OR FRUSTRATION

When an individual is faced with a barrier to the attainment of a goal, we say that he is thwarted. A mental or overt adjustment then becomes necessary. The thwarted individual either (1) continues to try to reach the goal, (2) compromises the goal, (3) distorts the original goal, or (4) withdraws entirely from the goal. These reactions take various forms and are given different names. A brief description of these ways of reacting to thwarting will be presented in the following discussions.

Continued activity to reach the goal. A boy may try to make the baseball team. If, after failing during his first year in high school, he continues in his effort, we say that he has not faltered from his goal. The girl who attempts to secure the approval of some boy at school may persist in writing notes to him expressing her admiration for him. Both the boy and the girl will have certain variations in their responses. These variations may lead to success on some subsequent trial. We admire their perseverance, although we would be critical if they continued to make an ineffective response to the situation. Fixation that does not allow for variations or careful study and interpretation of the situation is certainly not desirable. What are factors that make for fixity or fluidity of behavior? Two factors noted by Robinson are:

1. The amount of time spent in trying to solve a problem will vary directly with the degree of the individual's assurance that he will ultimately succeed.
2. The amount of time spent in a given activity is inversely related to the number of alternative promising activities which the individual knows are open to him.[25]

Other conditions that affect the rigidity or flexibility of behavior, when thwarted, are:

3. How important the goal is to the person. The amount of time spent will be in direct proportion to the importance the individual attaches to the goal.
4. The amount of time spent on an activity will vary in direct proportion to the ability of the individual to find other possible responses.
5. The amount of time spent in an effort to solve a problem will be in direct proportion to the extent to which the individual feels that he must continue his efforts in order not to "lose face," either with himself or with others.

A second form of continued activity is that of altering the response. If the adolescent girl finds that her continued effort to win the approval of a certain boy by writing notes fails, she may resort to some other form of behavior—for example, indifference. This is an indication that the girl has lost faith, as a result of failure, in the first method. It is not likely that she will continue this altered response, in case it fails, as long as she did the first response, since she has already begun to lose confidence in her ability to finally reach the goal. Random responses usually appear when the individual lacks insight into the situation. If the problem is not understood, or if the adolescent feels incompetent, trial-and-error behavior is likely to result.

Setting forth a substitute goal. If the adolescent boy is unable to make the baseball team he may decide to quit his efforts and strive to achieve success as a Boy Scout or in some special activity at school, other than baseball. This process of substituting another goal for the one that is blocked is sometimes referred to as *compensation*.

Compensation may be carried on consciously and appear as a direct attack on the problem of attaining satisfaction through a substitute goal. In this case the basic need has not changed, but is satisfied through another activity. Sublimation is a substituted form of behavior, which may be classified as a form of compensation. This involves those reactions, performed perhaps unconsciously or with no particular plan, by which the individual takes advantage of opportunities around him for satisfying a need or want. His desire for adventure may lead to the development of a theme on some adventurous trip, or to an interest in certain types of literature. The possibilities for sublimation will depend, largely, upon the opportunities offered by the adolescent's environment and by his experiences in meeting difficult situations. The weakness of this as a behavior mechanism stems mainly from the fact that it is seldom based upon insight but depends upon the nature of the environmental stimulation and adolescent's past experiences in meeting frustrations.

There are certain distinct advantages in substituting one goal for another, when such a substitution is based upon adequate information and sound principles. For the adolescent girl who is unable to make grades high enough for entrance into teaching, a substitute goal may be the only possible constructive reaction. Thus, substitution may take the form of a compromise with the original goal. The substitute behavior of the adolescent girl may be that of assisting in recreational programs for children, or even in household work, where her main task is that of looking after one or more children. Sometimes the substitute or compromise takes the form of *identification*. In this case the individual's aspirations and concepts of self are in some manner identified with certain people or institutions. The adolescent boy may not be able to make the baseball team but speaks freely of "our team," and how "we" are going to win a conference championship or title. The girl, through her clothes, may be able to identify herself with certain individuals or groups that she admires. Through this identification the ideal self is at least in part realized.

One type of substitution or compromise involves the abandonment of the satisfaction of one basic need for another. An example is the case of the adolescent girl who, unable to satisfy the desire for the approval of boys, turns to books or music in order to satisfy a desire for achievement. Such a substitution leads to a poorly balanced personality, since certain developmental tasks are accomplished while others are not. It is in connection with such problems that adolescents need guidance and help. The adolescent who continues to make substitutions by retreating to a few areas may develop self-confidence in those areas but may be seriously lacking in others.

Falsifying the goal. The most common method used to falsify the goal is *rationalization*. This may be noted in the explanation frequently used by adolescents for their failure to make good grades. In place of admitting an unwillingness to give an adequate amount of time to their studies or to some other condition responsible for low grades, the student may rationalize by saying that he wants to be an "all-round guy," not a bookworm. The boy who is unsuccessful in making the baseball team may rationalize by saying that he doesn't want to be an athlete anyway, since most athletes are "dumb." This represents a sort of *sour-grapes mechanism*. Rationalization serves as a self-justification device, and is perhaps designed to preserve the ego.

A common form of rationalization is that observed in the case of the girl who failed to be elected "May Queen." She says, as her reason for this failure, that her father is just a clerk and she doesn't have the "pull" that the elected girl has. This placement of the blame on someone else or on some condition in one's environment is known as *projection*. The home and school should discourage projection, since its effects are, in general, undesirable and do not lead to the actual solution of the problem encountered. This may be noted in one who blames his troubles on others, believes that various groups are constantly opposed to him, is suspicious of the actions and motives of others, and fails to recognize his own limitations.

Evasion or withdrawal. Through evasion the individual shields himself from having to face a difficulty or from the unpleasantness associated with frustrations and conflicts. *Suppression,* a form of forgetting, is one of the convenient means of evasion. By this procedure the individual protects himself from the thoughts of an unpleasant experience associated with the thwarting of some need or want. This is ordinarily done in an unconscious manner and becomes habitual through use. The high school student easily forgets to prepare an unpleasant assignment. There is evidence from many sources that unpleasant experiences are forgotten to a greater degree than pleasant ones.

One form of evasion frequently found among preadolescents and adolescents is *daydreaming*. Many boys and girls, unsuccessful at school or in their social life, find refuge in a "dream world"—a world of fantasy. Lewin describes personalities as varying along a dimension of reality-irreality.[26] The distinction between fact and fantasy is not always clear to the small child. With increased mental maturity and education the child becomes better able to distinguish fact from fantasy; however, he may on many occasions find his dream world more pleasant than the real world. Through fantasy he is able to shape the world and the happenings according to his own liking. Also, it is relatively easy to attain the ideal self in a world of fantasy. Mary's need for social acceptance, which has been seriously aggravated by the bad manners she has developed, may lead her into a world of fantasy whereby she finds herself very popular with her peers or the winner in some contest.

Sulkiness or "pouting" of some children is an example of the escape mechanism practiced during the early years that sometimes continues into and beyond the adolescent years. The prime danger involved in the development of such methods of responding to thwartings is that they may become the habitual mode of reacting to frustrations.

Regression is a form of escape in which the individual withdraws from the frustration as it exists and seeks to satisfy his needs in a more childlike manner. The crying of the adolescent girl and the childish mischief or "show-off" behavior of the boy may be thought of as examples of the use of regression. The refusal of parents to let their children grow up, through overprotection given them during preadolescence and adolescence, often leads to this form of behavior.

Many adolescents utilize an escape mechanism when a conflict arises at school. This has been described by Josselyn as follows:

> . . . Too many adolescents, for example, who are hostile toward authority, rebellious against it, or feel trapped by it, attempt to deal with these feelings by escaping from the authority of the school, only thereby to expose themselves to the authority of the job foremen. They are unable to strive for the long-time goal of equipping themselves for work in which they would be required to bow to authority. Likewise, in instances in which there is a need to be defiant, the adolescent too often chooses the escape pattern of leaving school rather than a pattern which would not make it necessary for him to lose the benefits from schooling.
>
> The escape aspect of the adolescent's response accents the importance of instituting therapy with the disturbed adolescent before he reaches the age at which he can logically choose actual escape from school in his efforts to handle this conflict. Thus, the urgency of helping adolescents to resolve such conflicts derives not solely from the nature of the conflict; in fact, the resolution of adolescence in many cases might itself erase the conflict's most crippling aspects. However, if an adolescent attempts to resolve the conflict by discontinuing his education, this solution may have a more seriously crippling effect on his future than would an inadequate resolution of the conflict.[27]

The rational approach. One of the fundamental mental hygiene principles is the willingness and ability of the individual to face reality, and to be honest with the self. If one is to meet a frustrating situation successfully he must recognize it as a problem that calls for a rational rather than an emotional approach. There are times when the individual may find that withdrawal is the best procedure to follow. The student of music may find that he is seriously limited by lack of talent. Thus, he is faced with compromise or withdrawal. The decision he makes will depend upon such factors as: (1) strength of the motive or goal in music, (2) strength of other goals or motives, (3) financial and other circumstances relating to various goals, and (4) the methods which have been successfully used in the past in meeting such problems. The adolescent should be guided in *facing reality* and in accepting conditions as they are rather than as he would like them to be. This does not mean that he should abandon a goal as soon as some frustrating condition appears. On the contrary, the situation should be carefully appraised and a decision made upon the basis of a rational understanding of the self in relation to the problem.

The rational approach will demand that the individual know himself and know the situation with which he is confronted. Aggressiveness directed toward overcoming a difficulty when there is a good likelihood of success should be encouraged; displaced aggressiveness based upon emotions should be discouraged. It is the function of education to help individuals solve their probelms through the use of problem-solving techniques. This means that infantile outbursts, intellectual evasions, aggression against others, and continuous daydreaming should be replaced with understandings, problem-solving techniques, self-restraint, self-evaluation, and a willingness to face reality in dealing with difficult situations.

SUMMARY AND CONCLUSIONS

The increased complexity of our social order has brought about a greater demand for guidance and training, if growing boys and girls are to be able to meet satisfactorily the conditions they will face tomorrow. However, *growing up* itself is accompanied by many problems. These relate to various aspects of the adolescent's life and are very real and significant to the individual concerned, although they may appear trivial to the mature adult. A number of students of adolescent behavior have concerned themselves with the problems of adolescents. Studies show that home and school problems loom large in the lives of growing boys and girls. The consequences of these problems are important in connection with adequate personal and social adjustments of adolescents.

The nature of adolescent problems varies with social and living conditions. Problems among preadolescents will be related, in a large degree, to their personal needs, whereas those of older boys and girls are more often connected with social needs. The possibilities of frustration increase with maturity and the expansion of the needs and wants of adolescents. The major sources of frustration listed in this chapter are cultural demands, the home situation, the social-class status, and the school. These sources do not operate separately. It is the combined influence of these and other forces in the adolescent's environment that operate to produce a well-adjusted or poorly-adjusted personality. Throughout this study of the adolescent it has been emphasized that personality is a result of the interaction of hereditary factors and potentialities and many environmental forces.

This chapter has emphasized the importance of successful adjustment during the adolescent years. Various symptoms of maladjustment appear when there is a failure in the socialization process. The persistence of these symptoms is of greater importance than the mere appearance of the symptoms. Behavior mechanisms, resulting in many cases from trial-and-error experiences, are manifested by the individual and are definitely indicative of an effort to adjust to frustrations or conflicts. The mechanisms described in this chapter are common forms of behavior, and no doubt in many cases necessary forms of behavior. They are used by the stable, the unstable, and the neurotic. They do not suddenly appear in an individual's life; neither do they occur in some haphazard manner. Concerning these Warters has stated:

> They are learned habits acquired over a period of time through the process of social interaction. The individual learns them through imitation of others and through the guidance and instruction provided him directly or indirectly by others. He often acquires them, as he does many other habits, through the trial-and-error method. Once he discovers that a particular mechanism is a useful way to adjust to thwarting, he is likely to try it again when he again meets thwarting. Should at another time the mechanism not prove successful, he will first try altering it and then perhaps, if necessary, try changing it entirely.[28]

THOUGHT PROBLEMS

1. Compare the adjustment problems of boys and girls. How do you account for the differences?
2. Observe a child in school several times and note any symptoms indicative of maladjustments. Are these symptoms more or less universal among children? Elaborate upon the significance of any observations on this point.
3. Study the category of needs reported by Lucas and Horrocks from their factorial study of adolescent needs. How do these fit into the hierarchy of needs theory proposed by Maslow?
4. List in order of seriousness what you believe to be the major causes of *failure in socialization*. Describe some individual in whom there has been a pronounced failure in socialization. Give any causes that you believe might have contributed to this failure.
5. List the outstanding adjustment problems of adolescents in the "Home Life" area. What factors or conditions sometimes aggravate these problems?
6. Perhaps everyone has feelings of inferiority in some ways, which may or may not be based upon reality. Consider several acquaintanceships along with yourself for these feelings of inferiority. What seems to be the major sources of such feelings of inferiority? What sex differences might one expect to find?

7. Observe several adolescents for evidence of infantilism. Note particularly evidence of the manifestation of the following types of infantile behavior (Rate each subject on a five-point scale: 1. *rarely,* 2. *occasionally,* 3. *half of the time,* 4. *frequently,* 5. *most of the time*):
    1. Showing off, or attempting to attract attention by some unusual form of behavior
    2. Lack of consistency in behavior activities
    3. Refusal to face reality
    4. Extreme manifestations of selfishness
    5. Easily given to crying
    6. Easily given to outbursts of anger
    7. Manifestations of jealousy
    8. Childhood excuses
    9. Avoidance of difficult tasks

SELECTED REFERENCES

Anderson, J. E., *The Psychology of Development and Personal Adjustment.* New York: Holt, Rinehart & Winston, Inc., 1949, Chaps. 17 and 18.

Jourard, Sidney M., *Personal Adjustment.* New York: The Macmillan Company, 1958, Chaps. 6 and 7.

Patty, W. L., *Personality and Adjustment.* New York: McGraw-Hill Book Company, 1953.

Sappenfield, B. R., *Personality Dynamics: An Integrative Psychology of Adjustment.* New York: Alfred A. Knopf, Inc., 1954.

Smith, H. C., *Personality Adjustment.* New York: McGraw-Hill Book Company, 1961, Chaps. 5, 11, and 13.

Staton, Thomas F., *Dynamics of Adolescent Adjustment.* New York: The Macmillan Company, 1963, Chap. 4.

Wattenberg, W. W., *The Adolescent Years.* New York: Harcourt, Brace & World, Inc., 1955, Chap. 20.

NOTES

[1] A. H. Maslow, *Motivation and Personality* (New York: Harper & Row, Publishers, 1954), pp. 80-122.

[2] Kurt Lewin, "Behavior and Development as a Function of the Total Situation," in *Manual of Child Psychology,* 2nd ed., ed. D. L. Carmichael (New York: John Wiley and Sons, Inc., 1954), p. 959. Reprinted by permission.

[3] C. M. Lucas and J. E. Horrocks, "An Experimental Approach to the Analysis of Adolescent Needs," *Child Development,* 31 (1960), 479-87.

[4] The *SRA Youth Inventory* and the *Examiner Manual* are published by Science Research Associates. These are copyrighted by Purdue Research Foundation.

[5] H. H. Remmers, "Cross-cultural Studies of Teen-agers' Problems," *Journal of Educational Psychology,* 53 (1962), 254-61.

[6] R. L. Mooney, "Surveying High School Students' Problems by Means of a Problem Check List," *Educational Research Bulletin* 22 (March, 1942).

[7] Paul M. Smith, Jr., "Problems of Rural and Urban Southern Negro Children," *Personnel and Guidance Journal,* 39 (1961), 599-600.

[8] Ronald S. Wilson, "Personality Patterns, Source Attractiveness, and Conformity," *Journal of Personality,* 28 (1960), 186-99.

9 J. J. Brownfain, "Stability of Self-conception as a Dimension of Personality," *Journal of Abnormal and Social Psychology*, 47 (1952), 597-606.

10 G. H. J. Pearson, "A Survey of Learning Difficulties in Children," *Psychoanalytic Study of the Child* (New York: International Universities Press, 1952), VIII, 337.

11 R. G. Kuhlen and M. Arnold, "Age Differences in Religious Beliefs and Problems during Adolescence," *Pedagogical Seminary and Journal of Genetic Psychology*, 65 (1944), 291-360.

12 S. R. Laycock, "Towards Mental Health for Exceptional Children," *Journal of Exceptional Children*, 16 (1950), 136-38, 151.

13 H. Deutsche, *The Psychology of Women* (New York: Grune & Stratton, Inc., 1944), Vol. I.

14 I. Josselyn, "The Ego in Adolescence," *American Journal of Orthopsychiatry*, 24 (1954), 228.

15 A. Schoeppe, "Sex Differences in Adolescent Socialization," *Journal of Social Psychology*, 38 (1953), 175-85.

16 Paul M. Smith, "Personality Differences of Rural and Urban Southern Negro Children," *Dissertation Abstracts*, 19, No. 5 (1958), 1019.

17 D. B. Boder and E. V. Beach, "Wants of Adolescents: I. A Preliminary Study," *Journal of Psychology*, 3 (1937), 505-11.

18 G. J. Mohr, "Psychiatric Problems of Adolescence," *Journal of the American Medical Association*, 137, Part 2 (August, 1948), 1590.

19 E. Heinz, "Adjustment Problems of Class Status, *Phi Delta Kappan*, 30 (1949), 290-93.

20 D. Segel, *Frustration in Adolescent Youth* (Washington, D.C.: Federal Security Agency, Bulletin No. 1, 1951).

21 Joseph Resnick, "A Study of Some Relationships between High School Grades and Certain Aspects of Adjustment," *Journal of Educational Research*, 44 (1951), 321-40.

22 Norman E. Gronlund and Walter B. Holmlund, "The Value of Elementary School Sociometric Scores for Predicting Pupils' Adjustment in High School," *Educational Administration and Supervision*, 44 (1958), 255-60.

23 Sister M. A. Martin, "Social Acceptance and Attitude toward School of Mentally Retarded Pupils in Regular Classes" (Ed.D. Dissertation, University of Southern California, 1953).

24 Karl C. Garrison, *Growth and Development*, 2nd ed. (New York: David McKay Co., Inc., 1959), p. 424.

25 E. E. Robinson, "An Experimental Investigation of Two Factors which Produce Stereotyped Behavior in Problem Situations," *Journal of Experimental Psychology*, 27 (1940), 394-410.

26 Kurt Lewin, *Field Theory in Social Science* (New York: Harper & Row, Publishers, 1951).

27 Irene M. Josselyn, "The Problem of School Dropouts," *Children*, 9 (1962), 194-96.

28 J. Warters, *Achieving Maturity* (New York: McGraw-Hill, Inc., 1949), p. 209.

12

THE
HYGIENE
OF
ADOLESCENCE

Advanced knowledge in the various sciences has provided an increased interest in man and an increased understanding of his behavior at different periods of life. The accumulated knowledge of the forces that affect the growth of boys and girls has given renewed courage to those who would combat certain conditions that appear to affect adversely their physical and mental well-being. Today the term *hygiene* has taken on a very familiar meaning and is constantly used by the minister, teacher, doctor, juvenile-court judge, social worker, and nurse.

This chapter is concerned with health problems of adolescents. Although physical health is important during adolescence, much of the emphasis is on mental health.

MENTAL HEALTH

The significance of mental health. The first half of the present century witnessed important developments in medicine. Remedies and preventive measures were discovered for dealing with contagious diseases; the dread of pneumonia, once the number one killer, practically disappeared; infant mortality was considerably reduced; the average span of life was lengthened; and the ill effects of a number of deteriorative diseases reduced. Social workers, teachers, and others concerned with child training were made more conscious of the mental health problems of children. However, understanding of mental disease did not increase along with that of physical disease.

Mental health has too frequently been considered simply the absence of mental illness. However, when we turn our attention to populations outside the hospitals and clinics we find much mental trouble. The study by Leighton revealed the seriousness of the problem. He found psychiatric impairment among at least 37 per cent of a sampling of the population of a Canadian town.[1] The major causes of rejection by the Selective Service during and following World War II, were psychoneurotic disorders and serious emotional disturbances.

Although psychiatry in its earlier days emphasized responsibility and volitional control, and dealt almost exclusively with mental diseases, prevention of such diseases has gradually received more and more attention. With increased knowledge and understanding of the growth and development of the personality, especially in the area of the emotions, it was recognized that the best preventive measure against an adult personality disorder or maladjusted condition was a well-integrated personality during childhood.

Extent of mental health problems among adolescents. Some are unable to cope satisfactorily with adolescent stresses and strains; thus maladjustments and neuroses appear. There is, however no clear line between adjustment and maladjustment, nor is there any infallible method for determining the extent of maladjustments existing among a group of adolescents.

Various estimates have been made of the number of people who are mentally or emotionally ill to the extent that their condition interferes with normal living. Conservative estimates place this around 10 per cent of the total population.[2] More than a third of the four to five million men rejected or discharged as unfit for service in World War II, "and over 40 per cent of the discharges have been for neuropsychiatric reasons."[3] That maladjustments appear among school children and adolescents is borne out by one study conducted with third- and sixth-grade boys and girls as subjects.[4] Of the 1499 children studied, 287 or 19.1 per cent were picked out as seriously maladjusted. The prevalence of maladjustment was higher among the sixth-grade children than among those of the third grade. Of each 100 sixth-grade boys, 29 showed poor adjustment; for each 100 sixth-grade girls only 13 were regarded as poorly adjusted. Perhaps the early training which emphasizes conformity to the social code among girls better prepares them for the rigidity of a school program.

It is generally estimated that half the hospital beds in the United States are occupied by patients suffering from mental and nervous disorders. Modern medicine reveals that many of the basic difficulties of those complaining of physical ills are to be found in mental and emotional conditions. Psychiatrists estimate that from 40 to 60 per cent of all physical illness is a result of or is complicated by unresolved emotional conflicts.[5] The extent of mental and emotional conditions has steadily increased, despite medical advancements and improved living standards. Various explanations have been offered for this, including better diagnosis, increased population, and increased tension resulting from the demands of civilization.

The extent of maladjustments among adolescents enrolled in schools is much greater than the ordinary teacher would ever realize. The teacher is not expected to be a psychotherapist or a psychiatrist with responsibility for diagnosing and treating every problem that appears in her room. She can, however, use the clinical point of view in recognizing that a child's problem behavior is symptomatic of some problem. The moody child, the aggressive child, and the nonsocial child have adopted certain modes of behavior as the most satisfactory way thus far found for meeting certain life conditions. The understanding and sympathetic teacher may be able to determine some of the needs of the individual and thus help him in meeting his problems and directing his efforts into positive and useful channels. In nearly all school situations, however, there are cases that should receive the attention of a psychiatrist or a school psychologist, if such attention is available. The failure of the teacher to detect symptoms of maladjustments may lead to such serious consequences as murder, moral degeneracy, or suicide.

The substantial number of mentally imbalanced adolescents is documented by figures on suicides and suicide attempts during adolescence. Toolan noted a steadily increasing incidence beginning at age 8.[6] According to Tuckman and Connon, it is the sixth leading cause of death

Table 12-1

DIAGNOSIS OF PERSONALITY
CHARACTERISTICS OF ADOLESCENT
SUICIDE CASES

(*Toolan*)

Childhood schizophrenic	12%
Schizophrenic reaction	33
Personality pattern disorder	10
Personality trait disorder	25
Transient situation reaction	2
Mental deficiency	4
Neurotic reaction	16

among those 15 to 24 years old.[7] Toolan noted that although attempted suicide is higher among females, actual suicides are higher among males. The majority of adolescents committing suicide are students. The circumstances precipitating the attempt most frequently reported by those in the Tuckman and Connon study involved conflict in the home over household chores, keeping of hours, school attendance, homework, choice of friends, personal appearance, or relatives. Family disorganization and the factors usually associated with family breakdown characterized a large percentage of attempted suicides.

One of the reasons why studies of suicides among children and adolescents have been overlooked is the erroneous notion that youngsters are gay and free from depression states. This is not true; the majority of the adolescents studied by Toolan were diagnosed as character and behavior disorders. The results, presented in Table 12-1, show that over 50 per cent were diagnosed as schizophrenic reaction and personality disorder. Toolan points out that, "When these patients are studied in more detail, however, they show more symptoms of depression; restlessness, boredom, compulsive hyperactivity, sexual promiscuity, truancy, behavioral difficulties at home, and running away from home."[8]

Conflicts and adjustments. When the emotional conflicts of childhood are not solved in a satisfactory manner, they lead to symptoms of neuroses. Many of the difficulties experienced by adolescents and postadolescents are simply a continuation of these persistent unsolved problems of childhood—in many cases actually accentuated by changed social conditions and physiological maturation. Another group of problems experienced during adolescence may more correctly be labeled adolescent problems, since their origin is closely related to the development and ripening of the sex drive. The appearance of an increased sex drive may seriously affect the harmony established between the socializing forces and the dynamic self. Thus, conflicts may appear between these forces and the ideals and concepts relative to the self that have developed during the years of growth. These conflicts appear in the form of feelings of guilt, depressed states, anxieties, and the like. The adolescent resorts to various forms of behavior in an attempt to resolve these conflicts. Open rebellion against parental restrictions may appear for the first time in the individual's life. When this is not feasible, more subtle procedures involving lying and deception may be resorted to. Withdrawal behavior, regression, and reversion to an earlier, more secure pattern may follow.

Mullen analyzed the apparent frustrations of two groups of high school youths: those who had dropped out of school under conditions of truancy, and those remaining in school who were referred to the Child Study Bureau of the city because of their disorderly behavior in the classroom.[9] The data presented in Table 12-2 indicate that adolescents who have histories of school truancy or classroom disorder also have many physical handicaps, come from homes presenting an excess of social and family problems, and are often poorly adjusted with their peers. Both

Table 12-2

PERCENTAGE INCIDENCE OF CERTAIN FACTORS AS CITED IN CASE HISTORIES
OF TWO SELECTED GROUPS OF ADOLESCENTS

(After Mullen)

	Truants	*Discipline problems in classroom*
Educational factors		
Repeated grade or grades	53.0	55.0
Interrupted attendance	26.7	19.9
Reading disability	9.8	20.3
More than one year over-age for grade placement	35.4	42.4
Physical factors		
Defective teeth	43.4	35.5
Defective vision	34.9	29.4
Ear, nose, or throat condition	17.8	16.0
Poor nutrition or general health	8.6	10.0
Behavior and personality factors		
Poor work habits	25.1	51.9
Lack of self-confidence	19.6	13.4
Nervousness, hyperactivity	7.6	19.5
Aggressive, antisocial behavior	5.0	27.7
Attention-getting devices	3.6	19.0
Habits of lying or stealing	9.7	4.8
Withdrawn, unsocial nature	5.6	4.8
Temper tantrums	1.8	6.1
Family factors		
Broken home	48.5	37.7
Step-parent in home, now or formerly	16.3	13.0
Crowded home	10.0	7.4
Unwise parental direction	27.9	27.7
Inadequate parent	12.7	14.7
Parent or sibling delinquent or criminal	6.2	2.6

types of adolescents suffer from educational retardation. An interesting aspect of this study appears when a comparison is made between factors present among the school truants and those with classroom disorders. In general, the school truants have more home problems, whereas grade retardation and reading disability appear more prevalent among the pupils with classroom disorders. The influence of position in the family seems to be less among adolescents than among preadolescents.

Some case studies indicate that maladjustments involve deep-seated emotional disturbances. These disturbances turn in different directions. Some of them tend toward *unsocialized aggressive tendencies,* observed in bullying, fighting, defiance of authority, and the like. Some have been termed *socialized delinquency behavior,* which is characterized by group activities contrary to established rules, such as group stealing, truancy from school, acts of mischief, and generally unwholesome gang activities. Others tend toward *overinhibited tendencies* revealed in shyness, seclusiveness, daydreaming, jealousy, and the like. The direction the maladjustment takes will depend in a large measure upon social forces in one's environment—the general pattern being exemplified by those with whom the individual is in social contact. Hewitt and Jenkins conclude from a study of these types:

> In each of the three behavior-situation pattern relationships there appears to be some evidence that not only is the behavior in question "provoked" by a peculiar type of frustration, but the general pattern of behavior itself is exemplified by other persons with whom the child is in close contact. Thus the resulting type of maladjustment would appear to be a "rational" reaction of the child to his distorted environment in a double fashion.
>
> Inasmuch as the behavior is rational in this sense, arises from a more or less identifiable type of circumstances, and represents a fundamental warping of the child's personality in a particular direction, the therapeutic implications must necessarily differ from those involved in other forms of maladjustment. That is, the three types of behavior distinguished in this analysis would seem to demand rather strikingly different methods of treatment. Both the pattern of *unsocialized aggressive* behavior and that of *overinhibited* behavior appear to involve deep seated emotional disturbances, but in different directions and for different reasons. Social delinquency, on the other hand, appears to involve the identification of loyalties and a positive response to the numerous deviation-pressure patterns displayed in the child's environment.[10]

Unsocialized aggressive behavior. The unsocialized aggressive type of behavior is seldom found among girls, since they are under considerable pressure from their parents and peers to conform to well-established patterns. These forms of behavior do appear among boys, especially those suffering from what has been termed an "inferiority complex." The aggressive behavior is usually a compensatory mechanism. The case of Jerry illustrates unsocialized aggressive behavior.

> Jerry is 14 years of age and below average in intelligence and achievement. His IQ on the *California Test of Mental Maturity* was found to be 82. Jerry is a slow reader, but appears to enjoy reading comic books and western stories. He also prefers cowboy movies and watches western stories on television. Jerry is small for his age group and is usually seen with younger and smaller boys whom he sometimes bullies, although he usually attains a satisfactory adjustment with them through bragging about his adventures. In one case he told the group about visiting his uncle who owned a ranch down in Florida and how he rode a wild horse.
>
> Boys of his own age and grade hesitate to choose him in their sports, since he is not an asset to the team. He doesn't brag around them, since they would laugh at him and ridicule him. He is considered a show-off by his teachers,

and displays very little interest in girls, although, he was reported to have pulled the hair of one girl, whom he appears to admire more than the others. In general Jerry avoids all social activities, especially if they involve girls. He uses many attention-getting devices in class, the most common being his eagerness to answer questions, although he seldom knows the correct answer. He proves himself to be a nuisance in general by his endless "acting up" methods of behavior.

Jerry has around 100 Indian arrow heads in a collection he started a few years ago. This hobby he values very highly and enjoys making certain that everyone knows that his collection is the biggest and best in the school and community. He claims that it is worth several hundred dollars.

Overinhibited tendencies. The commonest response to rejection among adolescent girls is withdrawal from social situations. The same response is also sometimes found among boys, although they more frequently display belligerent behavior. Withdrawal or seclusiveness takes on various forms. The psychological pattern for seclusiveness, just as other forms of behavior, originates as a response to a motive or stimulus. Shyness is an outstanding characteristic of a large number of preadolescents and adolescents.

Timidity is well illustrated in the case of a preadolescent girl described by Rivlin.[11] The method of handling the case through encouraging participation has been used by many teachers, and has been found to be very successful.

Stella, a 10-year-old pupil in the fourth grade, was referred to the school mental hygiene committee because she was "Very retiring, extremely quiet. She does not volunteer answers in class and does not play with other children." The family background was good and her work and conduct marks were excellent. Her I.Q. was 111. The teacher appointed Stella leader of playground games and made a definite attempt to induce her to speak freely in class.

In the course of the lesson the teacher asked her a question, any answer to which was tenable. During a geography lesson she was asked, "Do you think you could be happy if you had to live in Africa?" The response called for is a simple one and need cause even the most timid child little embarrassment. Whatever answer is given can be commented on favorably by the teacher. "It would be difficult for us to learn to like Africa," or "We really can't tell how we would like it," would be acceptable. Stella responded by shrugging her shoulders. The children were then asked to tell why one didn't know how pleasant or unpleasant life in Africa could be. Probably for the first time in her school career the girl was treated to the sight of the entire class working on an answer she had given, a flattering situation. Stella was then asked which of these reasons she had in mind when she expressed her opinion. Since many possible answers had just been suggested by the other pupils and were still on the blackboard, it was not difficult for her to offer an appropriate answer, even though she may not have had any definite thought in mind when she first responded to the teacher's question.

This procedure was followed for several days until Stella grew accustomed to speaking in class and to having her answers taken seriously by teacher and pupils. About a week later, after an easy question had been asked, the teacher looked at the girl in an encouraging and expectant manner till the youngster sensed the teacher's belief that she had something worth offering to the others.

Socialized delinquent behavior. While withdrawing, recessive personality traits may be serious from the viewpoint of mental health, it should be realized that the possession of certain aggressive types of conduct may also seriously handicap an adult in making adjustments. Ellis and Miller point this out when they state:

> Present standards of society impose requirements for certain types of behavior and exact retribution from transgressors. Offenders who steal are in serious difficulty (if caught). The person who violates these standards of social conduct certainly is handicapped in his success in making adjustments to the social group. Such traits as impudence, impertinence, and temper outbursts are frowned on in adult society, and the person who habitually exhibits them is unpopular with his associates and finds difficulty in making happy adjustments in his contacts with society.[12]

At adolescence occurs the first stage of the development of such habit systems as, when carried to an extreme, will bring the individual into direct conflict with the rules and regulations imposed by society. With the onset of such social conflicts we have a mental hygiene case or a case of delinquency—a case of undesirable behavior, growing directly out of earlier failures in social adjustment. Earlier failures have many and varied causes depending upon the inherent qualities of the individual, the peculiarities in the situation, and the habit systems established earlier in life. Moreover, since their growth is gradual and continuous, habit patterns tend to become integrated into larger units, thus creating a specific type of disposition or attitude. It is therefore difficult to say at just what point in the life of the adolescent the wrong elements developed and became integrated into larger units.

PHYSICAL HEALTH DURING ADOLESCENCE

Death from disease is extremely low during adolescence. Cancer, including leukemia, is the current leading cause of death from disease during this period. Tuberculosis is relatively unimportant as a cause of death among teen-agers, the incidence rate rising and falling with living standards. A study of the materials presented in Table 12-3 shows that accidents account for almost one-third of the causes of death among children aged 1 to 14.[13] Among individuals aged 15-24, accidents account for more than half of the deaths. Cancer is the second leading cause of death in this age group, followed by homicide, suicide, heart disease, and malformations respectively.

Diseased conditions which have a long-range effect appear frequently

Table 12-3

LEADING CAUSES OF DEATH AMONG CHILDREN AGED
1 TO 14 YEARS, 1962
(*Source: National Vital Statistics Division.*)

| | Death rate per 100,000 | | |
	Males	Females	Total
All causes	68.3	52.4	60.5
Accidents	27.7	15.8	21.9
Motor-vehicle accidents	10.6	6.4	8.5
Cancer	8.4	7.2	7.8
Congenital malformations	5.7	5.7	5.7
Pneumonia	5.7	5.2	5.4
Gastritis, enteritis	1.2	1.1	1.2
Heart disease	1.0	1.1	1.0
Meningitis	1.1	0.9	1.0

during the teen years. Congenital malformations, round shoulders, and spinal curvatures, for example, may develop at this time. Furthermore, owing to the frequency of exposure to somewhat dangerous environmental situations, deforming accidents are likely.

Headaches, eye troubles, indigestion, respiratory troubles, malformation of bones, and infections are especially prevalent among adolescents. These conditions result in a large measure from conditions and activities imposed upon them through our customs and institutions. Acne is a hazard to a good complexion among adolescents, three-fourths of whom have it to some degree during pubertal development.

Table 12-4

CAUSES FOR REJECTION OF YOUNG MEN ENTERING THE ARMED FORCES IN WORLD
WAR II
(*After Kleinschmidt*)

Causes	Per Cent	Causes	Per Cent
Dental defects	20.9	Venereal diseases	6.3
Eye defects	13.7	Ear defects	4.6
Cardiovascular diseases	10.6	Food defects	4.0
Hernia	7.1	Lung defects, including tuberculosis	2.9
Mental and nervous diseases	6.3	All others	24.5

The Iowa survey of nutrition problems among school pupils revealed that poor teeth was the most conspicuous physical defect.[14] Also, according to Kleinschmidt, the two main causes for rejections of young men entering the armed forces in World War II were dental defects and eye defects.[15] Table 12-4 shows that these, combined with cardiovascular diseases and hernia, account for more than half of the total. It is well known that these conditions do not suddenly develop as the boy reaches 17 or 18 years of age. They are closely related to diet and the care of the eyes at home and at school.

Health problems of adolescents. Until the beginning of adolescence, the child has usually had some reasonable guidance and discipline; his hours of sleep and meals, along with his appetitive habits, have been observed and provided for. But with the onset of adolescence, and with group situations playing an increasingly prominent part, there is a tendency to live in conformity with group desires and activities, which quite commonly involve smoking, drinking, and irregular hours of eating and sleeping. There is an enormous increase in the daily calorie needs of the adolescent as he progresses toward maturity. Results from the 5-year statewide survey in Iowa, referred to on page 45, revealed that children eat enough meat, potatoes, fats, bread, and cereals, but not enough milk, fruit, and vegetables.

Fifteen to 20 per cent of all adolescents are heavy enough to be fullfledged medical problems. The major causes for obesity are (1) heredity, (2) emotional need for food, (3) individual differences in the way the body uses food, (4) bad food habits, and (5) lack of exercise. The key to weight control is motivation. If the adolescent realizes that weight control is essential for the satisfaction of his personal and social needs he is likely to do something about his weight. Also, if he is confronted with good examples of weight control in his daily life he will probably develop desirable food habits. Motivation to reduce cannot be forced upon the adolescent but must come from within. Group therapy, in which overweight adolescents are brought together under capable leadership to talk about their common problem, has been found to successfully supply such motivation.

Accidents are the greatest single threat to the life and health of adolescents. Mortality studies show that accidents account for almost onehalf the deaths of teen-agers, with motor vehicle fatalities leading the list.[16] Drownings, excluding those associated with small boat accidents, rank second as a cause of accidental death among boys aged 5-14. Fires and explosions constitute the only category of accidents to take a larger toll among girls of school age than among boys. The materials presented in Figure 12-1 show, however, that the mortality rate from accidents among children ages 5-14 steadily declined during the decade from 1949 to 1959.

Need for a functional health program. The schools could probably make no greater contribution to the welfare of the nation than to assume a reasonable amount of responsibility for the mental health and for the

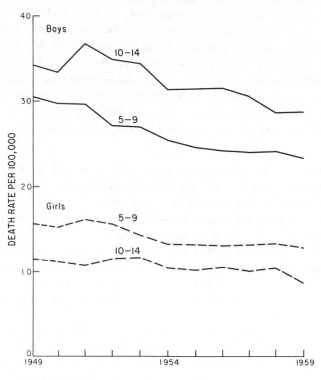

Figure 12-1

MORTALITY FROM ACCIDENTS, AGES 5-14, BY SEX,
UNITED STATES, 1949-1959
(*National Vital Statistics Division, National Center for Health Statistics*)

personality adjustments of growing boys and girls. It is through the agency of the school that enlightened influences can best operate for the development of wholesome personalities and of well adjusted individuals. The schools should more closely adhere to the old Greek maxim, "a sound mind in a sound body." At the end of the Renaissance and the Reformation, education stressed intellectuality and gave little consideration to the physical and mental health of students. It has been only within recent years that the emphasis has begun to change and that efforts have been made to develop the physical well-being of growing boys and girls.

An educational program should have as its first concern the development of the individual, which demands that the schools provide a functional health program. Very often health education either has been neglected in our schools or has not been organized and presented in a way to become effective in the lives of the pupils. The health program should include more than a periodic examination, a course in hygiene, some formal physical education acitvities, and an athletic program that touches the lives of only a small percentage of high school pupils. Rather, it should function throughout all the school activities, and should have as its objectives the development of healthy individuals, desirable health attitudes and habits, and a recognition on the part of the pupils of the nature and importance of sanitation and community health problems. The general aims and responsibilities of the school health program may be summarized as follows:

1. Provide a healthy environment for pupils and teachers. This involves elements related to the school program and the emotional tone of the school as well as to good sanitary conditions.

2. Have a planned program and facilities for taking care of accident victims at school and for cases of sudden illness.

3. Offer courses in driver education so as to develop among high school students good driving habits and a favorable attitude toward safety programs, traffic laws, and other matters relating to safety.

4. Cooperate with other agencies in teaching swimming, safety measures, and first aid.

5. Teach pupils facts relative to the causes of diseases, the ways diseases are spread, and the known methods of preventing diseases.

6. Provide periodic health examinations of pupils and teachers, and keep a cumulative record of the findings and recommendations.

7. Give special attention to those in need of medical or dental care. Where the pupils are not financially able to provide for their needs, the community should use its resources for this purpose.

8. Provide special educational programs adapted to the needs of the handicapped.

9. Cooperate with the community in health programs and in the control of contagious diseases.

10. Provide for in-service growth of teachers so that every teacher will recognize his responsibility for the maintenance of good health on his part and the promotion of good health habits and attitudes among the pupils. However, the specific responsibility for health courses and coordination of all school health facilities with community health programs should be that of a special teacher.

CONDITIONS AFFECTING MENTAL HEALTH

That there is a close relationship between physical and mental health has been recognized for many years. There are many studies which show that bodily limitations and malnutrition adversely affect the emotional stability of the growing child. Conversely, the mental attitude and emotional characteristics of the child will affect his physical well-being.

Mental hygiene must begin during childhood. If we are to understand the mental hygiene of adolescents, it is necessary to study the influences that have thus far affected them. The mother who allows the child to satisfy his needs through temper tantrums, or the mother who assumes a domineering role and forces the child to withdraw, fails to develop habits of initiative and self-control. Such a child, unless his behavior is modified by some trying experiences with other children, will probably adjust with difficulty to a world in which responsibility and self-control are essential.

It should be remembered, however, that only probabilities can serve as guides. And, although most of the difficulties encountered during adolescence can be traced at least in part to early childhood experiences, it would be a fallacy to conclude that all childhood disturbances lead to adolescent difficulties. The life development of the individual is not predictable by such a simple cause-and-effect formula. Many persons with unfortunate childhood experiences pass through adolescence without undue difficulties. Blos has pointed out that:

> The storms of this period are not the result of single causes; they arise, rather, from various pressures coinciding in time. For example, a boy of 14 whose overdeveloped body is going through a phase of rapid growth may weather his adolescence without trouble; he is more likely to develop difficulties if, at the same time, he is experiencing the added strain of a family break-up. On the other hand, the girl whose physical development progresses very satisfactorily and smoothly is in a favorable position to work out the relationship problems which have been with her for many years.[17]

The school and mental hygiene. Almost all mental hygiene societies are using the schools as agencies for furthering their work; in fact, nearly all suggestions connected with mental hygiene work include the use of the school in the program. Also, health clinics—designed rather to aid the child in adjusting the phases of his personality than to study behavior problems present in connection with environmental situations—are constantly held at schools to aid in the preservation of the health and sanity of youth.

No doubt many cases in need of mental hygiene treatment will never come to the attention of a child-guidance clinic, a psychiatrist, or any other person or organization formally interested in these problems, but will have to be dealt with largely through a trial-and-error process carried on unconsciously in the home or school. The child spends the major portion of his time in the home and the school, where these problems are sure to be encountered in either a characteristic or a disguised form. Concerning this, Ryan states:

Mental health through education will be much farther advanced if the school becomes aware of its active function in community living and works systematically with other agencies, including churches and "character-building agencies," social workers, group education workers, the health forces, and other elements seeking a more wholesome life for human beings as individuals and as members of the community. Instead of insisting upon their traditional separateness, the schools should welcome any movement to pool their resources with those of other developmental agencies in the community working in one way or another in behalf of mental health.[18]

A program of mental hygiene should be considered in every school. Any program should include the following elements:

1. Teachers trained in the principles of child and adolescent psychology and of mental health.

2. A psychophysical study of every beginning pupil.

3. A reorganization of primary grades in harmony with the interests and nature of children, along with an opportunity for more systematic and careful observation.

4. A consideration of the integrative nature of the various agencies dealing with the training and development of children.

5. The development of schools and classes to care for the handicapped and deficient.

6. The focusing of attention upon the causes underlying maladjustments, rather than upon behavior disorders as such.

That education is most hygienic which provokes and promotes the child's innate abilities and disposes him to be a good citizen. Hence educators, by developing well balanced personalities among their pupils, may influence the ultimate mental vigor and health of the nation. Until the center of attention of the school is shifted from subject matter to pupils—to human beings—little progress will be made.

Mental hygiene of the teacher. The large number of studies dealing with the successful teacher and personality adjustments of teachers attest to the importance attached to the influence of the teacher in the development of boys and girls. However, the complexity of the problem of ascertaining desirable teacher characteristics has added difficulty to determining the mental hygiene of the teacher. The report by Ryans of the efforts of the staff of the Teacher Characteristics Study throws considerable light on the characteristics of the effective teacher.[19] From "critical incidents" in teaching, some examples of behavior were found which described the activities of the effective teacher. The following descriptive terms were noted in this study:

1. Is alert, appears enthusiastic and interested in pupils and classroom activities.
2. Is cheerful, optimistic.

3. Exhibits self-control, not easily disturbed, well-organized.
4. Likes fun, possesses a sense of humor.
5. Recognizes and admits own mistakes.
6. Is fair, impartial, and objective in treatment of pupils.
7. Is patient.
8. Shows understanding and sympathy in working with pupils. . . .

The teacher's feelings and attitudes toward the learner, parents, and other teachers are closely interwoven with his feelings about himself and his attitudes toward teaching. His own conflicts, anxieties, and attitudes are projected into his interpersonal relationships. Sister Amatora studied the personalities of teachers and their pupils in a group of city and rural schools in grades 4 through 8.[20] She found a significant similarity between the pupil and teacher personality in over half the scales employed. Long term studies of the behavior pattern of pupils show that the influence of teacher personality persists beyond the period of contact with the teacher. Thus, the maladjusted teacher will have a detrimental effect upon the lives and mental health of many growing boys and girls. Garrison, Kingston, and McDonald have pointed out that the teacher will be psychologically adequate to the extent that:

1. He *is* himself, accepting his strengths and weaknesses realistically. He is not smug nor complacent nor unreasonably conforming.
2. He has realistic goals, aspirations, and ideals for himself and others. He has a vision which keeps him dynamic, alive, alert, and positive.
3. He can adequately satisfy his need "to know": to know himself; to understand human personality in its psychological aspects; to know the elements of his profession, its subject matter, techniques, and purposes; and his ability to find satisfaction in continuing to be a learner relative to himself, his profession, his students, and the entire environment of his universe.
4. He can feel adequately about his relationships with himself, the learner, his fellow teachers, his family and community associations, with his fellow man and his Creator.
5. He can be finely balanced in his independence-dependence relationships. This balance involves the handling of negative emotions and maladjustments, the self-respect that can combine conformity with creative professional contribution, and the freedom and security that is basic to flexibility of personality pattern.
6. He can love adequately. This involves respect for human dignity, sincere acceptance of individuals in personal relationships, ability to create a warm and constructive partnership with each student, and the synthesis of all these in levels of motivation corresponding to the levels of integration consonant with an adequate and mature personality . . ."[21]

The importance of religion. As the child grows into adolescence he needs some integrating ideal to supplement or replace his parents as the objects of faith and trust. He needs to have some conception of the universe and his place in it. Religion supplies this world-view. By furnishing the individual with a faith in God and a belief in ideals, it gives him the courage to meet the problems of his world. Man need not reject any aspect of the self, but should accept the self in its totality as part of the plan of his creation. Healthy self-acceptance also requires a realistic view of the self. If the adolescent is unable to accept his real self, he is likely to develop unrealistic compensatory devices.

The importance of the community. Various places of recreation in the community have an important bearing on the mental and physical health of adolescents. In many communities and cities, adolescents are able to secure cigarettes through legal or illegal sources. The question here is not whether or not the smoking of cigarettes in itself is harmful to growing boys and girls, although the preponderance of evidence thus far points to their ill effects; it is more a question of their availability to those who are not yet mature enough to exercise good judgment in their use. Also, it is often a matter of the method of securing cigarettes, or whiskey, and the manner in which they are used that contributes to their undesirability for adolescents.

When school is dismissed for a day or more, it has commonly been observed that crime and mischief increase. Although most high school boys and girls have a limited amount of money to spend, much of it is likely to be spent in places of vice, especially on the part of boys, if such places are available in the community. Doctors, juvenile courts, and police can attest to the problems facing many adolescents in our cities where places of vice are widespread, liquor available to adolescents, and dope peddlers ready to prey on the inexperience and weaknesses of boys and girls. The problem of juvenile alcoholism and drug addiction is becoming increasingly serious in many urban areas, and has assumed national importance.[22] For many years such activities as drinking, smoking, and sexual expressions were forbidden to early adolescents. However, widened social contacts, improved living standards, and increased educational opportunities and experiences of adolescents have tended to bring about a sort of permissive age delineation for these activities. The extent of this permissiveness varies from area to area, but the adolescent zealously guards his new freedoms and adopts readily the standards of urban adults, modifying them to fit into an adolescent peer culture. Thus he insists upon the right to begin smoking at 14 or 15, to drive the car at 15 or 16, or to take a cocktail at 16 or 17. These figures are arbitrary, and will certainly vary from group to group. In the case of drinking, adolescents will seldom be worse than their adult counterparts, although because of their lack of experience they may at times use less discretion.

Drug addiction among adolescents has become serious enough that national legislation has been adopted in an effort to cope with it. Falstein states:

Seliger has pointed out that of the drug addicts admitted in 1951 to the Federal Narcotics Farm at Lexington, Kentucky, about 20 per cent were under 21, whereas six years ago the proportion was 3 per cent.[23]

Although the removal of the forbidden aspect of these indulgences usually results in a decreased desire for them, the community cannot afford to make these easily accessible to adolescents. Actually alcoholism among adolescents is quite infrequent. The importance of community agencies and recreational facilities to provide for the needs of adolescents will be discussed at length in Chapter 15.

HEALTHFUL PERSONAL LIVING

The adolescent who has satisfactorily solved the varied problems of growing up has also solved the problem of healthful personal living. However, there is no simple formula for healthful personal living. Each adolescent is different, with his own unique heredity, body build, mental and emotional characteristics, and life history, but some criteria have been set forth for positive mental health: adequate perception of reality, ability to adjust to inevitabilities, ability to master resolvable difficulties, attainment of need satisfaction without injury to others, ability to set forth and strive toward attainable goals, and the development of a unified and harmonious philosophy of life.

Developing a feeling of security. Adolescents seek both independence and security. Individuals do not at this age give up their childhood *in toto,* neither do they refuse to grow up. The adolescent wants to make his own decisions, to have his own spending money, and to choose his own friends. However, these new responsibilities bring with them fears of failure: fears of making the wrong decisions or choosing the wrong friends.

The adolescent needs to feel secure with his peers. There is considerable evidence that feelings of insecurity often have their roots in infancy. This need stems from the physiological drive connected with hunger and the sustenance of life itself. Whenever this need is disturbed, the infant will display various forms of anxiety. He may develop such symptoms as eating or sleeping disturbances or general apathy. As he grows older he may become increasingly aggressive or stubborn. Security for the adolescent is enhanced through social participation and through successful achievement. It is closely related during this period to acceptability by one's peers—something very much desired and needed during adolescence.

Need for belongingness. Very closely related to the feeling of security is the *feeling of belongingness.* The adolescent needs to feel that he is an integral part of the peer group as well as a member of a family group. His parents may not look and act as other parents do, but they are his parents and he belongs to the particular family group. He "belongs" not by virtue of what he does or does not do but by virtue of the particular person he happens to be. This feeling of belongingness furnishes him with a sense of security essential to good mental health. *Affection* goes along with this belonging. The need for affection as the child begins to move away from the family circle finds its satisfaction in close friendships found outside the home. The adolescent must achieve independence and ultimately break away from the close ties of the family circle. This break with the family has been referred to as achieving independence or emancipation. As he grows older, he will become more and more aware that he is a member of the peer group and will come to look more and more to the peer group for approval and affection. This does not mean that he should turn entirely away from the home, but rather that he should expand his horizon of interests and activities and gradually emancipate himself from the close family ties that were so binding and so important during the early years. It is not well in most cases for children of great difference in chronological or physiological age to form too close a friendship. This is true during the adolescent years more than at any other time of life, since differences stand out far more at this period than later. But contacts with others with similar interests, understandings, and problems are most important in the development of well-adjusted and well-balanced personalities.

Developing a sense of personal worth. Habits of initiative and responsibility tend to give an individual self-confidence and a feeling of personal worth. Such habits are developed gradually through practicing activities in which opportunities for the use of initiative and responsibility are present. The discovery and development of the latent abilities of the adolescent constitute a more important function than the recognition of abnormal behavior tendencies. It is on such a basis that a sense of personal worth is gained. The child who is constantly told that he is "good for nothing" will soon be just about that—good for nothing. Through satisfaction that comes from successful achievement, the child comes to feel that he is really good for something. As the child develops, he should come to recognize his abilities better, and to believe in himself and his abilities. This is what we sometimes call "self-confidence." He should be provided with situations in which he helps to plan for cooperative living —a living of sharing and participation by all the members. When his personal contributions are recognized and accepted, he eventually feels himself an accepted member of the group.

Self-confidence develops from the individual's learning through experience that he can do certain things satisfactorily. It is contingent upon his being able to do things well enough to satisfy his standards of achievement. These standards have developed largely as a result of what is expected of him. Thus, the individual should be given responsibilities in harmony with his abilities. The child who is encouraged to enter upon a curriculum not commensurate with his or her abilities is certainly not educationally adjusted. The child who is encouraged to direct his ambitions toward something out of harmony with his general aptitudes is not vocationally adjusted. Such conditions will contribute to the ill health of a child. Everyone should be given tasks that require effort and initiative, but the efforts required should yield returns in the form of success. Success in various tasks becomes a great motivating force for further effort in the same general direction. It is well known that the dull child who is not kept busy owing to his inability to understand work, and the bright child who is not kept busy owing to his ability to perform work quickly and with ease, are potential problem cases. From these sources arise many disciplinary problems. Sherman presents a splendid illustration of the prestige and better adjustment attained by a high school boy through his interest in collecting:

> He was below the class average scholastically, and had failed in two subjects. He evidently was suffering from many conflicts of inferiority. He complained that the teachers paid little attention to him, that he was not popular in school, that his parents accused him of laziness because his grades were below standard. When asked if he had any trait which made him superior to others he brightened. He said that some of the boys were becoming interested in him because he had a number of antiques. For the past six months he had spent his allowance on antiques—miniatures, swords, coins, stamps. He said that he was studying their history and that he expected to become an expert in that type of work.
>
> Through the possession of antiques this boy gained the prestige he was unable to attain in other ways. Attention from other students was a strong incentive to further interest in antiques. The attention from his fellow-students tended to decrease his feeling of inferiority in regard to his scholastic attainment.[24]

Understanding one's sex role. Parents are responsible for giving the child instruction on sex suited to his age and his needs, as well as giving him training in proper habits. The needed information should be given gradually, in proportion to the child's curiosity and capacity for understanding it. The information given the child of 5 or 6 will be different from that given a child of 12, both in form and in certain features of content, but the one should be in harmony with the other. The child should feel perfectly free to ask his parents for information and he should feel confident that they will tell him the truth. His inquiries should be treated with candor because they are motivated by a natural unemotional curiosity. In this way the child will build up the right attitude toward sex and be prepared for puberty.

During the adolescent stage the sex role develops so that a satisfactory relationship with the opposite sex should be attained. A healthy attitude will be maintained if the problems that arise at this time are treated positively and constructively. Concerning this, Gardner states:

. . . One does not limit this identification merely to the biological role the youth must prepare himself to assume in adult life without serious conflict, but includes too all of the roles—dominant and subsidiary—that society insists he must have if the boy is to be a definite male or the girl a definite female. With all the dangers, actual or alleged, factful or fanciful, that have been outlined for youth by adults or by colleagues, and in the light of all the deliberately contrived or silently condoned ignorance in respect to these sexual roles, it is a never-ending surprise to all of us, I am sure, that the adolescent ever performs this task in development or ever becomes a reasonably conflict-free adult.[25]

Developing social consciousness. At first the child is more or less oblivious to most of the culture that surrounds him, although he reacts within his limits to certain aspects of it from the very beginning of life. His behavior is largely concerned with providing for his physical needs—eating, sleeping, exercising, and the like. Social consciousness is almost, if not wholly, lacking at this early period of life. The real beginnings of social consciousness are to be found in the activities of groups of children at play during the early school years. As they grow they come to realize what the group expects of them, and how they must behave with respect to the various members of the group.

Preadolescence is a period when heightened social consciousness is manifested in the formation of groups, gangs, and clubs. There is an extension and intensification of this during the adolescent period. If the adolescent is to secure and maintain a well-adjusted personality, he must develop out of this early egocentric nature into a social being who recognizes and appreciates the personalities of others, and who is anxious to become a part of his peer group.

Achieving a consistent and unified philosophy of life. As the individual develops into adolescence he should have made a beginning in the development of some concepts of the nature of the world in which he lives and of some purposes of life. It is here that faiths and truths related to actual living may be able to function most effectively. The adolescent needs help in the development of some consistent attitudes that will give meaning to life. There are elements in life that make it difficult to reconcile various teachings in a way that will develop a unified viewpoint. The adolescent may know enough science to block his acceptance of a traditional religious concept but may not know enough to synthesize the two. In an effort to reconcile the two, he encounters a third. These various concepts create confusion and conflicts. The relation between good mental health and a sound philosophy of life is inextricable. Kagan points out, "Recent psychiatric studies lead to the conclusion that where there is hope there is greater success in enduring pain, in healing and prolonging life. Hope vanishes when the need to belong, the need to be loved and the need to believe are unmet."[26]

SUMMARY

Life has been described as a continuous process of change and adjustment. The newborn infant is faced with adjustment problems as he emerges from the sheltered life within the mother to an expanded social and physical environment. As he develops out of the stage of infancy, new problems arise and additional needs and wants appear. The manner in which the child learns to meet frustrations will be extremely important in connection with adjustments during adolescence.

In our culture, growth into adolescence is accompanied by certain demands upon the individual. In the first place, he is required to accept more responsibility and, thus, to achieve increased independence. Secondly, he must effect a transition from interest in group activities to interest in members of the opposite sex. Thirdly, he must adjust to his own capacities and limitations. Fourthly, he must learn to face reality.

Adolescence has been described as a period of danger for mental and physical health. Many health hazards appear at this age, and the adolescent needs guidance in meeting them. Childhood is regarded as the golden period for mental hygiene. Attitudes essential for desirable adjustments are in the formative stage at this time. Many of these are sufficiently formed to act as an aid or barrier to successful adjustments at a later stage.

The basis for the new impulses of adolescence is the development of the visceral organs of the body, and especially the sex and related glands. This development no doubt does much to give the adolescent a better and fuller understanding of his relation to others, and an admiration for those of the opposite sex. In fact, he experiences a new and heightened sensitiveness to all the phases of his personal and social environment. As was suggested in previous chapters, he now begins to heed the general approval of those about him; he begins to make a more careful inventory of his own personal qualities, and may easily develop a keener and more extensive display of achievement, in conflict with the fear of failure and thus of social disapproval or ridicule. This effort to adjust in harmony with the maturing self presents many vital problems to adolescents. Harmonious personal and social adjustment will depend largely upon (1) ability and willingness to accept the *self,* (2) feeling of well-being (ego-involvement), (3) the satisfaction of needs for security, independence, and social approval.

THOUGHT PROBLEMS

1. Look up further meanings of the term *mental hygiene.* Why is it impossible to separate mental hygiene from physical hygiene?

2. Show how the stress and strain of modern life may affect the physical and mental health of adolescents.

3. What are some of the major problems of the hygiene of adolescence? Are any of these problems peculiar to this specific period of life?

4. Consider several teachers of your acquaintance and evaluate their mental hygiene relationships in connection with their classroom contacts. What problems or difficulties most frequently appear among this group of teachers?

5. Show how the needs and principles involved in healthful personal living are interrelated.

6. What barriers does the adolescent often face in understanding and accepting himself?

7. What are some essentials for the development of a consistent and unified philosophy of life? What agencies or forces have been most helpful to you in the achievement of such a philosophy of life? What values have these had for you?

8. Just what is your interpretation of the phrase "the clinical point of view"? Why is it desirable for teachers to have this point of view?

9. Show how mental hygiene problems follow the developmental idea presented throughout this text.

10. Suggest ways by which the cultural environment of your community could be made more conducive to good mental health.

11. It has been suggested that children and adolescents are being used today as status symbols for their parents. Show how this operates. How might this affect the mental health of children and adolescents?

12. Read carefully the case of Stella cited in this chapter. What are some possible conditions that might lead a 10-year-old girl like Stella to develop such a degree of timidity? Evaluate the method used by the teacher to help Stella.

13. Consider some community of your acquaintance. What are the major health hazards and problems of the community? Evaluate the school health program in light of the items summarized in this book.

SELECTED REFERENCES

Cole, Luella, *Psychology of Adolescence,* 6th ed. New York: Holt, Rinehart & Winston, Inc., 1964, Chap. 6.

Gallagher, J., and M. D. Roswell, *Emotional Problems of Adolescents.* New York: Oxford University Press, 1958.

Garrison, Karl C., Albert J. Kingston, and Arthur S. McDonald, *Educational Psychology.* New York: Appleton-Century-Crofts, Inc., 1964, Chap. 19.

Hollingshead, A. B., and F. C. Redlich, *Social Class and Mental Illness.* New York: John Wiley & Sons, Inc., 1958.

Howard, Wilbur K., *The Fracture Zone.* New York: Friendship Press, 1962.

Hurlock, Elizabeth B., *Adolescent Development,* 2nd ed. New York: McGraw-Hill Book Company, 1955, Chap. 3.

Joint Commission on Health Problems of the National Education Association and the American Medical Association, *School Health Services.* Washington: National Education Association, 1953.

Opler, Marvin K., ed., *Culture and Mental Health.* New York: The Macmillan Company, 1959.

Wattenberg, W. W., *The Adolescent Years*. New York: Harcourt, Brace & World, Inc., 1955, Chap. 7.

Young, Kimball, *Personality and Problems of Adjustment*. New York: Appleton-Century-Crofts, Inc., 1952.

NOTES

[1] D. C. Leighton, "The Distribution of Psychiatric Symptoms in a Small Town," *American Journal of Psychiatry*, 112 (1956), 716-23.

[2] W. C. Menninger, *Psychiatry: Its Evaluation and Present Status* (Ithaca: Cornell University Press, 1948), p. 98.

[3] F. A. Weiss, "Physical Complaints of Neurotic Origin," in *An Outline of Abnormal Psychology*, eds. G. Murphy and A. J. Backrach (New York: Modern Library, Inc., 1954), p. 267.

[4] A. R. Mangus and J. R. Seeley, "Mental Health Problems among School Children in an Ohio County," *Understanding the Child*, 18 (1949), 74-79.

[5] *The Mental Health Programs of the Forty-eight States: A Report to the Governor's Conference* (Chicago: Council of State Governments, 1950), p. 216.

[6] James M. Toolan, "Suicidal Attempts in Children and Adolescents," *American Journal of Psychiatry*, 118 (1962), Part 2, 719-824.

[7] Jacob Tuckman and Helen E. Connon, "Attempted Suicide in Adolescents," *American Journal of Psychiatry*, 119 (1962), Part 1, 228-32.

[8] James M. Toolan, *op. cit.*, p. 721.

[9] F. A. Mullen, "Truancy and Classroom Disorders as Symptoms of Personality Problems," *Journal of Educational Psychology*, 41 (1950), 97-109.

[10] L. E. Hewitt and R. L. Jenkins, *Fundamental Patterns of Maladjustment, The Dynamics of Their Origin* (Springfield, Ill.: State of Illinois, 1946), p. 91.

[11] H. N. Rivlin, *Educating for Adjustment* (New York: Appleton-Century-Crofts, Inc., 1936), p. 375.

[12] D. B. Ellis and L. W. Miller, "Teachers' Attitudes and Child Behavior Problems," *Journal of Educational Psychology*, 27 (1936), 508.

[13] *Accident Factors*. Published by the National Safety Council, 1963.

[14] "School Children in Iowa Lack Calcium, Vitamin C," *Public Health Reports*, 70 (1955), 177.

[15] E. E. Kleinschmidt, "Meeting Today's Health Problems," *Phi Delta Kappan*, 26 (1943), 12.

[16] Metropolitan Life Insurance Company, *Statistical Bulletin*, 12 (1961), 5.

[17] P. Blos, "Adolescence, Its Stimulations and Patterns," *Childhood Education*, 18 (1941), 83.

[18] C. W. Ryan, *Mental Health through Education* (New York: The Commonwealth Fund, 1938), p. 304.

[19] D. G. Ryans, "The Investigation of Teacher Characteristics," *Educational Record*, 34 (1953), 383.

[20] Sister M. Amatora, "Similarities in Teachers and Pupil Personality," *Journal of Psychology*, 37 (1954), 45-51.

[21] Karl C. Garrison, Albert J. Kingston, and Arthur S. McDonald, *Educational Psychology* (New York: Appleton-Century-Crofts, Inc., 1964), p. 500.

[22] E. I. Falstein, "Juvenile Alcoholism: A Psychodynamic Case Study of Addiction," *American Journal of Orthopsychiatry*, 23 (1953), 530-51.

[23] *Ibid.*, p. 550.

[24] M. Sherman, *Mental Hygiene and Education* (New York: David McKay Co., Inc., 1934), p. 173.

[25] George E. Gardner, "Present-day Society and the Adolescent," *American Journal of Orthopsychiatry*, 27 (1957), 511.

[26] Henry E. Kagan, "Psychotherapy as a Religious Value," *Journal of Counseling Psychology*, 6 (1959), 265.

PART FOUR

SOCIAL FORCES AFFECTING THE ADOLESCENT

13

THE
ADOLESCENT
AT
HOME

*All happy families resemble one another; every unhappy family is unhappy
in its own way.*   TOLSTOI

HOME INFLUENCES

The outstanding fact emerging from studies of adolescent behavior
and personality is the extent of home influences. The home provides not
only for the physical needs of the growing individual but also for such
psychological needs as affection, security, and belongingness; parents furnish the growing individual with models of behavior.

Importance of early home influences. The home's influence is greatest during the preschool years. Frequently, habits are formed in later
years that may not seem to be of the same lineage as habits acquired
earlier; but the influence of the latter must not be underestimated. Habits
are built upon habits, and the earlier habits are likely to give something
of their form to the later. This tendency is well illustrated by Rosenheim's descriptive analysis of a 13-year-old boy who lacked parental affection during the early years of his life; as a result, he had never learned to
show affection for others, and was unable to get along with other boys
and girls of his age.[1] Remedial treatment and guidance produced some
good results; in spite of this, however, the influence of the early home
environment remained constant and more or less pervasive. This influence
was especially noticeable in the boy's lack of social responsiveness, and
thus in his failure to establish desirable social relations with others; he
also lacked steadfastness to ideals and good behavior standards. Satisfac-

266

tory adjustments are related less to the education of the parents, the size of the family, or the socio-economic level than to the extent to which basic human needs for affection, security, status, and belongingness are satisfied.

Emotional climate. Among the ingredients of a favorable emotional climate is a family in which each member is accepted as a unique personality. Such a family is happy. In such a home parents reflect their own feelings of adequacy, with neither assuming a dominant role. This is readily transmitted to the growing child.

A study reported by Peterson involving data from 616 adolescent girls indicated that mother-daughter relations were not adversely affected by the mother's employment.[2] This is in harmony with results obtained by Roy relative to the ill-effects of the employment of mothers on adolescent behavior. He presents the following conclusions from his study:

> 1. The children of employed mothers seem to do more household chores than the children of nonemployed mothers. . . .
> 2. The employment of the mother does not seem to have any adverse effect on the social activities of the children. . . .
> 3. The employment of the mother does not generally lower the academic performance or aspirations of the children. . . .
> 4. The general fear that delinquency would increase due to the employment of the mother was not borne out. . . .[3]

It appears, therefore, that it is the nature of the relationship rather than the amount of time spent together that is most important.

There is evidence from a number of studies that when a high degree of parental role differentiation exists in middle-class American society, it contributes to emotional and social maladjustments among children and adolescents.[4] However, distinct parental role differentiation is more characteristic of the lower class than of the middle class. This may account in part for the greater number of maladjustments among girls from lower-class homes where sex-role differentiation on the part of parents is greatest.

A favorable emotional climate is one in which the needs of adolescents are met. This does not mean that the adolescent is able to have everything he wants, rather the adolescent's basic physiological needs are met. In addition he is able to be himself without suffering undesirable results. He can at times revert to a more childlike nature or can rise to the level of the adult.

There is evidence from a study reported by Bartlett and Horrocks that adolescents from homes where one parent is deceased tend to receive less recognition and affection from adults.[5] Thus, they tend to seek attention from the opposite sex in order to compensate for this condition. This frequently presents a problem and a hazard to the adolescent, particularly the adolescent girl.

The home as a transmitter of attitudes and values. It was pointed out in Chapters 8 and 9 that attitudes and values are soaked up from the milieu in which one has grown and learned. This is rather clearly shown in a study by Berdie in which the values of parents whose children planned to go to college were compared with those of parents whose children did not plan to go.[6] Although both groups recognized the financial rewards of a college education, the former emphasized a love of learning and the importance of college education for one's personal development, whereas the latter did not. The high school youth who develops a strong desire for a college education in the face of no encouragement from his parents is an exception rather than the rule.

Table 13-1

COMPARISON OF BRIGHT HIGH-ACHIEVING WITH BRIGHT UNDER-ACHIEVING HIGH SCHOOL BOYS ON THE "FAMILY RELATIONS SCALES"
(Morrow and Wilson)

	Per cent above median		
Scale title	*High* (N-48)	*Low* (N-48)	*p*
Family Sharing of Recreation	69	44	.02
Family Sharing of Confidence and Ideas	63	35	.01
Family Sharing in Making Decisions	60	44	ns
Parental Approval	73	33	.001
Parental Affection	60	42	ns
Parental Trust	60	25	.001
Parental Approval of Peer Activities	71	42	.01
Student Acceptance of Parental Standards	52	25	.01
Student Affection and Respect toward Parents	58	44	ns
Lack of Parental Overrestrictiveness	56	29	.01
Lack of Parental Severity of Discipline	69	42	.01
Lack of Parental Overprotection	52	56	ns
Lack of Parental Over-insistence on Achievement	63	46	ns
Parental Encouragement of Achievement	60	40	.05
Harmony of Parents (N-40)	63	48	ns
Regularity of Home Routine	52	46	ns
Over-all Family Morale	67	33	.001

Middle-class boys and girls may conform to school expectations because of the consistent reinforcement of middle-class standards and goals by all the character-building agencies with which they come in contact—their homes, their play groups, their schools, and their churches. Many of the values that are important in maintaining the position of their families in society are the values which the school stresses: higher education, the adherence to the "social amenities," leadership, and responsibility in dealing with others.

The few studies of the relation between family life and achievement in high school have indicated a positive relationship between student achievement and happy home life. A study reported by Morrow and Wilson compared the family relations of bright high-achieving and under-achieving high school boys.[7] Several types of information about family relations were obtained from the students through questionnaires. The students' family relations were also evaluated by 16 self-report *Family Relations Scales*. The results are presented in Table 13-1. High-achievers more often than under-achievers described their families as sharing recreation, ideas, confidence, and in making decisions. They also described their families as approving, trusting, affectionate, encouraging but not pressuring in achievement, and not overly severe in discipline. The over-all family morale was considerably higher for the high-achievers. The results supported the hypothesis that good family morale fosters academic achievement among bright high school boys by fostering positive attitudes toward teachers and toward school and interest in intellectual activities.

Influence of siblings. Whether or not the older member of the family is a boy or girl will influence the personal-social development of the younger child. For example, Koch suggests that a boy with a much older sister tends to be more dependent and withdrawn than a boy with a much older brother.[8] In the study by Koch, children with brothers were rated as more competitive, ambitious, and enthusiastic than were children with sisters. Koch concludes:

> The interaction of the three variables, child's sex, ordinal position, and sibling's sex was significant in the case of the traits, leadership and exhibitionism, and near significant at the five per cent level in the case of jealousy. The first born in opposite sex pairs were rated higher in jealousy, exhibitionism, and leadership than were those in same-sex pairs, while among second-born the differences were usually in the opposite direction, though less marked. The differences between boys with a younger sister and boys with an older sister were conspicuous. The former tended to be the more jealous, exhibitionistic, and inclined to lead. Boys with a younger sister also showed more jealousy, exhibitionism, and leadership than did girls with a younger sister or boys with a younger brother.[9]

Also boys with only sisters are somewhat more feminine in their preferences and activities than are boys with only brothers or with both brothers and sisters.[10]

PATTERNS OF PARENT BEHAVIOR

Studies of different families show a wide variation of parental behavior patterns in a given community. These behavior patterns reflect first of all the parental behavior patterns which the present-day parents experienced as children and adolescents. The attitudes and behavior patterns of parents toward a child reflect not only their beliefs and under-standings about children but also their satisfactions, frustrations, and feelings. Their ideas and beliefs combined with their emotional expres-sions produce a wide variety of parental behavior which may be observed in the interaction of parents and children. In one study the *Fels Parent Behavior Scales* were used to secure ratings of parent behavior.[11] These ratings were subjected to careful statistical treatment and clusters of re-lated variables were obtained from a table of intercorrelations. In many cases these syndromes were combined into a single larger syndrome. The three central syndromes noted from this statistical treatment were labeled, *Democracy in the Home, Acceptance of the Child,* and *Indulgence.* Other syndromes of less importance noted were *Severity, Nagging, Intellectual-ity, Hustling,* and *Personal Adjustment.* Eight types, based upon combina-tions of these three main variables, were noted and described. These are:

Actively rejectant	Acceptant indulgent
Nonchalant rejectant	Acceptant-casually indulgent
Casually autocratic	Acceptant-indulgent-democratic
Casually indulgent	Acceptant democratic

Rejectant patterns. Nonchalant or casual rejection may result from the busy life of the parents. Active rejection may result from psychologi-cal disturbances, as was the case of the McKane home:

Mrs. McKane is fundamentally a selfish, egocentric woman who evaluates events and people in terms of the extent to which they contribute to her own satisfaction. She takes child bearing and rearing as a matter of course but is fundamentally irritated by children. When her child Betty was 6 months old she remarked: "I hate to sit and hold her . . . I don't care to hold babies."

For Mrs. McKane the model child is the quiet, unobtrusive one. She im-poses her will upon Betty, demanding that she develop rigid standards of be-havior in terms of her liking. This strictness and harshness in punishment serves to keep down immediate annoyances and conflicts from Betty. She ap-pears to go out of her way to be frustrating and caustic to Betty. If Betty starts out the door, she says: "I suppose that you will leave the screen door open." If Betty is eating ice cream, she says: "I suppose that you will spill that down the front of your dress." Her behavior indicates clearly an active resentment and hostility toward the child.

Not only is Mrs. McKane severe and hostile toward the child, she is also inconsistent. An act that will bring forth severe punishment on one occasion may go unnoticed the next day, depending largely upon Mrs. McKane's mood. Mrs. McKane's own peace of mind sometimes drives her to protect her chil-dren against possible outside harm. This is also evidence of her selfish nature. She dominates her husband through threats of taking her children and leav-ing him.

After Betty reached 6 years of age Mrs. McKane's earlier inconsistent treat-ment seemed to become more one of continued coldness and indifference. Dis-like alternated with heated conflict. From this time on the mother is rated as extremely rejecting and hostile toward the child. Betty's reaction to this has been to withdraw and stubbornly resist, in a passive manner, adult authority. At school her superficially docile nature cannot be criticized, but in a situation requiring action or a response she retreats into an almost inaudible reply, "I don't know." Her teachers fail to understand her and are unable to break through her withdrawal, her passive resistive nature.[12]

Casual types of parent behavior. There are parents whose behavior would be classified as neither rejectant nor acceptant. Such parents may be inconsistent in that they accept the child at one time and reject him at a later period. There are also parents of the casual type who tend to be consistently mild and casual in their emotional relationship with the child. Two general types of casual behavior are listed: (1) casually autocratic, and (2) casually indulgent.

The picture of the casually autocratic pattern is different from that of the common concept of the autocratic home in that the parents are not so cold and efficiently autocratic. However, a strict autocratic home restrains a warm relationship between parents and children. The parents' authority is considered superior to that of the child at all times and in all areas. However, the casually autocratic parent does not insist upon strict conformity at all times. In comparison with the democratic home, these homes are more chaotic, maladjusted, restrictive, inactive, obtuse, and hostile. These restrictive influences tend to constrict the intellectual growth of the children and thus inhibit the development of such characteristics as originality, initiative, curiosity, and resourcefulness.

There is no strong persistent motivation that determines the behavior of the casually indulgent. Such parents are indulgent with the children of the household because they usually find it the easiest way. Such a pattern is described by Baldwin and others in the case of the Roberts household:

> Mrs. Roberts has no explicit philosophy of child care to guide her in her treatment of Evelyn, beyond a statement made to one visitor that her mother had always restricted her and that she intended to be a friend to her children. The Roberts family makes no attempt to protect Evelyn from all the difficulties of her environment, nor does it go out of the way to gratify all of her wishes and desires but merely indulges her at its own convenience. Their relationship with each other is wholesome and psychologically healthy; in relation to Evelyn they are inclined to let matters run their course. If Evelyn ignores the request of her mother to put away her clothes nothing further is said or done. They will permit Evelyn to do things that they do not approve of, provided they feel that Evelyn is getting enjoyment from the act. Outside the home Evelyn is somewhat timid and at the same time outstandingly aggressive. These are her methods of establishing contact with children. This preschool behavior has continued into the grade school, and makes her relationship with other children precarious. It will seriously complicate her school adjustments and will be felt more keenly in her social adjustments as she progresses into the preadolescent and adolescent years, when peer approval becomes increasingly important.[13]

Acceptant patterns. Acceptant homes have been classified into three types: (1) those which fit the indulgent syndrome but do not fit the democratic, called *indulgent* homes; (2) those which fit the democratic syndrome but not the indulgent, called *democratic* homes; and (3) those which fit both the indulgent and democratic syndromes, called *democratic-indulgent*. The general picture of the democratic home is one of good adjustment without undue attention to specific members of the family. The policy is one of freedom in which the parents respect the individuality of each other and of the children of the family. Emotionally the democratic parents tend to be objective, but above the average in affection and rapport. While rapport is generally good in the indulgent home, child-centeredness is ever present. The democratic-indulgent home combines the features of these two groups. It appears to strike a mean between a cold objective attitude and indulgence. It should be emphasized, however, that these are not clearly divisible types. All combinations and degrees of these features are to be found among acceptant homes.

The Jameson home, described by Baldwin and others, falls in the acceptant-democratic group, but is referred to as a scientific-democratic home, since the parents deal with problems around the home in a cold scientific manner and at the same time apply the philosophy of human relations involving the different members of the family in planning and policy making. The workings of democracy are carefully adapted to the children's ages and capacities:

Dale, at the age of 5, was voicing his opinion about the menu, his play life, and other matters relating to his daily schedule of activities. His choices were not subjected to subtle adult coercion, although it was openly explained to him that there were certain decisions that must be made by adults. The policy of directness was part of the technique of dealing frankly and honestly with particular problems. The "family council" method has been adopted to handle Dale's school-age adjustments in a democratic manner. Mrs. Jameson appears scientifically incapable of expressing warmth and affection toward Dale. Even when he was scratched by a cat at the age of 3 years, he received no special attention or sympathy from his mother. Companionability on the intellectual level characterizes the parent-child relations, rather than caresses and a feeling of warmth.

Mrs. Jameson has been very anxious for Dale to excel other children of the neighborhood; therefore her treatment of him has been partially motivated by this desire. He is furnished with every opportunity for experimentation, exploration, and the use of insight. As a small child he was urged to look for incongruities, to make criticisms, and to ask questions about things he did not understand. In his speech and language development he is quite precocious. The richness of his imagination and the originality of his play made him stand head and shoulders above the other children of his grade school group. Caught in the fervor of war activities, he was at an early age able to identify all the U.S. plane models.

Even more striking than his precocity has been his violent, uninhibited aggressiveness toward society. He seems to fear no one. He seeks no quarter and gives none. He will kick, strike, and bite his teachers, his relatives, and even innocent bystanders with great ferocity. This need for defiance and aggressiveness is born probably of his insecurity and lack of emotional warmth with his mother and fostered by the completely premissive atmosphere of the Jameson home. His entrance into school and contacts with schoolmates has brought about an improvement in his behavior. The desire for social approval which becomes even greater as he grows into adolescence may bring about a modification of his behavior toward a more realistic balance of conformity and freedom.[14]

Family authority patterns. The authoritative pattern found in the home refers to the controlling power relative to the activities of the family.[15] This control may be exercised in a number of ways; although, since there are only two parents, there can be only three general divisions of parental control. Authority may be in the hands of the mother, the father, or may be divided in some manner between the two. In the investigation by Ingersoll, based on an intensive study of 37 homes, the major types listed in Table 13-2 were observed. A brief description of these types should be useful in arriving at a clearer understanding of parental roles and authority patterns.[16]

In the mother-controlled family the husband is passive, being somewhat indifferent to his wife and leaving the problems of child rearing to her. He appears to prefer men's companionship to that of his wife and children. On the other hand, the wife has a tendency to disparage marriage in general and men in particular. Sometimes the affectional attachments in the home are split, the father favoring some children and the mother

Table 13-2

TYPES OF AUTHORITY PATTERNS

(*After Ingersoll*)

Mother-controlled—autocratic pattern of authority
Mother-led—democratic pattern of authority
Balanced control:
    Equalitarian—democratic pattern of authority
    Equalitarian—indulgent pattern of authority
    Equalitarian—laissez-faire pattern of authority
    Equalitarian—conflicting pattern of authority
Father-controlled—autocratic pattern of authority
Father-controlled—pseudo-autocratic pattern of authority
Father-led—democratic pattern of authority

---

others. Decisions regarding family policy are jointly made with the mother assuming the lead. There is warmth and affection in the family, with the children usually showing the greatest attachment to the mother, who is generally regarded as the stronger personality. The parents prepare the children jointly for increased participation in planning and policy-making relative to matters of the home.

In an equalitarian control pattern, the parents have worked out a unified system of authority based on a common philosophy of family life. This philosophy is most frequently found among college-educated parents, although it may be found in varying degrees among all groups. Authority over the various spheres of home and family life in the equalitarian family, for the most part, is jointly shared except in certain areas where one partner is felt to be more capable than the other. The equalitarian-democratic pattern of authority guides children from early dependency to a place of responsibility and individuality in the family group. The children are encouraged to become self-reliant and independent of parents as they approach adulthood and grow in independence and ability to make decisions regarding themselves. The equalitarian pattern of authority may take on other forms such as indulgence toward children, neglect of children, or inconsistent behavior.

In the father-led family the pattern of authority is democratic. Family policy is apparently unified with the husband's leadership being more frequently followed. The wife manages the home and rearing of children to conform to joint policy and in line with the husband's expectations. There is an affectional relation in the family with the wife apparently more emotionally secure than the huband. There are many variations in the father-led pattern of authority, with the father-controlled being toward the extreme, and being of an autocratic nature. The father-dominated home in its extremity is characterized by a severe type of husband-father control. The husband expects to be master of the household. He sets the family policy and makes the major plans and decisions. Conflicts between husband and wife are often unresolved, since the husband insists on having his way. As a parent, this husband is autocratic, erratic, and unpredictable.

The laissez-faire families are characterized by a father who delegates the major tasks of rearing the children to the mother. The mother, on the other hand, sets up fairly definite standards for child behavior but neither she nor the father enforces their rules and regulations. The children do almost as they please and as a result show little respect or consideration for their parents. Familism in these homes is at a minimum and affection is usually casual. Everyone goes his own way. Neither husband nor wife goes out of his way to adjust to the other's needs, but evidently take each other's differences for granted.

Influence of the family pattern. Data bearing on the relationships of parental authority patterns and personality adjustments were gathered from 4310 high school seniors of the State of Washington.[17] A questionnaire including a check list of 250 problems was used for gathering the data. The problems were grouped into seven areas of adjustment and comparisons were made between the number of problems checked by boys and girls from democratic, intermediate, and authoritarian pattern homes. The problem areas included family, personal, social, boy-girl relations, school, vocational, and morals and religion. In all seven areas, the young people from the authoritarian homes checked the most problems, although the differences were greater in some areas than in others.

Table 13-3

PERCENTAGE OF TEEN-AGERS LIVING IN DEMOCRATIC, INTERMEDIATE, AND AUTHORITARIAN FAMILIES CHECKING FAMILY PROBLEMS LISTED
(*After Landis and Stone*)

Problem	Sex	Family Administrative Pattern		
		Democratic	Intermediate	Authoritarian
Quarreling in the family	Boys	9.9	11.8	27.8
	Girls	12.7	16.2	37.0
Getting to use the car	Boys	22.3	25.0	34.8
	Girls	11.7	14.3	11.4
Getting along with my parents	Boys	5.7	10.6	17.2
	Girls	8.4	10.8	24.2
Getting Mother to understand my problems	Boys	4.2	5.7	10.6
	Girls	6.5	12.1	26.3
Getting Dad to understand my problems	Boys	10.4	10.9	17.7
	Girls	12.5	16.0	20.6
I have to work to buy things	Boys	12.0	21.6	27.0
	Girls	3.2	11.3	18.8
Having no regular allowance	Boys	5.7	8.2	16.9
	Girls	8.6	12.6	21.2
Don't have much spending money	Boys	6.8	7.9	11.4
	Girls	4.7	7.1	15.0
Wish I had my own room	Boys	6.2	6.0	11.4
	Girls	11.4	12.2	15.6
Treated like a child at home	Boys	4.8	6.1	11.6
	Girls	5.0	7.2	14.4
Folks ridicule my ideas	Boys	3.1	4.5	9.3
	Girls	2.2	3.1	14.3
Can't bring friends to my home	Boys	2.3	3.5	8.3
	Girls	3.1	4.9	13.3

⌐The two problems that showed the greatest difference were "quarreling in the family," and "getting along with my parents." The "desire to leave home" was more pressing among both boys and girls from authoritarian homes than from democratic and intermediate homes. The sex differences, shown in Table 13-3, are interesting. These problems were significantly greater among girls from authoritarian homes, especially from the city, than among any other group. This no doubt stems from the greater protection the authoritarian home in the city attempts to give the girl. An indication of the restriction on the social life of boys and girls from rural areas is shown by the per cent checking the problem "not much chance to do what others do." This is shown in Table 13-4. Farm boys and girls from democratic homes did not mention this as often as did city boys and girls from authoritarian homes.

The results of this study, supported by findings from related studies, suggest that adolescents in democratic homes have fewer adjustment problems than those in authoritarian homes. They enjoy a closer relationship with their parents and experience fewer frustrations. Furthermore, boys and girls from democratic families have a happier condition for social growth and development through guidance in social participation rather than restriction and prohibition. Perhaps the greatest superiority of the democratic home over the autocratic is that it substitutes cooperation for commands and thus enhances the developing ego and growth toward independence of the adolescent.

Table 13-4

PERCENTAGE OF TEEN-AGERS CHECKING PROBLEM: "NOT MUCH CHANCE TO DO WHAT OTHERS DO" (SOCIALLY) *(After Landis and Stone)*

Family administrative pattern	Farm	Town	City	Total
		(Boys)		
Democratic	5.2	3.6	3.1	3.8
Intermediate	5.4	5.5	3.4	4.5
Authoritarian	14.2	7.4	5.5	8.6
		(Girls)		
Democratic	3.2	5.2	2.3	3.3
Intermediate	7.6	3.9	4.2	4.9
Authoritarian	12.9	9.9	6.9	9.2

Family pattern and adolescent personality structure. A study by Peck was designed to measure the relationship between important elements in personality structure and certain characteristics of family emotional and control patterns. Intercorrelations were obtained between selected characteristics of the adolescents' personality structure and family ratings. Peck concluded:

> 1. Ego strength occurred in association with a family life which was characterized by stable consistency and warm, mutual trust and approval between the parents and between parents and child.
>
> 2. Superego strength was partially related to ego strength, but was chiefly related to the regularity and consistency of family life. It was *not* systematically related to severely autocratic rearing; or, at least, there appeared to be two different kinds of superego, produced in two different ways: (1) a strong, rigid, compartmentalized superego created by sternly autocratic rearing; and (b) a strong superego which was closely knit with ego functions, open to rational appraisal, and created by consistent, democratic, nonsevere rearing in a trustful, approving family. This interpretation rests, of course, on the qualitative case studies.
>
> 3. Generalized friendliness and spontaneity appear to be allied and to be associated with a lenient, democratic family atmosphere. Probably because the family background may or may not be allied with ego strength and superego strength.
>
> 4. The hostility-guilt complex might reasonably be considered a hostile but dependent unresolved Oedipal complex. It tends to occur in association with a severely autocratic, untrusting, and disapproving family.[18]

PARENT-ADOLESCENT ADJUSTMENT

As the adolescent assumes more independence and more authority over his own life he frequently runs into conflicts with his parents. The boundaries of his freedoms are not clearly defined. Parents and teen-agers look at life and adolescent behavior with different perspectives; problems that are extremely important to adolescents are unimportant to parents. The two generations are concerned with different problems. Parents' emotional stress caused by their adolescent children is real. Levy and Monroe state:

> Their children, parents complain, have suddenly become impossible. Affectionate, dutiful daughters treat their homes like a hotel. They sleep there and occasionally "grab a meal," but their real life is lived elsewhere. They fly into a fury when mother mildly suggests helping with the dishes. Johnny's conversation is almost exclusively of the "gimme" variety.[19]

The adolescent views his parents. The adolescent strives for increased independence, primarily because its achievement means he has reached adulthood—grown-up, self-sufficient, and able to chart the world of his own. Any blocking of this goal results in frustration with accompanying hostility toward those who blocked it. It is at this point that he frequently comes into conflict with his parents. This was noted by Landis in his study of 4310 high school seniors by means of a problem check list.[20] The number of problems checked varied with the type of home controlled, those from authoritarian homes checking the greatest number of problems. The results are shown in Table 13-5. In all experience areas, the child from the authoritarian home checked the most problems with the girls tending to check more problems than boys.

The adolescent's view of his parents is closely related to the control pattern of the parents. He becomes critical and sometimes actually hostile toward them when his prestige with peers or personal esteem is challenged. Wider contacts with peers and adults enable him to make comparisons. The results frequently cause him to lose confidence in his parents, since he had earlier conceived of his parents as ideal. Sometimes the child from

Table 13-5

SUMMARY OF AREAS IN WHICH PROBLEMS WERE CHECKED AND THE NUMBER OF PROBLEMS CHECKED BY TYPE OF HOME (*Landis*)

| Problem Areas | Sex | Number checked by young people by family type | | |
		Demo-cratic	Inter-mediate	Authori-tarian
Personal	Boys	3.5	3.6	4.4
(33 in check list)	Girls	4.2	4.5	5.1
Family	Boys	2.9	3.3	5.1
(63 in check list)	Girls	3.2	3.9	6.5
Social	Boys	1.8	1.9	2.5
(30 in check list)	Girls	1.9	2.4	2.7
Boy-girl relations	Boys	2.0	2.2	2.7
(34 in check list)	Girls	2.2	2.6	3.0
School	Boys	2.2	2.4	3.0
(30 in check list)	Girls	2.2	2.5	3.0
Vocational	Boys	2.9	2.9	3.4
(30 in check list)	Girls	2.6	3.1	3.2
Morals, religion	Boys	2.2	2.4	2.5
(30 in check list)	Girls	2.4	2.9	3.0

the lower culture is actually ashamed of his parents. Such was the case of Celia.

One day while walking home from school a very poorly dressed man stopped his well-worn automobile and called to her. Celia tried to ignore him, but he was insistent. So, she got in the automobile with him and he drove away. The next day some of her friends asked her who the man was with whom she had ridden away on the previous day. She told them that he was an old man who worked for them, doing odd jobs on certain occasions. Actually the man was Celia's father.

The adolescent who is insecure with his peers is more likely to be ashamed of any shortcomings or unfavorable home conditions than the one who is secure. This frequently accounts for the critical attitude of some adolescents toward their parents. Many adolescents take an ambivalent attitude toward their parents, seeing them as affectionate dictators.

Attitudes toward parents. In one study involving 730 fifth-grade students, boys reported less satisfactory relations with parents than girls.[21] Also, children saw their mothers in a more favorable manner than their fathers. Several factors may account for the latter. First, the mother usually spends more time with the children, since the father is often away from home at work. However, this may change to some degree as more mothers are employed. The father's interest in his work and civic affairs is often a barrier to good father-son relations. Fathers often become so engrossed in their professional or business activities that they neglect their family. The son is then denied the male image needed during the growing years. The results of such a relationship are frequently disastrous. Case studies of delinquents from the middle-class home show that in most cases these boys lacked a close association with their father. Neglect by the father often leads girls to leave home or to marry early.

Parent standards versus peer standards. The successes and failures of adolescents are judged largely by teen standards rather than by those of parents, teachers, or other adult leaders. This means that the parent of today has only 12 to 14 years in which to give the child the judgment necessary for adult responsibilities. Those who fail to acquire this during the period of childhood and early adolescence are at the mercy of their peers. Many adolescents are lost in the freedom of the teen-age world and are unable to cope with its demands for self-sufficiency. The case of Lydia is an example of an individual overprotected in early life and suddenly thrown into a life for which she was unprepared:

> Lydia was a bright, attractive girl with a keen desire for acceptance and social approval, but at the age of 15 she was too shy and distrustful of herself to make a place for herself with boys and girls of her age.
> Having lost her mother at the age of 6, she was brought up by her father and an elderly grandmother. The father did not care to have people around, and the grandmother was made very nervous by the normal activity of children.
> In such an environment Lydia had little opportunity for learning to get along with age-mates. Furthermore, she had no opportunity for developing the self-confidence necessary to enable her to play a significant role with those she wanted as friends. Her age-mates failed to understand her and made little effort to become better acquainted with her. It was little wonder that she warmly accepted any attention offered her. This condition led to an affair with an aggressive and irresponsible high school boy of 17.

Identification with parents. Although modern technology has produced a way of living where fathers often fail to share in home responsibilities and social contacts with their children, the father's part in the character development of adolescents is important. However, the majority of boys at some time in their lives identify themselves with their father and those who have done so to a great extent tend to adjust to peer groups more satisfactorily than those who have never been close to their fathers. The importance of the father-figure is well illustrated in an adolescent girl's diary: "My fifteenth birthday was a wonderful experience to me. My mother was staying with her sick sister. So, my father took me out to dinner at a swell place where they had a delightful floor show." The father, however, failed to see the importance of the experience. To his friends at the office he stated: "What a night I had last night. My wife was away, so I had to try and entertain that restless adolescent daughter of mine on her fifteenth birthday."

According to psychoanalytical theory, the identification process for girls is more complex than for boys. The boy's task is that of accepting the male role which is fairly well defined, while the girl may select or be compelled to assume one or more of several possible roles. The preschool girl frequently identifies closely with the father, especially if he is an active participant in home life. Fathers are less demanding of their preschool daughters than of their preschool sons. Thus, the father frequently gives the daughter considerable affection and protection, even during the preschool period.

It seems that it is more important for adolescent boys to identify with their father than for girls to identify with their mother. Working with fifth through eighth grades in an upper-middle-class school Susan Gray[22] found that there was no real difference in the adjustment of girls with high or low mother identification. The reason for this lies perhaps in the masculine prestige factor in Western cultures; the feminine role of the mother lacks this prestige factor. Furthermore, the feminine role is not so clearly defined—hence mothers may reject the role they play in our culture and provide roles that are inconsistent and unclear for their daughters.

Gilmore[23] found that nonachievers had poor relations with both father and mother, and were more dependent and passive. The achieving student had a much happier relationship with his father, a closer identification with his mother, and a marked quality of independence.

Sources of conflict. The results of a study reported by Landis show that girls more frequently disagree with their parents than boys, except about school work.[24] The summary of proportions of high school seniors checking 11 common areas of "frequent disagreement" is presented in Table 13-6. Authoritarian parents are much more often in disagreement with their children and adolescents over common issues that arise in the family than democratic parents.

One of the most interesting and far-reaching studies dealing with adolescent conflicts is that conducted by Block.[25] She found that the conflicts adolescents have with their parents (in her study, mothers) were in

Table 13-6

SUMMARY OF PROPORTIONS OF YOUNG PEOPLE CHECKING 11 COMMON AREAS OF "FREQUENT DISAGREEMENT" WITH PARENTS

(*Landis*)

Areas of disagreement	Sex	Percentage of "frequent disagreement" with parents by family administrative pattern:		
		Democratic	Intermediate	Authoritarian
My spending money	Boys	20.2	28.8	39.4
	Girls	16.0	22.7	38.6
My friends	Boys	3.6	9.4	11.1
	Girls	3.9	10.4	23.1
My choice of clothes	Boys	6.6	9.2	11.9
	Girls	5.4	9.3	14.3
My attitude toward my parents	Boys	8.9	13.2	24.7
	Girls	11.5	15.8	34.1
My outside activities	Boys	13.8	22.7	27.8
	Girls	13.8	19.5	28.5
My school work	Boys	21.6	28.4	31.8
	Girls	8.0	12.7	15.6
My future plans	Boys	13.5	17.5	20.2
	Girls	12.1	19.5	25.5
My share of the work around the house	Boys	26.2	24.7	40.4
	Girls	27.4	27.6	40.3
My social life	Boys	8.2	15.8	22.7
	Girls	9.1	12.8	27.2

many cases the basis for most of the disturbances in their lives. Over a period of five years, 528 junior and senior high school boys and girls were interviewed. By means of a questionnaire, an index of the conflicts that high school students are facing was obtained. A list of 50 problems indicated by the students was then studied. The problems most frequently encountered and the percentage of boys and girls reporting them are presented in Tables 13-7 and 13-8.[26]

Most conflicts were due to differences in opinion over personal appearances, habits, and manners. Vocational, social, recreational, and educational choices also caused some contention. The 8 items most frequently checked by the adolescent boys also appeared among the first 20 checked by girls, indicating that many problems were common to boys and girls. There were, however, some problems peculiar to each sex. A careful study of the items listed in Tables 13-7 and 13-8 will show the nature of such problems. The largest percentage of conflicts occurred in seventh-grade girls and in eighth-grade boys.

Table 13-7

THE TWENTY ITEMS MOST FREQUENTLY CHECKED BY ADOLESCENT BOYS THAT WERE SERIOUSLY DISTURBING FACTORS IN THEIR RELATIONSHIPS WITH THEIR MOTHERS

(After Block)

Won't let me use the car	85.7%
Insists that I eat foods which I dislike but which are good for me	82.4
Scolds me if my school marks are not as high as other people's	82.4
Insists that I tell her exactly what I spend my money for	80.0
Pesters me about my table manners	74.8
Pesters me about my personal manners and habits	68.5
Holds my sister or brother up as a model for me	66.9
Objects to my going automobile riding at night with boys	65.7
Won't let me follow a vocation in which I am interested	64.5
Complains about my hands or neck or fingernails being dirty	55.7
Won't give me a regular allowance	54.1
Teases me about my girl friends	51.3
Brags about me to other people	50.1
Embarrasses me by telling my friends what a good son I am	49.8
Objects to my going automobile riding during the day with boys	49.0
Makes a huge fuss over friends of mine whom she likes	34.3
Talks baby talk to me	33.4
Won't let me take subjects I want in school	32.9
Insists that I be a goody-goody	32.2

When parents are cognizant of the sources of such conditions, they are in a better position to substitute guidance and understanding for conflict and contention. Younger adolescents, especially, have difficulty in seeing any reason for many of the protective conventions of society. To insist upon obedience merely for the sake of obedience to some authority will have no value in the development of moral courage, but will, on the other hand, invite conflict and deception. As Butterfield points out:

> When adolescents are reaching out to establish and enlarge their prestige with boy and girl friends they are likely to resent anything which restricts their efforts to win favor with such persons. The friendships of youth are precious and when apparently senseless social customs threaten to limit their enjoyment, youth readily adopts a defiant attitude.[26]

Conflicts regarding the proper night hours appear to be among the most common sources of friction between parents and adolescents. The Lynds report that 45 per cent of 348 boys in the upper grades of the high school and 43 per cent of 382 girls who replied to their questionnaire argued with their parents over late hours.[27] The cause is usually the difference between the standards of the parents and the standards of the children's social group. Faced with this difficulty, parents all too often resort to scolding and complaining; they fail to give plausible reasons why they want their children to come in earlier, and neglect to set up incentives for obedience or to provide a workable plan whereby the children may be able to satisfy their needs for social life and still come in at a more reasonable hour at night. Most young people are pleased to cooperate when they realize that a plan proposed is a fair one and for their own best interests.

Liccione's investigation of adolescent girls' changing family relationships emphasized the age trends in adolescent, daughter-parent relationships.[28] Fathers demand more of their sons than of their daughters. In contrast, more daily care is taken of daughters. Boys are taught from a relatively early age to be independent, whereas girls are frequently coddled.

The projective method was used by Liccione in studying parent-daughter relationships. He showed 12 *Thematic Apperception Test* cards to groups of 50 girls, aged 9, 11, 12, 15, and 17, then analyzed their stories to identify themes relating to parent-daughter relations. The results showed that the girls were more frequently at odds with their mothers than with their fathers. This may be accounted for by the greater number of contacts that the mother has with the daughter and by the widespread practice, especially among middle-class families, of leaving the daughter's disciplining and counseling to the mother. The largest amount of tension in the mother-daughter relationship existed at age 15. The

Table 13-8

THE TWENTY ITEMS MOST FREQUENTLY CHECKED BY ADOLESCENT GIRLS THAT
WERE SERIOUSLY DISTURBING FACTORS IN THEIR RELATIONSHIPS WITH THEIR
MOTHERS
(After Block)

Objects to my going automobile riding at night with boys	87.4%
Scolds me if my school marks are not as high as other people's	85.9
Insists that I eat foods which I dislike but which are good for me	83.8
Insists that I take my sister or brother wherever I go	82.3
Insists that I tell her exactly what I spend my money for	81.2
Spends most of her time at bridge parties, etc., and is rarely ever at home	78.0
Holds my sister or brother up as a model to me	75.8
Won't let me use the car	70.8
Pesters me about my personal manners and habits	70.0
Insists that I go with friends of her choice	69.7
Nags about any little thing	66.4
Objects to my going automobile riding during the day with boys	66.4
Teases me about my boy friends	65.7
Fusses because I use lipstick	64.6
Pesters me about my table manners	63.9
Worries about my physical health	58.8
Objects to my going to dances	58.8
Insists that I be a goody-goody	57.8
Won't let me take subjects I want in school	56.1
Refuses to let me buy the clothes I like	55.6

least amount of father-daughter tension was at age 13; the greatest at 17. This may be a result of the daughter's desire for independence and the father's reluctance to recognize her increasing self-reliance. A problem frequently encountered by early-maturing girls from middle-class homes is described by one postadolescent girl:

> All of my sisters and I developed sooner than the girls we were thrown with in our class at school. We were what is referred to as early maturers. We were very conscious of our new self and the garments we had to wear. We were, I think, more interested in dating than most of the other girls. We were allowed to date only on week-ends and then had to double date and be in by 11 o'clock unless it were a very special occasion. Such an occasion did not appear

often and it bothered us to have to be in at what we considered such an early hour.

Teen-ager's complaints. The first and foremost complaint of teen-agers is that parents are dictatorial. They sometimes cut off discussions with "I don't want to hear any more about that," or appeal to children's sympathy by saying, "You are driving me mad," or "You are driving me to my grave." Often, parents blindly make rules and decisions. To stop a romance, they will punish, deny permission for a normal request, or inflict new-made rules. Further discussion is not permitted; neither is there an appeal from the ruling.

Havemann asked teen-agers from various parts of the country about their complaints against parents.[29] The most common complaints follow:

1. Adults refuse to recognize that teen-agers are human beings with feelings, dignity and pride of their own.

2. Teen-agers claim that parents often fail to observe even the most elementary rules of courtesy. For example, they often think nothing of scolding their children in front of friends.

3. "Sometimes parents act as if you weren't even alive." One girl said, "You'll be sitting right there in a roomful of company and your parents will start talking about you." "You're supposed to sit there as if you were a little machine or something."

4. Parents also seem to have a special knack for embarrassing teen-agers in front of their dates.

5. Parents are completely contemptuous of their property rights. They assume that no teen-ager really can own anything, that adults are the sole owners of everything in the family, the supreme givers who can also take away.

6. Even the best parents have a tendency to meddle far too much in the romances of their children.

7. On social matters, too many mothers and fathers consider it a personal reflection if their sons and daughters are not good mixers.

8. Overambitious fathers and mothers expect too much of their children. Often the complaint centers around the report card.

9. Parents have a way of making their decisions and issuing their edicts without really thinking about the effect on their sensitive youngsters.

10. Many parents insist that their children are going to grow up by their golden rules, regardless of what everybody else is doing.

11. Teen-agers often feel that privacy is denied them.

EMANCIPATION: GROWTH TOWARD MATURITY

The task of emancipation is far more difficult than that implied by the statement: "The child should increasingly become more independent as he grows toward maturity." Equipping and guiding the child is complicated by the following:

1. Parents' unwillingness to relinquish authority
2. The failure of parents to guide the child and adolescent in developing habits of responsibility

3. The existence of small families whereby much attention and attachment is centered on each child

4. The prolongation of economic dependence on the home

5. The attitudes of parents toward adolescent behavior and parental controls

6. Conflicting loyalties on the part of adolescents.[30]

Evaluating adolescent emancipation. We should be able to evaluate the extent to which emancipation has been accomplished in a given adolescent. Dimock has furnished a technique for estimating the degree of emancipation.[31] He first compiled a list of several hundred items of conduct and activities that were characteristic of dependence and independence. After the completion of the list, it was submitted to about one hundred judges—psychologists, educators, sociologists, and parents. These judges evaluated each item and the 120 most important ones were included in the final test. A sample of this E. F. P. Scale by which the degree of independence can be estimated is presented in Table 13-9.

Table 13-9

ILLUSTRATIVE ITEMS OF THE EMANCIPATION SCALE
(*After Dimock*)

	Boy's E. F. P. Scale		
Item	*What I do*	*What I want to do*	*What my parents want me to do*
Decide things for myself	Yes No ?	Yes No ?	Yes No ?
Do what my father or mother decides on every question	Yes No ?	Yes No ?	Yes No ?
Depend on my parents to buy all my things for me	Yes No ?	Yes No ?	Yes No ?
Spend my allowance as I choose	Yes No ?	Yes No ?	Yes No ?
Pick out and buy my own clothes	Yes No ?	Yes No ?	Yes No ?

From the scale, Dimock turned next to a study of the factors that condition emancipation. Chronological age was found relatively unimportant with a correlation of .14 between emancipation scores and age. Physical characteristics such as height and weight, on the other hand, were quite significant.

Emancipation is evidenced from an analysis of movie attendance of children. As the child grows older there is a decline of movie attendance with members of the family but an increased attendance with friends and others. The greater independence of the boys at all age levels is evident here.

If we employed Dimock's E. F. P. Scale to determine a boy's degree of emancipation and we found that he is still psychologically unweaned, what would be some characteristics of his behavior? First, he would constantly seek the advice and help of others simply because he cannot act or think independently. His mother has always been near to shield him from burdensome tasks and difficult decisions. Help in school and supervised study are both necessary for him to keep up with his classmates. He is incapable of following printed instruction without having someone there to explain each step. Again, if forced to leave home for a visit, he suffers nostalgia to the extent that he loses his appetite and is unable to sleep. Perhaps this lad profoundly desires to become independent but does not know how. As a shield for his attachment to his parents he indulges in dramatic overcompensations such as getting drunk or using profanity. These radical behavior patterns are his outlets to show his independence.

Looking into the future, we see the instability and unhappiness of an unweaned individual. He is not able to get along with the employer because he expects extra sympathy and "giving in" to his whims. Many a marriage has been wrecked owing to this same condition. The case may be that of an only child who constantly seeks the advice of an overanxious mother. It is not necessarily the mother who spoils the child. A case called to the attention of the writer illustrates this quite adequately.

> Jane, an orphan child brought up outside the orphanage, was cared for by an older sister. The older sister accepted full responsibility for Jane's clothes, education, and late love affairs. This was so complete that, even after marriage, Jane still consulted with her about things. Owing to varying circumstances, Jane finally came to make her home in an adjoining town near the older sister. She called her older sister almost daily over long-distance. Jane tried to see her at least each week. As a result of various social problems arising, she eventually found herself under the complete control of the older sister and finally wrecked her own home due to this complete *infantilism* accentuated by the ever-present dominance of the sister.

Principles of establishing independence. Learning to let go means, for the adolescent, the art of *relinquishment*. He is confronted with the task of throwing off childhood habits of blind obedience, dependence, and desire for protection. His emancipation from almost complete supervision to independence cannot and should not take place in too short a period. Rather, this should be a gradual process, begun during childhood by the parents and developed through carefully planned education for *initiative* and *responsibility*. With the adolescent caught between new urges and old habits, one cannot help but realize his deep need for sympathetic understanding and wise handling.

What, then, are some desirable procedures to follow in developing a child into a socially adequate and responsible youth? This is not a simple question; neither is there a single key that will answer it. That habits of independence should begin in childhood has already been suggested. With further development, responsibilities and privileges should be increased. The growing child should be given spending money to use as he wishes. He should be given greater freedom in the selection of his friends. The parents can function very effectively here through early training in ideals; for the present situation they can provide encouragement and an adequate setting for desirable friends whom the child has chosen. The family budget will in itself tend to put a limit on the amount of spending money the adolescent may have. Close supervision of how the money is spent tends to create tensions and frustrations which largely defeat the purpose of a weekly allowance. Robert Frost expressed this idea thus:

> Never ask of money spent
> Where the spender thinks it went.
> Nobody was ever meant
> To remember or invent
> What he did with every cent.[32]

The present-day adolescent needs more spending money than adolescents of a generation or more ago. A study reported by Esther Prevey showed that boys were provided with valuable experiences and training in the handling of money by their parents more often than girls were given such training.[33] This difference appeared in the various parental practices studied, but was most pronounced in connection with experiences in earning money and in being a party in the discussions of the family financial status, expenses, and plans involving money. Follow-up studies of later money habits of the subjects studied revealed a positive relationship between parental practices in training children in the use of money and the ability to handle their financial activities successfully in early adulthood.

Not only are parents prone to thrust their ideals and manners of life upon their children literally in the form of a blueprint, but they may lay out certain vocational plans and try to make their children conform to them. Sometimes such plans are conceived of in terms of the parents' own weaknesses, their rationalizations, or still some other element in their make-up that is without a logical basis. The vocational plans of the adolescent should be made by the adolescent himself, with the aid, of course, of suggestions and information that may be obtained from the wisdom and understanding of those with whom he is in contact. Parents may—and in many cases do—have their own notions about what studies should be pursued in school, and many almost force their child (a developing adolescent) to study particular school subjects without his understanding the reasons for such demands. It is in matters of such choices that parents can best serve as advisers; their advice becomes valid to the extent that emotions and feelings are controlled and reason and understanding, based upon fairness and truth, are used. Consider the following case:

> Morris, a boy of 15, managed to play truant from school for two full months before being discovered. His feat involved considerable lying, interception of mail, forging a report card, and general deception. Previously Morris had been an unusually satisfactory son and pupil. An only child, he was reared in a household consisting of parents, grandparents, uncles, and aunts. He was an affectionate, obedient child, thoughtful of the adults, and especially close to his parents, who were deeply attached to each other and to him. He had friends, was reasonably well liked by other boys throughout his childhood, but was more sober-minded than most of his companions, and of his own choice spent much of his free time reading or in recreational activity with his adult relatives. His parents had thought that they understood him thoroughly and had his full confidence. Actually, a small issue had, before the truancy, unconsciously become the symbol of the increasing dilemma of this boy and his parents.
>
> At about fourteen Morris had begun to be interested in the music of name bands, and soon afterward wanted to learn to play the trumpet. Though his parents recognized that he had musical talent and though there was money for instrument and lessons, they feared that Morris would want to form or join a band and that such a band would be the center of a whole section of his life that they could not share with him. Accordingly, they refused permission, rationalizing their refusal by claiming that he needed all his spare time for study. Later they weakened that argument to some extent by encouraging him to take a part-time job in the neighborhood drugstore.
>
> When Morris was just 15, he was thrown into a mild depression by the sudden death of a favorite uncle who had represented support of those individual interests that he was unable to affirm in the face of his parents' opposition. Nothing seemed worth doing, and when in the fall a school companion promised an excuse and suggested that they cut school to hear a famous band, he agreed. When, later, the excuse was not forthcoming, Morris continued to play truant, listening to records and attending theaters, all the while in such great conflict over what he was doing that it was eventually a relief to have his deception detected.[34]

In the choice of sweethearts and finally of a mate, parents often find themselves in disagreement with their children. Though well-meaning and eager for the boy or girl to choose wisely, the parent cannot make the choice for the youth. Again, the role of the parent should be that of a counselor; his counsel will be effective insofar as he has been willing to serve as an impartial and ever-helpful adviser in the various difficulties and problems that the adolescent faces. Adolescents will welcome suggestions and help, even in matters relating to the choice of a mate, when such help is given in a spirit of sincerity and fairness, motivated by a desire to aid them in finding the greatest harmony and happiness as a result of the choice made.

There is, therefore, a need for a carefully planned program integrated by the schools, churches, and homes in guiding the developing adolescent boys and girls. Many parents are unaware that conflicts exist, and when they are aware of them, they do not in most cases understand the sources of such conflicts. Home situations that take their toll in the form of parental nervousness, family discord, and childhood unhappiness can best be dispelled by studying the underlying sources of such troubles. This was the aim of the study by Block. As a result of this study a program was formulated and its effectiveness proved. Some important characteristics of the program are:

> A comparative study of the interviews with children and their mothers demonstrated that many situations producing apparently similar problems were very different in their causal elements. A careful investigation of the total clinical picture of 69.3 per cent of the children in the seventh grade complaining about their mothers nagging them about what they wear and how they dress showed that the basic cause of the nagging was different for different children. Since no two problems are identical, the home and school must realize that the methods of treating one child exhibiting a definite behavior pattern may be opposite from the method applied to another child exhibiting the same behavior pattern. Each child must be studied by his parents and teachers as an entity in relation to his peculiar physical, mental and emotional make-up and his environmental influences.
> An analysis of the interviews revealed the need and desire on the part of parents for a better understanding of the problems of adolescents and for cooperative effort to help boys and girls solve these problems. Parent discussion groups, parent-teacher meetings, personal interviews between parents and advisers, interviews with parents, children, and advisers helped to bring the school and home into a very close and cooperative relationship. Teachers were able to obtain clearer understandings of pupils and adjust their methods to the needs of each child. Administrators and supervisors were better able to distribute children intelligently to curricula and extra-curricula offerings that were interesting and challenging to them and to adjust the curriculum in the light of the felt needs of the group. Many children were better able to take advantage of the opportunities offered in the high school; others who had exhibited undesirable tendencies were recognized earlier and were so guided that their attitudes in many cases were modified into socially acceptable behavior. Parents and teachers worked together in defining, interpreting, and planning experiences for children which would be most conducive to well-balanced, satisfying, and challenging experiences for the child. As a result, children were less disintegrated by varying philosophies of treatment as is so often the case when the home, school, and community fail to define mutually a philosophy.[35]

The role of discipline. Attitudes of parents toward discipline shape children's personalities. As a child grows into adolescence his need for severe discipline lessens. However, some form of discipline—punishment, scolding, or deprivation—is necessary. Its effectiveness will depend upon the existing parent-adolescent relationship, parental attitudes, reaction of the adolescent to discipline, and consistency of the discipline. Consistency is far more important than either harshness or laxity. However, if the parent is going to err in either direction, it is better to be too lax than too strict.

Boys and girls view differently rules set forth at home, whether in an authoritarian or a democratic home. Boys consider them as a means of restricting behavior likely to lead to trouble; girls, as a means of directing and channeling energy. Elizabeth Douvan noted that more girls than boys felt that children might be able to manage their own lives.[36] She also noted that whereas 25 per cent of the boys studied questioned parental restriction, not with hostility, but with freedom that implies a right to question, only four per cent of the girls reacted in this manner. Boys are more inclined to break rules and justify such breaking of rules. The girls were more evasive about having broken rules, implying the purity or conformity expected of them.

SUMMARY

The adolescent is a product of all that has gone on before; no one ever outgrows his childhood. He develops physically, mentally, and emotionally, but he never escapes the influence of his earlier years. Early years become preparatory periods for adult living. They are fundamental as a stabilizing force in molding the individual into an adaptable member of the society in which he is to live. Sometimes the process of training is deficient and the child carries infantile traits into adulthood. "The immature adult is seen to be selfish, wilful, petulant, impulsive, and in other ways objectionable to society."[37]

Important differences may be observed in the manner in which parents deal with their children and adolescents. There is, however, a trend toward more democratic practices in the home. This does not mean that no controls are present, but rather that controls are conducted through a family council or through interaction of all members of the family. Where democratic controls are practiced, better personal and social adjustments among adolescents appear.

The causes of conflict between the child and the parents are many, but the failure of parents to realize that the child is growing up is the major one. The tendency of parents to thrust their exact pattern of conduct and ways of behaving on the child is also generally present. The child may become selfish and wilful under the protection of wealth. The daughter grows up without any sense of responsibility under the dominance of a very strict father. The only child may be pampered and spoiled by an adoring aunt or grandmother. The social pattern in the home will do much to affect the child's social and emotional development. A domineering and ill-tempered father keeps the child ill at ease and repressed. Vacillating and inconsistent authority and punishment will present a condition of bewilderment for the growing child. These childhood patterns become fixed and tend to persist into adult life.

THOUGHT PROBLEMS

1. Just what do you understand the term *emancipation,* as used in this chapter, to mean? What is its significance in relation to adjustment problems?
2. Present a descriptive case of personality maladjustment due to unfortunate or undesirable family conditions.
3. Consider the family patterns of some of your friends. Compare your observations of the characteristics of these friends with whaat one might expect from generalizing from the results of the study by Helen L. Koch.
4. How do you account for the underestimation of the role of the father that one frequently encounters? Give evidence from studies and from your observations that the father's role is important.
5. Consider some adolescents that are happy and apparently well adjusted. What are some of the special characteristics of their home life?
6. It has often been stated that the most important single factor making for satisfactory adjustments among adolescents is the *attitude of the parents.* What do you regard as desirable attitudes? Be specific.
7. Formulate a chart showing symptoms of rejection displayed by the rejected child, and symptoms displayed by the rejecting parents.
8. What were the major home conflicts you experienced as an adolescent? What influences, if any, do you consider that these have had on your present social adjustments and independence?
9. List 10 items that would furnish a basis for the estimation of one's degree of emancipation or achieving independence. Using these items as a basis for measuring the degree of independence achieved, study the degree of emancipation of two or more adolescent boys or girls of your acquaintance.

SELECTED REFERENCES

Bossard, J., *Parents and Child: Studies in Family Behavior.* Philadelphia: University of Pennsylvania Press, 1953.

———— and E. S. Boll, *Ritual in Family Living.* Philadelphia: University of Pennsylvania Press, 1950, Chaps. 2-5, and 8-9.

Duvall, Evelyn Millis, *Family Development.* Philadephia: J. B. Lippincott Co., 1957, Chap. 2.

Horrocks, John E., *The Psychology of Adolescence,* 2nd ed. Boston: Houghton Mifflin Company, 1962, Chaps. 2 and 3.

Remmers, H. H. and D. H. Radler, *The American Teen-ager.* Indianapolis, Ind.: Bobbs-Merrill Company, Inc., 1957, Chap. 4.

Rogers, Dorothy, *The Psychology of Adolescence.* New York: Appleton-Century-Crofts, 1962, Chap. 8.

Symonds, P. M., *The Dynamics of Parent-child Relationships*. New York: Bureau of Publications, Teachers College, Columbia University, 1949.

Wattenberg, W. W., *The Adolescent Years*. New York: Harcourt, Brace & World, Inc., 1955, Chaps. 9, 10, and 22.

NOTES

[1] F. Rosenheim, "Character Structure of a Rejected Child," *American Journal of Orthopsychiatry*, 12 (1942), 480-95.

[2] Evan T. Peterson, "The Impact of Maternal Employment on the Mother-daughter Relationship," *Marriage and Family Living*, 23 (1961), 355-61.

[3] Prodipto Roy, "Maternal Employment and Adolescent Roles: Rural-urban Differentials," *Marriage and Family Living*, 23 (1961), 348-49.

[4] Philip E. Slater, "Parental Role Differentiation," *American Journal of Sociology*, 67 (1961), 296-311.

[5] Claude J. Bartlett and John E. Horrocks, "A Study of the Needs Status of Adolescents from Broken Homes," *Journal of Genetic Psychology*, 93 (1958), 153-59.

[6] R. F. Berdie, *After High School What?* (Minneapolis: University of Minnesota Press, 1954).

[7] William R. Morrow and Robert C. Wilson, "Family Relations of Bright High-achieving and Under-achieving High School Boys," *Child Development*, 32 (1961), 501-10.

[8] Helen L. Koch, "Attitudes of Young Children Toward Their Peers as Related to Certain Characteristics of Their Siblings," *Psychological Monographs*, 70, No. 426 (1952).

[9] *Ibid.*, p. 48.

[10] Daniel G. Brown, "Sex-role Preference in Young Children," *Psychological Monographs*, 70, No. 421 (1956).

[11] A. L. Baldwin, J. Kalhorn, and F. H. Breese, "Patterns of Parent Behavior," *Psychological Monographs*, 58, No. 3 (1945). The descriptions presented of the different parent behavior patterns are based on this study. (Permission of *Psychological Monographs* and the American Psychological Association.)

[12] *Ibid.*, pp. 22-24. The case of Betty is adapted from this study.

[13] *Ibid.*, pp. 31-32.

[14] *Ibid.*, pp. 46-48.

[15] H. L. Ingersoll, "A Study of Transmission of Authority Patterns in the Family," *Genetic Psychology Monographs*, 38 (1946), 225-302.

[16] *Ibid.*, pp. 287-93. The description here presented is adapted from this source.

[17] P. H. Landis and C. L. Stone, *The Relationship of Parental Authority Patterns to Teen-ager Adjustments* (Pullman, Wash.: State College of Washington, Rural Sociology Series on Youth, Bulletin No. 538, 1952).

[18] Robert F. Peck, "Family Patterns Correlated with Adolescent Personality Structure," *Journal of Abnormal and Social Psychology*, 57 (1958), 350.

[19] John Levey and Ruth Munroe, "The Adolescent and His Happy Family," *The Adolescent* (New York: The Dryden Press, 1953), p. 549.

[20] Paul H. Landis, "The Ordering and Forbidding Technique and Teen-age Adjustment," *School and Society*, 80 (1954), 105-6.

[21] G. R. Hawkes, L. G. Burchinal, and B. Gardner, "Preadolescents' View of Some of Their Relations with Their Parents," *Child Development*, 28 (1957), 293-99.

[22] Susan W. Gray, "Perceived Similarity to Parents and Adjustment," *Child Development*, 30 (1959), 91-107.

[23] John V. Gilmore, "A New Venture in the Testing of Motivation, *College Board Review*, 15 (1951), 221-26.

[24] Paul H. Landis, *op. cit.*

[25] V. L. Block, "Conflicts of Adolescents with Their Mothers," *Journal of Abnormal and Social Psychology*, 32 (1937), 192-206.

[26] O. M. Butterfield, *Love Problems of Adolescence* (New York: Emerson Books, Inc., 1939), p. 33.

[27] R. Lynd and H. Lynd, *Middletown in Transition* (New York: Harcourt, Brace & World, Inc., 1937).

[28] John V. Liccione, "The Changing Family Relationships of Adolescent Girls," *Journal of Abnormal and Social Psychology*, 51 (1955), 421-26.

[29] Ernest Havemann, "The Teen-ager's Case Against Parents, *McCall's* (November, 1956), p. 45.

[30] See C. E. Meyers, "Emancipation of the Adolescent from Parental Control," *Nervous Child*, 5 (1946), 251-62.

[31] H. S. Dimock, *Rediscovering the Adolescent* (New York: Association Press, 1937), p. 145.

[32] From *Complete Poems of Robert Frost*. By permission of the publisher. Copyright, 1930, 1949, by Holt, Rinehart & Winston, Inc. Copyright, 1930, 1949, by Robert Frost.

[33] E. E. Prevey, "A Quantitative Study of Family Practices in the Use of Money," *Journal of Educational Psychology*, 36 (1945), 411-28.

[34] N. R. Ingraham, "Health Problem of the Adolescent Period," *The Annals of the American Academy of Political and Social Science* (November, 1944), p. 131.

[35] V. L. Block, *op. cit.*, pp. 204-5.

[36] Elizabeth Douvan, "Independency and Identity in Adolescence," *Children* (Published by United States Department of Health, Education and Welfare, September-October, 1957).

[37] C. S. Bluemel, *The Troubled Mind* (Baltimore: The Williams & Wilkins Co., 1938), p. 468.

14

THE
ADOLESCENT
AND
HIS PEERS

In the previous chapter it was pointed out that with the advent of the adolescent period boys and girls tend to break away from the home and seek the company of peers. One of the oustanding needs of adolescents is peer approval. The importance of peer relations, the nature of adolescent friendships, problems of dating and sex, and related problems involving peer activities during adolescence will be discussed throughout this chapter.

ADOLESCENT PEER RELATIONSHIPS

Importance of peer relations. We have a tendency to explain a child's behavior on the basis of his family and the organized institutions that he has been associated with—thus minimizing the importance of the experiences of boys and girls with each other in their day-by-day activities. Peer relations during adolescence are extremely important. Such developmental tasks as learning to get along with age-mates and acquiring a satisfactory sex role can be satisfactorily achieved only through good peer relations. It is with their peers that adolescents have opportunities to intimately share their problems and experiences, and it is from their peers that they are able to find sympathy and relatively complete understanding. Through *doing* they learn to cooperate, give and take, and clarify their sex role.

Adolescent peer culture. The subculture which characterizes the behavior of American teen-agers developed as a result of the failure of society to clearly define the roles of adolescents. It delineates his world from that of the adult world where he is neither prepared nor permitted to enter. Adolescents use various means to maintain their subculture and to exclude adults from it. Thus, when parents and teachers cannot understand the behavior of teen-agers, the adolescent realizes that he has succeeded in developing a world of his own. The members of this subculture carry out a distinct ritual as a symbol of their initiation: they wear the clothing dictated by their peers; they follow certain codes of social conduct; and they communicate in a language all their own. This ceremony tends to set the group apart from and serves as a means of excluding adults. Many fads appear. Some of these are given for Iowa teen-agers in an article dealing with the "Profile of Youth."

> One crowd of girls trade single shoes at school in the morning as a friendship gesture; a gang of fellows wear peaked white railroad engineers' hats for everything from gym class to dance dates; one basketball team sports athletic socks with bright red tops. Both fellows and girls wear ribbed white number socks, with class numerals stamped on turned-down cuffs.[1]

Adolescents exclude adults from their group indirectly by the use of slang and reminders such as "Oh, this is just for us kids." The group remains somewhat constant for a number of years during the growing life of the adolescent, but new members are continuously being admitted from the younger group, and older ones drop out for one reason or another.

Conformity to peer culture. Adolescents growing up in the United States are confronted with a variety of behavior codes. They frequently have no reliable frame of reference by which they can judge their behavior or that of others. When a conflict arises between a teen-ager and a parent or adult leader the common excuse is, "Everyone else is doing it." Such a reply is understandable when we consider the difference between the peer culture and that of adults. The conflict exists because there is no general agreement on an appropriate behavior pattern.

Conformity to peer culture or group norms has often been associated with good emotional adjustment. In a study by Langner, designed to test this hypothesis, various clinical and social-psychological tests were administered to a sample of 600 school pupils from the fourth to the twelth grade, one-third of whom were Indian, one-third white Protestant, and one-third Spanish or Mexican.[2] The results revealed that, although conformity to peer group behavioral norms was positively correlated with emotional adjustment, deviance did not necessarily indicate maladjustment. Several factors made it possible for the individual to deviate from the peer group norms and not suffer an emotionally bad consequence. Deviance brought maladjustments mainly when such deviation separated the individual from the group, automatically cutting off an important source for the satisfaction of certain needs of the individual and producing an "isolate." Those who had friends but thought they had none were most seriously disturbed, i.e., the feeling of isolation was a greater determinant of maladjustment than actual isolation, indicating further the importance of the individual's concept of the *self*.

However, the popular youngster who uses his energy to conform to the goals and values of the group may be doing so at the expense of the development of a unique personality. Many such youngsters are filled with anxiety about their own success or being accepted by the group. Thus, they may show a fine adjustment to the group yet lack self-confidence and inner security. Such was the case of Joe:

> Joe is a normal 13-year-old boy in the seventh grade of a new junior high school. On the basis of a sociometric test he is rated as one of the most popular members of his class, and is president of his class. Many parents hold Joe up as a model for their son to follow or for their daughter to date. Psychological tests show Joe to be a troubled boy, filled with anxiety and fear of failure. He sees himself as one unable to do as well on most tasks as others. He has strong feelings of aggression and hostility that he does not express. He is extremely careful to conform and be friendly with everyone in order to cover up his inner fears and hostilities toward others.

Adolescent friendships. Availability of social contacts and mutual satisfaction of needs were found by Reader and English to be the most important variables in adolescent female friendships.[3] Girls with similar interests and tastes would thus appear more likely to be able to satisfy these mutual needs. This is in harmony with results obtained from the California growth studies of adolescents.[4] Responses were obtained to the question "What kind of people do you like to be with best?" At all levels studied, the majority of boys and girls preferred to be with their own age groups, although the results presented in Table 14-1 show that many adolescent girls (girls in the ninth, tenth, eleventh, and twelfth grades) indicate a desire to be with people a few years older. This no doubt stems from the greater physiological maturity of a large percentage of girls at these grade levels (in comparison with the boys at the same levels).

A study of the friendship fluctuations of rural adolescent boys and girls was conducted by Thompson and Horrocks.[5] In this study 421 boys and 484 girls living in rural areas were studied over a two-week period. They found an increase in the stability of friendships from age 10 to 17. No significant difference in friendship fluctuations was observed between boys and girls. This increased stability of friendship during the adolescent years does not provide support for the hypothesis early advanced by Hall and others that adolescence is a period characterized as one of "storm and stress," and instability.

A second study of friendship fluctuations, conducted by these same investigators, compared urban and rural adolescent girls.[6] The 969 sub-

jects used in this study were obtained from two cities in New York state
and from one city in Pennsylvania. The individuals selected were from
6 to 12. An attempt was made to select girls from families of approximately average socio-economic status; a similar attempt was made in the
case of the rural adolescents in the study made at an earlier date. A comparison of the rural and urban boys in their fluctuations indicates a
slightly greater stability in friendships among urban than among rural
adolescents, although the difference is not statistically significant. Figure
14-1 shows the relationship between age and the percentage of boys and

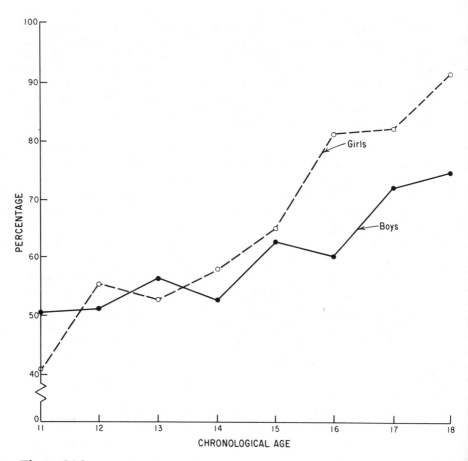

Figure 14-1

THE RELATIONSHIP BETWEEN CHRONOLOGICAL AGE AND PERCENTAGE OF BOYS
AND GIRLS CHOOSING THE SAME PERSON AS THEIR BEST FRIEND ON TWO OCCA-
SIONS SEPARATED BY A TWO-WEEK INTERVAL

(*After Horrocks and Thompson*)

girls choosing the same person as their best friends. For both boys and girls there is a decided tendency toward an increased stability of friendship, with the girls showing the greater increase.

Table 14-1

RESPONSE OF ADOLESCENTS TO THE QUESTION, "WHAT KIND OF PEOPLE DO YOU LIKE TO BE WITH BEST?"

	5HL6	6HL7	7HL8	8HL9	9HL10	10HL11	11HL12
				Boys			
Grown people (grown-ups)	1	1	1	3	0	0	0
People younger than I am	0	3	7	1	1	1	1
People about my age	86	80	89	87	89	85	95
People a few years older than I am	7	14	4	10	10	17	17
I would rather be by myself	6	1	0	1	1	0	0
				Girls			
Grown people (grown-ups)	4	6	1	1	1	0	0
People younger than I am	3	1	1	1	0	0	0
People about my age	82	85	94	78	69	62	56
People a few years older than I am	3	8	6	25	36	42	50
I would rather be by myself	8	3	1	1	1	0	1

This is no doubt closely related to the more democratic nature of boys and the greater tendency on the part of girls to form small "cliques" and have a single friend. These data further indicate that one of the characteristics of growing up is that of maintaining more stable friendships.

Adolescent cliques. Gangs and cliques characterize the adolescent age. When the 14-year-old adolescent daughter is asked where she has been, she may reply: "Oh, I have just been down the street with the gang." In this case she refers to her small group, a sort of self-sufficient unit. The study of friendship formation among Elmtown's youth furnishes worth-while information on this problem.[7] This study was designed to test the hypothesis that the social behavior of adolescents is related to the place their families occupy in the social structure of the community. This midwestern community consisting of some 10,000 inhabitants was found to be stratified into five classes. The group studied consisted of 369 boys and girls between the ages of 13 and 19 inclusive. This provided a good cross section of the teen-age group. These cliques, made up of one's peers, have an important influence on the activities of their members. Social pressure in these groups operates to channelize friendships and set forth behavior standards within limits permitted by the social system.

The dual operation of the parents and peers in the clique is well illustrated in the case of Joyce Jenson's (class III) relationship with her clique and especially with her friend Gladys Johnson (class III), reprinted from the Elmtown study.

> We influence each other a lot. She influences me almost as much as my parents do. I listen to them, especially when it comes to choosing friends, but I don't agree with everything they tell me. I've had them really give me the dickens about going around with some girls I wanted to go with or maybe Gladys did. Most parents don't want their kids running around with certain other kids, and they'll give them advice and they'll follow it or they won't, but when my folks put the foot down on me I listen.
>
> I know that the folks give me good advice, but sometimes they just don't understand what kids want to do, and they think we ought to act like they acted twenty years ago. My parents, especially my mother, influence me in what I do, but Gladys probably influences me as much or more.
>
> I don't want to run any of the kids down, but there are certain girls here who are just not my type and they're not Gladys's type; they'd like to run around with us, but we don't let them.
>
> Pauline Tryon (class IV) and her bunch would like to run around with us, but we turn our backs on them because they run around all night, cut school, and hang out down at Blue Triangle.
>
> There are some kids we'd like to run around with, but they don't want us to go with them. Gladys and I would like to go around with "Cookie" Barnett (class II) and her bunch, or the G. W. G.'s, but they snub us if we try to get in on their parties, or dances, or date the boys they go with.

An analysis of the 1258 clique ties observed in the study of Elmtown's youth revealed that approximately three out of five are between boys or girls of the same class position, two out of five are between adolescents who belong to adjacent classes, and one out of 25 involves individuals who belong to classes twice removed from one another. The detailed study of close ties disclosed that from 49 to 70 per cent of all clique ties are with class equals. It also reveals that when a class I boy or girl crosses a class line, and about one-third do, a member of class II is likely to be involved. Likewise, when a class II boy or girl crosses the class line, he moves into class I or class III. Thus, we note that the polar classes are largely isolated one from another insofar as intimate, personal, face-to-face relations are concerned.

Isolates. Among boys and girls at this age level are those who are termed "isolates." These boys and girls for one reason or another have no close ties with other members of the group. In a study by Wisenbaker 66 ninth-grade girls were asked to list their first four choices of friends.[8] Some results of this study are presented in the sociogram of Figure 14-2. These results are typical of what one would expect to find among a group of high school girls. Several closely knit cliques were observed. The socio-

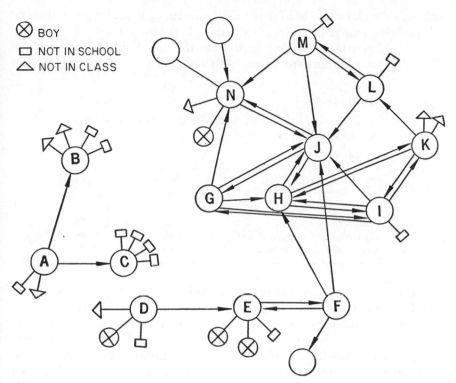

Figure 14-2

gram shows that several girls were chosen by no one or by just one person. A study of isolates shows that no single pattern characterizes them. The isolates of Wisenbaker's study failed to participate in class projects of various kinds and displayed a lack of confidence and experience in activities involving social skills. The nonisolates were found to be more stable emotionally, to have fewer absences from school, to have a greater variety of interests, to be more interested in being with people and sharing experiences, to participate in class and extraclass activities to a greater degree, and to come from homes with higher cultural standards.

   Traits associated with acceptability. Closely related to the formation of friendships is the problem of being popular with the group. The desire for popularity is very strong among most adolescent boys and girls. In one study a sociometric test was administered to 340 junior high school pupils.[9] The test requested each pupil to choose five associates whom (1) he would like to sit near in class, (2) he would most like as classmates next year, and (3) he would most like to play with in his neighborhood after school. The relation between pupils' social acceptability in these three areas is shown in Table 14-2. The results indicate that sociometric status in the classroom is a fairly reliable index of a pupil's general social acceptability among his peers at the junior high school level.

The importance of class status for the social development of the individual was emphasized in an earlier chapter. It has been observed

Table 14-2

RELATIONSHIP BETWEEN SOCIOMETRIC STATUS SCORES
IN THREE SITUATIONS

(Gronlund and Whitney)

Scores correlated	*Mean correlation*	*Standard deviation*
Classroom and school	.72	.04
Classroom and neighborhood	.67	.08
School and neighborhood	.78	.09

that beliefs, attitudes, moral practices, and values vary with class status. The traditional high school operates so as to instill middle-class ways of behaving and values in the students. The established church in the community also tends to uphold middle-class standards, with the general result that it often fails to reach lower-class children. Pope noted some interesting differences in peer culture prestige values of 12-year-olds from contrasting socio-economic backgrounds.[10] Fighting, physical domination, and "loudness" were more acceptable among those from the low than among those from the high socio-economic group. The "little lady" of the high group is likely to be a buoyant, high-spirited girl. Pope states:

> The high group of both sexes expect their members to show an appropriate tendency to conform to adult standards within the classroom. They also show a positive evaluation of certain conventional rules of decorum when attending parties and dances with the opposite sex. These qualities are not at all stressed by the low socio-economic groups. It is perhaps in these two respects that we find the most significant differences.[11]

Feinberg, Smith and Schmidt attempted to determine whether adolescent boys at three economic levels would use similar descriptive terms to characterize the peers they accepted or rejected.[12] Over 2400 adolescent boys between the ages of 13 and 15, drawn from schools representing three different family income levels in New York City and its suburbs were used as subjects. The results of the study are summarized in Table 14-3. A study of the traits presented shows that in many areas of personality the three income-level groups were in general agreement about their standards for acceptance and rejection. The similarity of the middle and low economic levels in so many areas indicates that these boys had many similar values about their peers. All income groups agreed in characterizing accepted peers as intelligent, fair, able to take a joke, good company, athletic, quiet, conscientious, and honest. There would no doubt be significant differences in the ways different groups would regard the actual manifestations of these traits. In the high income group, but not in the middle and low groups, cooperativeness, leadership, participation in activities, cheerfulness, and good scholarship were highly valued for acceptance. All groups agreed in describing rejected peers as pesty, noisy, conceited, silly, and sissy.

Table 14-3

TRAITS CONSIDERED IMPORTANT AT VARIOUS ECONOMIC LEVELS
(*Feinberg, Smith, and Schmidt*)

	High	*Middle*	*Low*
Two-way[a]	Intelligent vs. stupid Sociable vs. unfriendly Quiet vs. noisy Athletic vs. unathletic Honest vs. dishonest Kind vs. mean Cooperative vs. uncooperative	Mind own business vs. pest Quiet vs. noisy Conscientious vs. lazy	Sociable vs. friendly Mind own business vs. pest Plays fair vs. plays unfair Quiet vs. noisy Kind vs. mean Trustworthy vs. unreliable
Bonanza[b]	Plays fair Witty Helpful Conscientious Good company Gets along well with others Leader Cheerful Good scholar	Intelligent Sociable Plays fair Witty Athletic Helpful Good company Talks well Gets along well with others Common interests Good manners Pleasant, agreeable	Intelligent Witty Athletic Helpful Good company Conscientious Talks well Common interests
Blackball[c]	Pest Conceited Silly Immature No activities	Conceited Silly Sissy Always in trouble Always fighting	Conceited Silly Sissy Always in trouble Always fighting

[a] Two-way. Attention is paid to both the positive and negative aspects.
[b] Bonanza. Concentration is just on the positive aspects. The negative aspects are disregarded.
[c] Blackball. Concentration is just on the negative aspects of the trait.

Desire for social approval. Sex, notions of self, and the like play a prominent part in the individual's growth and development. It is through these that the group is able to establish and maintain uniformity in manners, styles, and interests. The force of public opinion tends to cause the adolescent to accept readily the standards and customs of the social group; because of public opinion the individual endeavors to further his position in life, and takes pride in his success. The desire for social approval becomes integrated early with the major biological forms of motivation of sex and hunger, the natural tendencies of the individual becoming so modified as to gain it. The very fact that this desire is operating in the life of the individual is evidence that he is becoming a full-fledged member of the social group.

"In the higher forms of social integration, the dominance often goes out of the hands of a single man and is crystallized into law, customs, traditions, and social sanctions. . . . In most social organizations there is a limit to the powers of the dominant person, idea, custom, or force."[13] Now if we begin to study these limitations, we shall probably find homogeneity to be the main force. As the child reaches maturity and becomes more and more a social rather than an individual creature, the force of the role and opinion of the group grows stronger, and is especially prominent in the development of social consciousness. But if the adolescents of the group are homogeneous, the customs, rules, and so forth will play a still more important role than they would otherwise. Homogeneity itself depends upon communicability, similarity of interests and beliefs, and—especially—similarity of general racial features. When this homogeneity exists, control and social integration are more easily effected—a fact that should be carefully observed by those in charge of our educational practice and by those dealing with clubs and group programs designed for adolescents.

Again, the desire for social approval might be thought of in connection with more complex adjustments in the life of the adolescent. Let us consider the "sweet girl graduate" from high school just prior to her graduation, and assume that she desires a certain graduation dress and other novelties that will blend with each other and with her general make-up. The images of these articles as they would appear on her constantly run through her mind. She imagines her friends' approval of this attractive outfit; she imagines herself winning Jack's attention, which she desires greatly. But the economic conditions of her family are such that she cannot purchase the clothes, and she therefore must either do without the costume or find some means as yet unknown to purchase them. Thus one will find adolescents and postadolescents often willing to resort to questionable devices in order to win the approval of their friends. Here we find the girl resorting to various devices in order to appear sexually attractive to the boy she admires. The beautiful wearing apparel will help her to become more attractive, and she recognizes that Jack is quite fond of such a type of costume; she may therefore deprive herself of the movies, other amusements, and even food in order that she may be able to buy what she considers necessities. Again, even petty crimes or mis-representations may be resorted to in order to win social approval. The average high school girl's ego complex is well developed around certain erotic tendencies, and these become more powerful as they involve the approval or disapproval of the male sex.

HETEROSEXUAL INTERESTS AND ACTIVITIES

As interest in the peer group grows, interest in activities involving parents declines. The youngster no longer wants to accompany his parents on a picnic or camping outing, unless members of his age-group are present. This changed relation frequently produces much anxiety on the part of parents and if conflicts are to be avoided they must revise their expectations of their preadolescents and adolescents. Since there is no clear-cut pattern set forth in our society for youngsters to follow at this age they adopt the pattern of their peers. This may not be in harmony with the pattern expected of them by their parents. Materials bearing on the resultant parent-adolescent conflicts were presented in Chapter 13.

Heterosexuality. The study by Harris and Tseng reveals important changes in attitudes toward members of the opposite sex as the individual grows from childhood into adolescence.[14] Using a sentence completion method of studying children's and adolescents' attitudes toward peers they were able to compute "negative," "positive," and "neutral" attitudes.

By combining percentages of boys and girls in each grade who gave responses of a particular classification, the investigators were able to draw curves expressing certain trends in attitude changes. Boys' attitudes toward other boys and girls are shown in Figure 14-3. The favorable and neutral responses are shown in this figure. The attitudes of girls toward other girls and boys are shown in Figure 14-4. The curves for boys' attitudes show that approximately two-thirds of the boys gave positive responses to other boys at all grades. Boys are at all grade levels more positive to boys than to girls. Taking into account the proportion of neutral attitudes, boys in the middle grades are more favorable than unfavorable in their attitudes toward girls. The decline at the tenth grade perhaps indicates a growing interest in particular girls with a slightly declining interest in girls in general. There was, however, throughout the grades a fair proportion of boys who gave a negative completion response to the general stimulus, "Most girls ————."

A noticeable trend in girls' attitudes was the increase in negative response to other girls following the ninth grade. This is probably an indication of the competitiveness of girls for boys' attention during the adolescent years. The investigators state, "Perhaps girls personalize their feelings more toward their own sex in adolescence, while boys shift more toward neutrality, and do not move into negative feelings." A wide

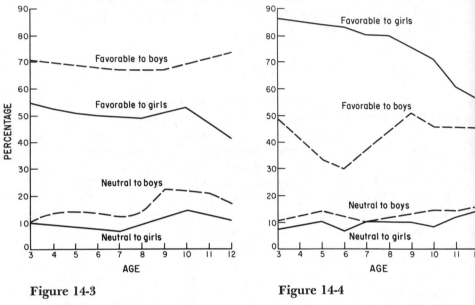

Figure 14-3

BOYS' ATTITUDES TOWARD PEERS

Figure 14-4

GIRLS' ATTITUDES TOWARD PEERS

range of reaction patterns relative to the opposite sex exists in adolescents, and it is very difficult to generalize concerning the reactions of the group as a whole. However, since the sexual urge is present in every individual and probably begins to function influentially, if indirectly, quite early in life, it is evident that the differences between the reactions of various adolescents result from the direction that this urge has been given, rather than its mere existence. The presence of this urge may be observed in the responses of two ninth-grade girls to the statement, "List what you would like to have *now* more than anything else:

"I would like to have more than anything—one certain BOY!"

"I would like a real nice boy friend."

Heterosexuality itself can be properly established only by social contacts with members of the opposite sex, and in these contacts two environmental conditions are essential: first, members of the opposite sex must be of sufficient numbers, of appropriate age, and of attractive personal qualities; second, an intelligently encouraging attitude is necessary on the part of parents and others concerned with the individual's guidance and welfare. If these essentials are absent, the child may emerge from adolescence with warped and shameful attitudes toward sex matters that may encumber him permanently.

It has been observed that, in some species of animals, characteristic patterns of behavior appear *de novo* when pubertal changes in the primary and secondary sexual characters and accessory organs of sex are most in evidence. Among the primates in particular, a limited amount of sexual play is said to appear prior to the pubertal changes. In either case it can be said that the sexual drive is greatly augmented as the time of somatic puberty approaches, and that it continues to grow in strength for some time thereafter by virtue of factors of maturation and of sexual contacts and experiences. Since the sexual drive is at heightened strength as a result of the development processes at work, the manifestation of increased sexual activities and sexual play by adolescents is to be expected. The savage youth was prepared to gain his living by the time the sex drive ripened. In contrast, it has already been revealed that in a civilized community most adolescents are in school when this happens, and that economic security and independence are still a dream. It is therefore not possible for the 14- or 15-year-old boy or girl to enter into economic pursuits in order to support a family; moreover, customs as well as laws do not permit him to do so; and yet, there has been no significant change in the period of the onset of the sex drive.

Dating during adolescence. Dating practices among preadolescents have undergone important changes during the past two decades. The great amount of shyness, timidity, and antipathy toward members of the opposite sex has given way to dating and going steady on the part of a large percentage of preadolescents. Frequently such dating, especially prevalent among middle-class suburban families, is encouraged or fostered by mothers anxious for their daughters to be popular and not to be left out of social events. The extent of dating by high school students will depend upon the customs, living conditions, social backgrounds, and special interests of the particular age-group concerned. Seniors date more than freshmen, and report chaperonage less frequently. This no doubt reflects their greater social and physical maturity and the increased willingness of their parents to allow them, as they grow older, to associate freely with members of the opposite sex.

The importance of social class may be observed in the dating activities of adolescents as well as in other aspects of their activities. The intra- and interclass dating patterns closely parallel the clique patterns. In the study of Elmtown's youth (16-year-old youngsters) no dates are observed between members of class II and members of class V.[15] In this case the social distance between the classes is too great. On the other hand, 61 per cent of the dates belong to the same class; 35 per cent to an adjacent class; and 4 per cent to a class separated by one intervening class. The association of class with class is clearly illustrated in Figure 14-5. This chart shows that the boy is more willing than the girl to date someone in a lower class structure than himself, or has more opportunity to do so

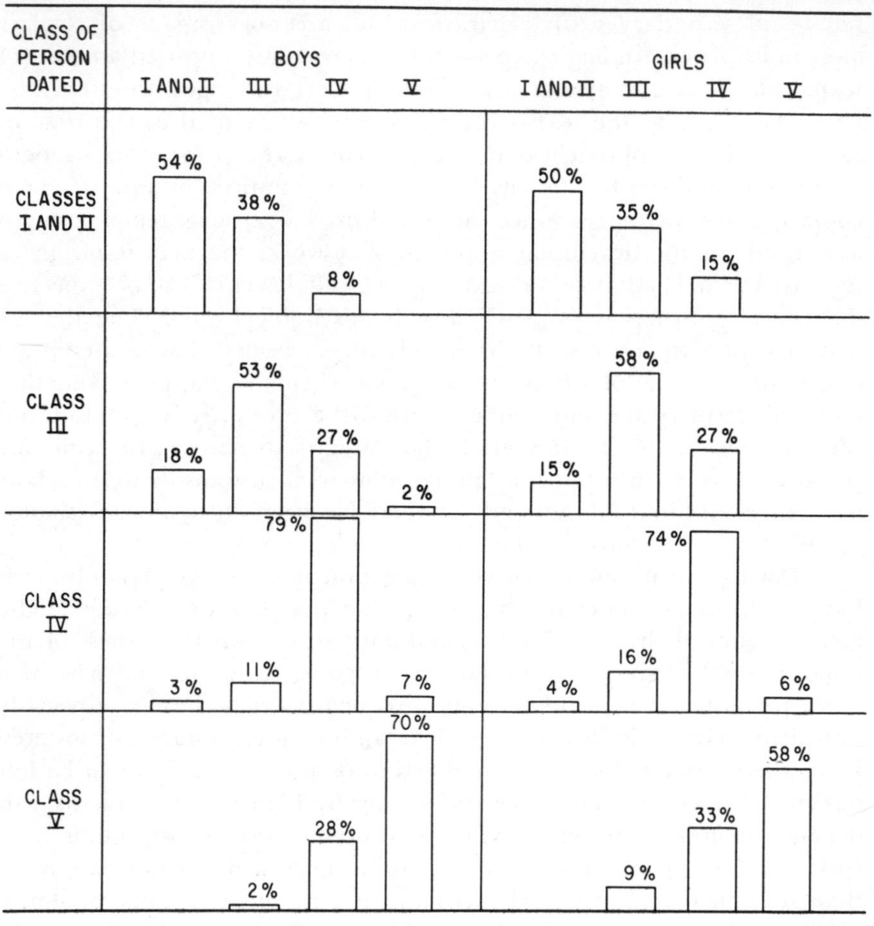

CLASS OF PERSON DATED	BOYS				GIRLS			
	I AND II	III	IV	V	I AND II	III	IV	V
CLASSES I AND II	54%	38%		8%	50%	35%	15%	
CLASS III	18%	53%	27%	2%	15%	58%	27%	
CLASS IV	3%	11%	79%	7%	4%	16%	74%	6%
CLASS V		2%	28%	70%		9%	33%	58%

Figure 14-5

INTRA- AND INTERCLASS DATING PATTERNS OF BOYS AND GIRLS OF ELMTOWN
(*After Hollingshead*)

since he is the one that takes the initiative in the dating. Many factors may be introduced to show why the boy dates in a class position below his more often than a girl does. The fact remains that when an Elmtown boy dates outside his class position the chances are two to one that he dates a girl in a class below his; when the girl dates a member of a different social class, the chances are two to one that she dates in a class above her own.

A nationwide sample of 2500 high school students was studied to determine the attitudes of teen-agers toward dating practices.[16] The students were first asked to rate a list of 25 items from the standpoint of their importance in making or accepting a date. The seven that were rated highest are, in order of rank, as follows:

> Is physically and mentally fit
> Is dependable, can be trusted
> Takes pride in personal appearance and manners
> Is clean in speech and manners
> Has pleasant disposition and sense of humor
> Is considerate of me and others
> Acts own age, is not childish

Although there was a close agreement by boys and girls in the ratings given the various items, there were some differences noted in the expected direction. Males regarded cooking ability as important, whereas females stressed the importance of financial support. In addition, males gave greater stress to physical appearance, whereas females gave greater stress to moderation regarding intimacy, parental approval, and consideration toward others. There were some interesting differences in the patterns of objectionable behavior listed. Males were in general characterized as being less inhibited and more careless, thoughtless, disrespectful, sex-driven, and louder than their dating partners. On the other hand, females were characterized as being less natural and more touchy, money-minded, unresponsive, childish, and flighty than their dating partners.

Personality traits liked and disliked. The personality traits liked and disliked by adolescents in their peer opposite-sex associates will vary to some degree with age and cultural conditioning. This problem was studied by Crow with 2540 girls and 2360 boys, representing a cross section of junior high school and senior high school students in New York City as subjects.[17] The results presented in Table 14-5 show personality leading the list of traits of girls admired by boys. They also emphasize good looks, neatness, consideration of others, good manners, appropriate dress, and good talking and listening. The results presented in Table 14-6 show that personality traits of boys admired by girls are quite similar to those presented in Table 14-5. An analysis of the data gathered shows further that the younger teen-agers (12-14 years) emphasized physical characteristics and overt behavior, whereas the more mature teen-agers (16-18 years) stressed attitudes and behavior associated with inner motivations and character traits.

A few of the younger boys said that they did not like anything about girls. Many girls expressed a liking for older boys. They dislike boys who are sloppy, extreme in dress, conceited, and poor sports. Boys in their later teen years seem to admire girls who are even-tempered, lively, less intelligent than the boy (not stupid), good listeners and talkers, and relatively modest. The notion of the superiority of the male has largely disappeared as a result of coeducation and other activities where girls participate on an equal basis with boys. Also, the roles of the sexes are not so clearly defined as they were several decades ago. Both changes have contributed to the similarity of the traits liked by adolescent boys and girls in their opposite-sex peer.

Table 14-5

PERSONALITY TRAITS OF GIRLS ADMIRED BY BOYS

(*Crow*)

Good personality	Good manners
Good-looking—beautiful face, dress and figure	Acts her age
Look nice in a bathing suit	Ability to dance
Neatness and cleanliness	Courtesy
Helpful to others	Politeness
Consideration for others	No show-off
Appropriate dress	Interest in hobbies of boys
Good talker	Modest, but not shy
Dependable	Act grown-up, not like a baby
Good listener	Clean-minded
Friendliness	Able to take a joke

Table 14-6

PERSONALITY TRAITS OF BOYS ADMIRED BY GIRLS

(*Crow*)

Good personality	Clean shaven and hair cut
Good-looking—not necessarily handsome	Clean-minded
Good character	Kind, generous, tall
Neatness	Acts his age
Clean and appropriate dress	Has a sense of humor
Intelligent	Not too shy
Good conversationalist	Honest and fair
Consideration for a girl's wishes	Respect for rights of girl
Respect for girls—not fresh	Punctuality
Willingness to take a girl on dates	Not to try to be a big shot
Boy to be older than girl	Able to get along with others
Good manners	Has self-control
Good-natured	The way he kisses
Smart in school	Good listener

THE SEX LIFE OF ADOLESCENTS

A mistaken assumption often made is that the problem of the expression of the sexual drive appears as a newly structured problem with the advent of puberty. The child is guided and forced by parents, teachers, and social custom to establish certain controls, thereby limiting the expression of various bodily or sensual pleasures associated with the sexual drive. These controls, both direct and indirect, are directed toward a control of varied infantile and childhood forms of behavior related to the sexual drive, as distinguished from the more complex nature of the drive as it appears during adolescence. Thus adolescence is a period during which this drive is normally directed toward varied forms of heterosexual behavior whose biological purpose is reproduction.

Studies of trends in sexual behavior, notably those conducted by Kinsey and his associates, attest to the strength and importance of the sex drive among men and women.[18] The development, control, and direction of the sex drive during the adolescent years presents problems that are challenging to all the social forces concerned with the training and guidance of adolescents.

Self-assertion before the opposite sex. Self-assertion in the form of self-display before members of the opposite sex has been observed among sexually maturing male animals as well as among adolescent boys. During the mating season there seems to be an overstock of energy that is stored up in animals and is released in the various courting acts that are initiated in response to specific stimulations. In certain species, notably among birds of prey, both male and female show this exuberance, and it is quite common to find it expressed through wonderful flying performances, circlings around each other, and calls peculiar to the kind. The male's showing-off before the female is particularly spectacular. Doubtless a feeling of pleasantness arises from these performances, owing to the growth and maturation of physical structures and reflex co-ordinations and the general release of bodily tensions.

Darwin gives a most striking picture of display by male peacocks and pheasants—their gorgeous crests and tails are given the optimum display before the female.[19] He further writes that the Angus pheasant appears to observe carefully the female's responses to his show; this could be explained adequately not as a result of some instinct of pride but rather as pride that has developed from experience and from the structures of the organism that are now coming to fruition. This courting among various animal types involves activities somewhat subsidiary to sexual ends, and playful exercise is a consequence of superfluous energy that becomes in part directed toward members of the same species and of the opposite sex.

In the human race this assertive tendency can also be seen. Witness the young adolescent, with his daring spirit, overexertion, and constant display of strength and skill. His situation is similar to that of Darwin's pheasant. And the same can be said of the female of the human species: her feminine manners, her shyness, and her persistent efforts to outwit her rivals are all manifestations of this same tendency. In order to reach normal adult stature the adolescent must pass, during these years that comprise the adolescent period, from a stage characterized by infantile and childhood expressions of the sex drive built primarily around the self to that of heterosexuality involving sex consciousness in relation to members of the opposite sex.

General internal changes prevalent during sexual excitation have an emotional tone and cause a general restlessness that involves the whole of the organism's behavior. During this state there is, in addition, a general lowering of the blood pressure. The sacral division of the autonomic nervous system is, it will appear, operating more than normally, and this unusual operation tends to direct excessive quantities of blood and glandular secretions into channels which—although they are often not so recognized—are directly related to the sex emotion. These changes are a result of profound visceral and glandular changes and, as we have noted, tend to affect all behavior of the organism.

Not all members of the sexes are attractive to the opposite sex, nor does the same person make an equal appeal to all. Beauty, good manners, "feminine qualities," health, education, and "personality" are but a few characteristics listed by boys as desirable in girls. Feminine good looks are usually listed as most essential to sex attraction, but their evaluation will differ from decade to decade. During the latter part of the nineteenth century curves were deemed the ideal of beauty; but within a period of 25 or 30 years thereafter, curves seriously lost vogue. To draw conclusions, one need only to examine the styles of the past, whether of a century or several centuries, and compare them with each other and with those of today. Girls of former times had, indeed, their sex appeal; they were adored, surely. But if a girl were to appear today with their manners and dress, she would at best be viewed as a curiosity.

The generalization that might be made from these facts is that the current vogue in costumes, manners, language, interests, cosmetics, hairdressing, and so forth makes for sex appeal among those contemporarily on the scene, but that if this vogue is revived later, its followers may be considered ridiculous. The modern mother who insists that her daughter imitate her in dress, manners, and interests either fails to recognize this truth or refuses to live according to its principle. When the facts are rightly understood, we may rightly appraise the value of clothes, appearance, manners, and other subjects of controversy.

The response of the adolescent boy or girl to what is strange or forbidden must not be overlooked, for both curiosity and self-assertion are important in the motivation of conduct. Familiarity with an individual will tend to lessen the sex appeal of that individual. Thus, if the "new girl" in the community has a somewhat different sex appeal, she will have an advantage over the others. Fickleness is indeed characteristic of sexual phenomena, especially in adolescence; and, it may be observed, changes of style serve to augment it by renewing elements of "strangeness." On the other hand, the spirit of self-assertion, which has already been noted as related to sexual life and which we shall consider further at a later point in this study, leads to love-making in the face of great obstacles. Thus *forbiddance* and *self-assertion* are often present in behavior as a combination that should not be ignored—especially by parents. Because of this combination, troubles often develop between parents and children in connection with courtship and marriage.

Adolescent crushes. Adolescent crushes are very common and should not be looked upon with too much fear and anxiety on the part of parents and teachers. Some of these, however, involve intimate and prolonged relations between members of the same sex and should be given special consideration. Perhaps the most undesirable feature of these continued crushes is that they deprive the individuals concerned of the opportunity for normal, healthy development of broad social contacts with members of both sexes, which are very important during this period of life. These crushes are more frequently found among girls than among boys, and sometimes appear among individuals of different age levels, as was the case of Alice.

Alice was a very attractive, intelligent young girl, 16 years of age, who was causing her parents a great deal of concern because she had developed a very resentful attitude toward authority, was extremely antagonistic toward all suggestions, and seemed hypercritical toward life in general. This young person had lived rather a secluded life and had made but few contacts with young people, either boys or girls. Then very suddenly she had developed an intense admiration for a girl who was somewhat older than herself and who came from a somewhat lower social and cultural level. The older girl was flattered by Alice's attentions, invitations, letters, and gifts, and clung quite as closely to Alice as did Alice to her.

All attempts on the part of Alice's parents to meet this problem, first by teasing and ridicule, later by threats, punishments, and deprivations, served no useful purpose. They did nothing more than make this young person feel that the object of her devotion was being maligned and persecuted. It was never suspected by the family that the girl herself had a good many conflicts over this relation, that she was eager to broaden her contacts, and that she was extremely desirous of having friends among boys as well as girls. On account of the circumstances under which she had been brought up and a certain inherent shyness and diffidence, a special effort had to be made on the part of her parents to help her meet the young people among whom such friendships could develop. This they were perfectly willing to do when they understood the emotional nature of the problem.[20]

As indicated in the case of Alice, attempts to break up the crush were met with antagonism and rebellion. There is an intense loyalty on the part of the parties concerned toward each other. Criticisms from family and friends are met with resentment. In the end, these intense crushes are self-eliminating. A wider range of contacts and experiences on the part of one or both members is one of the most effective ways of meeting these problems.

Going steady. Dating practices vary with culture and social class. Over the past two decades the social swirl has engulfed teen-agers with the result that dating and going steady has become widespread. In some high schools it is estimated that two-thirds of the students go steady, despite objections voiced by parents, teachers, ministers, priests, and other adult leaders. Two objections have been raised to the custom of going steady. In the first place, continuously keeping company with the same person of the opposite sex frequently leads to sexual intimacies. The Roman Catholic church in particular emphasizes this danger, particularly on the part of immature youngsters. A second objection is that the teen-ager needs contact and social experiences with different members of the opposite sex in order to understand it better and to be able to make a sounder decision on marriage later.

The Youth Research Institute has observed the romantic teen-ager at close range through nationwide surveys of young people's activities, preferences, and opinions. Most feel insecure and ill-prepared to fill the parts they are pressured to fill. "Going steady" occurs mainly because of group pressure or for the social approval and prestige it gives. Socially ambitious mothers, in particular, are anxious for their daughters to be popular. To such mothers, having a desirable date is an indication of prestige and popularity. Going steady is also a guarantee on the girl's part of a date for any social function she may attend. Two reasons have been listed by teen-agers for going steady. The first is that they may feel "in love" with each other and enjoy each other's company to the exclusion of others. The second is that it insures them with a date for different social occasions. A large number have doubts about the custom, however, and feel caught in a subculture in which they have little control.

Petting. Problems relating to dating, "going steady," and petting are not new, except for the fact that they are more in evidence than formerly. Also, petting is more widely practiced and accepted among so-called "nice" people as an aspect of dating. It is no longer reserved for the family parlor, or even for some secluded spot. In the automobile, at the beach, in the school corridors, at the movies, and in other public places wherever adolescents appear, petting may be observed. The fact that adolescents feel free to carry on a reasonable amount of petting in public, and often in the presence of their parents, is an indication of the less cramped and inhibited feelings on the part of modern adolescents about the whole subject of sex and changed attitudes about the roles of the sexes. This has no doubt resulted in a healthier comradeship among boys and girls. It seems likely that petting is being utilized more and more as a sublimation.

The problem of petting has increased the necessity for sex guidance and the need for a favorable attitude of boys and girls toward sex as an important aspect of human life and existence. Thus, parents, teachers, and others are more and more removing the cloud of secrecy which has so often surrounded the subject of sex.

The problem of sex is but one aspect of the life of the adolescent, but it is an aspect that should be dealt with honestly and frankly. Adolescents, like many adults, are in a state of confusion about sex codes. In literature, on television and radio, at the movies, in the classroom, at home, and at church they are bombarded with codes that are at variance with each other. Furthermore, members of a single group of boys and girls may have different codes. Thus, in our democratic spirit, each adolescent has to unravel from these a code that is acceptable to himself and not too much at variance with that of his peers. Jane is faced with many problems relative to petting. Where can she secure information to help her solve these problems? To whom can she turn for sound guidance and understanding? How can she maintain standards and retain friends of the opposite sex?

There is no single American sex pattern that furnishes Jane with an answer to these problems, as in primitive tribes. A code of conduct which has a large following among high school girls is that petting is all right if it takes place within the context of a stable affectional relationship but not if done with "just anyone." With such a code the girl enters into heavy petting without the result of having a guilty conscience. Jane needs guidance in the development of secondary sexual behavior that will satisfy her needs and tend to reduce sexual tension in ways that are socially acceptable and satisfying to her.

Some misconceptions about sex. Many misconceptions about sexual development and the sex drive appear among different groups. In the early years of life the sex impulse appears to act rather vaguely and indirectly, although one must not conclude that it is absent or dormant prior to the onset of puberty. The relationship between conduct during the earlier years of life and later sex life is not clear, but there is evidence that sex is somewhat related to the love behavior of the young child. With the development of the sex glands, and the maturation of the individual both physically and socially in a social world, many factors may operate to cause behavior resulting from the release of certain drives to deviate from a normal or socially acceptable course. Some of these factors are: repression, ignorance, sex phobias, disgust, curiosity, or some other conditions emotionally toned. It is during the stage of the operation of such factors that trial-and-error behavior occurs. The subject will try many methods of adjusting himself sexually, and some of his efforts may result in perversions—habits that are undesirable either because they will bring ultimate personal dissatisfaction or because they interfere with normal social relations.

There have been a number of investigations bearing on the frequency of masturbation and other sexual aberrations. The frequency of such aberrations varies so much from group to group that it would be unsafe to generalize widely from these studies. One of the most widespread misconceptions among preadolescents and adolescents about sexual activities is that masturbation is likely to have serious physical and mental aftereffects. There is little if any evidence that masturbation among adolescents is actually harmful, although this does not mean that it is to be encouraged. Actually masturbation is quite common; therefore, if it were very harmful the ill effects would be more observable. The study by Ramsey revealed that masturbation among boys sometimes began during the preschool period and by the age of 12, 73 per cent admitted engaging in it, and by the age of 15, 98 per cent had had such an experience.[21]

The studies of girls do not reveal such a high percentage engaging in masturbation, although the figures are sufficiently high to be alarming, were the practice so serious in nature.

Homosexuality. Homosexuality, sometimes referred to as homoerotism, refers to a personality whose sexual interests are inclined toward members of his own sex rather than the opposite sex. Although differences in physical make-up and balance between male and female hormones exist between adolescents of the same sex, there are also certain environmental factors that contribute toward homosexuality.

Cline reports that among the Arabs of Siwah the boy may pass his youth as the homosexual partner of an older friend of the family.[22] At maturity, in addition to normal marriage, the boy becomes a homosexual partner to a younger boy. In Western civilization environmental pressures sometimes operate to make adolescents deviate sexually. However, due to hormone differences not all adolescents of the same sex would be affected to the same degree by such pressures. Some boys may be made very effeminate in their behavior by mothers who persist in treating them as they would their daughters. The overprotected girl shielded in a strict girls' school has only the opportunity to associate with girls and to satisfy her sexual needs through these associations. These experiences may lead the adolescent boy or girl to desire homosexual stimulation and gratification. The data by Ramsey showed that approximately one-fourth of the adolescent boys studied admitted engaging in homosexual play.[23] With many of them this was merely a matter of experimentation. Most of them will return to heterosexual behavior once the opportunity is afforded them to do so. This is indicated by the fact that the incidence of homosexual behavior among adults is relatively low. One study conducted with college students reported that only one-tenth of the group had vague fears of homosexuality or actually engaged in it.[24] The extent of homosexuality found in a group of adolescents and postadolescents will depend upon a number of factors, such as cultural norms, early sex experiences, opportunities to socialize with members of both sexes, general recreational opportunities, and the nature of the guidance given to them.

Need for guidance. A number of students of adolescent psychology have emphasized the need for guidance of boys and girls in understanding and dealing with sex problems. It was pointed out in Chapter 8 that a large percentage of boys and girls obtain their first information about sex from sources other than the home, teachers, ministers and priests, and the like. These findings have led church leaders, educators, and social workers to become concerned, with the result that some churches, schools, and other agencies have developed programs designed to meet this problem.

The importance of recreation in the lives of boys and girls is more important today than at any time in the past. The social activities that permeate much of the club work and the extra-school life of adolescents are important avenues for the development of desirable boy-girl relationships. Through social affairs, boys and girls are given the opportunity of working together. Thus, opportunities develop for a division of responsibilities on the basis of sex. Girls make cookies and decorate tables in home economics classes, while boys aid by making things in the shop. Many communities are alert to the interests and needs of adolescents. Recreation centers are being opened in which a reasonable amount of supervision is provided.

Units of study in natural science give worth-while information about the birth and care of living things. In the same way, the social sciences provide an understanding of man's institutions, customs, and ways of living. Through ordinary classroom activities and school programs, materials may be presented and problems projected, provided the teachers do not take a "taboo" attitude toward a discussion of any problems that may have a direct bearing on sex education. In addition there is much information and literature that bring the students into closer contact with some of the problems directly related to social relationships between boys and girls. Many family problems are well illustrated in such books as Undset's

Kristin Lavransdatter, Maugham's *Of Human Bondage,* and Galsworthy's *Forsyte Saga.*

It is in misinformation and in inadequate information that the sources of many sex problems lie. When such a condition has existed and the child is further shielded from contacts of a wholesome nature with members of the opposite sex as he grows into adolescence, he acquires distorted ideas and attitudes toward sex. Many of the present-day sex problems among growing boys would be solved at an early period if conditions and customs provided for early mating as a means of sexual release. However, this is contrary to the customs, morals, philosophy, and institutions of our civilization.

The problems that have been presented throughout this study are important not only in relation to the present social and sex adjustments of adolescent boys and girls, but also in connection with their adjustments in family life in the years ahead. Guidance and training of youth toward a well-adjusted and happy family life has been too often left to chance. This is, no doubt, an important factor affecting the extent of maladjustments in home and family living. Concerning the importance of early childhood experiences and training for family life, Cochrane has stated:

> It is not too much to say that the ability to establish meaningful relationships and to find satisfaction in family life through marriage is largely conditioned by childhood experiences and by the acceptance of masculinity or femininity and sex differences by the individual.[25]

SUMMARY

The attainment of a satisfactory role among peers is a task faced by the child as he moves out of childhood into adolescence. The failure to attain a satisfactory role presents a critical problem to the adolescent. Studies have revealed several important findings relative to a child's relation to his peers:

1. The child desires the approval of his peers.

2. The relative importance of peer approval increases as the individual grows into adolescence.

3. Preadolescents and adolescents like to imitate their peers or those slightly older than they are.

4. Good peer relations during preadolescence are perhaps the best assurance available for good peer relations during adolescence and post-adolescence.

5. Early adolescence is accompanied by the formation of cliques. These cliques play an important part in satisfying certain felt needs of adolescents.

Problems of social approval, making friends, being popular, being accepted, and the like are real to most growing boys and girls. Since they feel that their parents either do not understand and appreciate them or are often critical of them in relation to their activities, and since they are unable to secure the needed help and guidance from their teachers, they seek help and sympathy from their peers.

The ripening of the sex impulses at this stage is accompanied by a changed attitude toward members of the opposite sex. No longer does a boy look upon a girl his own age as someone to be avoided; he now sees her as a personality whose admiration he desires. The development of this changed attitude is a natural concomitant of the ripening sex drive.

Adolescents have, as one of the major problems of their development, identification of themselves fully with the role—masculine or feminine—characteristic of their sex, an identification that began during infancy, when parents and friends made simple distinctions between boys and girls. It is necessary for the individual to learn to play his sex role, if he expects to be acceptable to members of the opposite sex. The infant is born without any awareness of sex or knowledge of its functions. Early in life, however, he learns that boys are treated differently from girls; he becomes familiar with the sex characteristics of his own body, and identifies himself with those characteristics; he accepts the attitudes of others concerning what is masculine and what is feminine; and if his sexual life and social contacts are normal, he eventually adjusts to his own and to the opposite sex in a satisfactory manner. The establishment of desirable heterosexual relations is an important part of social maturity.

Those working with adolescents should not judge them by their voice, body build, or special mannerisms, but both boys and girls should be guided in the achievement of their sex role. They should be encouraged to make themselves attractive to members of the opposite sex, to participate in heterosexual activities, and to realize that deviants from heterosexual interests are regarded by society as abnormal.

THOUGHT PROBLEMS

1. What is the general significance of the findings presented in this chapter dealing with the stability of adolescent friendships? How would you account for the sex differences presented?
2. Do your observations and experiences corroborate the findings presented in this chapter relative to the dating practices and activities within special class groups? What bearing does this have on the stability and continuity of class structure?
3. How would you account for the high degree of loyalty manifested by adolescents to their peers?
4. What are some of the barriers that adolescents often set up to exclude adults from their activities?

5. What do you consider the major values to be derived by adolescents from good peer relations? To what extent do such values enter into the lives of adults? How would you account for any differences to be noted here?

6. What is meant by the operation of *subculture?* Show how this operates among adolescent boys and girls?

7. What do studies indicate about the cause, nature, and dangers of "crushes"? Are these more common among adolescent boys or adolescent girls? How would you account for this?

8. What are some of the reasons why the "petting problem" may be more acute today than was the case 50 years ago? Cite evidence for changed attitudes toward matters related to sex.

9. Study someone of your acquaintance who is indifferent or antagonistic toward the opposite sex. What reasons do you think are back of his (or her) outward behavior?

10. What are the major causes of homosexuality in our society? Discuss the seriousness of homosexuality among adolescents. Among adults.

SELECTED REFERENCES

Block, Herbert A. and Arthur Niederhoffer, *The Gang: A Study in Adolescent Behavior.* New York: Philosophical Library, Inc., 1958.

Bromley, D. D. and F. H. Britten, *Youth and Sex.* New York: Harper & Row, Publishers, 1938.

Butterfield, O. M., *Love Problems of Adolescence.* New York: Emerson Books, Inc., 1939.

Hollingshead, A. B., *Elmtown's Youth.* New York: John Wiley & Sons, Inc., 1949, Chap. 9.

Horrocks, John E., *The Psychology of Adolescence,* 2nd ed. Boston: Houghton Mifflin Company, 1962, Chaps. 5-7.

Malm, M. and O. G. Jamison, *Adolescence.* New York: McGraw-Hill Book Company, 1952, Chap. 6.

Neisser, E. G., *When Children Start Dating.* Chicago: Science Research Associates, 1951.

Rogers, Dorothy, *The Psychology of Adolescence.* New York: Appleton-Century-Crofts, 1962, Chap. 9.

Strang, Ruth, *The Adolescent Views Himself.* New York: McGraw-Hill Book Company, 1957, Chap. 8.

Wattenberg, W. W., *The Adolescent Years.* New York: Harcourt, Brace & World, Inc., 1955, Chaps. 11 and 14.

Whyte, W. F., *Street Corner Society.* Chicago: University of Chicago Press, 1943.

NOTES

[1] "Iowa Teen-agers Step Out," *Ladies Home Journal* (August, 1949), p. 43. Copyright 1949 by the Curtis Publishing Company.

[2] Thomas S. Langner, "Normative Behavior and Emotional Adjustment" (Ph.D. Dissertation, Columbia University, 1954).

3 N. Reader and H. B. English, "Personality Factors in Adolescent Friendships," *Journal of Consulting Psychology*, 11 (1947), 212-20.

4 C. M. Tryon, *Inventory I: Social and Emotional Adjustment* (University of California Press).

5 G. G. Thompson and J. E. Horrocks, "A Study of the Friendship Fluctuations of Rural Boys and Girls," *Journal of Genetic Psychology*, 69 (1946), 189-98.

6 J. E. Horrocks and G. G. Thompson, "A Study of the Friendship Fluctuations of Urban Boys and Girls," *Journal of Genetic Psychology*, 70 (1947), 53-63.

7 A. B. Hollingshead, *Elmtown's Youth* (New York: John Wiley and Sons, Inc., 1949).

8 M. A. Wisenbaker, "A Study of the Factors Related to Social Isolation among High School Girls with Implications that Social Adjustment May Be Improved" (Master's Thesis, University of Georgia, 1952), p. 32.

9 N. E. Gronlund and A. P. Whitney, "Relation between Pupils' Social Acceptability in the Classroom, in the School, and in the Neighborhood," *School Review*, 64 (1956), 267-71.

10 B. Pope, "Socio-economic Contrasts in Children's Peer Culture Prestige Values," *Genetic Psychology Monographs*, 48 (1953), 157-220.

11 *Ibid.*, pp. 216-17.

12 Mortimer B. Feinberg, Max Smith, and Robert Schmidt, "An Analysis of Expressions Used by Adolescents at Varying Economic Levels to Describe Accepted and Rejected Peers," *The Journal of Genetic Psychology*, 93 (1958), 133-48.

13 M. A. May, "The Adult in the Community," in *The Foundations of Experimental Psychology*, ed. C. Murchison (Worcester, Mass.: Clark University Press, 1929), p. 782.

14 Dale B. Harris and Sing Chu Tseng, "Children's Attitudes Toward Peers and Parents as Revealed by Sentence Completions," *Child Development*, 28 (1957), 401-11.

15 Hollingshead, *op. cit.*, pp. 221-32. Figure 14-3 is reprinted by permission from *Elmtown's Youth* published by John Wiley & Sons, Inc., 1949.

16 H. T. Christensen, "Dating Behavior as Evaluated by High School Students," *American Journal of Sociology*, 57 (University of Chicago Press, 1951-52), 580-86.

17 Lester D. Crow, "Teen-age Traits, Interests, and Worries," *The Educational Forum*, 21 (1956), 423-28. By permission of Kappa Delta Pi.

18 A. C. Kinsey, *et al.*, *Sexual Behavior in the Human Male* (Philadelphia: W. B. Saunders, 1948); ———, ———, *Sexual Behavior in the Human Female* (Philadelphia: W. B. Saunders, 1953).

19 C. Darwin, *Expression of the Emotions in Man and Animals* (New York: Appleton-Century-Crofts, 1873).

20 *Guiding the Adolescent* (Children's Bureau, Federal Security Agency, Publication 225, 1946), p. 73.

21 G. V. Ramsey, "The Sex Information of Younger Boys," *American Journal of Orthopsychiatry*, 13 (1943), 347-52.

22 W. Cline, *Notes on the People of Siwah and El Garah in the Libyan Desert*, No. 4 (Menosha: General Series in Anthropology, 1936).

23 G. V. Ramsey, "The Sexual Development of Boys," *American Journal of Psychology*, 56 (1945), 230.

24 C. C. Fry, *Mental Health in College* (New York: The Commonwealth Fund, 1942).

25 H. S. Cochrane, "Emotional Aspects of Social Adjustment for the Child," *Mental Hygiene*, 32 (1948), 586-95.

15

THE ADOLESCENT IN THE COMMUNITY

The growing child lives and learns in his total environment. His behavior patterns and personality development cannot be understood apart from the cultural background in which he lives and learns. Figure 15-1 provides a perspective of the broadening of the child's social horizon with growth and development into and through adolescence.[1] The family group furnishes the major portion of environmental stimulation during the early years. During the preadolescent years play groups and gangs furnish considerable stimulation. With further growth the social horizon broadens so as to include many secondary groups, with the larger cultural pattern of the community exerting an ever-increasing influence.

This chapter deals with the following general topics as they relate to adolescent development and behavior: (1) the community structure, (2) adolescent needs and the community, and (3) adolescent participation.

THE COMMUNITY STRUCTURE

Changing community organizations. The social structure of American communities has undergone pronounced changes as a result of technology. For two centuries America was predominantly rural, with scattered towns which served as trading centers. As late as 1890, 72 per cent of the population was classified by the U. S. Bureau of Census as rural. However, the 1960 census showed that the urban outnumbered the rural nonfarm and rural farm population in all sections of the country, except in certain limited areas. Over half of these urban dwellers live in 14 metropolitan areas.

322

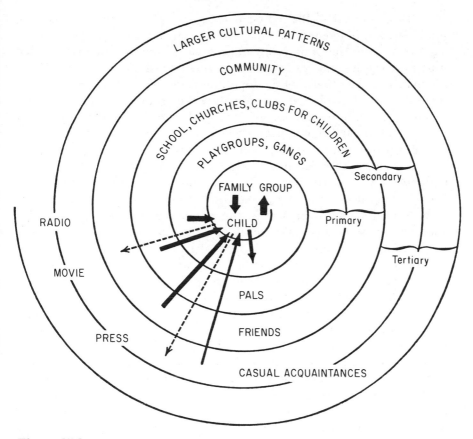

Figure 15-1

THE WIDENING OF THE CHILD'S EXPERIENCE AND THE RESULTING INTERACTION. THE THICKNESS OF THE ARROWS REPRESENTS THE PROBABLE RELATIVE IMPORTANCE OF THE INTERACTION BETWEEN THE CHILD AND THE VARIOUS INDIVIDUALS AND GROUPS

(*After Brown*)

The two World Wars accentuated certain population movements already under way during the first decade of this century. The result of this has been to increase the population of the metropolitan areas, to decrease the total farm population, and to develop more heterogeneous communities within and near the cities. This urban movement has taken place at a rapid pace, transforming the life, cultural interests, and values of a large percentage of our population. Many moral and social conflicts have developed as a result and new problems have arisen, which either did not appear or were not significant in the lives of the preceding generation.

Rural and urban life represent today, in spite of their approaching similarity, vast differences in value systems that create unique problems of adjustment for American youth. The greatest number of discontented American youth seems to be found in small towns. Their preference is for cities and the suburbs of metropolitan areas. The difficulties of life in the small town for youth are explained by the age structure of the typical population group. In most sections the small town is dominated by older people, widows, and retired people who are frequently opposed to change, and of little interest to young people.

Cultures within cultures. Within almost every community one will find diversity of occupations, religions, and organizations. These have been developed to fill the needs required of a more complex way of life. Also, local differences characterize American communities. These differences appear in the occupations of the people, cultural activities, religious life, economic standards, and educational levels. The social structure of the community affects adolescents in many ways, depending largely upon where their families fit into this structure.

Social stratification. Three variables were used by Reissman for measuring class position—occupation, income, and education.[2] He found that regardless of the variable used there was a greater degree of participation and involvement in the community by the higher-class group. That is, individuals from this group read more widely, attended church more regularly, belonged to more organizations, and held office more frequently in these organizations. The lower class, on the other hand, was less active in community affairs, and showed a startling lack of ideals and knowledge of the affairs and social mechanisms of the community.

The nature of family and church participation differs with different cultures. This may be observed in the types of social and recreational programs found in lower- and middle-class cultures. Significant differences may be observed in the nature of the school and out-of-school activities engaged in by teen-agers from different cultural backgrounds. The middle-class children in general make up the Boy and Girl Scouts and frequently take advantage of YMCA programs, whereas lower-class children are frequently found in clubs sponsored by some civic group or clubs for "underprivileged children." A significant minority of lower-class children do, however, participate with middle-class children in middle-class organizations. It is in this manner that these children learn middle-class attitudes and behavior which lead to upward social mobility.

An outstanding feature of the activities of upper-class children is their relative exclusiveness. Upper-class children attend summer camps too expensive for the majority. They travel to resort areas and stay at hotels patronized by a select group. They often attend schools with others from exactly the same background; they are in many ways protected from the rough edges of life. However, they frequently lack lower-class children's close association with their parents.

Whereas the activities of upper-class adolescents tend to be exclusive, those of the middle class may best be described as selective. Middle-class children and adolescents are required, because of financial considerations, to use public facilities. They are usually found in public and parochial schools, public parks, and other public areas. However, a selective process is continuously operating among middle-class adolescents and their parents. Parents try to choose the parks, the playground areas, and the forms of entertainment on the basis of middle-class culture and values. Especially in modern suburbia, they tend to be more discriminating and put greater pressure upon their children to achieve and move ahead socially than do lower-class parents. In suburbia, success is usually defined in terms of moving ahead; failure as not moving ahead. Parental anxieties and pressures are frequently very great among middle-class families, creating problems for teen-agers who are unable to fulfill the expectations of their parents.

Lower-class children have residual activities. They pursue the forms of play available to them such as those at the nearby playground or at welfare services. They are not protected from the difficulties of life. Individual competition in athletics, physical strength, and stamina are often in evidence. There is frequently little parental supervision, and few barriers to their growth in responsibility are set up by their parents. Parental expectations are seldom high.

Some influences of suburbia. The suburban way of life is first of all a segregated one. Housing developments have made for social-class segregation, since the homes of any one development usually fall within a somewhat limited price range. Children in the lowest class live in the abandoned area of the city that becomes the slum area. Here is civilization at its worst, a breeding place for juvenile crime. In contrast, the different suburban areas are made up of different social-class groups. The children of a particular suburban area tend to go to school together and to a church where there is again social-class segregation. Within a middle-class suburban community there are strong pressures for conformity. The parents are preoccupied with "keeping up with the Joneses," and the adolescents are supposed to achieve and behave in certain prescribed ways.

The suburbs are to a marked degree dominated by young people. Young parents, children, and teen-agers make up the population. The traditional familial ties are largely absent. Grandparents, aunts, and uncles seldom live in close proximity. Thus, youth is isolated from the past family culture. Children grow up in a protective environment. By the time adolescence is reached they have absorbed the mores and values of the adult society. They look upon themselves as privileged individuals and adopt the attitudes and patterns of behavior of the adults. "Going steady," drinking, and other activities of suburban adults become their way of life. Also, an outstanding feature of their life is the tendency to conform. Conformity brings security—an important need of adolescents. Concerning the problems of adolescents reared in suburbia, Barclay states:

> The adolescent reared in such a way and in such a setting is likely to enter high school advanced in a number of ways, prematurely so in a few, but almost a babe in the woods where some of the sterner realities of life are concerned.
>
> At a time when he most needs something solid to hold to, something clear-cut to strive toward, he finds himself adrift in a world dedicated to leisure and "the good life," in a community with no firm tradition, among adults unsure of their own values, looking to one another even as their adolescents do for standards of acceptability.[3]

The role of the community. The importance of community forces and conditions in the development of teen-age boys and girls is hard to evaluate. There is much evidence that, with the decline in size and function of the family unit, forces within the community have assumed a more important role; consequently, at some point, the growing individual comes face to face with problems that are not solved on the basis of authority or of sentiment, as are problems arising at home. The importance of the home and community in the development of character was well stated many years ago by John Dewey when he wrote:

> In its deepest and richest sense a community must always remain a matter of face-to-face intercourse. This is why the family and neighborhood, with all their deficiencies, have always been the chief agencies of nurture, the means by which the dispositions are stably formed and ideas acquired which lay hold of the roots of character. The Great Community, in the sense of free and full intercommunication, is conceivable. But it can never possess all the qualities which mark a local community.[4]

Favorable personal and social development will not take place in a vacuum. Neither will these result from too limited experiences. The adolescent must be given an opportunity to make social contacts outside the home and immediate neighborhood, to accept responsibility, and to display a reasonable amount of initiative in order to develop the personal and social self.

The community operates in a variety of ways in affecting the behavior and development of adolescents. In the first place, it is characterized by somewhat common patterns of behavior which are both taught to and forced upon the adolescents. In the second place, the community furnishes the adolescents with answers to questions of conduct, morals, and life's purposes. Not only are these answers furnished by the various forces and agencies of the community, but they insist upon their being accepted. Since the community is less compact than the neighborhood, however, the answers to these problems are more varied in nature. Thus, the adolescent is given some choice by the community in following certain patterns of behavior or accepting certain ways of life. The more homogeneous the community the less choice there will be for the adolescent.

A third way in which the community affects adolescents is through its cultural content. The language spoken in the community makes a deep impact upon the adolescent at an early age. The likes and dislikes, prejudices, tastes, and appreciations of the adolescents are to a marked degree a result of community influences. There is usually little conflict between the influences of the home and community, since most of the homes are in themselves largely products of the community or some similar community. Some types of communities offer better cultural content than do others. This is reflected in the libraries, churches, entertainment facilities, and schools. In general, rural people do not have the culture of urban people.

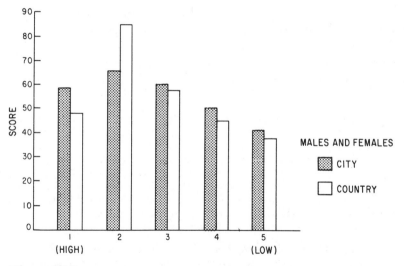

Figure 15-2

PERFORMANCE ON INTELLIGENCE TEST OF FIFTH-GRADE CHILDREN FROM DIFFERENT SOCIAL CLASS GROUPS IN THE CITY AND COUNTRY (*Young and Tagiuri, Tesi and Montemagmi*)

There are wide differences in the economic and cultural levels of different communities. A community composed largely of families in the lower cultural levels will provide different conditions for growth of adolescents than a community composed largely of families in the middle and upper cultural levels. Studies by Davis,[5] Anastasi,[6] and others show a significant relationship between social class and intelligence test scores. Differences have also been noted in educational expectations of parents, recreational opportunities, cultural activities and opportunities, and the nature of social and religious programs available. A study reported by Young and Tagiuri used fifth-grade children from Florence, Italy and the surrounding rural areas as subjects.[7] The results of an intelligence test administered to these children showed that boys in the city obtained higher scores than girls, whereas in rural areas, the situation was reversed. This indicates something of the complexity of the problem. The results presented in Figure 15-2 show that, except for class 2 (upper-middle-class), city children made higher average scores than rural children. Results obtained from American children give similar results, although exceptions may be noted due to wide variations in the social structure and cultural opportunities making up different communities.

ADOLESCENT NEEDS AND THE COMMUNITY

Due to indifference or lack of finances many communities provide no facilities for youth activities and no opportunities for youth to partici-pate in adult activities. Teen-agers frequently complain of the lack of something to do. The following testimony of a 15-year-old in an industrial area of a southern town of 35,000 is representative of the feelings of many teen-agers.

> In our community there is nothing to do over the week-ends except to go to church on Sunday. Some of the people of the community helped us set up a place which was a sort of gathering place for teen-agers where there were soft drinks, sandwiches, and music. Some of the kids of the community got angry because they closed the place at 11:30 on Saturday nights and just about wrecked the place. I was a Cub Scout for a while, but that didn't last. The physical education teacher was the main one that pushed this. He got a job somewhere else. When someone starts something it doesn't last. He can't get help from enough people to make it go.

The suburban adolescent's needs are just as acute as those of the adolescent in an industrial or rural area. Frequently his community, al-though made up of handsome homes, has failed to provide out-of-school facilities and services. Libraries, museums, park areas, and theaters are as lacking as they are in most run down city slum areas. The community developed as a means of satisfying the needs and aspirations of middle-class adults with little consideration given to the needs of children.

Effects of science and technological developments. A disturbing aspect of our technological culture is the lack of a balance between stimulation from movies, television, and other media and active outlets in the pleasures sanctioned for young people. Concerning this, Erickson has stated:

. . . With the passing of the western frontier and the accelerated appearance of automatic gadgets, young people have become increasingly occupied with passive pursuits which require little participation of mind and body—being conveyed rapidly through space by machines and watching violent fantasies at the movies or on television—without the possibility of matching the passive experience with active pursuits. When an adolescent substitutes passivity for the adventure and activity which his muscular development and sexual drives require, there is always the danger of explosion—and I think that this accounts for much of the explosive, unexpected, and delinquent acts on the part of even our "nice" young people.[8]

Need for conformity. The need for conformity is an outgrowth of the teen-ager's desire for peer approval. Conformity in American culture, however, is not confined to teen-agers; it may be observed in adults. Because of the nature of adolescent culture it appears to be more pronounced among teen-agers. In their urge to find security through similarity, some adolescents become stereotyped in behavior and ideals. They form cliques for self-protection and security, and they follow the fads of the group to assure themselves that they belong. Some points relating to conformity among teen-agers help us to better understand the function of conformity at this stage of life. Some of these may well apply to both teen-age and adult societies:

1. Conformity may be conceived of as an expression of the basic need to belong. The strange dress, peculiar hair styles, and teen-age lingo are signs to teen-agers and to others that they are part of the "in-group."

2. Conformity in itself is not necessarily good or bad. Adolescents can conform to the high values and ideals of the group, and thus gain support for worthy moral and ethical codes of behavior. A society of nonconformists would be unable to work together; they would be unable to cooperate on common tasks and would fall apart because of their wide differences. One of the strengths of a good youth program is the support which its members can find for their own living by conforming to the standards of the group.

3. Extreme conformity is frequently a sign of insecurity. Teen-agers who pattern their whole lives upon group goals and standards are usually extremely concerned about their position in the group. Such was the case of Joe:

Joe is a 13-year-old boy in the seventh grade of a new junior high school. He rates as one of the most popular members of his class, and is its president. Many parents hold Joe up as a model for their son to follow or for their daughter to date. Actually, psychological tests show Joe to be a troubled boy, filled with anxiety and fear of failure. He sees himself as one unable to do as well on most tasks as others. He is extremely careful to conform and be friendly with everyone in order to cover up his inner fears and hostilities toward others.[9]

Need for identity. During adolescence the individual begins to seek more remote sources of explanation, sources that lie outside the confines of his family and community. He often tries to find a coherent code of ethics or a religious philosophy to explain the divergent practices of people and even the conflicting tendencies that he discovers within himself.[10] Instead of the adventure stories of his former years, he turns his attention to biography and fiction, in which he can explore personal relationships vicariously and find men and women to represent ideal portraits of himself as well as ideal persons by whom he would like to be loved and respected. As the adolescent becomes gradually aware of social forces outside the range of his immediate experience, he may identify himself with national and international political issues and form passionate attachments to broad movements in social philosophy or art.

The adolescent's desire to relate himself to the wider culture is a potential source of development toward maturity. It indicates that he is moving from dependence to independence.

Hard though it is to achieve, the sense of identity is the individual's only safeguard against the lawlessness of his biological drives and the autocracy of his overweening conscience. Loss of identity, loss of the sense that there is some continuity, sameness, and meaning to life, exposes the individual to his childhood conflicts and leads to emotional upsets.

Sense of responsibility. American society demands, among other things, that an adult have a sense of responsibility. A sense of responsibility may be defined as the capacity to meet obligations in a manner satisfactory to oneself and to external reality. The obligations may be imposed from without by some external authority, or they may be imposed from within. The ability to meet an obligation imposed from within demands more maturity than meeting one imposed by external circumstances.

A sense of responsibility requires a combination of characteristics. First, the individual must have well-defined ego boundaries and be able to recognize himself as a person, separate and distinct from other people. Secondly, he must have made a firm identification with his parents. And lastly, he must have the ability to form adequate object relationships—to be able to love other people, understand them and their needs and desires, and hate and be angry under realistic circumstances. An individual with these characteristics is able to deal both with his instinctual impulses and with the external world; he has a well-functioning superego reinforced by a set of ideals—the ego ideal—and by identification with the traits of many other people besides his parents. Such a person is able to take responsibility for the results of his acts.

Four sets of pressures are involved in the development of a sense of responsibility: (1) the ways in which the adult world—parental, scholastic, and communal—pressures the adolescent to take responsibility; (2) the ways in which the adult world refuses to permit him to take responsibility; (3) the standards set for the adolescent by the adult world; and (4) the adolescent's own desire or lack of desire to be responsible.[11]

Sense of integrity. The sense of integrity is also essential for social development in adolescents. In every culture the dominant ideals—honor, courage, faith, duty, purity, grace, fairness, self-discipline—become at this stage the core of the personality's integration. The individual, in Erikson's words,

> becomes able to accept his individual life cycle and the people who have become significant to it as meaningful within the segment of history in which he lives. . . . Integrity thus means a new and different love of one's parents, free of the wish that they should have been different, and an acceptance of the fact that one's life is one's own responsibility. It is a sense of comradeship with men and women of distant times and of different pursuits, who have created orders and objects and sayings conveying human dignity and love. Although aware of the relativity of all the various life styles that have given meaning to human striving, the possessor of integrity is ready to defend the dignity of his own life style against all physical and economic threats. For he knows that, for him, all human dignity stands or falls with one style of integrity of which he partakes.[12]

In each developmental phase it is clear that organic and social factors converge to create a crisis for the maturing ego. At one time, it is rapidly emerging sensory and muscular abilities pitted against social demands for conformity and acquiescence. At another, it is the physiological and emotional changes of adolescence and the necessity for decisions regarding adult roles. At each stage there are physiological and cultural forces operating that affect the needs and behavior of the individual.

ADOLESCENT ACTIVITIES

School and peer groups have taken over many functions once performed by the family. In addition, church programs have been modified to aid in the educational and socialization program of children and youth. Many American children are being brought up in a piecemeal fashion—the home having a specific function, the school its function, the scouts their function, and the church its function: education and discipline are relegated to the schools, recreation and skills to the playgrounds and different youth groups, and ethical and spiritual guidance to the church. These conditions stem from the failure to make new experiences relevant to old in a rapidly changing society. The adolescents in our cities live in the midst of a paradoxical situation—a life with material comforts and living conditions never before known to man, but a life all too often without purpose and direction.

Despite the breakdown of the influence of the home, teen-agers regard the home and school as the major forces that have affected their lives. They yearn for money and a car.[13] Many of them are eager to get an education and a good position in life. They frequently participate in youth organizations and church activities. They admire family life and express a desire for a happy home. These are important facts about youngsters that seldom make the headlines.

Formation of groups and gangs. At the age of adolescence boys and girls become highly interested in forming groups, societies, gangs, and clubs; and these are indeed truly representative of the "gang" stage of life. Scientific investigations show that as a rule the members of a gang are likely to be of about the same level of intelligence. The members usually come from within a certain limited geographical area, as is the case in the selection of chums among adolescent boys. The gang is in the main a neighborhood affair. Through it individuals are affected by the behavior patterns of others and tend to influence the formation of behavior patterns in others by their own activities. The group is generally homogeneous in its desires, likes, and dislikes; social uniformity in ideals and attitudes tends to develop in accordance with general activities. Loyalty to different members of the group reaches a high pitch and may even surpass the loyalty earlier established to such ideals as honesty and truthfulness.

The structure and behavior of a gang is molded in part through its accommodation to its life conditions. The groups in the ghetto, in a suburb, along a business street, in the residential district, in a midwestern town, or in a lumber community vary in their interests and activities not only according to the social patterns of their respective milieus but also according to the layout of the buildings, streets, alleys, and public works, and the general topography of their environments. These various conditioning factors within which the gang lives, thrives, and develops may be regarded as the "situation complex," within which the human nature elements interact to produce gang phenomena. So marked is the influence of such factors as bodies of water, hills, and ravines in determining the location and character of gang activities that in Cleveland juvenile delinquents have been classified on this basis.

Gangs represent the spontaneous efforts of boys to create a society for themselves where none exists adequate to their needs. Boys derive from such association experiences that they do not get otherwise under the conditions that adult society imposes—the thrill and zest of participation in common interests, more especially in corporate action, in hunting, capture, conflict, flight, and escape. Conflict with other gangs and the world about them furnishes the occasion for many of their exciting group activities.

The gang functions with reference to these conditions in two ways: It offers a substitute for what society fails to give; and it provides a relief from suppression and distasteful behavior. It fills a gap and affords an escape. Thus the gang, itself a natural, spontaneous type of organization arising through conflict, is a symptom of disorganization in the larger social framework.

As individuals become affiliated with different groups in the school, the church, and the community in general, there may be conflicting loyalties. This is especially true for those who are members of minority groups, for the larger and more inclusive community organizations and agencies are likely to foster ideals and attitudes dominated by the majority element. The problem of adjustment is more difficult for minority groups—since it is fraught with more chances for conflicts—than for members of the majority group or groups. Concerning the role of the gang for such adolescents, Erickson states:

> A gang may be an important refuge and outlet for certain youths from minority groups who cannot identify proudly with their parents nor with the dominant urban culture which rejects them. The impulse which makes them come together in gangs where they can feel they are understood and respected, where they can gain a sense of belonging and learn cooperation, is often basically healthy.[14]

Club activities. During the early adolescent years girls seem to be more organizationally oriented than boys of the same age. As shown in Table 15-1, only 32 per cent of the girls belong to no club, whereas 41

Table 15-1

COMPARISON OF GROUP MEMBERSHIPS OF
EARLY ADOLESCENT BOYS AND GIRLS

Number	Boys 11–13 Years	Girls 11–13 Years
None	41%*	32%
One	38	35
Two	15	21
Three	4	8
Four	1	3
Five	—	1
Six	—	—
Seven or more	—	—

* These are given to the nearest per cent and do not add up to 100.

per cent of the boys do not belong.[15] Girls also belong to more clubs at the same time than boys. Significant differences appear in school activity groups, church groups, and informal groups. Several factors may be offered to account for these differences: In the first place, girls are more mature and at this early adolescent age seek friendships with others. Secondly, girls appear to be more interested in social activities and groups as a means of satisfying their desire for belonging. Thirdly, the club membership of this study did not include participation on organized teams. Boys are more given to sports and team activities than girls, and are more democratic in their relations with team members.

In looking at the types of clubs to which boys belong we note a shift from ages 11 to 13 to ages 14 to 16, although the per cent in each of these

Table 15-2

TYPES OF GROUP MEMBERSHIP OF EARLY- AND LATE-ADOLESCENT BOYS

Types	*11–13 Years* *Per cent*	*14–16 Years* *Per cent*
National activity clubs	44	45
Boy Scouts	25	16
YMCA, YMHA	4	8
Farm groups—4-H, etc.	10	14
Boys' Clubs of America	3	2
Cub Scouts	1	—
Other	1	5
School activity clubs	18	38
Glee club, band	4	7
Art, photography clubs	—	1
Clubs organized around one school course, scholastic clubs	4	11
Athletic clubs (not teams)	1	8
Class clubs, student body groups	3	2
Other	6	9
Church groups	18	33
Social and informal clubs	2	7
Miscellaneous clubs	2	2
None	41	31
Not ascertained	—	—

age ranges belonging to some type of national organization remained about the same. As shown in Table 15-2, the greatest change is in the percentage belonging to the Boy Scouts. In the school and church groups there are also great differences shown with increased age. Approximately twice as many older adolescents belong to school activity and church groups as younger adolescents. Part of this increase results from the greater availability of clubs and group organizations for older adolescents. However, a larger percentage of 11 to 13-year-old girls belong to clubs than boys, except for Boy or Girl Scouts.

Most popular leisure-time pursuits. The ways boys and girls spend their leisure time is an indication of the nature and direction of their interests. A survey of ninth- and tenth-grade students of the Evanston Township High School (Illinois) showed that the average time spent watching television was 2.75 hours per day.[16] Several other surveys have yielded similar results. There is evidence that the attraction of TV diminishes some after the newness tends to wear off. Witty refers to an unpublished study made at Glencoe, Illinois, which showed that the average time spent

Table 15-3

MOST POPULAR LEISURE ACTIVITIES AS RANKED BY ADOLESCENT BOYS, ACCORDING TO AGE

(*After Bibb*)

	Age of boys reporting			
Activity	*14*	*15*	*16*	*17*
Participating in sports	1	1	1	1
Attending movies	2	2	3	2
Attending social affairs	4	5	—	8
Attending sports	3	3	4	4
Attending parties	5	10	10	7
Talking	6	3	2	3
Playing games	7	7	5	—
Doing homework	8	9	9	6
Walking	9	—	7	—
Fixing things	10	4	6	—
Attending church affairs	—	8	—	9
Riding	—	6	8	10

by seventh graders at first was 3 hours per day. After 18 months this average was reduced to 1.8 hours. A number of studies show that most boys are more enthusiastic about TV than girls. This perhaps stems from their intense interest in sports presented over television.

The most popular leisure activities of adolescent boys and girls were

Table 15-4

MOST POPULAR LEISURE ACTIVITIES AS RANKED BY
ADOLESCENT GIRLS, RANKED BY AGE
(After Bibb)

Activity	Age of girls reporting			
	14	*15*	*16*	*17*
Talking	1	1	1	1
Attending movies	2	2	2	2
Participating in sports	3	6	5	7
Attending school affairs	4	3	3	3
Listening to phonograph	5	—	8	—
Attending church affairs	6	10	7	—
Doing homework	7	5	9	5
Attending parties	8	4	4	6
Going for walks	9	—	—	—
Dancing	10	8	6	10
Riding	—	9	10	—
Walking	—	7	—	8
Playing games	—	—	—	4

studied by Bibb with 1042 Rockford, Illinois, high school students as subjects.[17] Participation in sports ranked highest among the boys at all the grade levels studied. The results, shown in Table 15-3, show that boys prefer attending movies and social affairs next to participating in sports. The most popular leisure activities of girls, presented in Table 15-4, are talking, attending movies, and participating in sports.

As boys and girls pass through pubescence they display a progressive increase in interest in heterosexual activities. Dancing ranked first as the most popular leisure activity of heterosexual groups 15, 16, 17, and 18 years of age (see Table 15-5). Listening to the radio and watching TV programs are activities frequently engaged in by adolescent boys and girls together.

Leisure activities and socio-economic status. A number of studies have shown that different socio-economic groups in the United States have different cultures, although these cultures share a common American culture including language, political attitudes, interest in sports, food habits, and the like. Thus, one will find groups of adolescents culturally alike in some ways and culturally different in other ways. Kobrin noted that:

> Adolescents generally are expectedly responsive to the norms and values of the adult society which they seek to enter. However, since they are excluded from participation in the serious concerns of the adult society, adolescents have no opportunity to use these norms and values in the flexible and realistic way characteristic of adults.[18]

Table 15-5

MOST POPULAR LEISURE ACTIVITIES OF HETEROSEXUAL
GROUPS AS REPORTED BY ADOLESCENT BOYS AND GIRLS,
ACCORDING TO AGE
(After Bibb)

Activity	Age of boys and girls reporting				
	14	15	16	17	18
Playing games	1	3	2	4	3
Dancing	2	1	1	1	1
Listening to phonograph	3	2	3	2	—
Participating in sports	4	6	4	10	2
Attending movies	5	4	6	5	—
Talking	5	5	5	3	5
Attending school affairs	7	10	10	9	—
Attending parties	8	9	9	7	—
Attending sports	9	8	7	6	—
Riding	10	7	8	8	4

YOUTH PARTICIPATION IN COMMUNITY ACTIVITIES

Service activities of youth. It has been suggested that there is more
wasted energy among teen-agers than among any other group in our
society. There are, however, many services that teen-agers can perform
that will be most useful to society and valuable to those involved. Prior
to 1956, New York City hospitals refused to accept volunteers under 18,
since they were considered too irresponsible for doing tasks around the
hospital. In 1956, when there was a lack of adult volunteers to assist the
Red Cross Bloodmobile program, a group of high school youngsters were
recruited. Margaret Hickey reports the results of recruiting teen-agers and
how this program has expanded in New York City.[19] In the summers of
1957-61, more than 5000 youngsters gave from two to five days a week of
their time. Another 4000 helped without pay in city playgrounds, day-
care centers, homes for the aged, Red Cross chapters, and with blood-
mobiles. The teen-agers were provided free Red Cross uniforms when
necessary and carfare to and from their work when needed. The volunteers
came from all social classes—exclusive private schools and from slum areas.

The volunteer bureaus run by community health and welfare councils in hundreds of cities help thousands of teen-agers find summer jobs
with no pay.[20] However, these jobs pay tremendous wages in experience,
in enhanced opportunities for admission to college, in new friendships,
and in a sense of feeling wanted and needed in the world. In the Boston
area, for example, the School Bureau of the United Community Services
listed for the summer of 1963 over 100 types of jobs available to high

school and college students. Teen-agers frequently find their future careers through these jobs.

Junior workers do not seem to find the different jobs monotonous and worthless but feel that they are performing valuable services. This seems to give them a sense of worth that helps to inspire an attitude of courtesy and confidence. Concerning their work at the hospital, the director of volunteers at Roosevelt Hospital states:

> A young teen-ager doesn't react to tragedy the way an adult does because it's something he's never personally experienced. When he sees a crippled child, or someone old and blind, he doesn't put himself in their shoes. He doesn't *identify* with the patient. I've seen a 15-year-old girl walk over to a deformed infant and pick him up in the most natural, loving way you can imagine. As far as she's concerned, it's simply a child in need of love, and she responds wholeheartedly, without false sentimentality.[21]

Such tasks help satisfy certain needs of adolescents. Here is an example of the energies of youth being spent in constructive activities rather than destructive or useless activities. Concerning this, Dr. McLaughlin, Director of the Public Education Association of New York City pointed out:

> Our experience with New York City teen-agers has proved that kids are starved for interesting, essential work. In volunteer jobs they quickly learn that money isn't as important as they once thought and that giving money to charity is never as valuable as giving oneself.[22]

Community participation. Grambs set forth the following postulate regarding community influences on youth group formation:

> Civically-oriented self-governing youth groups probably cannot develop or survive without community help and localized institutional support. A study of the influences of communities on adolescents reveals this postulate to be sound. Where active community help and institutional supports are lacking delinquent and quasi-delinquent activities appear in an effort of adolescents to overcome adult barriers and give expression to their own needs. However, through adults and adult-sponsored institutions adolescents can when adequately motivated find a positive place in the community life as junior citizens of the community.[23]

Communities of any class can, if they wish, provide educational programs designed to prepare the adolescent to fit the communities' needs, and promote wholesome leisure-time outlets for recreation, avocation and diversion. Since even in this age of high mobility the majority of people stay within a small radius of their home communities, the coordination of the educational program of a community with the community's needs becomes a matter of importance, especially to the adolescent who should become the instrument for meeting these needs as well as having the community meet his needs. Worthy answers by the community to adolescents' questions concerning conduct, morals, and life's purposes require facilities for youth to implement those answers and give substance to them.

Enlarging the scope of participation. Most community activities for youth have been of a service nature. There is a need to enlarge the scope of work opportunities for teen-agers. The extended use of the community as a laboratory in education should help in providing opportunities for youth to participate in conferences, study groups, work camps, radio and television programs, community projects, civic programs, and international exchange of ideas. A movement in this direction was taken in the spring of 1958 when 60 teen-agers (leaders) met in New York City in a consultation called by the Committee on Youth Services of the National Social Welfare Assembly.[24] The young people were asked about ways to get youth to participate more freely in community activities. Through group discussions the young people came to the conclusion that only a small percentage of young people actively participated in community affairs. They expressed much concern about youth participation and indicated that it was their opinion that from 90 to 95 per cent of youth would definitely be interested in participation if they had the proper guidance and encouragement. They further expressed the belief that even the 10 per cent that would not be interested might be reached if the right kinds of appeals were made.

Contributions of youth. Adults have much to gain from working with youth on community projects. Surveys show that in many communities youths are participating in varied projects. Some of these are described by Wright:

> It is well then to take a look at life throughout the United States to see what are the major forces affecting the well-being of communities and then to ask, Can youth help? This does not mean to ignore those needs related to youth per se, such as the ever-present need for additional recreational facilities, but rather to accept the fact that any major public issue in one way or another not only has some bearing upon the degree to which young people can grow to their fullest stature as citizens but may itself benefit from the freshness and frankness of the young.
>
> Among the many problems facing our country today are a number in which young people have a direct stake. In regard to public-school integration, they are the ones who have firsthand experience. Their awareness, insights, and hopes in relation to their own abilities might also be taken into account as plans are developed for improving educational opportunities and school curricula and facilities.
>
> Our Nation's difficulties with other countries might even be eased somewhat if the natural openness of youth and their ability and willingness to see through outward differences to the inner similarities in people could be fostered. A 17-year-old girl, who spent a summer in Germany on a scholarship saw this when she said: "In 2, 3, or 4 years we'll be the airline hostesses, military personnel, trainees for diplomatic service, and tourists. If we could have more opportunities now to get to know youth in other countries who will

also be moving into these areas of responsibility, we'd save a lot of time in achieving a wholesome working relationship, which is so essential to real international cooperation and good will."

A group of 17 Y-Teens and 8 adults working on plans for the 1959 National Y-Teen Conference on Youth's Role in National and World Affairs emphasized the importance of young people's finding ways to express the goals of our Nation to the world in other than material aid. They pointed out that urging young people to build their skills in all the arts and languages could make a vital contribution in "presenting to the world the real face of America."

Some guidelines for analyzing how young people might appropriately contribute to any particular project might be found in estimating the degree of ability and knowledge required for various elements of the task; the quality and nature of experience necessary to bring reality to the approach; the abilities and skills needed to accomplish the goal; and the interrelationships that might enhance the work in process and bring the added benefits of good human relations and understanding at its completion.

Some Projects

Young people and adults are already working together in a number of projects to find ways of involving youth in local, national, and world concerns. Several national youth-serving organizations have advisory councils of youth constituents, which meet with national planning groups to evaluate programs and participate in the development of new programs. The National Council of Churches of Christ in the United States of America included young people as fully accredited delegates in a recent "high level" conference on the church and world order. Y-Teens are now recognized as full members of the YWCA, with opportunity to attend triennial national conventions as delegates. The Michigan Youth Advisory Council, composed entirely of young people, has initiated a program that bears on the well-being of the state as a whole, including projects to promote summer employment for youth; traffic safety; and improvement of the labor, educational, and recreational conditions of migrants.

The Wisconsin Youth Committee for Community Youth Participation, open to all young people through a county-district-state structure, is officially recognized as the channel for the expression of young people's opinions on public affairs. With adult consultation provided by the State Department of Public Welfare the committee attempts to draw youth into community affairs by providing clearinghouse services and by holding an annual state conference for the exchange of ideas and experience. Its state committee, chosen by the young people in district elections, works closely with the Wisconsin Committee on Children and Youth, a body of adults and young people appointed by the Governor, which has among its responsibilities the promotion of local youth councils. To help such councils inject vitality into adult-youth partnerships, the youth members of the Governor's committee have prepared the pamphlet "Youth Participation on the March," containing pointers for successful youth participation with adults in planning.

For several years young people in California have participated in the planning and deliberations of the Governor's youth conferences. The 1958 Conference on Youth Participation in Community Affairs offered an opportunity to discuss a wide range of interests including the family, the school, the church, jobs for youth, the motor age, delinquency prevention, community affairs, accomplishments of youth, and youth fitness. The report of the conference indicates that youth and adults entered freely into discussion and that there seemed to be acceptance of the need for partnership on the part of each. Reported one work group: "Youth and adults have something to share with each other. Neither group has all the answers. The important thing is developing good relationships and moving together with mutual trust and respect."

Principles for Success

As groups in towns and cities work to achieve more extensive and vital youth participation in community affairs, it is well to consider some of the factors that may help and those that may hinder their efforts. These might be identified by a consideration of the following questions:

1. What experiences in family living, school, church, and community groups will help young people become ready and willing to take part in the real issues of living?

2. As young people are helped to participate in community affairs, what are their motivations and expectations?

3. If young people seem unwilling to take responsibility in various phases of community life, what is the basis for their reluctance? What can be done to help them discover their own potential for participating in community life in a way that will have meaning for themselves and be of benefit to the community?

4. If adults invite youth to participate, what are the adult motivations and expectations?

5. As youth participates, how much should adults expect of them?

The role of the adult—singly and as an identifiable segment of the community—is an important key in the discovery, release, and utilization of the skills and potential of youth. It is important for those promoting adult-youth partnership to understand and accept some of the natural breaches between adolescents and adults, and find ways for them to work together in spite of these. The natural idealism and enthusiasm of youth along with the fact that most young minds are as yet uncluttered by the fears and prejudices that beset adults can bring an effective enthusiasm, not usually supplied by adults alone, to the tackling of many important tasks. Adults working to bring youth into meaningful participation in community affairs need an understanding of adolescent behavior, hopes, and aspirations, as well as an understanding and acceptance of themselves and their own strengths and limitations. They also need to have a knowledge of the elements at work in the community that enhance or hinder effective relationship, and to possess skill in helping people to work together in groups.[25]

The Wisconsin Committee on Children and Youth suggested several basic principles for successful youth participation:

In predominantly adult groups there must be enough youth to lend support to each other.

No youth group can function satisfactorily without mature adult support and guidance.

When youth are sitting in with adults, extra time must be taken to keep the youth informed.

Adjustments must be made in meeting times, places and methods when youth are being brought into adult programs—but also the inverse is true.

Whether youth or adults, special effort must be made to stay in contact with the people represented.

Youth must assume responsibility for showing adults what is desired of them. Sometimes, the nonparticipation of adults is a conscious effort not to take over.

Time must be allowed for both planning and evaluation if youth are going to learn by participating.[26]

The value of cooperation was well stated by a classroom teacher in the St. Louis public schools:

This faith in cooperation—belief that people working together to manage their own affairs is the best kind of control—has its roots in the social philosophy of democracy and is the essence of our American heritage. Yet, even though our society accepts this philosophy verbally, many of its institutions reveal that force and not the "will of all" is the guiding principle.[27]

SUMMARY

Changed social and economic conditions have resulted in profound changes in the organization and activities of the community. The increased leisure time of boys and girls has presented a definite challenge to the communities to provide recreational opportunities and better guidance of boys and girls, especially during the adolescent years. Materials have been presented in this chapter showing the activities of adolescents in the community and some of the needs for the community to provide better educational and recreational facilities for boys and girls as they grow through adolescence toward complete maturity.

A few pieces of lumber, some glue, and nails is not a table. Likewise, a collection of boys, girls, and adults is not a community. There must be some common interests and needs, mutual confidence and understanding, association and sharing a common lot, if there is to be a true community. Morgan has said in this connection: "In a true community many activities are shared by the same people. This unified living results in deeper social roots and more unified personalities."[28]

The summer camp has come into use as a means for providing for the recreational, health, and educational needs of adolescents. Increased leisure has presented a problem and a challenge. It is important that this time be not wasted, but used as a road to health, efficiency, and morality. Without a purpose or goal, free time may bring the adolescent in contact with vice, crime, and unconventional practices. But if his community offers libraries, museums, school activities, sports, hobby groups, church groups, "Y" settlement houses, playgrounds, movies, and parks, there is less chance that he will divert his energy into undesirable channels.

THOUGHT PROBLEMS

1. What are the main features of a community? Describe some community of your acquaintance, showing the presence of these features.

2. What are some of the new conditions and problems faced by the child in his community adjustments?

3. Show how conflicting loyalties sometimes develop as the individual becomes affiliated with various groups of the community.

4. What are some class distinctions found in a community of your acquaintance? Show how individuals may move from one class to another. What are the major barriers to such mobility?

5. Study the statement by Erickson, page 333, about the function of the gang. Show how this operates in connection with some gang of boys or girls of your acquaintance.

6. Describe the community facilities for recreation in some community with which you are especially acquainted.

7. Analyze the nature and function of one of the teen-age recreation centers discussed in some fairly recent number of *Recreation* magazine.

8. List the youth-serving agencies with which you are familiar. Look up data in a recent number of the *World Almanac* or some other source concerning the number of individuals enrolled in certain organizations with which you are familiar.

9. What are the major conclusions you would draw from the materials dealing with leisure activities and socio-economic status of children and adolescents? What are the implications of these findings for the planning of a recreation program for adolescents?

10. What are some of the major changes in the recreational interests of boys and girls from 10 to 16 years of age? (Review materials from Chapter 7 for additional information on this exercise.)

11. List what you consider to be the most important values that the adolescent derives from wholesome recreational activities.

12. What do you consider the role of the school to be in providing recreational facilities for adolescents? How can the church function in this connection?

SELECTED REFERENCES

Centers, R., "The American Class Structure," in T. M. Newcomb, E. L. Hartley, *et al., Readings in Social Psychology.* New York: Holt, Rinehart & Winston, Inc., 1947.

Cole, Luella, *Psychology of Adolescence,* 6th ed. New York: Holt, Rinehart & Winston, Inc., 1964, Chap. 22.

Hollingshead, A. B., *Elmtown's Youth.* New York: John Wiley & Sons, 1949, Chap. 7.

Jersild, Arthur T., *The Psychology of Adolescence,* 2nd ed. New York: The Macmillan Company, 1963, Chap. 14.

Kramer, D. and M. Karri, *Teen-age Gangs.* New York: Holt, Rinehart & Winston, Inc., 1953.

NOTES

1 F. J. Brown, *The Sociology of Childhood* (Englewood Cliffs, N.J.: Prentice-Hall, Inc., 1939).

2 L. Reissman, "Class, Leisure, and Social Participation," *American Sociological Review*, 19 (1954), 76-84.

3 Dorothy Barclay, "Adolescents in Suburbia," *Journal of the National Education Association*, 48 (1959), 11.

4 John Dewey, *The Public and Its Problems* (New York: Holt, Rinehart & Winston, Inc., 1927), pp. 211-12.

5 Allison Davis, *Social Class Influences upon Learning* (Cambridge: Harvard University Press, 1952).

6 Anne Anastasi, *Differential Psychology*, 3d ed. (New York: The Macmillan Company, 1958).

7 Harben B. Young and Renato Tagiuri, G. Tesi, and G. Montemagmi, "Influence of Town and Country upon Children's Intelligence," *British Journal of Educational Psychology*, 32 (1962), 151-58.

8 Erik H. Erickson, "Youth and the Life Cycle," *Children* (March, 1960), p. 47.

9 Garrison, Karl C., *Before You Teach Teenagers* (Philadelphia: Lutheran Church Press, 1962), p. 141.

10 Peter Blos, *The Adolescent Personality* (New York: Appleton-Century-Crofts, 1941), pp. 260-61.

11 H. J. Gerald and M. D. Pearson, *Adolescence and the Conflict of Generations* (New York: W. W. Norton & Company, Inc., 1958), pp. 145-49.

12 Erik H. Erickson, *Problems of Infancy and Childhood* (New York: Josiah Macy, Jr., Foundation, 1950), p. 55.

13 Karl C. Garrison, "Youth Survey: From Now to 2015" (Unpublished Data, Educational Psychology, University of Georgia, 1964).

14 Erik Erickson, *Young Man Luther* (New York: W. W. Norton & Company, Inc., 1958), p. 219.

15 *A Study of Boys Becoming Adolescents* (Ann Arbor, Mich.: Survey Research Center, Institute for Social Research, University of Michigan, 1960). A report for the National Council, Boy Scouts of America, of a national survey of boys in the 11 to 18 year age range.

16 Paul Witty, "Television and the High School Student," *Education*, 72 (1951), 242-51.

17 F. G. Bibb, "A Study of the Associates and Leisure-time Activities of 1,042 Rockford, Illinois Adolescents" (Master's Thesis, Indiana State Teachers College, 1950).

18 Solomon Kobrin, "Sociological Aspects of the Development of a Street Corner Group: An Exploratory Study," *American Journal of Orthopsychiatry*, 31 (1961), 687.

19 Margaret Hickey, "New York City's Teenagers," *Ladies Home Journal* (February, 1962), pp. 6, 11.

20 "What Will Your Teenager Do This Summer?" *Parent's Magazine* (May, 1963).

21 Margaret Hickey, *op. cit.*, p. 11.

22 *Ibid.*, p. 11.

23 Jean D. Grambs, "The Community and the Self-governing Adolescent Group," *Journal of Educational Sociology*, 30 (1956), 94-105.

24 *Report of Consultation on Youth in Community Affairs* (New York: National Social Welfare Assembly, Committee on Youth Services, 1958).

25 Sara-Alyce P. Wright, "Youth Participation in Community Affairs," *Children*, 6 (1959), 140-43. Most of the materials included under this topic are taken from this source.

26 *Youth on the March* (Madison, Wisc.: Wisconsin Committee on Children and Youth, 1958).

27 D. C. Bohn, "Teachers Share in Administration," *Educational Leadership*, 5 (1948), 429.

28 A. E. Morgan, "The Community," *Journal of the National Education Association*, 34 (1945), 55.

16

THE
ADOLESCENT
AT
SCHOOL

*What goes into the training of youth
emerges in the life of the nation.*[1]

INTRODUCTION: PROBLEMS AND PURPOSES

The institution of the school has evolved in all highly civilized societies. In a democratic society such as ours, it holds an outstanding and
dominant place. The estimated school-age population (5-17 years) in October 1963 was 48,342,000, while the enrollment in public elementary and
secondary schools reached a peak of 40.2 millions.[2] If we add to these the
number attending private schools it will be noted that approximately 90
per cent of the children and adolescents 5-17 years of age are enrolled
in school. The increased birth rate of World War II, which has continued
well beyond the middle of the century, along with the increased percentage of boys and girls of high school age remaining in school, is destined to increase considerably the enrollment in our high schools. The
number of high school graduates and population 17 years of age, 1900 to
1960, with projections to 1970 is shown in Figure 16-1. These data show
that the number of high school graduates grew from a relatively small
number in 1899-1900 to almost 1,700,000 in 1959-60. The projected growth
to 1970 would place the number of high school graduates in 1969-1970
around 2,700,000. There has also been a remarkable increase in college
attendance so that by 1965, over 1,000,000 students will be enrolled in
two-year colleges compared to 267,000 in 1940. The total enrollment in
colleges is expected to reach approximately 7,000,000 by 1970.

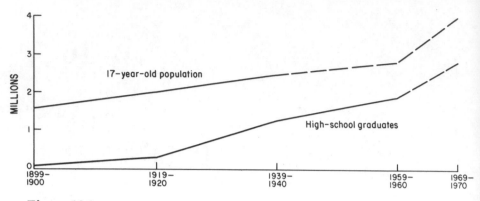

Figure 16-1

NUMBER OF HIGH SCHOOL GRADUATES AND POPULATION 17 YEARS OLD, 1900
TO 1960, WITH PROJECTION TO 1970

*(Based on: (a) U.S. Department of Health, Education, and Welfare, Office of Education.
"Statistical Summary of Education 1955-56." Biennial Survey of Education in the United
States, 1954-56. Washington, D.C.: Government Printing Office, 1959, p. 32. (b) U.S.
Department of Commerce, Bureau of the Census. School Enrollment: October 1959.
Current Population Reports, Population Characteristics, Series P-20, No. 101. Washing-
ton, D.C.: the Bureau, May 22, 1960, p. 8. (c) Unpublished figures of the U.S. Depart-
ment of Health, Education, and Welfare, Office of Education. NEA Research Division.)*

The twentieth century has also witnessed a pronounced increase in
leisure-time activities and a decrease in child labor. Our notion of what
constitutes child labor has changed enormously during the course of the
past century. Slightly over a century ago (1842) the State of Massachusetts
specified that children under 12 years of age should not work more than
10 hours per day. However, the first minimum-wage law, passed by Pennsylvania in 1848, established a 12-year minimum age for workers in textile mills. This was a higher minimum than that provided a few years
later in Connecticut and Massachusetts. The concern during this period
was over the control of the hours of labor for children rather than adolescents. There was little concern about child-labor legislation for adolescents until a fairly recent date. Thus, child labor in industry was at its
peak in 1910. At that time approximately 30 per cent of the 14- and 15-
year-old boys and girls were listed as gainfully employed, while many
others worked on the farms and at other tasks and did not attend school
regularly. Furthermore almost one million youngsters under 14 years of
age were gainfully employed. The steady decrease in the number of children employed each year since 1910, together with the corresponding increase in the number in school, is a reflection of the growth of the concept
that universal education is needed for intelligent and efficient citizenship.

Why adolescents quit school. Although the American theory of education maintains that the public school system, extending through the secondary school, is designed to serve all the boys and girls, a very large percentage of teen-agers drop out before completing high school. Most dropouts occur around the age of 16, or following the end of the compulsory school period. Actually, dropping out of school is usually a result of a long series of failures. Many dropouts play "hookie" from school several years before they leave. These boys and girls display little interest in any aspect of the school program. Cook concluded from a study of factors related to withdrawal that measurable differences exist between withdrawals and nonwithdrawals.[3] No single factor or simple combination of factors distinguished absolutely between the two groups.

The reasons given by students and those given by school counselors, presented in Table 16-1 are in many cases quite different. The interviews between the counselor and withdrawing student frequently revealed hidden forces at work affecting the student's attitude toward school. In many cases there was a tendency on the part of the withdrawing student to conceal the influence of scholastic failure, grade retardation, home and family difficulties, or feelings of rejection by giving as his reason for withdrawal some thinly veiled rationalization.

Table 16-1

REASONS FOR WITHDRAWAL AS STATED BY WITHDRAWING STUDENTS AND THOSE GIVEN BY THE SCHOOL COUNSELOR, BASED ON CLINICAL JUDGMENTS

(*After Cook*)

Reasons given by students	Per cent	Reasons given by counselor	Per cent
Going to work	39.6	Failure and retardation	34.9
Don't like school	20.9	Home circumstances	28.1
Married: Male	4.6	Marriage	20.29
Female	16.3		
Failing courses	9.4	Conflicts with teachers	7.2
Needed at home	4.6	Feelings of rejection	9.6
Left home	2.3		
Administrative request	2.3		

Youths who drop out of school may not be sure of the exact forces operating to cause them to do so. They know only that they are dissatisfied with school. Adverse school experiences or dissatisfaction with school was found to be an important factor in a study conducted by Wolfbein in Cleveland, Ohio.[4] Both boys and girls rated this higher than did the teachers. Dropping out of school, like delinquency, cannot usually be attributed to isolated causes. Case studies show that this behavior is usually a reaction to a total situation, as was the case of Tom:

> Tom was the youngest of four children. His parents owned a small farm. His father worked at varied jobs in the winter and at other times of the year when he was not busy cultivating his small farm. Tom's mother showed some anxiety for the education of the children. However, the father was quite luke-warm to the idea. Neither of Tom's two brothers nor his sister had finished high school. Tom was in the ninth grade, and was doing satisfactory work in all of his classes except English. Since he lived more than ten miles from school and rode to school on the school bus, he was unable to remain after school and take part in athletic practice and activities. Also, Tom didn't have as much money to spend as most of the children. Thus, Tom found little at school to interest him or to challenge his interests and abilities. A caustic remark by his English teacher relative to the grammar Tom used in a written composition was the final factor that caused Tom to remain out of school. At first his parents were unaware that he was not attending school. Later they found out that Tom had merely been riding into the village where the school was located and catching the school bus at the end of the school day and riding back. By this time Tom had gotten so far behind with his school work that he could not be persuaded by his mother to return to school.

Education and class status. With the constantly increasing number of adolescents remaining in school, teachers and school officials are confronted with problems that did not exist several decades ago. An important problem, often not recognized by the teachers and others concerned with the school program, is that of reconciling its middle-class point of view and values with the lower-class culture of so many of its pupils. This failure on the part of the schools creates conditions that drive the lower-class student from high school. The writer observed a case in which the small-town school had expanded and a number of boys and girls from the rural area were transported to school by bus. Several of these students had not had the social and cultural opportunities of the average child. They were at first unable to enter into many of the social aspects of the school life. The teachers tended to ignore them and the students, through their cliques, built up barriers that excluded the farm children from their activities. Most of the underpriviliged rural group dropped out of school. At a later date the school district was further expanded to include a much larger group of rural boys and girls. The program was expanded to provide vocational agriculture, industrial arts, home economics, and commercial courses. Many of these students were able to find courses and activities that were of interest to them. Perhaps a changed point of view was adopted by the teachers, without their realizing it, and after a few years the valedictorian and vice-president of the senior class came from the group of rural students.

A study of school retention among Elmtown youth shows that the dream of equality of educational opportunity is to a large extent a myth.[5]

Table 16-2

SCHOOL ENROLLMENT OF ELMTOWN YOUTH
ACCORDING TO CLASS STATUS

(After Hollingshead)

	In school		Out of school	
Class	Number	Per cent	Number	Per cent
I	4	100.0	0	00.0
II	31	100.0	0	00.0
III	146	92.4	12	7.6
IV	183	58.7	120	41.3
V	26	11.3	204	88.7

This is shown in the analysis of the per cent of adolescents from each of the five socio-economic cultural classes found in Elmtown presented in Table 16-2. There are two rather widespread misconceptions about the problem of school leavers. First, there are many upper-class city dwellers who pass up the problem by pointing out that these leavers are from the rural areas. Surveys conducted at Elmtown and other points show that this is not the case. The great preponderance of school leavers appear among the underprivileged groups in our rural areas, towns, and cities. The second misconception relates to the time of school leaving. The Elmtown study shows that despite compulsory school laws requiring boys and girls to remain in school until they are 16 years of age, 74 per cent of the 345 young people out of school in the spring of 1942 had dropped out before they had reached their sixteenth birthday. Neither the Elmtowners nor the school authorities were aware of the large number of young pople who had dropped from school. Such a condition may become even more exaggerated in a larger urban area.

Although differences in educational opportunity are apparent to any careful observer, differences in motives, goals, aspirations, and attitudes toward school are also extremely important to the teacher and to others concerned with the educational program. A study by Coster dealt with the relationship between specific attitudes toward school and level of income.[6] A questionnaire containing a morale scale and a house and home scale was administered to approximately 3000 pupils in nine central and south central Indiana high schools. The items pertained to the school teachers, school program, other pupils, and the value of an education.

Low income pupils were not so sure of parental interest in school work as other pupils; whereas practically all pupils from high income homes indicated that they felt their parents were interested in their school work. The high income pupils expressed a greater interest in continuing their education, and a greater confidence in being able to get the kind of job they wanted. The pupils in all groups reacted favorably to the value of education. The low income pupils, however, reacted more favorably to the utility value of education than to the enrichment values.

SCHOOL PROBLEMS OF ADOLESCENTS

Maladjustments at school. Educational problems loom large in the lives of adolescents. Problems relating to failure in school, how to study, pupil-teacher relationships, and the like, apparently appear in the lives of many high school boys and girls. Materials from the California adolescent growth studies, presented earlier, show that a large percentage of preadolescents, adolescents, and postadolescents disliked elements in the school situation that indicated unfair practices on the part of teachers and snobbish as well as overly aggressive and dominating attitudes and practices on the part of their classmates. In general the boys checked many more items related to the curriculum and program than did the girls. Dullness and lack of interest as well as lack of value (as viewed by the students) in the subject matter were checked in many cases at all stages of development by approximately 50 per cent or more of the boys and slightly fewer girls.

The results of investigations of school problems of adolescents show that a large percentage of boys and girls from the lower social status group express dissatisfaction with the school program. When this is coupled with the fact that a large percentage of dropouts, as revealed in Table 16-1, quit school because of dissatisfaction, we are forced to the conclusion that dissatisfaction with school operates among a large percentage of adolescents. It appears evident that a large percentage of adolescents, particularly from the lower social class, feel that the typical high school is unrealistic and offers little to them of special value.

A study reported by Jackson and Getzels dealt with the differences in psychological functioning and classroom effectiveness of two groups of adolescents—those who are satisfied with their recent school experiences and those who are dissatisfied.[7] Two groups of students enrolled in a midwestern private school identified by means of a *Student Opinion Poll* instrument as satisfied and dissatisfied were used as subjects in this study.

The results indicated first that dissatisfaction with school appears to be part of a larger picture of psychological discontent rather than a direct reflection of inefficient functioning in the classroom. Each of the test instruments designed to measure psychological health or adjustment was effective in distinguishing satisfied from dissatisfied students. Results on the negative adjective check list presented in Table 16-3 show that although both groups checked negative adjectives when asked to describe their feelings, the dissatisfied students checked negative adjectives more frequently than the satisfied students. Furthermore, interesting sex differences may be noted. It appears that "dissatisfied girls are somewhat less likely than dissatisfied boys to use negative adjectives involving implicit criticism of others. Dissatisfied boys, on the other hand, are less likely than dissatisfied girls to be distinguished from their satisfied counterparts by the use of adjectives *not* involving implicit criticism of others." Boys more often than girls project the cause of their discontent upon the world around them so that teachers and other adults are seen as rejecting and lacking in understanding.

Table 16-3

NUMBER OF SUBJECTS CHOOSING NEGATIVE ADJECTIVES WHEN ASKED TO DESCRIBE TYPICAL CLASSROOM FEELINGS (*Jackson and Getzels*)

	Boys		Girls	
Adjectives	Dissatisfied (N 27)	Satisfied (N 25)	Dissatisfied (N 20)	Satisfied (N 20)
Inadequate	19	16	17	7**
Ignorant	19	13	15	2**
Dull	25	16*	16	9*
Bored	24	13**	20	13**
Restless	20	15	19	9**
Uncertain	20	21	17	13
Angry	15	4**	13	4**
Unnoticed	19	5**	7	4
Unhelped	18	8*	9	6
Misunderstood	16	5**	5	2
Rejected	12	3**	4	0
Restrained	17	2**	9	3*

* Statistically (Chi Square) significant at the .05 level.
** Statistically (Chi Square) significant at the .01 level.

The child who is successful in school is quite often looked upon as a model; such success is regarded as a crowning achievement of will power, tenacity, desirable drives, and good mental habits and powers. That this is true in a great many cases is not questioned here; but when such an achievement is attained at the expense of a well-balanced personality, it is fraught with danger and should be looked upon with suspicion. The writer is reminded of a case that came within his observation a few years ago:

A girl, referred to here as Josephine, had always been a good student. She enjoyed her work at school and spent most of her time working with the assigned lessons. She was third from the top in a class of more than 30 pupils in the sixth grade. Since she was about average in intelligence (the Standard Revision of the Binet Test gave her an IQ of 107), she had to spend most of her time at work on her lessons in order to make the mark and hold the position in her class toward which her aims were always pointed. Her parents as well as friends and kinspeople commented favorably to her about her schoolwork, and this was an added urge to keep trying. From observations of this girl for a period of five years following this first general observation, it has become apparent that the girl is not developing her social qualities as she should. She has a very narrow range of interests; though a leader in her schoolwork she is not a leader among the group of girls of her class, nor has she given just consideration to her health and general appearance. It is unlikely that she will be able to go to college (unless her continued academic drive operates in this connection). Although she is not a problem case of any kind, she has not developed the various phases of herself that would serve her well in difficult situations or enable her to adapt herself to the groups with which she will come into contact during the course of her life.

Problems outside school have taken on an added importance within recent years. The high school student's behavior will be largely affected by the conditions and forces he meets outside the school environment. It makes a great deal of difference whether the boy or girl comes from a home where the social climate is happy and wholesome or where it is unhappy. Although it is not easy for school authorities to investigate problems arising from home and community conditions, an awareness of the nature of these conditions will enable them better to understand adolescent problems originating in situations and conditions outside the school.

The effects of nonpromotion. The notion that school standards must be upheld at "all costs" has gradually given way to the view that the individual pupils must be given first consideration. Naturally, there are a few cases where repeating a subject might be the most desirable procedure to follow, usually because the student involved is a normal, well-adjusted individual, who because of excessive absences, accidental conditions, or some other attenuating circumstances failed to make progress commensurate with his ability. In general, however, the factors that contributed to poor learning when the subject was first taken tend to operate when the subject is repeated.

A second objection to a policy of repeating a subject or grade concerns the personal and social effects upon the individual student. Nonpromoted students have fewer friends and are less popular with their classmates than are those regularly promoted.[8] Since retarded children are older than their classmates, they are on the average larger and stronger; however, teachers rate them low on most personality traits.[9]

Educational counseling will be concerned with the promotion of learnings commensurate with the abilities and needs of the individual pupils. In order to effectively counsel students whose achievement is low in comparison with their abilities, the counselor or teacher must be familiar with the causes of underachievement. Serene arrived at the major causes of underachievement by a group of high school students through interviewing them and analyzing their school records.[10] A summary of the causes is presented in Table 16-4. The list of causes shows the problems that must be met by high schools if they are to help students reach the level of achievement they are capable of reaching. Closely related to this problem is that of grades and promotion, a problem that has constantly plagued teachers.

Table 16-4

ESTIMATED CAUSES OF UNDERACHIEVEMENT BY HIGH SCHOOL STUDENTS

(*After Serene*)

Cause	Frequency
Lack of study	78
Poor planning and organization	56
Television	32
Not scholastic conscious	28
Dislike of subjects	22
Health and other physical reasons	18
Parental apathy	18
Social activities, dancing, skating, etc.	17
Study space lacking in the home	17
Work outside home	16
Poor home conditions, parents divorced or separated	15
Extracurricular activities	9
Poor grade school background	8
Poor reading habits	7
Dislike of teachers	6

Case studies in educational maladjustments. A better understanding of the operation of varied factors in producing educational maladjustments should result from a careful study of the two cases that are here presented.

CASE STUDIES

The case of Sonia

Sonia was a difficult person to find in school. She stayed home the equivalent of 51 days in half-day sessions during her years in senior high school and, when she was there, she was so expert at evading school regulations on any pretext that she just never seemed to be in the place to which she was assigned. She flitted about the halls with permission slips to go to the library, the typing laboratory, the nurse's office, or to any other spot in the building. She failed to do assignments and often arranged to be absent from classes on the days when they were due so that she had an alibi when the work was not done. Only one teacher followed through sufficiently to recognize what she was doing, and in that class she received her only failing grade. She came sufficiently close to failure so frequently that she ranked only 329 in a graduating class of 353. Sonia's grades are shown on the chart presented in Figure 16-2;

SUBJECT	GRADES 9		10		11		12	
English	C²	C²	D²	C²	D²	F	—	D
Amer. History					D²	D²		
Civics	C²	C²						
Amer. Problems							D²	C
Algebra	D²	D²						
Geometry			C²	D²				
Biology					D²	D²		
Physical Ed.	*Credit*		*Credit*		*Credit*		*Credit*	
Home Economics							C²	
Typing					C²	D²	C² *Dropped*	
Shorthand					D²	D²		
Junior Business	C²	C²						

Figure 16-2

MARKS GIVEN SONIA DURING HER FOUR YEARS IN HIGH SCHOOL

the numbers next to each grade indicate the degree of effort, (1) being high, (2) average, and (3) low.

In only one subject in one semester was Sonia's effort rated as excellent. She had started a course in clerical training, and because she liked the teacher and the subject seemed practical, she went right to work. As the work became more demanding in the second semester, her interest waned and she returned to her old practices. Sonia had very definite feelings about courses and teachers. She liked bookkeeping but not the teacher of that subject. She disliked geometry *and* the teacher of geometry. She refused for a week to attend the class in American problems to which she had been assigned because she did not like the teacher, and she might have missed graduation with her class had she not been permitted to transfer to another section. She disliked history because it was too difficult, but she admitted that she did not try very hard in that class. She disliked typing because of the speed tests, in which she said she got very nervous because one error counted so much against her. She said that she was forced to drop shorthand because she could not keep up with the speed of the other members of the class. She said that she would fail a course rather than give an oral report on it.

The pattern of behavior that she exhibited in classes carried over to other activities. When she was sent out to work in an office in a work-experience program for school credit, she did not like the brick floors and green shades in the room. And she did not like her fellow workers because "they were too catty and they did not like me because I wouldn't be catty, too." She did not like a part-time job as a store clerk and left it soon after she began.

When asked how her friends would describe her, Sonia said that they would say she was selfish and that she wanted her own way. She indicated that she was getting along better with her friends since she had stopped telling them what she thought about them. She encouraged the attentions of a boy who drove an expensive car but said that she was just leading him along without serious intentions to get the privileges which his plentiful supply of cash provided, and that she was dating other boys without his knowledge. She had many quarrels with her parents and she seemed unhappy about not getting her own way at home. As leader of a gymnasium class for younger girls, she was happy when she was a boss. Her nickname of Pouting Pansy seemed often to fit well.

That Sonia had physical assets was freely admitted by everyone. She was generally described as good-looking of face and figure, and she had learned to make the best of these features. Her grooming was immaculate and she used very good judgment in make-up, coiffure, and dress. The general visual impression that she presented called up such words as slender, petite, pretty, glamorous, and chic. It seemed possible that she could fulfill her desire to model.

Although Sonia had many quarrels with associates, her activities were largely social. She did some sewing, although she said she became very impatient in the process, and she did very little reading. She went to all dances at the youth center ("I couldn't get along without them") and was likely to appear at all strictly social functions. School organizations did not appeal to her, and she joined only one club, the Future Business Leaders of America, membership in which was mandatory for all students in the commercial course. One close friend, a girl who also wanted to become a model, accompanied her in most of her social activities.[11]

The case of Teddy

The huskiest boy in his class, Teddy was known to everyone for his prowess with the shotput and discus and as one of the solid blocks in the football line. Uninterested in matters academic and unhappy about "sitting still as much as they want you to do in school," Teddy almost became a dropout. Several times it appeared that he would succumb to the pleas of his friends to go out West and get away from high school, but he did "sweat out a diploma." When he left after his four years of travail, he was very uncertain about the wisdom of having stayed and about his future.

Perhaps Teddy's lack of interest in school could be traced to the fact that he always had trouble with words and with reading. His test scores, when he saw them, seemed only to verify what he had known about himself. He was very unhappy because English was a required subject. "I am not interested," he said, "in stories and poetry, and I can see no reason why I should have to read them and talk about them in class." He disliked even his classes in woodwork because marks were determined by written tests rather than by what had been accomplished manually in the shop.

Teddy's grades are shown on the chart presented in Figure 16-3. His school

SUBJECT	GRADES 9	10	11	12
English	D^2 B^2	D^2 C^2	C^2 C^2	C^2 C
Amer. History			D^2 C^1	
Civics	C^2 D^2			
Amer. Problems				C^2 D
Algebra			C^2 D^2	
Biology		C^1 C^1		
Physics				C^2 C
Physical Ed.	Credit	Credit	Credit	Credit
Agriculture	D^1 C^1			
Industrial Arts	C^2 D^2			
Woodwork		D^3 D^3		
Mechanical Drawing		D^2 D^1	C^2 C^2	D^2 D

Figure 16-3
MARKS GIVEN TEDDY DURING HIS FOUR YEARS IN HIGH SCHOOL

activities were confined to athletics. He was a member of the track and football squads for three years. He did say that he would have liked to be in the choir (prevented by a conflict in schedule with athletic activities), but he rejected invitations to join any other organizations. When he was asked what new school activities would attract him, he said, "Driving and shooting lessons."

Much of Teddy's leisure time was taken up with a motorcycle, which he had bought with his own earnings. Riding his motorcycle and participating in sports filled most of the time left after school, athletic practices, and 15 hours of work each week. He listed football, swimming, and ice skating in that order as the things he liked to do most in his spare time, with dancing and hiking as "once-in-a-while" interests.[12]

INTERGROUP RELATIONS AND ATTITUDES

Kinds of intergroup relationships. The attitudes of teen-agers toward different groups determine the nature of intergroup relations. Intergroup relations include a wide range of problems. These may be observed in all phases of life. For example, "cliques" are formed at school, cleavages may appear at church between adolescents from different schools or from different suburban areas; rivalry frequently develops between different groups for power or prestige in the class or group structure.

One kind of intergroup relationship frequently observed is that involving our social-class structure. Adolescents from the so-called lower class are frequently left out or considered crude and impolite. Many individuals at one time or another have the feeling of being part of a minority group. One-half the adolescents sometimes encounter a great deal of intergroup hostility. The younger and immature adolescents are frequently left out of many social activities pursued by older adolescents. Minority racial groups may not be accepted by the majority group. Boys often feel that girls receive preferential treatment at school, although this sometimes operates in reverse. Newcomers do not feel welcomed by the older members of the group, and are not completely accepted.

Intergroup problems and conflicts can be to a large extent avoided when the teacher shows a sympathetic and understanding attitude toward all members of the group. Sometimes the teacher may call on someone from the class to volunteer to help the newcomer get better acquainted with the group, or help the neglected teen-ager by cooperating in some activity with him. In one week-day church school class the teacher had different teen-agers tell about the birthday celebrations in their families. A girl with an Indian background told of a tradition in her home in which the meals and other surprises were carefully planned unknown to the person whose birthday was being celebrated. Such experiences give children who often feel "left out" opportunities to participate, thereby increasing their self-esteem and feeling of belongingness.

Peer recognition. The school and peer group are recognized as important socializing agents. Their collaboration in promoting activities at school common to their social goals is an important aspect of the student's daily life. A study reported by Jones dealt with some of the factors which influenced a student's participation in different activities at school.[13] A comparison was made of students frequently mentioned in the high school newspaper with those seldom mentioned. The paper was devoted exclusively to the reporting of school affairs. It served much as an "official house organ," reflecting the interests, activities, and values of the student group. Five hundred and forty issues (covering a three-year period) were read and all mentions tabulated for the 122 members who attended the high school through the 10th, 11th, and 12th grades. The weighing of the news items was derived from the composite judgment of staff members who were intimately acquainted with the school.

The relationship between maturity level and recognition status in the high school paper is shown in Figure 16-4. None of the late-maturing

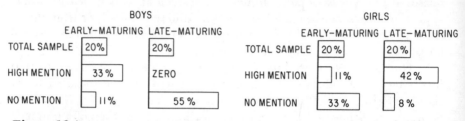

Figure 16-4

A COMPARISON OF THE PRESTIGE POSITION OF EARLY- AND LATE-MATURING SENIOR HIGH SCHOOL BOYS AND GIRLS

boys appeared in the high prestige group, whereas 55 per cent of them were in the "no mention" group. A reversal of prestige position, in relation to maturity level is shown for girls. Early-maturing girls fell more frequently in the "no mention" group. Since in this particular peer subculture athletic skill among girls had little prestige value, it is not surprising that the early-maturing girls were not at an advantage in being frequently mentioned. Several boys in the "high mention" group were athletic supporters; others were well known as leaders of the school paper or had some other prestige position with their peers.

Behavior problems. Responses were obtained by Kingston and Gentry from a total of 288 white high school principals and 132 Negro high school principals in Georgia to a questionnaire dealing with the types of student behavior most frequently of concern to them.[14] These responses were gathered from principals of segregated schools. Both Negro and white principals reported similar patterns of problem behavior in general. As shown in Table 16-5 the types of misbehavior most commonly encountered among the 420 high schools in Georgia were failure to do homework, congregating in halls, truancy, smoking at school, inpertinence and discourtesy to teachers, and cheating. The principals were also requested to indicate the class status of the pupils displaying the greatest incidence of misbehavior. Behavior problems were most frequently reported among members of the freshman class, with the incidence being 62.85. The sophomore class accounted for 21.42 per cent of the problem behavior. The excessive percentage of problem behavior in the freshman year and the small percentage for the junior and senior years may be partially explained by the very high dropout rate in Georgia, which at the time of this study was second highest in the United States. Thus, a large percentage of problem behavior pupils dropped out upon reaching their sixteenth birthday—the end of compulsory education in Georgia in 1961.

Table 16-5

TYPES OF STUDENT BEHAVIOR MOST FREQUENTLY OF CONCERN TO HIGH SCHOOL PRINCIPALS OF GEORGIA
(*Kingston and Gentry*)

Student behavior	Per cent
Failure to do homework and other assignments	66.66
Congregating in halls and lavatories	41.19
Truancy	33.80
Smoking in school or on grounds	30.71
Impertinence and discourtesy to teachers	22.38
Cheating on homework	20.23
Cheating on tests	18.09
Destruction of school property	17.14
Stealing small items	14.28
Obscene scribbling in lavatories	12.38
Using profane or obscene language	5.00
Lying of a serious nature	4.52
Stealing (money, cars, etc.)	4.04

Since the main function of the school is the education of youth, academic training is the area in which teachers have a very positive influence in the growth of adolescents. Each teacher is dedicated to imparting as much knowledge in his particular subject as he is capable of imparting. Quite frequently there is bidding for the student's time among the teachers. The student is given so much homework or involved in so much activity connected with one subject that he does not have time for others. Since the days of Sputnik the academic disciplines have added more and more required subjects for the academically talented and excluded electives that would help the student determine his vocational and avocational choices. The students are caught in the educational controversy. Some are forced to make choices based on avoiding pupil-teacher conflicts, especially when teachers of required subjects are involved.

NEEDS AND GOALS

Many changes have been made in the high schools during the past century. From the adult point of view most of these seem to be for the better. Just how well the modern high school is helping the youth to learn the things they feel a need of learning is still quite questionable. Perhaps we should seriously reflect upon the words of one teen-ager:

> Dad says I can quit school when I'm fifteen and I'm sort of anxious to because there are a lot of things I want to learn how to do and as my uncle says, I'm not getting any younger.[15]

Ralph W. Tyler in the 1960 White House Conference report named three educational tasks appropriate for the schools. One of these was to provide learning based substantially on the arts and sciences. Another was the learning of complex and difficult things that require organization of experience and distribution of practice over considerable periods of time. A third was to provide learning where the essential factors are not obvious to one observing the phenomenon and where principles, concepts, and meanings must be brought specially to the learner. This kind of learning is uniquely possible in the school rather than in the less organized conditions of other agencies.

In an article for the *Saturday Evening Post* the young author and former teacher, John Wain, enumerates some goals of education:

> An education, of whatever kind, has failed if it has not managed to stimulate in the student that kind of intellectual curiosity which will naturally lead him year by year, to extend his knowledge. And also it should give him the necessary basic information to build on; not only factual information but skills of a kind that do not show themselves in a parade of facts. How to find the knowledge he wants; how to marshal information; how to consider a subject dispassionately, brushing away the dust and cobwebs that naturally will form over any subject that has lain in his mind for a few years, among the lumber of his own prejudices and personal emphases.[16]

Education and technology. Since the school is often so completely separated from the world of work, the adolescent may emerge with a store of abstract knowledge, but with very little notion about life itself. It is also likely that those who immersed themselves most completely in their studies are the ones most unfit for the ordinary day-to-day activities. Furthermore, there is such a long time lag between the learning of certain facts and their application that the student must be motivated by various extrinsic and artificial incentives. The cry of unreality is raised against the school system by many who would integrate the school more closely with life. Many reforms have been proposed as the real solution to the problem. The real trouble seems to have developed as a by-product of technology. Technology has brought about an economic condition wherein the labor of children is no longer needed for the production and distribution of goods. Thus, children and adolescents are required to remain in school for a considerably longer period of time. However, preparation for employment has become one of the important goals of education. Both direct and indirect vocational education have become a part of the high school pattern. Such an education must not be too narrowly conceived. The individual must be prepared to live a full life as well as make a living.

Improving the cultural level. That something can be done to motivate and improve the level of achievement by the culturally deprived group in school is verified from many studies bearing on this problem. This was noted in a study described by Krugman.[17] The child from the low socio-economic class frequently entered school seriously handicapped and the gap between his progress and that of a child from the middle class increased. Krugman approached the problem by *not* relying entirely on verbal intelligence tests, but rather on individual psychological examinations, nonverbal intelligence tests, and simple subjective rating procedures. Teachers searched for clues of ability. Students tended to live up to higher expectations. Since elementary intelligence tests are less verbal, they provide better estimates of ability. Attempts to raise educational aspirations and choices were begun in the elementary schools. Teachers worked to use educational and guidance approaches to help the children raise their opinions of themselves. As students succeeded where they had formerly failed and as they sensed greater acceptance by the school personnel, they showed greater pride and marked improvement in behavior. Motivation alone was not enough to raise educational achievement. Neither were normal teaching procedures and class size. No more than 15 were in a class. Expense in experimentation was not spared. Intensive guidance service with no more than 150 students assigned to one high school counselor was necessary. The students were brought to recognize the need for exerting sufficient effort to succeed; standards were not lowered. Students accepted the challenge and expressed gratitude for being a part of the experiment. In order to raise the cultural level it was found that lack of experience instead of bad taste was the problem to be solved. Financial help was secured to provide firsthand experiences on weekends. The students' cultural backgrounds were carefully interwoven with these experiences so that their pride in themselves and their groups increased as they learned about other cultures. Trips to museums, Broadway theatres, the Metropolitan Opera, Carnegie Hall, scientific laboratories, libraries, and college campuses were enthusiastically participated in and enjoyed. It was no longer "square" or "sissy" to attend a symphony concert. Boys were not "queer" if they carried paperbacks which they bought for a nominal fee and retained as their own. Such efforts are expensive but not so expensive as failure, loss of educated manpower, delinquency and crime, maladjustment and mental illness. The success of the project led Krugman to conclude that schools can compensate to a considerable degree for the meager backgrounds of the culturally deprived child and adolescent.

Healthy living. Children and adolescents from all class levels have creative urges. The need for self-expression is universal. Different avenues are available for the self-expression of adolescents. The lack of such an expression by adolescents in the creative arts has been observed by a number of students of child and adolescent psychology.

The school presents opportunities for physical growth. Soft, easy living; quick, satisfying snacks; hurried, frenzied fatigue do not need to be the order of the day. The cafeteria with its hot lunch program and the absence of food vending machines can do a great deal for satisfying nutritional needs. Health and food classes can teach diet and health and can motivate the children to develop healthy bodies. Learning to budget time and selecting rewarding and satisfying activities can reduce frenzied living. The efforts of all who work with adolescents will be needed to direct their abundant energy into satisfying and useful channels. Health and physical education teachers as well as others concerned with the guidance of adolescents must face this problem of healthy living by first of all setting forth good examples. Leisure time furnishes opportunities for adolescents to engage in activities that promote individual development, self-expression, and healthy living.

Concern with moral and spiritual values. The importance of moral and spiritual values was emphasized in earlier chapters. The school cannot divorce itself from the teaching of moral and spiritual values, even if it should desire to do so. By popular demand religious growth is left to the homes, the churches, and the parochial schools. In all behavior the school can foster that based on right which gives the individual a feeling of well-being and teaches him to be considerate of the happiness and welfare of others. The examples set by teachers and others as authority figures, the emotional climate of the school, the program of the school, and the integration of the teachings at school with those of other agencies in the community are extremely important in the teaching of attitudes, ideals, and values. A case reported by Chazan shows some of the results that may appear from a conflict of parents in handling a boy, and the role that the guidance center and school had in helping him.

> Case 48 (a boy of 14 with a Terman Merrill IQ of 155) was referred for examination because of his persistently difficult behaviour in school. He was sullen and morose, defiant and disobedient, although said to be well behaved at home. The material conditions of the home were good but there was much conflict between the parents over handling the boy. The mother was indulgent with him, although she herself had a generally aggrieved attitude; the father was very authoritarian in manner. The boy suffered from frequent attacks of bronchitis, and had missed some schooling as a result. In addition he had been quite outstanding at the primary school stage, and since his transfer had resented the competition he found in the grammar school.
>
> The mere fact of his referral for examination to a child guidance centre

had an effect on his behaviour, and he responded quickly to help and advice. He was able to complete his grammar school course with success.[18]

The academically talented. Identification of the academically talented student and establishing his educational needs is an important task of teachers. Concerning their characteristics, Bish states:

> . . . Most of these students learn quickly without much drill, organize data efficiently, reason clearly, and show an interest in a wide range of abstract concepts. As a rule they are above average in their use of vocabulary and reading skills.
> Creativity and originality are often distinguishing characteristics. These children are generally persevering. They are capable of a considerable amount of independent study, possess more than the normal amount of stamina, and are usually above average physically.[19]

The increased college attendance is reflected in the increased percentage of academically superior high school students who go on to college.[20] The estimates made by Berdie indicated that about 50 per cent of the superior students were going on to college in the early fifties. McDaniel and Forenback's study involved the top 15 per cent of Kentucky's 1959 high school seniors who participated in a statewide testing program.[21] The findings indicated that 76 per cent of the students from the top 15 per cent of the class entered college. Simmons found from a study of academically superior high school students in Georgia that 88 per cent planned to attend college and that approximately the same percentage actually entered college in the fall following their graduation.[22] This study supports the trend for an increasing percentage of academically superior students to attend college. The relationship of background factors related to college attendance indicated some significant differences between superior students who entered college and those who did not enter college. The following factors were significantly related to college attendance:

1. Student Aptitude Test scores
2. Yearly income of the family
3. Extent of student-parent discussion of college plans
4. Occupational level of the father
5. Educational level of the father
6. Educational level of the mother
7. Parental attitude concerning student's college attendance
8. Number of siblings, particular older siblings
9. Size of high school attended
10. Presence of a guidance counselor in the high school
11. Extent of student-faculty discussion of college plans
12. Type of institution preferred for post high school training
13. Preference regarding the attending of a local junior college

14. Preference for a job rather than college after high school

15. Marital status was for girls highly significant

16. Preference for the armed forces rather than college was for boys highly significant.

Stivers conducted a study in a midwestern high school in a city of 40,000.[23] Research was centered on the top 25 per cent of the boys and girls in the tenth grade. The final group was made up of 86 students, 45 girls and 41 boys. Each student was questioned directly and indirectly about his plans for school and work. On the basis of the responses, students were classified as "motivated for college," and "not motivated for college." His study disclosed that the students who were well motivated for college at the tenth grade level were not significantly higher in social class but did have a significantly greater need for achievement. Basically the significant differences between the motivated and nonmotivated students were in the number and variety of persons who held up the goal of higher education. It was found that the higher motivated group had a higher composite score on tests of ability to succeed in school. The students who wanted to go to college had a higher score on the communality scale of the *California Psychological Inventory*. They also had a higher score on the achievement-via-independence scale of the *California Psychological Inventory*.

The results of a study by Morrow and Wilson support the hypothesis that bright, high-achieving high school boys engage in more sharing of activities, ideas, and confidences; are more approving and trusting, affectionate, and encouraging (not pressuring) with regard to achievement; are less restrictive and severe; and better accept parental standards.[24] Thus, family morale seems to foster academic achievement among bright high school boys by fostering positive attitudes toward teachers and school and interest in intellectual pursuits.

The nonacademic pupil. The traditional academic high school program has not proved appropriate for the increased percentage of boys and girls enrolling in our high schools. Sando studied problems encountered by high school pupils, especially those who dropped out of school during their sophomore and junior years.[25] The sophomores were asked the following question: "What kind of problems do you have that you would like some help with?" Some answers given were: "I couldn't get along with some of the kids"; "My problem is how to act, how to dress at a banquet, how to act among adults"; "The teachers are too wrapped up in the mass, not the individual." Twenty per cent felt history was least valuable—the same things being repeated again and again. Many English teachers have encountered the reaction: "Why should I study this? I ain't going to need it." Complaints frequently made by nonacademic students regarding science is that it is meaningless or too difficult to understand. It appears most likely that for today and tomorrow the most difficult task facing those responsible for the education of high school boys and girls is that of providing an educational program and educational goals for a large percentage of those in the lower socio-economic groups. All too often the motives held up by teachers for them to remain in school are unreal, or at least unimportant to these boys and girls.

The migrant adolescent. Perhaps the most educationally deprived group of children and adolescents are those whose parents are migrant workers, frequently working on farms as seasonal workers. Such children tend to enter school late, move from one school to another, and drop out of school at an early age. Their achievement is usually under the fourth grade, and the illiteracy rate among them is high.[26] Studies and surveys of migrant children indicate that they and their parents are seriously retarded educationally, although their native intelligence may be that of an average population sample. Most migrant families do not spend more than five or six months in any one place. A 1961 report from New Jersey states:

> Though complete data are not available, school reports from several states show that possibly as few as 1 in 50 enter high school and fewer than this graduate. Consequently vocational training courses and school guidance services usually offered in the high school are virtually out of reach of these youngsters.[27]

Hard-to-reach adolescents. Educators and social workers often refer to the "hard-to-reach" teen-ager. In school these teen-agers have a record of poor or failing work. They are either unresponsive or hostile to teachers and other adults who try to help them. Out of school, their record may show theft, traffic violations, and sexual irregularities. These boys and girls constitute the bulk of the discipline problems in school, and frequently run afoul of the law.

Hard-to-reach teenagers are sometimes called slow learners. Most of them have intelligence quotients between 75 and 90. Depending upon the type of community and type of school, half to three-fourths of teen-agers in this IQ range do passable work, but most of the remainder constitute the hard-to-reach adolescents. In a study by Havighurst, four-fifths of the students with IQs between 75 and 90 came from families in the lowest third of the community in socio-economic status; 37 per cent came from broken homes.[28]

The plight of these hard-to-reach boys and girls is the result of three failures: their families, the school, and society. Nearly every one of them comes from a poor family environment. They have been reared in an atmosphere accompanied by parental conflicts. The father or mother may have been given to excessive drinking, law breaking, or sexual promiscuity. Thus, one or both parents have presented a poor model to the children.

The crucial need is to improve family life. But this task is exceedingly difficult since it means changing the outlook and behavior of mothers and fathers whose own childhood and youth followed this same pattern. Somehow, this vicious circle must be broken.

Whether or not the family life is improved, many children will still be slow learners. For many of them, school will be a source of discouragement and frustration. Somehow, schools must find a way to work with these teen-agers. Society in general, apart from its influence on home and school, can take steps to clear the path to growing up in a decent environment for such children and adolescents. Thus, the challenge is not just to the school but to all forces in the community concerned with developing citizens for tomorrow.

SUMMARY AND EDUCATIONAL IMPLICATIONS

Materials relative to school survival rates show a high mortality rate, especially after the age limit for compulsory school attendance. In many cases the school curriculum and program are not designed for teen-agers of low intelligence or low academic aptitude and interest. There is some evidence that radio and television are offering advantages to teen-agers from an inferior cultural background that they did not formerly have. The school, in general, upholds the standards and teachings of our middle-class culture. Most of the teachers and a very large proportion of the school programs are closely affiliated with our middle-class culture. Thus, adolescents from a lower social class culture are frequently handicapped in school, where they are expected to adjust to a middle-class culture and to learn middle-class ways of behaving.

The problem of providing for the needs of *all the pupils* when they reach the secondary school age is a difficult one. This will require, first of all, teachers who realize that the school exists for all the pupils, not just for those with good scholastic aptitude. Second, there is a need for a diversified school program. A good school program will furnish materials and procedures in harmony with the needs and abilities of all the pupils. Some of the contemporary problems with which the schools are faced may be listed as follows:

1. The educational effects of increased production resulting from science and technological developments

2. The educational problems created by increased leisure time

3. The educational impact of changed world conditions resulting from the applications of science and technology

4. The uses that might be made of television, radio, motion pictures, and modern travel in a more complete educational program

5. Problems involving increased equality of opportunity as an ideal of a democratic society

6. Problems arising from the merging of various racial, religious, and social-economic groups in a comprehensive high school and college program

7. How to work most effectively with the home, church, and other agencies in the guidance of children and adolescents

8. Problems involving educational, moral, social, and vocational guidance of adolescents.

THOUGHT PROBLEMS

1. List in order the factors you consider most important in the increased school enrollment.
2. Show from some case of your acquaintance how school success is not sufficient.
3. How does the school aid in the expansion of interests? Illustrate.
4. Elaborate on the meaning and significance of the following statement: "In the future, schools will be more closely integrated with the life of the community than they were in the past."
5. It has been stated that, "Education comes out of all kinds of experiences and affects all phases of one's life." What effect should the acceptance of such a viewpoint have on the work of the schools?
6. How would you account for differences in the reasons given for withdrawal from school as stated by students and counselors? From your experiences what three factors account for most students' dropping out of school before graduation?
7. What are some of the major problems of the culturally deprived teen-ager in high school?
8. Study carefully the cases of Sonia and Teddy. What are the individuals' assets and limitations? What are the major problems encountered at school? What are some special needs?
9. It has been suggested that the biggest problem facing the high school teacher is finding means of motivating a large percentage of students who find no values in the learning experiences imposed upon them at school. What are the implications of this for the teacher?

SELECTED REFERENCES

Cole, Luella, *Psychology of Adolescence,* 6th ed. New York: Holt, Rinehart & Winston, Inc., 1964, Chaps. 23-28.

Friedenberg, Edgar Z., *The Vanishing Adolescent.* Boston: Beacon Press, 1959.

Jersild, Arthur T., *The Psychology of Adolescence,* 2nd ed. New York: The Macmillan Company, 1963, Chap. 16.

Rogers, Dorothy, *The Psychology of Adolescence.* New York: Appleton-Century-Crofts, 1962, Chap. 11.

Strang, Ruth, *The Adolescent Views Himself*. New York: McGraw-Hill Book Company, 1957, Chaps. 7 and 13.

Wattenberg, W. W., *The Adolescent Years*. New York: Harcourt, Brace & World, Inc., 1955, Chaps. 12 and 24.

Wittenberg, Rudolph M., *Adolescence and Discipline*. New York: Association Press, 1959, Chap. 14.

NOTES

1 Message of President S. C. Garrison to the graduating class at George Peabody College of Teachers, August 22, 1939.

2 Carol Joy Hobson and Samuel Schloss, "Enrollment, Teachers, and School Housing." Highlights from the fall 1963 survey of public schools, *School Life* (January-February, 1964), p. 18.

3 Edward Cook, "An Analysis of Factors Related to Withdrawal from High School Prior to Graduation," *Journal of Educational Research*, **50** (1956), 191-96.

4 Seymour L. Wolfbein, *The Transition from School to Work: A Study of the School Leaver* (Washington, D.C.: Bureau of Statistics, U.S. Department of Labor, Government Printing Office, 1959).

5 A. B. Hollingshead, *Elmtown's Youth* (New York: John Wiley & Sons, Inc., 1949). Elmtown is a fictitious name given to a midwestern town of around 10,000 population. Table 16-2 is reprinted by permission.

6 John K. Coster, "Attitudes Toward School of High School Pupils from Three Income Levels," *Journal of Educational Psychology*, **49** (1958), 61-66.

7 Philip W. Jackson and Jacob W. Getzels, "Psychological Health and Classroom Functioning: A Study of Dissatisfaction with School Among Adolescents," in *Studies in Adolescence*, ed. Robert E. Grinder (New York: The Macmillan Company, 1963), pp. 392-400.

8 R. D. Anfinson, "School Progress and Pupil Adjustment," *Elementary School Journal*, **41** (1941), 507-514; C. Saunders, *Promotion or Failure for the Elementary Pupil* (New York: Bureau of Publications, Teachers College, Columbia University, 1941).

9 A. R. Mangus, "Effects of Mental and Educational Retardation on Personality Development of Children," *American Journal of Mental Deficiency*, **55** (1950), 208-12.

10 M. F. Serene, "An Experiment in Motivational Counseling," *Personnel and Guidance Journal*, **31** (1952-53), 319-24.

11 J. W. M. Rothney, *The High School Student* (New York: The Dryden Press, 1953), pp. 103-8.

12 *Ibid.*, pp. 61-66.

13 Mary C. Jones, "A Study of Socialization Patterns at the High School Level," *The Journal of Genetic Psychology*, **93** (1958), 87-111.

14 Albert J. Kingston and Harold W. Gentry, "Discipline Problems and Practices in the Secondary Schools of a Southern State," *The Bulletin of the National Association of Secondary School Principals*, **45** (1961), 34-44.

15 S. M. Corey, "The Poor Scholar's Soliloquy," *Childhood Education*, **20** (1944), 219-20.

16 John Wain, "Dilemma of Youth," *Saturday Evening Post* (June 17, 1961), p. 48.

17 Morris Krugman, "The Culturally Deprived Child in School," *Journal of the National Education Association*, **50** (1961), 23-24.

18 Maurice Chazan, "Maladjusted Children in Grammar Schools," *British Journal of Educational Psychology*, **29** (1959), 198-206.

19 Charles E. Bish, "The Academically Talented," *Journal of the National Education Association*, **50** (1961), 33.

20 R. Berdie, "After High School—What?" (Minneapolis: University of Minnesota Press, 1954).

21 E. D. McDaniel and Mary S. Forenback, *Kentucky's Top 15 Per Cent, A Study of*

the College Attendance Patterns of Superior High School Students (Lexington, Kentucky: Special Research Report, Kentucky Cooperative Counseling and Testing Service, University of Kentucky, 1960).

[22] Norvelle G. Simmons, "College Going Plans and Actual College Attendance of Academically Superior High School Seniors in Georgia" (Ed.D. Dissertation, University of Georgia, 1963).

[23] Eugene Stivers, "Motivation for College in High School Boys," *The School Review* **66** (1958), 341-50.

[24] William R. Morrow and Robert C. Wilson, "Family Relations of Bright High-achieving and Under-achieving High School Boys," *Child Development,* **32** (1961), 501-10.

[25] Rudolph Sando, "Education of the 'Non-academic' Pupil in Secondary Schools—This They Believe," *California Journal of Secondary Education,* **31** (1956), 45-49.

[26] George E. Haney, "Problems and Trends in Migrant Education," *School Life* (July, 1963), pp. 5-9.

[27] Curtis Gatlin, *The Education of Migrant Children in New Jersey* (Trenton, N.J.: Department of Labor and Industry, 1960), p. 2.

[28] Robert J. Havighurst, "The Hard-to-Reach Adolescent," *School Review,* **66** (1958), 125-32.

17

EDUCATIONAL
AND
VOCATIONAL
GUIDANCE

He that hath a trade hath an estate; and he that hath a calling hath an office of profit and honor.   BENJAMIN FRANKLIN

There is an ever-increased use of scientific procedure in the ordinary life activities of man. This increase has brought with it changed modes of living, changed occupational conditions, more widespread leisure, increased luxuries, and a change in our socio-economic structure. All these have had an important influence upon family relations, peer activities, community enterprises, educational and religious programs, work opportunities, and the economic needs and conditions of adolescents and youths.

The materials presented throughout the previous chapter indicated the educational needs and problems of adolescents. A review of the materials of this chapter shows that:

(1) Adolescents are beset with many problems, and need help and guidance in their efforts to solve their problems.

(2) Many young people lack the information needed for making sound decisions, especially about occupations.

(3) Services for counseling young people and giving them adequate assistance in the solution of their problems are in many instances woefully inadequate.

(4) The problems involved in choosing a vocation are extremely complex and cannot be solved by a rule-of-thumb method.

(5) There is a great need for an opportunity for young people to secure work experience as part of their training, as well as for occupational orientation.

Increasing the holding power of the school. The increased secondary school enrollment presents a major problem to those concerned with the education and guidance of boys and girls. In the previous chapter it was pointed out that many drop out of high school before graduation. If the schools are to adequately serve all youth, conditions and provisions must be such that they will remain in school and thus develop their abilities and acquire skills and understandings essential for solving the problems they will meet as mature adults. There is evidence that the modern secondary school is reducing the number of early school leavers. An important factor is a conviction on the part of the school staff that high schools should serve all the youth. Unless this conviction guides the action of the school personnel, the high school will be a selective institution where a large percentage of students will attend only until they reach the legal school-leaving age.

A second essential, closely allied to that of the attitude of teachers and others toward the function of the school, is that of providing adequate counseling services. By improving and extending the counseling services, the needs of the various groups of students needing special assistance will be more nearly met. Each pupil should know well at least one teacher or counselor and feel free to approach such a person concerning his problems. Studies show that a good counseling program inevitably reduces the number of dropouts. It was pointed out in the previous chapter that educational problems loom large in the lives of many high school boys and girls. Effective school counseling will help boys and girls meet these and other problems with increased understanding and solve them more intelligently. A good counseling program will also require a flexible curriculum. The case of Teddy, presented in the previous chapter, could have been solved more readily if the curriculum program had been more flexible, especially that phase of it concerned with testing and grading. Pupils not qualified for either vocational or academic courses might choose general courses. Miller refers to one system where 3250 pupils who could have left school to go to work were retained by a system of instruction apparently attractive to them.[1] A fourth feature that should prove helpful in increasing the holding power of the school is the provision of school-work projects, under which pupils spend part of their time at school and part on the job under the supervision of trained coordinators. Such projects furnish valuable educational experiences for the students as well as financial assistance needed by many.

A fifth means of increasing the holding power of the high school is to provide diagnostic services, along with the counseling and educational program, for students with special needs. The educationally and mentally retarded pupils are too often branded as failures because of their inability to do the work prescribed for them. Penny noted that the dropout rate in one study was 14.5 per cent for good readers and 50 per cent for poor readers, with the peak of dropouts occurring in the tenth grade.[2] A marked disparity was noted between the reading age and mental age, indicating that many of the dropouts were not working up to their potential ability. Teamwork in diagnostic testing, counseling, and teaching services will have a beneficial effect upon retaining students in schools for a longer period of time.

Closely related to the diagnostic services is the need for research on the nature and causes of dropouts. The dropouts, as well as the graduates, represent our human resources. They are the products of our schools. The pupil personnel program should, as part of its responsibilities, conduct follow-up studies of these students. This can be done by means of questionnaires and interviews, depending largely upon the purpose of the study and the personnel available for conducting it. Such follow-up studies have two major functions: (1) to help the individual through guidance and further training, and (2) to serve as a basis for revising the school program.

EDUCATIONAL GUIDANCE

It was pointed out earlier in this chapter that a large percentage of high school students drop out of school before graduation. Various reasons have been given to account for these dropouts. Studies show that a large percentage of these are maladjusted. There are also many students who remain in school until they graduate although they are frequently emotionally disturbed or socially maladjusted. There are also the covert dropouts, who present a subtle problem to educators. They are described as individuals who remain in school and pass the course requirements, thus fulfilling their parents' expectations. They have no particular goals, and display little initiative or responsibility. Remaining in school is the easiest and most secure way out for them. One of the main differences between these youngsters and many capable youngsters who drop out is in their home relations. These covert drop outs usually come from middle-class homes and feel secure in their home environment as long as they follow the desires and expectations of their parents. These conditions have led to an increased interest in the guidance of boys and girls in the solutions of their problems and in making better personal, social, educational, and vocational adjustments.

Importance of guidance. The expansion of guidance facilities is one of the important characteristics of a modern high school program. The chief methods of providing guidance are through school counselors, home-room teachers, classroom teachers, assembly programs, special orientation courses, career days, visiting teachers, and special resource agencies outside the school. The major objective for counseling is usually considered that of helping students form sound judgments in the solution of their educational, vocational, personal, social, recreational, and religious problems. There is no one person who may be designated as the one who should do all or even a major portion of the counseling; neither is there any one best procedure for counseling. However, there are certain principles for organizing and administering counseling activities which will tend to expedite the work and to help students better solve their problems.

The diversity of problems that may come to the attention of the counselor or teacher presents them with a real challenge. These problems indicate the need for resource materials and people to help teachers and others in their counseling activities, and to help adolescents in solving their problems. In order to determine the activities and duties of school counselors Hitchcock secured data from 1282 counselors representing 1255 schools throughout the United States.[3] The materials presented in Table 17-1 show the duties now performed by these counselors. Hitchcock found that the majority of counselors are now utilizing public rela-

Table 17-1

PERCENTAGE OF 1282 COUNSELORS PERFORMING CERTAIN DUTIES
(*After Hitchcock*)

Duty	*Per cent*
Helping pupils adjust to school	95
Assisting pupils who are failing course work	91
Assisting pupils with course planning	94
Referring pupils in need of specialized help	89
Assisting pupils with occupational plans	96
Gathering information about pupils	94
Making notes of interviews	90
Helping pupils appraise strength and weakness (educationally and vocationally)	92
Assisting pupils with in-school placement	87
Securing part-time jobs for pupils	81
Assisting school leavers with next steps (i.e., college, trade school, jobs, etc.)	84
Assisting pupils with leisure-time placement	62
Administering group tests	94
Administering individual tests	89
Administering sociometric tests	40
Interpreting test results to pupils individually	92
Assisting pupils who are emotionally maladjusted	91
Assisting pupils who are socially maladjusted	90
Assisting pupils with moral and religious problems	85
Assisting pupils who are juvenile delinquents	82

tions media in their work. The counselors also work closely with teachers, administrators, and other youth-serving individuals and agencies, although many of them felt that this should not be a part of their responsibility. Three important factors emerging from this study may be summarized as follows: (1) A very large percentage of counselors are called upon to deal with a diversity of student problems. (2) Counselors are called upon to perform a wide range of tasks, and must work closely with teachers, administrators, and parents. (3) The duties of the counselor carry him outside the school, as he attempts to help students with such problems as job placement, emotional, social, and religious adjustments, and assisting school leavers with next steps.

A democratic system of education should provide opportunities for each child to develop his abilities and potentialities. Individual guidance on the part of the teacher is essential if this goal is to be reached. The dull child, the neuropathic child, the defective child, and the gifted child alike should receive consideration in our school program. Complete recognition of individual differences means a recognition of these deviations in intelligence, in aptitudes, in temperament, as well as in goals and purposes in individual cases.

Counseling the individual pupil. Counseling is as old as formal education, if not older. It has recently been described as "a personal and dynamic relationship between two people who approach a mutually defined problem with mutual consideration for each other to the end that the younger, or less mature, or more troubled, of the two is aided to a self-determined resolution of the problem. . . ."[4] Counseling is primarily an individual matter and is more apt to be successful when conducted on that basis. In connection with the school environment it implies greater maturity and understanding on the part of the teacher or adult. In a study of 1500 15-year-old boys in Detroit, 82 per cent wanted adult companionship and counsel.[5] Those who had least companionship and poor family adjustment were most eager for this adult counseling. Counseling is not synonymous with interviewing, since the latter is a technique for some specific purpose. Referring to Wrenn, we find the following diagrams with explanations:

A too common type of interview is information and advice given, thus:

Counselor ————————→ Student

A less common and sometimes quite justifiable interview is the information-getting situation, thus:

Counselor ←———————— Student

The interview as it should be used in counseling must be represented:

Counselor ←———————→ Student

Educational, vocational, and personal-social problems loom large in the lives of adolescents. Too often social and personal problems are not given the attention and consideration they deserve. It is only when these reach the teacher or administrator that they are recognized. There, they have usually been treated as behavior activities, without much consideration of the drives back of them.

The need for "belongingness" or being accepted is very important during the adolescent years. Teachers must be aware of this need, and must recognize the problems of adolescence as real, even though they may appear trivial to the adult. This ability to understand the nature of the problems of others is a prerequisite for counseling. When the problems of others are considerably removed from one's own life, the ability to understand such problems becomes more difficult of attainment. Adolescents' problems are not synonymous with the problems of a teacher on the job. This in itself presents a challenge to the teacher, if his work in the guidance and direction of adolescents is to be effective:

> Each boy and girl in the classroom wants to be accepted as a unique individual. He wants to be accepted *as a person* and not for what he can accomplish. Students like to think of a teacher as someone whom they can trust. To violate a confidence will freeze the channels of human relationships immediately. What might seem insignificant and unimportant to the teacher may be of vital importance to the child.[6]

Importance of records. A basic principle of guidance is that we must secure definite information about the individual before effective plans can be formulated to meet his needs. The kinds of information that should be useful for instructional and guidance purposes and that should be included in the cumulative record have been listed by Dugan as follows:

AREAS OF INFORMATION	MEANS OF APPRAISAL
1. Scholastic aptitude	Previous grades, psychological tests of ability and achievement
2. Scholastic achievement and basic skills	Previous grades, standardized and teacher-made achievement tests, survey and diagnostic tests of basic skills, school activities, and work experiences
3. Special abilities: clerical, mathematical, artistic, and the like	Special aptitude tests, interviews, and evaluation of previous achievement or performance (work experiences, hobbies, extracurricular activities)
4. Interest and plans	Autobiographies, interest inventories or tests, stated interests, interviews, previous achievements, and both work and leisure activities
5. Health and physical status	Physical examination, health history, observation, attendance record and nurse follow-up, and family consultation

6. Home and family relationships	Observation, anecdotes, rating scales, interviews, autobiographies, themes, check lists and adjustment inventories, reports from employers, group workers or group leaders, and parent conferences
7. Emotional stability and social adjustment	
8. Attitudes	Student questionnaires, home contests, interviews, themes, autobiographies and other documentary information, and standardized rating scales
9. Work experiences	Record of employer, reports of vocational counselor, interviews, and student questionnaires.[7]

Previous school experience is not by any means an absolute, safe basis for the prediction of future development. However, the pupil's response to certain types of courses, his areas of high and low achievement, and his participation in extracurricular activities all show definite trends that are a source of help to the counselor. Records should be kept on mental and educational growth from time to time. Educational achievement tests furnish records of growth in the school subjects.

Techniques for use in securing information on aptitudes and abilities are manifold. Such tests, however, may be dangerous in the hands of an untrained person. Some occupations require only a special type of intelligence while others demand only skills of some particular type. Facts about past activities, interests, health, and educational growth should serve as valuable information on a cumulative record. Through interviews, questionnaires, tests, rating devices, and observations, information is obtained. When it is organized in an understandable and usable manner, such information should serve as a basis for more accurate guidance and counseling of adolescent boys and girls.

The chief advantage of the cumulative record is the possibility of combining the separate items it contains into an integrated picture of the whole individual. The meaning of various patterns of interest records, as well as of patterns of abilities and activities, and ways of combining these most effectively are matters demanding further study. Concerning the importance of having such information available, in order to assist the students in their educational problems, Strang has stated:

> Assistance to students must be thorough but not superfluous. One cannot have too much information about a student, but one can give him too much advice. His present level of maturity must be ascertained; his values, goals, aims and purposes recognized and respected. Counseling, in part, is instruction in self-direction. It is a process, not a conclusion.[8]

VOCATIONAL ASPIRATIONS AND OPPORTUNITIES

Aspirations for attending college, finishing high school and going to work, or dropping out of school relate to the adolescent's total background. The influence of friends on college attendance is shown in a study of high school graduates in Wisconsin. Seventy-five per cent of the graduates going to college said that their friends were planning college attendance; 71 per cent of those getting jobs and not planning to attend college reported their friends were getting jobs.[9] Classmates, peers, and friends have an important bearing on the adolescent's educational plans. Simpson and others studied the educational plans of boys from a Piedmont town of North Carolina.[10] The results, shown in Table 17-2, reveal that most boys whose fathers' occupations are in the higher scale plan to go to college, whereas only 16.4 per cent of those whose fathers' occupations are in the lowest of the four occupational groups plan to go to college. The educational choices made while in high school vary with the occupational background of the students. In the study by Simpson and others a positive relationship was found between the son's expected future earnings and the present earnings of his father.

The majority of boys and girls from the upper- and middle-class groups have educational and vocational objectives. This is not true of those from the lower occupational groups. Adolescents from the middle class who aspire to a manual vocational objective are apt to have selected a skilled occupation. Their intelligence test scores and educational records

Table 17-2

SON'S COLLEGE PLANS AND HIGH SCHOOL CURRICULUM BY FATHER'S OCCUPATION

(*Simpson* et al.)

Son's plan and curriculum	Level of father's occupation*			
	A	B	C	D
	(per cent)			
A. College plans				
Don't plan to go to college	2.1	12.5	28.1	37.7
I may or may not go to college	8.5	20.1	33.1	23.0
Will go if I can afford	8.5	12.5	17.5	23.0
Definitely plan to go	80.9	54.9	21.3	16.4
B. High school curriculum				
College preparation	88.3	72.3	39.6	35.0
Vocational	11.7	27.7	60.4	65.0

*A = executives, proprietors and professionals.
 B = administrative personnel, minor professionals, clerical and sales, technicians.
 C = skilled manual employees.
 D = machine operators, semiskilled and unskilled workers.

are definitely inferior to those aspiring to white-collar occupations. They are significantly more impulsive, submissive, and concerned with overt activity than boys from the same home background who choose to remain at that occupational level.

The majority of high school seniors from the manual home background have adopted white-collar vocational aspirations. These boys occupy a position midway between the manual aspirants and the white-collar-background boys choosing white-collar vocations. Their intelligence test scores are superior to those choosing manual vocations but inferior to those of the stable white-collar group. They are characterized by restraint and thoughtfulness. They are also more concerned with overt activity. The boy who is stable at the manual occupational level or who is moving downward is, conversely, impulsive and much concerned with overt activity. The notion that upward mobility is a result of poor adjustment is not supported by this study. Rather, it appears that such boys are well adjusted at school and have adopted many of the values found among the white-collar group.

Factors and conditions affecting vocational choices. What are the factors that contribute to one's choice of a vocation? Wilson reported a study of the vocational preferences of secondary-school pupils in the county of Middlesex, England.[11] The pupils were asked to give their vocational choice and also the reason for such a choice. "Liking the work" was the most important reason given by both boys and girls. Girls gave greater consideration to working conditions than did the boys, while boys ranked "prospects for promotion," and "good pay" higher than girls did. A questionnaire dealing with reasons for vocational choice was administered to 929 high school students.[12] The percentage of reasons given for the selection of certain vocational areas is presented in Table 17-3. The three reasons most frequently mentioned by boys were interest in work, security, and personal advancement; the three most frequently given by girls were interest in work, service to others, and interest in people.

In a survey conducted by the national Girl Scout organization it was found that one-third of the girls wanted to go to college.[13] In their job plans, they expressed a desire for steady employment, interesting work, and pleasant people to work with. High pay and promotion ranked much lower. Only two per cent of the girls wanted to run their own business.

Mental ability and vocational aspirations. Many factors affect the vocational preferences of adolescents. This may be noted in the distribution of IQ quintiles of boys who expect to go on to college, shown in Table 17-4.[14] There is a progressive increase in the percentage of boys who expect to go on to college in each of the five occupational classes studied. For example, whereas only four per cent of boys in the lowest quintile of the group whose fathers are skilled laborers or service workers expect to go on to college, 40 per cent of those in the upper (fifth) quintile expect to go on to college. These data furnish evidence that mental ability is a factor related to vocational choice, but is only one of a number of factors.

Table 17-3

THE PERCENTAGE OF TOTAL REASONS GIVEN AS
A BASIS FOR THE SELECTION OF CERTAIN
VOCATIONAL AREAS
(Powell and Bloom)

Motivating Factor	Boys	Girls
Interest in work	36.2	27.4
Ability to do the work	6.1	4.3
Interest in people	3.4	15.2
Personal advancement	7.0	3.9
Offers security	11.9	6.0
Service to others	5.3	17.4
Adventure and travel	4.3	5.1
Creative idealism	5.3	4.0
Plan to marry	.1	5.8
Armed services	2.7	.6
Previous experience	3.6	2.6
Variety within the work	1.5	.6
Need education	.4	1.4
Religious	.9	.6
Social prestige	.6	.7
Same work as father	3.3	.5
Parental influence	1.6	1.0
Miscellaneous	2.5	1.9
No reason given	5.2	2.9

Vocational aspirations. A 1960 poll of youth's attitudes conducted by the Purdue Opinion Panel revealed that 58 per cent aspired to enter some professional field.[15] This is a disproportionate number when one considers the percentage of people qualified to be professional men. Aspirations to and actually entering a field are quite different. This was brought forth in a study reported by Moreland.[16] The results of his study indicated that the majority of children of textile workers will ultimately enter mill work, even though they may express aspirations to the contrary. Only 3.5 per cent of mill children in school in 1948 said that they wanted to work

Table 17-4

PERCENTAGE OF BOYS WHO EXPECT TO GO TO COLLEGE BY IQ AND
FATHER'S OCCUPATION

(Kahl)

Father's occupation	IQ		Quintile (percentiles)			
	1	*2*	*3*	*4*	*5*	*All quartiles*
Major white collar	56	72	79	82	89	80
Middle white collar	28	36	47	53	76	52
Minor white collar	12	20	22	29	55	26
Skilled labor and service	4	15	19	22	40	19
Other labor and service	9	6	10	14	29	12
All occupations	11	17	24	30	52	27

in the mill. However, by 1958, 52.3 per cent of them had become cotton mill workers.

Class status and vocational aspirations. There is evidence from many studies that the social and economic status of the family is an important factor in the vocational choices of adolescents. Data on the vocational preferences of junior high school students and their parents' occupational levels were gathered and studied by Krippner.[17] He found from his study the following relationships:

> . . . At all occupational strata (except the highest), the fathers apparently suggested careers that would boost their sons slightly above their own job level.
> 1. Fathers whose occupational level was 1.00 suggested that their sons enter occupations with an average level of 1.00.
> 2. Fathers whose occupational level was 2.00 suggested that their sons enter occupations with an average level of 1.87.
> 3. Fathers whose occupational level was 3.00 suggested that their sons enter occupations with an average level of 2.20.
> 4. Fathers whose occupational level was 4.00 suggested that their sons enter occupations with an average level of 2.90.
> 5. Fathers whose occupational level was 5.00 suggested that their sons enter occupations with an average level of 3.67.

A careful study of the aspirations of Elmtown's youth showed that job opportunities are closely associated with the class position of the boy or girl seeking the job.[18] The family influence is such that class II boys and girls are given a preferable type of employment when they are employed at all; class V and to a lesser extent class IV boys and girls must take what they are able to get with respect to full-time or part-time employment. The net result of this is that general office and clerical jobs are assigned to class II and class III boys and girls, whereas menial odd tasks around stores, factories, and other places of employment are left to boys and girls of class IV and of class V.

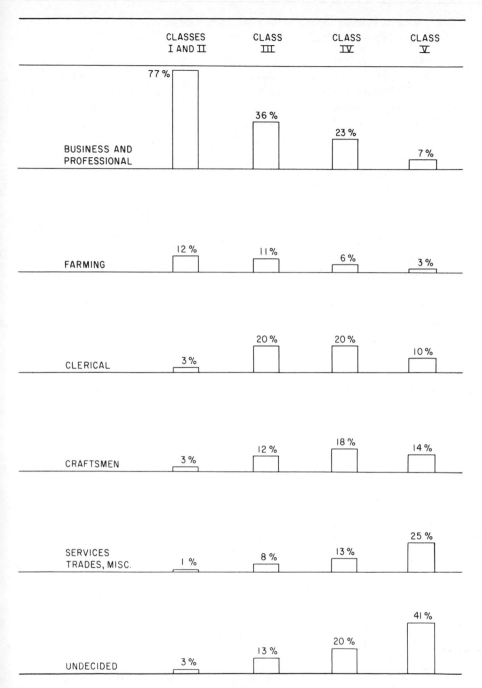

Figure 17-1

VOCATIONAL ASPIRATIONS OF ELMTOWN'S YOUTH BY CLASS AND OCCUPATIONAL GROUPS

(*After Hollingshead*)

Each adolescent in the Elmtown study was asked to name the job or occupation he would like to follow at maturity. The results, presented in Figure 17-1, show the vocational choices by class for the different occupational groups. The adolescent boys of class I and class II wish first to be business and professional people (77 per cent) and second to be farmers. The girls wish to get married. Class III has somewhat similar desires, although only 36 per cent aspire to be professional and business people. The choice in the clerical area looms large with this group, a choice that no doubt reflects the influence of the adult vocational pattern that prevails among a large number of this class. The large increase between class II and class III in the undecided column indicates that many of these youngsters are unable to reconcile their aspirations with their abilities and opportunities. Many adolescents in class III aspire to a higher vocational level than that followed by their parents, but are not able to see their way clear, financially and otherwise, for securing the training needed to enter into such a vocation. There is a continued sharp increase among the undecided as we move from class III to a study of the choices in class IV and class V.

Class V presents a vocational-choice pattern that is almost opposite to that of class I and class II. Uncertainty (41 per cent) stands out as significant in this group. Many miscellaneous vocations such as animal trainer, juggler, and the like were listed by this group. In the craftsman group, containing 14 per cent, is included the largest percentage of those who have made specific plans for their future. Farming as an occupation shows little appeal to this group. A follow-up would no doubt show that a still closer relationship exists between the occupations actually chosen and followed and the class status. Needless to say, most of the girls will become housewives; although in this study their preferences were about equally divided between business and the professions and clerical work. The girls appear to be oriented toward fields of endeavor that will require some or much technical training, although a large percentage of them will never obtain such training.

Despite the credos we may use with respect to our democratic ideals and practices, anthropological and sociological research has shown that individuals acquire certain anxieties and assume characteristic roles to some extent because of their class membership. Also, these studies have shown that there is a certain mobility in our class structure, although this is certainly not as great as most people would claim. Furthermore, it is well known that occupations are very important in determining class status, because of a number of characteristics associated with certain occupations, such as nature of the work, extent of power, nature of associates, training and educational requirements, income, security, and the like.

Concerning their role in the development of attitudes and anxieties, Levin has stated:

> In terms, therefore, of the relationships between given occupations and their common class status, certain attitudinal and belief requirements may be expected to be associated with the various occupations. It would not even be rash to assume that many of the emotional and personality requirements of various occupations are fundamentally based on class status factors and not on job requirements, as such. Thus, the professional is expected to appear, behave, feel and think quite differently than the skilled worker, and even more differently than the semiskilled worker or unskilled worker. The stereotyped hierarchical classification of vocations is essentially a reflection of their class-conferring characters.
>
> In a relatively mobile class society in which the vocations have class-conferring potency, it is obvious that ego-involvement with respect to occupational achievement would be high for many. Occupations must be selected, consciously or otherwise, in terms of their value in either maintaining the present class membership, if that is adequate to the individual's level of class aspiration, or in terms of their value in facilitating the individual's climb to the class considered higher, if he is motivated to do so.[19]

Occupational choices and opportunities. Occupational choices have been so affected by the social factors that they are out of harmony with occupational demands. This becomes evident from a further study of choices commonly made by high school boys and girls. The influence of parents on the choice of the occupation of their children has been re-

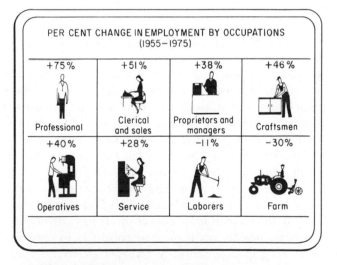

Figure 17-2

PER CENT CHANGE IN EMPLOYMENT BY OCCU-
PATIONS, 1955-1975

*(1955 U.S. Census Bureau, 1975 U.S. Department of
Labor Estimates. Prepared by NAM)*

vealed in a number of general studies. Kroger and Louttit give the results from a questionnaire study of 4543 boys in four technical and academic high schools.[20] About 90 per cent of the boys expressed vocational choices. A majority indicated choices higher than those of their fathers. When compared with census figures, 70 per cent of the boys indicated a preference for types of work engaged in by only 35 per cent of those gainfully employed today.

Every teacher concerned with counseling students about their vocational aspirations should have information concerning occupational demands and trends. As late as 1870, more than one-half of all American workers were engaged in agriculture. According to the 1950 census approximately 10 per cent of the workers were classified as farmers, farm managers, foremen, and farm laborers (except unpaid). The continued mechanization of farming during the past decade has reduced the per cent of people engaged in farming, but there have been substantial increases in those engaged as clerical workers, craftsmen, service workers, and machine operators. Data and estimates relative to the employment of workers in major occupational groups, presented in Figure 17-2, reveal something of the nature of occupational changes taking place and occupational opportunities for youth during the next decade. The upgrading of jobs will place a heavier demand upon the education of youth, and the greater variety of jobs will create a greater need for vocational counseling.

VOCATIONAL NEEDS AND ATTITUDES

Educational demands. There is considerable evidence that the increased demand for universal education on the secondary level is not a result of the demands of various occupations and jobs. This is not to be interpreted to mean that there is no need for universal education on the secondary level; it means rather that such a need must be related to factors, bearing upon increasing complexity of our social order, and not to actual demands of a vocational nature. However, as the average educational level of the young people entering the labor market is raised, those who leave high school without graduating will find themselves competing for jobs with individuals with more education. It has already been pointed out that employers consider many of these youths as too immature, undependable, or lacking in experience. A manager of several filling stations recently explained to the writer his reasons for hiring only helpers who had finished high school. He stated:

> The high school graduates are more eager to make good.
> They can be depended upon to be on the job at the time they are supposed to be there.

They are more intelligent and are thus able to assume responsibility when the need arises.

They are courteous to the customers and help to build up my trade.

A comparison of boys and girls who finish high school with those who do not reveals some interesting and significant differences. Although one should be careful in drawing conclusions about causation from association there is evidence from case studies as well as from group comparisons that additional schooling has desirable effects upon the character and personality of the boys and girls as well as upon their knowledge, skills, and understanding. In one study, data were obtained by means of the "guess who" test on sixth- and ninth-graders and analyzed to show contrasts between those who later completed and those who failed to complete high school.[21] Among the sixth-graders those who later dropped out of school acted "older" than other sixth-graders. They also were quiet, unpopular, sad, less friendly, less cheerful, and less enthusiastic than those who remained to graduate.

Vocational needs of youth. The fundamental differences between the problems of livelihood faced by the youth of a generation or more ago and those faced by today's youth have been presented in earlier chapters. These changed conditions have brought with them changed vocational needs. To a marked degree, the vocational pace of the worker is governed by social forces about him or the machine in the factory. The worker must be able and ready to perform the task and meet the demands placed upon him by the various forces and conditions present in a technological society. On the job he is likely to be called upon to do some specialized task, which usually requires very little formal training. Thus, the vocational needs of the worker cannot be thought of in terms of the acquisition of specific skills alone. The new worker brings with him to the job attitudes, habits, outlooks, moral codes, health, and civic qualities that have important bearings on his success on the job. Industry, dependability, ability to follow directions, good personal and social adjustments, and the ability and willingness to cooperate in a common task are attributes that a youth should acquire while in school, if he is to succeed on the job.

Skills requiring dexterity, speed, strength, and endurance are increasingly being taken over by machines. This makes the manager's role a specialized intellectual one usually associated with college or university training. The task of the worker has changed to that involving vigilance and good judgment. Welford has summarized his analysis of the trends as follows:

Although automatic methods may reduce the immediate part played by human operator, they leave human beings in certain key positions in which the mental load upon them may be heavy and the effects of their actions far-reaching. The human link in the system thus becomes more and not less important than it was before.[22]

Interviews with youths will verify that, if a student once drops out of school, he is not likely to go back again. The decline of the need for unskilled workers and the decreasing demand for semiskilled workers, shown in Table 17-5, indicate that the school dropout is not likely to find steady employment.[23] Thus, many young people who drop out of school enter blind-alley jobs, or wander for years after they leave school from one job to another. The vocational needs of adolescents may be summarized as follows: (1) a better understanding of their own aptitudes and limitations, (2) occupational information—including occupational opportunities and job requirements, (3) vocational training, both in school and

Table 17-5

PER CENT OF WORKING POPULATION IN MANUAL
OCCUPATIONS
(*Wolfbein*)

Year	All manual workers	Skilled (craftsmen and foremen)	Semiskilled (operative and kindred workers)	Unskilled (except farm and mine)
1900	36	11	13	12
1930	40	13	16	11
1950	41	14	20	7
1960	37	13	19	5
1970	36	13	18	5

through work experiences, and (4) the opportunity to use their abilities once developed, i.e., the right to a job. If these needs are to be satisfied, there must be more vocational guidance in our schools. Guidance is based upon a recognition of the existence of individual differences and the philosophy of freedom of choice. The field of guidance has been divided into six comprehensive areas: (1) occupational information, (2) cumulative records, (3) counseling, (4) survey of training opportunities, (5) placement, and (6) follow-up.

Education and employment. The ability of young people to embrace the opportunities for employment that will appear during the next decade will depend to a large extent upon the type of education and training they receive. Figure 17-3 shows that a young person's chances for steady employment will be substantially less if he does not have at least a high school education.[24] The rising level of educational demands of different

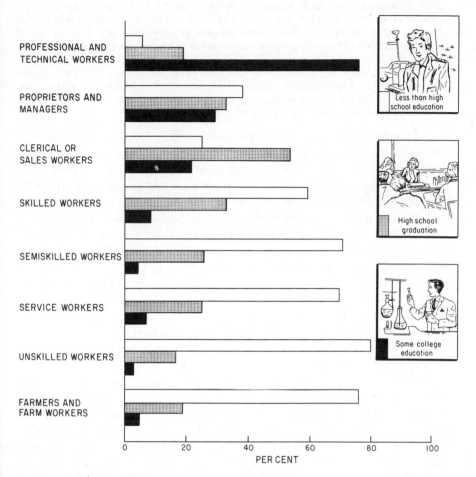

Figure 17-3

EDUCATION BY OCCUPATION, 1950-60

(Manpower, Challenge of the 1960's, *Study of Manpower in the United States*. [*Washington: United States Department of Labor, 1960*], *p. 17*.)

jobs makes it imperative that American youth graduate from high school or trade school, if they expect to find steady employment. The changing educational demands have presented educators with a dilemma. This has been set forth in a report by Whitlock and Williams as follows:

Whether to train young workers broadly as some employers want, or to train them in a specific skill as other employers desire, offers a dilemma to educators who are currently trying to prepare noncollege-bound graduates for transition from high school to work. Current indications are that vocational curriculum planners must choose between preparing students for specific employment within a given locality or providing broad programs of general training that will prepare students for successful on-the-job training in any section of the country and in a variety of occupations. In either case there is need for research to determine the best program of vocational education from school to school and community to community. Because jobs will change during the lifetime of most future workers, it is necessary that constant reassessment of vocational education be made.[25]

In connection with the organization and planning of vocational courses, it has been pointed out that "there is increasing recognition that highly specialized types of vocational education should be reserved until the period immediately prior to the time when the pupil leaves the full-time school, and that in many cases the young person can better come back for specialized vocational courses after he has made a beginning in some suitable occupation."[26] It has been proposed that the reorganized secondary school curriculum should involve the specific activities that high school youth are now experiencing, subject to guidance and integration of these experiences with materials related to different aspects of the school program. There are two types of such activities found in most communities that can be used for this purpose. One of these is made up of the gainful occupations; the other involves civic-social participation.

A survey of the work opportunities in almost any community, under normal conditions, will reveal a great number of jobs well within the capacities of high school youth, and, at the same time, educationally valuable, if conducted under the supervision and guidance of competent school authorities. There is perhaps no limit to what can be done in this connection. However, it is obvious that difficulties may arise relative to child-labor legislation or to conflict with labor organizations. If this work is conceived to be an educational adventure and if precautions are taken to safeguard the pupils from exploitation, one part of the difficulty will have been overcome. Furthermore, if the public recognizes that the work is done as part of the school program, and is not a procedure for supplying cheap labor, the second problem can be overcome as well.

Most educators today feel that work experiences contribute to the high school student's education. Values, skills, and understandings are secured through these experiences that cannot be otherwise acquired. If such experiences do have important educational values, a fundamental question appears: Should not the school find ways to make these benefits available to a larger segment of the high school population? Another fundamental question related to this problem is: How can teachers and counselors help boys and girls get the greatest educational benefits from their work experiences?

VOCATIONAL GUIDANCE

It has already been pointed out that today's job world has become highly specialized and extremely complex. There are over 30,000 different occupations to be found in our industrial economy. This makes the adolescent's task of selecting the kind of work that he desires to pursue much more difficult than it was when our economy was primarily agricultural. Also, the different jobs require varying amounts and kinds of training. This places a burden upon the schools to try to provide the training that is needed for different kinds of work. There is also the problem of helping students better understand their abilities and characteristics and of providing them with information and experiences about the world of work that will help them make sounder vocational decisions. Thus, the problem of vocational guidance has become extremely important in a modern school program designed for the needs of today's youth.

Criteria of vocational success. If vocational success is one of the aims set forth for education, we must determine what is meant by this term. During the early part of this century *earnings and output* were commonly used as a basis for evaluating vocational success.[27] However, during the late twenties and early thirties other criteria were introduced. *Advancement,* the rate of progress made in moving into a better position, became an important criterion. This is quite different from earnings and output, since the emphasis is now on suitability for a higher or more advanced job. During the depression of the 30's, the ability to hold a job was often used as a measure of vocational success.

During this period also rating scales were introduced, and the success of the individual was often judged by *ratings* from a supervisor or from one serving in some such capacity. Despite the fact that ratings are not dependable, they served to broaden the base for estimating success. Then, too, the emphasis was shifted from earnings, output, or achievement to the worker as an individual. This early emphasis upon achievement was reflected in the aims of education and in the purposes of vocational guidance during this period. In a large percentage of cases the focus is still on achievement rather than on the adjustment and satisfaction of the individual concerned.

The emphasis of school psychologists and mental hygienists has brought forth a reappraisal of the meaning of success. They have pointed out that success should be thought of not wholly in objective terms but in a personal and subjective manner. Success in terms of earnings would have meant little to Gandhi. Social position has meant little to many of our great scholars. Prestige is unimportant to the recluse. Individual goals and values should be considered in judging success from a subjective standpoint. Super has suggested that since success in American culture is so often measured by achievement, we should probably use a new term. His emphasis upon *adjustment* as a criterion to be used by teachers in evaluating the results of teaching and guidance is worthy of special study and consideration. In this connection he presents the following definition of vocational adjustment:

> In the fullest sense of the term, vocational adjustment implies that the individual has opportunity to express his interests, use his abilities, achieve his values, and meet his emotional needs.[28]

If teachers and counselors would shift their emphasis from the traditional emphasis upon success in terms of advancement to that of success in terms of vocational adjustment, the individual student would find realistic values and increased satisfaction in his school work and better vocational adjustment after he leaves school.

Need for vocational guidance. Choices that have vocational implications must be made during the adolescent years; failure to make a decision during this time is actually a decision by default. Most boys and girls do not have a clear-cut vocational plan and need help in making educational and vocational choices. The vocational-guidance counselor is usually able to help the individual better assess his own aptitudes, characteristics, and needs. In addition, he will be able to furnish information about job requirements, employment opportunities, working conditions, and other matters relating to different jobs or careers.

Although vocational guidance has been assigned to the high school period there is considerable evidence that it takes place over a period of years. Ginzberg, Ginsburg, Axelrad, and Herma identified three periods in the process of occupational choice.[29] The first period is one of fantasy choices and coincides with the early elementary school years. During the adolescent years tentative choices, frequently unrealistic, are made. At this time choices are based largely upon interests with little consideration of the requirements of the occupation. As the individual grows emotionally and mentally he begins to recognize his own assets and limitations and frequently revises his choice more in harmony with his newly recognized abilities as they relate to the requirements of the occupation. Super and Overstreet conclude from follow-up studies conducted with ninth-grade pupils that it is frequently premature to require ninth-graders to make specific vocational choices.[30] Education at this stage should be concerned with helping pupils make preliminary choices of a broad nature that will "keep as many doors open as possible for as long a time as possible."[31]

Not only is the discussion presented here true for young men, but similar factors are also valid for high school girls. In the past, vocational guidance has been meager, and almost exclusively for men, but today it is reaching into the lives of girls. Observe the large number of girls occupied in various pursuits; notice the many lines of endeavor in which women engage. With the inclusion of so many activities in woman's domain has come their acceptance as desirable social positions, and thus they have become generally occupied by young women. Vocational guidance, then, has a prominent appeal for the young women of tomorrow. The opportunities for girls in the professions, the world of science, and even in engineering have increased enormously during the past two decades. The changed role of women presents a problem for the school counselor in counseling girls on vocational opportunities.

Changes in the life activities, and particularly in the vocational activities, of women during the past century have been accompanied by innumerable problems for the adolescent girl. Cultural norms relating to the nature of the feminine role have been established. These norms have been passed down as part of our social heritage. Specifically, the male expects the female to play this feminine role.

The other role, introduced as a result of women's entrance into many vocational fields, tends to eliminate the factor of sex and the sex role. Here the girl is encouraged to study hard in school so that she can enroll in a certain school for nurses. The father and mother may point with pride to their daughter, who is now a laboratory technician at some reputable hospital. These contradictions of roles present problems for adolescent and postadolescent girls. It is with her family and through boy friends in particular that she is confronted by these contradictions. The writer observed this in a study of the problems of adolescents, referred to in Chapter 10. One of the most common problems added by girls to the check list was: "Wondering whether or not I will ever get married." In discussing these inconsistencies in relation to the girl's adjustments, Komarowsky stated:

> . . . Generally speaking, it would seem that it is the girl with a "middle-of-the-road personality" who is not happily adjusted to the present historical moment. She is not a perfect incarnation of either role but is flexible enough to play both. She is a girl who is intelligent enough to do well in school, but not so brilliant as to "get all A's"; informed and alert but not consumed by an intellectual passion; capable but not talented in areas relatively new to women; able to stand on her own feet and to earn a living but not so good a living as to compete with men; capable of doing some job well (in case she does not marry or otherwise has to work) but not so identified with a profession as to need it for her happiness.[32]

Task of the counselor. The vocational choice of the adolescent and the task of the counselor relative to an individual's vocational choice on a higher occupational level than that occupied by his father should be carefully studied. To many counselors and most secondary school teachers, social mobility is a virtue that should be given encouragement. The American dream that if a child works hard he will be able to climb from an underprivileged place on our cultural ladder to a privileged place has infiltrated their thinking. Often boys and girls with the ability and aspirations to move up the socio-economic ladder become frustrated because they are stymied in their efforts and blocked by circumstances beyond their control. There are also many boys and girls with good ability, who, with drive and willingness to postpone certain immediate needs and satisfactions, could move into an occupation requiring aptitude or ability and training, but lack the aspirations to make the sacrifices and efforts necessary for such training. Such was the case of James.

> James' father was dead. His mother taught the first grade in a mill village. Since she assisted with the recreational program she was given a comfortable home in which to live without having to pay rent. James was the older of two children. He had access to the family car and learned to play his roles as a boy and a member of the community. His mother was ambitious for him to go on to college after finishing high school. However, none of James' close friends were planning to continue further schooling. James was better than an average student in high school. His ambition, however, was to finish high school, secure a job as a clerk in a store in a nearby town or city, and purchase a sport-model automobile. With some sacrifice and drive on the part of James he could have gone on to college and received additional training for a higher occupational level. Lack of aspirations for additional education prevented James from seeking further training.

The task of the counselor is not that of deciding what James and others should do. Rather it is to help adolescents make sounder decisions in their efforts to solve their problems. Specifically his task may be summarized as follows:

1. To help the adolescent decide whether or not he should try for a higher occupational level
2. To encourage certain individuals in their aspirations and to discourage others
3. To help students arrive at sounder values as a basis for formulating their vocational decisions
4. To help the majority of students find satisfactions through vocational adjustments within their own occupational levels
5. To assist teachers in their efforts to help students make sound decisions and arrive at good vocational adjustments.

The vocational guidance of handicapped pupils presents special problems. The handicapped adolescent must have an understanding of his own abilities and limitations, and, secondly, he must have information about the requirements of various occupations.[33] A study of 1000 students of the Hawthorne Junior High School in San Antonio, Texas, reported that 144 had an IQ below 80. However, only 33 per cent of these selected a semiskilled job, and none selected an unskilled job. After completing a course in occupations, 48 per cent of the original group of 144 lowered their choice of occupation to a level nearer their true abilities.

Rehabilitation programs and demands for manpower during national crises have opened up a great variety of jobs for the physically handicapped. Employers have found that, partially because of their handicapped condition, they are more dependable on certain types of jobs than are the nonhandicapped workers. Thus, vocational training in the modern school is not limited to the physically able adolescents. However, good vocational training programs must be accompanied by vocational counseling which will consider the whole individual in connection with particular vocational pursuits.

The use of intelligence and aptitude tests. The two major uses made of intelligence and aptitude tests in today's schools are (1) to determine what level of schoolwork may be best suited to the individual, and (2) for vocational guidance. The majority of tests used for these purposes are group intelligence tests. These tests are sometimes classified as verbal and nonverbal tests. In some cases, notably the *California Test of Mental Maturity*, both verbal (language) and nonverbal (nonlanguage) test items are included, making it possible to obtain both verbal and nonverbal IQ's. It was pointed out in Chapter 4 that positive correlations ranging from .30 to .70 are usually obtained between group intelligence test scores and scholastic grades. The relationship is sufficiently close that some students of measurement have referred to group verbal tests of intelligence as scholastic-aptitude tests. Since educational and vocational guidance are closely interrelated, scholastic-aptitude evaluations become extremely important in a modern vocational guidance program.

A number of studies have shown a low relationship between intelligence-test scores and occupational choice. This is to be expected, since intelligence is only one of a number of interrelated factors related to good occupational adjustment. There is a likelihood, however, that many adolescents aspire to occupations beyond their intellectual abilities, while many more are satisfied with occupations requiring far less intelligence than they have. This may be noted in the distribution of IQ quintiles of boys who expect to go on to college, shown in Table 17-4. These data show that over half of the boys in the lowest quintile (20 per cent) expect to go on to college. Various studies show that going to college is an aspiration of most parents of adolescents as well as adolescents from our middle-class homes.

The use of interest inventories. The testing movement brought with it attempts to appraise not only the abilities of students but also their interests and personality. It has already been suggested that vocational counseling must be concerned with the whole person, not just his aptitudes and skills. Interest inventories have been developed which may be useful to the counselor in helping students determine more accurately their areas of highest and lowest interests.

Three groups of high school students were used in one study of the relation of scores on vocational-interest inventories to vocational choices.[34] Scores were obtained from 115 tenth-grade boys and 117 tenth-grade girls on the *Kuder Preference Record*. These students were also requested to rank the nine vocational areas measured by the Kuder test for their vocational preferences. Correlations were then obtained between these rankings and the inventory rankings. The correlation for the boys was .59 and for the girls .50. A comparison of the first three choices of the students with the three highest-ranking areas on the *Kuder Preference Record* showed that the first choices of the boys were within the three highest scores in 90 per cent of the cases. The results presented in Table 17-6 show that this relationship is not so close for the girls. The first three choices of the girls were the highest score on the Kuder test in 70 per cent of the cases.

These results have been corroborated by other studies bearing on this problem. Data presented in Chapter 7 showed that vocational inter-

Table 17-6

THE RELATIONSHIP BETWEEN THE
VOCATIONAL CHOICES OF TENTH-GRADE
STUDENTS AND THEIR SCORES ON THE *Kuder
Preference Record*

| Choice | Rankings of scores made on the Kuder Preference Record | | | |
	1	2	3	Total
(Boys)				
First	67	15	8	90
Second	17	44	12	73
Third	10	16	17	43
(Girls)				
First	40	22	11	73
Second	17	22	14	53
Third	13	15	17	45

ests as measured by interest inventories showed considerable changes from grade 9 through grade 12. Actually the correlation between scores on different vocational inventories is only around .50, indicating a lack of agreement for the specific areas. The value of vocational interest inventories lies in pointing out several areas of interest rather than any one area. This is brought out in a study of the stability of high school students' interests in science and mathematics.[35] Data were available from administering the *Kuder Preference Record* at the ninth-grade level and again after the same students had completed three or more years of high school training. The results indicated that, to a great extent, if interest in science or interest in mathematics ranks high at the ninth-grade level, it is likely to rank high in grade 12. However, over-all predictability for the particular rank is not high. Of 29 students whose interest ranked highest in science at grade 9, only 13 had science as the highest ranking area at grade 12. Although this and other studies fail to substantiate the claim that interest scores furnish a reliable basis for predicting the talent of an individual, such data when utilized cautiously with other data should be useful to the teacher and vocational counselor in the educational and vocational guidance of high school boys and girls. Interest inventories lack the concreteness essential for making sound vocational choices, however. Counselees persist in remaining human beings.

Total personality versus isolated-traits viewpoint. It was pointed out in Chapter 8 that personality should not be regarded as so many traits functioning in an isolated manner. Vocational guidance has moved from a consideration of isolated variables to that of viewing the counselee as a total personality engaged in solving a vocational or related problem. Thus the original "numerical counselee" has become a dynamic human being, equipped with emotions, aspirations, aptitudes, attitudes, interests, and values. He is functioning in a society where certain values, mores, and cultural patterns exist. These impinge upon him in such a way as to determine his aspirations, concepts of himself and others, and his role as a member of the social group.

The assumption has at times been made that different jobs require different but rather specific vocational patterns. Studies of successful workers will show that this is not the case. One will find successful welders, farmers, teachers, nurses, and the like with varying personality patterns.

New role of vocational guidance. The goal of vocational guidance has taken on a new meaning, with the words *vocational adjustment* being substituted for vocational success. Career planning, counseling, aptitude testing, placement, and follow-up work are subgoals in this process of helping the individual make good vocational adjustments. Gellman states: "The criterion for success or failure of vocational counseling is the degree to which it facilitates individual adjustment to work within the limits imposed by the vocational pattern and socio-economic factors."[36] The shift in the goal to vocational adjustment means that the counselor must consider not only the individual's fitness for the job but also on-the-job conditions and problems that might affect the individual's personal and vocational adjustment. In this connection personal adjustment may not always be essential for vocational adjustment, although good personal adjustment should help one in his vocational adjustment.

Methods in vocational guidance are changing in that more emphasis is being given to the observations and study of individuals in actual work situations, or situations that simulate reality. "Interviewing must deal with the meaning of work to the individual, his attitude toward work, the values sought in a work situation, and the psychological limits within which an individual functions."[37] It seems unlikely that any real substitute can be used for actual work experiences at tasks, in exploratory courses in school or in part-time work out of school. These experiences furnish the student with the foundation needed to better understand occupational information and vocational counseling encountered in the school program. It furnishes the counselor with a more realistic basis for evaluating and changing behavior.

SUMMARY

Vocational training is a function, a resultant of technological developments, economic changes, and social forces. It is based upon a recognition of the value of the individual as a member of a social group. Within the social group is variety, caused by the specialization of labor, and this calls for vocational guidance and training to the end that each individual may be successful and adjusted in his place in the world of work.

There is no unanimity of opinion concerning the effects technological developments are having upon the concept of the function of schooling. In many cases, such as in that of the specialization found on the assembly line, the need for training in specific vocational skills has decreased. It appears that there is now a need for a broader conception of vocational training, which will include character and personality development. Furthermore, the increased complexity of our social and economic structure has increased the need for considering training in citizenship as part of the vocational training program.

Some important trends may be noted in the guidance program. In the first place the adolescent functions as a unit. One cannot divorce one aspect of guidance from all other aspects. The goal of vocational guidance has been defined in terms of facilitating vocational adjustment. A vocational-guidance program developed in accordance with modern trends presented in this chapter will provide the following to all adolescents and youth whether in school or on the labor market: counseling, placement, vocational adjustment, and guided work experience.

THOUGHT PROBLEMS

1. List some of the basic factors to be considered in a sound vocational guidance program.
2. How has technological development affected the nature of vocational training? Illustrate your answer by reference to some jobs with which you are acquainted.
3. Study the materials presented in Table 17-2. What are the implications of these data for the teacher? For the counselor?
4. What conclusions would you draw from the data presented by Kahl? What implications do these data have for teachers and counselors?
5. What is the new role of the vocational counselor? In what ways is this different from the old role?
6. What do the results of the study of the vocational choices of Elmtown's youth from the different class groups indicate? How would you account for these results?
7. It has been suggested that one of the difficult problems of adolescents in our culture is the lack of a definite occupational identity. What advantages arise from this condition? What are some problems that emerge as a result of this?
8. What are the most important factors that influence youth's choice of a vocation? What should be the role of the teacher and counselor in this connection?
9. What are the major vocational needs of youth? What bearing should these have on the school program?
10. Discuss the place of intelligence and aptitude tests in vocational guidance. Why have intelligence tests been referred to as scholastic-aptitude tests?

SELECTED REFERENCES

Ginsberg, E., et al., Occupational Choice: An Approach to a General Theory. New York: Columbia University Press, 1951.

Hamrin, S. A. and B. B. Paulson, Counseling Adolescents. Chicago: Science Research Associates, 1950.

Hollingshead, A. B., Elmtown's Youth. New York: John Wiley & Sons, Inc., 1949, Chap. 11.

Jersild, Arthur T., The Psychology of Adolescence, 2nd ed. New York: The Macmillan Company, 1963, Chap. 17.

McKinney, Fred, Counseling for Personal Adjustment. Boston: Houghton Mifflin Company, 1958, Chap. 11.

Rogers, Dorothy, The Psychology of Adolescence. New York: Appleton-Century-Crofts, 1962, Chap. 13.

Staton, Thomas F., Dynamics of Adolescent Adjustment. New York: The Macmillan Company, 1963, Chap. 15.

Veness, Thelma, School Leavers. London: Methuen & Co., Ltd., 1962.

Warters, J., *Techniques of Counseling*. New York: McGraw-Hill Book Company, 1954.

Wattenberg, W. W., *The Adolescent Years*. New York: Harcourt, Brace & World, Inc., 1955, Chap. 19.

NOTES

[1] L. M. Miller, "How Can a High School Increase Its Holding Power of Youth?" *Bulletin of the National Association of Secondary School Principals*, 36, No. 185, (1952), 117-25.

[2] Ruth C. Penny, *Reading Ability and High School Drop-outs* (New York: Bureau of Publications, Teachers College, Columbia University, 1956).

[3] W. L. Hitchcock, "*Secondary School Counselors and Their Job in the United States*" (Ed.D. Dissertation, Oregon State College, 1953).

[4] C. G. Wrenn, "Counseling with Students," *Thirty-seventh Yearbook of the National Society for the Study of Education, Part I* (Bloomington, Ill.: Public School Publishing Company, 1938), p. 121.

[5] K. W. Layton, "Guidance Needs of Detroit's 15-Year Old Pupils," *Occupations*, 15 (1936), 215-20.

[6] E. C. Morgenroth, "Relationships between Teachers and Students in Secondary Schools," *Progressive Education* (April, 1939), 248-49.

[7] W. E. Dugan, "Counseling in the Modern Secondary-school Program," *Bulletin of the National Association of Secondary School Principals*, 35 (1951), 15.

[8] Ruth Strang, *Counseling Techniques in College and Secondary School* (New York: Harper & Row, Publishers, 1937), p. 130.

[9] J. Kenneth Little, "The Wisconsin Study of High School Graduates," *Educational Record*, 23 (1959), 123-28.

[10] Richard L. Simpson, David R. Rorsworthy, and H. Max Miller, *Occupational Choice and Mobility in the Urbanizing Piedmont of North Carolina* (Chapel Hill, N.C.: Institute for Research in Social Sciences, Cooperative Research Project No. 722 [8403], University of North Carolina, 1960).

[11] Mary D. Wilson, "The Vocational Preference of Secondary Modern School Children," *British Journal of Educational Psychology*, 23 (1953-54), 97-113, 163-79.

[12] Marvin Powell and Viola Bloom, "Development of and Reasons for Vocational Choices of Adolescents through the High School Years," *Journal of Educational Research*, 56 (1962), 126-33.

[13] Dorothy C. Stratton, "Interpretations of the Findings of the National Study of Adolescent Girls," *National Association of Women Deans and Counselors Journal*, 21 (1957), 18-20.

[14] A. Kahl, "Educational and Occupational Aspirations of 'Common Man' Boys," *Harvard Educational Review*, 23 (1953), 186-203.

[15] R. D. Franklin, S. G. Grazino, and H. H. Remmers, *Report of Poll 59 of the Purdue Opinion Panel: Youth's Attitudes toward Industrial Relations* (Lafayette, Ind.: Purdue University Division of Educational Reference, 1960).

[16] J. Kenneth Morland, *A Follow-up Study of the Mill-village Sections of Kent* (Chapel Hill, N.C.: On file in the institute for Research in Social Science, University of North Carolina), p. 8.

[17] Stanley Krippner, "Junior High School Students' Vocational Preferences and Their Parents' Occupational Levels," *Personnel and Guidance Journal*, 41 (1963), 590-95.

[18] A. B. Hollingshead, *Elmtown's Youth* (New York: John Wiley & Sons, Inc., 1949). Figure 17-1 is based on data from the book. Reprinted by permission.

[19] M. M. Levin, "Status Anxiety and Occupational Choice," *Educational and Psychological Measurement*, 9 (1949), 29-38.

[20] R. Kroger and C. M. Louttit, "The Influence of Fathers' Occupations on Vocational Choices of High School Boys," *Journal of Applied Psychology*, 19 (1935), 203-12.

[21] Raymond G. Kuhlen and E. Gordon, "Sociometric Status of Sixth- and Ninth-

graders Who Fail to Finish School," *Educational and Psychological Measurement,* 12 (1952), 632-37.

22 Alan T. Welford, "Egronomics of Automation," *Problems of Progress in Industry* (London: Department of Scientific and Industrial Research, No. 8, Her Majesty's Stationery Office, 1960), p. 59.

23 Seymour L. Wolfbein, "The Outlook for the Skilled Worker in the United States: Implications for Guidance and Counseling," *Personnel and Guidance Journal,* 40 (1961), 334-39.

24 James M. Whitlock and Billy J. Williams, *Jobs and Training for Southern Youth* (Nashville, Tenn.: Southern Education Studies, George Peabody College for Teachers, 1962).

25 *Ibid.,* p. 7.

26 F. W. Reeves, *Youth and the Future* (Washington, D.C.: American Council on Education, 1942), p. 139.

27 Donald E. Super, "The Criteria of Vocational Success," *Occupations,* 30 (1951-52), 5-9.

28 *Ibid.,* p. 8.

29 E. Ginzberg, S. W. Ginsburg, S. Axelrad, and J. L. Herma, *Occupational Choice and Approach to a General Theory* (New York: Columbia University Press, 1951).

30 D. E. Super and P. L. Overstreet, in collaboration with C. N. Morris, W. Dublin, and M. B. Heyde, *The Vocational Maturity of Ninth-grade Boys.* Career Pattern Study Monograph Two (New York: Bureau of Publications, Teachers College, Columbia University, 1962).

31 *Ibid.,* p. 158.

32 M. Komarowsky, "Cultural Contradictions and Sex Roles," *The American Journal of Sociology,* 52 (1946), 189.

33 A. T. Allen, "Cogs in the Occupational Wheel," *Occupations,* 20 (1941), 15-18.

34 T. Kopp and L. Tussing, "The Vocational Choices of High School Students as Related to Scores on Vocational Interest Inventories," *Occupations,* 25 (1947), 334-42.

35 G. G. Mallinson and H. V. Dragt, "Stability of High School Students' Interest in Science and Mathematics," *School Review,* 60 (1952), 362-67.

36 W. Gellman, "The Role of Vocational Guidance in Counseling Youth," *School Review,* 62 (1954), 159.

37 *Ibid.,* p. 159.

18

JUVENILE DELINQUENCY

‒ Although there is little exact knowledge of undetected delinquency, there is evidence that it is extensive. Considerable delinquent behavior never comes to the attention of the courts. Also, the extent of delinquency depends partly upon the definition used. This chapter is especially concerned with the extent, nature, and trend of juvenile delinquency. Special attention is given in the latter part of the chapter to the personal characteristics of juvenile delinquents and the forces and conditions that tend to lead to juvenile crime.

DEFINITIONS AND EXPLANATIONS

⇐ From a social point of view delinquency means any form of behavior detrimental to the well-being of society. Such a definition, however, does not provide for any practical limits. Actually, juvenile delinquency is a legal term. In most states a juvenile delinquent is an individual under 18 years of age who is adjudged guilty of violating the law. Thus, it can readily be seen that the great majority of problem adolescents would not be officially designated as juvenile delinquents. In a broad sense of the word, our schools and other social agencies are concerned with all problem behavior, including that frequently classified as delinquent.

Quasi-delinquents. If delinquency is defined in terms of wrong doings alone, acts of mischief, or breaking the law, then almost every adolescent is a delinquent. In American culture many activities by youth are regarded as part of their way of life. This may be noted in connection with high school parades without a permit, bonfires, and escapades that are regarded as harmless although not in keeping with the letter of the law. The quasi-delinquent is defined by Kvaraceus as "a rather well-integrated youngster who makes a mistake or who misses his target only to do injury to others."[1] Left to himself he will usually work out his problem and develop in a normal manner. The high school youngster celebrating a football victory who accidentally injures some bystander or the Halloween prankster who defaces his neighbor's shrubbery is by no means a true delinquent, although he may have commited acts that may be classed as delinquent. If these and others who commit acts of mischief are classified as delinquents the number of children and adolescents classed as such will be doubled several times. Help is needed in distinguishing pseudo- or quasi-delinquents from true delinquents. An attempt will be made later in this chapter to better describe the nature and characteristics of those classified as true delinquents.

The extent of juvenile delinquency. One factor that determines the extent of delinquency is the enforcement of the law. If traffic violations were not enforced, there would then be no violators apprehended and thus no traffic delinquents. Some of the increase in juvenile delinquency may result from changes in definition, laws, or enforcement of laws. Stealing apples from the fruit vendor today is likely to bring the adolescent to a court, whereas stealing apples from the farm orchard a half century ago was not likely to.

Whether an adolescent comes to the attention of the court today is influenced markedly by community and parental attitudes toward the adolescent's behavior. The data presented in Figure 18-1 represents the number of cases disposed of by juvenile courts at different periods. For reasons already stated, juvenile court statistics, when taken by themselves, do not reveal the full extent of delinquency. The data in Figure 18-1 do give us some notion about the seriousness of the problem.[2] Data presented in different parts of this chapter furnish valuable information about the forces and conditions that contribute to delinquency. However, caution should be observed in making generalizations from a study to conditions significantly different from those in which the particular study was conducted.

Basic explanations of juvenile delinquency. The development of explanations of delinquent behavior seems to have gone through three fairly distinct phases. These have been referred to by Tappan as: "a prescientific mystical period, an early modern particularistic era, and a contemporary quasi-scientific empirical period."[3] In each of these, however, there has been considerable variation in the nature of the explanation brought forth by its exponent, although there is a special feature characteristic of each of these explanations that makes such a classification possible. Since our treatment of juvenile delinquency in this chapter will not be especially concerned with the first two explanations, only a brief description of them will be presented.

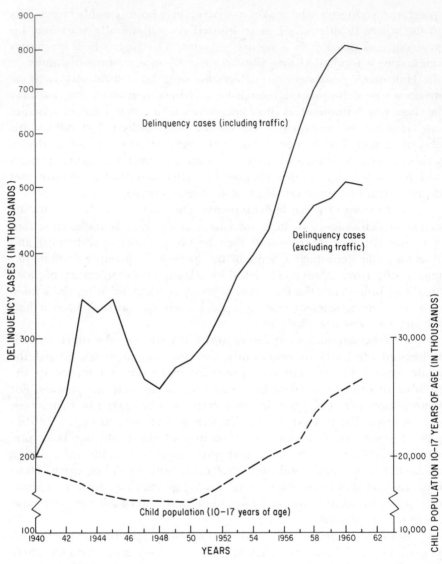

Figure 18-1

TRENDS IN JUVENILE COURT DELINQUENCY CASES AND CHILD
POPULATION 10-17 YEARS OF AGE 1940-1961 (SEMILOGA-
RITHMIC SCALE)

The mystical concept ascribed delinquent behavior to some force outside of and beyond the individual, such as evil spirits. Such spirits might, however, inhabit the body and thus affect one's actions. There were many varieties of this concept; but they were similar in the one respect just mentioned. The mystical concept held sway for many centuries. Its influence was extremely great until about a century ago. Beginning, however, around the middle of the nineteenth century, a series of deterministic explanations appeared. These were also referred to as particularistic, since they attempted to explain a specific behavior act on the basis of some particular factor. The exponents of the various deterministic viewpoints were aided in their explanations by objective testing techniques and statistical procedures. The particularists followed the pattern set forth by the mystics in oversimplifying the basis for delinquency. Adherents to the particularistic concepts appeared with many different causal interpretations, such as heredity, climate, endocrines, frustration, religion, ignorance, broken homes, slums, health, and the like. In fact some of the adherents would rely on less inclusive particulars, such as movies, comics, modern jazz, and other factors or conditions of a like nature.

With the greater use of scientific techniques combined with critical studies of the various theories that had been propounded by the particularists, it was soon recognized that these explanations were oversimplified. Thus, the theory of multiple causation has gradually come to be accepted by a large number of students of juvenile delinquency. A great deal of statistical work has been conducted in an effort to determine the relative importance of various factors in producing delinquency. The multicausal notion has revealed that crime results from many complicated factors, and that its prevention is not as simple as some of the earlier particularists had indicated. This theory, however, should not be viewed in a mechanistic manner. These various factors do not operate separately. The hyperthyroid adolescent lives in a home and neighborhood. His overactivity will be affected by the nature of his home, his size, his financial circumstances, his intelligence, and the neighborhood conditions. The girl is reared not simply in a poverty-stricken home, but in a neighborhood of a certain type. How she reacts to her home conditions will be affected by her emotional characteristics, her intelligence, her body build, the quality of her neighborhood, the attitudes of her parents, and many other factors too numerous to list. In the discussions of the influence of various factors on the development of delinquent behavior, one should realize at all times that these do not act separately upon the growing individual. There is a definite interrelationship existing at all times between all the forces or conditions that affect the behavior of the individual.

Another basic explanation supports the hypothesis that juvenile delinquency fulfills a number of psychological functions for the adult population. The irritating adolescent and the annoying delinquent afford the adult a handy target, or scapegoat for his aggressions. We no longer have the wartime scapegoats; it is no longer fashionable to manifest direct hostility toward ethnic or religious groups; and when the surge of anti-Negro feeling gradually subsides, many groups will vilify the delinquent. The public, suddenly awakened to its second place in the race to the moon, has pounced on the school and the adolescent nonlearner as the archvillians. Also, the popular writers of stage, screen, radio, and the press have exploited and built up a terrifying image of the adolescent delinquent. Most of these products are geared to the adult market, but they are also seen and read by the adolescents, so the distorted picture begins to actualize itself. Even many parents and teachers expect bizarre, norm-violating behavior; youth discovers what is expected and then accommodates adult anticipations.[4]

Psychological types of delinquency. Attempts have been made to ascribe special characteristics to delinquents. In a fairly recent study of the psychiatric aspects of juvenile delinquency, Donet concluded that delinquency is a bio-social phenomenon, the common psychological denominator of which is a feeling of insecurity.[5] Case studies of delinquents reveal that these boys and girls have the same basic need and, in general, face the same problems as nondelinquents. Any attempt to draw a clearcut line between delinquents and nondelinquents will be fraught with many difficulties.

A number of recent studies have furnished a useful basis for studying delinquents. On the basis of data gathered from the records of 1110 white male juvenile delinquent probationers of the Cook County Juvenile Court, Reiss was able to isolate three psychological types of delinquents: (1) the relatively integrated delinquent, (2) the delinquent with markedly weak ego control, and (3) the delinquent with relatively defective superego control.[6] Hewitt and Jenkins classified delinquents as (1) socialized, (2) unsocialized, and (3) maladjusted or withdrawn.[7] The classification given by Kvaraceus is quite similar to that given by Hewitt and Jenkins: (1) the emotionally disturbed and neurotic, (2) the socialized, and (3) the unsocialized.[8]

The *integrated delinquent* is relatively well adjusted and will in all probability become an emotionally mature adult. These are socialized delinquents and show no symptoms of maladjustments other than the delinquent act. They are classified by some psychiatrists as "normal," although individuals of this group are repeatedly engaged in delinquent acts.[9] The range of behavior of this group is wide, ranging from stealing an automobile for joy riding to selling protection to younger children or committing a holdup with a loaded pistol. The case of Walter H. illustrates one who is a "normal" or integrated delinquent.

Walter H., the second of two brothers, was 13 years of age. He played hookey from school frequently and was part of a gang of boys who stole from department stores. He frequently came home late at night. His father deserted his mother soon after he was born.

Results on psychological tests given at different periods showed an IQ range from 74 to 88. The lowest score was made on a verbal test of intelligence, while the highest score was made on a nonverbal type. Walter's school record was very poor. His older brother was in the tenth grade and doing satisfactorily in his schoolwork. He also assumed considerable responsibility for his own needs as well as certain family needs.

The center of Walter's life activities and interests was the gang of boys he ran with in and out of school. His home offered little of interest to him. His mother worked in a textile plant in an effort to provide for the family's needs. Her work and social life visiting with her neighbors occupied most of her time. Walter had no educational goals and looked upon school as an unfortunate or unhappy experience which he had to endure. He maintained a friendly relationship with his older brother, who regarded him as a young and irresponsible member of the family. He was friendly with his teacher and the school counselor as long as they did not pressure him about his schoolwork and activities.

The delinquent with markedly *weak ego control* is generally regarded as an insecure person with low self-esteem or as a highly aggressive and hostile person. These delinquents make up the maladjusted group in the threefold classification of Hewitt and Jenkins. They tend to withdraw from social participation and are often "lone wolf offenders." A case described by Topping illustrates a confused delinquent.

Harold, white, 14½. One of probably identical twins, of a family of seven children. When he was four, his mother died and his father deserted. The twins, two brothers, and a sister were placed in an orphanage where they remained four years, until the sister died. The other twin became delinquent. Harold stated his own delinquent conduct was due to his desire to be with his brother. His studied efforts to emulate the gangster smack of adolescent theatricals. He has a warped and scarred personality and is capable of deadly attack. Bitter hostility and a philosophy of futility became an integral part of his personality. Outstanding in his reaction were disappointment and bitterness arising from the loss of his parents; dread of being thought a sissy by his twin; loss of emotional security through separation from his siblings; determination to rejoin his twin by becoming delinquent.[10]

The type of delinquent referred to as having *defective superego controls* has not developed the social-conforming behavior of our middle-class society. These delinquents are characterized by emotional immaturity. Kvaraceus as well as Hewitt and Jenkins refer to them as "unsocialized delinquents." However, they may be socialized with respect to their own peer group. An important task faced by adolescents, as they grow toward maturity, is that of reconciling their individual desires and characteristics with the demands of society. We honor the hero who is daring, we magnify power and speed, and we glorify the machine for what it can do. However, the adolescent is cautioned to drive the automobile at a restricted speed, and not to take chances by chasing other cars on curves or on the brow of a hill. The difficulty of the emotionally immature adolescent to reconcile these demands and conditions may be observed in the reckless driving of many youths. A 15-year-old boy, referred to by Hirschberg as B. S., illustrates the operation of emotional immaturity in producing delinquent behavior:

> B. S. A small, thin 15-year-old boy of dull-normal intelligence. The fourth in a family of five children, two of whom have records of delinquency. Urban environment, high delinquency area. Associates with undesirable companions and spends most of his time on the streets. Goes to movies four times a week. Mother states he is interested in movies and athletics. School conduct "fair" and does passing work in spite of truancy. Subject disabilities in English and arithmetic. Goes to church regularly but has stolen while in church. In court for burglary (twice) and some petty stealing. Has run away from home, is unmanageable and disobedient. Stubborn attitude in court.
>
> When the psychiatrist had examined this boy he wrote: "From the intellectual standpoint one knows that B. is capable of better reasoning and a better sense of values than this incident demonstrates. However, he does not formulate his attitudes and thinking on an intellectual basis. So he explains his deviations by saying 'I do these things because I am just stupid,' yet he does not want us to think of him in terms of being stupid. Rather he is inclined to be quite insistent that his points and requests should be given serious consideration. It is all part of the emotional immaturity of the boy, one who carries hostility within him, and when his emotional impulses and requests are not met, then his hostility shows forth. He is nearly 16 years old, and he acts the part of a 13-year-old insofar as judgment, sense of values, etc. are concerned."[11]

SEX AND JUVENILE CRIME

Despite the fact that there is almost no type of antisocial behavior committed by one sex that is not committed by the other, rather pronounced differences in the modal trends of the delinquencies of the two sexes exist. Here again it appears that such differences as exist are not inherent but only reflect the interaction of the various elements peculiar to the personalities of each sex.

Although juvenile crime is still dominated by boys there has been a pronounced increase of juvenile crime among girls. According to Travers, the boy-girl ratio of delinquency throughout the United States was approximately 5:1 until 1958.[12] Since that date there has been a decline in this ratio along with an increase in juvenile crime, indicating that juvenile delinquency is reaching ever-different segments of the teen-age population. During the past two decades there has been a gradual and continuous increase in traffic violations and in running away from home. The "hot-rod" drivers have produced some real traffic hazards and traffic problems in some of our large cities. If adolescents are to be permitted to drive, they must develop a greater sense of responsibility.

Sex offenses bring many more girls than boys to the courts. It was suggested in Chapter 7 that changes have come about in the sex lives of growing boys and girls, affecting various types of behavior, including sex behavior itself. Thus, it is becoming increasingly difficult to determine just which sex acts may be regarded as delinquent forms of behavior. Some analytic investigations of crimes committed by girls have indicated, in fact, that sex is much more prominent in their commitments than records show. Many families would say "ungovernable" when the real delinquency is probably sex offenses. It appears, further, that in many cases of ungovernability or running away, the sex offense is probably prominent. Although a fairly large number of girls are affected, and immorality is admitted by a rather high percentage according to some studies, very few of the delinquent girls have fallen to the level of prostitution. For various reasons boys of the adolescent age are seldom placed in institutions because of sex experiences, and this is especially true for heterosexual experiences. They, on the other hand, have been held more responsible for their own support, have probably been less protected in the home than the girls, and are faced with certain needs that they attempt to satisfy; hence they develop habits of stealing more than girls.

Although stealing is far less common among girls than among boys, it occurs sufficiently often to be given special study and consideration. The causes are numerous, but frequently appear in connection with selfadornment and being well dressed. Thus, many adolescents yield to the temptation of shoplifting or petty thieving in the stores, colleges, and boarding homes. Out of 7500 confessed shoplifters in the fall of 1962 in Alexander's New York stores, 3500 were teen-agers, the majority of whom were girls. Macy's, with department stores across the country, reports that shoplifting among teen-agers has greatly increased since World War II, with girls in the majority. Shillito's, a leading department store in Cincinnati, reports that 78.2 per cent of shoplifters apprehended were under 18 years of age —45 girls to 33 boys. Shoplifting clubs have cropped up in some areas, composed largely of girls: ". . . most experienced store-protection experts agree that girl shoplifters are apt to steal in pairs, occasionally in groups of three or four. Boys usually work alone."[13]

INTELLIGENCE AND CRIME

No criminal type. It is quite generally believed that most delinquents are feeble-minded or that delinquency and feeble-mindedness parallel each other. This belief is exceedingly unfortunate, because objectively obtained and carefully interpreted data do not substantiate it. It arose before modern intelligence tests had been developed or put into such actual, widespread use as would enable those using them to know the true meaning or import of data obtained. Lombroso's now thoroughly disproved idea that there is a definite criminal type did much to make people feel that delinquents and criminals were qualitatively different from those not so branded by the law. His discussion of the stigmata of the criminal type and his description of it as being possessed of "the characters of primitive men and of inferior animals" went far toward making that part of the general public which is attentive really feel that the criminal and delinquent surely must be set apart as a separate type.[14]

Goring very conclusively demonstrated the falsity of Lombroso's concept of special physical stigmata, and is himself probably in part responsible for the previously mentioned current concept. In fact, though he denies it, he really took over Lombroso's qualitative position, simply substituting the term "defective intelligence" for Lombroso's "defective physique." Lombroso believed that the characteristics that he described were of an atavistic type, and thus inherited; and Goring, as previously mentioned, states that heredity and intelligence are the two main factors that differentiate the criminal from the noncriminal type. Since Goring's method of classifying prisoners by intelligence was wholly subjective, one cannot rely very much on its results.

Goddard's early work. In America, Goddard, more than anyone else, is responsible for the quite prevalent idea in some circles that the delinquent is defective. Contrary to his thought, the fact that any one element of personality is associated with crime is not proof in itself that such an element is the sole factor responsible for crime. Granted that mental deficiency is related to inferior social and environmental status, that a preponderance of crime exists in congested sections of inferior social and environmental status in our cities, and that therefore an abundance of crime is committed by those of defective mental ability—granted this, it does not follow from the mere association of the factors that mental defectiveness is itself a cause of the crime.

Goddard concludes from some rather early studies:

> Every investigation of the mentality of criminals, misdemeanants, delinquents, and other antisocial groups has proved beyond the possibility of contradiction that nearly all persons in these classes, and in some cases all, are of low mentality. . . . The greatest single cause of delinquency and crime is low-grade mentality.[15]

Error in sampling. A number of investigators early pointed out that factors of intelligence and socio-economic status operate to select delinquents that are brought before the juvenile courts. It is quite doubtful if we at any time have a truly representative group that can be labeled "juvenile delinquents." Since this is the case, we should exercise caution when we assume that the mean IQ of delinquents is between 80 and 90. A number of different investigators have presented data showing the average IQ of juvenile delinquents. The discrepancies found between the results from these studies may be explained on the basis of differences in sampling. To be sure, there is evidence from these studies that a larger percentage of boys and girls of low-grade intelligence appear before the juvenile courts than would be expected on the basis of chance. However, Mann and Mann point out:

> A closer approximation to a general rule is that delinquents having an IQ below 90—because of low intelligence, because of the area from which they come, or for some other reason or reasons—are more likely to be caught in their delinquencies than those whose IQ is higher.[16]

If one bases his conclusion on children already committed to institutions, it is probably true that intelligence superiority among delinquents is rather rare. (Of course, it must be remembered that this group is not the entire body of delinquents in any state; the entire delinquent group, if *all* delinquents are considered, comes very close to being the entire population.) Among institutional cases the per cent of intelligence quotients in excess of 100 is small as compared with the per cent less than 100; however, for every intelligence quotient below 70 in the penal institution there can be found dozens or more of comparably low-ability persons not in such an institution—and, from the standpoint of behavior activities, no more deserving of being there than the general average of the population. It is probably true, and in most cases proper, that many juvenile-court judges try to salvage from the human wreckage that is brought to their courts as many as possible who appear promising or capable of recognizing the nature and consequences of antisocial behavior—those who can profit from mistakes and thus give promise of making more adequate adjustments under some sort of supervision outside institutions. But these individuals are in most cases not retarded mentally and are therefore not counted among the institutional cases. Hence, counting methods decrease the average mental ability found in our institutions.

In evaluating the findings reported by various investigators of the intelligence of juvenile delinquents, an answer should first be sought to the questions: (1) What evaluation device was used for determining the level of intelligence of the delinquents? (2) Whom did the investigator test? Juvenile-court cases? Institutionalized cases? Cases referred to a psychological or guidance clinic?

There is evidence from many sources that educational retardation, leading to dissatisfaction with school and truancy from school, is often the beginning stage of juvenile delinquency.

One study of the scholastic achievement of 345 boys committed to an institution for juvenile delinquency revealed a median retardation in reading of five years. In arithmetic, the retardation was even higher, slightly more than six years.[17] More than 90 per cent of the group indicated a distinct dislike for school. The *United States Public Health Serv-*

ice Classification Test was used as a basis for measuring the intelligence of these boys. The range and distribution of intelligence quotients obtained from this test for the 345 boys is shown in Table 18-1.

Table 18-1

DISTRIBUTION OF INTELLIGENCE
QUOTIENTS OF DELINQUENT BOYS
(*After Eckenrode*)

Intelligence group	IQ range	Per cent
Superior	120-134.9	4.35
High Average	110-119.9	11.89
Average	90-109.9	51.69
Low Average	80- 89.9	17.68
Inferior	50- 79.9	14.40

One study was concerned with differences in the components of intelligence of delinquents and nondelinquents as revealed in the verbal and performance aspects of the *Wechsler-Bellevue Scale*.[18] The delinquents were inferior to a control group of nondelinquents in verbal intelligence, while the two groups resembled each other closely in performance intelligence. A distribution of verbal and performance IQ's of the 500 delinquents is shown in Figure 18-2. The delinquents do better in those tasks in which the approach to meaning is direct in nature rather than through symbols. They are, in general, inferior in vocabulary and information. This is a source of difficulty for them in much of the learning emphasized in the traditional school program. Thus, the nature of the test used affects the intelligence quotient obtained. Since the delinquent is frequently retarded in his schoolwork, he is seriously handicapped on tests involving language activities and reading materials. In spite of the fact that the various investigators have used different techniques for evaluating the intelligence of delinquents and have in many cases tested subjects in which different criteria have been used for classifying them as delinquents, their data agree in certain respects as follows:

(1) There are more mental defectives among the delinquents tested than among unselected groups of children.

(2) The average intelligence-test scores of children brought before the courts or institutionalized is less than the average for unselected school children of the same age level.

(3) The average educational retardation among the children regarded as delinquent is greater than that for public school children in general.

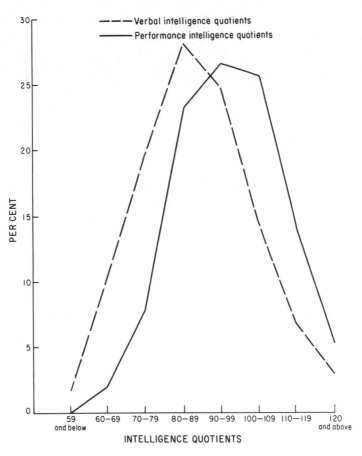

Figure 18-2

DISTRIBUTION OF VERBAL AND PERFORM-
ANCE IQ'S OF 500 DELINQUENT BOYS
(*Glueck and Glueck*)

(4) There are delinquents with high levels of intelligence as well as delinquents with low intelligence levels.

(5) In line with item 4, we note that the distribution of IQ's among juvenile-court cases tends to follow the normal probability curve (see Figure 18-2).

MALADJUSTMENTS AND DELINQUENCY

It was emphasized earlier in this chapter that delinquent acts result from a multiplicity of factors operating in a unitary manner. Delinquent behavior may serve to express hostile retaliatory feelings against an institution, a society, or a person. The boy who breaks the window of the school building may be showing his resentment of the treatment received from the teacher or his classmates. Juvenile delinquent acts may be employed to resolve certain inner conflicts—aggressive acts release tension. The boy who breaks out the window panes of the school building may find this an avenue for releasing tension resulting from a conflict between failure in his school activities and a desire for approval from his teachers, parents, or classmates. Juvenile delinquency may result from frustrations. The boy who is unable to attend the school dance may seek release from the tension thus developed by harming certain individuals attending or damaging property somewhat related to the dance. The girl who persists in indulging in sexual activities may be striving to satisfy a need for status or affection that is being denied her in the normal life pursuits.

Self-concept and juvenile delinquency. Reckless, Dinitz, and Kay have pointed to a good or poor concept of self and others, as manifested by 12-year-olds, as a basis for predicting juvenile delinquency.[19] They suggested that a child or adolescent with a good self-concept has a sort of built-in insulator against juvenile delinquency, while the individual with a poor concept of the self frequently succumbs to delinquency. He finds security and acceptance in the juvenile gang, which in our cities has frequently become the most effective and rewarding group of a particular neighborhood. With this group he is able to protect his ego and prove his worth from episode to episode, in accordance with the code of the gang.

A study reported by Lively, Dinitz, and Reckless dealt with the stability of the direction of socialization in adolescents, 12 to 15 years of age.[20] A total of 1171 students from the sixth, seventh, eighth, and ninth grades supplied usable information. The socialization scale consisted of 46 items from the *California Personality Inventory*. The results, presented in Table 18-2, show the mean scores by grade, sex, and area (good or bad). A score of 30 or above was considered as representing a veering toward socialization whereas a score below 30 was less favorable. The results indicate a trend toward stability of scores from 12 to 15 years of age. There was also a constancy in the differences between boys and girls and between good and poor neighborhoods.

These findings give much assurance to those working with teenagers. In view of the fact that the direction of socialization and a favorable self-concept have been found to have insulation value against a propulsion toward delinquency, stability in the direction of self-concept and socialization becomes very important in the prediction and control of delinquency. Concerning the task of the behavioral scientist the investigators state:

. . . He can attempt to fortify the favorable components, so as to strengthen the insulation against delinquency, although this is probably not necessary.

He can also attempt to change the unfavorable direction of socialization and self-concept in those children who are veering toward delinquency, an effort which would amount to mobilizing the child to internalize values, norms, goals, expectations, responsibilities, limits, status, belongingness, identification, alternative approaches—concepts which in turn would steer him away from delinquency, provided there is no basic damage and no basic antisocial character formation. . . . The task ahead is to design a program which will enable the 12-year-old child who is spotted as showing an unfavorable direction of self to strengthen this self and to develop defenses against pressures, pulls, and pushes.[21]

Table 18-2

VARIATIONS IN MEAN SOCIALIZATION SCORES BY GRADE, SEX, AND AREA OF RESIDENCE

(*Lively, Dinitz, Reckless*)

	Grade 6			Grade 7			Grade 8			Grade 9		
	N	M	SD	N	M	SD	N	M	SD	N	M	SD
Sex												
M	92	35.5	6.4	156	36.2	6.6	153	34.4	7.3	154	33.8	7.8
F	100	38.7	6.3	168	39.4	6.1	172	38.9	6.9	176	38.8	7.2
CR		3.5			6.4			7.1			6.2	
Area												
G	95	38.4	6.3	175	38.8	6.1	177	37.8	7.2	176	37.4	7.3
B	97	35.9	6.8	149	36.8	6.7	148	35.6	7.3	154	35.5	7.5
CR		2.6			2.8			2.7			2.3	

Code: M = male, F = female, CR = critical ratio, G = good, B = bad.

Defensive behavior and delinquency. Defensive behavior frequently takes the form of aggressive behavior in an attempt to cover up an inadequacy. This means that many delinquencies originate in mechanisms such as attention-getting and compensation. This aggressive behavior of a serious nature in delinquents shows many pattern factors such as:

1. The individual has no basis for maintaining self-esteem, such as love or proper attention.

2. He is overly-motivated to secure recognition and admiration, either from his peer-group, or from older delinquents.

3. He is driven by anxieties originating in physical, social, and intellectual inferiorities, and can gain satisfactions from the feeling that his aggressive behavior gives.

4. Quite often he has developed a deep hostility toward his parents, and employs his delinquent behavior as a means of hurting and punishing them.

5. Flagrant sexual delinquency among girls is thought to be a re-

sponse to an unsatisfied need to have someone love them and pay attention to them.

An adjective checklist of 75 words was used by Shippee-Blum to compare the ego strength of rebellious and cooperative adolescents. Each subject was asked to mark as true (1) the adjectives which described him as he really was, (2) all adjectives which described his father as he (the adolescent) saw him, and (3) those which described his mother correctly. On the adjective checklist the rebels "revealed unrealistic self-regard, which differed from the realistic self-appraisal of the cooperatives. Rebels were found to regard themselves more highly than they regarded their parents; cooperators admired their parents more than themselves."[22]

Personality characteristics. Healy and Bronner compared 105 pairs of delinquents and their nondelinquent brothers or sisters on certain personality characteristics.[23] The delinquent in this study is distinguished from his nondelinquent brother by his marked feelings of inferiority, ascendant behavior, restlessness and hyperactivity, and greater number of nervous habits. His dislikes for school and his teachers are plainly revealed. He displays the picture of an insecure individual attempting to satisfy certain unfulfilled needs through aggressive acts, belligerency, showing-off, excessive movie attendance, and the like.

Through statistical treatment of data from questionnaire items previously shown to differentiate between delinquents and nondelinquents, Peterson, Quay, and Cameron determined the personality and background factors related to delinquency.[24] Three personality dimensions were ob-

Table 18-3

PSYCHOPATHIC FACTORS THAT DIFFERENTIATED DELINQUENTS FROM NONDELINQUENTS

(Peterson, Quay, and Cameron)

Factor	Loading
1. The only way to settle anything is to lick the guy	64
2. Winning a fight is more fun than anything	62
3. The people that run things are usually against me	62
4. Cops usually treat you dirty	61
5. If you don't have enough to live on its OK to steal	60
6. A lot of times its fun to be in jail	54
7. The only way to make big money is to steal it	53
8. A person is better off if he doesn't trust anyone	52
9. If the cops don't like you, they will get you for anything	51
10. Life usually hands me a pretty raw deal	48

tained from this study. The first of these was characterized by a number of psychopathic qualities. Tough, amoral, rebellious qualities are obviously implied by the 10 factors presented in Table 18-3.

Impulsive, antisocial tendencies along with expressions of regret, depression, and other negative feelings characterized behavior among many delinquents. This factor is interpreted as neurotism and bears a close resemblance to the type of delinquent sometimes labeled as the "Disturbed Delinquent." The 10 items with the heaviest loading are presented in Table 18-4. The third group of items, presented in Table 18-5 are characterized by a feeling of "inadequacy." Studies show that many delinquents are characterized by a history of failure, which leads to feelings of inadequacy. This group of delinquents may be closely identified with those suffering from an inferiority complex.

Table 18-4

FACTORS CLASSIFIED AS "NEUROTICISM" THAT DIFFERENTIATE DELINQUENTS FROM NONDELINQUENTS

(Peterson, Quay, and Cameron)

Factor	Loading
1. I often feel that I am not getting anywhere in life	68
2. Sometimes I used to feel that I would like to leave home	56
3. I seem to do things that I regret more often than other people do	56
4. I have often gone against my parents' wishes	55
5. My parents often disapproved of my friends	54
6. I sometimes wanted to run away from home	52
7. I often feel as though I have done something wrong or wicked	52
8. I don't think I'm quite as happy as others seem to be	51
9. People often talk about me behind my back	48
10. With things going as they are, it's pretty hard to keep up hope of amounting to something.	47

Table 18-5

FACTORS CLASSIFIED AS "INADEQUACY" THAT DIFFERENTIATE DELINQUENTS FROM NONDELINQUENTS

(Peterson, Quay, and Cameron)

Factor	Loading
1. I have never been in trouble with the law	—43*
2. I am behind at least a year in school	41
3. I'd quit school now if they would let me	39
4. When I was going to school I played hooky quite often	38
5. When something goes wrong I usually blame myself rather than the other fellow	35
6. I hardly ever get excited or thrilled	34
7. I enjoy work as much as play	31
8. My folks move (or used to move) from place to place a lot	30

* A negative sign indicates that a false response is associated with the positive pole of the factor.

THE HOME AND JUVENILE DELINQUENCY

Cultural anthropologists have been interested in cultural factors which contribute to the low incidence of stress and violence among adolescents in some cultures as opposed to the greater incidence in American culture. Hsu, Watrous, and Lord pointed out the following from their study of this problem:

> . . . The most striking difference, in fact, between the Chinese-American adolescents in Hawaii and white American adolescents on the mainland is the absence of overt rebellion against authority. The "big fight" with parents is lacking. The Chinese in Hawaii are simply not troubled by adolescent difficulties. Both police files and interviews with parents and social workers suggest that the "problem adolescent;" when found, is an exception.[25]

Interaction of the individual and social factors. Growth and development at any period of life must be evaluated in terms of the nature of the individual organism and the various forces that have operated in the organization and direction of growth. The study by Healy and Bronner shows how individual and social factors operate together in producing juvenile delinquents. Intensive studies were made of delinquents in Boston, New Haven, and Detroit. Those who had nondelinquent siblings were selected for special study, since a control group with social backgrounds similar to that of the offenders was available for study and comparison. The importance of the home and community background is evidenced by the fact that in only 22 cases of the 153 delinquents studied did they find the delinquent living in a favorable situation with reference to the following:

1. Reasonably good home conditions from the viewpoint of stability, normal recreational conditions, and normal physical needs and comforts

2. Reasonably good attitudes of the parents from the viewpoint of freedom from family friction, normal attitude toward child care and treatment, and law abiding

3. Normal neighborhood from the viewpoint of freedom from direct influences leading toward juvenile crime.

Parental attitudes. It was pointed out in Chapter 10 that an important source of frustration for many adolescents is the unwillingness of parents to "let go." A thwarting of the quest for independence is closely related to the early development of many juvenile crimes. It has been observed that at 10 or 11 years of age around 70 per cent of girls and 60 per cent of boys find greatest pleasure in the home and prefer to spend most of their leisure time there. With the onset of puberty, the wider range of interests, and broadened social activities, adolescents begin to find more pleasures outside the home. Parents should not deplore this fact, but, instead of thwarting adolescent desires, should aid the growing boy and girl in his or her emancipation from the dependency of childhood. Testing the hypothesis that parental attitudes are closely related to juvenile delinquency, the Gluecks investigated the kinds of parental discipline employed in the homes of delinquents and nondelinquents.[26] It was observed that parents of delinquents resorted to punishment and to a lesser extent to reasoning than did the parents of nondelinquents. It was further noted that mothers of delinquents were inclined to be lax and erratic in their discipline, while fathers were erratic, lax, and overstrict. Both the mothers and fathers of nondelinquents displayed firm but kindly measures of discipline. Sometimes the delinquent behavior of the adolescent is reinforced by parents who consciously or unconsciously sanction the delinquent activity of the individual. Such was the case of Jack reported by Baittle:

> An example is Jack, who was a popular member of the group. He was constantly involved in serious fighting with other boys and was expelled from school many times. His father frequently boasted of getting into trouble when he was Jack's age, and refused to recognize the seriousness of his son's fighting. He felt Jack would straighten out as he himself had. Moreover, the father felt that Jack could not possibly compete with his own delinquencies in adolescence, and therefore blinded himself to what the boy was doing. The mother, although verbalizing wishes to impose controls on Jack, could not because of her conscious fear of hurting him. Unconsciously, she wished the boy to get into trouble and be punished, and he acted this out.[27]

The Gluecks have given us a measuring device designed to indicate the possibility of future delinquency in a particular child. Their instrument is made up of factors having to do with parent-child relationships. The five factors making up the subcategories of the prediction table are shown in Table 18-6.[28]

Character and personality adjustment of parents. A factor closely related to parental attitudes is the character of the parents. It has been pointed out that the child is imitative; especially does he imitate those whom he considers authorities. He comes to feel that their acts are an endorsement of such types of behavior. Imitation and suggestion in connection with drinking, immorality, or lawlessness aid in the establishment of delinquent tendencies in adolescent boys and girls. In a study by Lumpkin the delinquent girls' parental background was found to be very unfavorable.[29] Social defective tendencies such as crime, alcoholism, and sexual irregularity appeared 443 times in 189 families. In the study by Glueck and Glueck comparisons were made between the parents of delinquents and nondelinquents with respect to physical, mental, and emotional handicaps.

Table 18-7 shows that the parents of delinquents are more burdened

Table 18-6

THE GLUECK SOCIAL PREDICTION TABLE

Social factor	Failure score
1. Discipline of Boy by Father	
Overstrict	71.8
Lax	59.8
Firm but kindly	9.3
2. Supervision of Boy by Mother	
Unsuitable	83.2
Fair	57.5
Suitable	9.9
3. Affection of Father for Boy	
Indifferent or hostile	75.9
Warm (including overprotective)	33.8
4. Affection of Mother for Boy	
Indifferent or hostile	86.2
Warm (including overprotective)	43.1
5. Cohesiveness of Family	
Unintegrated	96.9
Some elements of cohesion	61.3
Cohesive	20.6

with serious physical ailments, mental retardation, emotional disturbances, drunkenness, and criminality than are the parents of nondelinquents.[30] Thus, 39.6 per cent of the fathers of delinquents and 48.6 per cent of the mothers suffered from serious physical ailments, as compared with 28.6 per cent of the fathers of nondelinquents and 33 per cent of the mothers. Over 60 per cent of the fathers of delinquents drank to the point of intoxication, as compared with 39 per cent of the fathers of nondelinquents. More than three times as many of the mothers of delinquents drank excessively, as compared with the mothers of nondelinquents. Delinquency and crime were also present far more among the parents of the delinquents.

Family breakdown and delinquency. For many years the broken home has been pointed to as one of the main causes of juvenile delinquency. To substantiate this claim many studies of home backgrounds have appeared. These studies almost without exception show broken homes in the background of a large percentage of delinquent children. We should be extremely careful, however, in the interpretation of these studies. The broken home is, in most cases, the climax of a long series of events and simply indicates underlying adjustments that affect all members of the family. There is evidence that it is not the broken home so

Table 18-7

HISTORY OF SERIOUS PHYSICAL AILMENTS, MENTAL RETARDATION, EMOTIONAL
DISTURBANCES, DRUNKENNESS, AND CRIMINALITY OF FATHER AND MOTHER
(*After Glueck and Glueck*)

	MOTHER				
	Delinquents		*Nondelinquents*		*Difference*
Condition	*Number*	*Per cent*	*Number*	*Per cent*	*Per cent*
Serious physical ailments	243	48.6	165	33.0	15.6
Mental retardation	164	32.8	45	9.0	23.8
Emotional disturbances	201	40.2	88	17.6	22.6
Drunkenness	115	23.0	35	7.0	16.0
Criminality	224	44.8	75	15.0	29.8
	FATHER				
Serious physical ailments	198	39.6	143	28.6	11.0
Mental retardation	92	18.4	28	5.6	12.8
Emotional disturbances	220	44.0	90	18.0	26.0
Drunkenness	314	62.8	195	39.0	23.8
Criminality	331	66.2	160	32.0	34.2

much as the factors often associated with this condition—especially among
the lower economic groups in which separation is a standard or an acceptable way of living. Thus, a broken home has a different connotation.
Campbell presents evidence that it is the tension, neglect, and poverty
accompanying broken-home conditions that cause an increased percentage
of delinquency in these groups.[31] Based upon the records of 604 juvenile
delinquents of both sexes, Hirsch interprets the results as showing broken
homes a consequence of constitutional abnormalities and temperamental
instabilities of parents rather than a direct cause of delinquency.[32] Many
siblings of delinquents from broken homes are untouched by this factor.

Economic factors. It has been observed that the amount of juvenile
delinquency is closely related to certain economic conditions. Delinquency
increases both in times of extreme prosperity and during periods of depression, with the lowest rate in a period of fairly normal economic conditions. Burgess noted that there was a high correlation between juvenile
delinquency areas and low family income.[33] He reports that in such cities
as Chicago, Cleveland, Columbus, Richmond, and Boston juvenile delinquency rates are closely related to such economic factors as the family
being on relief, dependency, nonsupport, unemployment of father, and
level of rent paid. Poverty seems to bring with it or to include factors
closely related to delinquent behavior. We usually find crime, disease,
ignorance, and vice associated with poverty.

It is probable that a careful study of homes broken by the death of one parent would indicate that such a circumstance is apt to result in behavior difficulties in the children from families less favored financially more than in children at the other end of the economic scale. The death of the father in a laborer's family usually burdens the mother and the older children with the responsibility of furnishing a livelihood. Often no insurance or other form of security is available. The mother must be away from home during many hours of the day, so that close supervision is impossible. In such a situation it is not easy for the parent to establish a relationship of close confidence with the children, which is vitally necessary to harmonious home life.

Even when both parents are alive, the poverty-stricken home presents a tremendous handicap to rearing the children as well-adjusted individuals. Often the father must work long hours without sufficient nourishment and recreation. His temper and training do not fit him for considerate handling of descipline situations and the result is constant tension. The children in such a family are denied the comforts and luxuries that some of their companions at school enjoy, with the result that many resort to dishonest means to attain these advantages. The death or desertion of the father in such a situation is the final stroke that brings on the more adverse conditions.

Overcrowding. Another home condition somewhat closely related to many of those already considered is overcrowding. This is especially likely to occur in circumstances of poverty and leads to stealing. Congested living conditions within the home or neighborhood may also throw children into undue contact with sexual stimulation and thereby result in increased immorality. A follow-up study of 207 boys, who as 10-year-olds in 1948 had been the subject of complaints to the Detroit police, showed that only 43 of these had had any contact with the police in 1950.[34] A comparison was then made between the repeaters and the nonrepeaters on items recorded at the time of the first contact with the police. Having two or more brothers, living in an apartment or rooming house, and having a reputation as "Peck's Bad Boy" seemed to best differentiate the repeaters from the nonrepeaters. This is shown in Table 18-8.

Other casual home conditions exist that cannot be considered here; nor is there ample space to consider even the major studies that have been made of the subject. Rejection, the mother's being forced to work, lack of educational advantages, lack of recreational facilities, the broken home, and undesirable companions in relation to the home are all potent factors. However, there is considerable evidence from various studies that the most important home factor that influences the growing boys and girls is the relationship existing between parents and children, and between the chil-

Table 18-8

SOME COMPARISONS BETWEEN REPEATERS AND NONREPEATERS

(After Wattenberg and Quiroz)

Item	Repeaters N 43		Nonrepeaters N 164	
	No.	Per cent	No.	Per cent
Poor marks or failing school	16	37	45	27
Two or more brothers	27	63	53	32
Apartment or rooming house	11	26	19	12
Reputation as normal	21	49	122	74
Reputation as "Peck's Bad Boy"	20	47	32	20

dren themselves. The importance of favorable and consistent attitudes of parents in relation to adolescent problems cannot be overemphasized.

NEIGHBORHOOD CONDITIONS

Congested neighborhoods. The detrimental effect of bad home conditions is usually supplemented by undesirable neighborhood influences. In the first place, congested home conditions are closely related to congested neighborhood conditions. It has been found from various studies that crime is relatively higher in populous territories. In Maller's study of juvenile delinquency in New York City, it was observed that delinquency is largely concentrated in certain underprivileged areas.[35] High delinquency areas are characterized by (1) low rents, (2) low educational level of the adults, (3) excessive retardation of pupils in school, (4) poor recreational facilities, (5) overcrowded conditions, (6) high adult crime rate, and (7) lack of organized activities for adolescents. These conditions are similar in nature to the results obtained from surveys in other cities. These studies indicate that delinquent areas fall into the following general types: (1) deteriorating residential areas in which business establishments are being organized, (2) manufacturing areas, and (3) districts characterized by an unstable population.

Delinquents are given to stealing rides, hopping trucks, and roaming about the streets after dark far in excess of nondelinquents. Delinquents are more frequently found within the lower-class group. The individual brought before the courts is often a person rejected or neglected, both by his parents and by the community. The lower-class delinquent usually does not have the orientation toward developing a regard and respect for attitudes of foresight, self-control, responsible independence, and desire to achieve that is found in the middle-class range; nor does he have the opportunity or the training in the fundamental emphases on taste, manners, good form and family reputation of the middle- and upper-class patterns.

Much of the delinquency of lower-class teen-agers is due to their attempt to adhere to behavior patterns, standards, and values of their subculture. Among lower class adolescents, focal concerns are centered around trouble, toughness, endurance, physical prowess, "outsmarting the other guy," fate and luck, desire for autonomy with dependency needs, excitement, escape from boredom and monotony, and the like. Attitudes, values, concerns, and ideals are contagious, and necessarily so for in order that the youth be accepted into his segment of society, he must adopt the behavior patterns of that society. Thus, the youth born into this lower class society must make these concerns his own, and with a choice of alternative forms of behavior his decision is frequently on the side of norm-violating behavior.

Delinquent gangs. The gang furnishes the teen-ager with a pattern of life that satisfies certain basic needs. The adolescent who feels unwanted at home or who is unable to identify himself with organized activities at school or elsewhere, drifts naturally into a gang. In fact, if a boy lives in a certain neighborhood where gang activities flourish, he is well-nigh forced to join a gang for self-protection. Although gangs are made up largely of boys, in New York City three out of four teen-age gang wars are caused by girls.[36] Although these girls are not members of the all-male gangs, they associate with them and are frequently a source of conflict between opposing gangs, leading the boys to commit crimes ranging from misdemeanors to murder. These gang girls are promiscuous, truant, and violent. They are petty thieves, alcoholics, dope addicts, prostitutes. They give birth to illegitimate children, smuggle deadly weapons, and transmit venereal disease. A broken home, poor parent-child relationship, a slum neighborhood, lack of recreational facilities—all these factors contribute to the making of a gang girl. Without a favorable adult identification, and with a failure to satisfy her psychological needs otherwise, she shifts her allegiance from socially acceptable activities to those of the gang.

A study of the records of 5878 boys between the ages of 12 and 16 contacted on complaint of Detroit police revealed that gang members are more likely to come from "easy-going" homes and low neighborhoods than are nongang members.[37] The gang members were also more likely to come from substandard homes and racially mixed neighborhoods, which at the time of the study tended to be less well-to-do. The nongang group had a higher proportion of youngsters living in good neighborhoods. Gang activities thrive in neighborhoods where no provisions have been made for meeting the need for achievement, for belongingness, and ego enhancement.

The general characteristics and spirit of the neighborhood and community are thus most important factors in the cause and prevention of juvenile delinquency. There is evidence from many sources that organized educational, recreational, and work programs help in the prevention of delinquency. The need for such programs is borne out in the study by the Gluecks of the play places of delinquents and nondelinquents, presented in Table 18-9.[38] Almost all (95.2 per cent) of the delinquents, as compared with 58.4 per cent of the nondelinquents, hung around the street corners, while 86.8 per cent of the delinquents as compared with 14.2 per cent of the nondelinquents sought their recreation in neighborhoods at a considerable distance. A larger percentage of delinquents than nondelinquents played in vacant lots, on the waterfront, and in railroad yards. On the other hand, a much lower percentage of delinquents spent part of their leisure time at home and on the playgrounds.

Table 18-9

COMPARISON OF PLAY PLACES OF DELINQUENTS AND NONDELINQUENTS
(*After Glueck and Glueck*)

Description	Delinquents		Nondelinquents		Difference
	Number	Per cent	Number	Per cent	
Street corners	476	95.2	292	58.4	36.8
Distant neighborhoods	434	86.8	71	14.2	72.6
Vacant lots	232	46.4	135	27.0	19.4
Waterfronts	152	30.4	79	15.8	14.6
Railroad yards	102	20.4	5	1.0	19.4
Poolrooms, cheap dance halls, and the like	76	15.2	4	0.8	14.4
Home	208	41.6	466	93.2	—51.6
Playgrounds	147	29.4	305	61.0	—31.6

THE SCHOOL AND DELINQUENCY

Its enlarged function. The school is becoming a potent force in the development and guidance of individual boys and girls into useful and worthy citizenship. It is sometimes thought of as one would think of a life insurance policy, except that in this case the state pays the premiums and is expecting returns in the form of better and more useful citizenship. One assumption here is that a citizen trained for earning a living will be a better citizen; the other is that a democratic state cannot afford to be controlled by the will of an ignorant *demos*.

Although the schools are playing an increasingly important role in the training of future citizens, they are also in many cases contributing to

juvenile delinquency. Some of the major problems faced by adolescents
have been listed in earlier chapters as school problems. It has been pointed
out that many adolescents are almost doomed to failure because of an
inadequate program, while another large group find themselves at odds
with the teachers and school administration because they are not interested in, and in many cases actually dislike, the program in which they
are required to participate at school. We note that the first step of many
juvenile delinquents is truancy from school. Teachers and administrators
must concern themselves with the causes of truancy, since truancy is so
closely related to stealing and to sex offenses. The study by Williams shows
the importance of truancy in relation to juvenile delinquency. His study
is based on the results from 98 cases referred to a clinic during the school
year 1944-45. Truancy, stealing, incorrigibility, and sex misdemeanors
were the chief reasons for referring half the cases. There were few cases,
however, where one factor alone was noted. Truancy was the chief complaint in 21 cases and there was a history of truancy present in 33 other
cases. A further study of the 98 cases showed that certain factors seemed to
favor truancy. Listed in order of frequency, these were: (1) poor parental
control, (2) no goal, (3) gangs, (4) pushed against a low IQ, (5) low economic status, with desire to keep up with others as to style and dress,
(6) inability to keep up with the progress of the class after a severe illness,
(7) punishing parents, and (8) dislike of teacher.[39]

Kvaraceus lists several characteristic functions of a good school that
in their fulfilling act and react in a positive and negative fashion to spark
anti-social aggressions and delinquency. Such functions and their reactions
are:

1. The maintenance of ordered patterns of living in daily experiences; the
delinquent is devoid of systematic living
2. Demanding self-denial, self-control, self-restraint, and a focus on distant
goals; the delinquent has not had the chance to acquire these concepts
3. Authoritarian control; the delinquent detests authority in any degree
4. Enforced attendance through the twelfth grade; the delinquent usually
drops out
5. Presents the virtues of fair play, honesty, cleanliness and good clean
speech; the delinquent considers these virtues as weaknesses
6. Places a high priority on abilities of verbalization and abstraction; the
delinquent may not cultivate these abilities
7. Functions as a center for learning, not a community convenience for the
emotionally disturbed and socially maladjusted; some delinquents may be in
the wrong institution.[40]

Numerous authorities have outlined various functions and criteria
for school administrators in the rehabilitating of delinquents and for
diagnosing predelinquents within the school program. It is not within
the scope of this study to undertake such a task. If the school program is

well integrated with the life of the community, if the values of the teachers coincide with those of the community, and if there is a democratic and harmonious working relationship established between the pupils and teachers, the school will be a powerful agency for preventing juvenile delinquency and for developing desirable and wholesome personalities.

Effects of failure. More and more the problem of individual variation is receiving attention in an endeavor to interpret better the cause-and-effect relations in the development of behavior. The importance of this is brought forth in a study by Wattenberg of factors associated with repeating among preadolescent delinquents.[41] The records of 90 "repeaters" were compared with those of 235 boys showing only one police contact. Repeating was found to be closely associated with poor school work, low intellectual ability, membership in unruly gangs, and reputation for trouble. The seriousness of continued school failure is supported by data reported by Zabolski in which a comparison is presented of 50 delinquent boys with a mean age of 15.5 years with a control group of 50 nondelinquent boys.[42] The delinquent boy presented a psychological deficit. His behavior was attributed to a series of inadequacies or failures. It was a positive form of socially unaccepted behavior made in an attempt to overcome certain unsolved problems.

The school delinquent. School delinquents have been described by Kvaraceus as being educationally bankrupt. Their report cards show marginal or failure marks, and they read poorly. The importance of reading in the school and out-of-school adjustments of teen-agers is brought forth in the results of a study by Kvaraceus designed to forecast delinquency. He concludes:

> Junior high school youngsters who fall into the lowest or poorest reading group tended to show a heavy preponderance of norm violations. Reading ability, whether it be cause or effect, must be taken into account as a potential factor closely tied in with the delinquent symptom.[43]

The delinquent's attitudes toward school are heavily charged with hate and hostility; they change schools frequently; truancy is frequent or habitual; leaving school as soon as the law will allow is the rule; membership in special classes for atypical students is more often observed; they seem to enjoy little feeling of belonging in the classroom; they rarely participate in volunteer extra-curricular activities; they tend to be the bullies on the playground, and they take their frustrations out on school property.

SUMMARY

Throughout this volume there has been a continuous emphasis on the general concept that the development of behavior patterns is a result of forces and conditions both within and without the individual. The adolescent has been described as a dynamic individual in a state of transition from childhood to adulthood. His behavior at any particular time arises from a multiplicity of causes and conditions. Delinquent behavior, according to this viewpoint, is thus regarded as symptomatic of a great variety of conditions—among them physical conditions, emotional states, socio-economic status of the home, recreational needs and opportunities, educational attainments, relationships with peers, social and personal adjustments, and guidance. The personality structure of delinquent boys is often an adjustive reaction resulting from failure to satisfy their needs through socially acceptable channels. A consideration of the types of delinquents presented early in this chapter in the light of the factors associated with delinquency might lead to a better clarification of how certain syndromes or patterns of factors may operate to produce a particular type of delinquent.

Sex alone does not cause delinquency; psychoneurotic tendencies alone do not cause delinquency; inferior intelligence alone does not cause delinquency. It is not inherited; environment considered as an entirely isolated factor cannot give the whole story of delinquency. Delinquents differ from nondelinquents in a number of significant ways. However, one should be cautious about making generalizations from individual cases. The roots of delinquency are usually in the home. An outstanding characteristic of many delinquencies is a history of failure. Delinquents are often retarded and/or not accepted by their classmates. The needs of the delinquent are not different from those of nondelinquents but may be more pronounced. The home, school, church, and other youth-serving agencies should consider the needs and problems of youth in any prevention and rehabilitation program.

THOUGHT PROBLEMS

1. List in order of importance the 10 factors that you believe to be most closely associated with juvenile delinquency.
2. Describe some case of a juvenile delinquent that is familiar to you. Can you give the factors in his life that are probably responsible for his behavior?
3. Elaborate on the thought that "badness" in behavior is symptomatic of a great variety of conditions affecting the individual.
4. Account for the increase in crime despite the development of public education.
5. Point out how three boys, each of whom had stolen a baseball glove, might have been motivated by different conditions or forces? Just what is the significance of this in relation to the treatment that should be accorded these three boys?
6. List several common misconceptions about the nature, characteristics, and problems of the juvenile delinquent.
7. Make a list of behavior expressions that should be looked upon as sympto-

matic of potential delinquency. What values should an understanding of these symptoms have for the teacher and parent?

8. Consider some juvenile delinquent of your acquaintance. Present a simplified case study of this individual, showing his family background, school achievements and record, peer relations, neighborhood activities and interests, and other personal information about the individual.

9. Report on gang activity in your community or from your readings and observations. In what ways is the community responsible for gang mischief?

SELECTED REFERENCES

Cole, Luella, *Psychology of Adolescence,* 6th ed. New York: Holt, Rinehart & Winston, Inc., 1964, Chap. 19.

Coward, Richard A. and Lloyd E. Oblin, *Delinquency and Opportunity: A Theory of Delinquent Gangs.* New York: Free Press of Glencoe, Inc., 1960.

Friedlander, Kate, *The Psycho-analytical Approach to Juvenile Delinquency.* London: Routledge & Kegan Paul, Ltd., 1959.

Kvaraceus, William C., *Juvenile Delinquency* (What Research Says to the Teacher Series, No. 15). Washington, D.C.: Department of Classroom Teachers, National Education Association, 1958.

———— and Walter B. Miller, *Delinquent Behavior. Vol. I: Culture and the Individual.* Washington, D.C.: National Education Association, 1959.

McCord, W. and J. McCord, *Origins of Crime.* New York: Columbia University Press, 1959.

Neumeyer, Martin H., *Juvenile Delinquency in Modern Society.* New York: D. Van Nostrand Co., Inc., 1952.

Robison, Sophia, *Juvenile Delinquency: Its Nature and Control.* New York: Holt, Rinehart & Winston, Inc., 1960.

Rogers, Dorothy, *The Psychology of Adolescence.* New York: Appleton-Century-Crofts, 1962, Chap. 14.

Roucek, Joseph S., *Juvenile Delinquency.* New York: Philosophical Library, Inc., 1958.

Salisbury, H. E., *The Shook-up Generation.* New York: Harper & Row, Publishers, 1959.

Steiner, Lee, *Understanding Juvenile Delinquency.* Philadelphia: Chilton Company—Book Division, 1960.

NOTES

1 William C. Kvaraceus, *Juvenile Delinquency, What Research Says to the Teacher Series,* No. 15 (Washington, D.C.: Department of Classroom Teachers, National Education Association, 1958), p. 10.

2 *Juvenile Court Statistics—1961* (Washington, D.C.: Children's Bureau Statistical Series 69, U.S. Department of Health, Education and Welfare, 1962).

3 P. W. Tappan, *Juvenile Delinquency* (New York: McGraw-Hill Book Company, 1949), p. 74.

4 William C. Kvaraceus and Walter B. Miller, *Delinquent Behavior.* Vol. 1, *Culture and the Individual* (Washington, D.C.: National Education Association, 1959), pp. 25-31.

5 L. Donet, *Psychiatric Aspects of Juvenile Delinquency*. World Health Organization Monograph Series No. 2 (Geneva: World Health Organization, 1951).

6 A. J. Reiss, "Social Correlates of Psychological Types of Delinquency," *American Journal of Sociology*, 17 (1952), 710-18.

7 E. Hewitt and R. L. Jenkins, "Case Studies of Aggressive Delinquents," *American Journal of Orthopsychiatry*, 11 (1941), 485-92.

8 William C. Kvaraceus, *op. cit.*, p. 11.

9 F. Schmidt, "The Rorschach Test in Juvenile Delinquency Research," *American Journal of Orthopsychiatry*, 19 (1947), 151-60.

10 R. Topping, "Case Studies of Aggressive Delinquents," *American Journal of Orthopsychiatry*, 11 (1941), 485-92.

11 R. Hirschberg, "The Socialized Delinquent," *The Nervous Child*, 6 (1947), 464.

12 J. F. Travers, "Schools and Delinquency," *Education*, 80 (1960), 304.

13 Don Wharton, "Newest Crime Wave—Shoplifting," *Family Weekly* (March 17, 1963), pp. 8-9.

14 C. Goring, *The English Convict* (London: Her Majesty's Stationery Office), p. 13. Quoted from an address delivered by Lombroso in 1906 before the Congress of Criminal Anthropology at Turin.

15 H. H. Goddard, *Human Efficiency and Levels of Intelligence* (Princeton, N.J.: Princeton University Press, 1920), pp. 72-73.

16 C. W. Mann and H. P. Mann, "Age and Intelligence of a Group of Juvenile Delinquents," *Journal of Abnormal and Social Psychology*, 34 (1939), 351-60. A review of the average IQ's found by various investigators is presented in this study.

17 C. J. Eckenrode, "Their Achievement in Delinquency," *Journal of Educational Research*, 43 (1949-50), 554-58.

18 Sheldon Glueck and Eleanor Glueck, *Unraveling Juvenile Delinquency* (New York: Commonwealth Fund, 1950), pp. 198-201.

19 Walter C. Reckless, Simon Dinitz, and Barbara Kay, "The Self Component in Potential Delinquency," *American Sociological Review*, 22 (1957), 566-70.

20 Edwin L. Lively, Simon Dinitz, and Walter C. Reckless, "Self Concept as a Predictor of Juvenile Delinquency," *American Journal of Orthopsychiatry*, 32 (1962), 159-68.

21 *Ibid.*, p. 167.

22 Eva Marie Shippee-Blum, "The Young Rebel Self-regard and Ego-ideal," *Journal of Consulting Psychology*, 23 (1959), 44-50.

23 W. Healy and A. F. Bronner, *New Light on Delinquency and Its Treatment* (New Haven: Yale University Press, 1936), pp. 73-78.

24 Donald R. Peterson, Herbert C. Quay, and Gordon R. Cameron, "Personality and Background Factors in Juvenile Delinquency as Inferred from Questionnaire Responses," *Journal of Consulting Psychology*, 23 (1959), 395-99.

25 Francis L. K. Hsu, Blanche G. Watrous, and Edith M. Lord, "Culture Patterns and Adolescent Behavior," *International Journal of Social Psychiatry*, 7 (1960-61), 43.

26 Glueck and Glueck, *op. cit.*, p. 131.

27 Brahm Baittle, "Psychiatric Aspects of the Development of a Street Corner Group: An Exploratory Study," *American Journal of Orthopsychiatry*, 31 (1961), 708.

28 Glueck and Glueck, *op. cit.*, p. 261.

29 K. D. Lumpkin, "Factors in the Commitment of Correctional School Girls in Wisconsin," *American Journal of Sociology*, 37 (1931), 222-30.

30 Glueck and Glueck, *op. cit.*, p. 100.

31 M. W. Campbell, "The Effect of the Broken Home upon the Child in School," *Journal of Educational Sociology*, 5 (1932), 274-81.

32 N. D. M. Hirsch, *Dynamic Causes of Juvenile Crime* (Cambridge, Mass.: Sci-Art Publishers, 1937).

33 E. W. Burgess, "The Economic Factor in Juvenile Delinquency," *Journal of Criminal Law, Criminology, and Political Science*, 43 (1952), 35.

34 W. W. Wattenberg and F. Quiroz, "A Follow-up Study of Ten-year-old Boys with Police Records," *Journal of Consulting Psychology*, 17 (1953), 309-13. By permission of the *Journal* and the American Psychological Association.

35 J. B. Maller, "Juvenile Delinquency in New York City," *Journal of Psychology*, 39 (1936), 314-28.

36 Abner Sundell, "Report of the Gang Girl," *American Girl*, Special Edition (May, 1961), p. 44.

37 William W. Wattenberg and James J. Balistrieri, "Gang Membership and Juvenile Misconduct," *American Sociological Review*, 15 (1950), 744-52.

38 Glueck and Glueck, *op. cit.*, p. 162.

39 E. Y. Williams, "Truancy in Children Referred to a Clinic," *Mental Hygiene*, 31 (1947), 405.

40 Kvaraceus, *op. cit.*

41 William W. Wattenberg, "Factors Associated with Repeating among Preadolescent Delinquents," *Journal of Genetic Psychology*, 84 (1954), 189-95.

42 F. C. Zabolski, "Studies in Delinquency: Personality Structure of Delinquent Boys," *Journal of Genetic Psychology*, 74 (1949), 109-17.

43 William C. Kvaraceus, "Forecasting Delinquency: A Three-year Experiment," *Exceptional Children*, 27 (1961), 434.

PART FIVE

THE
END
OF
ADOLESCENCE

19

FROM
ADOLESCENCE
TO
MATURITY

The superior man is liberal toward others' opinions, but does not completely agree with them; the inferior man agrees with others' opinions, but is not liberal with them. CONFUCIUS

During the period of growth and development, new needs are continuously appearing in the individual's life, while certain earlier needs are modified or lose their potency. The development into adolescence introduces a different self and different concepts of self. Old goals are reorganized and new goals are introduced. Growth toward maturity brings with it increased abilities and independence along with increased demands and responsibilities. Certain developmental tasks appearing with the onset of adolescence are extended. At the same time, the maturing adolescent is confronted with other developmental tasks. Some of the tasks appearing during late adolescence and postadolescence which will be presented in this chapter are those relating to vocational adjustment, marriage and marital adjustments, becoming a citizen in a democratic society, and developing a more unified philosophy of life.

Young people or postadolescents can roughly be divided into three groups, based upon their experiences of moving into adulthood. The first group consists of those who follow a long course of educational training before moving into a self-supporting state. These are the young people who go on to college, and in increasing numbers into graduate and professional schools. Many of these marry in their early twenties but continue their education. The second group is made up of adolescents who meet with difficulties and frustrations in their achievements. These boys and girls generally drop out of school at the age of 15 or 16 after a history of frustration, failure, and frequent difficulties with school or legal authorities. A third group that has been steadily growing in numbers consists of those who finish high school or a trade school and then go to work. This group enters fully into the adult world between the ages of 17 and 19.

GROWTH TOWARD MATURITY

Psychologically and sociologically, adolescence ends when the individual attains a consistent and comparatively widespread level of maturity in his drives, interests, and behavior patterns. The development of such maturity is gradual in nature, so that one cannot state a specific time when this is reached for a particular individual. In general most individuals attain this degree of maturity during the teen years. However, many individuals do not attain this maturity at this time. Still others never arrive at a high level of social and ethical maturity.

The maturing adolescent. Throughout preceding chapters it has been emphasized that as the child grows into the period of adolescence, following that of childhood, he is truly entering upon a new sphere of activity. He is reaching into a new social atmosphere, his maturing physiological nature is asserting itself along new channels, and new impulses are arising. It has furthermore been pointed out that behavior is not explicable wholly in terms of the stimulus-response hypothesis but rather in terms of the individual as a whole. This includes, in the case of the adolescent, his biological and sociological past, as well as the momentous present.

The adolescent, with his rapid physiological changes, with his new type of physical potency, with his increased physical strength and vigor, with his growing impulses relative to others, is not the same organism that responded to various stimuli during infancy and childhood; because of his organic changes his responses to various stimuli are quite different from what they were just a few years ago. At age 4, Tom will call to Mary, a neighbor's child, to climb over the fence and play in the sand pile with him. At the age of 17, Tom will likely be calling over the phone rather than over the back fence. This time the call will be for an automobile ride, a dinner dance, or a swim in the lake. The impulses prompting the call over the back fence to play in the sand and those prompting the call over the telephone to go for a ride or a stroll are different; the interests of a maturing organism have replaced those of the playful child.

Thus behavior changes somewhat in harmony with the physiological changes that are taking place at this period; also, with such changes in behavior activities Tom and Mary face increasing responsibilities and increasing needs for adequate adjustments to a changing condition in their own life and environment. To express it analytically, the drives of both Tom and Mary have undergone pronounced changes. This is a clear illustration of the development of heterosexuality.

Reaching social maturity. Maturity is often looked upon as full physical development. A conception of adolescence that pervades much of our culture is that based upon social maturity. The boy or girl who has reached an advanced stage in his social relations may be said to have progressed beyond that of childhood. The degree of one's development beyond the self and his ability to enter into the activities of the group cooperatively is a good measure of social development. Certainly there are some behavior activities that characterize the socially mature person, although not all adults display these characteristics. Thus, social maturity is a relative term. The typical adolescent tends to display these characteristics to an increased degree as he passes into the postadolescent stage. Some characteristics of the socially mature person may be listed as follows:

1. Exercises mature judgment on crucial problems and issues
2. Is able to carry on cooperative activities on a fair and sound basis
3. Assumes personal responsibility for his actions
4. Has a wide range of friends, chosen on a sound basis
5. Displays independence in judgment and actions, but with due regard for the rights and opinions of others
6. Able to take an objective attitude toward the *self*
7. Able to adjust to different situations—practices a certain amount of "role flexibility"
8. Thinks and plans in terms of long-time goals rather than the immediate
9. Is not self-centered in his conversation and in his actions
10. Evaluates issues and problems in terms of the welfare of the group rather than how it is going to affect the *self*.

An overambitious parent may be an important factor in deterring the social and emotional development of adolescents toward maturity. The case of Andrew is an excellent example of how an ambitious father with very dominant ideas created a situation that worked to the disadvantage of the emotional and social development of a 16-year-old boy:

Andrew had lost his mother very early in life and had been brought up by a kindly, affectionate relative, who undoubtedly was a bit too much concerned about his health, manners, and personal appearance. In spite of this, however, he developed in a most satisfactory way. His schoolwork was a bit better than the average, he excelled in athletics, enjoyed reading good books, and developed as a sort of hobby his flair for writing a bit of poetry.

Andrew's father was very enthusiastic about his son's athletic abilities and spurred him on to greater activity in this particular field. With reference to his literary interests, however, he was quite intolerant and left no stone unturned to humiliate this boy about what he called his "sissified" indulgence.

He finally had him transferred to a school where greater emphasis was put on athletic ability; but instead of being stimulated to greater effort in baseball and football, Andrew became more and more absorbed in his reading and poetry.

As might have been expected, his behavior antagonized the father and soon caused a real gulf between the two. The boy became argumentative and later resentful and defiant toward what he felt was unjust domination on the part of his father. He also complained that the latter no longer understood him. The emotional state that was created in the boy by this antagonism toward his father, however, dulled his enthusiasm for his schoolwork and his athletic activities, and even for his hobbies, and he had such a severe slump that he was on the verge of flunking out of school. It was necessary to have frequent interviews with both the father and the son over a period of several weeks before the former began to appreciate his son's needs, leaving him free to build his life around his own personality rather than around his father's ambition.[1]

Intellectual maturity. It has been emphasized throughout the previous chapters that the adolescent develops as a whole—a unified personality. Intellectual maturity cannot be separated from other aspects of maturity. One of the outstanding differences between the child and the mature individual is the way they react to remote or long-term goals. The immature individual is best motivated by goals that are within his reach over a relatively short period of time. Any planning based on long-term purposes loses its force early and is thus short-lived. The more mature individual is able to maintain a steady course of action for a longer period of time. The following account of the vocational planning of a mentally superior 17-year-old boy is a manifestation of intellectual and emotional maturity:

> My father died when I was 10 years old, and left me a sufficient amount of money to provide for my college education. My mother has encouraged me during the course of the past several years to study pharmacy when I enter the state university.
>
> This year I am graduating from high school and must soon decide what I will take when I enter college. Last week I had a long talk with our vocational counselor. At that time I told him of my mother's wishes about my professional future. He asked me some questions about my interests and what I would like to be doing 10 or 15 years from now. Thus, I have been doing lots of thinking about what I would like to be doing at that time. There are some things that I know that I don't want to be doing, so I am trying to decide between business, pharmacy, and teaching.
>
> I have some literature dealing with a number of different fields of work, and have been reading some of it. Maybe after I have read more about the requirements of these different occupations, I will be able to make up my mind. Anyway, I am planning on going to the university this fall and will enroll in the liberal arts school. My counselor told me that the first year's work was basic anyway, and that I could make up my mind further after this first year. I don't want to put this off too long, though, for I think a fellow should decide soon after he goes to college just what field of work he is going to prepare to enter.[2]

The problem of what constitutes intellectual maturity was studied in one case in which 56 college instructors listed traits that they thought were indicative of intellectual maturity.[3] The traits listed are presented in Table 19-1. A study of these traits shows that college instructors emphasize rational judgment, critical attitudes, independence in thought, ability to apply knowledge, and a wide range of information as characteristics of the intellectually mature person.

Table 19-1

TRAITS LISTED AS CHARACTERISTIC OF INTELLECTUAL MATURITY
(*After Eckert*)

Forms rational judgments uncolored by emotional tones
Is able to perceive relations and correlate materials
Shows a critical, evaluative attitude toward problems
Is independent in his thought and work
Possesses a wider background or experience in the field than do other students
Shows initiative in intellectual work, suggesting problems and asking intelligent questions
Is able to apply his knowledge, utilizing general principles in specific situations
Is open-minded, able and willing to assimilate new ideas
Readily comprehends new facts and ideas
Has a sense of values, or a philosophical point of view
Has insight, separates the fundamental points from the unimportant, and sees the implications of problems
Possesses a tolerant attitude toward other people's work and ideas
Is able to suspend judgment until more evidence is found.

ADOLESCENCE AND THE WORLD OF WORK

Work in teen-age culture. The American teen-ager is primarily a consumer rather than producer. It is true that many teen-agers work hard at school in atheltic programs, club activities, planning social events, customizing automobiles, and in varied teen-age projects. These, however, have little economic value and are not subject to the discipline and control of the adult world at large.

Those teen-agers who do participate in the labor market do so as marginal producers, usually in connection with part-time jobs which fit into the adult world but do not deprive them of the contacts and influences of teen-age culture. Some jobs are to a very marked degree teen-age jobs such as the paper route, mowing lawns, helping Saturdays at the community grocery store, baby-sitting, shoveling snow, picking berries in the summer, and other part-time or seasonal occupations. Many teen-agers also find employment at camps or resorts.

Part-time employment of teen-agers may be said to have three important functions. First, it furnishes many with needed money that would not be available otherwise. To others it supplements the small allowance provided by parents who have to live on a rather limited budget. Secondly, gainful employment has educational value in that it trains the individual for holding down a job by actually participating in the world of work. Third, gainful employment helps to satisfy certain basic needs. This may be observed in a study reported by Scales and Hutson with 150 Negro boys of the Hill District in Pittsburgh as subjects.[4] In grade placement the boys ranged from seventh to twelfth grades. Two-thirds were from broken homes. The developmental tasks that gainful employment helped to accomplish, as identified by responses of the boys, are shown in Table 19-2. The four most important satisfactions the boys obtained from gainful employment were in order of frequency as follows: (1) feeling of independence, (2) feeling of growing up, (3) improved relations with family and parents, and (4) status with peers.

Table 19-2

DEVELOPMENTAL TASKS THAT GAINFUL EMPLOYMENT HELPED TO ACCOMPLISH

(After Scales and Hutson)

Developmental task	Per cent
Establishing economic independence	68.0
Achieving emotional independence of parents and other adults	48.0
Acceptance of the proper sex role	20.0
New relations with peers	20.0
Accepting, desiring, and achieving socially responsible behavior	3.3
Selecting and preparing for an occupation	0.7
No developmental task identified	7.3

The first job. The first job is a milestone in the life of the individual. It provides him with the opportunity for achievement and the extension of his independence. A wrong start—getting fired, finding the job too difficult, clashing with the foreman or management—is a frustrating experience for the young worker and may adversely condition him toward a working life. It is very important for the young worker to make satisfactory vocational adjustments, since the world of work is destined to play an important role in his life activities. The vocational needs of youth must be recognized and dealt with in a realistic manner if the transition from school to work is to be a satisfactory one. The story of Jean indicates that graduation from high school does not necessarily assure one of a job or even a satisfactory vocational orientation.

Jean was an attractive girl of 18 with intelligence, poise, and considerable musical ability. She not only completed high school but spent six months in college. She had two months' experience in sales work before going to college, and her parents gave their approval and financial support to her education.

Yet Jean was "in a quandary as to where to turn." She did not like her brief experience in selling. But she was also dissatisfied with the music course she took in college, because she considered it would not lead to practical employment. Jean had no interest in returning to school for a business course, however. She was marking time with a Saturday job in a downtown department store, and would have welcomed counseling from any source that could have helped her get a sense of direction.[5]

‾The level of the first job of the young worker will depend primarily upon his educational level and the social status of his home. The study by Simpson and others dealt with problems related to occupational choice in the Piedmont section of North Carolina, an expanding industrial area.[6] The results, presented in Table 19-3, show the levels of first jobs in relation to educational level and father's occupation. First of all it may be noted that almost half of the workers whose fathers were in occupations C and D (the lower occupations) were not high school graduates, whereas less than 20 per cent of the workers whose fathers were in occupations A and B (the higher occupations) were not high school graduates.

A further study of Table 19-3 reveals that the young workers whose fathers were in the higher occupational groups more frequently obtained their first jobs in the higher occupational groups, whereas those workers whose fathers were in the lower occupational groups tended to gravitate

Table 19-3

LEVELS OF FIRST JOBS OF WORKERS BY CERTAIN CHARACTERISTICS OF THEIR ORIGINS

(*Simpson*, et al.)

Characteristic	Per cent of workers whose first job was in each level				
	A	B	C	D	N
Father A or B					
Worker—h. s. education	36.4	40.9	3.0	19.7	132
Worker—not h. s. educ.	0.0	27.8	8.3	63.9	36
Father C or D					
Worker—h. s. education	6.2	38.1	6.2	49.5	97
Worker—not h. s. educ.	0.0	6.4	7.4	86.2	94

A = executives, proprietors and professionals
B = administrative personnel, minor professionals, clerical and sales, technicians
C = skilled manual employees
D = machine operators, semiskilled and unskilled workers

toward jobs in the lower occupational groups. This condition was remarkably true despite similarities in educational attainment. Thus, the nature of the first job of the young worker is not only affected by his educational attainment but also by his cultural background.

Adolescents at work. The part that work occupies in the lives of adolescents varies widely from section to section of the United States as well as with different socio-economic groups. Also, the employment status of youth is affected by general economic conditions. Employment of individuals 14 to 17 years of age was at a low ebb during the Depression years before World War II. The employment demands of the war and postwar years changed this picture so that the number of adolescents at work more than tripled the number at work during the prewar years.

Technological advancements have produced problems related to unemployment that fall heaviest on teen-agers. It was estimated in 1962 that some 2,500,000 of the 10,800,000 teen-agers enrolled in senior high schools would leave before graduation.[7] Many authorities expect this to increase to 7,500,000 or 8,000,000 before 1970. Most of these will perhaps never find desirable permanent employment. Concerning this, Wolfbein states:

> . . . The high school dropout makes relatively the biggest contribution to our current unemployment figure—with jobless rates as high as 30 per cent. Needless to say, his prognosis in the job market of the future is negative indeed. Even when employed, the dropout gets the low-paying jobs down at the bottom of the occupational ladder.[8]

Many factors operate in connection with the employment of adolescents and the kinds of work they do. In the cities the work may be confined largely to cooperation in a few simple household duties, or it may involve any of the full-time or part-time jobs open to individuals in particular age-brackets. The declining number of people engaged in farming and the development and use of labor-saving devices in the homes have reduced considerably the opportunities for adolescents to work.

Attitudes of high school students toward the job and work. Studies show that high school students have not only aspirations about the kinds of work they would like to do, but rather definite attitudes toward different aspects of the working situation. This was observed in a study by Payne of high school students in rural and urban areas of Georgia.[9] The boys from rural areas were significantly less favorable to the idea of their wives' working after marriage than were the boys from urban areas.

A study conducted for the Girl Scouts by the Research Center of the University of Michigan Institute for Social Research involving a scientifically selected sample of approximately 2000 girls revealed some useful information about the vocational aspirations of adolescent girls. In their jobs they want steady employment, interesting work and nice people to work with. The results shown in Tables 19-4 and 19-5 show that opportunity for promotion and to be a leader rank low among the things regarded by girls as important about a job.[10] This is to be expected, since for girls, a job and a career are usually secondary to marriage and a family. For boys the important things about a job are most likely to deal with income, opportunity for promotion, and security.

The attitudes of students toward membership in labor unions will vary with their home and community backgrounds. However, these attitudes have a bearing on their vocational adjustments. In the Michigan

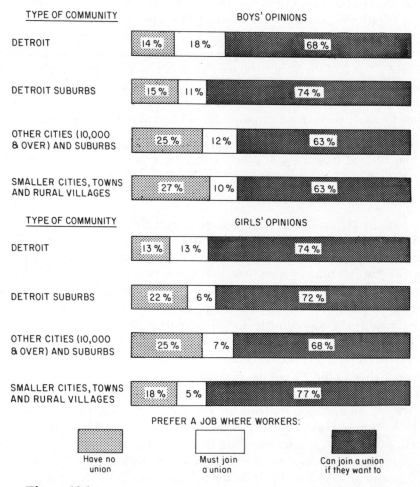

Figure 19-1

COMPARISON OF OPINIONS OF STUDENTS FROM DIFFERENT TYPES OF COMMUNITIES ABOUT UNION MEMBERSHIP

study the attitudes of students in Detroit and other areas were studied and some interesting comparisons made.[11] An interpretation of the findings, shown in Figure 19-1, must take into consideration the fact that Detroit is an automobile manufacturing city where labor unions are very impor-

Table 19-4

WHICH OF THESE THINGS ABOUT A JOB WOULD BE MOST IMPORTANT TO YOU? WHICH NEXT MOST IMPORTANT?*

	Age			
	14–16		Over 16	
	First choice	Second choice	First choice	Second choice
A steady job	29%	29%	18%	26%
Interesting work	24	33	27	41
Nice people to work with	31	22	34	24
High pay	5	2	4	1
Be your own boss	1	2	1	1
Outdoor work	1	**	—	1
Be looked up to by others	1	3	3	1
Be a leader of people	1	**	1	1
Good chance for promotion	1	2	7	4
A job in hometown	3	1	3	—
Not ascertained, sixth or seventh grader, or no second choice	5	5	2	—

* Totals to more than 100 per cent because some girls gave more than one response.
** Less than one half of 1 per cent.

Table 19-5

OCCUPATIONAL CHOICE: STATUS ASPIRATIONS*

	Age		
	Under 14	14–16	Over 16
Professional (doctor, teacher, arts)	32%	30%	29%
Secondary professional (nurse, fashion model, stewardess)	40	38	29
Business	**	1	2
Entertainment	4	2	2
White collar	32	41	49
Personal service	4	6	7
Manual	5	2	5
Housewife	5	2	3
Two or more job choices given	30	28	27
Not ascertained, don't know, other	4	2	3

* Totals to more than 100 per cent because some girls gave more than one response.
** Less than one half of 1 per cent.

tant in connection with almost all phases of human activity. The results show that over 60 per cent of the boys and girls from all communities indicated that they would prefer a job where they could join the union if they wanted to. Interestingly enough, girls were as favorably disposed toward union membership as boys, and in the Detroit area were apparently more favorably disposed.[12] It has already been suggested that one should not generalize too widely from results such as these. They do appear to indicate, however, that in a large city where a large percentage of workers belong to a union the high school boys and girls are quite likely to take a favorable attitude toward union membership.

Why young people fail at work. When young people drop out of school they are usually faced first with the task of securing employment. Once they have obtained employment, they are faced with the task of holding on to their job or of securing a better position. The New York State Employment Service has assembled information dealing with these two problems.[13] The following reasons have been given for why young people fail to obtain jobs: attitudes and behavior, appearance, unrealistic wage demands, insufficient training, applying for a job with friends or relatives, impatience and unwillingness to adapt to entry requirements, reluctance to change from school to business conditions, acquiring a reputation for unreliability, and oversensitiveness about a physical defect. Some case studies presented from the Employment Service files show how some of these factors or conditions operate:

Sandra Z., first applied at an NYSES office at the age of 16. She said she needed a job urgently because she was living with a sister since her parents had moved to California. It was then extremely difficult to find employment for girls under 18 and several contacts with this applicant were necessary before an interview could be arranged.

When she reported to the employer, and he told her the wages, she immediately replied that friends advised her not to work for those wages and that she wasn't interested.

The employer contacted the counselor and said he would not hire this applicant under any circumstances. Her attitude and manner were so unsatisfactory that he felt that she should not be referred again.

Harvey B., 18, and a high-school graduate, completed a general course and had four months' experience as a canvasser, demonstrating kitchen utensils for sale in the home. He also had some experience as a floor boy in a fur-coat manufacturing plant. He preferred wholesale sales rather than canvassing but lacked experience or product knowledge. Harvey was told that to enter the wholesale sales field he would have to be ready to perform some sales and stock duties to learn something about the product the firm sold. Harvey balked at this idea. He felt that with four months' canvassing experience he could start right in with a sales job. He insisted that he should not have to put up with the "menial" aspects of stock work. Complete refusal to start at the beginning made Harvey practically impossible to place. Until he is prepared to perform all the duties of a beginning sales worker in the wholesale field it will not be possible to refer him to the kind of job he wants.

The reasons listed by the New York State Employment Service why young workers fail to hold jobs are: unrealistic wage demands, impatience and unwillingness to adapt to entry requirements, ignorance of labor-market facts, insistence on own concept of job duties, failure to notify employer of absence, inability to get along with others, lack of sense of responsibility, attitude and behavior on the job, and misrepresentation. Some case studies presented from their files show how some of these factors or conditions operate:

L.N., 19, left high school after his junior year two years ago because he was just "bored with schoolwork." Because he is neat and well-spoken he has been able to get several jobs. He held none for long, however. His primary interest, he says, is "getting a job that lets me move about." Just now he wants to get a Florida resort job because he has never been south. He has no interest whatever in getting a job and holding it. With this attitude, he admits he is finding it more and more difficult to get jobs. When he tells employers his work history they are reluctant to hire him because, as one employer said, they could not depend on a "job hopper," because of the cost of training.

Unless L.N. can choose a field of work and stick to it, he will find that only the less desirable casual jobs will be open to him. He will have lost his opportunity to secure permanent and worth-while employment.

Donald T., 18, is serious, cooperative, and neat. His father owns a garage and Donald got experience working part time and summers until he completed eighth grade. Then he left school and worked a year as a mechanic's helper. He quit because of long hours and low pay. On the basis of an excellent reference from this employer the applicant was accepted by another garage at a very good salary and shortly after the placement was made, the new employer called to say that the applicant was exactly what he wanted. Customers liked him so well he was getting tips above his attractive salary. He worked three months and was suddenly discharged.

It was learned that the young man, left alone one day, had crashed a motorcycle into the garage wall, damaging the motorcycle and badly injuring his hand. He said he was gassing the motorcycle for a nearby gas station and since the motor was running he wanted to "kill an urge" to try out a motorcycle.

YOUTH AND MARRIAGE

There is some evidence that the sex drive reaches its maximum during this period; however, the effects of technology and the demands for increased schooling have tended to prolong the period of adolescence and youth so that the individual is unable to assume the responsibilities of family life during the postadolescent period. This has had a profound effect upon our social and moral structure, although many parents, teachers, religious workers, and others would like to remain blind to the changed conditions. This has no doubt so affected the sexual lives and practices of the present generation that many activities that were seriously frowned upon by those of a few generations ago are quite widely accepted today. It appears that a democratic society is faced with one of two choices in this connection. Either we must recognize the fact that the sex drive is powerful during this period and that guidance rather than repression of adolescents in their social activities must be followed, and that increased sexual activities will be found where such a program is not instituted, or we must provide in some way for earlier marriages. As a result of changed social, economic, and cultural conditions changes have taken place in boy-girl relations, and the age of marriage has steadily declined. According to the Statistical Abstract of the United States issued by the Bureau of Census the median age at first marriage of American men and women dropped from 24.6 and 21.2 years in 1920 to 22.8 and 20.3 years in 1961.

Falling in love. Most young people have two main goals: first, finding a suitable life occupation, and second, getting married and establishing a family. These do not necessarily come in this particular order, for we note that falling in love appears in the lives of most teen-agers at one time or another. This is another milestone in the lives of adolescents, and is preliminary to a major decision relative to a mate and family. It is not always easy for young people actually to know when they are in love. Being in love is very intangible, and may not affect all individuals in the same manner. The element of physical attraction is much stronger in some than in others. Also, some individuals have learned to play their sex role much better than others. Love in modern American courtship represents respect and comradeship to a higher degree than perhaps at any other period. The aspect of love involving partnership grows and develops through the enjoyment of common experiences. Similar tastes, ideals, aspirations, and outlooks are most important in the development of wholesome comradeship.

Becoming engaged furnishes a couple with the final opportunity to make their choice relative to marriage. However, prior to engagement many adolescents find it to their advantage to have a "steady," someone they can count on to accompany them to a dance or other event. One of the most important arguments against "going steady" is that such a practice may keep adolescents from becoming better acquainted with a larger number of the opposite sex. It is important for adolescents to become acquainted with a large circle in order that choices may be made from a wide range of individual personalities. A nationwide study of girls between 11 and 18 years of age revealed that most girls are dating by the time they are 16.[14] And, although "going steady" is a pattern of many girls, 50 per cent of the girls included in this survey indicated that they dated more than one boy (Table 19-6). Dating doesn't necessarily mean that the youngsters are in love, although it frequently leads to falling in love. It is at this point that dating between couples of mixed faiths becomes a problem, especially if parents object to such marriages. Studies do indicate that such marriages are more likely to end up in divorce than marriages between members of the same faith. Similarity in background, religion, culture, and educational level tend to make for stability of

Table 19-6

SUMMARY OF DATING PATTERNS OF ADOLESCENT GIRLS

	Age				
Dating pattern	*11 & under*	*12*	*13*	*14–16*	*Over 16*
R dates	4%	12%	30%	72%	91%
R is engaged	—	—	—	1	2
R goes steady	—	2	2	12	29
R dates one boy, does not "go steady"	1	3	5	8	10
R dates different boys	3	7	23	51	50
R mixes with boys, does not date	46	60	51	21	8
R neither dates nor mixes	50	27	18	7	1
Not ascertained	—	1	1	*	*

* Less than one half of 1 per cent.

marriages. Common goals, attitudes, and values also contribute to harmonious marriages.

Courtship practices. Marriage among adolescents has steadily increased. This presents a serious economic and psychological problem to many adolescents and sometimes a difficult social problem to their parents and the community. Adolescents are criticized by adults for excessive petting, but adults seem to have forgotten their drives and behavior during adolescence. What are the courtship practices of adolescents, especially those that go steady?

Some materials bearing on this problem were presented in Chapter 14. Considerable data have been gathered relative to premarital sexual relations of adolescents and youth. The Kinsey study revealed class differences, with premarital sexual relations significantly more frequent among adolescents of the lower class.[15] Out of 615 couples studied by Burgess and Wallin, 274, or 45 per cent, admitted intercourse with their spouse before marriage.[16] These results are supported by findings from studies dealing with the per cent of brides pregnant at the time of marriage. The results presented in Table 19-7 indicate that many youth marriages are caused by pregnancy or fear of pregnancy. The inability of the young couples to discuss this problem with parents frequently leads to secret marriages, the girl running away from home, or, in extreme cases, suicide.

Table 19-7

PER CENT OF YOUTH BRIDES PREMARITALLY PREGNANT

Subjects and study	Per cent
1425 high school students in California (Landis)[17]	44
58 Iowa high school students (Burchinal)[18]	40
New Haven (Hollingshead and Redlich)[19]	40
296 girls under 19 (Moss and Gingles)[20]	31
20,981* Women of England and Wales (Landan)[21]	70.5
Copenhagen, under age 20** (Holm)[22]	82.9

* First birth less than 8 lunar months after marriage.
** First birth less than 7 lunar months after marriage.

Factors influencing dating and marriage. In Chapter 14 it was pointed out that 16-year-olds tend to date from the same economic class. It was found that the small community furnished many opportunities for young people to meet each other and learn something of each other's interests and characteristics; the large city failed to provide these close associations. A relatively large number of individuals residing in cities find their marriage partner through their jobs, through common professional or religious activities, or within a few blocks of where they reside. Proximity provides for contacts, and this is the first essential for marriage in a society

Table 19-8

CUMULATIVE DATA SHOWING THE EFFECT OF RESIDENTIAL PROPINQUITY ON MARRIAGE SELECTION

Number of blocks apart	Philadelphia	Per cent New Haven	Duluth
Same address	12.64	6.42	5.67
One block or less	17.18	9.42	8.00
Two blocks or less	23.26	14.12	11.33
Three blocks or less	27.46	17.32	15.33
Four blocks or less	30.56	20.84	17.66
Five blocks or less	33.58	23.84	20.66
Ten blocks or less	42.32	36.57	30.99
Fifteen blocks or less	48.00	44.16	37.32
Twenty blocks or less	51.94	51.33	42.65

where individuals make their own choice of a marriage mate. The schools, churches, and other community agencies oftentimes furnish the opportunities for young people to meet each other. Data from three studies have been assembled and presented in Table 19-8.[23] In two of these studies over half of the marriages were between couples living within 20 blocks of each other.

While there is an association between residential propinquity and mate selection, it should be emphasized that other factors operate to produce dating and marriage. Davie and Reeves reported that "in a vast majority of cases marriage is an ingroup affair, that is, the two contracting parties tend to be of the same race, nationality, religion and socioeconomic status."[24] In a study reported by Zubrack a school-wide survey was conducted, designed to determine what personality traits or other factors were regarded as most important to those thinking of selecting a marriage partner.[25] Data were obtained from over 700 boys and girls ranging from ages 13 to 20 and representing grades 8 to 12 from Haddon Heights High School in New Jersey. The items which were regarded as important, listed in order of importance were as follows: emotional love, emotional maturity, agreeable personality, same religion, physical attractiveness, common interests, financial responsibility, intelligence, and family background.

In analyzing the results, a breakdown into individual age-groups exhibited no significant differences in rating of choices. These responses seem to parallel those cited in similar surveys of a more inclusive nature. Since the romantic complex is so dominant in the lives of adolescents, the "family background" factor is pushed to the bottom of the list of factors. This rejection of the need for a good family background may be a reflection of the breakdown of family tradition as an important factor and may imply that the adolescent is groping toward independence of family control.

There has been a pronounced trend since World War II towards earlier marriages, especially on the part of girls. Teen-age marriages were formerly confined largely to the lower socio-economic group. However, this is no longer the case. As many as one-fifth of the undergraduate college students in this country are married; more than half of these have children. Financial difficulties are a common problem. Parental aid to young couples is often forthcoming, but frequently with strings attached. Students who work, attend classes, and make a home are likely to be so exhausted physically and emotionally that they are unable to do any of these tasks well. The arrival of children is considered a serious crisis because of the additional problems it entails. If both parents are emotionally mature, and are willing to share homemaking responsibilities with lowered standards of living, these marriages can, however, become strong unions. Two-thirds of the couples interviewed in a 1959 study reported that, given the opportunity to make the decision again, they would repeat their campus marriage.[26]

Youth and the family. As boys and girls advance toward maturity their outlook extends beyond the self and their mate toward having children of their own. This observation is borne out by data on marriages and children, especially during critical times. During World War II, the government in effect subsidized marriage and families for men in service. This removed many of the economic handicaps of marriage and raising a family for men in service, while higher wages removed many similar economic problems encountered by civilians. As a result, the age of marriage was lowered and the birth rate increased. There is also a likelihood of certain changes in values. The past generation may be regarded as a generation that looked to science and technology to solve most if not all of the major problems. Two world wars, a Korean conflict, and unsettled world conditions have brought many people to realize that these forces alone will not produce happiness, security, and a good life for all.

Children are no longer taken for granted in our society. Most young couples are eager to have children as shown by the birth rate among young people despite widspread birth control information. A study conducted by Remmers and Shimberg approximately two decades ago showed that 98 per cent of boys and girls consider that children were essential to an ideal family.[27]

Although the problems of marriage and raising children have become more complicated as a result of technological developments and urbanization, it seems likely that youth is better prepared biologically for bearing children and psychologically for rearing children than older adults. The marriage of youth is too often postponed, or, if not postponed, the bearing of children is postponed until the parents can get ahead financially. Social and economic conditions tend to militate against childbearing and training during the most desirable years.

YOUTH AND CITIZENSHIP IN A DEMOCRATIC SOCIETY

The role of learning is extremely important in the preparation of adolescents and youth for citizenship in a democratic society. Attitudes toward freedom, work, politics, government, laws, and human relations are learned. The fact that every year a million or more teen-agers are in trouble with the police is likely to cause many to lose sight of the many millions who like Elizabeth Evans (a 1954 winner of the Voice of Democracy contest) have never encountered trouble with the law. In defense she writes:

> I am 17. . . . I've never set a fire, robbed a gas station, or beaten a defenseless old man. In fact, I don't even know anyone who has. But every year a million American teen-agers just like me—oh, some a few years younger and some a few years older, some from families a little larger or a little smaller than mine, . . . but, basically a million kids *just like me*—are in trouble with the police. . . .

Sure, it's a problem. It's one of the biggest problems facing America today. But sometimes I wish someone would think of the 95 per cent of us who aren't delinquents. Because we're here, too. And we're the ones who will be the scientists and the editors and the clergymen and the statesmen 10 and 20 and 30 years from now. We're the ones who'll be pushing most of the nation's baby carriages and growing its food and selling its shoes and making its automobiles. We're the one's who'll be electing its leaders and filling its churches, and, if necessary, fighting its wars.

Our job is to stay on the right track until we reach maturity. It's hard at any time, under any circumstances. It's harder in 1955. And it's hardest of all when headlines continually scream and radios constantly blare that young America is going to the dogs. . . .

Basically we aren't a bad generation. We couldn't be. We started out the same way everyone does—as babies. . . . But living has been at best a difficult and insecure thing; at worst an insurmountable wall of bewilderment and frustration. . . .

What's the answer? What will determine the kind of men and women we'll be and the kind of world we'll make? What is it that our generation needs most of all? There are hundreds of theories: more preventive mental hygiene, strong law enforcement, stricter divorce laws, better recreation programs, more schools and more teachers, censorship of television and movies and magazines, the old-fashioned hairbrush. . . . I know what our generation needs, what we need more than laws or courts or recreation centers, more than better schools or better entertainment or better discipline—no matter how much we may need all of those—We need someone to believe in us.[28]

The challenges that youth face. There is today among youth a lack of challenging social and civic goals. This has been noticed among senior high school students of Georgia. Among their major concerns about the future in 1962-63 were:

When will we reach the moon?
What will things be like in 2,000 A. D.?
Will there be another World War?
Will the United States still be a great power in 2,000 A. D.?
Will the communists finally win out?[29]

Ours is not an age of dreams and adventure—except for a small group interested in space travel. Concerning the effect of this age on youth, Bettelheim states:

The buoyancy of youth is fed by the conviction of a full life to come, one in which all great things are theoretically available. But one cannot believe in the good life to come when the goal is suburbia. One cannot realize one's values by climbing the ladder of the business community, nor prove one's manhood on the greens of the country club. . . . Neither our conviction that the West is declining nor our fear that atomic destruction will wipe man from the earth . . . offers much hope for assertive self-realization, now or ever . . . youth does not create its own cause for which it is ready to fight. All it can do is to embrace causes developed by mature men . . . age provides the direction but youth the leadership and fighting manpower.[30] *Bell*

What are adequate social goals for an age of plenty? What are civic responsibilities in a democratic society such as ours? What are the responsibilities in an age where developments in space and travel have made this one world? Youth must exercise progressively higher levels of competency and understanding of present and future problems in his own society and all over the world. He will be called upon to solve difficult problems involving human relations and human welfare that adults of the past have been unable to solve.

Some of the problems faced by adolescents as they approach maturity and accept the responsibilities of citizenship in a democratic society have been stated by Allport:

1. The new generation of students will have to face an ever increasing domination of life by science, by technology, and by automation. . . .

2. The new generation will have to recognize the impossibility of living any longer in a state of condescension toward the colored peoples of the world (about three-quarters of the world's population). Centuries of comfortable caste discrimination and segregation are from here on impossible to maintain.

3. The coming generation will have to deal with a population explosion whose predicted magnitude staggers our imagination.

4. It will need a complete understanding of world societies and their marked differences in values. In the past, we could be politely ignorant of such places as Africa, Latin America, and Asia in a way that is no longer possible.

5. It will have to create a world government or, at least, an effective confederation to forestall the threat of thermonuclear war.

6. As if a planetary view were not difficult to achieve, the coming generation may have to develop an interplanetary point of view. . . .[31]

Youth in politics. Teen-age culture is insulated from influences of the adult world. Teen-agers in the United States lack interest in politics. Many reasons have been offered to account for this. It appears that the best explanation is that this is not an integral part of teen-age culture— the issues affect them only indirectly.

Studies of the attitudes of teen-agers, however, show that they reflect those of their family and community background. They display many of the prejudices of their homes and communities. Polls of the political opinions of teen-agers show that social class markedly affects their opinions.[32] The results of such polls indicate that lower-class teen-agers are more likely than middle- and upper-class teen-agers to be liberal on issues involving government and private ownership and control but they tend to be more conservative about civil liberties.

However, young people of today have certain characteristics which tend to distinguish them from their counterparts of previous decades. Today, the average youth is considerably better informed on national and world problems than he was 40 or 50 years ago. Secondly, young people do not believe in party loyalty to the same degree that their fathers did. "Stand by the party no matter what they espouse or whom they elect" has lost its appeal. Furthermore, the typically American, pervasive interest in experimentation has entered the political field, bringing with it the hint to youth that it is entitled to propose a better design even though that design may be opposed by past experience. It should be pointed out again that young people need guidance in these activities, in order that democratic ideals, democratic ways of behaving, and self-determination may become a part of the self.

The voting age was lowered to 18 in Georgia in 1943. A study of the activities of youthful voters during the first 10 years of this law revealed that they behaved very much like their elders. In "hot elections" more voters go to the polls and vote along the general lines of family and community interests. A lowering of the voting age brought forth a wave of young voters at first. It has been observed that political clubs are more active in the schools and colleges of Georgia than in neighboring states. In some cases students are given instruction in the operation of voting machines. Former Governor Arnall, who sponsored the law in Georgia, has pointed out, "Actually, young people take a more active interest in politics because they study it in school and want to become active at once."

Table 19-10

RESPONSES OF HIGH SCHOOL STUDENTS TO THE QUESTION: "IF YOU HAD TO GIVE UP ONE OF THESE THINGS, WHICH WOULD YOU BE LEAST WILLING TO GIVE UP? WHICH WOULD YOU BE MOST WILLING TO GIVE UP?"

	Least willing	Most willing
Freedom of speech	46.0%	.9%
Freedom of religion	36.5	1.8
The right to vote	5.2	6.4
Trial by jury	3.8	3.9
The right to change jobs if you want to	3.0	20.8
The right to earn more than $3,000 a year if you can	2.3	59.8
Don't know	3.2	6.4

Youth and the freedoms. Freedom is an American tradition. The cry of "freedom" has played an important role throughout our history—both in war and in peace. The results of the 1942 *Fortune* survey of the opinion of American high school youth was most encouraging to those who believe in the principles of our democratic government. They reveal that youth has an ardent devotion to liberty, and indicate quite definitely that its devotion to liberty's ideals is more related to the things for which our forefathers fought than to conditions that have evolved as a result of industrial and technological developments. The results, presented in Table 19-10, show that 82.5 per cent would be least willing, of all freedoms, to give up that of speech or of worship.[33] This is most noteworthy at a time in our history when ideological conflicts engulf the world.

The importance of cultural demands has been emphasized throughout our study of adolescents. Also, it has been emphasized that attitudes, ideals, and values are acquired. A 60-item questionnaire was used to test the agreement of a sample of 3000 high school pupils with concepts from the *Bill of Rights, Communist Manifesto,* and certain fascist principles.[34] A positive correlation was found between adherence to democratic principles and higher socio-economic status, higher level of mother's education, factual information, urbanity, and higher grade level.

American parents encourage their youngsters to be creative and ambitious and to think many things out for themselves. This encouragement of young people to be independent creates problems for both the young and their parents. Independence from parents means they must seek security elsewhere, primarily through a closer affiliation with their peers. The American adolescent is therefore far more likely to be influenced by the wishes, desires, and behavior of his peers than, for example, the Chinese adolescent who from an early stage is gradually inducted into adult society. The lack of a close identity of American adolescents with adults creates problems of adjustment to the adult social and economic standards. These difficulties may, however, serve as an advantage. Hsu, Watrous, and Lord state:

> The white American youth, because of discontinuity between their early and later experiences, sometimes come to the position of responsibility with an idealism far less known among their counterparts in China. American youths tend to go out to improve things, to fight towards a better living, or at least to do things differently from their parents and to explore unknown possibilities.[35]

Cultural changes (economic, social, political, etc.) may result from either external or internal pressures. Internal pressure for change is ever present when there are differences in outlook between successive generations such as we find in America, especially among urban families. Adolescent instability, unrest, and idealism frequently displayed in youth movements and youth demonstrations may be thought of as outgrowths of the American discontinuity between generations. This will insure cultural change. The nature of this change will be considerably affected by educators, religious leaders, and others concerned with the training of these young people for citizenship in a free society.

Education for world citizenship. Education for world citizenship can only be brought about when world citizenship becomes part of the goal of society, and particularly the goal of teachers, parents, and others concerned with the guidance of youth, for both now and for the future. Training for world citizenship, like training in democratic ways of living, cannot be relegated to some special department of the school; it will require the attention and consideration of every teacher of every subject, coordinated with ideals and practices in the home, at church, and in other community activities.

American boys and girls must be trained to detect the economic fallacies that led us toward imperialism at one decade and into isolation a generation later. They must come to understand that favorable conditions for trade will provide opportunities for other nations to pay for our goods by selling us their goods in exchange. They must be given an understanding of how our technology operates, and how it has affected our way of living. They must come to see that the various agencies of production are so complex and interrelated that, without planning and regulation, economic chaos would result. They must be shown the possibility and necessity of a full life for all members of our society.

DEVELOPING A CONSISTENT PHILOSOPHY OF LIFE

It was pointed out in Chapter 2 that an important developmental task of adolescents is that of developing a philosophy of life. The role of the church in character development and the development of a philosophy was emphasized in Chapter 9.-Within recent years educators have come to realize that science alone fails to furnish youth with adequate answers to many of their problems. Worldwide events during the past several decades have shown clearly that science does not furnish man with a code of ethics or some standards to guide him in his human relations.-The youth problem has loomed large on the American scene during and since World War II. It has even caught the attention of the U.S. Congress. The importance of inculcating worthy ideals, sound values, good character, and a sound philosophy relative to the nature, purpose, and destiny of man has been ascribed to by competent leaders in all walks of life. The best means of developing these attributes is the challenge facing the home, church, school, community, and other agencies concerned with the guidance and training of adolescents and youth.

The previous chapters have pointed out the influence of various forces and conditions on the development of the adolescent. It has been suggested that a better integration of the various forces and a better understanding of the function and activities of the different agencies by each of the other agencies concerned would make their work more meaningful and purposive.

Autocratic, democratic, and laissez-faire controls. The effects of autocratic and democratic control on the home and on community life have been discussed in earlier chapters. One of the most important means of preparing boys and girls for participation in democratic ways of life is to provide them with opportunities for participating in the various institutions concerned with their guidance and development. However, the relationship between autocracy, democracy, and complete individual freedom is poorly understood by the average counselor, teacher, and parent. The relationship is usually thought of as following a linear scale, at one end of which is laissez-faire and at the other autocracy. Democracy is then thought of as a form of control falling around the midpoint between these extremes. That such a notion is incorrect has been well illustrated by Lewin.[36] According to his concept, these forms of control should be perceived as a triangle. Since both democracy and autocracy are types of leadership involving controls, they are somewhat similar. These, then, can be perceived of as being on a straight line. Autocracy presents that type of leadership in which all the controls are highly centralized. In the case of complete democracy these controls lie in the voice and action of the people. The line between autocracy and democracy represents a continuum—showing all degrees from complete leadership responsibility and control to complete group responsibility and control. This relationship is illustrated in the triangle of Figure 19-2. Autocracy and democracy diminish and converge at *LF,* which represents laissez-faire. At this point there is an absence of both democracy and autocracy; there is complete individual freedom and perhaps chaos.

Concerning the role of authority, Stevenson states: "With love and understanding children can be trusted to live up to the ideals and standards of the home and society. But this love must be accompanied by the kind of authority that teaches a child that there are governing principles that set limits for his behavior."[37] Unless the adolescent has learned during childhood that life activities are governed by limiting principles, he is poorly prepared to accept the responsibilities of maturity.

The best protecton against the encroachment of autocratic controls in our national life is for homes, clubs, schools, churches, and other institutions to operate in a democratic manner. Adolescents could then learn that with freedom goes responsibility, that controls are essential if a harmonious social order is to exist, and that if they desire to make their own choices they must be willing to accept responsibilities involved in such choices. In a democracy controls must be established in the hearts of men. Thus, habits of control must begin during the early years of life and become an integral part of *the self* as the individual grows into maturity.

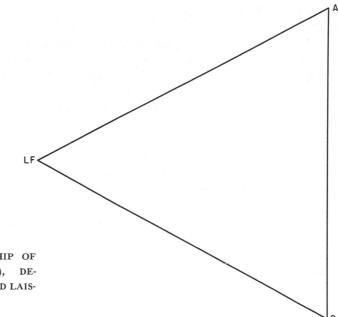

Figure 19-2

THE RELATIONSHIP OF
AUTOCRACY (A), DE-
MOCRACY (D), AND LAIS-
SEZ FAIRE (LF)
(*After Lewin*)

Growth in self-control and self-direction. One of the unfortunate conditions that has developed out of our modern technology is the lack of an opportunity for adolescents to exercise judgments and accept responsibilities for which they are capable, except in time of war when 18-year-olds are called upon for hazardous, adventurous, and responsible tasks. This is readily passed off with the notion that it is better for them to remain in school in order to prepare for greater responsibilities. Thus, he is forced to develop a world largely of his own where he engages in athletic contests, scholastic endeavors, and varied leisure-time pursuits. His world is neither the make-believe world of the child nor the real world of the adult.

Two fallacies appear in connection with such a technique for handling adolescents. In the first place, adolescents are mature or near the stage of maturity and feel the need for asserting themselves as members of the larger social group. When they are denied the opportunity for participating in the affairs of the world about them, they create a society all of their own with all of its comedies, tragedies, and pitfalls. Second, one does not develop habits of initiative and civic responsibilities by merely following through a course of study in high school and college. The need for opportunities to function as young citizens in our society is being recognized by some agencies and institutions. Where such opportunities have been provided youth, the results have been good citizenship, better homes, and improved communities. Materials bearing this out were presented in Chapter 16.

Adolescent boys and girls use various means to bring about their independence of parental control. It is difficult for many parents to relinquish their authority. The school and other agencies also find themselves playing an authoritarian role, and thus fail to provide for the adolescent's need for achieving independence and maturity. The problem of how to get more experience in self-discipline and group cooperation (essentials for effective citizenship in a democratic society) in responsible and significant activities is thus made a difficult one. A summary of the needs of the established social forces as they affect the adolescent includes:

1. A better understanding for parents of the importance of late childhood and early adolescence as a basic period for training in responsibility and self-discipline

2. A recognition by parents of the characteristics and needs of adolescents as a basis for providing for their achievement of independence and status, and for preparation for adult responsibilities

3. High schools of a democratic nature concerned with providing worthwhile learning experiences in which the students shall have a responsible share in planning

4. High schools concerned with the development of cooperative, responsible citizens, schools that will furnish genuine experiences in self-government in matters that directly concern the lives of the individual students

5. Community enterprises that will furnish opportunities for adolescents to plan and execute activities of a wholesome nature which provide for the moral, social, and personal growth of adolescents—with the church functioning effectively in providing opportunities and guidance in recreational, social, and spiritual development of adolescents

6. The cooperation of the industrial and business life of the community in providing rich and extensive opportunities for adolescents to explore the world of work, which would provide these boys and girls with a basis for making sounder decisions relative to their educational and vocational plans.

SUMMARY

The development of youth with the interests, attitudes, ideals, and values essential for happy and harmonious living in a democratic society will require more than platitudes, more than textbook assignments in the schools, and more than political or religious creeds. This will require teamwork on the part of all persons and agencies concerned. The home as the beginning point has been emphasized throughout our study of the adolescent. Just as the experiences of the early years prepare for the elementary school years, the experiences of preadolescence and adolescence prepare the growing individual for youth and maturity.

The adolescent years have been described as those during which individuals normally achieve considerable independence. At this age they assert themselves in various ways by throwing over tradition in general and questioning the teaching of their parents, school teachers, and religious leaders, who tend to despair over the indifference and the rebellious attitude of these adolescents. School authorities often look with disdain at this age, wishing that they could by-pass adolescents except for athletic events. Thus, this age has been commonly labeled a problem age. A more careful study of the situation seems to lead to a different characterization of this age for boys and girls. This seems to be the age when society, largely as a result of technology, fails to provide a place for them, except in a very artificial manner in connection with sports and school events.

The effects of science and invention are being felt in almost all parts of the world, and are creating world, rather than individual, problems. The education of boys and girls demands that consideration be given to these problems, and that training for *world citizenship* be one of its goals. Again, if democracy is to survive and function effectively for the well-being of all the people, the school must accept its challenge, and provide students with the information, skills, and attitudes that will equip them to meet the problems of tomorrow. Youth must be trained to pass sound judgment on national and international issues and policies; and it must be equipped with values consistent with a philosophy of worldwide brotherhood.

This chapter has emphasized that growth from adolescence to maturity presents certain problems. Some of these are an extension of earlier problems; others are largely new. The postadolescent is faced with the problem of preparing for and securing a job, and of breaking almost completely away from former home ties and establishing a home of his own. This latter problem usually means finding a mate and raising a family. The fact that so many vocational and marital maladjustments appear indicates that the problems involved are serious and complex, requiring guidance. There is also the problem of developing a consistent philosophy of life. This may be said to be an extension of this same problem which appeared earlier in the individual's life. With maturity the individual finds that there are many problems in life that he has not been able to solve satisfactorily through his own efforts alone. He finds many questions are not adequately answered through textbooks at school. He finds himself in need of some standard to guide him in evaluating his behavior in everyday activities. Thus, he attempts to arrive at a somewhat consistent philosophy of life so as to make his own life more complete and more harmonious.

Many adults seem to have forgotten their aspirations, behavior patterns, and interests during the teen years. They are in despair of the modern adolescent. If we can only take a long view of youth we can find hope and encouragement. Carl Sandburg seems to sense this in the following words:

> One thing I know deep out of my time: youth when lighted and alive and given a sporting chance is strong for struggle and not afraid of any toils or punishments or dangers or deaths.
> What shall be the course of society and civilization across the next hundred years?
> For the answers read if you can the strange and baffling eyes of youth.
> Yes, for the answers, read, if you can, the strange and baffling eyes of youth.[38]

THOUGHT PROBLEMS

1. Discuss the importance of adolescents as resources in a democratic society.
2. What is the significance to you of the findings relative to youth and the freedoms?
3. What do you understand the term *world citizenship* to mean? How is this problem related to education?
4. What are the major social changes that have resulted from technology? What are the implications of these changes to education?
5. What do you believe to be the function of the school in relation to problems of courtship and marriage? Give some specific things that the school might be able to do in fulfilling this function.
6. Grown-up behavior as distinguished from child behavior is presented in our society in very tangible terms. Give several illustrations of this.
7. Give arguments for and against lowering the voting age to 18 years.
8. How would you account for the trend toward earlier marriages? Give arguments for and against early marriages.
9. What do studies reveal about the effects of residential propinquity on the choice of a marriage partner? How is this affected by our modern educational program for adolescents and youth?
10. List what you consider to be the four outstanding characteristics of the intellectually mature person.
11. What are some things the school and community might do in preparing adolescents and youth for citizenship? Why is this more important today than was the case fifty years ago?

SELECTED REFERENCES

Jersild, Arthur T., *The Psychology of Adolescence,* 2nd ed. New York: The Macmillan Company, 1963, Chap. 19.

Overstreet, H. A., *The Mature Mind.* New York: W. W. Norton & Company, Inc., 1949, Chap. 2.

Pierce, W. C., *Youth Comes of Age*. New York: McGraw-Hill Book Company, 1948.

Rogers, Dorothy, *The Psychology of Adolescence*. New York: Appleton-Century-Crofts, 1962. Chap. 15.

Rothney, J. W. M. and B. A. Roens, *Guidance of American Youth*. Cambridge: Harvard University Press, 1950.

Warters, J., *Achieving Maturity*. New York: McGraw-Hill Book Company, 1949.

NOTES

[1] *Guiding the Adolescent* (Washington, D.C.: Children's Bureau, Federal Security Agency, Publication 22, 1946), pp. 39-40.

[2] Karl C. Garrison, *Growth and Development,* rev. ed. (New York: David McKay Co., Inc., 1959), p. 506.

[3] R. C. Eckert, "Intellectual Maturity," *Journal of Higher Education,* 5 (1934), 478-84.

[4] Eldridge E. Scales and Percival M. Hutson, "How Gainful Employment Affects the Accomplishment of Developmental Tasks of Adolescent Boys," *School Review,* 63 (1955), 31-37. By permission of The University of Chicago Press.

[5] "Hunting a Career: A Study of Out-of-School Youth in Louisville, Kentucky," *United States Department of Labor Bulletin, No. 115* (1949), p. 90.

[6] Richard L. Simpson, David R. Rorsworthy, and H. Max Miller, *Occupational Choice and Mobility in the Urbanizing Piedmont of North Carolina* (Chapel Hill, N.C.: Institute for Research in Social Sciences, University of North Carolina, Cooperative Research Project No. 722, 1960).

[7] Chandler Brossard, "Teen-ager Without a Job," *Look,* No. 5 (February 27, 1962).

[8] Seymour L. Wolfbein, "The Outlook for the Skilled Worker in the United States: Implications for Guidance and Counseling," *Personnel and Guidance Journal,* 40 (1961), 339.

[9] R. Payne, Unpublished data on file in the Department of Sociology, University of Georgia (1955).

[10] *Adolescent Girls; A Nation-wide Study of Girls between Eleven and Eighteen Years of Age* (Ann Arbor, Mich.: Survey Research Center, Institute for Social Research, University of Michigan, 1957), p. 239.

[11] *Youth and the World of Work* (East Lansing, Mich.: Social Research Service, Michigan State College, 1949), p. 11.

[12] *Ibid.,* pp. 14-15.

[13] New York State Employment Service, *Why Young People Fail to Get and Hold Jobs* (New York: Department of Labor, Division of Placement and Unemployment Insurance).

[14] *Adolescent Girls, op. cit.*

[15] P. H. Gebhard, W. B. Pomeroy, C. E. Martin, and C. V. Christenson, *Pregnancy, Birth, and Abortion* (New York: Harper & Row, Publishers, 1958).

[16] E. W. Burgess and P. Wallin, *Engagement and Marriage* (Philadelphia: J. B. Lippincott Co., 1953).

[17] G. T. Landis, *Building a Successful Marriage* (Englewood Cliffs, N.J.: Prentice-Hall, Inc., 1958).

[18] L. G. Burchinal, "Adolescent Role Deprivation and High School Marriage," *Marriage and Family Living,* 21 (1959), 378-84.

[19] A. B. Hollingshead and F. C. Redlich, *Social Class and Mental Illness* (New York: John Wiley & Sons, Inc., 1958).

[20] J. J. Moss and R. Gingles, "A Preliminary Report on a Longitudinal Study of Early Marriage in Nebraska," Paper read at the National Council of Family Relations at Eugene, Oregon (August, 1958).

[21] R. Landan, *Sex Life and Faith* (London: Faber and Faber, Ltd., 1945).

[22] A. Holm, *Monthly Statistical Review* (Copenhagen: City of Copenhagen, 1959).

23 J. R. Marches and G. Turbeville, "The Effect of Residential Propinquity on Marriage Selection," *The American Journal of Sociology*, **58** (1953), 592-95; M. R. Davie and R. J. Reeves, "Propinquity of Residence before Marriage," *American Journal of Sociology*, **44** (1939), 510-17; J. H. S. Bossard, "Propinquity of Residence before Marriage," *American Journal of Sociology*, **38** (1933), 219-24.

24 Davie and Reeves, *op. cit.*, 516-17.

25 Fred Zubrack, "Adolescent Values in Marital Choice," *Marriage and Family Living*, **21** (1959-60), 77-78.

26 David R. Mace, "The Many Costs of a Campus Marriage," *McCall's* (January, 1962), p. 126.

27 H. H. Remmers, and B. Shimberg, *The Purdue Opinion Poll for Young People* (Lafayette, Ind.: Purdue University Studies, Purdue University, 1949).

28 Elizabeth Evans, "In Defense of My Generation," *Journal of the National Education Association*, **44** (March, 1955), 139-40.

29 Karl C. Garrison, "Youth Survey: From Now to 2015 A.D.," Unpublished data on file, College of Education, University of Georgia, (1964).

30 Bruno Bettelheim, "The Problem of Generations," *Daedalus* (Winter, 1962). By permission of the American Academy of Arts and Sciences.

31 Gordon W. Allport, "Value and Our Youth," *Teachers College Record*, **63** (1961-62), 211.

32 H. H. Remmers and D. H. Radler, *The American Teenager* (Indianapolis: Bobbs-Merrill Company, Inc., 1957).

33 "The Fortune Survey," *Fortune* (November, 1942), p. 8.

34 H. H. Remmers, *et. al.*, "Does Youth Believe in the Bill of Rights?" *Purdue Opinion Panel*, No. 30 (Lafayette, Ind.: Purdue University, 1951).

35 Francis L. K. Hsu, Blanche G. Watrous, and Edith M. Lord, "Cultural Pattern and Adolescent Behavior," *International Journal of Social Psychiatry*, **7** (1961), 51.

36 Kurt Lewin, "The Dynamics of Group Action," *Educational Leadership*, **1** (1944), 195-200.

37 George S. Stevenson, Midcentury White House Conference on Children and Youth, Panel 15 (Washington, D.C., 1950).

38 Carl Sandburg, *Always the Young Strangers* (New York: Harcourt, Brace & World, Inc., 1953), p. 304.

APPENDICES

BIBLIOGRAPHY OF RECENT BOOKS DEALING WITH ADOLESCENTS

Bernard, Harold W., *Adolescent Development in American Culture*. New York: Harcourt, Brace & World, Inc., 1957. Social and cultural influences on the development of the adolescent are emphasized throughout this volume.

Bier, W. C., ed., *The Adolescent: His Search for Understanding*. New York: Fordham University Press, 1963. This is a third volume in a pastoral psychology series. The period of adolescence is viewed as a time when the individual is trying to understand himself and his parents as he strives for independence.

Blos, Peter, *On Adolescence, A Psychoanalytic Interpretation*. New York: Free Press of Glencoe, Inc., 1961. True to its title this volume is largely concerned with the psychoanalytical theory of adolescence.

Cole, Luella, *Psychology of Adolescence*, 6th ed. New York: Holt, Rinehart & Winston, Inc., 1964. The relevance of psychological considerations to the classroom situation is brought forth throughout this book. This textbook covers the major topics of adolescent psychology with case studies being widely used.

Coleman, James S., *The Adolescent Society*. New York: Free Press of Glencoe, Inc., 1961. The social systems of ten high schools in widely varied communities are described. The relationship of the attitudes, values, and achievement to the subcultures of the communities is shown.

Friedenberg, Edgar Z., *The Vanishing Adolescent*. Boston: Beacon Press, 1959. Its thesis is that adolescence as a stage of personal and social development is being crowded out in our present culture.

Gallagher, J. R. and H. I. Harris, *Emotional Problems of Adolescents*. New York: Oxford University Press, 1958. Emphasis is given to the adolescent as a person and the role of adults in dealing with him. The problem of adolescent identification is treated extensively.

Garrison, Karl C., *Before You Teach Teen-agers*. Philadelphia: Lutheran Church Press, 1962. Written for Christian leaders who work with teen-agers, consisting of six chapters: the young person in modern society, adolescent development, life involvements of personal nature, life involvements of interpersonal nature, life involvements in world and society, and you and the teen-agers.

Grinder, Robert E., *Studies in Adolescence*. New York: The Macmillan Company, 1963. Forty-five selections from the writings of authorities in psychology, sociology, and anthropology present a variety of viewpoints relative to adolescent behavior.

The Growing Years—Adolescence. Washington, D.C.: American Association for Health, Physical Education, and Recreation. Points out the understandings, attitudes, and skills adolescents need in order to lead a full and complete life and how the secondary school program can best meet these needs.

Hadfield, J. A., *Childhood and Adolescence*. Baltimore: Penguin Books, Inc., 1961. The author draws on his experience as a psychiatrist to give examples of children's behavior and difficulties and to make recommendations to parents, for whom the book is intended.

Hechinger, Grace and Fred M. Hechinger, *Teen-age Tyranny*. New York: William Morrow and Co., Inc., 1963. A critical analysis of the values and typical behavior of middle-class American teen-agers is presented. Special consideration is given to the moral and ethical implications of adolescent patterns of leisure-time activities, academic pursuits, attitudes toward possessions, television influences, and privileges of a dynamic and affluent society.

Hemming, James, *Problems of Adolescent Girls*. London: William Heinemann, Limited, 1960. The problems and difficulties of girls, based upon 3,000 letters written to a national weekly magazine, are presented.

Horrocks, J. E., *The Psychology of Adolescence: Behavior and Development*, 2nd ed. Boston: Houghton Mifflin Company, 1962. A reorganized and enlarged revision of the 1951 edition covering six major areas: the nature of adolescence, relations to others, delinquent behavior, development and growth, bases of behavior, and adolescent activities and interests.

Jersild, A. T., *The Psychology of Adolescence*, 2nd ed. New York: The Macmillan Company, 1963. A major theme of this book is that "a person who seeks to understand the adolescent will probably gain most if in the process he seeks to understand himself." Considerable attention is given to emotional development, social development, and self-fulfillment.

Kiell, Norman, *The Adolescent Through Fiction*. New York: International Universities Press, Inc., 1959. Various phases of the adolescent period are pointed out in examples from fiction. This volume shows how the work of the creative novelist and the psychologists merges.

Lorand, Sander, and Henry I. Schneer, eds., *Adolescents: Psychoanalytic Approach to Problems and Therapy*. Nineteen writers present current psychoanalytic knowledge of adolescent problems. Adolescence is viewed as a distinct stage of development, with specific analytic technique needed for dealing with the problems of this age group.

Mead, Margaret J., *From the South Seas: Studies of Adolescence and Sex in Primitive Societies*. New York: William Morrow & Co., Inc., 1939. A one-volume edition of three anthropological works: *Coming of Age in Samoa, Growing Up in New Guinea*, and *Sex and Temperament*.

Powell, Marvin, *The Psychology of Adolescence*. Indianapolis: Bobbs-Merrill Company, Inc., 1963. The emphasis is on the role of culture in personality formation. The roles of the home and school are emphasized. Case studies are used to illustrate principles.

Rogers, Dorothy, *The Psychology of Adolescence*. New York: Appleton-Century-Crofts, 1962. Various aspects of adolescent development are presented along with a treatment of the adolescent in his most common roles—in home, school, peer group, world of work, and in the adult world of which he is to become a part.

Salisbury, Harrison E., *The Shook-up Generation*. New York: Harper & Row, Publishers, 1958. This is a vivid account of the codes and behavior patterns of teen-age gangs. Although the importance of the home is given little attention, this is a fascinating study of the difficult problem presented in juvenile delinquency.

Schneider, A. A., *Personality Development and Adjustment in Adolescence*. Milwaukee: Bruce Publishing Co., 1960. This revised edition of an earlier publication consists of three parts: the physiology, psychology, and sociology of adolescence.

Seidman, Jerome M., ed., *A Book of Readings*, 2nd ed. New York: Holt, Rinehart & Winston, Inc., 1960. This is a revision of a 1953 compilation of readings. A diversity of well-chosen materials is presented, largely from publications since 1955.

Staton, Thomas F., *Dynamics of Adolescent Adjustment*. New York: The Macmillan Company, 1963. The emphasis is principally on theories and concepts of adolescent adjustments which have proved useful to the author of the book.

Strang, Ruth, *The Adolescent Views Himself*. New York: McGraw-Hill Book Company, 1957. Adolescents' own statements taken from hundreds of compositions dealing with adolescents' concerns about themselves furnished the author with useful materials relative to the inner world of teen-agers.

Symonds, P. M., and A. R. Jensen, *From Adolescent to Adult*. New York: Columbia University Press, 1961. This is a follow-up study of a group of adolescent boys and girls which shows a remarkable persistence of personality trends over a three-year period.

Wattenberg, W. W., *The Adolescent Years*. New York: Harcourt, Brace & World, Inc., 1955. The social influences on adolescents are discussed in various accounts and descriptions of the adolescent years.

Wilkins, L. T., *The Adolescent in Britain*. London: Central Office of Information, 1956. This publication is based on facts collected by a team of interviewers from a random sample of 1,390 male and 451 female adolescents aged 15-19 years.

Wittenberg, Rudolph, *On Call for Youth*. New York: Association Press, 1955. Explains the meanings of the ups and downs observed among adolescents and how grown-ups and teen-agers affect each other. It indicates further when and how adults can be of help.

MOTION PICTURES
RELATED TO THE
ADOLESCENT AGE*

Age of Turmoil (M-H, 20 min.). Teen-age boys and girls enact various sorts of behavior frequently associated with adolescence. Adolescence is depicted as an age in which the individual is absorbed in his own affairs and those involving peers.

Attitudes and Health (C-I-F, 10 min.). The importance of self-confidence and favorable attitudes to good health is demonstrated in the case of two girls.

Boy with a Knife (I-F-B, 19 min.). A case history from the files of a Los Angeles Youth Service Agency. A group worker attempts to reach a gang of boys from adverse home backgrounds who are headed for delinquency.

Discipline During Adolescence (M-H, 16 min.). The problems facing parents of adolescents, especially those related to discipline and restraint are shown.

The Dropout (N-E-A, 29 min.). This is a story of youngsters who leave high school without graduating. It shows how the community through remedial reading programs, work experiences, and other community and educational activities may attack the dropout problem.

Emotional Maturity (M-H, 20 min.). The effects of lack of control in the case of an adolescent boy entrusted with valuable property are shown. The behavior of an adolescent boy is traced back to parental treatment as a child.

---

* Sources of the films used in the appendix:
Athena—Athena Films, 165 West 46th Street, New York, N.Y.
C-I-F—Coronet Instruction Films, 65 East South Water Street, Chicago, Ill.
E-B-F—Encyclopedia Britannica Films, 20 North Wacker Drive, Chicago, Ill.
I-F-B—International Film Bureau, Suite 308-316, 57 East Jackson Boulevard, Chicago, Ill.
M-H—McGraw-Hill Book Company, Text Films Dept., 330 West 42nd Street, New York, N.Y.
M-H-F-B—Mental Health Film Board, 168 East 38th Street, New York, N.Y.
N-E-A—National Education Association, 1201 Sixteenth Street, N.W., Washington, D.C.
N-F-B-C—National Film Board of Canada, 630 Fifth Avenue, New York, N.Y.
Y-A-F—Young American Films, 18 East 41st Street, New York, N.Y.

Family Circles (M-H, 31 min.). Both positive and negative aspects of the home-school relationships and the responsibilities of each for providing for the educational needs of boys and girls are shown.

Feeling of Hostility (M-H, 27 min.). The case history of a young woman who, lacking affection and security as a child, achieves some personal satisfaction through intellectual achievements. However, because of her unconscious feelings of resentment and hostility, she is unable to establish satisfactory personal relations with others.

Feeling of Rejection (M-H, 23 min.). The case history of a young woman who learned to avoid possible disapproval by withdrawing from normal competition and refusing to take independent action. The harmful effects of this form of behavior are shown and analyzed, and the benefits of group therapy in such cases indicated.

The High Wall (M-H, 32 min.). A case study of Tom, an insecure boy brought up in a rigid home life, is here presented. The influences of the rigid, demanding home are clearly portrayed in the behavior of Tom.

The Meaning of Adolescence (M-H, 16 min.). The meaning of adolescence and problems facing adolescents are here presented. Behavior traits characteristic of adolescents are clearly shown.

Meeting the Needs of Adolescents (M-H, 19 min.). This film presents constructive means which parents and teachers may use to help adolescents meet problems relating to achieving independence, boy-girl relations, self-discipline, and the attainment of wholesome attitudes.

Mental Health (E-B-F, 12 min.). Good health is carefully defined. The basic structure of personality is presented along with ways of maintaining good mental health.

Physical Aspects of Puberty (M-H, 19 min.). This film deals with the physiological changes of adolescence. The accompanying emotional and mental changes that occur at this time are also shown.

Problem of Pupil Adjustment, "The Dropout" (M-H, 20 min.). Some characteristics of the high-school program that led Steve Martin to drop out of school are shown along with suggested ways of improving the program by relating the work to the interests and needs of boys and girls.

Problem of Pupil Adjustment, "The Stay-In" (M-H, 19 min.). The problem of dropouts is solved when a life adjustment program is instituted. Classes fitted to the needs and interests of high school pupils are shown.

The Quiet One (Athena, 67 min.). This is a pathetic story of a sick boy in a slum environment who has broken completely from reality and is struggling toward recovery.

Social Acceptability (M-H, 20 min.). The problems faced by the adolescent girl who is rejected by her classmates at school and the effects of this rejection upon her personality are shown.

Social Development (M-H, 16 min.). Presented here is an analysis of social behavior at different age levels and the reasons underlying the changes in behavior pattern as the child develops. At different age levels there is a definite organization of social behavior which demands guidance and understanding from adults if conflicts are to be avoided.

Social-sex Attitudes in Adolescence (M-H, 22 min.). Various stages in the development of social-sex attitudes are depicted through a well-devised chronological story dealing with the marriage of a young couple. Flashback aspects of earlier experiences show how certain attitudes develop.

The Story of a Teen-age Drug Addict (Y-A-F, 16 min.). A case history of a young high school boy who has become a helpless slave to heroin. The treatment, problems involved, and rehabilitation program are vividly presented.

The Teens (N-F-B-C, 28 min.). Earlier and later adolescence are depicted through the activities of a family which has several teen-agers. The parents' roles in guiding the teen-agers through their varied problems are stressed.

ANNOTATED BIBLIOGRAPHY OF POPULAR LITERATURE

Popular literature touching upon adolescence presents in a vivid manner the problems faced by real adolescent boys and girls as they grow toward maturity, although the stories themselves may be pure fiction. Since such books give a detailed and perhaps more realistic interpretation than scientific compilations of facts in a textbook, they should be of value to the reader in helping him to understand the significance of the adolescent period.

There are many books dealing with this period of life. The following list is by no means complete. In its compilation, the writer made an extensive survey of the field, and the list is the result of a selective process. Some of the books to be found in it deal with *growing up* in general. Others deal with the adolescent over a short period of time, and still others are concerned with some special problem of the adolescent years. The extent to which the social setting of the adolescent is introduced varies considerably—depending upon the authors' points of view, interests, and purposes. From this bibliography, presented in annotated form, the reader will be able to find materials relative to adolescence that will be of interest and value to him.

Aldis, Dorothy, *All Year Round*. Boston: Houghton Mifflin Company, 1938. The influence of a mother's triumphs and mistakes upon her three children. The nervous condition of a four-year-old and the skillful treatment of an adolescent daughter are among the many interesting things sympathetically treated by the author.

Armstrong, Margaret, *Fanny Kemble*. New York: The Macmillan Company, 1938. This book furnishes a vivid picture of Victorian child psychology, revealing its differences from modern views. When Fanny's family can do no more with her, they turn her over to a boarding school; this treatment contradicts all modern practices.

Athas, Daphne, *Weather of the Heart*. New York: Appleton-Century-Crofts, 1947. The problems and difficulties of two adolescent girls living at Kittery Point are presented in a fascinating manner.

Baker, Dorothy D., *Young Man with a Horn*. Boston: Houghton Mifflin Company, 1938. Here is an example of innate ability strong enough to carry a youth from the confines of a poor environment to the heights of success. His interest in books and music helped him to ignore hardships.

Berry, Wendell, *Nathan Coulter*. Boston: Houghton Mifflin Company, 1960. A novel of the Coulter family in the Kentucky tobacco country and the growth to manhood of Nathan, their youngest son.

Blanton, Margaret Gray, *The White Unicorn*. New York: Rudo S. Globus, Inc., 1961. A heartening story of a young girl whose early life was shattered by the death of her mother but who learns to cope with the world that unfolds before her.

Burress, John, *Apple in a Pear Tree*. New York: Vanguard Press, 1953. The hero is Jeff, an eleven-year-old boy, whose mother has married a second time. His efforts to assert himself and grow up on a farm are not at first understood by his stepfather; however, in time his efforts are accepted at full value.

Childs, Marquis W., *The Cabin*. New York: Harper & Row, Publishers, 1944. This is a sympathetic story of the life of a thirteen-year-old boy one summer on a middle western corn farm. Tragedies unfold and are successfully met.

Cleary, Beverly, *The Luckiest Girl*. New York: William Morrow & Co., Inc., 1958. A teenage girl's point of view on being 16 years of age and popular with her peers.

Corbett, Jim, *Jungle Lore*. New York: Oxford University Press, 1953. A fascinating story of a boy's adventures in the Indian jungles.

Cormack, Maribelle, and Pavel L. Bytovetzeski, *Swamp Boy*. New York: David McKay Co., Inc., 1948. The story revolves around the life and experiences of sixteen-year-old Clint Sheppard of the Okefinokee swamp of Georgia. Clint has been taught the love of the swampland by Tom, a Seminole Indian, who is the recognized leader of the community. Clint's problems of adjusting to town ways of living along with those of the swamp environment are interesting as well as amusing.

Cronin, A. J., *The Green Years*. Boston: Little, Brown & Co., 1944. *Green Years* is a stirring story of Robert Shannon from 8 to 18. Robert may be described as a waifish little boy, depending upon his grandfather for affection and security.

Curie, Eve, *Madame Curie*. New York: Doubleday & Company, Inc., 1933. A convincingly accurate, though brief, record of the scientist's childhood and the conditions and reverses which made her shy, nervous, overemotional, and mature for her age but which could not squelch her genius.

Davis, Christopher, *First Family*. New York: Coward-McCann, Inc., 1961. A study of an adolescent Negro born in an upper-middle-class suburban neighborhood whose parents use him to resolve some of their problems.

Doan, Daniel, *Crystal Years*. New York: Abelard-Schuman Limited, 1953. A story of a fourteen-year-old boy, Roy Martin, whose family moves from Boston to New Hampshire. The efforts of Roy to fit into his school environment are hampered by the snobbery of the family.

Dornfield, Iris, *Jenny Ray*. New York: The Viking Press, Inc., 1962. Jenny is a very real, moving character surrounded by a mixture of good and bad. This is a good combination of realism and fantasy.

Doyle, Helen M., *A Child Went Forth*. New York: Gotham Book Mart, 1934. During her whole childhood Helen adjusts to situations from which there is no escape. The strength of character she develops by overcoming these obstacles enriches her whole life.

Eustis, Helen, *The Fool Killer*. Garden City, N.Y.: Doubleday & Company, Inc., 1954. This is the story of a twelve-year-old boy who runs away from his foster parents and after many adventures finds a good home.

Farrell, James T., *Father and Son*. New York: Vanguard Press, 1940. A lengthy but impressive story of the development of Danny O'Neill from adolescence up to the age of 19. The realism presented reveals the author's understanding of human nature.

————, *No Star Is Lost*. New York: Vanguard Press, 1938. Like *Studs Lonigan*, this book portrays a boy's struggles with and defeat by his environment. The lack of adjustment of the school to the needs of the community it serves is also evident.

————, *Studs Lonigan*. New York: Vanguard Press, 1932. This story presents a sociological study of the influences of a vigorous but often unfortunate environment upon Studs Lonigan, a son of middle-class Chicago.

Field, Isobel, *This Life I've Loved*. New York: David McKay Co., Inc., 1937. Isobel Field's story furnishes a study of the effect which a change of environment had upon her childhood, and the way her experiences in a mining camp influenced her life in a large city.

Frank, Anne, *Diary of a Young Girl* (translated from the Dutch by B. M. Mooyaart). New York: Doubleday & Company, Inc., 1952. Two years from the diary of a thirteen-year-old Jewish girl, hiding from the Nazis.

Fuentes, Carlos, *The Good Conscience*. New York: Ivan Obolensky, Inc., 1961. This is a sombre story of an adolescent, heir to power, torn between the reality of his family's world and the idealism of his youth.

Geijerstam, Gösta of, *Northern Summer* (translated from the Norwegian by Joran Birkeland). New York: E. P. Dutton & Co., Inc., 1938. The author has succeeded in picturing the happy development of children in a family living on a Norwegian island. Free from social conventions, and aided by the enthusiasm and guidance of their parents, they live naturally and happily together.

Gibbs, A. Hamilton, *The Need We have*. Boston: Little, Brown & Co., 1936. Denny at 14 impresses one as the impish, young-for-his-age result of an over-sheltered childhood, and then as a prodigiously mature mind of adult level with insight, judgment, and subtlety.

Gold, Herbert, *Therefore be Bold*. New York: The Dial Press, Inc., 1960. This book is concerned with the joys and trials of adolescents. It is written with much humor and displays much fantasy.

Gunnarsson, Gunnar, *Ships in the Sky*. New York: Bobbs-Merrill Company, Inc., 1938. Although the life of a child in Iceland must of necessity be quite different from that of children in our country, this book presents a valuable picture of how a child develops in lonely regions where the family is his whole society.

Hagedorn, Hermann, *Edwin Arlington Robinson*. New York: The Macmillan Company, 1938. As the youngest child in the family, Edwin Arlington Robinson was neglected, but was probably saved from maladjustment by his play life with the neighborhood gang. Although not encouraged by others, his poetic talents developed naturally.

Havighurst, Walter and Marion M. Boyd, *Song of the Pines*. New York: Holt, Rinehart & Winston, Inc., 1949. Nils Thorsen, a Norwegian boy, joins a group of pioneer settlers at the age of 14. His inventive genius is a source of help to these Wisconsin pioneers in their lumbering activities.

Jaynes, Clare, *Early Frost*. New York: Random House, 1953. A book about Lann Saunders, a young girl of divorced parents in a boarding school. The problems she is confronted with are largely those of an adolescent dealing with elders.

Kehoe, William, *A Sweep of Dusk*. New York: E. P. Dutton & Co., Inc., 1945. The material of this volume revolves around the problems of an oversensitive adolescent reared by an overbearing mother. The material is drawn from the author's own experiences.

L'Engle, Madeleine, *The Small Rain*. New York: Vanguard Press, 1945. This is a touching story of the problems encountered by a young and talented artist during the adolescent years. Her disillusionments are characteristic of the life of many adolescents filled with zeal and ambition.

Llewellyn, Richard, *How Green Was My Valley*. New York: The Macmillan Company, 1941. A dramatic story of the struggles of a boy against the odds of poverty and class distinction in a mining area. His difficulties, privations, and thwartings are presented in an understanding manner.

Low, Elizabeth, *High Harvest*. New York: Harcourt, Brace & World, Inc., 1948. Life for fifteen-year-old Suzanne on a Vermont mountain farm is not easy. However, Suzanne finds happiness and satisfaction from the outlets available.

McCullers, Carson, *The Member of the Wedding*. Boston: Houghton Mifflin Company, 1946. Frankie, a twelve-year-old girl, was lonely and bored until she learned of her older brother's wedding. She is driven to steal, throw knives, date a soldier, and threaten suicide. In the end Frankie finds a sympathetic friend.

Maugham, Somerset W., *Of Human Bondage*. New York: Modern Library, Inc., 1940. From a protected, pampered childhood, Philip Cary is placed under the guardianship of his disciplinary uncle. Lack of understanding at home and humiliation caused by the ridicule of his club foot by his schoolmates and teachers make him supersensitive and unhappy.

Maxwell, William, *The Folded Leaf*. New York: Harper & Row, Publishers, 1945. This is a story of the friendship begun by two normal boys at the age of 15. The conditions which draw them together and the unfolding events of their friendship make the book an interesting as well as perceptive portrayal of human relationships.

Miller, Sidney, *Roots in the Sky*. New York: The Macmillan Company, 1938. Through poverty and nationality difficulties these children of Jewish-American stock have many chances, if not justifications, for going wrong. The unifying kinship and loyalty to standards upheld by the Jewish religion help avert a tragedy.

Mitchell, William Ormond, *Who Has Seen the Wind*. Boston: Little, Brown & Co., 1947. The story of a boy, Brian O'Connal, from 4 to 12 in a small prairie town.

Morris, Hilda, *The Long View*. New York: G. P. Putnam's Sons, 1937. This author is interested in showing how Asher Allen was influenced by his sober Quaker environment and a forced pride in his family name.

O'Moran, Mabel, *Red Eagle, Buffalo Bill's Adopted Son*. Philadelphia: J. B. Lippincott Co., 1948. The story of Red Eagle, a young Choctaw Indian boy, and his pioneer adventures.

Parrish, Anne, *Poor Child*. New York: Harper & Row, Publishers, 1945. A tragic story of a twelve-year-old boy in need of security and affection, which takes place in a household where he is neither loved nor understood.

Pratt, Theodore, *Valley Boy*. New York: Duell, Sloan, & Pearce, Inc., 1946. *Valley Boy* is a series of character sketches as seen through the eyes of Johnny Birch, a ten-year-old boy. Johnny is a sensitive, lonely lad seeking affection and security outside his home.

Raphaelson, Dorshka W., *Morning Song*. New York: Random House, 1948. The story of a fifteen-year-old girl's efforts and problems as she attempts to support her neurotic mother and younger brother presents an interesting and touching picture of adolescence and family life.

Rawlings, Marjorie Kinnan, *The Yearling*. New York: E. P. Dutton & Co., Inc., 1938. Jody's solitary environment leads him instinctively to find companionship in nature. His father's influence helps the boy to develop a strong character.

Ricks, Peirson, *Hunter's Horn*. New York: Charles Scribner's Sons, 1947. Life and values in postbellum North Carolina are presented in this novel. Uncle Benjamin's grandnephew falls in love with a girl from a poorer class and presents problems for all concerned.

Robertson, Eileen A., *Summer's Lease*. Boston: Houghton Mifflin Company, 1940. This is a psychological study of a sensitive boy who is further handicapped by weak eyesight. Depicted are the trials and pains of the boy as he tries to cope with problems accentuated by refined but unsuccessful home conditions.

Rölvaag, Ole E., *Peder Victorious*. New York: A. L. Burt Co., Inc., 1938. This sensitive, inquisitive Dakota boy is too eager to grow up, is old for his age, and lives through emotional periods approaching maladjustment. A contrast between two teachers is especially well done. Like a number of other authors, Rölvaag criticizes the effects of certain religious experiences upon children.

Rubin, Louis D., *The Golden Weather*. New York: Atheneum Publishers, 1961. The spring and summer of 1936 in Charleston, S.C., as seen by Omar Kohn, a thirteen-year-old Jewish boy.

Sandburg, Helga, *The Owl's Roost*. New York: The Dial Press, Inc., 1962. The teen-ager is portrayed through the encounters of the Olson children and their friends.

Shanks, Edward, *Tom Tiddler's Ground*. Indianapolis: Bobbs-Merrill Company, Inc., 1934. Tom Florey's high intelligence helps him to advance quickly in school in spite of himself. The antagonistic attitude of Tom's father toward his progress does not extinguish the boy's determination to escape from the confines of his home town.

Shaw, Lau, *Rickshaw Boy*. New York: Reynal & Hitchcock, Inc., 1945. An adventure story of a Chinese boy whose dream of happiness is to own a rickshaw.

Singmaster, Elsie, *Isle of Que*. New York: David McKay Co., Inc., 1948. A seventeen-year-old youth is faced with the problem of caring for his mother and sister when his older brother enters military service. He overcomes early fears and difficulties and develops a real sense of responsibility.

Smith, Betty, *A Tree Grows in Brooklyn*. New York: Harper & Row, Publishers, 1943. A colorful presentation of the childhood and youth of Francie Nolan, her family, and her friends. There is beauty and wholesomeness intermingled with plain realism in the problems faced by Francie as she strives to find for herself a place of usefulness in a larger social environment.

Smith, Vian, *Pride of the Moor*. New York: Doubleday & Company, Inc., 1962. Novel about a boy and a horse that will appeal to all who are interested in animals.

Speare, Elizabeth G., *The Witch of Blackbird Pond*. Boston: Houghton Mifflin Company, 1958. The theme of this historical novel involves a young girl's difficult but somewhat successful battle against bigotry.

Sperry, Armstrong, *The Little Eagle—A Navajo Boy*. New York: Holt, Rinehart & Winston, Inc., 1938. An adventure story of a fourteen-year-old Navajo boy in the setting of the Arizona canyons. The warm relations of his home life help him adjust to changed values and cultures encountered in the modern government school.

Spring, Howard, *My Son, My Son!* New York: The Viking Press, Inc., 1938. Parental attempts to shape the lives of two boys result in tragedy. One-sided personalities fail to fit the sons for adult life. Lack of understanding by the parents seems to have an effect upon the characters of all the children.

Stafford, Jean, *The Mountain Lion*. New York: Harcourt, Brace & World, Inc., 1947. This is a symbolic representative of evil in which the novel is centered in a girl in her late childhood and adolescence.

Steele, William O., *The Perilous Road*. New York: Harcourt, Brace & World, Inc., 1958. A Southern boy adventures into the Union army camp with perilous results which help him to realize the bitterness of war.

Strong, Leonard, *The Seven Arms*. New York: Alfred A. Knopf, Inc., 1933. This novel, concerning the life of a large family of children, reveals characters ranging from one extreme to the other. Included are the extrovert, bossy, thoughtful, daydreaming, weak, dependent, independent, and delicate types of children whose characters react upon one another.

Summers, Hollis, *City Limit*. Boston: Houghton Mifflin Company, 1948. The story of the dilemma of a high school boy and girl who are driven into marriage by social criticisms and pressures. The idealism of youth is clearly revealed in contrast to the rigidity of the elders of a Kentucky community.

Tarkington, Booth, *The Fighting Littles*. New York: Doubleday & Company, Inc., 1941. The author gives an interesting and oftentimes humorous presentation of the conflicts between youth and parents. The teen-age children appear as real characters in their revolt against parental controls.

————, *Little Orvie*. New York: Grosset & Dunlap, Inc., 1933. This is a commendable handbook of how to get results opposite to what you want in dealing with children. Popularized through clever handling are the problems of nagging, thwarting, comparison with other children, discussion of child in his presence, shaming, and so on.

Tunis, John, *The Kid from Tomkinsville, Illinois*. New York: Harcourt, Brace & World, Inc., 1940. A sports story with Roy Tucker, a small-town boy, as the principal character. There is a strong emphasis upon community ideals brought forth in the efforts, mistakes, and triumphs of Roy.

Van Etten, Winifred, *I Am the Fox*. Boston: Little, Brown & Co., 1936. Through lack of understanding and individual treatment by her elders, Selma Temple develops many misconceptions and fears.

West, Jessamyn, *Cress Delahanty*, drawings by Joe Krush. New York: Harcourt,

Brace & World, Inc., 1953. The story sketches the problems of an adolescent girl, growing up on a California ranch, from her twelfth to her sixteenth year. The book portrays Cress with her growing pains and the anguish of her parents.

Wolfe, Thomas, *Look Homeward, Angel*. New York: Modern Library, Inc., 1934. This is the story of the childhood and early youth of Eugene Gant. The theme is the development of the artist into a person, the making of the lonely and solitary genius. Eugene is a voyager in quest of self-realization.

Wouk, Herman, *City Boy: The Adventures of Herbie Bookbinder and His Cousin, Cliff*. New York: Simon and Schuster, Inc., 1948. A refreshing and readable novel of an eleven-year-old Bronx boy. The adventures of Herbie and his cousin at home, school, and elsewhere are vividly recounted.

INDEXES

INDEX
OF
AUTHORS

INDEX
OF
SUBJECTS